What They Said
in 1985

What They Said®

In 1985

The Yearbook Of World Opinion

Compiled and Edited by

ALAN F. PATER

and

JASON R. PATER

MONITOR BOOK COMPANY, INC.

To

The Newsmakers of the World . . .

May they never be at a loss for words

SEVENTEENTH ANNUAL EDITION

Printed in the United States of America

Library of Congress catalogue card number 74-111080

ISBN number: 0-917734-13-0

WHAT THEY SAID is published annually by Monitor Book Company, Inc., Beverly Hills, California. The title, "WHAT THEY SAID," is a trademark owned exclusively by Monitor Book Company, Inc., and has been duly registered with the United States Patent Office. Any unauthorized use is prohibited.

Preface to the First Edition (1969)

Words can be powerful or subtle, humorous or maddening. They can be vigorous or feeble, lucid or obscure, inspiring or despairing, wise or foolish, hopeful or pessimistic . . . they can be fearful or confident, timid or articulate, persuasive or perverse, honest or deceitful. As tools at a speaker's command, words can be used to reason, argue, discuss, cajole, plead, debate, declaim, threaten, infuriate, or appease; they can harangue, flourish, recite, preach, discourse, stab to the quick, or gently sermonize.

When casually spoken by a stage or film star, words can go beyond the press-agentry and make-up facade and reveal the inner man or woman. When purposefully uttered in the considered phrasing of a head of state, words can determine the destiny of millions of people, resolve peace or war, or chart the course of a nation on whose direction the fate of the entire world may depend.

Until now, the *copia verborum* of well-known and renowned public figures—the doctors and diplomats, the governors and generals, the potentates and presidents, the entertainers and educators, the bishops and baseball players, the jurists and journalists, the authors and attorneys, the congressmen and chairmen-of-the-board—whether enunciated in speeches, lectures, interviews, radio and television addresses, news conferences, forums, symposiums, town meetings, committee hearings, random remarks to the press, or delivered on the floors of the United States Senate and House of Representatives or in the parliaments and palaces of the world—have been dutifully reported in the media, then filed away and, for the most part, forgotten.

The editors of *WHAT THEY SAID* believe that consigning such a wealth of thoughts, ideas, doctrines, opinions and philosophies to interment in the morgues and archives of the Fourth Estate is lamentable and unnecessary. Yet the media, in all their forms, are constantly engulfing us in a profusion of endless and increasingly voluminous news reports. One is easily disposed to disregard or forget the stimulating discussion of critical issues embodied in so many of the utterances of those who make the news and, in their respective fields, shape the events throughout the world. The conclusion is therefore a natural and compelling one: the educator, the public official, the business executive, the statesman, the philosopher—everyone who has a stake in the complex, often confusing trends of our times—should have material of this kind readily available.

These, then, are the circumstances under which *WHAT THEY SAID* was conceived. It is the culmination of a year of listening to the people in the public eye; a year of scrutinizing, monitoring, reviewing, judging, deciding—a year during which the editors resurrected from almost certain oblivion those quintessential elements of the year's *spoken* opinion which, in their judgment, demanded preservation in book form.

WHAT THEY SAID is a pioneer in its field. Its *raison d'etre* is the firm conviction that presenting, each year, the highlights of vital and interesting views from the lips of prominent people on virtually every aspect of contemporary civilization fulfills the need to give the *spoken* word the permanence and lasting value of the *written* word. For, if it is true that a picture is worth 10,000 words, it is equally true that a verbal conclusion, an apt quote or a candid comment by a person of fame or influence can have more significance and can provide more understanding than an entire page of summary in a standard work of reference.

The editors of *WHAT THEY SAID* did not, however, design their book for researchers and

v

PREFACE TO THE FIRST EDITION (1969)

scholars alone. One of the failings of the conventional reference work is that it is blandly written and referred to primarily for facts and figures, lacking inherent "interest value." *WHAT THEY SAID*, on the other hand, was planned for sheer enjoyment and pleasure, for searching glimpses into the lives and thoughts of the world's celebrities, as well as for serious study, intellectual reflection and the philosophical contemplation of our multifaceted life and mores. Furthermore, those pressed for time, yet anxious to know what the newsmakers have been saying, will welcome the short excerpts which will make for quick, intermittent reading—and rereading. And, of course, the topical classifications, the speakers' index, the subject index, the place and date information—documented and authenticated and easily located—will supply a rich fund of hitherto not readily obtainable reference and statistical material.

Finally, the reader will find that the editors have eschewed trite comments and cliches, tedious and boring. The selected quotations, each standing on its own, are pertinent, significant, stimulating—above all, relevant to today's world, expressed in the speakers' own words. And they will, the editors feel, be even more relevant tomorrow. They will be re-examined and reflected upon in the future by men and women eager to learn from the past. The prophecies, the promises, the "golden dreams," the boastings and rantings, the bluster, the bravado, the pleadings and representations of those whose voices echo in these pages (and in those to come) should provide a rare and unique history lesson. The positions held by these luminaries, in their respective callings, are such that what they say today may profoundly affect the future as well as the present, and so will be of lasting importance and meaning.

Beverly Hills, California

ALAN F. PATER
JASON R. PATER

Table of Contents

Editorial Treatment

ORGANIZATION OF MATERIAL

Special attention has been given to the arrangement of the book—from the major divisions down to the individual categories and speakers—the objective being a logical progression of related material, as follows:

(A) The categories are arranged alphabetically within each of three major sections:

Part One: "National Affairs"

Part Two: "International Affairs"

Part Three: "General"

In this manner, the reader can quickly locate quotations pertaining to particular fields of interest (see also *Indexing*). It should be noted that some quotations contain a number of thoughts or ideas—sometimes on different subjects—while some are vague as to exact subject matter and thus do not fit clearly into a specific topic classification. In such cases, the judgment of the Editors has determined the most appropriate category.

(B) Within each category the speakers are in alphabetical order by surname, following alphabetization practices used in the speaker's country of origin.

(C) Where there are two or more quotations by one speaker within the same category, they appear chronologically by date spoken or date of source.

SPEAKER IDENTIFICATION

(A) The occupation, profession, rank, position or title of the speaker is given as it was *at the time the statement was made* (except when the speaker's relevant identification is in the past, in which case he is shown as "former"). Thus, due to possible changes in status during the year, a speaker may be shown with different identifications in various parts of the book, or even within the same category.

(B) In the case of a speaker who holds more than one position simultaneously, the judgment of the Editors has determined the most appropriate identification to use with a specific quotation.

(C) Nationality of the speakers is given only when it is relevant to the specific quotation.

THE QUOTATIONS

The quoted material selected for inclusion in this book is shown as it appeared in the source, except as follows:

WHAT THEY SAID IN 1985

(A) *Ellipses* have been inserted wherever the Editors have deleted extraneous words or overly long passages within the quoted material used. In no way has the meaning or intention of the quotations been altered. *Ellipses* are also used where they appeared in the source.

(B) *Punctuation and spelling* have been altered by the Editors where they were obviously incorrect in the source, or to make the quotations more intelligible, or to conform to the general style used throughout this book. Again, meaning and intention of the quotations have not been changed.

(C) *Brackets* ([]) indicate material inserted by the Editors or by the source to either correct obvious errors or to explain or clarify what the speaker is saying. In some instances, bracketed material may replace quoted material for the sake of clarity.

(D) *Italics* either appeared in the original source or were added by the Editors where emphasis is clearly desirable.

Except for the above instances, the quoted material used has been printed verbatim, as reported by the source (even if the speaker made factual errors or was awkward in his choice of words). Special care has been exercised to make certain that each quotation stands on its own and is not taken "out of context." The Editors, however, cannot be responsible for errors made by the original source, i.e., incorrect reporting, mis-quotations, or errors in interpretation.

DOCUMENTATION AND SOURCES

Documentation (circumstance, place, date) of each quotation is provided as fully as could be obtained, and the sources are furnished for all quotations. In some instances, no documentation details were available; in those cases, only the source is given. Following are the sequence and style used for this information:

Circumstance of quotation, place, date/Name of source, date:section (if applicable), page number.

Example: *Before the Senate, Washington, Dec. 4/The Washington Post, 12-5:(A)3.*

The above example indicates that the quotation was delivered before the Senate in Washington on December 4. It was taken for *WHAT THEY SAID* from *The Washington Post*, issue of December 5, section A, page 13. (When a newspaper publishes more than one edition on the same date, it should be noted that page numbers may vary from edition to edition.)

(A) When the source is a television or radio broadcast, the name of the network or local station is indicated, along with the date of the broadcast (obviously, page and section information does not apply).

(B) An asterisk (*) before the (/) in the documentation indicates that the quoted material was written rather than spoken. Although the basic policy of *WHAT THEY SAID* is to use only *spoken* statements, there are occasions when written statements are considered by the Editors to be important enough to be included. These occasions are rare and usually involve Presidential messages and statements released to the press and other such documents attributed to persons in high government office.

INDEXING

(A) The *Index to Speakers* is keyed to the page number. (For alphabetization practices, see

Organization of Material, paragraph B.)

(B) The *Index to Subjects* is keyed to both the page number and the quotation number on the page (thus 210:3 indicates quotation number 3 on page 210); the quotation number appears at the right corner of each quotation.

(C) To locate quotations on a particular subject, regardless of the speaker, turn to the appropriate category (see *Table of Contents*) or use the detailed *Index to Subjects*.

(D) To locate all quotations by a particular speaker, regardless of subject, use the *Index to Speakers*.

(E) To locate quotations by a particular speaker on a particular subject, turn to the appropriate category and then to that person's quotations within the category.

(F) The reader will find that the basic categorization format of *WHAT THEY SAID* is itself a useful subject index, inasmuch as related quotations are grouped together by their respective categories. All aspects of journalism, for example, are relevant to each other; thus, the section *Journalism* embraces all phases of the news media. Similarly, quotations pertaining to the U.S. President, Congress, etc., are in the section *Government*.

MISCELLANEOUS

(A) Except where otherwise indicated or obviously to the contrary, all universities, organizations and business firms mentioned in this book are in the United States; similarly, references made to "national," "Federal," "this country," "the nation," etc., refer to the United States.

(B) In most cases, organizations whose names end with "of the United States" are Federal government agencies.

SELECTION OF CATEGORIES

The selected categories reflect, in the Editors' opinion, the most widely discussed public-interest subjects, those which readily fall into the over-all sphere of "current events." They represent topics continuously covered by the mass media because of their inherent importance to the changing world scene. Most of the categories are permanent; they appear in each annual edition of *WHAT THEY SAID*. However, because of the transient character of some subjects, there may be categories which appear one year and may not be repeated the next.

SELECTION OF SPEAKERS

The following persons are always considered eligible for inclusion in *WHAT THEY SAID*: top-level officials of all branches of national, state and local governments (both U.S. and foreign), including all United States Senators and Representatives; top-echelon military officers; college and university presidents, chancellors and professors; chairmen and presidents of major corporations; heads of national public-oriented organizations and associations; national and internationally known diplomats; recognized celebrities from the entertainment and literary spheres and the arts generally; sports figures of national stature; commentators on the world scene who are recognized as such and who command the attention of the mass media.

The determination of what and who are "major" and "recognized" must, necessarily, be made by the Editors of *WHAT THEY SAID* based on objective personal judgment.

Also, some persons, while not generally recognized as prominent or newsworthy, may have nevertheless attracted an unusual amount of attention in connection with an important issue or event. These people, too, are considered for inclusion, depending upon the specific circumstance.

SELECTION OF QUOTATIONS

The quotations selected for inclusion in *WHAT THEY SAID* obviously represent a decided minority of the seemingly endless volume of quoted material appearing in the media each year. The process of selecting is scrupulously objective insofar as the partisan views of the Editors are concerned (see *About Fairness*, below). However, it is clear that the Editors must decide which quotations *per se* are suitable for inclusion, and in doing so look for comments that are aptly stated, offer insight into the subject being discussed, or into the speaker, and provide—for today as well as for future reference—a thought which readers will find useful for understanding the issues and the personalities that make up a year on this planet.

ABOUT FAIRNESS

The Editors of *WHAT THEY SAID* understand the necessity of being impartial when compiling a book of this kind. As a result, there has been no bias in the selection of the quotations, the choice of speakers or the manner of editing. Relevance of the statements and the status of the speakers are the exclusive criteria for inclusion, without any regard whatsoever to the personal beliefs and views of the Editors. Furthermore, every effort has been made to include a multiplicity of opinions and ideas from a wide cross-section of speakers on each topic. Nevertheless, should there appear to be, on some controversial issues, a majority of material favoring one point of view over another, it is simply the result of there having been more of those views expressed during the year, reported by the media and objectively considered suitable by the Editors of *WHAT THEY SAID* (see *Selection of Quotations*, above). Also, since persons in politics and government account for a large percentage of the speakers in *WHAT THEY SAID*, there may exist a heavier weight of opinion favoring the philosophy of those in office at the time, whether in the United States Congress, the Administration, or in foreign capitals. This is natural and to be expected and should not be construed as a reflection of agreement or disagreement with that philosophy on the part of the Editors of *WHAT THEY SAID*.

Abbreviations

The following are abreviations used by the speakers in this volume. Rather than defining them each time they appear in the quotations, this list will facilitate reading and avoid unnecessary repetition.

ABC: American Broadcasting Companies
ABM: anti-ballistic missile
ABT: American Ballet Theatre
ACLU: American Civil Liberties Union
AFL: American Football League
AFL-CIO: American Federation of Labor-Congress of Industrial Organizations
AIDS: acquired immune deficiency syndrome
ANC: African National Congress
ANZUS: Australia, New Zealand, United States defense treaty
BBC: British Broadcasting Corporation
CBS: Columbia Broadcasting System (CBS, Inc.)
CCC: Civilian Conservation Corps
CEO: chief executive officer
CFC: chlorofluorocarbons
CIA: Central Intelligence Agency
CNN: Cable News Network
CPA: certified public accountant
DEA: Drug Enforcement Administration
DH: designated hitter
DOD: Department of Defense
DOT: Department of Transportation
EPA: Environmental Protection Agency
FBI: Federal Bureau of Investigation
FCC: Federal Communications Commission
FDA: Food and Drug Administration
FDIC: Federal Deposit Insurance Corporation
F.D.R.: Franklin Delano Roosevelt
FSLIC: Federal Savings and Loan Insurance Corporation
GM: General Motors Corporation
GNP: gross national product
IBM: International Business Machines Corporation
ICBM: intercontinental ballistic missile
IDF: Israeli Defense Forces

IRA: Irish Republican Army
IRS: Internal Revenue Service
KGB: Soviet secret police
MIA: missing in action
MIRV: multiple independently targeted re-entry vehicle (missile)
m.p.h.:   miles per hour
NATO: North Atlantic Treaty Organization
NBA: National Basketball Association
NBC: National Broadcasting Company
NCO: non-commissioned officer
NEA: National Education Association
NFL: National Football League
NPA: New People's Army
NUM: National Union of Mineworkers
OAS: Organization of American States
OMB: Office of Management and Budget
OPEC: Organization of Petroleum Exporting Countries
PAC: political action committee
PBS: Public Broadcasting Service
PLO: Palestine Liberation Organization
PR: public relations
R&D: research and development
SALT: strategic arms limitation talks
SBA: Small Business Administration
SDI: strategic defense initiative
SEC: Securities and Exchange Commission
TV: television
TWA: Trans World Airlines
UC: University of California
UDF: United Democratic Front
UN: United Nations
UNESCO: United Nations Educational, Scientific and Cultural Organization
UNITA: National Union for the Total Independence of Angola
U.S.:   United States
U.S.A.:   United States of America
USFL: United States Football League
U.S.S.R.:   Union of Soviet Socialist Republics
USTA: United States Tennis Association
VCR: video cassette recorder

V-J: Victor in Japan
WPA: Works Progress Administration
ZANU: Zimbabwe African National Union
ZAPU: Zimbabwe African People's Union

Party affiliation of United States Senators, Representatives and Governors—

    D: Democrat
    R: Republican

The Quote of the Year

Surely one of our highest charges in teaching is to teach what we ourselves have loved: The Call of the Wild, Beautiful Joe, Treasure Island, Swiss Family Robinson, Huckleberry Finn. If we remove this kind of content from our courses, we take away the very things that make students love to be students, and which lead to the improvement of skills. We should want every student to know how mountains are made, and that for most actions there is an equal and opposite reaction. They should know who said, "I am the state," and who said, "I have a dream." They should know about subjects and predicates, about isosceles triangles and eclipses. They should know where the Amazon flows, and what the First Amendment means. They should know about the Donner Party and slavery, about Shylock, Hercules and Abigail Adams; where Ethiopia is, and why there is a Berlin Wall. They should know a little about how a poem works, how a plant works and what "if wishes were horses, beggars would ride" means. They should know the place of the Milky Way and DNA in the unfolding of the universe. They should know something about the Convention of 1787 and about the conventions of good behavior. They should know a little of what the Sistine Chapel looks like and what great music sounds like. In certain places in America, there is a great zeal to remove certain things from study. Let us match that zeal for exclusion with a zeal for inclusion. As we decide what to teach our children, let us remember the advice of Wordsworth: "What we have loved, others will love, and we will teach them how."

—WILLIAM J. BENNETT
Secretary of Education of the United States; before National Press Club, Washington, March 27.

PART ONE

National Affairs

Presidential Inaugural Address

Delivered by Ronald Reagan, President of the United States, at the Capitol, Washington, January 21, 1985.

Senator Mathias, Chief Justice Burger, Vice President Bush, Speaker O'Neill, Senator Dole, Reverend Clergy and members of my family and friends, and my fellow citizens:

This day has been made brighter with the presence here of one who for a time has been absent. Senator John Stennis, God bless you and welcome back.

There is, however, one who is not with us today. Representative Gillis Long of Louisiana left us last night. And I wonder if we could all join in a moment of silent prayer.

Amen.

There are no words to—adequate to express my thanks for the great honor that you've bestowed on me. I will do my utmost to be deserving of your trust.

This is, as Senator Mathias told us, the 50th time that we, the people, have celebrated this historic occasion. When the first President, George Washington, placed his hand upon the Bible, he stood less than a single day's journey by horseback from raw, untamed wilderness. There were four million Americans in a Union of 13 states.

Today we are 60 times as many in a Union of 50 states. We've lighted the world with our inventions, gone to the aid of mankind wherever in the world there was a cry for help, journeyed to the moon and safely returned.

So much has changed. And yet we stand together as we did two centuries ago.

When I took this oath four years ago, I did so in a time of economic stress. Voices were raised saying that we had to look to our past for the greatness and glory. But we, the present-day Americans, are not given to looking backward. In this blessed land, there is always a better tomorrow.

Government and Freedom

Four years ago I spoke to you of a new beginning, and we have accomplished that. But in an-

other sense, our new beginning is a continuation of that beginning created two centuries ago when, for the first time in history, government, the people said, was not our master. It is our servant; its only power that which we, the people, allow it to have.

That system has never failed us. But for a time we failed the system. We asked things of government that government was not equipped to give. We yielded authority to the national government that properly belonged to states or to local governments or to the people themselves. We allowed taxes and inflation to rob us of our earnings and savings and watched the great industrial machine that had made us the most productive people on earth slow down and the number of unemployed increase.

By 1980, we knew it was time to renew our faith, to strive with all our strength toward the ultimate in individual freedom consistent with an orderly society.

We believed then and now there are no limits to growth and human progress when men and women are free to follow their dreams. And we were right. And we were right to believe that. Tax rates have been reduced, inflation cut dramatically, and more people are employed than ever before in our history.

We are creating a nation once again vibrant, robust and alive. But there are many mountains yet to climb. We will not rest until every American enjoys the fullness of freedom, dignity and opportunity as our birthright. It is our birthright as citizens of this great republic.

And if we meet this challenge, these will be years when Americans have restored their confidence and tradition of progress; when our values of faith, family, work and neighborhood were restated for a modern age; when our economy was finally freed from government's grip; when we made sincere efforts at meaningful arms reductions by rebuilding our defenses, our economy, and developing new technologies helped preserve peace in a troubled world; when America courageously supported the struggle for individual liberty, self-government and free enterprise throughout the world and turned the tide of history away from totalitarian

3

darkness and into the warm sunlight of human freedom.

My fellow citizens, our nation is poised for greatness. We must do what we know is right and do it with all our might. Let history say of us, these were golden years—when the American Revolution was reborn, when freedom gained new life and America reached for her best.

Our two-party system has solved us—served us, I should say, well over the years, but never better than in those times of great challenge, when we came together not as Democrats or Republicans but as Americans united in the common cause.

Adams and Jefferson

Two of our Founding Fathers, a Boston lawyer named Adams and a Virginia planter named Jefferson, members of that remarkable group who met in Independence Hall and dared to think they could start the world over again, left us an important lesson. They had become, in the years spent in government, bitter political rivals. In the Presidential election of 1800, then years later, when both were retired and age had softened their anger, they began to speak to each other again through letters.

A bond was re-established between those two who had helped create this government of ours.

In 1826, the 50th anniversary of the Declaration of Independence, they both died. They died on the same day, within a few hours of each other. And that day was the Fourth of July.

In one of those letters exchanged in the sunset of their lives, Jefferson wrote, ''It carries me back to the times when, beset with difficulties and dangers, we were fellow laborers in the same cause, struggling for what is most valuable to man, his right of self-government. Laboring always at the same oar, with some wave ever ahead threatening to overwhelm us, and yet passing harmless, we rode through the storm with heart and hand.''

Well, with heart and hand let us stand as one today: one people under God determined that our future shall be worthy of our past. As we do, we must not repeat the well-intentioned errors of our past. We must never again abuse the trust of

working men and women by sending their earnings on a futile chase after the spiraling demands of a bloated Federal establishment. You elected us in 1980 to end this prescription for disaster. And I don't believe you re-elected us in 1984 to reverse course.

The Economy

The heart of our efforts is one idea vindicated by 25 straight months of economic growth: freedom and incentives unleash the drive and entrepreneurial genius that are the core of human progress. We have begun to increase the rewards for work, savings and investment; reduce the increase in the cost and size of government and its interference in people's lives.

We must simplify our tax system, make it more fair, and bring the rates down for all who work and earn. We must think anew and move with a new boldness so every American who seeks work can find work; so the least among us shall have an equal chance to achieve the greatest things—to be heroes who heal our sick, feed the hungry, protect peace among nations and leave this world a better place.

The time has come for a new American emancipation, a great national drive to tear down economic barriers and liberate the spirit of enterprise in the most distressed areas of our country. My friends, together we can do this, and do it we must, so help me God.

From new freedom will spring new opportunities for growth, a more productive, fulfilled and united people and a stronger America, an America that will lead the technological revolution and also open its mind and heart and soul to the treasuries of literature, music and poetry, and the values of faith, courage and love.

A dynamic economy, with more citizens working and paying taxes, will be our strongest tool to bring down budget deficits. But an almost unbroken 50 years of deficit spending has finally brought us to a time of reckoning.

We've come to a turning point, a moment for hard decisions. I have asked the Cabinet and my staff a question, and now I put the same question to all of you. If not us, who? And if not now, when? It must be done by all of us going forward with a program aimed at reaching a balanced budget. We can then begin reducing the national debt.

I will shortly submit a budget to the Congress aimed at freezing government program spending for the next year. Beyond this, we must take further steps to permanently control government's power to tax and spend.

We must act now to protect future generations from government's desire to spend its citizens' money and tax them into servitude when the bills come due. Let us make it unconstitutional for the Federal Government to spend more than the Federal Government takes in.

We have already started returning to the people and to state and local governments responsibilities better handled by them. Now, there is a place for the Federal Government in matters of social compassion. But our fundamental goals must be to reduce dependency and upgrade the dignity of those who are infirm or disadvantaged. And here a growing economy and support from family and community offer our best chance for a society where compassion is a way of life, where the old and infirm are cared for, the young and, yes, the unborn, protected, and the unfortunate looked after and made self-sufficient.

Minorities

Now there is another area where the Federal Government can play a part. As an older American, I remember a time when people of different race, creed or ethnic origin in our land found hatred and prejudice installed in social custom and, yes, in law. There's no story more heartening in our history than the progress that we've made toward the brotherhood of man that God intended for us. Let us resolve: There will be no turning back or hesitation on the road to an America rich in dignity and abundant with opportunity for all our citizens.

Let us resolve that we, the people, will build an American opportunity society in which all of us—white and black, rich and poor, young and old—will go forward together, arm in arm. Again, let us remember that though our heritage is one of blood lines from every corner of the earth, we are all Americans pledged to carry on this last best hope of man on earth.

Peace and Defense

And I have spoken of our domestic goals, and the limitations we should put on our national government. Now let me turn to a task that is the primary responsibility of national government—the safety and security of our people.

Today we utter no prayer more fervently than the ancient prayer for peace on earth. Yet history has shown that peace does not come, nor will our freedom be preserved, by good will alone. There are those in the world who scorn our vision of human dignity and freedom. One nation, the Soviet Union, has conducted the greatest military buildup in the history of man, building arsenals of awesome offensive weapons.

We've made progress in restoring our defense capability. But much remains to be done. There must be no wavering by us, nor any doubts by others, that America will meet her responsibilities to remain free, secure, and at peace.

There is only one way safely and legitimately to reduce the cost of national security, and that is to reduce the need for it. And this we're trying to do in negotiations with the Soviet Union. We're not just discussing limits on a further increase of nuclear weapons. We seek, instead, to reduce their number. We seek the total elimination, one day, of nuclear weapons from the face of the earth.

Now for decades we and the Soviets have lived under the threat of mutual assured destruction; if either resorted to the use of nuclear weapons, the other could retaliate and destroy the one who had started it. Is there either logic or morality in believing that if one side threatens to kill tens of millions of our people, our only recourse is to threaten killing tens of millions of theirs?

I have approved a research program to find, if we can, a security shield that will destroy nuclear missiles before they reach their target. It wouldn't kill people, it would destroy weapons. It wouldn't militarize space, it would help demilitarize the arsenals of earth. It would render nuclear weapons obsolete. We will meet with the Soviets hoping that we can agree on a way to rid the world of the threat of nuclear destruction.

RONALD REAGAN

World Freedom and Democracy

We strive for peace and security, heartened by the changes all around us. Since the turn of the century, the number of democracies in the world has grown fourfold. Human freedom is on the march, and nowhere more so than in our own hemisphere. Freedom is one of the deepest and noblest aspirations of the human spirit. People worldwide hunger for the right of self-determination, for those inalienable rights that make for human dignity and progress.

America must remain freedom's staunchest friend, for freedom is our best ally, and it is the world's only hope to conquer poverty and preserve peace. Every blow we inflict against poverty will be a blow against its dark allies of oppression and war. Every victory for human freedom will be a victory for world peace.

So we go forward today a nation still mighty in its youth and powerful in its purpose. With our alliances strengthened, with our economy leading the world to a new age of economic expansion, we look to a future rich in possibilities. And all of this is because we worked and acted together, not as members of political parties, but as Americans.

My friends, we live in a world that's lit by lightning. So much is changing and will change, but so much endures and transcends time.

History is a ribbon, always unfurling; history is a journey. And as we continue on our journey we think of those who traveled before us. We stand again at the steps of this symbol of our democracy, or we would've been standing at the steps if it hadn't gotten so cold. Now, we're standing inside this symbol of our democracy, and we see and hear again the echoes of our past.

A general falls to his knees in the hard snow of Valley Forge; a lonely President paces the darkened halls and ponders, ponders his struggle to preserve the Union; the men of the Alamo call out encouragement to each other; a settler pushes west and sings a song, and the song echoes out forever and fills the unknowing air.

It is the American sound: It is hopeful, big-hearted, idealistic—daring, decent and fair. That's our heritage, that's our song. We sing it still. For all our problems, our differences, we are together as of old. We raise our voices to the God who is the author of this most tender music. And may He continue to hold us close as we fill the world with our sound—in unity, affection and love. One people under God, dedicated to the dream of freedom that He has placed in the human heart, called upon now to pass that dream on to a waiting and a hopeful world.

God bless you and may God bless America.

The State of the Union Address

Delivered by Ronald Reagan, President of the United States, at the Capitol, Washington, February 6, 1985.

Mr. Speaker, Mr. President, distinguished members of the Congress, honored guests and fellow citizens. I come before you to report on the state of our union. And I am pleased to report that, after four years of united effort, the American people have brought forth a nation renewed—stronger, freer and more secure than before.

Four years ago, we began to change—forever, I hope—our assumptions about government and its place in our lives. Out of that change has come great and robust growth—in our confidence, our economy and our role in the world.

Tonight, America is stronger because of the values we hold dear. We believe faith and freedom must be our guiding stars, for they show us truth, make us brave, give us hope and leave us wiser than we were. Our progress began not in Washington, D.C., but in the hearts of our families, communities, workplaces and voluntary groups, which, together, are unleashing the invincible spirit of one great nation under God.

Economic Growth

Four years ago, we said we would invigorate our economy by giving people greater freedom and incentives to take risks, and letting them keep more of what they earned.

We did what we promised, and a great industrial giant is reborn. Tonight we can take pride in 25 straight months of economic growth, the strongest in 34 years; a three-year inflation average of 3.9%, the lowest in 17 years; and 7.3 million new jobs in two years, with more of our citizens working than ever before.

New freedom in our lives has planted the rich seeds for future success:

For an America of wisdom that honors the family, knowing that, as the family goes, so goes our civilization;

For an America of vision that sees tomorrow's dreams in the learning and hard work we do today;

For an America of courage whose servicemen and women, even as we meet, proudly stand watch on the frontiers of freedom;

For an America of compassion that opens its heart to those who cry out for help.

We have begun well. But it's only a beginning. We are not here to congratulate ourselves on what we have done, but to challenge ourselves to finish what has not yet been done.

We are here to speak for millions in our inner cities who long for real jobs, safe neighborhoods and schools that truly teach. We are here to speak for the American farmer, the entrepreneur and every worker in industries fighting to modernize and compete. And, yes, we are here to stand, and proudly so, for all who struggle to break free from totalitarianism; for all who know in their hearts that freedom is the one true path to peace and human happiness.

Visions and Dreams

Proverbs tells us, without a vision, the people perish. When asked what great principle holds our union together, Abraham Lincoln said, "Something in [the] Declaration giving liberty, not alone to the people of this country, but hope to the world for all future time."

We honor the giants of our history not by going back, but forward to the dreams their vision foresaw. My fellow citizens, this nation is poised for greatness. The time has come to proceed toward a great new challenge—a Second American Revolution of hope and opportunity; a revolution carrying us to new heights of progress by pushing back frontiers of knowledge and space; a revolution of spirit that taps the soul of America, enabling us to summon greater strength than we have ever known; and a revolution that carries beyond our shores the golden promise of human freedom in a world at peace.

Let us begin by challenging conventional wisdom: There are no constraints on the human

7

mind, no walls around the human spirit, no barriers to our progress except those we ourselves erect. Already, pushing down tax rates has freed our economy to vault forward to record growth.

In Europe, they call it "the American Miracle." Day by day, we are shattering accepted notions of what is possible. When I was growing up, we failed to see how a new thing called radio would transform our marketplace. Well, today many have not yet seen how advances in technology are transforming our lives.

In the late 1950's, workers at the AT&T semiconductor plant in Pennsylvania produced five transistors a day for $7.50 apiece. They now produce over a million for less than a penny apiece.

New laser techniques could revolutionize heart bypass surgery, cut diagnosis time for viruses linked to cancer from weeks to minutes, reduce hospital costs dramatically and hold out new promise for saving human lives.

Our automobile industry has overhauled assembly lines, increased worker productivity and is competitive once again.

We stand on the threshold of a great ability to produce more, do more, be more. Our economy is not getting older and weaker, it's getting younger and stronger; it doesn't need rest and supervision—it needs new challenge, greater freedom. And that word—freedom—is the key to the Second American Revolution we mean to bring about.

Tax Reform

Let us move together with an historic reform of tax simplification for fairness and growth. Last year, I asked then-Treasury Secretary Regan to develop a plan to simplify the tax code, so all taxpayers would be treated more fairly, and personal tax rates could come further down.

We have cut tax rates by almost 25%, yet the tax system remains unfair and limits our potential for growth. Exclusions and exemptions cause similar incomes to be taxed at different levels. Low-income families face steep tax barriers that make hard lives even harder. The Treasury Department has produced an excellent reform plan whose principles will guide the final proposal we will ask you to enact.

One thing that tax reform will not be is a tax increase in disguise. We will not jeopardize the mortgage interest deduction families need. We will reduce personal tax rates as low as possible by removing many tax preferences. We will propose a top rate of no more than 35%, and possibly lower. And we will propose reducing corporate rates while maintaining incentives for capital formation.

To encourage opportunity and jobs rather than dependency and welfare, we will propose that individuals living at or near the poverty line be totally exempt from federal income tax. To restore fairness to families, we will propose increasing significantly the personal exemption.

And tonight, I am instructing Treasury Secretary James Baker—I have to get used to saying that—to begin working with congressional authors and committees for bipartisan legislation conforming to these principles. We will call upon the American people for support, and upon every man and woman in this chamber. Together, we can pass, this year, a tax bill for fairness, simplicity and growth making this economy the engine of our dreams, and America the investment capital of the world—so let us begin.

Tax simplification will be a giant step toward unleashing the tremendous pent-up power of our economy. But a Second American Revolution must carry the promise of opportunity for all. It is time to liberate the spirit of enterprise in the most distressed areas of our country.

Minority and Youth Employment

This government will meet its responsibility to help those in need. But policies that increase dependency, break up families and destroy self-respect are not progressive, they are reactionary. Despite our stride in civil rights, blacks, Hispanics and all minorities will not have full and equal power until they have full economic power.

We have repeatedly sought passage of enterprise zones to help those in the abandoned corners of our land find jobs, learn skills and build better lives. This legislation is supported by a majority of you. There must be no forgotten Americans. Let us place new dreams in a million hearts and create a

8

new generation of entrepreneurs by passing enterprise zones this year.

Tip [Speaker of the House Thomas P. O'Neill, Jr.], you can make that a birthday present.

Nor must we lose the chance to pass our Youth Employment Opportunity Wage proposal. We can help teen-agers who have the highest unemployment rate find summer jobs, so they can know the pride of work, and have confidence in their futures.

We will continue to support the Job Training Partnership Act, which has a nearly two-thirds job placement rate. Passage of tuition tax credits and education and health-care vouchers will help working families shop for services they need.

Our Administration is already encouraging certain low-income public housing residents to own and manage their own dwellings. It is time all public housing residents have that opportunity of ownership.

The federal government can help create a new atmosphere of freedom. But states and localities, many of which enjoy surpluses from the recovery, must not permit their tax and regulatory policies to stand as barriers to growth.

Let us resolve that we will stop spreading dependency and start spreading opportunity; that we will stop spreading bondage and start spreading freedom.

There are some who say that growth initiatives must await final action on deficit reductions. The best way to reduce deficits is through economic growth. More businesses will be started, more investments made, more jobs created and more people will be on payrolls paying taxes. The best way to reduce government spending is to reduce the need for spending by increasing prosperity. Each added percentage point per year of real GNP growth will lead to a cumulative reduction in deficits of nearly $200 billion over five years.

Spending and Deficits

To move steadily toward a balanced budget we must also lighten government's claim on our total economy. We will not do this by raising taxes. We must make sure that our economy grows faster than growth in spending by the federal government. In our fiscal year 1986 budget, overall government program spending will be frozen at the current level; it must not be one dime higher than fiscal year 1985. And three points are key:

First, the social safety net for the elderly, needy, disabled and unemployed will be left intact. Growth of our major health care programs, Medicare and Medicaid, will be slowed, but protections for the elderly and needy will be preserved.

Second, we must not relax our efforts to restore military strength just as we near our goal of a fully equipped, trained and ready professional corps. National security is government's first responsibility, so, in past years, defense spending took about half the federal budget. Today, it takes less than a third.

We have already reduced our planned defense expenditures by nearly $100 billion over the past four years, and reduced projected spending again this year. You know, we only have a military industrial complex until a time of danger. Then it becomes the arsenal of democracy. Spending for defense is investing in things that are priceless: peace and freedom.

Third, we must reduce or eliminate costly government subsidies. For example, deregulation of the airline industry has led to cheaper airfares, but on Amtrak taxpayers pay about $35 per passenger every time an Amtrak train leaves the station. It's time we ended this huge federal subsidy.

Our farm program costs have quadrupled in recent years. Yet I know from visiting farmers, many in great financial distress, that we need an orderly transition to a market-oriented farm economy. We can help farmers best, not by expanding federal payments, but by making fundamental reforms, keeping interest rates heading down and knocking down foreign trade barriers to American farm exports.

We are moving ahead with Grace Commission reforms to eliminate waste and improve government's management practices. In the long run, we must protect the taxpayers from government. And I ask again that you pass, as 32 states have now called for, an amendment mandating the federal government spend no more than it takes in. And I ask for the authority used responsibly by 43 governors to veto individual items in appropriations bills. Sen. Mattingly has introduced a bill permitting a two-year trial run of the line-item veto. I hope you will pass and send that legislation to my desk.

RONALD REAGAN

Nearly 50 years of government living beyond its means has brought us to a time of reckoning. Ours is but a moment in history. But one moment of courage, idealism and bipartisan unity can change American history forever.

Sound monetary policy is key to long-running economic strength and stability. We will continue to cooperate with the Federal Reserve Board, seeking a steady policy that ensures price stability, without keeping interest rates artificially high or needlessly holding down growth.

Government Regulations

Reducing unneeded red tape and regulations, and deregulating the energy, transportation and financial industries, have unleashed new competition, giving consumers more choices, better services and lower prices. In just one set of grant programs, we have reduced 905 pages of regulations to 31.

We seek to fully deregulate natural gas to bring on new supplies and bring us closer to energy independence. Consistent with safety standards, we will continue removing restraints on the bus and railroad industries; we will soon send up legislation to return Conrail to the private sector, where it belongs; and we will support further deregulation of the trucking industry.

Every dollar the federal government does not take from us, every decision it does not make for us, will make our economy stronger, our lives more abundant, our future more free.

Space and Science

Our Second American Revolution will push on to new possibilities not only on Earth—but in the next frontier of space. Despite budget restraints, we will seek record funding for research and development.

We have seen the success of the space shuttle. Now we are going to develop a permanently manned space station, and new opportunities for free enterprise. In the next decade, Americans and our friends around the world will be living and working together in space.

In the zero-gravity of space we could manufac-

Abortion

The question of abortion grips our nation. Abortion is either the taking of human life, or it

ture in 30 days life-saving medicines it would take 30 years to make on Earth. We can make crystals of exceptional purity to produce super computers, creating jobs, technologies and medical breakthroughs beyond anything we ever dreamed possible.

As we do all this, we will continue to protect our natural resources. We will seek reauthorization and expanded funding for the super-fund program, to continue cleaning up hazardous waste sites which threaten human health and the environment.

Rediscovering Our Heritage

There is another great heritage to speak of this evening. Of all the changes that have swept America the past four years, none brings greater promise than our rediscovery of the value of faith, freedom, family, work and neighborhood.

We see signs of renewal in increased attendance in places of worship; renewed optimism and faith in our future; love of country rediscovered by our young who are leading the way. We have rediscovered that work is good in and of itself; that it ennobles us to create and contribute no matter how seemingly humble our jobs. We have seen a powerful new current from an old and honorable tradition—American generosity.

From thousands answering Peace Corps appeals to help boost food production in Africa, to millions volunteering time, corporations adopting schools and communities pulling together to help the neediest among us at home, we have refound our values. Private sector initiatives are crucial to our future.

I thank the Congress for passing equal access legislation giving religious groups the same right to use classrooms after school that other groups enjoy. But no citizen need tremble, nor the world shudder, if a child stands in a classroom and breathes a prayer. We ask you again—give children back a right they had for a century-and-a-half or more in this country.

isn't; and if it is—and medical technology is increasingly showing it is—it must be stopped.

It is a terrible irony that while some turn to abortion, so many others who cannot become parents cry out for children to adopt. We have room for these children; we can fill the cradles of those who want a child to love. Tonight I ask the Congress to move this year on legislation to protect the unborn.

Schools

In the area of education, we're returning to excellence, and again, the heroes are our people, not government. We're stressing basics of discipline, rigorous testing and homework, while helping children become computer-smart as well. For 20 years, Scholastic Aptitude Test scores of our high school students went down. But now they have gone up two of the last three years.

We must go forward in our commitment to the new basics, giving parents greater authority and making sure good teachers are rewarded for hard work and achievement through merit pay.

Crime

Of all the changes in the past 20 years, none has more threatened our sense of national well-being than the explosion of violent crime. One does not have to have been attacked to be a victim. The woman who must run to her car after shopping at night is a victim; the couple draping their door with locks and chains are victims; as is the tired, decent cleaning woman who can't ride a subway home without being afraid.

We do not seek to violate rights of defendants, but shouldn't we feel more compassion for victims of crime than for those who commit crime? For the first time in 20 years, the crime index has fallen two years in a row; we've convicted over 7,400 drug offenders, and put them, as well as leaders of organized crime, behind bars in record numbers.

But we must do more. I urge the House to follow the Senate and enact proposals permitting use of all reliable evidence that police officers acquire in good faith. These proposals would also reform the *habeus corpus* laws and allow, in keeping with the will of the overwhelming majority of Americans, the use of the death penalty where necessary.

There can be no economic revival in ghettos when the most violent among us are allowed to roam free. It is time we restored domestic tranquility. And we mean to do just that.

Defense

Just as we are positioned as never before to secure justice in our economy, we are poised as never before to create a safer, freer, more peaceful world.

Our alliances are stronger than ever. Our economy is stronger than ever. We have resumed our historic role as a leader of the Free World—and all of these together are a great force for peace.

Arms Agreements

Since 1981, we have been committed to seeking fair and verifiable arms agreements that would lower the risk of war and reduce the size of nuclear arsenals. Now our determination to maintain a strong defense has influenced the Soviet Union to return to the bargaining table. Our negotiators must be able to go to that table with the united support of the American people. All of us have no greater dream than to see the day when nuclear weapons are banned from this Earth forever.

Each member of the Congress has a role to play in modernizing our defenses, thus supporting our chances for a meaningful arms agreement. Your vote this spring on the Peacekeeper missile will be a critical test of our resolve to maintain the strength we need and move toward mutual and verifiable arms reductions.

For the past 20 years we have believed that no war will be launched as long as each side knows it can retaliate with a deadly counter strike. Well, I believe there is a better way of eliminating the threat of nuclear war.

It is a Strategic Defense Initiative aimed ultimately at finding a non-nuclear defense against ballistic missiles. It is the most hopeful possibility of the nuclear age. But it is not very well understood.

Some say it will bring war to the heavens—but

its purpose is to deter war, in the heavens and on Earth. Some say the research would be expensive. Perhaps, but it could save millions of lives, indeed humanity itself. Some say if we build such a system, the Soviets will build a defense system of their own. Well, they already have strategic defenses that surpass ours; a civil defense system, where we have almost none; and a research program covering roughly the same areas of technology we're exploring. And finally, some say the research will take a long time. The answer to that is: "Let's get started."

Freedom and Democracy

Harry Truman once said that, ultimately, our security, and the world's hopes for peace and human progress, "lie not in measures of defense or in the control of weapons, but in the growth and expansion of freedom and self-government."

Tonight, we declare anew to our fellow citizens of the world: freedom is not the sole prerogative of a chosen few; it is the universal right of all God's children. Look to where peace and prosperity flourish today. It is in homes that freedom built. Victories against poverty are greatest and peace most secure where people live by laws that ensure free press, free speech and freedom to worship, vote and create wealth.

Our mission is to nourish and defend freedom and democracy, and to communicate these ideals everywhere we can.

America's economic success is freedom's success; it can be repeated a hundred times in a hundred different nations. Many countries in East Asia and the Pacific have few resources other than the enterprise of their own people. But through low tax rates and free markets, they have soared ahead of centralized economies. And now China is opening up its economy to meet its needs.

Foreign Trade and Aid

We need a stronger and simpler approach to the process of making and implementing trade policy and will be studying potential changes in that process in the next few weeks.

We have seen the benefits of free trade and lived through the disasters of protectionism. Tonight, I ask all our trading partners, developed and developing alike, to join us in a new round of trade negotiations to expand trade and competition, and strengthen the global economy—and to begin it in the next year.

There are more than 3 billion human beings living in Third World countries, with an average per capita income of $650 a year. Many are victims of dictatorships that impoverish them with taxation and corruption. Let us ask our allies to join us in a practical program of trade and assistance that fosters economic development through personal incentives to help these people climb from poverty on their own.

We cannot play innocents abroad in a world that is not innocent. Nor can we be passive when freedom is under siege. Without resources, diplomacy cannot succeed; our security assistance programs help friendly governments defend themselves, and give them confidence to work for peace. Congress should understand that, dollar for dollar, security assistance contributes as much to global security as our own defense budget.

Stand By Friends and Allies

We must stand by all our democratic allies. And we must not break faith with those who are risking their lives—on every continent, from Afghanistan to Nicaragua—to defy Soviet supported aggression and secure rights which have been ours from birth.

The Sandinista dictatorship of Nicaragua, with full Cuban Soviet-bloc support, not only persecutes its people, the church and denies a free press, but arms and provides bases for communist terrorists attacking neighboring states. Support for freedom fighters is self-defense, and totally consistent with the O.A.S. and U.N. charters. It is essential that the Congress continue all facets of our assistance to Central America. I want to work with you to support the democratic forces whose struggle is tied to our own security.

Opportunity in America

Tonight I have spoken of great plans and great

79 years ago, she lives in the inner city where she cares for infants born of mothers who are heroin addicts. The children born in withdrawal are sometimes even dropped on her doorstep. She helps them with love. Go to her house some night and maybe you see her silhouette against the window. She walks the floor, talking softly, soothing a child in her arms. Mother Hale of Harlem, and she, too, is an American hero.

Jean, Mother Hale, your lives tell us that the oldest American saying is new again: Anything is possible in America if we have the faith, the will and the heart.

History is asking us, once again, to be a force for good in the world. Let us begin—in unity, with justice and love.

Thank you and God bless you.

dreams. They are dreams we can make come true. Two hundred years of American history should have taught us that nothing is impossible.

Ten years ago the young girl left Vietnam with her family, part of the exodus that followed the fall of Saigon. They came to the United States with no possessions and not knowing a word of English. Ten years ago the young girl studied hard, learned English and finished high school at the top of her class. And this May, May 22 to be exact, is a big date on her calendar. Just 10 years from the time she left Vietnam, she will graduate from the United States Military Academy at West Point.

I thought you might like to meet an American hero named Jean Nguyen.

Now, there is someone else here tonight. Born

The American Scene

Robert M. Ball
Former Commissioner,
Social Security Administration
of the United States

1

. . . we seem to have moved into a period when our national leaders are teaching an extreme individualism that would make us forget our shared concerns . . . If each of us pursues a life dedicated to getting the most we can for ourselves, it will not automatically follow that the community will be better off. There is a law of reciprocal obligation. The community has given us the opportunity to succeed—although it is true that only we can seize that opportunity—and to the extent that we do succeed we owe something back. We owe the obligations of a responsible citizen to participate in the great decisions of our time. At the minimum, we owe the obligation to pay cheerfully for our fair share of government, the major expression of our collective enterprise.

At University of Maryland commencement,
June 9/The Washington Post, 6-21:(A)22.

Mikhail Baryshnikov
Ballet dancer

2

[On his adjustment to the U.S. after defecting from the Soviet Union 11 years ago]: Let's see, how American am I? Well, I'm not a Yankee fan or a Forty-Niner, and I don't like Coca-Cola or pink shirts. But I love television, fast cars and corn. That's pretty American.

Interview/Time, 7-8:88.

Mario M. Cuomo
Governor of New York (D)

3

We need people who understand how all the parts relate, who know that unless we infuse all our strivings and compassion with intelligent concern for the common good, then we will be just another rich and affluent society that struts and frets its hour on the world stage.

At Colgate University commencement, May 26/
The New York Times, 5-27:11.

4

[Supporting the idea of residents of one area of the country paying, through distribution of taxes, for projects in other parts of the country]: Is it right that the residents of New Jersey spend their money to subsidize farmers in Iowa? Why do Iowans contribute to mass transit in New Jersey? Why do the people of Alabama help build dams in the Northwest? And why do people in the Northwest help construct the Tennessee-Tombigbee waterway? A central idea at the heart of our republic [is] that we are one nation, not 50 nations, and that we are strongest when we stand together and help each other.

Before House Ways and Means Committee,
Washington, July 17/The New York Times, 7-18:23.

E. L. Doctorow
Author

5

. . . however bad things were in the 1930s—and they were very bad—people seemed to be more connected with their lives. They knew what was happening to them, whereas today we are so much appreciably better off—but some lines have been cut, some kind of circuit has flipped out in our self-perception . . . See, the thing about people in those days was that they sought to live morally, they had some connection with what they valued, with what's true and what's fair and what's just. [Today,] we have been making so many moral concessions in return for our comforts that something is broken somewhere in our national psyche. If that's true, you can understand why not only the writers are looking back but everyone is looking back, and why there's this sort of cultural ceremony of looking back to try to find that time when it all worked somehow.

Interview, Los Angeles/
Los Angeles Times, 12-11:(V)9.

Tom J. Farer
President, University of New Mexico

6

We Americans live more easily with vast differences in wealth and income than any other

15

(TOM J. FARER)

people in the West. We do so for two reasons. First, because our culture continues to nurture belief in political and social equality: The rich are not allowed to indulge the belief that they are in some sense morally superior or that they have a right to demand signs of deference. In fact, it is one of the characteristics of the American rich to pretend, even as they descend from large, shiny and conspicuously expensive cars under the canopies of conspicuously expensive hotels, that they are just good ol' boys who like lite beer no less than [sports stars] Dick Butkus and Bubba Smith who by now, one imagines, must be pretty well off themselves. The second reason we live fairly comfortably with large and manifest inequalities of wealth and economic power is a twinned belief in the possibility of social mobility and, consequently, in a connection between economic success and merit or, if not merit, at least luck, other than the luck of having been born rich, although even in that case, it is presumed that this generation's wealth is justified by the skill and hard work of its predecessors. There are those who argue that social mobility is largely a myth sustained by cheap novels, expensive movies, a handful of anecdotes and a desperate desire to believe . . . I suppose there is some truth to that charge. The achievements of our families do give us handicaps or advantages in the race of life. Nevertheless, it is not hard to be impressed by the evidence of social mobility over generations.

Commencement address, May 12/
The Washington Post, 7-11:(A)20.

John Fowles
Author

1

New York is an impossibly rich city. There is so much to do here that one does nothing, so much to buy here that one buys nothing. I read my way through the fat Sunday *New York Times* and it calls out "Consume more . . . consume more . . . consume more." I somehow feel places like New York are enormously rarified, isolated forms of human society. They're not real. It's not just flying to New York, it's flying to a different planet. If you fly to Los Angeles, it's another planet still.

Interview, New York/
The Washington Post, 9-12:(C)8.

Hayden Fry
Football coach, University of Iowa

2

I remember President Eisenhower made a statement once. Somebody asked him why he ever bought that farm of his in Gettysburg [Pa.]. He told them that all his life he wanted to take a piece of ground that really hadn't been cared for or cultivated or fertilized or watered, and work with everything he had and leave it in better condition than he found it. It's a simple statement, but I think maybe many men in life, regardless of their profession, have that inner urge to make a winner of a loser. That's the American way of life, I think. There's no challenge too big for anyone.

Interview, Iowa City, Iowa/
Los Angeles Times, 10-28:(II)13.

Lawrence H. Fuchs
Chairman of American Studies,
Brandeis University

3

What binds Americans to one another, regardless of ethnicity or religion, is an American civic culture. It is the basis for the *unum* in *E pluribus unum*. It is a complex of ideals, behaviors, institutions, symbols and heroes connected by American history and its great documents: the Declaration of Independence, the Bill of Rights, the Gettysburg Address. It is backed by a civil religion giving transcendent significance to those ideals. And it is the basis for accepting ethnic diversity while protecting individual rights. An American can be as ethnic as he or she wishes in private actions, but in public actions, the rules of the civic culture are binding.

Time, 7-8:33.

Harold H. Greene
Judge, United States District Court
for the District of Columbia

4

All we need to ask is, where is it difficult to get exit visas? Where are walls built to keep people in? Where is it dangerous even to communicate with the outside? When people are free to come and go as they please, America and its

(HAROLD H. GREENE)

freedom are most often their destination. There can be no greater vote of confidence, nor more meaningful election.

At naturalization ceremony, Washington, Feb. 12/The Washington Post, 2-13:(A)6.

George F. Kennan
Former United States Ambassador to the Soviet Union

1

A country of this size [the U.S.], with so many varieties of people, can be governed only by a very elaborate system of compromises that results in a least common denominator. It is primitive, inflexible and anchored in emotional states and prejudices . . . Probably the way this country is being ruled is the only way it can be ruled. But for a country to be ruled in this way disqualifies it for active participation in the world.

Interview/Esquire, January:75.

Ted Koppel
Anchorman, "Nightline," ABC-TV

2

The mass media are creating a market for mediocrity. We've diminished the incentive for excellence. In business, individual responsibility has been defused into corporate nonaccountability. Our criminal-justice system is becoming a playground for the rich and a burial ground for the poor. Unless we restore a sense of genuine value to what we do in each of our chosen professions, we will find that even the unprecedented flexibility of the American system can and will reach a breaking point.

At Middlebury (Vt.) College commencement/ USA Today, 6-3:(A)11.

Richard D. Lamm
Governor of Colorado (D)

3

While other countries have been investing in their future, we've been mortgaging ours. We train lawyers, accountants and real-estate sales-

men; they train scientists and engineers. They build factories; we build overopulent homes. The United States has not been disciplined enough to solve its problems.

Interview/USA Today, 10-23:(A)11.

4

The good news is that there is a capacity for renewal in our country. You look at the revolutions of our time—the civil-rights movement, the women's movement, the consumer movement, the environmental movement. Who would have imagined that, for all the problems, you could go to a law school today and 50 per cent of the students are women? You really are seeing how, once a democracy starts asking the right questions, it starts finding the right responses.

Interview/U.S. News & World Report, 12-16:60.

Arthur Mann
Professor of history, University of Chicago

5

One of the conditions of being an American is to be aware of the fact that a whole lot of people around you are different—different in their origins, their religions, their life-styles.

Time, 7-8:27.

Ronald Reagan
President of the United States

6

The family is the moral core of our society, the repository of our values and the preserver of our traditions . . . the safe haven where we've taught charity, generosity and love . . . In raising the next generation of Americans, the tired breadwinner and the exhausted homemaker are doing the essential work of our society.

At rally of his supporters, Washington, May 29/ Los Angeles Times, 5-30:(I)14.

7

I'm not optimistic about the future of America because I have a sunny disposition, and I'm not optimistic because I don't know the realities. I'm optimistic because I do know them. I'm optimistic because I have witnessed the American experience for more than seven dec-

(RONALD REAGAN)

ades, and I know that the American people can do anything.

At rally, Bloomfield, N.J., June 13/
The New York Times, 6-14:32.

1

[On the White House]: Sometimes I want to say to those who are still in school, and who sometimes think that history is a dry thing that lives in a book: Nothing is ever lost in that great house; some music plays on. I have been told that late at night when the clouds are still and the moon is high, you can just about hear the sound of certain memories brushing by. You can almost hear, if you listen close, the whir of [Franklin Roosevelt's] wheelchair rolling by and the sound of a voice calling out, "And another thing, Eleanor!" Turn down a hall and you can hear the brisk strut of a fellow [Theodore Roosevelt] saying, "Bully! Absolutely ripping!" Walk softly now and you're drawn to the soft notes of a piano and a brilliant gathering in the East Room, where a crowd surrounds a bright young President [John Kennedy] who is full of hope and laughter. I don't know if this is true . . . but it's a story I've been told. And it's not a bad one, because it reminds us that history is a living thing that never dies. A life given in service to one's country is a living thing that never dies.

At dinner after fund-raiser for John F. Kennedy
Library/Los Angeles Times,
6-27:(II)7.

2

[This] generation is subject to more information than any generation in history. Let me suggest one thing: don't let me get away with it. Check me out, but check everybody else out. Don't just take it for granted because you read it someplace or because someone stood up in a lecture course and told you from a lecture platform. Check it out. Don't be the sucker generation. You are the brightest and the best, and make sure that you are hearing the facts, not just somebody's opinions. And, as I say, that goes for me, too. Check me out.

Interview with college students, Washington,
Sept. 9/The New York Times, 9-11:6.

Donald T. Regan
Chief of Staff to the President of the United States

3

When you're born in America, so much comes free . . . You inherit a brilliant and decent political tradition, you get a rich and varied culture, you get the freedom to make your own decisions, you get a society that still accepts the validity of spiritual beliefs and spiritual values—and you get all of this for free, just because you showed up. The way I see it, public service is a give-back . . . something you give back to the country that made your success possible. I hope someday you'll go into public service, and make a contribution. You really *can* make a difference. A nation as free as ours is endlessly open to change, to new ideas and leadership. It's not a stagnant environment. If you want to improve it, you can. If you look at where we were 10 years ago, and where we are now, you realize how far we've come, and how open to improvement our country is.

At University of Pennsylvania commencement/
The Christian Science Monitor, 6-20:19.

Guy de Rothschild
Banker

4

Americans are much more open than Europeans. They're open to new ideas, to contradictions, to other habits and other cultures. They like foreigners and are interested in them. I tend to say that "Americans like the elephant from the other circus" . . . There's no self-consciousness in this country about having money. The richest people in the world are Americans, along with a few Arabs. America is philosophically Protestant. That means God rewards moral behavior in this world with material success. By contrast, my native France is a Catholic country, even for a Jew. The reward for being a saint is when you are dead, for which I'm in no hurry. So the jealousy toward those who make money is much smaller here [in the U.S.] than in France. People in the United States are generous compared to Europeans. The average American is prepared to help others. You ask something of someone, and they immediately tend to say "Yes." The average European, however, is at best neutral and at worst sullen. Certainly that's the case in France.

Interview/U.S. News & World Report, 8-12:48.

Civil Rights • Women's Rights

Morris B. Abram
Vice Chairman,
United States Commission on Civil Rights

1

[The realigned Civil Rights Commission has] halted an express train taking us to preferences for every special-interest group. We feel good—we feel we are the right and moral side of the debate and we feel doubly good that the [recent Presidential] election outcome and polls show we are consonant with the feelings of most of the American public on quotas and other race preference. My impression is that [President Reagan] is delighted that a Commission which previously raised certain expectations and supported preference based on race has now halted that express train and redirected our studies. We're heading to equal opportunity for all and special opportunity for none. That means equal chances and no guarantees of equal results for all.

Washington, Jan. 29/
The Washington Post, 1-30:(A)2.

2

There is sex-based discrimination in America, but it is declining. The repetitious charge that women earn only 60 per cent of what men earn in this country obscures the significant fact that women work less hours, have less seniority and work more intermittently.

Washington, April 11/
The New York Times, 4-12:1.

3

[Arguing against affirmative-action programs]: I believe the government has the responsibility to address the needs of citizens as they occur, regardless of race, color, creed or sex. This includes meeting the need for remedial training and education among those who need it. But I object strenuously to the government using a racial, religious or sexual test to confer benefits or opportunities, because this introduces into society the concept not of equal individual rights but of group rights. Groups do not have needs as such, only individuals within groups have needs . . . Moreover, in a society as diverse as ours, composed of many races, creeds and religious beliefs, to confer advantage upon any particular racial grouping introduces the prospect of the Lebanonization of U.S. society, the most dangerous and divisive force one can experience. This is a belief I have held for 40 years while I've been involved in the civil-rights movement.

Interview, Richmond, Va./
USA Today, 5-6:(A)10.

4

[Arguing against affirmative-action programs]: I oppose quotas because they create an ethnic spoils system for certain groups to grab more power for their members—at the expense of individuals outside the group. That's contrary to our civil-rights laws that guarantee equal protection of civil rights for *all* Americans, not just for blacks, women and other minorities . . . Any individual who proves that he or she has been subject to discrimination is entitled to compensation under our civil-rights laws. But the fact that one black or a hundred blacks have been discriminated against in the past doesn't mean that Joe White Man, who didn't discriminate, can be replaced or prevented from getting a job so that Joe Black Man, who may never have suffered any discrimination, can be appointed. I don't know of any legal basis for groups being entitled to compensation regardless of whether or not individuals in that group have suffered any discrimination.

Interview/U.S. News & World Report, 5-27:50.

Bella Abzug
Women's-rights activist;
Former United States Representative,
D-New York

5

[On remarks by U.S. Presidential Chief of Staff Donald Regan that women would not understand the issues to be discussed at the U.S.-Soviet summit meeting in Geneva]: It's not true

(BELLA ABZUG)

that women don't care and don't know. Women know a lot more than men want to concede. It simply re-emphasizes what a lot of people think about a lot of people in this [Reagan] Administration—that there's a lack of sensitivity and a total misunderstanding of a full partnership for women. Even if it was not meant that way, I deplore the carelessness.

Interview, Nov. 20/
Los Angeles Times, 11-21:(I)9.

John Agresto
Acting Chairman, National Endowment for the Humanities of the United States

1

A year and a half ago . . . [the Endowment] discussed what race-based goals and timetables did to our best principles, our highest ideals. We objected because goals, quotas, set-asides and timetables put an undue burden on the just principle of American equality—the principle that no one should be rewarded or penalized, preferred or held back because of race or sex or creed. We thought, and we still think, that this was an ideal that all Americans, male or female, black or white, would hope to see prosper. We were told that "goals" were more benign than "quotas," that one was "flexible" and acceptable, the other "rigid" and wrong. But we also know and have seen . . . that such goals inevitably become standards of measurement indistinguishable from quotas themselves. For our own part . . . we have even seen our agency criticized for not satisfying some abstract notions of racial or sex-based balance. But more: We objected to goals not only because they invariably degenerate into quotas but because, on a moral basis, they are indistinguishable from quotas; for they require us to judge people on the basis of their sex and race. No matter how "flexible," no matter how hortatory they may be, "goals" and "timetables" still suffer from the same fatal and regressive flaw: They ask us to take into account a person's sex or race when we look to fill our jobs. They ask us to perpetuate and promote distinctions based on race and color.

Before House Employment Opportunities Subcommittee, Washington/The Washington Post, 8-2:(4)18.

Bernard E. Anderson
Visiting Fellow, Woodrow Wilson School of Public and International Affairs, Princeton University

2

[On those who criticize affirmative-action programs]: During the past few years a group of black conservatives has emerged as prominent critics of social policies designed to help the disadvantaged. But this new ideology is a curious application of conservative principles. Conservative principles advise prudence and caution . . . but the new conventional wisdom leads in the opposite direction. It is legitimate to ask what is conserved when there are thousands of minorities looking for work and unable to find it. What is conserved when the hopes, the dreams and aspirations of the future of young people are cruelly dashed upon the rocks of unemployment? . . . [Quotas are proper when there has been] denial of basic rights. Affirmative action in all other instances means no more and no less than taking special pains to remove all vestiges of discrimination by making sure qualified minorities and women are included in the relevant applicant pool and are seriously considered for available positions . . .

Before National Urban League, Washington, July 24/The Washington Post, 7-25:(A)15.

Ben F. Andrews
Connecticut state president, National Association for the Advancement of Colored People; Chairman, Hartford County Republican Party

3

During [President] Reagan's second term, black leaders must act quickly and decisively. I see Democrats pulling back their support of black issues. I see Republicans reaching out to blacks. [We must] beat the bushes for black support at the state and local levels. Blacks can't keep complaining about the Administration and wait four years, hoping for another Democratic President some day.

Interview/The Christian Science Monitor, 2-11:9.

Polly Baca
Colorado State Senator (D)

4

The only way for blacks, Hispanics and women to influence politics in this country is

(POLLY BACA)

through the Democratic Party. Hispanics went through that with La Raza Unida 15 years ago and found that minorities lose by forming third parties. They don't work when you have a majority of voters who don't consider themselves minorities.

Feb. 11/The Washington Post, 2-12:(A)3.

Gary Bauer
*Under Secretary
of Education of the United States*

1

When pornography is protected in the name of "freedom," our children receive a very disturbing message—since pornography is allowed, it is all right. And when pornography is defended by an appeal to lofty Constitutional principles, our children receive an even more disturbing message—that pornography is one of the "blessings of liberty" that our Constitution seeks to protect . . . Pornography is a threat to our democratic way of life. It is also a threat to the larger cause of Western culture. Nothing is more outrageous than hearing the purveyors of filth wrap themselves in the Constitution and accuse millions of decent men and women in communities across the land of being a threat to liberty. They have it exactly backwards.

At conference sponsored by National Consultation on Pornography, Cincinnati, Sept. 5/ The Washington Post, 9-6:(A)2.

William J. Bennett
Secretary of Education of the United States

2

[On the busing of school children for racial balance]: I do not favor compulsory assignment of students by racial count. The studies I have read over the years suggest to me that this kind of compulsory assignment by race is not effective education. I was born in Boston and watched that situation and saw the pain it caused for people in both communities—the people being bused and the community where the children were bused. There's no firm or reliable evidence that compulsory assignment of students by race improves the education of the children who take

part in it . . . Desegregation as a social goal, as an ideal, we should not abandon. But to be so specifically compulsory about it, in ways that we have been, to turn it into social policy and social engineering, is not the way to do it.

Interview/USA Today, 3-15:(A)11.

Mary Frances Berry
*Commissioner,
United States Civil Rights Commission*

3

[Criticizing the current makeup of the Civil Rights Commission, saying the majority is too supportive of the Reagan Administration]: The vote is 6 to 2 on almost every issue. The message of the Civil Rights Commission to every President since its inception has been: "We're the watchdog and if we bite you, don't be upset." One of the first things I did after I was appointed was to criticize something Jimmy Carter did and he was the one who had appointed me. But these [current Commissioners] feel they should speak with one voice, as part of the Administration. In the history of the Commission that is unheard of.

The New York Times, 8-26:10.

Rose Elizabeth Bird
*Chief Justice,
Supreme Court of California*

4

The poor and minorities, whether religious or racial, are singled out as the object of anger and discrimination in our society not because they are the cause of the problems which are perceived, but because they are the least able to defend themselves from criticism and attack.

Before Community Relations Committee of Jewish Federation Council, Los Angeles, March 8/Los Angeles Times, 3-9:(II)6.

Andrew F. Brimmer
Economist

5

I believe [racial] discrimination still exists. It is not as rampant as it once was, but more than an echo still remains. However, we have reached the point where the cutting edge is not discrimination but capability, capacity, marketa-

(ANDREW F. BRIMMER)

bility . . . The fundamental is that you have to be able to do it. So while discrimination still exists as more than an echo, I don't think it is the primary task we have to face.

Before Joint Center for Political Studies, Washington, March 21/ The Washington Post, 3-22:(A)3.

William E. Brock
Secretary of Labor of the United States

1

I think this country is going to have some form of affirmative action for a considerable period of time into the future. There is a distinction which you can make between absolute numbers and quotas and so-called goals approaches. But we as a country have lived for 200 years with a major part of our population in remarkable disadvantage. And it takes some time to recover from that. Maybe we [this generation of white Americans] were not here then. But that does not change the obligation we have as citizens to respond to that situation.

News conference, Dallas, June 24/ The Washington Post, 6-25:(A)4.

2

[Saying the Reagan Administration and black America must improve their relations]: Those words "we" and "they" will not be in the vocabulary at the Labor Department. I can tell you what will be our key words—trust, listen, try, try again, determination, new ideas, open mind and open door.

Before National Urban League, Washington, July 23/Los Angeles Times, 7-24:(I)2.

3

What does [affirmative action] mean? . . . It does not mean heavy-handed government edicts on absolute numerical quotas . . . Affirmative action is a statement of national will, of intent, of integrity . . . Does it mean everyone who does business with this government has to take exactly the same steps? Of course not. That would be to deny all that this country is about. Does it mean that one can have goals? Yes. But those goals can be set in different ways to respond to different situations.

Before National Urban League, Washington, July 23/The Washington Post, 7-24:(A)8.

Tony Brown
Chairman, Council for the Economic Development of Black Americans; Founding dean, School of Communications, Howard University

4

The race problem will never be resolved so long as the black movement insists that white people give up a percentage of their standard of living. If we continue to do that, whites will always oppose us, and not necessarily out of racism, but out of self-interest.

Interview/USA Today, 10-22:(A)9.

John H. Chafee
United States Senator, R-Rhode Island

5

The first proposed equal-rights amendment was introduced in Congress in 1923. Now, more than 60 years later, we are still working to embody the essential principle of equal rights between the sexes in our nation's fundamental legal document: the Constitution. Discrimination based on gender continues in education, in employment and in the issuance of credit and insurance. And until they are made part of the Constitution, the legislative gains of recent years can be rescinded, eroded or simply not enforced.

Before the Senate, Washington, June 21/The New York Times, 6-27:12.

Henry Cisneros
Mayor of San Antonio

6

[On whether the 1980s is the "decade of the Hispanic" in the U.S.]: That's a lot of Madison Avenue hype. I don't think it is the decade of the Hispanic. There may be a decade after the year 2000 that is the decade of Hispanic achievement, but we [Hispanics] are so far off right now in terms of even what the black community has achieved in politics, the arts and sports, the

(HENRY CISNEROS)

news media, education, professions, economic achievement, that this is clearly not the decade of the Hispanic. It was never declared so by a Hispanic. It was declared so by the cover stories of national magazines.

Interview, San Antonio/USA Today, 12-9:(A)13.

Mary Jean Collins
Vice president,
National Organization for Women

1

The anti-abortion terrorists who have bombed or burned nearly 30 abortion clinics during the past year are not merely attacking real estate. These terrorist acts are attacks on women and can only be grounded in an utter disdain for women, their moral character and their choices about their lives.

At abortion-rights rally, Indianapolis, Jan. 22/Los Angeles Times, 1-23:(I)13.

James Conway
Associate director of equal opportunity,
National Association of Manufacturers

2

[Approving of government requirements for numerical goals in hiring minorities and women]: We believe that using numerical goals and timetables is something that business is comfortable with, something that has been a proven success over the last two decades and something that business would like to continue to use. Overall, we think it has worked.

The Washington Post, 8-16:(A)3.

Alan Cranston
United States Senator, D-California

3

[Criticizing those who oppose sanctions against South Africa as a protest against that country's apartheid system]: There seems to be, at the heart of the American ultra-right-wing movement, an undercurrent of racism that rises to the surface every now and then. I strongly suspect—and gravely fear—that that dirty undercurrent of racism is rising to the surface again in the tolerance of apartheid and the apparent lack of concern over the suffering of 23 million blacks.

Before the Senate, Washington, July 8/The Washington Post, 7-9:(A)16.

Mary Cunningham
Former vice president,
Bendix Corporation

4

Many women today are still their own worst enemy. They have been made to feel almost afraid of power. Women are still embarrassed to admit that they have power and to embrace its energy as something that can be very positive if implemented with a conscience. Many of us have spent so much time criticizing the external barriers to our advancement we haven't spent enough time tapping our innermost potential as human beings. Women have for centuries been recognized as talented listeners, nurturers, motivators, excellent communicators. These very qualities that we once were told were unbusinesslike are precisely the qualities that business needs most to tap human potential.

Interview/USA Today, 6-13:(A)9.

Jean Bethke Elshtain
Professor of political science,
University of Massachusetts, Amherst

5

The argument that abortion is a right necessary to the control over one's self is based on a social-contract model of society which presupposes that only independent, rational adults have rights, or needs to be met. Such a society is nothing more than a network of freely negotiated contracts between isolated Robinson Crusoes, a marketplace where we choose what we want, goaded by consumerism. [In such a society,] we enter parenthood with a shopping list of qualities we want in a child. So infanticide becomes both possible and permissible. But this model leaves out the bonds of caring and dependency you get in traditional family life. And it ignores the human life cycle, which all of us enter as dependents and most of us leave in the same condition.

Newsweek, 1-14:29.

Nanette Falkenberg
Executive director,
National Abortion Rights Action League

1

[Defending legalized abortions]: . . . we're talking about women who have a Constitutional right to an abortion and therefore a right to exercise that right unhindered. We are in danger as the focus shifts to an increasing discussion of medical and fetal technology and to the question of when life begins. We have to refocus on the women. Even in the difficult pregnancies, the late pregnancies, those are individual women making tough decisions under tough circumstances.

Interview/Ms., February:68.

Jerry Falwell
Evangelist

2

. . . the American people will not very long tolerate terrorism in this country, and that is why abortion is doomed. It is the ultimate kind of terrorism: the terrorism of defenseless, voiceless, helpless unborn babies. Let me give you my theological position. A person is one that is formed when two elements of life—a man and a woman—merge. At that very moment, according to many passages of the Bible, human life, a living soul, is formed. Life, I believe, begins at conception.

Before National Press Club, Washington,
Feb. 12/USA Today, 2-13:(4)9.

Geraldine A. Ferraro
Former United States Representative,
D-New York; 1984 Democratic
Vice Presidential nominee

3

[On her support of freedom-of-choice for abortions]: Because of my [religious] background . . . I think some people feel that my position on abortion is an absolute betrayal. It was never an issue for me before 1978. I opposed abortion, and that was it. But after I was elected to Congress, I honestly felt it was not right for me to impose my religious views on other people. And it's only a religious view that makes me opposed to abortion. I don't know at what point

24

a fetus becomes a baby, at what point it has feelings. None of us who are lay people do. In fact, doctors don't know . . . I said, "Okay, I'll accept all the church's teachings because I accept all the church's teachings, and God has given me the gift of faith." But how can I impose my religious presumption on somebody else? It is the worst issue to have to deal with . . . There will never be a Constitutional amendment passed in this country that eliminates abortion. If it got through the Congress, it would never pass the number of states needed to ratify it. The Right-to-Lifers are absolutely spinning the wheel. But they sure are vocal.

Interview/Ladies' Home Journal, May:193.

4

Yes, we lost an election [in 1984], but we [women] won a victory of spirit that will help our future. What it means for all of us is that the "Men Only" sign has been removed from the doors of the White House . . . [Women] know that we can walk in space, and we can teach our children to take their first steps. We can do all these things, or none of these things. We have widened the universe from which we pick the talent to lead the country. In fact, I would venture that in 1988 you are going to see a couple of women running in the primaries.

Before American Booksellers Association,
San Francisco/Los Angeles Times, 5-31:(V)1.

Mark S. Fowler
Chairman,
Federal Communications Commission

5

I don't agree with allotting or awarding radio and television licenses because of a person's skin color. That's discrimination. The idea that we discriminate against people or award preferences to others based on skin color is a loaded gun which can be pointed at minorities, who now enjoy those preferences, at some time in the future by someone claiming an urgent need to do so. The more correct and safe course is to say, "In America no one may be discriminated against, or others preferred, based on skin color. Period."

Interview, Washington/
The New York Times, 5-25:7.

John Hope Franklin
Professor of history,
Duke University

1

. . . I'm not certain we can accomplish a great deal as long as we're moving in the direction that we are moving now—namely, that the government has little or no role to play in equalizing opportunities and in protecting the rights of individuals or groups of individuals. One can only hope that there will come a time when we will recognize that the Constitutional rights can only be realized through government action.

Interview/USA Today, 2-22:(A)15.

William F. Gibson
Chairman, National Association for the Advancement of Colored People

2

The NAACP is taking off the gloves in relation to dealing with the Reagan Administration. For the past few years, we felt Mr. Reagan is a nice guy who doesn't know what's happening. Today we see a change. We see the kind of change where we'll be calling Mr. Reagan what he is. I've said some time ago he's basically a reactionary and racist. And we're preparing now to tell the story to the world.

News conference, May 17/
The Washington Post, 5-18:(A)4.

Judy Goldsmith
President,
National Organization for Women

3

[Supporting the right to have an abortion]: I believe, as do many people based upon their religious or personal ethics, that there is a person when a fetus is *born* and becomes a living person. I say without qualification that I will give greater rights to a woman than to a microscopic, fertilized egg. I will. I say that on the grounds that a woman can feel pain. A fetus cannot. A woman can hope for the best for those around her whom she loves. A fetus cannot.

Before National Press Club, Washington,
Feb. 12/USA Today, 2-13:(A)9.

4

[Criticizing anti-abortionists]: We must drive home the message to [President] Ronald Reagan, to the Supreme Court, to the Catholic hierarchy, to Jerry Falwell [of the Moral Majority] and to all the anti-abortion extremists that to elevate the value of insensate fetal life over that of women is a cynical perversion of compassionate human values. [The abortion issue] is our movement's movement of truth.

At National Organization for Women convention,
New Orleans, July 19/The Washington Post, 7-20:(A)2.

5

In the beginning [of the women's-rights movement] you get rid of most of the really disgusting, blatant forms of discrimination that are on the surface and that are the most easily seen and therefore the most easily dealt with and removed. But that's a very difficult point because then people say, "Well, what do you women want, anyway? You've got everything. You've got a woman up in space, you've got a woman running for Vice President—what more do you want?" What is left is the bedrock, which is much tougher, much harder to get at, and much more difficult to see. [Comparable worth, or pay equity is] an excellent example of bedrock. It is also an issue that has a dollar sign on it. This is where women always come up short, and where the fight for equality gets particularly hard.

Interview, New Orleans/
The Christian Science Monitor, 7-24:25.

Gary Hart
United States Senator, D-Colorado

6

This time of exceptional opportunity for black America is also a time of exceptional peril. Where we once had a Civil Rights Commission, we now have an agency determined to put civil rights *out* of commission. My message is this: We must not retreat one inch . . . We must never permit this [Reagan] or any other Administration to turn back the clock by tampering with voting rights and weakening the Civil Rights Act.

At Talladega (Ala.) College commencement/
USA Today, 6-3:(A)11.

Timothy S. Healy
President, Georgetown University

[On the decline in black enrollment at U.S. colleges]: Nationally, college by college and university by university, we are pushing equality of access onto the back burner. All of us acknowledge the ideal of integration, but our zeal for keeping access open, and for working at the integration of faculties, has slipped. In some institutions, it has disappeared.

Before American Council on Education/
The Washington Post, 7-6:(A)8.

1

Benjamin L. Hooks
Executive director, National Association for the Advancement of Colored People

Some Pollyannas would have us believe that racial discrimination has been eliminated from the fabric of American society. A look around the country will show that Jim Crow is alive and well in America, albeit in a slightly more subtle form.

Before House Education and Labor Committee,
Washington, March 7/The Washington Post, 3-8:(A)2.

2

[Criticizing Reagan Administration negative views of affirmative-action programs]: They [the Administration] are catering to the worst instincts of the American public, but they are hiding it behind mushy-mushy, goody-goody words: "color blind," "sex blind," "equity," fairness and justice," when in fact it is designed to perpetuate injustice and inequality.

At rally, Washington, May 7/
The New York Times, 5-8:13.

3

All this talk about "reverse discrimination" has convinced a lot of people that indeed affirmative action is reverse discrimination. Most people believe there ought to be equality of opportunity. If you ask them if they believe in reverse discrimination, the answer is no. This [Reagan] Administration is very adept in packaging their package in such a way as to make it appear it's

4

designed to open the doors to those to whom the doors have been closed.

News conference, May 17/
The Washington Post, 5-18:(A)4.

William Hudnut
Mayor of Indianapolis

[Supporting affirmative-action programs]: A lot of progress has been made with affirmative-action goals. Without them, we would regress into a situation where overt or covert discrimination against blacks, Hispanics and women would prevent them from taking their rightful place in the mainstream of community activity . . . The sponsors of the Civil Rights Act may have opposed quotas at the time, but subsequent history has shown that without goals we'll never get close to the dream of equal treatment for minorities, because that doesn't happen when nature takes its course. What happens is that the overwhelming majority of job opportunities goes to white males because they are the majority. Those same sponsors of civil-rights laws also said that the government has a special role to play as an advocate for the disadvantaged. I think it's morally obligatory that we make an extra effort for disadvantaged groups.

Interview/
U.S. News & World Report, 5-27:50.

5

Jesse L. Jackson
Civil-rights leader;
President, Operation PUSH
(People United to Save Humanity)

The climate in the country is cold for black people. It amounts to a cultural conspiracy . . . People are starting to look at blacks like maybe something is wrong with these people . . . There is nothing wrong with blacks demanding a humane foreign policy or sensible defense spending or protesting budget cuts that leave them unprotected or asking for a good education. We will not back down.

Interview, Washington, Feb. 10/
The Washington Post, 2-11:(A)13.

6

(JESSE L. JACKSON)

1

[Saying the Democratic Party is trying to attract more white voters at the expense of blacks]: There is a scheme to have the party prove its manhood to whites by showing its capacity to be unkind to blacks.

Interview/The New York Times, 2-13:15.

2

[On the 20th anniversary of the Selma, Ala., civil-rights marches]: When I think about Selma, I think about blacks not being able to drink water when we were thirsty. Whenever our spirits are down and our hearts are heavy, we can always return to this landmark and remember how far we've come.

At Brown Chapel African Methodist Episcopal Church, Selma, Ala., March 3/The New York Times, 3-4:1.

John E. Jacob
President, National Urban League

3

[The Reagan Administration] is the first Administration in memory in which government officials have been isolated from voluntary organizations representing America's poorest citizens [blacks] . . . If this Administration can institute "a new dialogue" with Russia, which it has called "an evil empire," it can institute a new dialogue with that part of America that has time and again proved by its blood, sweat and tears its loyalty to America . . .

*Washington, Jan. 16/
Los Angeles Times, 1-17:(I)17.*

4

In recent months, we have seen a concerted campaign to convince Americans that the reason for the black failure to support [the Reagan] Administration lies in the pro-Democratic sympathies of black leadership. But even the most superficial knowledge of the mood of black Americans indicates the answer lies elsewhere— in the policies of an Administration that blacks perceive as damaging to their deepest interests. There has been retrogression in the civil-rights area, with the government waging war on affirmative-action programs responsible for black breakthroughs in education and employment. There have been persistent cuts in social-service programs that the poor rely on for survival. The numbers of poor people have increased, in part because of those policies.

Jan. 16/The Washington Post, 1-29:(A)18.

Jerry J. Jasinowski
*Executive vice president,
National Association of Manufacturers*

5

[On an appeals-court ruling overturning a lower-court decision that had approved comparable-worth job-pay in Washington state]: We are elated. Setting different salary and wage rates for different occupations is simply not discrimination. Businesses will rest easier today knowing they won't be dragged into court based on the idea that jobs have some inherent worth regardless of market conditions.

Los Angeles Times, 9-6:(I)12.

Barbara Jordan
*Professor of public values and ethics,
University of Texas, Austin;
Former United States Representative, D-Texas*

6

Abortion has developed into an issue that is surrounded by conflict and difficulty, and it should not be. I think that we will get pulled out of the conflictual nature of the abortion issue once we get a rational and reasonable discussion under way between those who say we are pro-choice and those who say we are pro-life. They are both pro-life, as far as I am concerned. We have compromised on just about every other issue in this country that you can think of, and there will be some resolution and compromise on abortion.

Interview/Ms., April:112.

Jack Kemp
*United States Representative,
R-New York*

7

[Saying the Republican Party should pay attention to blacks and their representatives]:

27

(JACK KEMP)

You've got to talk to blacks, and you can't just talk to the ones who voted for you. You cannot be conscious of the problems facing blacks in America today without talking to the people who represent them.

U.S. News & World Report, 5-27:49.

Jeane J. Kirkpatrick
United States Ambassador/Permanent Representative to the United Nations

Any time a woman is involved in nontraditional roles, she is likely to encounter certain kinds of discrimination. And one also develops an ability to bear it in certain perspective. I go and read a good book, listen to some Bach, absorb myself in music.

Interview/Newsweek, 1-14:32.

1

My position on abortion is very much the traditional Protestant position. Basically, I believe abortion is always tragic, always to be avoided. But it is not invariably the worst possible evil in every situation. I would not call myself pro-choice, however, because pro-choice is the term associated today with readily available abortion and casual abortion counseling—really almost use of abortion as a form of contraception and family planning. And I think that is abominable and appalling on all grounds.

Interview/The Washington Post, 7-29:(A)13.

Madeleine Kunin
Governor of Vermont (D)

3

[On being a woman who ran for governor]: I think you do have a special hurdle to overcome. Sometimes I think the whole point of a woman running for high office, when that hasn't been achieved before, is to get people to really look at you for who you are and to put the whole gender question aside. That's easier said than done, because it doesn't really work that way. But that's what you want to achieve. In a sense, I think

that's what I achieved—that I could get people to focus on my qualifications and the issues, and that diminishes the obstacle of gender. The hurdle is mostly there because of lack of precedent. I don't think it's in and of itself a bias. I think it's a bias because nobody's used to the idea. Fifty years from now, it'll be less of a novelty.

Interview/The Washington Post, 2-18:(C)6.

Mickey Leland
United States Representative, D-Texas

4

[President] Reagan knows no black people. He has no sense of what it is to be black in America. I question whether he even has a black friend. He has no insight into the life and reality of blacks . . .

The Washington Post, 2-5:(A)3.

Ann F. Lewis
National director, Americans for Democratic Action

5

Women's work is underpaid because the reality of women's work was so long unrecognized and unorganized. We must speak out aggressively against the tactic of turning men and women against each other, of trying to blame working women for the failures of the economy to provide decent jobs for enough Americans. The fight is not between working men and women. It is between the real needs and aspirations of working people and the neo-elite selfishness of a would-be elite.

Before National Committee for Pay Equity/
The New York Times, 5-30:12.

C. Eric Lincoln
Professor of religion,
Duke University

6

The tone for the 1980s has already been set. I think the mood in the nation has been made quite clear. That mood seems to be characterized by a notice to the black, the poor and the dispossessed that we have come to the end of what the nation has come to perceive as a free ride for the underprivileged. From this point on, the nation

(C. ERIC LINCOLN)

fully intends to disallow any responsibility at all for those groups who are at the bottom of the economic and social scale. [President] Reagan's re-election has been interpreted as a mandate for the American people to turn back the clock. From this point on, it is crystal clear that blacks will have to fend for themselves—no matter who put them at a disadvantage, and no matter how long they have been kept there.

Interview/USA Today, 2-22:(A)15.

Glenn C. Loury
Professor of public policy,
John F. Kennedy School of Government,
Harvard University

1

Blacks continue to seek the respect of their fellow Americans. And yet it becomes increasingly clear that, to win the equal regard of their fellows, black Americans cannot substitute judicial and legislative decree for what is to be won through the outstanding achievements of individual black persons . . . For what ultimately is being sought is the freely conveyed respect of one's peers. Assigning prestigious positions so as to secure a proper racial balance . . . seems fundamentally inconsistent with the attainment of this goal . . . This is especially so with respect to the policy of racially preferential treatment, because its use to "equalize" can actually destroy the good which is being sought on behalf of those initially unequal.

Before National Urban League, Washington, July 24/The Washington Post, 7-25:(A)15.

Joseph E. Lowery
President, Southern
Christian Leadership Conference

2

[Criticizing U.S. Civil Rights Commission Chairman Clarence Pendleton for saying traditional civil-rights leaders are guilty of reverse racism]: Pendleton is simply echoing the charges made by racists for the last generation. It's the same old film, only now they've added color [Pendleton is black]. It's what the white citizens' councils and the diehard racists have been saying—cries of reverse discrimination, reverse racism—the only difference now is that it's coming in color . . . The original criticism of affirmative action came from white racists. It's the same old story now being sung by a black public official. Affirmative action is an intentional effort to close the gap. Government has a moral as well as Constitutional responsibility to try and close the gap because the gap was created by government policy.

Interview/USA Today, 3-8:(A)11.

3

What's really hurting the black community is the 15 to 24 per cent unemployment. What's really hurting [black] communities is the 50 to 65 per cent unemployment among black youths. What's really hurting the black community is that our immediate income is about 57 to 58 per cent of the median income of the white community. What's hurting the black community is that we're the last hired and the first fired. What's hurting the black community is the senseless use of police force in too many instances.

Interview/USA Today, 3-8:(A)11.

Connaught Marshner
Director,
National Pro-Family Coalition

4

The mind-set [of many feminist organizations] is, if you are a liberal and a Yuppie and a professional woman, then you qualify as a woman who deserves to benefit from feminism. If you are a conservative or a traditional-values woman, then you don't fit their idea of what a "woman" ought to be, so your concerns and your problems are of no interest to militant feminists. The kind of "woman" who is exalted in the feminist model is a woman who is a clone of a professional man—aggressive, college-educated, professional, climbing up the corporate ladder. The woman who wants to be a schoolteacher doesn't rate, because that's not one of the approved careers. And the homemaker is beyond contempt.

The Christian Science Monitor, 9-27:27.

30

William S. McEwen
Director of equal opportunity,
Monsanto Company

1

As the debate on affirmative action has emerged in recent years, much attention has focused on goals and timetables versus quotas. Industry does not believe that numerical goals for minority inclusion in the workforce, by themselves, constitute quotas. Business, particularly big business, sets goals and timetables for every aspect of its operations—profits, capital investment, productivity increases and promotional potential for individuals. Setting goals and timetables for minority and female participation is a way of measuring progress and focusing on potential discrimination. Industry recognizes, however, that goals and timetables can become masks for rigid quotas. We oppose any regulations that turn positive programs for measuring progress into unwielding rules on the number of minorities and women who must encompass the workplace. Yet, voluntary goals set by corporations for workforce participation should not be viewed as eroding equal-opportunity objectives. These goals are merely a recognition that ingrained prejudices remain in our society. Assuring equal opportunity, at least for the next few years to come, means we must be ever vigilant in facing these prejudices and overcoming them.

Congressional testimony, Washington,
July 10/The Washington Post, 8-16:(4)23.

2

[Saying affirmative action should continue]: Some say we don't need affirmative action; if we just find the most-qualified person, that will take care of the problem. But that assumes fairness; that assumes we always treat our employees equally, that we know how to choose the most-qualified person. That assumes we know how to minimize if not eliminate subjectivity as a human element in choice. But even if there were no minorities or women around, we don't know how to do that . . . There are people who say they believe in voluntary compliance [with non-discrimination laws]. But voluntary compliance does not work. If it did, Moses would have come down from the mountain with Ten Guidelines. But he came down with the Ten Commandments.

Interview, St. Louis/USA Today, 9-5:(4)8.

Edwin Meese III
Attorney General of the United States

3

[On criticism of his handling of civil-rights issues]: The interest of the civil-rights movement is being advanced every day by the Justice Department . . . I would consider myself in the forefront of the civil-rights movement in the country today . . . There is no one who is more adamant in defense of civil rights . . . more opposed to discrimination in any form . . . more the champion of minorities, and of all citizens for that matter, than I am.

Broadcast interview/
"This Week With David Brinkley,"
ABC-TV, 8-25.

4

[Arguing against quotas to further the employment of minorities]: For all intents and purposes, a new version of the separate-but-equal doctrine is being pushed upon us. [Those who advocate quotas as a means of remedying past injustice] will tell you that whatever discriminatory features such policies employ, that discrimination is benign; that it is benevolent. But you should not forget that an earlier generation of Americans heard from some that slavery was good not only for the slaves but for society. It was natural, they argued; it was a kind of benevolence . . . Counting by race is a form of racism. And racism is never benign, never benevolent. It elevates a perverted notion of equality and denies the original understanding of equality that is our national birthright. The idea that you can use discrimination in the form of racially preferential quotas, goals and set-asides to remedy the lingering social effects of past discrimination makes no sense in principle; in practice, it is nothing short of a legal, moral and Constitutional tragedy. The fact that discrimination occurred in the past provides no justification for engaging in discriminatory conduct, even if the stated reason is to undo the past wrongs . . . The person preferentially selected by means of race or gender classifications suffers no less indignity than the person excluded because of those classifications. Such classifications are wrong when they were used by governments to bestow advantages on whites and men; they have no greater claim of morality when

(EDWIN MEESE III)

the tables are turned. The vast majority of Americans today reject that idea that preferring some people for certain jobs because of their race or gender is right. There is no other way to say it: Discrimination is wrong.

At Dickinson College, Sept. 17/
The New York Times, 9-18:15.

James Meredith
Civil-rights activist

1

Integration is the biggest con job ever pulled on any group of people, any nationality in the world. It was a plot by white liberals to gain black political power for themselves and their wild ideas, and for a few black bourgeoisie who were paid to exercise leverage as black spokesmen. I've never heard any other black person say integration did one good thing for them . . . Have you ever heard of Irish, Poles, Germans, Italians and Jews being integrated? They go anywhere and just enjoy their rights. Why call it integration when black folks do the same thing? The people who started this integration thing knew that in 30 years they'd have the same thing, the same problem they could take advantage of. That was the object of the con job—to keep blacks separate.

At Ohio Wesleyan University/
The Washington Post, 2-23:(G)1.

Irene Natividad
Chairman, National
Women's Political Caucus

2

[On arguments that the women's movement is in the doldrums]: Look where we are today. The local [government] level is critical in order to create a pool of national candidates, and in state governments we have 18 women Secretaries of State, up from 9 a decade ago. We have 1,096 women state legislators, compared with 771 14 years ago. Last week an all-female city council was elected in Missoula, Montana. Does this look like a movement that's on hold or being eroded?

Interview, New York/
The New York Times, 7-6:18.

Richard M. Nixon
Former President of the United States

3

[Saying that while he objects to quotas for minority-group employment, he supports laws that require Federal contracts to go to minority businesses on a percentage basis]: That is different. The law provides that minorities receive certain percentages of contracts. That should continue. In the Eisenhower Administration, I was chairman of the President's commission on government contracts. It had the responsibility on a voluntary basis to get firms that had Federal contracts to have fair employment practices. It worked pretty well. I said then and I say now that all people pay taxes; therefore, all should have proportionate benefits from the taxes they pay.

Interview/USA Today, 10-21:(A)13.

Sandra Day O'Connor
Associate Justice,
Supreme Court of the United States

4

I worked hard to try to eliminate what I saw or judged as legal impediments in the way of letting women progress and meet their career goals. I think that after women got the right to vote, they pretty much sat down for a long period of time and packed their banners and stayed quiet. It wasn't until the '60s that women began to bring to the forefront the continuing concerns that they had about equal opportunity. I am sure that but for that effort, I would not be serving in this job, because people obtained a greater consciousness of the need for women in these positions.

Interview/The Saturday Evening Post, September:47.

Margaret Papandreou
Head of Greek delegation to
United Nations Women's Conference

5

[On criticism that international politics are being projected into the UN Women's Conference]: Why is it this conference becomes "politicized" when you discuss the rights of refugee women or racist violence experienced by women in South Africa? Is that any more political than the issues that are called "women's issues"?

(MARGARET PAPANDREOU)

. . . The women's movement is a political movement. It is a social revolution. It is about changes in society, changes that are global. This means it addresses itself to all issues that affect the daily lives of women. This also means that no one group of women can determine what are women's issues and foreclose discussion on non-women's issues, as that group defines them . . .

At United Nations Women's Conference, Nairobi, Kenya, July 12/The Washington Post, 7-15:(B)2.

Clarence M. Pendleton, Jr.
Chairman, United States Commission on Civil Rights

1

. . . [I agree with President Reagan] totally that black leaders out there are running a misery industry. Civil rights is not equal to social-welfare programs. But now the Urban League is attacking the President for destroying progress on civil rights because he wants to cut the [Federal] budget . . . The Urban League isn't a civil-rights group any more. It's into social and economic issues, and blacks have no more claim to the budget than any other group.

Washington, Jan. 31/The Washington Post, 2-5:(A)3.

2

The new racism is what whites and blacks are perpetrating upon black people. It's the continued clamoring by a lot of black leaders for preferences from an Administration, whether it be Republican or Democrat, that leads black people to assume that they are some special wards of the state in perpetuity . . . There is a belief that blacks and whites are not allowed to compete as equals. Therefore, it is expected that results are to be guaranteed without competition. The new racists believe that because there is no equality of results, blacks are still unequal.

Interview/USA Today, 3-6:(A)11.

Samuel R. Pierce, Jr.
Secretary of Housing and Urban Development of the United States

3

I think that a lot of the established black community has taken an attitude that they want to continue dealing in a way that this [Reagan] Administration doesn't want to. We are trying to reduce deficits and get things down to manageable shape, and others just want to have a giant giveaway program, and we are not going to do that.

Following Administration meeting with black leaders, Washington, Jan. 15/The New York Times, 1-16:43.

Muammar el-Qaddafi
Chief of State of Libya

4

[Speaking to black American servicemen]: This country [the U.S.] must be destroyed. They [white Americans] refuse to accept you as American citizens. This means you are obliged to create a separate and independent state. The whites force you to do this by refusing you in political and social life . . . You have the force, you have the soldiers. We are ready to give you arms because your cause is just. We are with you, don't worry. You have to trust us. We will fight together shoulder by shoulder. The final victory will be soon.

Satellite-transmitted speech from Libya to Nation of Islam convention, Chicago, Feb. 24/The New York Times, 2-26:16.

Joseph L. Rauh, Jr.
Civil-rights lawyer

5

To the extent that there is a valley in the efforts toward equality today, it results from a national fatigue based on the unprecedented efforts of recent decades. But one can hope—no, expect, that this too will pass, that batteries will be recharged and that increased racial tolerance will spark new gains of which future generations will be as proud as we are of ours.

At Clinch Valley College of the University of Virginia/The New York Times, 1-8:8.

Ronald Reagan
President of the United States

6

I know there are a number of leaders of various organizations that are coming forth all the time with reports that . . . somehow we've [the Reagan Administration] relegated the black

(RONALD REAGAN)

community to a second-class status. That's not our intent and that's not our practice. The people since we came here who got the jobs—more than one million of them are blacks who have left the unemployment rolls. It's true, they've had farther to go. But based on some of our past history and all, they're on an upward climb. And reducing inflation—there's been a benefit to people who, in the lower earning scale, it means a lot more to them. The number of blacks who are now getting college educations is far higher than it has ever been.

Interview, Washington, Jan. 17/USA Today, 1-18:(A)13.

1

As an older American, I remember a time when people of different race, creed or ethnic origin in our land found hatred and prejudice installed in social custom and, yes, in law. There's no story more heartening in our history than the progress that we've made toward the brotherhood of man that God intended for us. Let us resolve: There will be no turning back or hesitation on the road to an America rich in dignity and abundant with opportunity for all our citizens. Let us resolve that we, the people, will build an American opportunity society in which all of us—white and black, rich and poor, young and old—will go forward together, arm in arm. Again, let us remember that, though our heritage is one of blood lines from every corner of the earth, we are all Americans pledged to carry on this last best hope of man on earth.

Inaugural address, Washington, Jan. 21/The New York Times, 1-22:7.

2

[On his position against abortion]: I feel these days, as never before, the momentum is with us ... There are already signs that we've changed the public attitude on abortion. The number performed each year is finally leveling off. The general feeling that abortion is just a small, harmless medical procedure that's simply a matter of choice has almost disappeared. We're making progress. [We must continue working with those] who believe, as I do, that abortion is the taking of life of a living human being, that the right to abortion is not secured by the Constitution and that the state has a compelling interest in protecting the life of each person before birth.

To anti-abortion marchers, Washington, Jan. 22/Los Angeles Times, 1-23:(I)12.

3

[Some mainstream black leaders] are protecting some rather good positions that they have. And they can protect them better if they can keep their constituency aggrieved and believing that they have a legitimate complaint. If [blacks] ever become aware of the opportunities that are improving, they might wonder whether they need some of those [black] organizations.

Interview/Newsweek, 1-28:30.

4

The question of abortion grips our nation. Abortion is either the taking of human life or it isn't. And if it is—and medical technology is increasingly showing it is—it must be stopped. It is a terrible irony that while some turn to abortion, so many others who cannot become parents cry out for children to adopt. We have room for these children; we can fill the cradles of those who want a child to love. Tonight, I ask the Congress to move this year on legislation to protect the unborn.

State of the Union address, Washington, Feb. 6/The New York Times, 2-7:13.

5

[I] believed in affirmative action and civil rights before there were any things called affirmative action and civil rights. I was raised in a household in which the way you could really get in trouble with your mother and father was if you showed any evidences of prejudices against anyone. When I was a sports announcer, I was one of a small coterie that was trying to open baseball up to other races. And at the same time, I saw the misuse of [racial] quotas in the schools, hospitals and so forth. Today, affirmative action is being distorted to mean the reimplementation of quotas. That isn't what the civil-rights bill was all about.

Interview/U.S. News & World Report, 11-18:32.

Donald T. Regan
*Chief of Staff to the
President of the United States*

[Saying the issues to be discussed at the U.S.-Soviet summit meeting in Geneva are beyond the understanding of most women]: They're not . . . going to understand [missile] throwweights, or what is happening in Afghanistan, or what is happening in human rights. Some women will, but most women—believe me, your readers for the most part if you took a poll—would rather read the human-interest stuff of what happened.

Interview/The Washington Post, 11-25:(4)7.

1

William Bradford Reynolds
*Assistant Attorney General,
Civil Rights Division, Department
of Justice of the United States*

[On the possibility that schools are lowering their academic standards to make it easier for minority students to graduate]: If we are giving kids diplomas that are nothing but an empty piece of paper and sending them out into the work force to compete, that certainly disadvantages them in a considerable way . . . The schools, in the interests of avoiding accusations of discrimination and unfair treatment, are leaning over backwards to jimmy the numbers in terms of their graduating class. And, in so doing, they are doing a monumental disservice to a whole generation of students.

*Interview, Washington,
Sept. 20/The New York Times, 9-21:7.*

2

[Opposing job-hiring preferences and quotas for racial minorities]: In reality, there is only discrimination, pure and simple, whether it operates in forward gear or in reverse. There simply are no winners under a racially preferential program—however devised—only losers . . . Some of those who had been in the forefront of the battle for equal opportunity began to pursue policies calculated to compromise that principle for which so many had fought for so long. They embarked on a misguided venture to find short-

3

cuts to achieve the fruits American society has to offer. [As a result,] the cherished ideal of equality of opportunity gave way in many quarters to a drive for a new kind of equality—an equality of results. And civil-rights successes and failures came to be measured on the basis of statistical balance or imbalance.

*Before Rotary Club, Wilmington, Del.,
Oct. 31/Los Angeles Times, 11-1:(I)14.*

Yvette Roudy
Minister for Women's Rights of France

[Comparing the women's rights situation in France with that in the U.S.]: I believe that machismo in France is stronger. In the United States you have the great tradition of the pioneers. It's not an accident that it was Wyoming that first gave the right to vote to women. The women who came there made decisions; they fought; they were needed. Here [in France] the social customs are much more conservative because traditional structures are more deeply fixed. We also have the Catholic religion, which, I think it's true to say, has been less liberal toward women than the Protestants. We also have the Mediterranean influence, which is more sexist in its traditions than the north.

*Interview, Paris/
The New York Times,
7-1:19.*

4

Charles Silberman
Social scientist

What we have to keep in mind is that anti-Semitism [in the U.S.] is the fringe. It does not affect the crucial decision we make in our lives. It does not affect where we live, where we work, where we can go to school. [Americans] have shown themselves to be far more resistant to anti-Semitism than anyone had realized . . . On the one hand, American society has broken open to Jews in ways we never could have imagined a generation ago. On the other hand, many of us are worried. We are afraid that our success is going to reawaken old pools of anti-Semitism.

*Interview, New York/
Los Angeles Times, 9-9:(V)1,4.*

5

(CHARLES SILBERMAN)

1

[On why some Jews are opposed to affirmative-action programs for blacks, women, etc.]: If affirmative action is defined as numerical quotas, that has the same emotional resonance to Jews as calls for making this a Christian country. It's too reminiscent of the days when quotas kept Jews out. There's a visceral fear that if the notion that each group's place in the society is to be determined by its numerical representation in the population, this would have disastrous consequences for Jews. In many of the fields Jews have entered, they are not distributed evenly.

Interview/USA Today, 9-17:(A)11.

Eleanor Smeal
President-elect,
National Organization for Women

2

The leadership of the women's movement and the activists of the movement believe there's a need for a change and for greater activism. I think it's time to put a lot more heat on the right wing and the reactionary policies of the [Reagan] Administration. We've been good too long. It's time to go back into the streets and on to the campuses.

News conference, New Orleans,
July 21/The Washington Post, 7-22:(A)1.

Gloria Steinem
Editor, "Ms." magazine

3

The only functional difference between women and men is women's ability to give birth. Men have a desire to control that, whether it's an individual man who wants to determine the paternity of his child, or a nation that wants to decide how many workers and how many soldiers it should have, and perhaps also what class and what race should increase more than others. Whatever the motive, it's the desire to control women as the most basic means of production and the means of reproduction. That is the root of women's inequality.

Interview/USA Today, 5-20:(A)11.

4

The main problem young women have is that they don't think there is a [sexism] problem. But that is a function of youth. It means their dreams have not been taken away from them [yet]. They assume that they can do whatever they want to do. The women's movement is the one social movement in which you grow more radical with age.

Interview/USA Today, 5-20:(A)11.

5

The first stage of gaining majority support [for women's issues], majority hopes and dreams, is finished. We have a base of support. We don't have to prove that women are discriminated against. In general, we no longer have to document the problems. Now we are more able to report on the diverse solutions. The second stage involves beginning to change institutions. We now have major support for equal pay, which we didn't have 10 years ago. But we don't have equal pay. We have the idea of shared parenthood, but we don't have the institutional changes that would make shared parenthood possible. We don't have parental leave; we barely have maternity leave. We're just beginning to transform institutions so that new dreams will be real, practical choices.

The Christian Science Monitor, 9-26:27.

Clarence Thomas
Chairman, Equal Employment
Opportunity Commission of the United States

6

[Arguing against the idea of equal pay for different jobs of comparable worth]: Sole reliance on a comparison of the intrinsic value of dissimilar jobs which command different wages in the market does not prove a violation [of Federal civil-rights law]. We are convinced that Congress never authorized the government to take on wholesale restructuring of wages that we set by non-sex-based decisions of employers, by collective bargaining or by the marketplace.

Washington, June 17/The New York Times, 6-18:8.

7

[On the decline in black enrollment at U.S. colleges and whether potential students should blame the aid cutbacks instituted by the Reagan Administration]: It would service those students

35

(CLARENCE THOMAS)

if, instead of blaming the Reagan Administration, we went back and looked at what is happening in grammar schools and high schools. You may not be able to go to Harvard [because of budget cuts], but how much does it cost to go to [the University of the District of Columbia]? Blacks went to colleges, which were predominantly black colleges, for a hundred years without a lot of government support.

Interview/The Washington Post, 7-6:(A)8.

Kathleen Vick
*President, Association
of State Democratic Chairs*

[Saying the Democratic Party is more responsive to blacks than is the Republican Party]: Come election time, blacks can decide which party is most responsive. I'm not saying they don't have anywhere to go—they can do anything they want, including staying home—but it's not a close call with the Republicans. The record of the Democratic Party on black issues is clear.

Feb. 11/The Washington Post, 2-12:(A)3.

1

William A. Webb
*Commissioner,
Equal Employment Opportunity
Commission of the United States*

When somebody tells me they ought to get something because they're Irish and saw signs in Boston that said "Irish Need Not Apply" when they were in grade school; or that they are Italian and their grandfather could not get hired in New York; or that their ancestors were in slavery, I say, so what. This agency is not in the business of windfall legislation. We want to make people whole who have been damaged by discrimination.

The Washington Post, 2-13:(A)8.

2

John C. Willke
*President,
National Right to Life Committee*

[Criticizing the recent bombings of abortion clinics by people opposed to abortion]: If we were to adopt the evil tactics of those who promote abortion by using violence ourselves, we would destroy the very ethic that is the foundation of our pro-life movement.

The New York Times, 1-4:11.

Laval S. Wilson
Superintendent of Schools of Boston

It seems to have been the history of our country that when school systems become predominantly minority that the white population begins to decrease. Obviously, if you're going to have an integrated school system, you need to have white students as well as blacks and other minorities. I would hope that the Boston public schools would be able to provide a good quality educational program for *all* students. And once quality education becomes the priority, you'll find that parents who have their children in private parochial schools will place their kids back into the public schools.

Interview/USA Today, 9-9:(A)13.

4

Robert Woodson
*Director, Council for a Black Economic
Agenda; President, National Center
for Neighborhood Enterprise*

Racism could end tomorrow and the plight of the black underclass would not change. It would not increase their income, improve their health, or make their communities safer from crime. These issues could only be addressed by mounting strategies to improve their economic well-being . . . Blacks, unfortunately, have focused almost exclusively on civil rights for the past 20 years or so, as if applying civil-rights solutions would somehow translate into economic equity. It does not. Most groups in this society didn't start off trying to achieve political equity. They went for businesses. In every other group, the leaders of the community are business people. They are business leaders. Once they have made their stake in business, then they go into politics . . . If you have economic power, you vote every day with your money. If you have political power, you vote only once every two years. Now, you can have economic power and then gain political power. But political power does not translate into economic power.

Interview/USA Today, 1-24:(A)7.

5

Commerce • Industry • Finance

James Abdnor
United States Senator, R-South Dakota

1

[On the financial crisis of family farms]: I want to alert you to a clear and present danger, an America without agriculture the way we have known it. If we fail with agriculture, we will have a rural America without economic purpose and an America without its heritage. The continued failures of our farmers, our rural bankers, our Main Street merchants will ripple disastrously throughout the fabric of our national life for generations to come.

The New York Times, 2-13-13.

Frederick E. Balderston
Professor of business administration,
University of California, Berkeley;
Former Savings And Loan
Commissioner of California

2

[On the recent financial difficulties of savings and loans]: The problem is that there are occasional instances in which management may not have the competence to deal with complicated conditions in today's money markets, or it may simply be unlucky in the choices it makes . . . Institutions are pressured to get the highest yields they can on their investments; as a result, they may sometimes be attracted to financial opportunities that contain more risk than they anticipated.

Interview/USA Today, 3-12:(B)2.

Malcolm Baldrige
Secretary of Commerce of the United States

3

[On U.S. criticism of other countries' trade barriers]: People understand comparative advantage [in producing and marketing goods]. What they can't understand is other countries' closed markets in the face of our open markets. Considering the volume of trade between us, we don't have any restrictions to speak of, except the voluntary restraints on [Japanese cars], and there'll be a decision soon whether to keep that or not.

Interview, Washington, 2-21:(A)19.

4

If you don't allow American companies, from shoes to steel, to merge to get more efficient, you are going to see increases in protectionism, and that's not good for consumers. Businesses are not going to merge unless they are going to be better off.

Feb. 25/The Washington Post, 2-26:(D)4.

5

Right now, we're going through [trade] negotiations with the Japanese that are akin to peeling an onion: You get one layer off, and there's another layer underneath. It takes so long. We did have very good results for opening their markets for [U.S.] telecommunications [equipment]. I would say we got 95 per cent of what we wanted. There are other negotiations going on. With wood products, such as plywood and paper, we didn't get anything except a promise to look at the tariffs in three years. On electronics and on medical instruments and pharmaceuticals, we made some progress, but I wouldn't call it excellent progress by any means. It's not enough for Japan to *talk* about barriers being reduced. Because of this trade deficit and what it's doing to U.S. jobs, Congress wants to hear cash registers jingling before it's going to be satisfied. So I don't think the end of the story is going to be known until this fall or, perhaps, next year, when we get a real fix on how all our negotiations have gone and whether the Japanese are buying. I'm sure that this issue is not going to go away.

Interview/U.S. News & World Report, 5-13:50.

George J. Benston
Professor of accounting and finance,
University of Rochester

6

[Government banking regulators] don't do a very good job, and they never have. It's as though there's a pile of trash in the back of a bank with a lot of oil-soaked rags. They say, "Gee, that's a fire hazard." But as long as no one throws a match, the problem can go on for a long time. They protect the banking system and not the public.

The New York Times, 3-20:39.

Lloyd Bentsen
United States Senator, D-Texas

1

[Criticizing President Reagan's decision not to impose protectionist measures to defend the U.S. shoe industry against foreign imports]: It's just another sign that the Administration lacks a coherent, understandable strategy for dealing with our $150-billion trade deficit. When it comes to trade, there is a huge policy void, and it should surprise no one if Congress in coming weeks steps in and tries to fill it.

Aug. 28/The Washington Post, 8-29:(A)22.

James F. Bere
Chairman, Borg-Warner Corporation

2

We're the only country that doesn't have a strong public-private partnership. Philosophically, we have had an adversarial role between the two sectors. I think the public sector is ready to talk about this partnership because they see that the trade imbalance is causing enormous dislocations. But the private sector is not ready to talk. They think it would be synonymous with national planning, which they see as being inconsistent with free enterprise. I disagree. I think you can keep the best of democratic capitalism with a public-private partnership and at the same time you can facilitate fairness in international trade. We need something like a National Security Council for economics. I think our economic relations are as important as security.

*Interview/
The New York Times, 7-30:34.*

Howard L. Berman
*United States Representative,
D-California*

3

Of all the issues facing the members of the 99th Congress in this session, trade may be the most contentious. The trade deficit and what it says about the American economy is getting to be the great national issue of this time. There's a growing sense we have lost our economic supremacy.

Los Angeles Times, 9-9:(I)1.

John R. Block
*Secretary of Agriculture
of the United States*

4

[Advocating a more market-oriented agriculture and less reliance on government interference]: We are at a crossroads. If we stay on the same road we've been traveling, we will be headed for more government controls, more losses in the world marketplace, more limits on our opportunities and more cheap-food policies. And that spells nothing but more troubles on the farm.

*Before Sunkist Growers stockholders, Beverly Hills,
Calif., Jan. 16/Los Angeles Times, 1-17:(IV)1.*

5

[On Federal farm policy]: We've had 50 years of government intervention that hasn't solved the old problems and won't solve the new ones. It's obvious that we can no longer regulate supply, control surpluses and hold up farmers' prices with the law we've got now. If we keep trying to lower production to get better prices for our farmers, the rest of the world will continue to expand their agriculture and we'll lose even more of our foreign markets.

Interview, Washington/The New York Times, 1-23:1.

6

I'm painfully aware of the [financial] difficulties many farmers are having today. But I'm equally certain American agriculture has a great future if it's willing to compete for exports at world market prices. We can't do that if we continue with a farm policy built on false prices, false hopes and high dependence on the government.

*News conference, Washington,
Feb. 6/The New York Times, 2-7:8.*

7

[On the farm debt crisis]: Farmers are in trouble because of powerful international and national economic forces beyond the control of the Secretary of Agriculture, beyond the control of the President and beyond the control of Congress. We in agriculture built our own trap. We're all responsible—the farmers who bid up

(JOHN R. BLOCK)

the land; the so-called experts who said, "Buy another piece of land—they ain't makin' any more of it"; the lending institutions that couldn't shovel the money out the door fast enough; the public officials who encouraged us to increase production to feed a hungry world. We all fell into the trap and expanded too much and too fast. At the time, no one believed that the dollar would become so strong or that interest rates would be so high for so long. We didn't see the recent world-wide recession coming.

Interview/U.S. News & World Report, 2-18:63.

1

Two-thirds of American agriculture does not receive direct government support. The cattle business, the . . . swine business, too, is important, [yet] those two meat industries don't receive direct support. Two-thirds of agriculture goes it for the most part on its own. I would submit that that two-thirds that is for the most part on its own is probably healthier than the third that gets all the government support. That might be telling us something.

Broadcast interview/"Meet the Press," NBC-TV, 2-24.

2

Agriculture is restructuring now. More than 3 million acres of land were voluntarily taken out of crop production last year. Lower prices will reduce the incentive to bring new land into production. We'll see some casualties—there's no question about that. But a policy of gradually reducing the income transfers [price supports, etc.] to farmers—I emphasize *gradually*—is not going to break the industry. It will help agriculture during the transition that must occur if we're going to get supply and demand back into reasonable balance. We just can't keep producing for government warehouses.

Interview/U.S. News & World Report, 9-2:39.

3

William E. Brock
*Special Trade Representative
for the President of the United States*

We [the U.S.] are, by any measure, the most free-trade country in the world among the indus-trial nations. We take twice the share of imports from developing countries that Europe does and 7 1/2 times as much as Japan does. There just is no way that you can compare those two situations. Even where we have stepped back from pure free trade, we have done it very carefully and, frankly, in order to defend ourselves against the unfair practices of others—not simply for the basis of pure protectionism.

Interview/U.S. News & World Report, 4-8:72.

William E. Brock
Secretary of Labor of the United States

4

You can't hide from [foreign] competition behind the protection of the Federal government. The one thing you can't do is to say, "I want my job, and to keep my job I'm going to cause two other people to lose theirs." That's what protectionism does. Protectionism is shared misery.

Interview/USA Today, 10-28:(A)15.

George Bush
Vice President of the United States

5

[Criticizing calls in Congress for trade protectionism against imports from Japan]: Whatever walls we dream of building, it's not walls we'd get if we started to live out a nightmare like that. It's a cliff, and we'd find ourselves falling straight down to chaos.

*Address sponsored by Export-Import Bank,
April 9/The Washington Post, 4-10:(A)16.*

John Carlin
*Governor of Kansas (D); Chairman,
National Governors' Association*

6

[On the farm debt crisis]: It's a depression for all those who have been forced out through the bankruptcy door. We have communities that if you were to drive through today and could flash back to five or 10 years ago, yes, you would say we're on the brink of a depression. It is real. Without significant action, it's really going to be a sad situation, and one that's going to alter the face of this country.

Interview/USA Today, 2-27:(A)9.

WHAT THEY SAID IN 1985

Robert Crandall
Senior Fellow, Brookings Institution

[Arguing for removal of quotas on Japanese automobile exports to the U.S.]: It's hard to imagine the rationale for having them in the first place or for continuing them. If there is a rationale, it's to make our industry more competitive, and I don't see how they serve that purpose. The quotas are likely to alleviate pressure upon the U.S. industry to become more competitive. There are few examples of an industry becoming more competitive as a result of trade protection. I just don't see any truly beneficial effects of the quotas. Without them, you wouldn't be asking American consumers to subsidize Japanese producers. You wouldn't be asking American consumers who make less than $20 an hour to subsidize American car workers, who generally make more.

Interview/U.S. News & World Report, 2-4:44.

1

Edith Cresson
Minister of Industry and International Trade of France

If we discuss protectionism, we can say a lot of things. For example, a common [international] attitude should be taken toward Japan. Nobody can sell to Japan. The Japanese talk about the [high U.S.] dollar, which is certainly one part. But we [French] don't have the dollar and we can't sell [to Japan] either.

Interview/The New York Times, 5-28:28.

2

John Culbertson
Professor of economics, University of Wisconsin

The [Reagan] Administration's policy of permitting unlimited imports, rather misleadingly called "free trade," is ruinous to the country. It is causing us to lose desirable industries and jobs to other countries. We are losing steel, textiles, autos and even newer industries such as electronics and computers. So-called free trade is destroying America's industrial base and damaging our economic prospects . . . As usually applied, free trade means all countries permit unlimited imports. But the U.S. is virtually the only country now doing that—to its great disadvantage . . . . Those who advocate free trade do so in an imaginary world in which trade is balanced among countries and beneficial to all. We don't live in that kind of a world. The U.S. is suffering from a huge excess of imports.

Interview/U.S. News & World Report, 9-23:53.

3

Mary Cunningham
Former vice president, Bendix Corporation

The only [woman] chairman or president of a Fortune 500 company is Katharine Graham, who inherited that job at *The Washington Post.* Despite women's progress, there are internal and external barriers preventing women from rising to the next level in corporate America. The external ones are familiar: prejudice, outdated assumptions about women's competence, and overly protective employers who assume a woman wouldn't want to advance.

Interview/USA Today, 6-13:(A)9.

4

John C. Danforth
United States Senator, R-Missouri

[On U.S. trade with Japan]: I honestly believe that Japan has no interest whatsoever in doing anything other than shipping everything it can into our market, or anybody else's which will have it, and importing absolutely nothing.

Time, 3-25:54.

5

A return to [trade] protectionism would be a disaster for our country. It would threaten the jobs of one sixth of our work force, and it would destroy our farmers. It would increase consumer prices and reduce consumer choice. It would ruin our economy and the economies of our trading partners.

Nation's Business, June:48.

6

The [international trading] system depends on everybody playing by the rules. Violations

7

(JOHN C. DANFORTH)

have to be policed. If necessary, there has to be retaliation—yet we [the U.S.] don't retaliate. The options now are either to do nothing—just let imports come in and never protect Americans—or go to Congress and seek protection for specific sectors [of the economy] . . . I don't think it's protectionist to say that if the Japanese can sell telecommunications in our market, we should be able to sell it in their market, or for us to say that if we can't sell what we produce in other people's markets, we're going to retaliate. Otherwise, how do you expect them to make any concessions at all?

Interview/U.S. News & World Report, 9-16:23.

Carlo De Benedetti
Chairman,
Olivetti Corporation (Italy)

1

We have to remain number one in Europe and also become a major world leader. It may seem paradoxical to mention survival and expansion at the same time, but in our business [office machines] there is no future in becoming a second-, third- or fourth-ranked company. Either you win or you die.

Time, 5-13:48.

E. de la Garza
United States Representative, D-Texas

2

[Criticizing proposed changes in Federal farm legislation]: That phrase, "market oriented," has become a litany of the budget balancers. It just means lower supports and more hardship for the farmers. We're not going to circle the wagons and do nothing. But it's no good producing a radically new farm program that drives people off the land.

Interview/The New York Times, 1-23:9.

John D. Dingell
United States Representative,
D-Michigan

3

What policies could halt the erosion of our industrial base that is threatened by unfair and illegal foreign trade practices? One approach to address our massive trade deficit is an across-the-board import surcharge. It is the functional equivalent of a currency devaluation—and it raises revenue that could be used to reduce the Federal deficit . . . Some of us have been accused of being protectionist because we have insisted that free trade be fair trade. We were told that if we sought to protect our basic industries from unfair foreign competition, American exports would be cut off in retaliation. Well, the free-trade ideologues have had their way, and the export markets for agricultural implements, petrochemicals, machine tools and other goods have dried up—largely because of protectionist measures abroad. We might accept that the Japanese are very efficient. But by the definition of comparative advantage, a nation can't have a comparative advantage in *everything*.

At International Forum of Chamber of Commerce of the United States/Nation's Business, May:49.

Maurice Dingman
Roman Catholic Bishop of Des Moines

4

[On the debt crisis of family farms]: The scope of the present crisis is unparalleled, even in the 1930s. We're astounded at the rapidly escalating nature of the crisis. It is a disaster of astounding proportions. Equally astounding is the reaction of Federal officials who are unaware of or don't care about the gathering storm. We're dying . . . If we lose those family farmers and businessmen in small towns, we have lost the bedrock of democracy.

At meeting of Congressmen and Senators, Washington, Jan. 30/The Washington Post, 1-31:(A)8.

Robert J. Dole
United States Senator, R-Kansas

5

[On the current farm debt crisis]: We're certainly on the right track on farm credit. But, then, we've always been. The President [Reagan] offered this same farm debt restructuring plan last October, saying $650-million would be available for loan guarantees. Now we're saying that any amount, a billion dollars, two billion, whatever is needed, will be pro-

(ROBERT DOLE)

vided. There is no cap, no limit on this if the bankers agree to reschedule the farm loan in trouble, using the guarantees we've provided.

At State of the American Farm Conference, Washington, Feb. 24/
The New York Times, 2-25:9.

Thomas Donaldson
Professor of philosophy,
Loyola University, Chicago

What we're seeing, as corporations get larger and larger, is a breakdown in the lines of accountability. We've created some superstructures in business that are wildly complex, and we haven't tamed them yet.

Time, 6-10:57.

1

Thomas Donovan
Senior executive vice president,
Marine Midland Bank, New York

Banking is a mirror of society. If there is trouble in the bread belt, you can be sure banks serving the bread belt will reflect those difficulties.

U.S. News & World Report,
5-27:58.

2

Byron Dorgan
United States Representative,
D-North Dakota

[On the possibility of Reagan Administration cutbacks in financial support for family farms]: Do we care about a network of family farms in this country? The answer coming from this Administration is "no." They don't care if there are 2,000 or 3,000 family farmers or two or three agricultural corporations. That is the fundamental difference between us, who represent the farmers, and the Administration. They don't care how agriculture is structured.

News conference, February/
The New York Times, 2-12:8.

3

Arthur Dunkel
Director General, General Agreement
on Tariffs and Trade

I am always worried by the tendency to look at trade only from the point of view of bilateral balances. I am not denying that Japan's trade relations with the U.S., the European Community and others are a source of friction at present. However, some of the recent political rhetoric has rather overdramatized the difficulties, in my opinion. As for "doing something" about the trade imbalance with Japan, the search for effective trade action must recognize that the imbalance is primarily the result not of trade policies but of differences in the economies of these countries.

Interview, Geneva/U.S. News & World Report, 5-20:46.

4

Thomas F. Eagleton
United States Senator, D-Missouri

[In a debate over a proposed bill to curb shoe imports]: Not so long ago, it was said Missouri was first in shoes, first in booze and last in the American [baseball] League. Today, we are first in the American League but last in shoes. Only booze seems to be holding its own.

Before the Senate, Washington,
Oct. 24/The New York Times, 10-29:12.

5

Roger Enrico
President, Pepsi Cola USA

[On advertising]: In what other field can you set off on a journey without any idea of where you're going, arrive at your destination and have no idea where you are, return home and have no idea where you've been, and do it all on someone else's money.

At workshop sponsored by "Advertising Age"/
USA Today, 8-29:(B)2.

6

Thomas S. Foley
United States Representative,
D-Washington

. . . the [Reagan] Administration needs to pay some attention to the depression that exists

(THOMAS S. FOLEY)

in the farm country, to the rising river of credit problems that threatens literally a flood of foreclosures. We've got 300,000 or 350,000 farmers in the country that face bankruptcy. Now, I also think—and this is not a matter of making blame—but I also think the [government] farm programs could have been better administered with less money . . So I think now the farm outlays are going to have to take their place in freezing or generally reducing Federal expenditures; but with that framework, I think we can do a better job than the Administration is proposing for the future of agriculture.

Broadcast interview, Washington/
"Meet the Press," NBC-TV, 2-10.

Bernard A. Goldhirsh
Publisher, Inc.
and High Technology magazines

1

An entrepreneurial revolution is taking place throughout the business landscape. It has come into being because society has come to recognize the value, importance and productivity of the entrepreneurial business unit . . college graduates are redefining the relationship between risk and personal fulfillment. In the '60s, joining the Peace Corps was perceived as a far better option than starting a business. In many circles the idea of working to turn a profit was scorned, as if to say that those who were generating profits were not also generating products, jobs and playing a key role in the creation of a better economy. Now we have college graduates who aren't necessarily reaching for the hand of the first established company to come along and offering them security. They are thinking in terms of risk.

Before Advertising Club of Pittsburgh/
The Wall Street Journal, 6-20:26.

James Goldsmith
Chairman,
General Oriental Investments, Ltd.

2

The only reason a [corporate] merger is termed "hostile" is that top management doesn't like it. It's not hostile to shareholders. It's not

hostile to employees. Except for top bureaucrats, employees prosper in most cases. Management is uncertain of its future in a "hostile" bid, whereas it has negotiated its future in a "friendly" merger . . . Most mergers are done for good, strategic reasons. They improve the businesses. There's an element of synergy. The "bust up", takeover, I happen to believe, is a good thing, too. What you have is a tired conglomerate with a number of good assets—but the vigor is gone. Someone acquires a company like that, then sells the pieces. It is merely liberating the pieces . . . No excellent company is subject to a takeover. The only companies running that risk are those where the market, in its wisdom, thinks management is not making its assets work best. Either management itself takes the necessary steps to rectify the situation, or someone has to do it for them.

Interview/U.S. News & World Report, 7-22:57.

Alan Greenspan
Former Chairman, Council of
Economic Advisers to the President of
the United States (Gerald R. Ford)

3

I think it's quite remarkable that, throughout this period of rising imports, the forces of protectionism have not prevailed. The local-content bill, which looked to be the easiest to sell, is dead; the 20-per-cent import surcharge has failed. A remarkable maturity has emerged in the Congress not to be enticed by irresponsible protectionist moves.

Interview/U.S. News & World Report, 6-3:27.

Gerald Greenwald
Vice chairman,
Chrysler Corporation

4

[Arguing against lifting quotas on Japanese automobile exports to the U.S.]: With the cost advantage the Japanese have, there is no doubt in my mind that they could capture upwards of 40 per cent of the car market, compared with about 20 per cent now. Nearly 1 in 7 people in this country is employed, directly or indirectly, in our industry, and if the Japanese took another 20 points of the market, I guess we're talking about

(GERALD GREENWALD)

750,000 to 800,000 jobs . . . you can't ignore the real world. We've had four years of quotas, and they are working—600,000 jobs have been added in the automotive industry, and four Japanese companies have committed to build plants in the U.S., all as a direct result of the quotas.

Interview/U.S. News & World Report, 2-4:44.

Lloyd Hackler
President,
American Retail Federation

1

[On complaints by members of Congress about restrictive Japanese trade policies]: You talk to a fairly reasonable, logical fellow on [Capitol] Hill who understands the economic realities of trade, and he says: "I'll tell you what you do. You get those SOBs to start taking some of my constituents' beef and I'll quit complaining about them sending their cars over here" . . . Congress itself tends to be protectionist. They have to look out for their parochial interests. That's what they were elected for.

Los Angeles Times, 4-4-(I):1.

Gary Hart
United States Senator, D-Colorado

2

If the [trade] protectionist policies advocated by some in our [Democratic] Party are followed, we will see some short-term political gains . . . But in the long term, I think it is a political disaster for us, because it is wrong. It is not a good policy. And ultimately, over the long term, good policy is good politics. Sooner or later, if you are just cashing in on short-term chips, people are going to find that out.

To reporters, Washington/
The Christian Science Monitor, 10-16:28.

Fred L. Hartley
Chairman and president,
Unocal Corporation (Union Oil)

3

[Criticizing the increase in corporate takeovers]: It's important to understand that raiding is *not* going on because Unocal and all other integrated oil companies somehow suddenly need to be "restructured," as claimed by [industrialist] T. Boone Pickens . . . Carrying Mr. Pickens' line of reasoning to its extreme, we would end up with every large U.S. oil company being either merged, liquidated, or "decapitalized." This is obviously an impossible result, with impossible demands on the credit system. It's also a result that, even if partly achieved, would be severely damaging to the national economy and our nation's energy security. It could also lead to a reconcentration of our oil industry—pushing us back to the monopoly days of the Standard Oil trust . . . If the Russians had somehow quietly managed to murder five of the nation's leading oil companies, and were stalking the rest, I'm certain that Congress would be in an uproar, demanding action. But murder it has been, and murder it may be.

Before House Oversight Subcommittee,
Washington, April 2/
The Wall Street Journal, 4-3:35.

Richard E. Heckert
Vice chairman,
E. I. du Pont de Nemours and Company

4

Over the years we have developed an ideological hangup about free trade, as though it were the only acceptable and moral way to conduct our international affairs. We have accepted the theory of comparative advantage, not always noticing that good theory was being badly distorted in practice. Now we need a large measure of pragmatism. We need to realize that trade arrangements—of whatever kind—are only a means to an end. Our government has to give priority to its first duty, which is not to be a missionary for virtually non-existent "free trade," but to serve the interests of the public. Other governments do not practice free trade in their markets and never have. Some of them do have a comparative advantage that fits classical theory, but today much of the advantage comes not from that source but from the actions of governments working in alliance with industry. In this day and age, for the U.S. to pursue a unilateral free-trade

(RICHARD E. HECKERT)

policy, and ignore the actions of those governments, makes about as much sense as pursuing a unilateral disarmament policy.

Before Chemical Manufacturers Association, Houston/The Wall Street Journal, 6-6:26.

John Heinz III
United States Senator,
R-Pennsylvania

1

[On Japan's proposals to open his country to more U.S. products]: Prime Minister [Yasuhiro] Nakasone has just announced the sixth market-opening package in four years. None of the others has done much good and I suspect that the current one will have just about the same effect. I would argue that the time is long past for continued discussion and negotiations. These endless negotiations seem to have taken on the character of an elaborate con game, with the United States as the willing dupe. The Japanese have no incentive to make meaningful changes in their market structure because they are confident that we will never take any action against them.

The Washington Post, 7-31:(F)2.

Don Hewitt
Executive producer,
"60 Minutes," CBS-TV

2

[On criticism of his program by the corporate world]: If we're perceived as being against big business, well, we're a big business ourselves. We're probably a bigger business than what we usually report on. Business is anti-media. And the media are anti-business. There's a very simple reason. There are only two things a businessman ever wants said about himself: what he pays his advertising agency to say and what he pays his PR people to say. I would love to go through life, if I were a car company, with people thinking that everybody who worked for me was named Mr. Goodwrench [a General Motors advertising character]; or if I were a tobacco company, that people thought my middle name was low tar and nicotine. That's why businesspeople go up the wall: We play with their carefully manicured image.

Interview/Playboy, March:167.

Constance Horner
Associate Director,
Federal Office of Management and Budget

3

[On the Reagan Administration's desire to abolish the Small Business Administration]: We are seeking to reduce the role of the Federal government as a money lender. For 32 years, the SBA has been a political petty-cash drawer for special interests sponsored by the Executive and Legislative branches—mushroom processors, fishermen afflicted by changes in ocean currents, individuals affected by the devaluation of the Mexican peso. That's subsidy out of the taxpayers' pockets to businesses chosen by bureaucrats, not the market . . . The direct-loan and loan-guarantee activities of the SBA are not important to small business as a whole. Fewer than 1 per cent of small businesses receive SBA credit assistance; the other 99 get along nicely without it.

Interview/ U.S. News & World Report, 3-11:63.

Lee A. Iacocca
Chairman, Chrysler Corporation

4

[On how to reduce the imbalance favoring Japan in Japan-U.S. trade]: How about giving them a strategy like this: "Look, Mr. [Japanese Prime Minister Yasuhiro] Nakasone, I'm $37-billion a year in the hole to you, and that's just too big a ripoff, even for a friend. You think I've got a problem, but I've got news for you, friend: You've got a problem. It's $37-billion and it's growing, and that won't fly. I just set a goal for my team on the budget deficit: I want $50-billion out. And I'm giving you one for your team: $10-billion out next year, and then we'll set a plan for the second and third years. Tell me how you get there. Some more beef and oranges and telecommunications from our side, and a few less cars or video recorders from your side. Your call. If you can't work it out, I'll have a few suggestions for you. Do it, or the [U.S.] Congress will do it for both of us. Sayonara" . . . I'm no Communist, folks, but it's not Russia that's laying waste to my business and to most of the rest of business in this country. It's Japan. Our friend. While we

WHAT THEY SAID IN 1985

(LEE A. IACOCCA)

stack the missiles up in the front yard, all aimed at our enemy, our friend is taking over the back yard.

Before House Democratic Caucus, Washington, March 2/The New York Times, 3-5:12.

1

[Saying he advocates government action to protect U.S. markets against countries that limit U.S. imports]: I'm not very popular with the people around the White House any more. I told them, "Let's make sure we don't get hosed [on trade]." They don't like that. This [Reagan] Administration sees you either as a protectionist or a free-trader, with no shades in-between. And we're going to lose, as a country, for it.

Interview/Time, 4-1:38.

2

The first requisite in running a major corporation is the ability to pick good people, because you can't do anything alone. I look for eager beavers who do more than they're expected but who can work as a team. You have to motivate them, communicate with them in plain language so they know when they're doing something right and when they're doing something wrong. And you have to be a decision-maker. After all the information has been gathered, somebody has to decide. That's what being in charge is all about.

Interview/U.S. News & World Report, 5-20:68.

3

Right now, America is getting whipped [in foreign trade]. Your birthright as an American is to change things. When Americans get mad enough, they change things. Satisfied people don't change things. Until we fix the trade deficit, this country won't be able to compete. So get mad. Get mad at those people in Washington. Get mad at anybody who tells you you'll have to settle for less . . . [The U.S. trades] raw materials and foodstuffs for manufactured goods [from Japan]. Does the pattern sound a little familiar? It's the classic definition of a colony. That's what

46

de-industrialization and weak-kneed trade policies are doing for America. I hope it really makes you mad.

At Massachusetts Institute of Technology commencement, June 3/USA Today, 6-4:(A)1.

William Isaac
Chairman, Federal Deposit Insurance Corporation

4

[On the effect of recent bank failures on the FDIC]: The FDIC has sustained record losses over the past four years but, despite that, the fund has grown dramatically from $11-billion in assets in 1981 to $18-billion today. It has never been stronger or more liquid . . . Yes, we favor legislation requiring all [banks and savings] institutions to join FDIC or FSLIC. I sense a strong commitment for this on Capitol Hill now. I think [private insurance's demise] is coming anyway because most of the privately insured institutions are making application to FDIC or FSLIC. Nevertheless, I favor legislation to require it.

Interview/USA Today, 5-15:(B)1.

5

To me, the Federal deficit is the number one threat to the financial system today. There is virtually no problem in the financial system that wouldn't be substantially alleviated by an immediate, significant reduction in the deficit. It would bring interest rates down, and it would bring down the value of the dollar, making our products more competitive around the world.

Interview/U.S. News & World Report, 5-27:61.

William J. Janklow
Governor of South Dakota (R)

6

. . . we talk about getting government out of agriculture. It's not coming out, ever, and it's never been out of agriculture. Good Lord, if you go back to 1974 when the price of wheat went up high in the world markets—and in America you had $6.00 wheat—Gerald Ford, a Republican President, put an embargo on wheat and soybeans that couldn't leave this country—and that's

way American firms are doing business, driving more of them abroad and increasing the amount of outsourcing [buying components overseas].

The Washington Post, 2-8:(A)7.

Edward G. Jefferson
Chairman,
E. I. du Pont de Nemours and Company

3

The sharp appreciation of the dollar since 1980 has significantly undermined the competitive position of U.S. industry, imposing in effect a 50 per cent surcharge on American goods sold abroad and a comparable subsidy on imports sold in the United States. The total trade deficit is costing us more than 2 million jobs, and threatens the industrial base of the country. The loss of these jobs adds substantially to the Federal budget deficit.

At Conference on Technology and Economic Policy, Washington, Feb. 4/The Washington Post, 2-14:(A)18.

Edward Kane
Professor of economics and finance,
Ohio State University

4

[On the failure of Ohio's Home State Savings Bank and the subsequent decision by the Governor of Ohio to close a number of other banks to prevent runs on them by depositors]: The proximate cause of Home's failure was its gross overexposure in one credit, its accounts with a now-defunct government-securities dealer in Florida. But push it back a step. Why didn't the regulators in Ohio find ways of stopping them from doing this? Push it back further: Why didn't other banks in the system blow the whistle? They should have known that a failure would force their own deposit insurance premiums to go up.

The New York Times, 3-20:39.

Lane Kirkland
President, American Federation of
Labor-Congress of Industrial Organizations

5

[On the rise in corporate takeovers]: I think corporate raids are an outrage and a bloody

cy considerations, [it] had
te farmers; he absolutely
dent Jimmy Carter doesn't like what the Russians are doing in Afghanistan, so he puts an embargo on. That's, again, governmental policy. In addition to that, it's our government's official policy to prop up the nations of Argentina and Brazil, pouring money and wealth into those countries to develop an agriculture infrastructure that destroys and competes with the American farmer.

Broadcast interview/
"Meet the Press," NBC-TV, 2-24.

1

[Calling for Federal aid to debt-ridden farmers, and rejecting the Reagan Administration's policy of letting the free market work for farming]: What's wrong with asking the guy who drove over you with a truck for compensation . . . ? It's the national government that drove over these farmers. Get rid of the [Federal] deficit, and you won't have a farmer in town [lobbying for assistance] . . . [And] when you use agriculture or any industry as a tool of foreign policy [such as grain embargoes against certain countries], don't give me this bunk about a free market. It's never going to be a free market . . . So let's quit dreaming about it.

Washington, Feb. 26/
The Christian Science Monitor, 2-27:6.

Jerry J. Jasinowski
Senior vice president and chief economist,
National Association of Manufacturers

2

[On the U.S. foreign trade deficit]: It's reached a point of outrage. Business leaders across the spectrum regard the trade deficit and the problems that lead to it as on a parallel with the [Federal] budget deficit. It's pretty much across the board. It reflects the fact that we have a pretty healthy domestic recovery, at the same time that firms have made themselves extraordinarily more efficient, and yet we're losing markets. [The trade deficit] is radically changing the

(LANE KIRKLAND)

scandal. The object is for somebody to make a killing, pure and simple, and I see no virtue in it at all.

Time, 4-22:44.

Charles Kittrell
Executive vice president,
Phillips Petroleum Company

[Criticizing many corporate takeovers by investors]: The critical issue is whether we want to encourage the short-term speculator out for a quick buck over the long-term interests of our corporations. We oppose the kind of takeover activity now seen more and more because we believe it is an abuse of the free market . . . In our view, this activity is not in the national interest.

Before House Energy and Commerce subcommittee, Washington, Feb. 27/The Washington Post, 2-28:(B)1.

1

Nicholas Kominus
President, United States
Sugar Cane Refiners Association

[On foreign trade]: Protectionists talk about "fair" trade, whatever that might be. The only example of "fair" trade that I can cite appeared in an excellent editorial in the *World Sugar Journal,* which lambasted the sugar protectionists. That editorial referred to a schoolmaster in England. He mailed a note to all parents that stated, "If you promise not to believe everything your child says happens at this school, I'll promise not to believe everything he says happens at home." Now, that is a fair trade.

At conference sponsored by Organization of American States and Georgetown University, Washington/The Wall Street Journal, 1-4:10.

2

John Kotter
Professor,
Harvard Business School

It makes me sick to hear economists [tell management students] that their job is to "maximize shareholder profits." Their job is going to

48

be managing a whole host of constituencies, bosses, underlings, customers, suppliers, unions—you name it. Trying to get cooperation from different constituencies is an infinitely more difficult task than milking your business for money.

Newsweek, 9-16:54.

Thomas Labrecque
President,
Chase Manhattan Bank, New York

[On the entry into some banking functions, such as consumer financing, by non-banking companies]: When an executive says that he'd like to grow his business into "the largest financial institution in the world, financing people's cars, handling their mortgages, checking accounts and everything else for them," I sit up and take notice. When that executive's name is Roger Smith and his company is General Motors, it hammers home the fact that the banking business has changed and we'd better change along with it.

U.S. News & World Report, 5-27:60.

4

Robert Lawrence
Senior Fellow,
Brookings Institution

The basic principle—the so-called comparative advantage of nations—that motivated those advocating free trade under Adam Smith remains valid today. Nations gain by specializing through trade, both because producers gain from large-scale economies and consumers gain from being able to buy a broader range of goods. OPEC countries have an advantage because of natural-resource endowments, such as oil. The United States has an advantage because of human endowments, its highly skilled and knowledgeable labor force. China has an advantage in unskilled labor, so it exports textiles. The Japanese and Europeans have an advantage in small cars, which we [in the U.S.] buy . . . Our poor trade performance is not due to our free-trade policy. Rather, it reflects the strength of the dollar, which is related to the high interest rates caused by our record [Federal] budget deficits. It is pre-

5

(ROBERT LAWRENCE)

posterous to argue that protectionism by other countries has increased sufficiently to bring about the sharp drop in our trade balance over the past four years.

Interview/U.S. News & World Report, 9-23:53.

Lee Kuan Yew
Prime Minister of Singapore

1

[On the importance of free trade]: What is at stake is the issue of war and peace, and not the simple preservation of jobs in plants that are no longer competitive internationally. People now accept as commonplace the resurgence of the dynamic German and Japanese economies without military expansionism . . . Without free trade, we can imagine what would have happened had the energies of the German and the Japanese people in their quest for a better life been frustrated.

Interview, Washington/
The Washington Post, 10-15:(A)10.

Frank Luerssen
Chairman, Inland Steel Corporation

2

[Calling for a U.S. tax on foreign imports as a method of aiding the American economy]: It's my impression that the Europeans, and the less-developed countries, and the Japanese, and you name it, believe that this economy, the U.S. economy, is the most important economy in the world. They don't want to do anything to destroy or to weaken it substantially, because this is where they trade their goods.

Interview, Chicago/
The Christian Science Monitor, 8-15: 3.

Gordon S. Macklin
President, National
Association of Securities Dealers

3

There has in recent months been much comment, both in the press and in the governmental/regulatory community, about a feared "race to the bottom" among the securities marketplaces. Admittedly, there is more competition between the country's securities markets, but we

do not believe it to be inherently detrimental to the investing public. In fact, we believe there have been a number of public benefits that have resulted from this intermarket competition, in the areas of automation, information and market services to issuers.

Before House subcommittee on telecommunications,
consumer protection and finance, Washington,
May 22/The Washington Post, 5-23:(E)3.

Bill Marriott
President, Marriott Corporation

4

When the managers of corporations make decisions that are not good long-term decisions for their business, and then they go ask the government to bail them out, it's bad. This damages the credibility of business.

Interview/Business Week, 1-21:75.

Preston Martin
Vice Chairman,
Federal Reserve Board

5

I want to raise the radical notion that it is time for the [banking] industry and regulatory bodies, both Federal and state, to investigate with seriousness the feasibility of some kind of peer review or self-governance . . . We have arrived at a crossroads in the banking business which faces a future considerably different from the past. The challenges and opportunities confronting banks will continue to increase and bankers will be expected to step up to greater leadership roles in maintaining safety and soundness in the changing banking industry. Today's high-risk banking requires new approaches by the examiners. Industry self-interest, I would submit, also necessitates your involvement in self-regulatory and other solutions.

At conference sponsored by American
Banking Association, Washington, April 11/
The Washington Post, 4-12:(F)3.

Nobuo Matsunaga
Japanese Ambassador to the United States

6

[Arguing against trade protectionism by the U.S.]: We believe these kinds of protectionist

49

WHAT THEY SAID IN 1985

(NOBUO MATSUNAGA)

measures would undermine our trade relations. [There would be] reactions abroad in many other countries. Once it starts, I'm quite sure it will have a snowball effect . . . It is hard for us to accept the view . . . that this situation [the large U.S. trade deficit] is entirely and exclusively Japan's fault . . . Japan is a tough, competitive and quality-conscious market, but it is richly rewarding those American companies with the right product, the marketing ingenuity and the long-term commitment to see it through. It is not enough for Japan to dismantle its import barriers. Potential exporters to Japan still have to study the market and how to compete in it.

To reporters, Washington, Sept. 18/
Los Angeles Times, 9-19:(I)14.

J. Paul McGrath
Assistant Attorney General, Antitrust Division,
Department of Justice of the United States

1

Our policy permits more [corporate] mergers and, yes, it's messier than a regime in which almost no mergers were allowed, but that's the nature of competition . . . If you look at the host of hostile takeovers in the last several years, they were [of] companies that were undervalued [and then] increased dramatically in value. Their stock price went up as they sold off [unproductive assets] or they got better management. They [stock prices] stayed up. It was not just some back gnomes on Wall Street who benefited by hostile takeovers. It's your friends and neighbors. [Who loses?] Management sitting on assets, running divisions it has no competence to run. Overall, that company will be less efficient . . . its products more costly.

Interview/USA Today, 3-25:(B)2.

Peter J. McLaughlin
Chairman, Union Camp Corporation

2

The myth is that you can turn out more tons if you take off the quality-control restrictions. The truth is that you usually can make more by adhering to quality control. When you get close to

the edge of acceptance, you start getting rejects. A rejected roll of paper is just a waste of a lot of money and time.

The Wall Street Journal, 1-25:18.

John Melcher
United States Senator, D-Montana

3

If I were a dictator for a day? I would set up [farm] exports, provide more impetus on [farm] exports, and my policy would be to try to turn our production machine loose to try to meet the world's needs. This [Reagan] Administration is blatant in its belief that there are too many farmers in this country. There really are not. There simply isn't too much food in the world. We're blessed in the variety of foods we have and there's just a breakdown in supplying that food to people who need it. And I say that's a hell of a lot more important right now than whether we have Reagan's "Star Wars" defense or MX missiles.

Interview/The Washington Post, 11-2:(A)10.

Ruben Mettler
Chairman, TRW Corporation

4

The trade deficit has a very direct, immediate impact. There's an enormous distortion in our economy with import- and export-sensitive industries cutting back on investment in the U.S. because they can't compete . . . Competitiveness is a package of many things. It's quality, productivity, price availability and so forth. But clearly the biggest single head wind we face now is the strong dollar or the weak yen; the strong dollar or the weak European currencies.

Interview/U.S. News & World Report, 7-22:23.

Akio Morita
Chairman,
Sony Corporation (Japan)

5

Trade restrictions are dangerous in a free economic system. In truth, we are confused by American attitudes. Three years ago, Americans

Ralph Nader
Lawyer;
Consumer-rights advocate

2

[On the recent increase in corporate mergers and take-overs]: Very little rationale for them. In the old days, a company would try to give rational reasons, such as a company being acquired because it had a good distribution system or management. Now it's really empire-building. It's concentration of corporate and political power that is disruptive of communities and workers and is money that's not going into new investments and new productive activity.

Interview, Washington/The New York Times, 11-23:8.

Yasuhiro Nakasone
Prime Minister of Japan

3

There has been criticism against Japan that the country closes its market to foreign products and maintains an unfair policy. Other nations feel that they cannot leave that unfair situation as it is and that they should take some retaliatory measures. They feel that they should impose surcharges on goods from Japan—10 per cent or 15 per cent—so that they can block inroads of Japanese goods into their countries. If this materializes, Japan's exports would be suspended and the country would face a serious depression . . . If Japan doesn't change its trade measures, the United States Senate will take action. It passed unanimously a bill authorizing the President to stop imports of goods from Japan . . . If President Reagan has to take action under these bills, Japan's exports would be stopped. Japan would not be able to export its cars, television sets and machinery. Plants would have to close, and unemployment would rise sharply . . . The important thing is that we should give American businessmen an equal opportunity to compete fairly with their Japanese counterparts. Then, if they fail to do well in Japan, it is their responsibility, not ours.

Broadcast address to the nation, Tokyo,
April 9/The New York Times, 4-10:38.

4

Free trade is as fragile as glass; if we do not take care, even the slightest shock may shatter it to bits. Because free trade is premised upon

(AKIO MORITA)

said Japan should adopt voluntary export restrictions on automobiles. We did. Then the American manufacturers had a boom in business, and top management took big bonuses, which they are now enjoying. Three years passed. Now [U.S.] President Reagan says, "We don't want restrictions any more." So because of the big demand for Japanese automobiles in your country, Japan lets more autos be exported, and this causes a trade crisis. Meanwhile, General Motors and Chrysler come to Japan and seek to buy more Japanese automobiles under their names. As I said, this confuses us. Americans want us to decrease our exports. But the big American auto manufacturers, whose profits rise because of this, then want more Japanese autos for their own sake. This is an unfair, selfish attitude by American managers. If the balance of trade is so serious, why doesn't American management cooperate with us? Instead, they invest money in Japan or Taiwan and bring back more products, and make the imbalance worse.

Interview/
U.S. News & World Report, 7-29:52.

Robert K. Mueller
Chairman,
Arthur D. Little, Inc.

1

There's no shortage of people who want to get on boards [of directors of large corporations]. I have a file this deep where people write me and say, "How do I get on a board?" But the role of the board is not too clearly understood. People have two false notions: One is that it is an elite society and sort of doesn't do anything; the other is that it's kind of a subdivision of religion—that there's somebody up there who knows and solves everything. Neither of them is valid. One, it isn't an elite society; the other is that the board doesn't know any more than you and I know as individuals. The value system of a corporation is made up by those of us sitting around the table—our beliefs and our own value systems. Boards don't govern; people govern.

Interview/
U.S. News & World Report, 1-28:71.

WHAT THEY SAID IN 1985

(YASUHIRO NAKASONE)

competition, it inevitably inflicts pain on certain industries in every country. Yet if countries fall back on selfish national policies in an effort to avoid this pain, then clearly the entire structure of free trade will collapse. Like a powerful narcotic, protectionism may induce a feeling of temporary well-being in the industries it is supposed to protect. But protectionism not only saps the vitality of its users, it also begets further protectionism, and ultimately the world economy will lapse into a coma. Recognizing the need to match words with deeds, I am implementing a forceful program to make the Japanese market one of the most open in the world.

At United Nations, New York, Oct. 23/
The New York Times, 10-24:9.

James Newman
Vice chairman,
Booz, Allen & Hamilton

1

Many of the successful CEOs I know today are particularly people-developers. They're not people-oriented in the sense of a warm, developing person. But they know how to appreciate the talents that exist in people, and they know how to make the maximum use out of them. Now, when you get a CEO who is also very people-sensitive and a people-developing type, then you have a real star, because he will take the subordinate and really try to bring out his or her best . . . I've been asked if I advocate people working 14 or 16 hours a day. No, I don't *per se* and I would say the same on the workaholic theme. I don't advocate being a workaholic *per se*, but I do say the person who's going to get up the ladder is going to be someone who gets so dedicated to the assignment or job given him, is so caught up in it and so enthusiastically pursuing it, that he just will work the long hours.

Interview/USA Today, 4-24:(A)11.

William Norris
Chairman,
Control Data Corporation

2

There have been several studies recently showing that most [corporate] mergers don't

52

work. It's hard to get a good mix of companies even in a friendly environment, where things are carefully thought out. A hostile takeover has much less of a chance of working because there's very little planning before companies are smashed together . . . I've been saying for years that hostile takeovers undermine our competitive position in world markets. They often loot corporate treasuries, rob shareholders and disrupt the lives of employees and communities. They force management to sacrifice the development of new products and services for short-term gains. The pressure is to drain off equity and put the company in debt. Money then goes into paying interest, and paying interest is a lot less productive than spending it on innovation. The debt will have serious consequences in a recession; a lot of these companies will go under because they took on that enormous debt . . . In virtually every hostile takeover I'm familiar with, there have been losses of jobs. Also very bad is career disruption, particularly in middle management. All of that adds up to an adverse effect on communities.

Interview/U.S. News & World Report, 7-22:57.

Kenichi Ohmae
Managing director,
McKinsey & Co., Tokyo,
international consultants

3

[Saying consumer tastes are becoming increasingly similar around the world]: The global "Yuppie" has arrived. He awakes to music from his Sony radio, reaches for his Brazilian-grown coffee in a cup from Taiwan, rides down Otis elevators, climbs into his Porsche, turns on a Blaupunkt cassette player, and heads to work.

Interview, New York/
The Christian Science Monitor, 2-12:23.

Thomas P. O'Neill, Jr.
United States Representative,
D-Massachusetts

4

[Criticizing President Reagan's objection to a House bill to aid debt-ridden farmers]: Reagan can veto the bill, but he cannot veto the problem. The President seems determined to surprise and

(THOMAS P. O'NEILL, JR.)

disappoint the people who elected him. Maybe he wants the farmers to say "uncle" before he gives them the help they need.

Washington, March 5/Los Angeles Times, 3-6:(I)1.

Rudolf A. Oswald
Chief economist, American Federation of Labor-Congress of Industrial Organizations

1

I don't think pure free trade has ever existed anywhere in the world. Clearly, trade has always been restricted for national-security reasons. And it would seem that national security would include certain industries that may be necessary for long-term stability of a country.

The New York Times, 9-9:28.

Robert W. Packwood
United States Senator, R-Oregon

2

I believe in the inherent justice and economic benefits of free [international] trade. All nations and people benefit when the rules of comparative advantage are permitted to operate freely. These principles have not operated as expected in the case of Japan. The existence of complicated and deeply rooted Japanese [trade] barriers has altered the forces that normally guide an open market . . . What is puzzling about this situation is that the Japanese government should not recognize its own self-interest. A nation as heavily dependent on export markets as is Japan should behave in a manner intended to preserve those markets. Frankly, I am not interested in the explanation for Japan's endemic resistance to imports. Japan has important international obligations which require that Japan, not the rest [of] the world, discern a means of opening its markets.

Before the Senate, Washington, July 9/The New York Times, 8-24:5.

William S. Paley
Founder and former chairman, CBS, Inc.

3

[Lamenting the possible effects on CBS of a hostile takeover bid]: CBS is strong; CBS is

healthy. But that strength and health are the products of more than a half a century of careful, concerned nurturing by a great many very dedicated people. To throw this away would be a tragedy. To risk its loss would be to trifle recklessly with the company's future and with the public interest.

Interview, New York, April 30/ The New York Times, 5-1:29.

William E. Peacock
President, Hypertat Corporation; Former Assistant Secretary of the Army of the United States

4

Although society sets up rules to prevent unfair practices and the objective is not to destroy your competitors, business has much in common with war. Executives can learn a lot about running a successful enterprise by looking at the principles of war that have always guided victorious military campaigns down through history. There are basically nine of these principles, and they are taught in virtually every military academy in the world. These principles of war— and trade—can be recalled by using the acronym MOOSEMUSS. The first M stands for mass— concentrating your strength against an enemy's weak point. The first O is for objective: In war or in business you have to be clear on just what you want to accomplish. The second O represents offense—the notion that few competitions are ever won by being passive. S stands for simplicity—the importance of making your strategy clear to all employees. E represents economy of force: In business you use the fewest resources practicable to keep the operation functioning while concentrating on the objective. The second M is for the maneuver or strategy used—frontal assault, flanking attack, etc. U stands for unity of command—pinpointing responsibility. And the last two principles starting with S are surprise and security—the practice of timing while keeping your strategy secret.

Interview/U.S. News & World Report, 2-25:68.

Donald E. Petersen
Chairman, Ford Motor Company

5

[Arguing against removing the quotas on Japanese automobile exports to the U.S.]: When

53

(DONALD E. PETERSEN)

I think of the tremendous debate going on over the Federal budget deficit and our enormous trade deficit with Japan, it seems to me that we'd be shooting ourselves in the foot if we supported removing these restraints from the Japanese at this time.

Interview, Los Angeles,
Jan. 29/The Washington Post, 1-30:(F)1.

1

There's a very strong strain in this particular [Reagan] Administration to listen to classical economists. They talk about the parity of free trade, which, of course, doesn't exist anywhere in the world. That is a very serious problem we have in dealing with Washington at this time.

Interview, Los Angeles,
Jan. 29/The Washington Post, 1-30:(F)2.

John Phelan
Chairman,
New York Stock Exchange

I don't see the use of inside information as being anything near a widespread problem [in the securities business]. Instances of it are very limited. Nevertheless, you can't ignore it. If we and the Securities and Exchange Commission don't continue to attack head-on what does show up, there will be the perception of not having an open and fair market.

Interview/U.S. News & World Report, 1-14:74.

2

T. Boone Pickens, Jr.
Chairman and president,
Mesa Petroleum Company

3

If legislation restricting mergers and tender offers is ever enacted into law, the Securities and Exchange Commission should require that all stock certificates contain an appropriate bold-face legend: "Warning: It's the law—your ability to realize the highest price for these shares is severely restricted." Oftentimes, a takeover is the only way, or at least the quickest way, of dislodging a management that is unresponsive to market

developments and therefore unresponsive to shareholders. It is important that stockholders not be burdened with a management that cannot face up to or handle current problems. The mere threat of a hostile takeover attempt can perform a desirable disciplinary function and fosters enhanced corporate accountability to the shareholders. Management must never be allowed to become complacent or to forget who really owns the corporation.

Before House Energy and Commerce subcommittee,
Washington, Feb. 27/USA Today, 3-13:(A)8.

William J. Popejoy
Chairman,
Financial Corporation of America

4

I feel the whole trend of deregulation [of banks and savings institutions] went too far. Along the way, it was somewhat forgotten that in the final analysis, it is Uncle Sam's checkbook and the taxpayers' dollars that pay for the folly of insured financial institutions' management. I believe new rules should be put in place that provide safeguards against government deposit insurance paying for mismanagement. I am in favor of a program that would involve an "early warning accountability matrix." That accountability would be that each month at a directors meeting, the directors would be required to review this early warning matrix, and the early warning matrix could be a list of the salient risk factors of the institutions . . . One problem regulators have now is they don't know about these problems until they are out of control. If management is willing to take on greater risk, they should pay for [deposit insurance] with a higher premium.

Interview/The Washington Post, 1-2:(B)9.

William Proxmire
United States Senator, D-Wisconsin

5

[On the rise in corporate takeovers]: The rising tide of hostile takeovers threatens the very foundations of our American system. They undermine productivity, wreak havoc on entire communities and saddle well-managed companies with billions of dollars in excessive debt.

Time, 4-22:44.

Donald Ratajczak
Economist, Georgia State University

1

There's a legitimate role for government [to play in agriculture]. A farmer shouldn't go under because the rain doesn't fall this year.

Newsweek, 2-18:55.

Ronald Reagan
President of the United States

2

[On the farm debt crisis]: The situation we're facing today with those farmers is one other people in other lines of work have faced and it's the result of ending an era of building your business on expected inflation. And farmland, unfortunately, was one of those things that, in an inflationary world, zoomed in value. And then they borrowed on the basis of that as security. And when we were successful in bringing down inflation, one of the first things that happened was the nose-diving of that land.

Interview/The Wall Street Journal, 2-8:8.

3

[Saying he is vetoing a bill to help debt-ridden farmers]: Let's be clear on one thing. The bill I vetoed would not really help farmers. It's too late in the season for that. The bill is merely designed to convey the impression of helping farmers . . . The truth of the matter is, in need of immediate help are less than 4 per cent, or around 4 per cent at best, of all the farmers in the United States. Ninety-six per cent do not have liquidity problems . . . I've pleaded and warned repeatedly that just as your [America's] families don't have a blank check for whatever your needs may be, neither can government, and that means taxpayers, bail out every farmer hopelessly in debt, or every bank which made imprudent or speculative [farm] loans and bet on higher inflation.

Upon vetoing bill, Washington, March 6/The New York Times, 3-7:12.

4

[On the current Ohio savings-bank crisis]: I'm pleased to say that this is a matter of a group of savings and loans that had taken out either private or state insurance, had not availed themselves of the Federal insurance program, and it

is limited to Ohio. This is not a major threat to the banking system; there is no other problem of that kind anyplace else in the country that we're aware of. And the Federal Reserve has stepped in and said that they will keep the window open for loans on to those banks or those savings and loans—any of them that meet the requirements of collateral and so forth. And the loans will be available to them when they reopen. So that situation, I think, is being taken care of by the Federal government. There isn't anything else for the Federal government to do.

News conference, Washington, March 21/The New York Times, 3-22:10.

5

We have lived through the age of big industry and the age of the giant corporation, but I believe that this is the age of the entrepreneur, the age of the individual. That's where American prosperity is coming from now, and that's where it's going to come from in the future . . . We have to recognize it and encourage the brave men and women who are taking risks and investing in the future. They ought to be honored. But to invest your time and money and concern is a leap of faith, a profoundly hopeful act that says, "Yes, I have faith in the future. I am the future. The future is what I make of it."

At St. John's University, New York, March 28/The New York Times, 3-29:12.

6

[Turning down proposals for import quotas to protect the U.S. shoe industry]: Our economy is truly interwoven with those of our trading partners. If we cut the threads that hold us together, we injure ourselves as well. If our trading partners cannot sell shoes in the United States, many will then not be able to buy U.S. exports. That would mean more U.S. jobs lost. Thus we find that the true price of protectionism is very high indeed. In order to save a few temporary jobs, we will be throwing many other Americans out of work, costing consumers billions of dollars, further weakening the shoe industry and seriously damaging relations with our trading partners.

Santa Barbara, Calif., Aug. 28*/ The New York Times, 8-29:31.

WHAT THEY SAID IN 1985

(RONALD REAGAN)

1

A mindless stampede toward protectionism will be a one-way trip to economic disaster. That's the lesson of the Smoot-Hawley tariff in 1930, which helped to trigger a world-wide trade war that spread, deepened and prolonged the worst depression in history. And I know; I lived through that period. I have seen and felt the agony this nation endured because of that dreadful legislation. If we repeat the same mistake, we'll pay a price again. Americans whose jobs depend upon exports of machinery, commercial aircraft, high-tech electronics, and chemical products could well be the first targets of retaliation. Agriculture, an industry already in great difficulty, would be even more vulnerable. Protectionist tariffs would invite retaliation that could [deliver] an economic death blow to literally tens of thousands of American family farms.

News conference, Washington,
Sept. 17/The New York Times, 9-18:14.

2

[On the large current U.S. foreign-trade deficit]: From 1790 to 1875, this country, all that 85 years, ran a trade imbalance. And in those years we were becoming the great economic power that we are in the world today . . . [In the 1930s depression.] 25 per cent unemployment, the worst depression the world has ever known, we had a trade surplus every one of those 10 years until World War II ended the depression. So I think this [the current trade-deficit problem] has been exaggerated, and it isn't a case of us being a debtor nation. Another thing we don't count is that from abroad, that is not counted in our export figures, are the billions of dollars of foreign capital that has been invested in the United States, invested in our private industry, invested in our government bonds, if you will—things of this kind—because we are the best and safest investment in the world today.

News conference, Washington,
Sept. 17/The New York Times, 9-18:14.

3

. . . to make the international trading system work, all must abide by the rules. All must work to guarantee open markets. Above all else, free trade is, by definition, fair trade. When domestic markets are closed to the exports of others, it is no longer free trade. When governments subsidize their manufacturers and farmers so that they can dump goods in other markets, it is no longer free trade. When governments permit counterfeiting or copying of American products, it is stealing our future and it is no longer free trade. When governments assist their exporters in ways that violate international laws, then the playing field is no longer level and there is no longer free trade. When governments subsidize industries for commercial advantage and underwrite costs, placing an unfair burden on competitors, that is not free trade.

To business and government officials, Washington,
Sept. 23/The New York Times, 9-24:48.

4

Sometimes in Washington there are some who seem to forget what the economy is all about. They give me reports saying that the economy does this and the economy will do that. They never talk about business. And somewhere along the way these folks in Washington have forgotten that the economy is business. Business creates new products and new services. Business creates jobs. Business creates prosperity for our communities and our nation as a whole. And business is the people that make it work. From the CEO to the workers in the factories.

To business and government officials, Washington,
Sept. 23/The New York Times, 9-24:48.

Robert Reich
Professor of political economy and management, Harvard University

5

[On the increasing foreign investment in the U.S.]: In the short term, these kinds of foreign investments are probably good for the United States and American workers because they preserve jobs. In the long term, however, this relationship is not healthy for the U.S. economy simply because Americans working for foreign owners do not get the kind of technical learning they need to keep our country competitive internationally. They get only as much technical education and experience as the parent company is willing to parcel out to its foreign subsidiary here.

The New York Times, 12-31:9.

Donald Reid
Senior vice president, Wells Fargo Bank

1

The structure of the financial-services industry is in a period of enormous flux. With deregulation, it is necessary to conduct business in a different and more competitive manner. The most ethical bank is one that carefully and unselfishly balances the responsibilities it has to customers, shareholders, employees and communities where it is doing business.

U.S. News & World Report, 12-9:62.

Ronald Rhody
Senior vice president for corporate communication, Bank of America

2

Businessmen have to develop a thicker skin. Business leaders today are almost in the role of politicians, and they are going to be looked at, appraised and criticized. Sometimes the media may beat up on you—that comes with the territory.

Fortune, 3-4:68.

Louis R. Ross
Executive vice president, Ford Motor Co.

3

Training is the final key to survival for the North American auto industry. It also is the key to the individual survival of each North American automotive engineer. For by the end of the decade, the North American auto companies will be smaller companies. Pressure for lower-cost production will whittle down the domestic companies, and on a personal basis, too. Darwinism will prevail. Only the best people will survive.

The Wall Street Journal, 4-23:36.

Herbert M. Sandler
Chairman, Golden West Financial Corporation

4

[On the increased number of savings-and-loan failures in recent years]: It's a strange situation. Companies fall into three categories now: those that are extraordinarily healthy, a middle group of legitimate operators that are not very profitable, and another sector one might call the walking dead. They exist in name only. Their losses, when recognized, will be greater than their net worth. There are hundreds and hundreds and hundreds of them, of all sizes.

Interview, Los Angeles/The New York Times, 9-3:32.

Frederick M. Scherer
Professor of economics, Swarthmore College

5

[Criticizing the President's Council of Economic Advisers for their support of corporate takeover activity]: [Their views fail] to explain why business performance was good when there were few contested takeovers and poor when there were many. It ignores the "undervalued assets" explanation for takeovers. The stock market studies on which it relies are short-run in orientation. Longer-term analyses suggest different results. It fails to examine the actual behavioral changes following a takeover. It implicitly approves the short-run reward goals that drive tendering decisions. But short-run profit maximization leads to weaker, less competitive companies in the long run.

At Congressional hearing, Washington, March 12/The Washington Post, 3-13:(F)3.

Michael Schudson
Associate professor of sociology and communications, University of California, San Diego

6

Any social system needs to affirm itself and its values. It needs to say, "This is who we are, and we feel good about it." Advertising is a way we do this. Ads remind us that this is a country of private people, private ambitions, individual achievement and purportedly infinite material possibility. Ads remind us day after day of a world of choice, abundance and freedom. This focuses on very limited aspects of our lives, and the choice, freedom and abundance exists within very circumscribed, commercial categories. In that sense, ads are misleading, but in a way that says, "Let us affirm ourselves, and let us feel good about ourselves."

Interview/U.S. News & World Report, 1-28:62.

Ted Schwinden
Governor of Montana (D)

1

Agriculture over the last three or four months has had a level of media visibility unprecedented in my lifetime. Unfortunately, much of that is focused on the human stories that are out there—the failing farms, crying spouses, Ma and Pa going to the poorhouse. Now, there *is* a human side to the agricultural story. But even more important is the need for people and government to make some responsible, long-term policy decisions about the future of American agriculture . . . It all boils down to whether people think American agriculture is an industry worth saving in something like its present form. Farmers have to deal with the variabilities of weather, probably a grasshopper infestation again this year, the whims of a President who decided that we're mad over [the Soviet involvement in] Afghanistan or that we're going to sell secretly to the Soviets or some other darned thing. There has to be some certainty in a business as diverse and as important to this country as agriculture.

Interview/U.S. News & World Report, 6-24:(B)11.

Donald B. Shea
President,
United States Brewers Association

2

[Criticizing proposals to ban beer and wine advertising on TV]: To have a legitimate product removed from a legitimate medium is inappropriate. It is the same as saying because 50,000 people are killed in auto accidents each year you should ban automobile advertising. There's not a single product that cannot be misused. Even water and oxygen can be abused.

The New York Times, 1-15:21.

Alan K. Simpson
United States Senator, R-Wyoming

3

[On the farm credit crisis]: The bankers are in trouble because they were thinking in terms of inflated land values and thought the farmer could always subdivide his land into Sunnyville Acres—and that ain't happening. Now that it

58

isn't fun any more, they want the U.S.A. to be the banker for these farmers. This [Reagan] Administration has poured 63 billion bucks into agriculture programs—more than any other Administration—and it has not worked.

Interview/U.S. News & World Report, 3-11:23.

4

[On government aid to farmers]: I have not seen a thing . . . that would show me what we are really doing for the little guy in Oshkosh B'gosh overalls with the hoe in his hand. We play with the big-ticket guys, the rice cats, the corn cats, the wheat cats—all of them heavy hitters. Then we get up and talk about that poor little guy. I do not see anything going out to him at all. I just see the heavy money streaming out the door.

The Washington Post, 11-25:(A)5.

Roger Smith
Chairman, General Motors Corporation

5

[On his rise through the ranks at GM]: One of the given characteristics of a large company is that, when you start out [as an employee], you're just another runner in the pack. You've got to show somebody that you can do something better than someone else. From the beginning, I had relatively routine assignments. It took me nine years to get off the mark. When I first walked in the door downstairs, I certainly didn't holler, "Look out, here I come." No, I don't think anybody up here then was too worried about that ever happening.

Interview, Detroit/Nation's Business, February:32.

Edson Spencer
Chairman, Honeywell, Inc.;
Chairman, Advisory Council on
U.S.-Japan Economic Relations

6

[On U.S. efforts to open up the Japanese market to imported goods]: When all is said and done, the Japanese have come a very, very long way in recent years in making it easier to get into their market. There's a spirit in Japan of saying, "Let's open it up." In fact, they can point to all the things they've done. The unfortunate thing is

(EDSON SPENCER)

that the U.S. has had to drive hard, threaten and rattle cages to push the Japanese to do what they should do anyway . . . What is needed, perhaps more on their side than ours, is to understand that they have their own cultural structure, but they're in a world that is completely hostile to them in terms of dealing with that structure. Patience and education and constant talking on our side are the thing that's going to bring it home to them that they've got to make some changes in their style.

Interview/U.S. News & World Report, 4-22:34.

David A. Stockman
Director,
Federal Office of Management and Budget

1

[Arguing against Federal aid to farmers in debt]: For the life of me, I cannot figure out why the taxpayers of this country have the responsibility to go in and refinance bad debt that was willingly incurred by consenting adults who went out and bought farmland when the price was going up and thought that they could get rich, or who went out and bought machinery and production assets because they made a business judgment that they could make money.

Before Senate Budget Committee,
Washington, Feb. 5/Time, 2-18:24.

2

[Saying he favors the dismantling of the Small Business Administration]: Why should somebody who's got everything on the line—worked like a dog for his life's savings—have to compete with the new guy on the block who's got an SBA loan to set up a pizza parlor?

U.S. News & World Report, 3-11:14.

Robert S. Strauss
Former Trade Representative for the
President of the United States (Jimmy Carter)

3

. . . our American workers and our American farmers are in trouble now, and they're being criticized—lack of efficiency, we can't compete.

Our biggest problem is, our workers and farmers don't compete with workers and farmers in foreign nations; they're competing with governments. They're competing with governments, I say, because of the subsidies that [foreign] governments provide. Take a look at agriculture. Our sugar growers in this country are competing with a European sugar policy where the Europeans pay 26 or 27 cents for sugar. They dump it on the world market at 3 cents a pound. If you buy it at 27, dump it for 3, no way in the world our people can compete with that. We need a coherent trade policy in this country. Not just Japan—we've had enough Japan-bashing. All over the world we need a trade policy. We should begin at home.

Broadcast interview/
"Meet the Press," NBC-TV, 8-18.

Margaret Thatcher
Prime Minister of the United Kingdom

4

Protectionism is a danger to all our trading partnerships. For so many countries, trade is even more important than aid.

Before joint session of U.S. Congress, Washington,
Feb. 20/The Washington Post, 2-21:(A)9.

James R. Thompson
Governor of Illinois (R)

5

[On his recent trip to Asia to promote trade and investment in the U.S.]: For a long time I was reluctant to go, because I just didn't want to hear the perpetual criticism of "How much did your hotel room cost?" and "How much is this costing the state?" People believe foreign travel is exotic. If you're going to Detroit, that's okay; but if you go to Hong Kong, it becomes a "junket." Actually, foreign travel is one of the cheapest forms of economic development there is. We spent much less taking this delegation to the Orient than we'd spend on any other form of economic development, including tax abatement or job retraining . . . I finally said, "To heck with it—I'm going."

Interview, Chicago/
The Christian Science Monitor, 4-15:3.

Shoichiro Toyoda
President,
Toyota Motor Co. (Japan)

[Saying his industry's restraints on auto exports to the U.S. should be ended]: These voluntary restraints were a political decision made in May, 1981, as an emergency measure for two years—three years at the most—to help the American auto industry readjust itself. Although they were supposed to end after three years, the restraints were extended, for a maximum of one year, nominally as an interim measure . . . No one can doubt that the Big Three [U.S. auto companies] have recovered and that they have increased their international competitiveness . . . There is absolutely no reason for the voluntary restraints to be continued.

To foreign correspondents,
Tokyo, Jan. 24/
Los Angeles Times,
1-25:(IV)1.

1

Paul A. Volcker
Chairman, Federal Reserve Board

Banks and bank holding companies, and thrifts and their service corporations, are expanding interstate and into new product lines, including investment banking, real-estate development and insurance activities, whenever and wherever they can find room through new interpretations of Federal law or new state law. Non-bank entities—securities firms, insurance companies and commercial and retail organizations—are making inroads where they can into the banks' traditional franchise in deposit-taking and payments system. In the process, long-established policies set by the Congress are breaking down . . . Confusion abounds. Equity is lost.

Nation's Business, June:39.

2

James G. Watt
Former Secretary of the
Interior of the United States

We've got to quit subsidizing and giving welfare to business. That is wrong, whether we're

3

talking about banks or dairy farmers. Taxpayers' dollars should not be used to subsidize business.

Interview/U.S. News & World Report, 11-11:79.

William L. Weiss
Chairman, Ameritech, Inc.
(Midwest Bell telephone companies)

[Calling for decreased government regulation of telephone companies to permit them to enter other communications services in competition with other technology companies]: The rules will have to give way to reality sooner or later. The government doesn't sort these things out quickly. And if they see me always asking for what seems like an unfair advantage, I ain't going to get much slack. But if I'm willing to play the game, someday they'll realize we've all got to play by the same rules. Otherwise, we'd always be a discombobulated industry. Patient aggressiveness—it's an attitude that permeates this company. It would be nice to go home at night with a warm feeling of being a fully protected company, but it would probably take away our motivation to excel.

Interview, Chicago/
USA Today, 1-3:(B)3.

4

Pete Wilson
United States Senator,
R-California

There's a very high level of frustration [with President Reagan's stands on foreign trade]. Many of us who have been among the President's staunchest supporters think that the Administration has not been strong enough or tough enough as a trade negotiator. [The President has a] perception that going on and simply turning the other cheek [to unfair trade practices by foreign countries] will bring about free trade . . . He's erred on the side of too much restraint. There comes a time when you have to recognize you're being dealt with unfairly and take steps that are required to remedy the situation.

Washington, Sept. 4/
Los Angeles Times,
9-5:(I)8.

5

Timothy E. Wirth
United States Representative,
D-Colorado

1

[On his subcommittee's hearings into the increase in corporate takeovers]: We embark on this effort because we are told that the threat of corporate takeovers is forcing management to a short-term horizon and that research and development and long-term capital investments are short-changed in an environment where corporate managers worry about keeping stock prices high in the short term to avoid a takeover. We see that the threat of corporate takeovers is the driving force behind major corporate decisions. How can we hope to compete internationally if major corporate activity in this country is driven by takeover threats, not by the desire to build better products for the long term? Is this activity simple paranoia on the part of corporate managers? Does it reflect the desire of corporate managers to totally insulate themselves and protect their jobs? Or are corporate managers justified in taking steps to protect corporate assets from "raiders" whose desire, we are told, is simply to turn a quick profit in the market at the expense of companies, employees, other shareholders and the economy long term? Takeover activity could lead to a major change in the way we govern corporations in this country.

At subcommittee hearing, Washington/
Los Angeles Times,
4-14:(V)3.

Clayton K. Yeutter
President, Chicago Mercantile Exchange

2

[On his forthcoming Presidential nomination for U.S. Trade Representative]: There's no question that my basic philosophy in trade is 100 per cent in line with that of President Reagan. That is, an orientation toward a free and open system, but with a recognition that trade has to be fair. There has to be a level playing field out there. It's important for the U.S. to protect its own interest on trade issues, and that certainly does not put me in the protectionist category.

Chicago, April 3/
The New York Times,
4-4:36.

Clayton K. Yeutter
Trade Representative for the
President of the United States

3

[On dealing with the U.S. trade deficit]: If we were to go [the protectionist] route, as many members of Congress would like now to do, we may have legislation . . . taking effect about the time the dollar gets down to where we really become competitive overseas . . . If everybody else then retaliates, for we will have given them the basis for doing so, they'll close their markets to us at the very time we'll be ready to have an export surge. So we may totally shoot ourselves in the foot if we aren't careful . . . We do have a natural human tendency of wanting to blame someone else for our problems. It's always easier to find a scapegoat, and the Japanese are a ready target in this case because of the gigantic bilateral deficit we have with them . . . There are a lot of things the Japanese could, and should, do to ease this situation. Many areas of their economy are just not open to us or anybody else in the world in any real sense . . . But I do think we have overdone the rhetoric. It has become essentially a Japan-bashing exercise. Even if the bashing is deserved, we ought to look in the mirror because there are a lot of things we could be doing to get our own house in order.

Interview, Washington/
The Christian Science Monitor,
8-26:8.

4

. . . the United States has to be a major player in international trade. If we are to continue to advance our standard of living, it has to be done to a very major degree through international trade. We're not going to do it through major domestic economic growth. We have to tap some of the international demand. We've got to find market opportunities elsewhere in the world if we are going to sustain the kind of overall growth we'd like. We're in a global marketplace forevermore.

Interview/
Nation's Business,
October:66R.

WHAT THEY SAID IN 1985

John A. Young
President,
Hewlett-Packard Company

1

The world trading environment within which we're operating has changed dramatically. Fully 70 per cent of the goods manufactured in this country face competition from products made abroad. We are facing new competitors in Japan and the other nations of the Pacific Rim. We now do more trade with those nations than with all of Europe combined. We must not congratulate ourselves because our economy is outperforming Europe. Japan and her neighbors have created a new standard by which we should judge our competitiveness.

To reporters,
Washington, Feb. 13/
The Christian Science Monitor,
2-14:4.

James Zumberge
President, University of Southern
California; Member, California
Economic Development Corporation

2

[On American businessmen and foreign trade]: Time and time again, we go into an area, complacent and uninformed, and find ourselves outmaneuvered, out-negotiated and out of step . . . We can no longer assume that American-made goods and American-based services are so much in demand that all we have to do is send our sales people to the Far East with their sample cases and order books to build a backlog of new customers . . . [U.S. business has] widespread ignorance of the nations with whom we do business . . . One cause of our undoing has been a failure to use the knowledge available to us.

At trade seminar, Newport Beach, Calif./
Los Angeles Times, 3-1:(IV)3.

Crime • Law Enforcement

Georgette Bennett
Sociologist (specializing in police training and personnel)

1

[On stress experienced by police officers]: Many, when they peak in terms of cynicism, begin to resent all policy changes or new rules in the department which they perceive as being soft on criminals. They become frustrated with the criminal-justice system, the chain of command in the department. Some become rootless and freed from normal moorings and restraints. Some internalize and take it out on themselves, become alcoholics or suicides. Others, after years of being in a culture of violence, externalize by lashing out at others, the public, the people they arrest . . . Regardless of the training and admonitions new officers get in the police academy, once they are out in the field it is the old-timers who give them a wink and tell them, "This is the way things are *really* done, kid" . . . We give them a gun and the power of life and death, but they work in a system that infantilizes them. They are told when to wear a hot-weather or cold-weather uniform, how they can or cannot comb their hair. And it is a severely punitive system for any transgression. The result is that some learn to avoid risk and do nothing. Others become abusive or brutal.

Interview/The New York Times, 5-6:15.

William J. Brennan, Jr.
Associate Justice,
Supreme Court of the United States

2

[Arguing against capital punishment]: The calculated killing of a human being by the state involves, by its very nature, an absolute denial of the executed person's humanity. The most vile murder does not, in my view, release the state from Constitutional restraints on the destruction of human dignity . . . The fatal Constitutional infirmity of capital punishment is that it treats members of the human race as non-humans, as objects to be toyed with and discarded.

At Hastings College of Law, San Francisco,
Nov. 18/Los Angeles Times, 11-19:(I)13.

Lee Brown
Chief of Police of Houston

3

Young people who are coming into the [police] profession now have not had the discipline that officers in the past have brought with them, such as a military background; and they're products of a generation where the tolerance for certain things, such as drugs, is much greater than it was when I joined the police department.

U.S. News & World Report, 12-9:62.

Warren E. Burger
Chief Justice of the United States

4

During a 1983 tour of correctional institutions in the Scandinavian countries, a team of American professionals saw what had long been known: Prisoners there engage in productive work, something generally lacking in America's prison systems. Prison-industries employment levels in America average 10 per cent; in most Scandinavian prisons virtually all prisoners work. Prisoners must be given the opportunity to learn marketable skills, both to repay the government some of the costs of confinement and to train them for life after release. A Washington cabdriver put it this way: "Right now, prisons are like putting a shirt in water with no soap. Putting it in and taking it out. It's getting wet, but you ain't getting no dirt out."

The Washington Post, 1-4:(A)14.

Mark A. Cunniff
Executive director, National
Association of Criminal Justice Planners

5

[On prisons managed by private corporations]: I have a problem in terms of propriety. One of the state's basic functions is to pass laws and enforce them. Part of enforcing the law is to mete out punishment when people violate it. It's a sad statement when someone is found guilty and a government says, "We're going to send you to prison, but we don't feel we're competent enough to run the prison, so we're going to turn to the private sector and have them administer the punishment."

(MARK A. CUNNIFF)

Criminal justice reflects societal conflicts over values. The liberals tend to look at the social forces that cause crime, such as poverty and ignorance, while the conservatives tend to look at individual responsibility. I personally believe that as soon as we relinquish responsibility for our acts, democracy is seriously jeopardized. Democracy is based on individual accountability.

Interview, Washington/
The New York Times, 9-7-8.

1

Mario M. Cuomo
Governor of New York (D)

The real deterrent to crime is found not in draconian punishment or circumventing due process, but in the certainty of swift, sure justice. Determinate sentencing is a major element in restoring that certainty to . . . [the] criminal-justice system.

Introducing determinate-sentencing legislation,
Albany, N.Y., May 8/
The New York Times,
5-9:17.

2

Alfonse M. D'Amato
United States Senator, R-New York

[On crime in America and the public support of New York subway rider Bernhard Goetz who shot four alleged muggers]: We have lost domestic tranquility, and it's not just the subway. We are living in fear. We are the oppressed. People who see this understand the frustration of Goetz. They're not saying he did the right thing, but they understand him. It's frustration and outrage.

Before the Senate, Washington,
Feb. 6/The New York Times, 2-7:10.

3

Thomas D. Davies
Rear Admiral, United States Navy (ret.);
Former Assistant Director, Nuclear Weapons and Advanced Technology Bureau, Arms Control and Disarmament Agency of the United States

When we look at the terrorist record of the past few years, it is safe to conclude that sabotage of military and civilian nuclear facilities is at the top of the the danger list. The spectrum of [nuclear] targets for sabotage—at mines, enrichment and reprocessing plants, reactors, storage facilities, waste sites—is very broad, and the consequences of destruction or damage range from unpleasant to cataclysmic . . . The risk of theft of special nuclear materials and of weapons of their components is also very real. [Explosive materials are] always traveling—moving by air, sea, truck and railway from the mines to the enrichment plants, the fabricators, bomb assembly depots, power reactors, processing plants and storage. Transport of so much dangerous material in open commerce may well turn out to be the Achilles heel of the nuclear industry, a number-one target for terrorist theft.

The New York Times, 6-22:13.

4

Alan Dershowitz
Professor of law,
Harvard University

[On the recent case of a woman saying she lied when she accused a man of rape, for which the man spent eight years in prison]: Twenty years ago, jurors and police tended to have grave doubts about the testimony of rape victims. Then the pendulum started to swing the other way. This case may produce a healthier skepticism about the testimony of both parties, and that can only strengthen the legal system.

U.S. News & World Report, 5-27:52.

5

George Deukmejian
Governor of California (R)

[Calling for prisoners to work to pay for their incarceration]: Simple fairness suggests that these criminals should start footing the growing

6

(GEORGE DEUKMEJIAN)

bill for their support while they are in prison. I believe that every prisoner physically and mentally capable of working should be put to work and earn their keep just like the rest of us . . . Why should law-abiding citizens and the victims of crime foot the whole bill for the criminal? It should be the other way around . . . Currently, about 75 per cent of state prison inmates are engaged in some kind of work activity, but most perform only internal housekeeping chores. Very few participate in the prison-industries program, which has a far greater potential to provide relief for the taxpayers.

Before Lincoln Club, Sacramento,
Feb. 12/Los Angeles Times, 2-13:(I)3.

1

[On capital punishment]: I do feel it will deter some people. I recognize that it certainly will not deter everyone . . . And for those people who are not deterred, and who willfully and deliberately in premeditated fashion take the life of another, that is an appropriate punishment. And finally, I think if you believe life is sacred—and I do—I think we have to do everything that we can as a society to protect the lives of innocent people. And we have always had a graded form of punishment in our penal system. You pay a fine if you get a traffic ticket. You are sentenced to a couple of years in prison if you commit an assault. And when someone takes the life of another, that person is, in effect, going to forfeit their life.

Interview/Los Angeles Times, 8-20:(I)19.

Robert Gangi
Executive director,
Correctional Association of New York

2

[On determinate sentencing]: In most other states, with the notable exception of Minnesota, there has been an increase in prison commitments and overpopulation after a determinate sentencing scheme was adopted. There's been no evidence that harsher sentences have worked to reduce prison populations.

The New York Times, 1-15:10.

Alonzo H. Garcelon
President, National Rifle
Association of America

3

[Arguing against gun-control provisions such as gun registration]: Criminals normally get their guns by stealing them, either from a local armory or from the local gun store. They'll import them if they have to. You know, it isn't the gun that kills people. It's people that use guns that kill people . . . It's a myth to think that gun registration will curb crime. The criminal gets the gun he wants to use in the crime, regardless of what we have for a law. The only people who are going to obey gun-registration laws will be the law-abiding citizen, and what will that accomplish?

Interview/USA Today, 7-24:(A)11.

Rudolph W. Giuliani
United States Attorney for the
Southern District of New York

4

You have to hit organized crime at the very top, in the very middle and at the very bottom.

Newsweek, 3-11:27.

5

The thing you have got to do with the justice system is make it become a reality for the criminal, for the potential criminal. It has to get out on the street that if you get arrested, you are in a lot of trouble. Not if you are arrested that there are a hundred ways out and not much of a sentence . . . The criminal-justice system is a joke to potential criminals.

Interview, New York/
The Christian Science Monitor, 4-5:3.

6

[Saying banks should be wary of being used as money-launderers for criminals]: An institution with any self-respect wouldn't want to be used for furthering criminal activities. Banks and financial institutions should follow the know-your-customer rule. They should know what business the customer is in. If not, they should check it out. If you write down that

65

WHAT THEY SAID IN 1985

(RUDOLPH W. GIULIANI)

you're a baker, and then come in with $1-million every two or three weeks, then either you're the biggest baker in the United States or you lied.

The Washington Post, 5-24:(E)7.

1

[On white-collar crime]: If executives who make healthy salaries can't abide by the law, how do we expect the disadvantaged not to break the law?. . . . Corporate crime is a crime of greed and fear. The best way to combat it is to raise the fear.

Time, 6-10:57.

2

[On drug laws]: Look, we deal with the crime problem—which goes beyond the resources allocated to solve it—by prosecuting individual, representative cases as a means of deterring other crime. That strategy is working in containing our heroin problem, largely because our educational programs have reduced the population of users to a manageable size. Right now, the strategy isn't working as well with cocaine. But wouldn't our cocaine problem be catastrophic if we weren't making any effort at all? The answer is not to legalize cocaine and give people all they want, and at the same time go into schools and tell kids that cocaine is dangerous, don't use it. That's absurd. Give up on our drug laws and it will be almost impossible to mount an educational effort that will truly discourage drug use. And there is a moral question here as well. Do we want to live in a society that says, "Go ahead, pump all the drugs into your body that you want"?

Panel discussion, New York/
Harper's, December:48.

James Harmon
Executive director, President's
Commission on Organized Crime

3

Investigating money-laundering is an indirect way to get at the mob. We recognized pretty early that you've got to figure out a way to get at the economic benefits of organized crime.

Washington, March 24/
The Washington Post, 3-25:(A)9.

Philip W. Harris
Assistant professor of criminal
justice, Temple University

4

[On the recent resumption of capital punishment]: Everybody was worried about how the public would respond to executions once we really started killing people. The poll says it [the resumption] has increased strength for the death penalty. . . . There must be a pretty strong belief that the death penalty makes a big difference. If it didn't matter, then I think issues of fairness and discrimination would affect public opinion.

Los Angeles Times, 2-3:(I)8.

Patrick Healy
Director, Chicago Crime Commission

5

[Favoring the use of legal wiretaps by police]: Any time you've got wiretaps that are admissible as evidence, the trial is anticlimactic. If prosecutors can get past the defendants' motion to suppress, it's just a matter of time till the yellow bus takes them away.

Newsweek, 3-11:27.

Lois Haight Herrington
Assistant Attorney General,
Office of Justice Programs,
Department of Justice of the United States

6

Sexual-assault victims would be more likely to report the crime if they did not fear becoming entangled in the morass of an insensitive criminal-justice system. In many states, rape victims must literally pay for their crime. They are given the bill for the medical exam required to gather physical evidence. Burglary victims are not charged for collecting fingerprints. Why should sexual-assault victims be charged for collecting evidence?

The Washington Post, 5-24:(E)2.

Narcotics, labor payoffs, payoffs to public officials—the problem for them is always how to get rid of the cash. The common denominator is always cash.

Elizabeth Holtzman
District Attorney, Brooklyn, N.Y.

1

[Saying she does not support capital punishment]: I see in a more practical way, as a prosecutor, what I would say are the bad consequences of the imposition of the death penalty. Some of the homicide cases are very close cases. I think there's a strong possibility you would get more acquittals if there were a death penalty. Staff would be diverted by all the appeals. Also, while one always has to be prepared to make mistakes, one doesn't like to be in the position of making an irreparable mistake.

Interview/The New York Times, 3-13:14.

2

In Congress, I was not in favor of mandating sentencing, but since I've been here, I've seen the importance of it. When I came here, one of the things that concerned me very much was the leniency of sentences in some cases. Mandatory sentences are an important protection in terms of assuring there will be a just sentence—at least, there's a floor.

Interview/The New York Times, 3-13:14.

Brian Jenkins
Director, research program on subnational conflict and political violence, Rand Corporation

3

[On why terrorism has not flourished in the U.S.]: We have nothing that is equivalent to the [Spanish] Basque provinces in this country, with one exception—the island of Puerto Rico. And this society is not an ideological society: Marxism never really took root; Fascism in this country has never really been more than a costume party for social malcontents who like to wear hoods or arm bands. We have a very individualistic society; therefore, our violence tends to be individualistic—not ideological or collective.

Interview/USA Today, 3-13:(A)9.

Edward M. Kennedy
United States Senator, D-Massachusetts

4

The ready availability of lethal, concealable handguns undermines the fundamental effort to protect citizens from violent crimes . . . Instead of weakening handgun controls, we should be working to keep handguns from falling into the wrong hands, without jeopardizing in any way the legitimate sporting interests of our citizens or their interest in self-defense.

Washington, July 9/
Los Angeles Times, 7-10:(I)12.

Mark A. R. Kleiman
Resident fellow, Kennedy School of Government, Harvard University; Former Director of Policy and Management Analysis, Criminal Division, Department of Justice of the United States

5

. . . we have a drug problem not only because some people use drugs but because other people object to them, with the result that the United States now has a huge illicit drug industry. The damage a drug does may result as much from its illegality as from its pharmacology. Americans probably spend between $25-billion and $30-billion annually on illegal drugs. Only a small fraction of this money is earned by large criminal organizations. But virtually all of it represents the income of criminals: people who either buy and sell drugs on their own account or work for someone who does. The only significant expenses involve boats and planes, radio equipment, and lawyers' fees, bribes and the other expenses of getting out of legal trouble. The actual raw-material price is almost always trivial.

Panel discussion, New York/
Harper's, December:41.

Edward I. Koch
Mayor of New York

6

The two top priorities for us are education and law enforcement. If I had to deal with only one, if I had to make a choice, it would be to punish the criminals. Is it because I just want revenge? No. People are fed up, absolutely fed up . . . Nobody goes out and commits a crime because they are hungry today. It's baloney. Nobody goes out and commits a crime because there is no bread on the table. So why do people

(EDWARD I. KOCH)

overwhelmingly commit crimes? Because you have better odds of not getting caught than you do at the race track. If you have 500,000 or more felonies committed, only 100,000 of them end in arrests and only 2 per cent go to jail. Those are damned good odds.

Before State Committee on Sentencing Guidelines, New York, Feb. 14/The New York Times, 2-15:1,12.

C. Everett Koop
Surgeon General of the United States

Violence is every bit a public-health issue for me and my successors in this century as smallpox, tuberculosis and syphilis were for my predecessors in the last two centuries. Violence in American public and private life has indeed assumed the proportions of an epidemic.

Los Angeles Herald Examiner, 1-20:(A)1.

1

John C. Lawn
Deputy Administrator, Drug Enforcement Administration of the United States

Acts of violence, threats of violence [against DEA agents] are a clear indication that the pressure we're bringing to bear on traffickers is having an effect and that they're responding the only way they know how—by trying to provoke fear and intimidation. We have taken precautions in all overseas posts; we have established special working guidelines for our people. But the nature of our work and the sometimes corrupting environment makes absolute security of personnel impossible. But if traffickers are using fear and intimidation to test our mettle, they're going to find we test well.

Feb. 13/The Washington Post, 2-14:(A)30.

2

Patrick J. Leahy
United States Senator, D-Vermont

[Criticizing calls for the death penalty in espionage cases of Americans selling secrets to the Soviets]: Providing a death penalty for spies eliminates their incentive to cooperate and the

3

possibility of a trade with the Soviets. They [Soviets] aren't going to trade for spies if we send them in a casket.

U.S. News & World Report, 8-12:31.

Thomas F. McBride
Commissioner, President's Commission on Organized Crime

[Saying some of the largest labor unions are controlled by the Mafia]: Members of the big four internationals [unions] are some of the poorest, hardest-working, most unprivileged members of our society. They need active and vigorous union protection. But in too many cases their unions have become part of the machinery of exploitation.

At hearing on labor corruption and racketeering, Chicago, April 22/Los Angeles Times, 4-23:(I)4.

4

Jacqueline McMickens
Commissioner of Correction of New York City

In New York City there are 10,200 people in jail, and most of them are minorities. Most are males. When you take that kind of population out of a community, you're bound to hurt that community... Think of the number of people out of that community who are not being productive. We [blacks] are 10 per cent of this community and every man is valuable, every person is valuable. But those men have children, and when a man is away from one to five years, those children have no opportunity to have any kind of experience with their father. My father, my mother and my grandmother were the most important people in the world to me... But we have to take on crime in our community. We can't allow it to continue.

Interview/Ebony, May:130.

5

Edwin Meese III
Attorney General-designate of the United States

[Saying he opposes blanket U.S. economic sanctions on countries that produce or ship narcotics]: We have to look more carefully to see

6

(EDWIN MEESE III)

whether it will produce the right results, and that depends on a country-by-country analysis. In some cases, punitive efforts may be counter-productive, but in other cases it might work . . . The important thing is to push eradication programs, to push law-enforcement programs, to get their help in interdicting the export of narcotics from those countries. That can probably be achieved without imposing economic sanctions.

Interview, Washington, March 14/
The New York Times, 3-15-13.

Edwin Meese III
Attorney General of the United States

1

[Supporting capital punishment as a deterrent to murder]: I think that if we are able to spare the life of one innocent person in a robbery or a killing for hire or in some similar incident, it is worth . . . having capital punishment in every state of the union . . . [It is] a 100 per cent deterrent upon everyone on whom it's been successfully imposed . . . I don't say that facetiously, because there have been so many killers who have been sent to prison, then let loose and went out and killed again.

Before U.S. Chamber of Commerce, Washington,
April 29/Los Angeles Times, 4-30:(I)18.

2

[Saying states should have the right to impose the death penalty on those whose crime was committed when they were under 18 years of age]: You have kids becoming increasingly sophisticated—I suspect largely by watching television; they're just smarter, know more . . . There's no question you can have very vicious criminals at age 16 or 17. Unfortunately, the trend has been in that direction. Most of your violent crime is committed by people under 25 and a good portion of it by people under 18. So I think a state is justified at imposing a cutoff age for the death penalty at what they think is appropriate.

To "Los Angeles Times" editors and reporters,
Washington, Sept. 16/Los Angeles Times, 9-17:(I)4.

3

[Criticizing the Miranda decision which gives criminal suspects the right to have a lawyer present during police questioning]: The Miranda decision was wrong. We managed very well in this country for 175 years without it. Its practical effect is to prevent the police from talking to the person who knows the most about the crime—namely, the perpetrator. As it stands now under Miranda, if the police obtain a statement from that person in the course of the initial interrogation, the statement may be thrown out at the trial. Therefore, Miranda only helps guilty defendants. Most innocent people are glad to talk to the police. They want to establish their innocence so that they're no longer a suspect. Remember, Miranda has nothing to do with coercive or abusive police tactics. Those are outlawed by other cases. So it only has to do with the normal questioning of suspects, the people who have information about a crime.

Interview/U.S. News & World Report, 10-14:67.

Howard Metzenbaum
United States Senator, D-Ohio

4

If you're guilty of white-collar crime, there's a kind of protective cloak thrown around you. If you wear a white collar, you don't get prosecuted . . . The Justice Department drops the prosecution of [Teamsters Union president] Jackie Presser because he's an informant. An informant? Against whom? He's the biggest of the big. Do you drop prosecution against the biggest of the big to get [his uncle] Allen Friedman, who was a nobody?

At Senate Judiciary Committee hearing, Washington,
Sept. 12/The Washington Post, 9-13:(A)9.

Abner Mikva
Judge, United States Court of
Appeals for the District of Columbia

5

[On privately owned or operated prisons]: My initial reaction is, when you're dealing with people's problems, you ought to look at all conceivable ways to solve them. But the confusion between the objectives of the private and public sectors worries me. Are we looking for an institution to maximize its profits or promote justice?

The New York Times, 2-11:12.

Robert M. Morgenthau
District Attorney,
New York County (Manhattan)

We are much better off with determinate sentences. The whole philosophy behind indeterminate sentencing is you send people to prison to be corrected. The parole board then decides when someone is corrected. Experience has shown that people don't get corrected in prison.

The New York Times, 1-15:10.

1

Francis Mullen
Former Administrator, Drug Enforcement
Administration of the United States

[On foreign countries' involvement in the drug trade]: We can go on forever making a seizure here and there, but until the Mexicans themselves root out that corruption, I don't think we'll ever stop the flow of drugs from Mexico . . . We know that in [Syria's] Bekaa Valley the Syrian Army is facilitating heroin traffic. The Syrian government could stop that, but they haven't. The Cuban government could stop the transiting on their territory, but they haven't. You've got to know that [Cuban President] Fidel Castro sits down there and takes great delight in this.

Interview/Newsweek, 3-18:30.

2

Patrick V. Murphy
Former president, Police Foundation;
Former Police Commissioner
of New York City

As more and more blacks and Hispanics have become the mayors and police chiefs of the nation's largest cities, the police are adopting a very different approach. More and more, they are finding ways to work with the community, to spot the drug dealer and burglar and to actually prevent crime . . . It wasn't so long ago that the all-white, mostly male police departments in most cities were really there to enforce an informal but very real system of segregation. Real co-operation between the police and the policed was very rare.

Interview, Washington/
The New York Times, 6-5:12.

3

Ralph Nader
Lawyer; Consumer-rights advocate

[Saying white-collar "corporate criminals" usually get more lenient treatment by the courts than other law-breakers]: The more you steal, the less time you do, as long as you do it on the 20th floor. Very little will and resources are directed toward catching these corporate criminals. Very few are caught. Of the ones who are caught, most cop a plea. Of the ones who are convicted, many get probation or suspended sentences. Of those who go to jail, most get a country club of a prison.

Interview/The New York Times, 5-9:30.

4

William G. Nagel
Corrections specialist;
Former president, American Foundation

We as a people don't see the consequences of taking a person out of society, out of family, out of work, putting [him] in some forbidding place [prison], and not realizing that he comes out somewhere down the line a different person . . . And [he's] probably a more serious problem to deal with. So we respond to [one] problem by creating [another] . . . There is no evidence that severe sentences deter [crime] more [effectively] than short, sure sentences. In practice, benign handling equals less crime . . . Anyone who truly has compassion for the victim [of crime] . . . has to exercise that compassion by creating a criminal-justice system that does not brutalize the offender, so that he returns more apt to victimize the public.

Interview/The Christian Science Monitor, 1-25:21,22.

5

Ronald Reagan
President of the United States

There are apparently some centers of crime and places where criminals have found happy hunting more than others. But actually we've been making sizeable progress in the last few years with regard to law enforcement; for the first time, I think, since the crime statistics have been kept. In the last few years they have gone down; two years in a row in regard to serious

6

(RONALD REAGAN)

crime. So a lot of it, I think, depends on all of us and our insisting on law and order . . . There's a kind of an attitude in the whole structure of judicial and every place else in crime in which it seemed that we got overzealous in protecting the criminals' rights and forgot about the victim. And, I think, if we have stricter enforcement and stricter punishment, we'll continue to see [a] decline in crime.

News conference, Washington,
Jan. 9/The New York Times, 1-10:8.

1

Of all the changes in the past 20 years, none has more threatened our sense of national well-being than the explosion of violent crime. One does not have to have been attacked to be a victim. The woman who must run to her car after shopping at night is a victim; the couple draping their door with locks and chains are victims; as is the tired, decent cleaning woman who can't ride a subway home without being afraid. We do not seek to violate rights of defendants. But shouldn't we feel more compassion for victims of crime than for those who commit crime?

State of the Union address, Washington,
Feb. 6/The New York Times, 2-7:13.

2

Believe me, there is nothing I'd like better than to be remembered as a President who did everything he could do to bust up the syndicates and give the mobsters a permanent stay in the jailhouse, courtesy of the United States government.

To U.S. Attorneys, Washington,
Oct. 21/The Washington Post, 10-22:(A)5.

Oliver Revell
Executive Assistant Director
for Investigations, Federal
Bureau of Investigation

3

The U.S. is probably the most vulnerable to terrorism of any country in the world. Our borders are open. Once they are in the country,

there are no identity checks. They can travel freely. They can enroll in colleges, and the government can pay their way. The U.S. is a country that is virtually impossible to police. [On the other hand,] I think we're making the United States a very hard target. We have penetrated and prosecuted virtually every terrorist group that has operated in the U.S., using the law. That has given rise to the United States as not such an easy target.

The New York Times, 12-6:11.

Ramona Ripston
Executive director, American Civil
Liberties Union of Southern California

4

[On why the ACLU opposes capital punishment]: On civil-liberties grounds. We feel that it violates the Eighth Amendment prohibition against cruel and unusual punishment. Beyond that, I personally feel that one of the messages we send out when we execute someone is a violent message. Violence begets violence, and I think when the government acts in a violent way, it teaches people to act in a violent way. I also don't think it's a deterrent . . . Recent studies show that what matters most is the race of the victim. So if the victim [of the crime] is white and the perpetrator of the crime is a minority, the death penalty is almost certainly applied. The death penalty is used against poor people. It's used against minorities. So, in addition to the other reasons, it's applied in a very arbitrary and discriminatory manner.

Interview/USA Today, 11-14:(A)11.

Burton B. Roberts
Administrative Judge, Criminal Branch,
Supreme Court, Bronx County, N.Y.;
Former District Attorney, Bronx County, N.Y.

5

. . . people's *perceptions* of what's happening are as important as the reality. The media prefer to tell the public that crime is rampant, that it is continuing to rise, that people are afraid to go out at night. After all, that's what sells newspapers and makes exciting television. But the reality is that crime is going down: The streets are safer and the criminal-justice system

(BURTON B. ROBERTS)

is more effective. The politicians, meanwhile, find it convenient to blame the judges [for crime], and the judges climb into their ivory towers and don't respond . . . numerous social problems contribute to the crime rate, as do demographic factors. So why do politicians always point to the judiciary? Because blaming judges is much easier than looking in the mirror, easier than examining what has really happened to our inner cities.

Panel discussion/Harper's, May:42.

Thomas Sheer
Deputy Assistant Director, New York Office, Federal Bureau of Investigation

[On the FBI's strategy in fighting organized crime]: We've almost totally reversed a theory that you knock off La Cosa Nostra by the prosecution of single acts by individuals, by a numbers game of convictions. We're going after the enterprise itself, and shredding the hierarchy. We've matured.

Interview/The New York Times, 10-18:1.

1

Barry Slotnick
Lawyer

[On the attempted-murder indictment of his client, Bernhard Goetz, who shot four men he said were accosting him in the New York subway]: If the district attorney wanted, a grand jury would indict a ham sandwich. And today Bernie Goetz was the ham sandwich.

New York, March 27/
USA Today, 3-28:(4)1.

2

Tom Smith
Associate director, criminal justice section, American Bar Association

[On whether victims of crime can strike back at their assailants in self-defense, such as in the current case of a New York subway rider who shot four youths trying to rob him]: Everyone has a right to defend themselves, but the general law is that you have an obligation to retreat, to

try to avoid a confrontation. If met with force, you may retaliate only with an equal force. It depends on the circumstances; each state is a little bit different. If you are in fear for your life—a person is pointing a gun at you and says: "Your money or your life"—you may have justification to believe your life is in danger, and retaliate with lethal force. It's hard to make a judgment call in a split second . . . It is very dangerous and unwise for a person to attempt to take the law into their own hands unless they truly have no alternative and are truly in fear for their life.

Interview/USA Today, 1-3:(4)2.

3

Stephen S. Trott
Assistant Attorney General, Criminal Division, Department of Justice of the United States

[On the high rate of repeat offenders]: These findings graphically illustrate the enormous impact repeat offenders have on public safety and the criminal-justice system. [They] also give us some sense of how much additional crime could be reduced if criminals actually served the increased sentences which could be imposed under present law.

March 3/Los Angeles Times, 3-4:(I)11.

4

Ernest van den Haag
Professor of jurisprudence, New York University

In practice, the purpose of the drug laws is not to educate at all—if it were, I'd be in favor of them—but to restrict the sale of these substances. And *that* purpose the law has failed, and must fail, to achieve. Only from 5 to 10 per cent of all drugs entering the United States are intercepted. The price of seizing that tiny percentage is enormous, not only in direct law-enforcement costs but also in the corruption and social dislocation produced. The time has come to ask ourselves the question we asked about alcohol in the '20s: Wouldn't the money wasted trying to prohibit the stuff be more profitably spent on direct efforts to educate people about the dangers of drugs?

Panel discussion, New York/
Harper's, December:44.

5

Adam Walinsky
Lawyer; Former Chairman, New York
State Commission of Investigations

1

Over the last 20 years, politicians have had to rationalize their miserable record in coping with crime. Every police chief in America has learned to say that the causes of crime are "really," poverty, degradation, bad housing, unemployment—problems he cannot be expected to solve. Although they still use poverty as an excuse, politicians now talk more about drugs. Rather than devote any more resources to courts, police prosecutors and prisons in their own states, politicians blame the State Department for not getting tough with [drug-exporting countries such as] Turkey and Colombia.

Panel discussion/Harper's, May:46.

William H. Webster
Director,
Federal Bureau of Investigation

2

The excessive use of deadly force [by police] has represented one of the great problems in police-community relationships . . . The problem is we do not equip our police officers with anything except a lethal weapon to deal with a fleeing suspect. He can't stop him with a billy club, unless he can catch up with him. If we could put a man on the moon, we ought to be able to design an alternative weapon and supply our police officers with the ability to stop a fleeing suspect with less than lethal force. It's that simple. It seems to me that if you equip a police officer with an alternative weapon, he'll use it. If you equip him with nothing but a gun and a billy club, you put him to a terrible choice: let somebody go or use force that might kill him.

Interview/USA Today, 4-8:(A)9.

3

Our challenge continues to be the criminal enterprise, whether it's a group of terrorists, espionage agents or organized crime. We have made major inroads into such groups. Recent indictments in New York and elsewhere have reached to the very top of the organized-crime hierarchy. This has had a tremendously disruptive effect on what has been a sanctuary for significant wrongdoing. We also will do more in

labor racketeering to break up the unholy alliances between some corrupt labor leaders and organized-crime figures. This is a problem that has been around for a long time but is probably on the upswing, in part because we haven't focused as much on it. But drugs continue to be the number-one crime problem in the United States. We must maintain the momentum that has been developed in the last three years and not roll over and play dead to a problem that could change our society irrevocably for the worse.

Interview/U.S. News & World Report, 4-22:64.

Caspar W. Weinberger
Secretary of Defense of the United States

4

[On the recent cases of espionage and weapons-theft by Americans in the U.S.]: The fact that these things are surfacing can be attributed perhaps to greater enforcement efforts. All of them are reprehensible, [but] sadly you are going to have spies and thieves no matter what we do . . . Certainly, these are all very unhappy events, but I don't think they represent any letting down of the guard or anything like that. I think it is fortunate they are being caught when they are. Obviously, you try to learn lessons from each one of these things . . . We ought to be as careful as we can in the number of [security] clearances and in the people who have access [to secrets]. I don't have any illusion that that is going to cure the problem, but it narrows the target; it reduces the number of people who might be tempted.

To reporters, Washington, Aug. 8/
Los Angeles Times, 8-9:(I)6.

Stanton Wheeler
Director, studies on
white-collar crime, Yale University

5

Many white-collar criminals are first-time offenders who have records of contributions to their community and have often led exemplary lives. From that point of view, they deserve a great deal of leniency. On the other hand, they occupy positions of power and trust, and their violation of the law is significant. Judges try to weigh one interest against the other, and it's often a difficult job.

Time, 6-10:57.

Hubert Williams
Director of Police, Newark, N.J.

1

We can give up our Constitution in return for our safety. If you give police unfettered rights, I assure you that crime will drop. The price will be a garrison state. As a policeman, I think that is a price we cannot afford.

Time, 4-8:34.

2

When one out of every three American households is directly victimized [by crime] each year, it isn't long before everyone has either been a victim himself or had someone very close to him victimized. The problem is not just what crime does to people's lives; it is also what the fear of crime does to our society. As this fear feeds on itself, any decisive action to fight crime becomes less likely. People take strong collective action only when they have confidence in themselves and in their society. When people are afraid, they tend to act as individuals. The result is an increasingly atomized society. That's when people flock to the suburbs and buy the extra locks—or a gun.

Panel discussion/Harper's, May:44.

Pat Williams
United States Representative,
D-Montana

3

[On the use of lie detectors]: It is sadly ironic that criminals cannot be convicted by a polygraph but workers can be denied jobs, shamed and branded forever by these same machines.

USA Today, 8-7:(4)8.

James Q. Wilson
Professor of government,
Harvard University

4

Men are more likely to commit crimes than women. Part of the explanation may be that young boys are raised differently—but why is that? Partly it's that boys behave differently than girls, and there are growing signs this is linked to hormones that produce behavioral tendencies we have not understood. The lasting influence of sex-related hormones occurs before birth. Boys exposed in the womb to high levels of such hormones are likely to be especially active and aggressive. Of course, these biological tendencies interact in complicated ways with how the children are raised. But—and this is the important point—child rearing is not the whole story.

Interview/U.S. News & World Report, 9-30:54.

5

... many elderly people have stopped going out on the streets at night. One of the consequences of crime, I think, is that after it reaches a certain level, it turns the victims into prisoners by making them curtail their lives ... One of the reasons that the crime rate has come down in several cities is not that there are fewer criminals abroad, but there are more victims who have voluntarily locked themselves up so they can't be victimized.

Interview/USA Today, 11-13:(A)11.

Defense · The Military

Kenneth L. Adelman
Director, Arms Control and
Disarmament Agency of the United States

1

[On why the U.S. pursues new arms-control agreements with the Soviet Union when they violate existing ones]: We do this for several reasons. First, new arms-control agreements, if soundly formulated and adhered to, can serve U.S. interests. We should not abandon efforts to achieve effective and verifiable agreements that can increase U.S. and allied security and reduce the risk of war. Second, entering new negotiations does not in any way condone or ignore past Soviet behavior. Third, continuing to negotiate can give us leverage and another way for trying to get the Soviets to abide by existing agreements.

To reporters,
Washington, Feb. 1/
The New York Times,
2-2-3.

2

There is no trick at all in getting an arms-control agreement [with the Soviets]. That can be done tomorrow. We can sign up with the Soviet proposals, and if we don't want to sign up just for the Soviet proposal word for word, then kick the numbers way up so that it won't affect either force at all. Now, will it help strategic stability? No, it certainly would not. Would it leave the world safer? No, it would not. Would it have verification provisions? Not at all. Would it reduce nuclear weapons? No, it would not. But it would be an arms-control agreement. And that cheapens the whole process. That is not being sincere about arms control. [U.S. President] Ronald Reagan has been saying, "Let's have the process do something. Let's have it really help our security, really help reduce nuclear weapons. Otherwise, I'm just not going to buy on." And I think that's being serious about arms control.

Interview/
USA Today,
10-25:(A)11.

Sergei F. Akhromeyev
Military Chief of Staff
of the Soviet Union

3

It took seven years to negotiate the SALT II treaty. In the 1970s we saw the willingness of the United States to negotiate while defending its interests . . . Now we don't see this willingness. We see only willingness to force us to accept their proposals. The Soviet Union cannot negotiate on such a basis.

News conference/
Los Angeles Times, 11-17:(I)4.

Georgi A. Arbatov
Director, Soviet Institute of
U.S.A. and Canadian Affairs

4

I think our [Soviet] moratorium on nuclear testing, and proposal to the United States to join it, this ignited all the furors in Washington, and really they reacted with biblical wrath. I think it is because they [U.S. officials]—it's okay for them to have a bellicose Russia, and they get furious if they see a peaceful Russia—and not only they see it can be projected in this way to American minds, because it destroys somehow the image of [a Soviet] "evil empire" which was built with such care by present [U.S. Reagan] Administration in last year, and which is the foundation for the whole arms race and for the whole policy of the United States at the moment.

Broadcast interview, Moscow/
"Meet the Press," NBC-TV, 8-25.

5

[On why the Soviets have built up their nuclear forces]: There is something irrational in the course of the arms race. For rational people, 10 weapons are enough not to start war; maybe hundreds at the most. But when we see that the American side has a lot of these weapons and irrational strategies, then you must make other calculations. We learned also that you would never talk in a serious way until we acquired rough parity. It is not rational; the whole arms race is irrational. I am not working on building

(GEORGIA A. ARBATOV)

the nuclear arms race, so don't ask such questions from me. But these are the rules of this bloody business.

Interview, San Francisco/
Los Angeles Times,
9-27:(I)24.

1

[The Great Wall of China] never saved them from the Mongols; it didn't save them from the Manchurians. You have the same with the Maginot line. Now you have the same with the [U.S.] "Star Wars" [space defense] concept. Because . . . the same brain, the same research facilities which will work for defense will also work for annihilating this defense. We just cannot solve the security problem by a technical fix . . . We [know] you [the U.S.] are good guys, but we cannot trust you just on your word. And you also don't trust us on our word, though I can assure you that we are good guys . . . For thousands of years [technical security has only made] war more possible, accelerated the arms race and not [let] people see that the only way to security is . . . by political means.

ABC-TV's "Nightline" broadcast/
Newsweek, 12-2:47.

Les Aspin
United States Representative,
D-Wisconsin

2

There is some suspicion on my part that [when] they came into office, [the Reagan Administration] found the public was willing to spend an awful lot of money [on the military], and they didn't really have a coherent list of where the money should be spent. So they kind of scrambled around, took some programs off the shelf and blew the dust off them and asked the services to tell them what they wanted. But then the program didn't have as much coherence as it should have, especially in the early days, when they really had the bucks. So what I'm asking is, what is the evidence that we've improved our capabilities and our position vis-a-vis the Russians?

Jan. 31/The Washington Post, 2-1:(A)10.

3

If Democrats want to spend the rest of their careers writing op-ed pieces and giving lectures at universities, then we continue to stroke our anti-defense image. But if we want to make defense policy in the White House and Pentagon, then we had better stand for something. The voters are not attracted to national-security naysayers . . . The point is that we don't seem to stand for anything any more. In the debate that goes on daily in the newspapers and on the television screens, Democrats are not shown being for anything in the defense area. We are always against. We are the Doctor No of the defense debate.

At Henry M. Jackson dinner before
Coalition for a Democratic Majority, Washington,
April 17/The Washington Post, 4-18:(4)7.

4

The results [of President Reagan's increased defense spending] are discomforting and disconcerting, to say the least, for they indicate miniscule improvements—outside the personnel area—despite immense budgetary increases . . . Is Ronald Reagan doing with defense what he accused previous Administrations of doing with social welfare—just throwing billions at the problem, and then the statistics show that poverty remains rampant?

Washington, Oct. 6/
The New York Times, 10-7:5.

5

[Saying President Reagan's proposal for a space defense system cannot protect civilian populations]: [It] is a perfect bargaining chip [in arms-control negotiations with the Soviet Union] . . . The defense of missiles is something you can talk about because it is feasible. Population defense is not feasible, so we should negotiate it away.

Newsweek, 10-7:26.

Howard H. Baker, Jr.
Former United States Senator,
R-Tennessee

6

[Saying he supports development of a space defense system]: Let me tell you why: The whole

(HOWARD H. BAKER, JR.)

idea that we are going to protect this country by threatening to incinerate the Soviet Union is repugnant. One of these days we are going to have an accident. It may not be between the U.S. and the Soviet Union. But there will be an accident if we don't get this thing under control. And I don't know what the consequences will be. So the sooner we can get on with the business of trying to stand down offensive weapons systems and substitute in their place defensive weapons systems, the better off civilization will be.

To reporters/The Christian Science Monitor, 8-20:16.

Jack Brooks
United States Representative,
D-Texas

1

[Criticizing the use of lie detectors for certain Defense Department employees]: The polygraph is a dubious machine that could be used to threaten and intimidate hundreds of thousands of Federal workers at that agency. This is unnecessary and foolish. It may jeopardize national defense as well by exonerating professional "moles" [spies]. Good Soviet agents can be trained to fool the polygraph. But ordinary Americans are not so trained. The plan would brand innocent people and let professional spies get away scott free.

Interview/U.S. News & World Report, 2-25:44.

Harold Brown
Former Secretary of Defense
of the United States

2

It is very difficult for the U.S. to sustain a protracted conventional war for interests that aren't obviously vital to the American public . . . Senior military people have to give an honest answer about what can be accomplished under various levels of restriction. If they think it's a mistake, they can either go along or resign and take their case public. It's up to civilian officials not to hold the military responsible for outcomes that are determined by political restrictions.

The Wall Street Journal, 1-14:8.

3

People often demand too much of the arms-control process, asking it, in effect, to prevent nuclear war. Nuclear war can be prevented only by a strategy of deterrence, by keeping U.S. nuclear forces relatively invulnerable and by managing the Soviet-American political rivalry. What an arms-control agreement realistically can do is to limit the inflammation of U.S.-Soviet relations that would come from an unrestricted arms competition. It can also make our deterrent more secure by limiting threats to our forces. And it can do these things only in a modest way.

Interview/U.S. News & World Report, 1-21:33.

Stephen D. Bryen
Deputy Assistant Secretary of
Defense of the United States

4

[On the illegal transfer of U.S. defense technology to the Soviet Union]: Our biggest difficulty now is not so much what a neutral country or an advanced country will do. Generally, we're getting cooperation. The biggest problem we have is what we call transit—where an item is shipped from one country, perfectly properly, to another country, perfectly properly, repackaged and then sent on to the East . . . God forbid if we have to go to war some day. I wouldn't want my son facing superior equipment, or at least equipment as good as we've got, thanks to technology transfer.

Interview/
USA Today,
3-6:(B)6.

Dale Bumpers
United States Senator, D-Arkansas

5

[Complaining about Congress' voting for almost every weapons system proposed to it]: Weapons systems have gotten to be just like Rasputin—you can't kill them. It doesn't make any difference whether they work or not.

Before the Senate, Washington,
March 20/
The Washington Post, 3-21:(A)14.

McGeorge Bundy
Professor of history, New York University; Former Assistant to the President of the United States (John F. Kennedy and Lyndon B. Johnson) for National Security Affairs

1

If I had to pick just one lesson [from the Vietnam war], it would be: Ask yourself ahead of time about any adventure. How much is this game worth? We should also have asked more sharply what our prospects were . . . You can argue that we should have gone in to win and win fast. But my problem is that I don't know how to do that, even now. What we wanted was not to lose, but we didn't squarely face the question of the costs of that objective.

*The Wall Street Journal,
1-14:8.*

Michael I. Burch
Spokesman for the Department of Defense of the United States

2

[Defense] Secretary [Caspar] Weinberger feels that those who hope for, "success in bringing down the defense budget" really mean success in weakening the security of the country. Cutting defense does not solve the [Federal] deficit problem. Cutting defense means the loss of national security, the loss of jobs and the loss of taxes.

*Jan. 25/
The Washington Post, 1-26:(A)1.*

Frank C. Carlucci
Former Deputy Secretary of Defense of the United States

3

The biggest problem I have with the defense industry is their desire to expand their own program at the expense of the other fellow. As I've told them publicly, it's kind of like rearranging deck chairs on the *Titanic* . . . Maybe [I am] unrealistic and utopian, but certainly other industries have looked to the common good.

*The Washington Post,
4-1:(A)6.*

Lord Carrington
*Secretary General,
North Atlantic Treaty Organization*

4

[On U.S. President Reagan's proposals for a space defense system]: I would have to be deaf, blind and impenetrably stupid not to be aware of European concerns about the American Strategic Defense Initiative, and it is an important part of my job to ensure that these are understood and taken account of in Washington. It is important that allies on both sides of the Atlantic should be aware of the divisive potential of the SDI and take steps necessary to avoid the danger.

Los Angeles Times, 11-17:(I)4.

Konstantin U. Chernenko
President of the Soviet Union

5

[Criticizing the U.S. Reagan Administration's proposal for a space defense system]: To put it simply, the aim is to acquire a capability to deliver a nuclear strike [against the Soviet Union], counting on impunity, counting on an ABM shield to protect oneself from retaliation. This is the same old policy to achieve decisive military superiority with all the ensuing implications for peace and international security. I believe that makes it clear why we are so resolutely opposed to this concept and such plans. In substance, this is an offensive, or to be more precise, an aggressive concept. The aim is to try to disarm the other side and deprive it of a capability to retaliate in the event of nuclear aggression against it.

*Written response to interview questions,
Jan. 31/The Washington Post, 2-1:(A)10.*

Robert Cooper
Director of Advanced Research, Department of Defense of the United States

6

It's inevitable that military operations will be conducted in space, because that is a human activity and all human activities will be conducted in space.

*At symposium sponsored by American Academy of Arts and Sciences and the Planetary Society, Jan. 12/
The Christian Science Monitor, 1-15:36.*

Jim Courter
United States Representative,
R-New Jersey

1

[Supporting President Reagan's space-defense system proposal]: A world of defensive weapons will not suit Soviet military goals, and it will not suit the Soviet political and ideological strategy that relies on their strategic nuclear forces. It will, however, be a more stable world in which to compete with the Soviet Union, and it will be less prone to the risk of deadly escalation in the next crisis that we have to face. It will also be a world in which arms reduction is a more attainable goal. Without defenses, deep cuts in offensive forces could be risky, because the more we cut our offenses, the military significance of marginal cheating on arms-control limits increases. In this sense, strategic defense can act as an insurance policy.

At Woodrow Wilson School of Public Affairs,
April 1/The Washington Post, 5-14:(A)18.

Alan Cranston
United States Senator, D-California

2

[Criticizing the Senate's vote to fund the MX missile]: [The Senate has] thrown away money [on an] unnecessary piece of goldplated military junk that serves no useful military purpose and is intended solely to serve political perceptions.

Washington, March 19/
The New York Times, 3-20:1.

Jaime de Pinies
President,
United Nations General Assembly

3

. . . peace needs security. Security needs protection. And how are you going to achieve the security? Through armaments. And down the road we go to the armament race. And it's so unbelievable and so expensive. We are coming close to a trillion dollars. If only a small part would be designated to remedy the famine, to help the countries to develop, to advance further. Imagine!

Interview/
Los Angeles Times Magazine, 10-20:22.

Byron Dorgan
United States Representative,
D-North Dakota

4

[Arguing against Congressional approval for funding the MX missile]: Are the Soviets going to get upset by the American people spending money they don't have for a missile they don't need and putting it in silos that are vulnerable? We're stronger than the Soviets; we don't need it.

Before the House, Washington,
March 25/Los Angeles Times, 3-26:(I)5.

Laurent Fabius
Premier of France

5

[On U.S. proposals for a space defense system]: In opening up new fields for weapons, you risk dismantling an already delicate military balance. The position of France is that peace depends on a strong military balance and on re-establishing it when it is upset. There must be a constant effort to bring this balance to a lower level. Regarding the prospects opened up by [U.S.] President Reagan's Strategic Defense Initiative [the space defense system], I think that it is too early to arrive at definitive conclusions. In any case, there is nothing that could lead France to modify its own defense policy, which is based on its deterrent capacity.

Interview, Paris/Time, 3-25:51.

Bernard Feld
Professor of physics, Massachusetts
Institute of Technology; Editor-in-chief,
"Bulletin of Atomic Scientists"

6

The problem has been that somehow, once you have weapons, you can't reduce. We both—both sides—know these weapons can't be used, and at first it was seen that 200 of these [nuclear] weapons would be enough to ensure that the other side wouldn't use them. Then it was thought that for safety's sake we better double that to 400; then maybe safety required a factor of 10, to 2,000. A compromise was reached at 1,000. But, of course, the Russians started to catch up. Instead of stopping at 1,000, they had

(BERNARD FELD)

the assembly line going, and they went on to 1,500. Now the two sides have 40,000 or so. We seem to go on the theory, on both sides, that anything you can do, technologically, you better do.

Interview, Washington, Feb. 5/
The Washington Post, 2-6:(C)12.

Thomas S. Foley
United States Representative, D-Washington

1

The [Reagan] Administration's insistence that they have to have a 10 per cent increase in defense [spending], rising in out-years, is creating heartburn and dissatisfaction and anxiety among both parties. Let me emphasize, nobody's talking about cutting defense. Defense will rise in real terms under any budget that will be approved by the Congress. It's a question of how fast and how much. And when the rhetoric, sometimes, coming from the White House suggests that those in the Congress, Democrats and Republicans, want to slash defense, it gives the impression we're cutting back. We've had a steady buildup of defense in real terms. We're spending more in real terms today than we did at the height of the Vietnam war. That's inflation-adjusted dollars. So the question is, doesn't defense have to play part of the role in a cutback in these spending areas, and we think it does. That's shared in the House and the Senate, among Democrats and Republicans.

Broadcast interview, Washington/
"Meet the Press," NBC-TV, 2-10.

J. William Fulbright
Former United States Senator,
D-Arkansas

2

It is constantly reiterated that our interests and the Soviet interests are so inherently opposed that there is no possibility of normal, peaceful relations. This is said as a given, without reservation, with complete confidence that no reasonable man should question. Well, as one unreasonable man, I question it. It seems clear to me that our true interests are not served by the arms race and, that if it continues, it will lead

either to the gradual impoverishment of both superpowers or to armed conflict. If instead of endless negotiations about all manner of exotic arms, nuclear and conventional, we seriously considered the effects of a well-designed program of joint ventures in all possible fields of activity, we would recognize that nuclear weapons have made the ancient game of trial-by-battle obsolete and dangerous and that the competition must be transferred to a different arena, to a non-military arena where the competition could be vigorous but not fatal.

Interview, February/
Los Angeles Herald Examiner,
2-6:(A)11.

Barry M. Goldwater
United States Senator, R-Arizona

4

[Supporting increased defense spending]: In defense, the problems of cost overruns, program instability and forces unfit for combat that greeted the new [Reagan] Administration in 1981 have, to a great extent, been overcome.

Upon receiving honorary degree
from Georgetown University, November/
Los Angeles Herald Examiner, 12-1:(F)1.

[Saying that President Reagan's proposed space defense system should be developed jointly by the U.S. and the Soviet Union]: The President has on several occasions suggested that, if the project should prove feasible, he would be prepared to share the technology with the Russians, or, as he more recently put it, sell it to them "at cost." Instead of this rather casual and condescending promise for the future, it would be far more credible if the research of "Star Wars" were conducted jointly with the Russians from the outset. Such a joint venture would enhance the likelihood of success, reduce the cost to each party, and, of far greater importance, would remove the destabilizing effects of a unilateral program while contributing substantially to the development of trust and confidence. President Reagan insists that SDI is solely for defensive purposes, but the Russians obviously are not convinced.

3

(BARRY M. GOLDWATER)

They are achievements we should build on, not use as an excuse to do less.

At Senate Armed Services Committee hearing, Washington, Feb. 4/The New York Times, 2-5:8.

1

We are the only country in the world I know of that has four air forces, a navy with an air force and an army, an army with a navy and an air force, and an air force that doesn't have any boats yet [because] it hasn't been around long enough. The Constitution gives the Congress the responsibility to raise and maintain the armed services. But the Constitution also gives us oversight responsibilities, and I believe we have not paid enough attention to that responsibility.

The Christian Science Monitor, 10-17:36.

Mikhail S. Gorbachev
General Secretary, Communist Party of the Soviet Union

2

[Arms-control] negotiations between the Soviet Union and the United States of America will open in Geneva tomorrow. The approach of the U.S.S.R. to these negotiations is well known. I can only reaffirm that: We do not strive to acquire unilateral advantages over the United States, over NATO countries, for military superiority over them; we want termination, and not continuation, of the arms race and, therefore, offer a freeze of nuclear arsenals, an end to further deployment of missiles; we want a real and major reduction of the arms stockpiles, and not the development of ever new weapon systems, be it in space or on earth. We would like our partners in the Geneva negotiations to understand the Soviet Union's position and respond in kind. Then agreement will be possible. The peoples of the world would sigh with relief.

Upon his assuming leadership, before Soviet Communist Party Central Committee, Moscow, March 11/The New York Times, 3-12:6.

3

[Criticizing U.S. President Reagan's proposal for a space defense system]: I would describe as fantastic the arguments used to substantiate the militarization of outer space. They speak about defense but prepare for attack. They advertise the space shield but are forging a space sword. They promise to liquidate nuclear arms but in practice build up these arms and perfect them.

Interview/The New York Times, 4-8:4.

4

[On the current U.S.-Soviet arms talks in Geneva]: I get information from Geneva every day, and I'm not inspired . . . What do we see in Geneva today? Marking time. Geneva should not turn into a debate. Otherwise the teams in Geneva will be eating their way through piles of gold rubles, drinking coffee, sipping tea, while mountains of arms continue to be built.

At meeting with visiting members of U.S. Congress, Moscow/The Washington Post, 4-18:(A)30.

5

[Criticizing U.S. plans for a space defense system]: The Soviet Union, the Warsaw treaty countries, seek no superiority either on earth or in space. We are not striving to compete to see who will build a higher nuclear fence. But we shall prevent the military strategic parity from being upset. If preparations for "Star Wars" [the U.S. space defense system] go on, we will have no other choice but to take measures of response, including, of course, a buildup and improvement of offensive nuclear arms.

At dinner in his honor, Warsaw, Poland, April 26/The New York Times, 4-27:1.

6

[Criticizing the U.S. attitude at the current Soviet-U.S. arms-control talks in Geneva]: If our partners in the Geneva talks carry on their line, marking time at the sessions of the delegations, avoiding solutions to the problems for the sake of which they have gathered and using that time to intensify their arms-buildup programs in space, on land and on the seas, we will, of course, have to reassess the entire situation. We just cannot allow the talks to be used anew as a decoy, as a cover for military preparations the purpose of which is to insure the strategic supe-

WHAT THEY SAID IN 1985

(MIKHAIL S. GORBACHEV)

riority of the United States and its course of achieving world dominance.

Broadcast address to the nation, Dnepropetrovsk, U.S.S.R., June 26/The New York Times, 6-27:3.

1

[Criticizing U.S. plans for a space defense system]: Talk about its alleged defensive character is, of course, a fairy tale for the naive. The plan is to try to neutralize Soviet strategic weapons and to secure a possibility to deliver with impunity a nuclear strike at our country. This is the crux of the matter and we cannot help but bear this in mind. The Soviet Union, if it faces a real threat from space, will find effective means to counter it—and I can say quite definitely that no one should have any doubts about it.

Broadcast address to the nation, Dnepropetrovsk, U.S.S.R., June 26/The Washington Post, 6-27:(A)32.

2

[Saying his country is instituting a five-month moratorium on nuclear test explosions]: A moratorium is an important step on the way to an end to the further sophistication of lethal nuclear weapons. Besides, the longer the period without tests, the more rapid will be the process of "aging" of the stockpiled weapons. And finally, a moratorium creates more favorable conditions for reaching agreement [with the West] on the termination of nuclear tests and for making headway toward the elimination of nuclear weapons altogether.

Moscow, Aug. 13/ Los Angeles Times, 8-14:(I)5.

3

[Arguing against the proposed U.S. space defense system]: If this were done, then the scope of military rivalry would be considerably greater and the arms race could assume an irreversible direction. We are prepared to engage in radical cutbacks in nuclear weapons, provided that the door to unleashing an arms race in outer space be firmly slammed shut . . . I feel the [U.S.] President [Reagan] is committed to it personally,

but since he is a statesman responsible for the security of such an important state, we cannot understand his attitude . . . I said [to him during the summit meeting in Geneva]: "Mr. President, we are not naive. We are not simpletons . . ." It's now clear our response [to the U.S. space defense system] will be effective, less costly, and be put in place more rapidly, [although] we will not welcome this path.

News conference, Geneva, Nov. 21/ Los Angeles Times, 11-22:(I)5.

4

[Saying the U.S. should join the Soviet Union in a moratorium on nuclear testing]: The Soviet Union is prepared to take most resolute steps down to on-site inspection as regards control over the ending of nuclear testing. Our country has a stake in reliable and rigorous control no less than any other country. Under the present international conditions, given the deficit of mutual trust, verification measures are simply indispensable . . . Let us act so that 1986 should go down in history as the year when people mustered up enough common sense to rise above narrow motives and stop disfiguring their own planet.

To foreign diplomats, Moscow, Dec. 27/The New York Times, 12-28:3.

Charles E. Grassley
United States Senator, R-Iowa

The weakness of conservatives too often has been to equate a larger defense budget with a stronger defense. The evidence is clear—we're spending more and getting less in some cases than we did in the Carter years.

Washington, March 1/ The Washington Post, 3-2:(A)6.

Andrei A. Gromyko
Foreign Minister of the Soviet Union

6

[On the current U.S.-Soviet arms-control talks]: It is impossible to examine productively questions of strategic nuclear armaments and

(ANDREI A. GROMYKO)

intermediate-range nuclear weapons without considering questions of [the militarization of] space, outer space . . . The Soviet Union is ready not only to consider the problem of strategic armaments, but would also be prepared for their sharp reduction. On the other hand, if there were no advancement on the issues of outer space, it would be superfluous to discuss the possibility of reducing strategic armaments.

Broadcast interview, Moscow,
Jan. 13/The New York Times, 1-14:4.

Geoffrey Howe
Foreign Secretary of the United Kingdom

1

[On the U.S. proposals for a space defense system]: It would be wrong to underestimate the enormous technological expertise and potential of the United States. But there would be no advantage in creating a new Maginot Line of the 21st century, liable to be outflanked by relatively simpler and demonstrably cheaper counter-measures [that the Soviets might develop] . . . We must be especially on our guard against raising hopes that it may be impossible to fulfill. We would all like to think of nuclear deterrence as a distasteful but temporary expedient. Unfortunately, we have to face the harsh realities of a world in which nuclear weapons exist and cannot be disinvented.

Before Royal United Services Institute, London,
March 15/The Washington Post, 3-16:(A)23.

Fred C. Ikle
Under Secretary for Policy,
Department of Defense of the United States

2

[On President Reagan's proposed space defense system]: The Strategic Defense Initiative is not an optional program, at the margin of the defense effort. It's central. The one and one-fifth per cent of the budget that it requires for the coming fiscal year will build the very core of our long-term policy for reducing the risk of nuclear war.

Before Senate Strategic and
Theatre Nuclear Forces Subcommittee, Washington,
Feb. 21/The New York Times, 2-22:11.

Max M. Kampelman
Chief United States negotiator at
U.S.-Soviet arms-control talks

3

I'm a Democrat and I've never separated myself from that. And yet I don't know why being in favor of a strong national defense or highlighting a perception of the Soviet Union as a danger to democracy and our liberty should be called conservative. It was the hallmark of Franklin Roosevelt, Harry Truman, Jack Kennedy, Scoop Jackson and Hubert Humphrey. I think my position is consistent with the tradition of the Democratic Party and American liberalism.

Interview, Washington/
The Washington Post, 1-23:(D)1.

Viktor P. Karpov
Chief Soviet negotiator at
U.S.-Soviet arms-control talks

4

The [forthcoming U.S.-Soviet arms] negotiation affords an opportunity for productive work and reaching solutions aimed at preventing an arms race in space and terminating it on Earth after limiting and reducing nuclear arms and strengthening stability. Agreement on implementation of far-reaching measures in these areas would be an important step toward obtaining a truly historic goal—that of ultimately eliminating nuclear arms completely and everywhere . . . The Soviet delegation will be consistently guided by the principle of equality and equal security which precludes either party to the negotiations from gaining unilateral advantages.

Arrival statement, Geneva,
March 10/Los Angeles Times, 3-11:(I)10.

5

The U.S. "Star Wars" [space defense] program sharply reduces chances of reaching an agreement on disarmament issues. Renunciation of the development, including research, testing and deployment of space arms would open the way to radical reductions in nuclear arms. That is why nuclear and space arms must be considered and resolved in their organic interrelationship.

Geneva, May 29/
Los Angeles Times, 5-30:(I)5.

WHAT THEY SAID IN 1985

George F. Kennan
Former United States Ambassador to the Soviet Union

I start from a basic premise. First, that there is no issue at stake in our political relations with the Soviet Union which could conceivably be worth a nuclear war. Second, that there is no way in which nuclear weapons could conceivably be employed in combat that would not involve the possibility—and indeed the prohibitively high *probability*—of escalation into a general nuclear disaster. First use became irrational when the Russians developed the ability to respond in kind . . . They have already renounced first use in every way they conceivably could. They've done so unilaterally. They've done so publicly, and with every indication of meaning it. We are the ones who are dragging our feet. If there is no first use of these weapons, there will never be any use of them.

Interview/
Esquire, January:72.

1

George A. Keyworth II
Director, White House Office of Science and Technology Policy

Defense is off by itself. It has a job to do. In contrast to what many think, you don't spend on defense according to the wishes of the defense community. You spend on defense according to the challenges that you face from adversaries. If the Soviet Union builds and builds and builds, we are forced to respond. And that's what we are doing right now. We discuss defense R&D in one environment. We discuss non-defense civilian R&D in a completely different environment. It's the difference between the National Security Council and the Cabinet system, for example.

Interview, Washington/
The Christian Science Monitor, 1-22:17.

3

Edward M. Kennedy
United States Senator, D-Massachusetts

The [Reagan] Administration's own reckless military budget has eroded the consensus for a stronger, steadier defense effort. And much of the money has been misspent in a misguided strategic arms race. We have stockpiled a vast arsenal of expensive nuclear missiles and bombers; we are launching a distant, uncertain and perhaps destabilizing "Star Wars" [space defense] experiment—and yet we are short-changing the readiness and reliability of our conventional forces. We now find ourselves in the paradoxical position of lavishing more and more on national security, while becoming less and less sure of how secure we really are . . . Just as we should not let a child go hungry, so we should never starve our national defense. But today it is overfed; it consumes too much of our scarce resources; it weakens our economy and our security—and perhaps even the prospects for our survival. We cannot afford to slash the defense budget or to deny reasonable increases; but we cannot afford to bloat it, or to

84

Lane Kirkland
President, American Federation of Labor-Congress of Industrial Organizations

The AFL-CIO remains committed to a strong defense. But we are equally committed to a strong economy and social justice at home. We will, therefore, not support increased defense spending at the expense of programs that are vital to our domestic welfare. We strongly oppose the proposition that the security of this present generation ought to be paid for by future generations or that the security of the affluent classes in our society ought to be paid for by further stripping the neediest classes in our society.

Bal Harbour, Fla., Feb.19/
The Washington Post, 2-20:(A)3.

4

Henry A. Kissinger
Former Secretary of State of the United States

[Supporting President Reagan's proposal for a space defense system]: I think it is absurd to say

pay for it by sapping another essential element of our strength—our economic leadership.

At John F. Kennedy Presidential Conference, Hofstra University, March 29/The Washington Post, 4-2:(4)18.

2

(HENRY A. KISSINGER)

that the Soviets can have 10,000 anti-aircraft missiles and uncounted thousands of fighter planes against bombers, but one cannot have defense against missile warheads. That is an intellectual absurdity. I believe that it is impossible, for the indefinite future, to base the security of the West entirely on unopposed offensive forces. It will demoralize the public. It will undermine credible deterrence . . . Our position should be that defensive deployments will be related to offensive deployments [by the other side]. The lower the offense, the lower can be the defense. We are prepared now to accept limitations on defense, provided there are limitations also on offense . . . I don't think that it is possible to have a perfect defense, but, equally, I do not think it makes any sense to say that unless you can have a perfect defense, you can have no defense at all.

Interview, Washington/
Los Angeles Times, 6-16:(IV)2.

Edward I. Koch
Mayor of New York

1

[Criticizing proposed funding of the MX missile]: If you build a steel wall around this country and the people behind the wall you are defending are going into abject poverty and the government is perceived as the enemy, then what have you preserved, what have you defended, what have you saved?

At rally, Washington, March 26/
The Washington Post, 3-27:(A)6.

John F. Lehman, Jr.
Secretary of the Navy
of the United States

2

It is my personal belief [that] to get meaningful and substantial progress for the long term in arms control, that we must have on-site inspection techniques as part of that negotiation. The Navy stands ready to accept whatever intrusive means of arms-control inspection, including allowing Soviet inspection teams aboard our ships, whatever is negotiated.

Before Senate Armed Services Committee, Washington,
Feb. 6/The Washington Post, 2-7:(A)28.

3

[Criticizing a Congressional proposal to freeze defense expenditures]: We cannot continue to pretend and lie to the American people that we can meet our 40-some treaty commitments, that we can keep our economy afloat, that we can keep 90 per cent of the strategic minerals coming by sea from every continent and to keep the oil flowing, with a fleet that is reduced in readiness, size and manning that would be mandated by this [defense-spending freeze]. I cannot overstate the violence to our programs if what the [Senate] Budget Committee has done were ever carried through.

Before Senate Defense Appropriations Subcommittee,
Washington, March 7/The Washington Post, 3-8:(A)6.

4

It would be impossible for me or anyone at this table to accurately describe to you the system with which, and within which, we [in the military] must operate. There are thousands upon thousands upon thousands of officers and entities and bureaus that have been created over the years to deal episodically with aspects of defense. The Office of the Secretary of Defense, originally 50 people, is now 2,000 people. The Joint Staff, originally to be not more than 100 people, is now 2,000 people. The Office of the Secretary of the Navy, the Chief of Naval Operations and the Commandant of the Marine Corps, originally to be 300 people, is now 2,000 people. The Defense Logistics Agency, originally to be the "coordinator" of commodities, is now 50,000 people. There are 11 defense agencies, 9 joint and specified commands with staffs that run into the thousands each. These are the results, every one of them, of reform. Each was created in the name of "inter-service unity," "jointness" and "reform progress." What has been created over the last 40 years is an incredible, and unwieldy, "monster."

At Air-Sea-Space Exposition Banquet,
Washington, April 3/The New York Times, 4-6:8.

5

If we have to live with a zero-growth defense budget year after year, there's no way we can run a 600-ship Navy. If Congress insists on maintaining zero growth, we'll have to start later in this decade retiring ships early, putting a lot of

85

(JOHN F. LEHMAN, JR.)

them into mothballs—that kind of thing. We know what zero growth brings; we lived through it in the '70s. It brings a rapid upturn in resignations and a rapid drop in retention and recruiting.

Interview/U.S. News & World Report, 6-24:46.

Carl Levin
United States Senator, D-Michigan

Getting a fix on just how much [funding] the Pentagon really needs is like trying to nail Jell-O to a wall.

U.S. News & World Report, 5-27:10.

1

Robert C. McFarlane
Assistant to the President of the United States for National Security Affairs

For all of our modern experience in the SALT I, SALT II negotiations, this country was negotiating at a time when we had no new [weapons] systems. We had nothing that told the Russians that there is a reason why you should agree to reduce. They were watching a country which was not investing in modernization—no submarine-based missile for 13 years, no land-based missile for more than that, no bomber for 20 years. Why should the Soviets negotiate if we seem to be headed unilaterally toward restraining ourselves? Now we're in the midst of a modernization of each leg of our triad—land-based, sea-based and bombers. This provides powerful incentives for the Russians to say, let's put a cap on those American systems by going to the table and negotiating agreements to reduce on both sides. In short, we have incentives that we didn't have before.

Broadcast interview, Washington/
"Meet the Press," NBC-TV, 1-20.

2

Francois Mitterrand
President of France

Arms on earth—or even in space—can contribute to a certain balance. However, when you

3

talk about things that are cosmic [such as the proposed U.S. space defense system], that could mean the end of the 1972 agreements on the ABM's—not just the end of the agreements, but a move toward other types of weapons that I can't even go on to explain to you. France has already said it will not participate in this. France is interested in what goes on in space, and space should be put at the disposal of all mankind.

News conference, Paris,
Oct. 4/The New York Times, 10-5:4.

Brian Mulroney
Prime Minister of Canada

[Saying Canada supports the U.S. space defense system plan as a bargaining chip in the U.S.-Soviet arms-control talks]: That is one thing. It is another, quite another thing, to be invited [by the U.S.] to participate actively in a project [the space defense system] where you are not a big player, where you don't set the thrust and where you have no control over the parameters . . . It's one thing to reassert our commitment to our friend and to the strength of NATO. It's another for a country like Canada to go beyond that . . . What we do [regarding the space defense system] will be in the interest of Canada, as a sovereign nation, as a loyal ally and as a believer in freedom. Those are the criteria on which the decision will be made.

News conference, Baie Comeau, Quebec, Canada,
March 28/The New York Times, 3-29:4.

4

Paul H. Nitze
Special Adviser to the President of the United States for Arms-Control Negotiations

[On Soviet criticism of the proposed U.S. space defense system]: They are trying to cause us to abandon a research program which is comparable to a research program that they've had for many years. No, they're not bluffing. They're very expert in the field of propaganda . . . They would like us to unilaterally abandon a research program similar to the one that they have been conducting. They were the first ones to go into the field of particle-beam research; they were the first ones to go into the

5

(PAUL H. NITZE)

field of high-powered lasers. They'd like to have a monopoly in that field—and why not? If I were they, if I were on the Central Committee [of the Soviet Communist Party], I would agree: It's much better to have a monopoly.

Broadcast interview/
"This Week with David Brinkley," ABC-TV, 3-10.

1

[On U.S.-Soviet arms-reduction talks]: There clearly is a tendency in some quarters to believe that all of the responsibility for success or failure rests in the U.S. government and not the Soviet government, that Moscow's position is immutable and that, therefore, failure to reach an agreement must be the fault of the United States. Some people do look at it that way. It's completely unfair, but there is a danger that this view could gain force.

Interview/U.S. News & World Report, 7-22:36.

Sam Nunn
United States Senator, D-Georgia

2

[Saying military pensions may be too high]: I do think we need to take a look at the pension system . . . installed back in a period when pay was woefully inadequate, when we had a draft, when we basically had a totally different compensation system than we do today, and when, first and foremost, we had an enormous number of people actually serving in combat.

USA Today, 2-7:(A)2.

3

[On President Reagan's space-defense system proposal, or SDI]: It's not in trouble with votes [in the Senate] now, but neither was [the] MX [missile] two years ago. These are the kind of things you don't measure by votes—you put your nose in the air and smell. If you give it the old sniff test, there's an awful lot of uneasy feeling about SDI . . . I find very few people who are informed in this area in either party who even come close to the President's definition of SDI [as a system that will lead to the abolishment of

nuclear weapons]—and that's people who support the program. I think it's a trap. If you define it that broadly, when the public finds out—and they will, the American people are intelligent—that this is not achievable, then there's going to be disillusionment, and we're going to have SDI in trouble.

Los Angeles Times, 6-7:(I)4.

4

I've always feared that the volunteer [armed] forces, with its premium on pay and benefits, is creating a mentality moving away from patriotism and protection of one's country . . . I want the military to be paid well and I want them to be comfortable and their family to be well protected by health benefits. But I don't want that to be the main reason that people join the U.S. military, and I'm afraid that we have moved very far down that road. I think service in the military ought to be looked on as an opportunity to protect the country, to defend the homeland and to promote sufficient deterrence to preserve peace.

Interview, Washington, Aug. 2/
Los Angeles Times, 8-3:(I)23.

Richard N. Perle
Assistant Secretary of Defense
of the United States

5

To believe in far-reaching arms control with the Soviet Union in an adversarial position, you have to believe they'll change, change fundamentally, by reducing the prominence of military forces as a factor. I wish I saw a plateau on which relations would somehow even out, become more mutually accommodating. But I think it unlikely . . . The sense that we and the Russians could compose our differences, reduce them to treaty constraints, enter into agreements, treaties, reflecting a set of constraints and then rely on compliance to produce a safer world—I don't agree with any of that.

Interview/The Washington Post, 1-2:(A)20.

6

[Saying the U.S. always gives up more than it wins at arms-control talks with the Soviets]: [In

(RICHARD N. PERLE)

the forthcoming talks,] they're going to produce this mouse, and this mouse is going to scurry across the stage, and the press is going to say: "Well, was that it?" It's not a good situation for the West . . . a lot of controversy over who's to blame, why more progress wasn't made.

Los Angeles Times, 1-7:(I)13.

1

. . . we're concerned by the effect of anti-nuclear sentiment in a number of countries. Some of it, I think, is deliberately intended to disassociate those countries from the United States and from the protective umbrella that we have extended to those countries. Frankly, I don't see how in the long run we can ask the American people to bear the risks of war in order to defend allies who will have nothing to do with us when delicate issues like the movement of nuclear weapons is involved.

Television interview, Feb. 14/
The Washington Post, 2-15:(A)6.

2

[People] accept an image of the strategic relationship between the United States and the Soviet Union that is characterized by a spiraling arms race. And yet the facts are significantly different. The United States has today, deployed around the world, some 8,000 fewer nuclear weapons than we had deployed in 1967 . . . the megatonnage of this diminished American force is barely one-quarter of what it was in the late 1960s. Moreover, the Western alliance agreed, at a meeting in Canada a little over a year ago, to reduce further, by 1,400 weapons, the number of our nuclear weapons deployed in Europe. By contrast, we have seen in recent years consistent additions to Soviet nuclear forces: 8,000 new strategic warheads alone since 1969, when the SALT I negotiations got under way, 4,000 of which have been added since 1979 when the SALT II treaty was signed.

At Groupe de Bellerive conference, Geneva,
June 29/
The Wall Street Journal,
8-21:24.

David Pryor
United States Senator, D-Arkansas

3

[On the publicity about military cost-overruns and other defense-related abuses]: In the past, people thought that if you questioned military procurement, you'd be labeled a Communist sympathizer. Now if you go to a farm rally or senior-citizen center and you jump on the [defense] contractors and the Pentagon, you get your biggest round of applause.

News conference, Washington, May 8/
The Washington Post, 5-10:(A)23.

4

[On defense-industry overcharges to the military]: We see procurement horror stories—war profiteering in peacetime. We not only need a law with teeth, we . . . need a law with fangs.

U.S. News & World Report, 6-3:14.

Paul Quiles
Minister of Defense of France

5

[Criticizing the proposed U.S. space defense system]: The most optimistic predictions do not allow us to consider this a credible project, even for the next half-century. Science can make progress, sometimes very rapid progress, but it cannot work miracles. . . . A space defense risks becoming a new Maginot Line more costly than all such previous military projects.

Interview/The Washington Post, 12-18:(A)23.

Ronald Reagan
President of the United States

6

[Defending his proposed space defense system]: . . . all through history we've always been able to come up with a defensive weapon; isn't it worth researching to see if there isn't some weapon that is more humane and moral than saying that the only defense we have in the nuclear age is that if they kill tens of millions of our people we'll kill tens of millions of theirs. We're searching for a weapon that might destroy nuclear weapons, not the nuclear itself, destroy weapons, not people. And if we come up with

(RONALD REAGAN)

such a thing, then is the time to turn to the world, to our allies, possibly even our adversaries, and say, "Look, we now have this." And if we haven't by that time eliminated nuclear weapons entirely, this could be a big contributing factor to bringing that about.

News conference, Washington,
Jan. 9/The New York Times, 1-10:8.

1

For the past 20 years we have believed that no war will be launched as long as each side knows it can retaliate with a deadly counterstrike. Well, I believe there is a better way of eliminating the threat of nuclear war. It is a Strategic Defense Initiative [space defense system] aimed ultimately at finding a non-nuclear defense against ballistic missiles. It is the most hopeful possibility of the nuclear age. But it is not very well understood. Some say it will bring war to the heavens—but its purpose is to deter war, in the heavens and on earth. Some say the research would be expensive. Perhaps, but it could save millions of lives, indeed humanity itself. Some say if we build such a system, the Soviets will build a defensive system of their own. Well, they already have strategic defenses that surpass ours; a civil defense system, where we have almost none; and a research program covering roughly the same areas of technology we're exploring. And finally, some say the research will take a long time. The answer to that is: "Let's get started."

State of the Union address, Washington,
Feb. 6/Los Angeles Times, 2-7:(I)16.

2

National security is government's first responsibility, so, in past years, defense spending took about half the Federal budget. Today it takes less than a third. We have already reduced our planned defense expenditures by nearly $100-billion over the past four years, and reduced projected spending again this year. You know, we only have a military-industrial complex until a time of danger; then it becomes "the arsenal of democracy." Spending for defense is investing in things that are priceless: peace and freedom.

State of the Union address, Washington,
Feb. 6/The New York Times, 2-7:13.

3

[On whether he agrees with criticism of high military pensions]: No. I have to think this is a little different than any other pension program you want to name. They go into a profession in which they know that, in a matter of a certain number of years, that the physical requirements are such that they're going to be out. There is that—coupled with the sacrifice that is made by the military. I talked to a retired military officer. He had found other employment. But he told me that in the call of duty, for 20 of his 31 married years, he and his wife had not been together. He was out there in the world someplace.

Interview/The Wall Street Journal, 2-8:8.

4

[On the U.S.-Soviet arms-control talks in Geneva]: It's hard to be optimistic when you look back at the record. There have been some 19 offers and efforts by ourselves since World War II to seek control of this . . . and always the Soviet Union has resisted, even when they didn't have it and we had the monopoly. On the other hand, there are a couple of things that lead me to believe there's a possibility. Number one are their own words . . . One of them said to me, just between the two of us, he said, "Can we go on forever sitting on these ever-rising mountains of weapons?" and I said, "No, why don't we start reducing the mountains?" So what leads me to believe there's hope is not the idea that too often in the past when we've said, well, if they understand how nice we are, maybe they'll be nice, too. No, you'll get an agreement when it is to their practical interest also. They know they cannot match us industrially . . . And this leads me to believe that possibly they can see the practicality of this and do it.

Interview, Washington/Newsweek, 3-18:22.

5

[Calling for Congress to approve funds for the MX missile]: I believe that not only the Sovi-

WHAT THEY SAID IN 1985

(RONALD REAGAN)

. . . ets but our European allies view the current [U.S.] debate on the Peacekeeper [MX] as a key test of our resolve. If we fail, we'll be signaling to the world that on this key issue we are irresolute and divided. And the Soviet Union will see that in dealing with the United States, propaganda and stonewalling are much more profitable than good faith negotiations.

To members of Congress, Washington,
March 25/The New York Times, 3-26:12.

1

[On his proposal for a space defense system]: The Strategic Defense Initiative has been labeled "Star Wars." But it isn't about war, it's about peace. It isn't about retaliation, it's about prevention. It isn't about fear, it's about hope. And in that struggle, if you will pardon my stealing a film line [from the motion picture *Star Wars*], the force is with us . . . What could be more moral than a system designed to save lives rather than avenge them? What could be more peaceful than moving away from reliance on our ability to threaten global annihilation and toward reliance on systems which are incapable of threatening anyone?

Before National Space Club, Washington,
March 29/
The New York Times, 3-30:1,8.

2

Our first priority must always be our national security. The Soviets are far more dangerous today than during the '50s and '60s—periods in which we devoted far more to our defense. And they continue arming well beyond the defense needs of their country. Because of that threat, we must maintain modest but steady growth each year. Three per cent is the rock-bottom level we must maintain for effective deterrence to protect our security. Our plan will freeze the defense-spending share of our gross national product at 6.4 per cent for the next 3 years, a share well below the 8 to 9 per cent at the time of Eisenhower and Kennedy.

Broadcast address to the nation, Washington,
April 24/The New York Times, 4-25:15.

3

You will hear during your career that maintaining the military at peak readiness, keeping our forces trained and supplied with the best weapons and equipment is too costly. I say it is too costly *not* to be prepared. Today, as through our history, it is strength, not weakness, resolve, not vacillation, that will keep the peace. It is about time that those who place their faith in wishful thinking and good intentions got the word.

At U.S. Naval Academy commencement,
May 22/The New York Times, 5-23:14.

4

[On revelations of defense contractors charging too much for equipment they sell to the military]: We've moved forward to ferret out waste and inefficiency. That's why you hear stories about outrageously expensive hammers or bolts. We're finding the waste and cutting it out. Those press stories are actually success stories because, by and large, they represent our efforts to make the best use of our defense dollar.

At U.S. Naval Academy commencement,
May 22/The New York Times, 5-23:14.

5

[On Soviet criticism of his proposed space defense system]: It has been the Soviets who have built the world's most extensive network of civil defenses and the most widespread air defense system, who have deployed the world's only operational ABM and anti-satellite systems, and who have devoted extensive resources to investigating many of the same technologies we are now examining in our SDI [space defense] research . . . Soviet criticism of SDI is more than a little hypocritical. It is quite clear that the Soviets are intent on undermining the U.S. SDI program, while minimizing any constraints on their own ongoing strategic-defense activities.

Interview, Oct.21/The New York Times, 10-24:8.

6

[On his proposed space defense system]: . . . the United States seeks to escape the prison of mutual terror by research and testing that

(RONALD REAGAN)

could, in time, enable us to neutralize the threat of these ballistic missiles and, ultimately, render them obsolete. How is Moscow threatened if the capitals of other nations are protected? We do not ask that the Soviet leaders—whose country has suffered so much from war—to leave their people defenseless against foreign attack. Why, then, do they insist that we remain undefended? Who is threatened if Western research and Soviet research, this itself well advanced, should develop a non-nuclear system which would threaten not human beings, but only ballistic missiles? Surely, the world will sleep more secure when these missiles have been rendered useless, militarily and politically, when the Sword of Damocles that has hung over our planet for too many decades is lifted by Western and Russian scientists working to shield their citizens and one day shut down space as an avenue of weapons of mass destruction. If we're destined by history to compete, militarily, to keep the peace, then let us compete in systems that defend our societies rather than weapons which can destroy us both, and much of God's creation along with us.

At United Nations, New York,
The New York Times, 10-25:9.

John D. Rockefeller IV
United States Senator,
D-West Virginia

1

[Criticizing the Senate's vote to fund the MX missile]: The MX missile placed in existing silos looks like the worst of all worlds. A vulnerable, destabilizing first-strike weapon—in times of crisis, a prime target for the Soviets because of its size; a real temptation for us to "use it or lose it" because of its vulnerability.

Washington, March 19/
The New York Times, 3-20:14.

Toby Roth
United States Representative,
R-Wisconsin

2

At long last, Congress is finally addressing the problem of interservice rivalry in our armed forces. Wonderful. It is about time we are doing something about the Pentagon and the infighting that goes on there. The rivalry among the branches of our services—the Navy, Army, Air Force, Marines—is legendary, as anyone who has served in the armed forces can tell you. Most Americans believe that one branch of our armed forces would rather win a fight with another branch than win a battle with one of our nation's adversaries. Also, because of the sharp separation among our armed forces, there are endless duplications and unconscionable added costs. This is one of the reasons our defense budget is so high. The effectiveness of our military is also impaired because of the lack of communication and coordination among the branches. Yes, it is about time that the overweight Pentagon gets down into fighting trim, and that we are not caught flatfooted in an increasingly dangerous world.

Before the House, Washington,
Oct. 16/The New York Times,
10-22:10.

Donald H. Rumsfeld
Chairman, G. D. Searle & Company;
Former Secretary of Defense
of the United States

3

Over my years in public life, I have been asked again and again, "Where are the great leaders? Where are the giants today?" I answer, "They are there, and they will be there when they are needed. Let there be no doubt." And I ask in return, "Don't you suppose in the 1920s and the 1930s people also asked, 'Where are the great leaders? Where are the giants?'" We know now where they were. They were people whose names we had never heard, who were being paid a few thousand dollars a year, posted in dry, unpleasant forts all across the country and the world, moving their families every few years, bringing their children up in difficult circumstances, stuck in the same rank for eight, 10, 12 years, neglected by Congress, and whose patriotism, dedication and service were at great cost to themselves and their families, and were essentially without appreciation by the people, whom they served. It was not until World War II, when the need was urgent, that the people discovered

(DONALD H. RUMSFELD)

that the great leaders were there. Imagine our cause's good fortune that individuals of such character, stature, leadership qualities and dedication rose out of that difficult, rigorous and thankless environment. And when the call came, there, among that anonymous group, was a Dwight Eisenhower, an Omar Bradley, a Patton, a McAuliffe, a MacArthur, a Taylor, a Grunther, a Lemnitzer and an Abrams and others. And yes, there was a George Marshall, the mighty warrior, the man of peace. What a wonderful thing to say about the U.S. Army. Despite all the hardships, the lack of support, of recognition, or even awareness on the part of the people, when the need came, they were there. Doesn't it tell us something about an institution that can attract, develop, foster, retain, encourage and motivate individuals of that size?

Upon receiving George C. Marshall Medal
from Association of the U.S. Army/
The Wall Street Journal, 9-25:30.

1

Carl Sagan
Professor of astronomy and
space science, Cornell University

I'm not against the militarization of space. We have been militarizing space with reconnaissance satellites since the 1960s, and they're worth their weight in gold. It's the introduction of weapons into space that worries me very much. Space has become an arena for warfare, a kind of bloodless warfare, a kind of video-arcade warfare that is pure and clean. You get a very strong sense that this is not only easy but fun. We are at a clear branch point—a time at which the same set of technologies that can destroy us can also carry us to the planets and the stars.

At symposium sponsored by American Academy
of Arts and Science and the Planetary Society,
Jan. 12/The Christian Science Monitor, 1-15:36.

2

Patricia Schroeder
United States Representative,
D-Colorado

The President of the United States [Reagan], when he was running for office, pointed out there was an awful lot of waste in some social programs and really made one of his major platform speeches and many of his radio speeches about what he called Welfare Queens. Well, his Administration has come up with their own version of Welfare Queens. They are the defense contractors of America. The Office of the Inspector General of the Department of Defense tells us that now 45 of the top 100 American defense contractors are under criminal investigation of some sort. I find that shocking.

Before the House, Washington,
June 17/
The New York Times, 6-19:16.

3

Brent Scowcroft
Lieutenant General, United States Air
Force (retired); Former Assistant to the
President of the United States (Gerald
Ford) for National Security Affairs

[Criticizing President Reagan's proposed space defense system]: There are immense arms-control implications because it has been difficult enough to negotiate simply strategic offensive weapons agreements. When you throw defense in, it obviously makes it immensely more complicated... [It] is unlikely to be true [that a space defense system would facilitate nuclear-arms reduction, because] the most reasonable reaction is quite the opposite. And that, in a sense, is what happened in the late '60s and early '70s when the Soviets moved toward building an ABM system. We increased our offensive forces and went to MIRVs in order to maintain the ability to penetrate a defense. I'm not saying the other reaction couldn't take place, but I think it's not—and has not historically—been the normal reaction... It is difficult enough, given the kind of asymmetries between the U.S. strategic forces and the Soviets' strategic forces, to figure out what balancing reductions might be among bombers, submarine missiles and ICBMs. When you add the implications of the possible deployment of a defensive system, and how one has to deal with that and how one balances that off against the various offensive systems, it just gets very, very complicated.

Interview/Los Angeles Times, 2-7:(I)13.

John M. Shalikashvili
Brigadier General,
and Community Commander (Nuremberg,
West Germany), United States Army

1

The thing that keeps our Army together is the noncommissioned-officer corps. We are so structured, and our procedures are so set up, that the Army needs a strong, positive noncommissioned-officer corps. When you unravel that [as happened in the Vietnam war], you can't replace it with inexperienced second lieutenants or with youngsters who might have been handed the reins of a sergeant but in experience and maturity are still privates . . . If you are not prepared to go into combat in the best possible posture, then you stand up and raise your hand and say that something else has to be tried. If going into combat means you must do away with the glue, the NCO corps, which holds us together, then you better have serious second thoughts [about going].

Interview/The Washington Post, 4-16:(A)9.

Vladimir V. Shcherbitsky
Member, Politburo, Communist
Party of the Soviet Union

2

[Criticizing the proposed U.S. space defense system]: Today such a system could be defensive, but tomorrow it could become offensive. If the Soviet Union pursues this line, the Soviet Union will have to take adequate measures—offensive, defensive, but adequate to the measures of the United States . . . If you look at all the previous [arms-control] agreements, those agreements were a sum of compromises. We are ready to agree to a number of compromises. And if the United States government will go along in the same direction, then a solution based on a compromise could be reached and the people would breathe more easily.

To reporters after meeting U.S. President Reagan,
Washington, March 7/Los Angeles Times, 3-8:(I)1.

Eduard A. Shevardnadze
Foreign Minister of the Soviet Union

3

The heaviest burden on mankind's shoulders is the arms race, which is inexorably bringing us

closer to the edge of an abyss. It is our duty to stop and then to reverse it, to prevent it from spreading to space. The Soviet Union has countered the concept of "Star Wars" [the U.S. proposal for a space defense system] with the concept of "Star Peace" and of a lasting peace on earth. The Soviet Union is proposing a world without weapons in space. The Soviet Union is proposing a world where nuclear arms would be radically reduced and then eliminated altogether. The Soviet Union is proposing a world where the U.S.S.R. and the United States would set an example for other nuclear powers by stopping any nuclear explosions. The Soviet Union is proposing a world where the U.S.S.R. and the United States would renounce the development of new nuclear weapons, freeze their arsenals, and ban and destroy anti-satellite systems.

At United Nations,
New York, Oct. 24/
The New York Times,
10-25:6.

George P. Shultz
Secretary of State
of the United States

4

[On the Soviet Union's criticism of the proposed U.S. space defense system]: Behind the curtain that encloses Soviet society, free from the open debate we see in the West, a major strategic defense program has proceeded for decades. The current Soviet leaders know that. In the past 20 years, the Soviet Union has spent about as much on strategic defense as on their offensive nuclear forces. They know that. The Soviets have the world's most active military space program, last year conducting about 100 space launches, some 80 per cent of which were purely military in nature, compared to a total of about 20 U.S. space launches. The Soviets know that, too. They deploy the world's only ABM system, whose nuclear-armed interceptors and other components are undergoing extensive modernization. They are researching many of the same new technologies as we, and are ahead in some. And the Soviet Union has the world's only extensively tested and fully operational anti-satellite system. The Soviet leaders know full well their own efforts in these fields. Their

(GEORGE P. SHULTZ)

propaganda about American programs is blatantly one-sided and not to be taken seriously.

At United Nations, New York,
Sept. 23/The New York Times, 9-25:8.

1

[On U.S. plans to pursue a space defense system]: Our research program is, and will continue to be, consistent with the ABM treaty. The treaty can be variously interpreted as to what kinds of development and testing are permitted, particularly with respect to future systems. It is our view . . . that a broader interpretation of our authority is fully justified. This is, however, a moot point. Our SDI research program has been structured and, as the President has reaffirmed, will continue to be conducted in accordance with a restrictive interpretation of the treaty's obligations.

At meeting of North Atlantic Assembly, San Francisco,
Oct. 14/Los Angeles Times, 10-15:(I)9.

Gerard C. Smith
Former United States
arms-control negotiator

[Criticizing U.S. development of anti-satellite weapons, saying it would cause the Soviet Union to develop similar weapons]: In four or five years, if we both have this sort of killer, we, being more dependent on satellites than the Soviets, will be sorry we didn't choke this thing off. This is like shooting yourself in the foot to show resolve.

Los Angeles Times, 9-14:(I)6.

2

Sergei L. Sokolov
Minister of Defense
of the Soviet Union

[Criticizing the proposed U.S. plan for a space defense system]: The U.S. course of militarization of outer space will extremely negatively influence the military-political situation in the world and complicate, if not make impossible, solution to the problem of reduction of nuclear armaments. Our aim is an end to the arms race, full destruction of nuclear weapons every-

3

where . . . The so-called Strategic Defense Initiative of [U.S.] President Reagan is called "defensive" only for cover-up purposes, but actually it is aimed at the development of a new class of weapons—strike space systems . . . Neither the Soviet Union nor the United States has weapons in space at this time. Space militarization, endangering mankind, will begin when strike systems designed to hit objects in space from earth are placed there.

Interview/Los Angeles Times, 5-6:(I)1,13.

Richard Stillwell
Deputy Under Secretary for Policy,
Department of Defense of the United States

[Defending lie-detector tests for certain Defense Department employees]: Three and a half million persons hold defense security clearances. One hundred thousand are cleared for very sensitive information. We are testing 3,500 of those with access to the most sensitive. Unauthorized release of certain of this information could jeopardize lives or lose the U.S. an important strategic advantage. Some convicted spies have said they were told by Soviet handlers to avoid working for agencies that used polygraphs. The tests will give us a bit more assurance that we won't lose our most precious secrets.

Interview/U.S. News & World Report, 2-25:44.

4

David A. Stockman
Director, Federal Office
of Management and Budget

[Saying military pensions are too high]: I haven't been able to get anything done on military retirement. It's a scandal. It's an outrage. The institutional forces in the military are more concerned about protecting their retirement benefits than they are about protecting the security of the American people. When push comes to shove, they'll give up on security before they'll give up on retirement. Now, that's just another true fact of life, and I'll probably be in hot water for saying it. But I'm going to say it because it's about time it was said.

Before Senate Budget Committee, Washington,
Feb. 5/USA Today, 2-11:(A)10.

5

(DAVID A. STOCKMAN)

1

Big [budget] savings [in defense] come from canceling programs and reducing core structures, not from paper growth-rate exercises in which some of our distinguished legislators apparently are plugging in their locker combination like 0-3-3 or something of that sort. While every budget has its wiggles, and defense is no exception, none can be radically cut without sweeping policy and program changes. In the case of defense, these are not in the cards because the national-security risks would be too great—something that most of the Congress already knows full well and the rest will soon find out.

Before National Press Club, Washington, March 28/ The Washington Post, 3-29:(A)6.

Harry G. Summers, Jr.
Colonel, United States Army;
Strategic research analyst,
U.S. Army War College

2

There are two ways the United States traditionally uses force, two ways built into our Constitution. One is, the President under Article II of the Constitution, as Commander-in-Chief, uses force in response to immediate crisis, quickly in, quickly out—Thomas Jefferson in 1801, President Reagan in Grenada. And by and large the American people tend to rally around the President in a moment of crisis. So that's one use of military force . . . Without a declaration, short lived, immediate crisis, in and out. But the other way is under Article I of the Constitution, where it's a prolonged commitment of military force over time, and there the support of the people and the Congress are absolutely necessary. But in Vietnam, if you'll recall, both President Johnson and President Nixon tried to justify an Article I use of force, if you will, under their authority as under Article II, and that won't wash. It just won't wash.

Broadcast interview/ "Meet the Press," NBC-TV, 4-28.

Edward Teller
Nuclear physicist;
Senior research fellow, Hoover Institution, Stanford University

3

I believe we have classified too much. Secrecy is a measure that hurts our opponents a little and us a great deal . . . In nuclear weapons, where we had the greatest of secrecy, the Soviets are now ahead of us. In electronics, where we had very little government secrecy, we are way ahead of others, particularly the Soviets. It looks like an absurdity, but who is ahead depends not only on what they learn from us but on the speed of our own development.

Los Angeles Times, 4-10:(I)12.

4

The Soviets have civil defense; we have none. The Soviets have a defense around Moscow, which I believe in its present improved version will work. We have none. The Soviets have deployed what I consider one of the best candidates for a strategic defense weapon anywhere, that is a very powerful laser, on their Sari Shagan site . . . and we have none. They have done work; we have not. Who is ahead? Zero is less than any accomplishment, and we know that the Russians have accomplished a lot with lots of money and lots of hard work.

Broadcast interview/ "Meet the Press," NBC-TV, 7-28.

5

[On critics of the proposed U.S. space defense system]: There was a time when [those critics] opposed the hydrogen bomb because it was too terrible. Now they oppose the humane defense [program] because it is not terrible enough.

Broadcast interview/ The Christian Science Monitor, 9-30:15.

John G. Tower
United States arms-control negotiator;
Former United States Senator, R-Texas

6

[On whether U.S. testing of an anti-satellite weapon will affect the U.S.-Soviet arms-control talks in Geneva]: I think that the arms talks, the

(JOHN G. TOWER)

progress of the talks, the ultimate outcome is going to be driven by both sides' perception of their national interest. That's going to be the determining factor, not incidents that may occur along the line. The ultimate outcome will depend largely on the extent to which the Soviets perceive it to be in their interest to agree to radical reductions in offensive arms.

Broadcast interview/ "Face the Nation," CBS-TV, 8-25.

Henry Trofimenko
Head, U.S. foreign-policy section, Institute of American and Canadian Studies, Soviet Academy of Sciences

1

In the Pentagon's view, every weapon the Soviet Union has is "destabilizing"; every weapon the United States has is a "stabilizing" weapon. They said that the Soviet SS-16 missile was immediately destabilizing, but when the United States started to build MX missiles it was immediately stabilizing. Sometimes this game of numbers is designed to distract the people's attention from the greater problem of how do you ensure the security of your own country. In the present time of overabundance of nuclear weaponry, security ought to be ensured by mutual agreement on arms control, not through competition of one against the other.

Interview, Middlebury College/ Los Angeles Times, 1-13:(IV)2.

William L. Ury
Director, Nuclear Negotiation Project, Harvard University

2

[Nuclear-weapon] flight times are getting shorter and accuracy is getting greater, so the time [for] decision in time of crisis is shrinking. The thing that concerns me is that the pace of technology is outstripping the pace of the diplomats.

The Christian Science Monitor, 1-3:18.

Cyrus R. Vance
Former Secretary of State of the United States

3

[On President Reagan's proposed space defense system]: I am strongly opposed to committing ourselves to pursuing the strategic defense initiative beyond research . . . A leak-proof system is an unrealizable dream . . . [because] the means for defeating any defense of cities are too numerous. [Furthermore,] the Soviet reaction to the development and deployment of such a system will almost certainly be a large increase in the number of their offensive weapons, which we will then be compelled to match, and the arms spiral will be ratcheted upwards.

Before Senate Foreign Relations Committee, Washington, Feb. 4/The New York Times, 2-5:6.

4

We recognize that arms-control negotiations cannot and do not take place in a political vacuum . . . At the same time, however, if U.S.-Soviet political difficulties arise elsewhere in the world, we must be exceedingly cautious in attempting to link Soviet political behavior to the pursuit of arms-control agreements. There is no merit in our trying to impose such "linkage." Any particular arms-control agreement is either in our interest and should be pursued—or it is *not and should not.*

Before Senate Foreign Relations Committee, Washington, Feb. 4/U.S. News & World Report, 2-18:45.

John W. Vessey, Jr.
General, United States Army; Chairman, Joint Chiefs of Staff

5

We [in the military] know how to build forces. We think we know how to employ them. But choosing the time and place is a political decision. We have some ideas about whether it's right or wrong. We ought to make those ideas known but recognize that it's a political decision . . . All of us have to recognize that the ultimate decision is the President's. He's Commander-in-Chief. It's our business to advise and tell him; then, when he makes his decision, to carry it out.

Interview, Washington/ The New York Times, 9-3:12.

(JOHN W. VESSEY, JR.)

1

[Supporting U.S. development of a space defense system]: It is the duty of governments to protect their citizens. Therefore, it is a logical fallacy to say, "We will protect you by threatening to annihilate those who threaten to annihilate you." That's fine, until it happens. Then all you can do is avenge your own annihilation. So the idea of protecting the population with a Strategic Defense Initiative—an anti-missile system in outer space—makes uncommonly good sense if we can do it. And in time, we will be able to do it. We need to develop such a system to keep the seamless web of deterrence intact.

Interview/U.S. News & World Report, 10-21:40.

Michael Vlahos
*Coordinator of security studies, Foreign
Policy Institute, Johns Hopkins University*

2

[Supporting Reagan Administration plans to develop and test an anti-satellite weapon]: If we don't undertake some development, we will be in miserable shape. It's not just a bargaining chip [in arms-control negotiations with the Soviets]. We must ask ourselves if delaying the test would serve any useful purpose. A gesture of good-will on our part in the wake of the enormous Soviet effort might be a sign that we were so soft in our negotiating position that we would forfeit the right to reach an agreement with the Soviets. This isn't an act of bravado—it is a very prudent step.

Los Angeles Times, 8-23:(I)21.

John W. Warner
United States Senator, R-Virginia

3

[On the forthcoming U.S.-Soviet summit meeting]: You can look at the history of summitry and cast doubt on it, but you can't cast doubt on the proliferation of nuclear technology, particularly as it relates to weapons and the enormous arsenals that both nations have now amassed. The whole world is now held at bay by virtue of these ever-expanding nuclear arsenals. And if we can begin to lower the level of the arsenals—that is, substantial reductions on both sides—in a fair, equitable, verifiable and, I

would like to add, enforceable, arms agreement, then I think there will be a great reassurance spread across this Earth.

*Broadcast interview/
"This Week With David Brinkley," ABC-TV, 9-1.*

Paul C. Warnke
*Former Director, Arms Control and
Disarmament Agency of the United States*

4

[Criticizing Reagan Administration plans to conduct tests of an anti-satellite weapon]: The Soviets have no effective anti-satellite capability. Their system is a low-orbiting one with no rapid-firing capability and it does not work well. We have more capability with our space shuttle than they have with their system. This demonstrates that arms control in the Reagan Administration is dominated by those who are opposed to arms control.

The Christian Science Monitor, 8-22:3.

Caspar W. Weinberger
*Secretary of Defense
of the United States*

5

To achieve success [in arms-control talks with the Soviet Union] we must continue our strategic modernization program and demonstrate our resolve to stay strong. It was that resolve that brought the Soviets back to the negotiating table, and that resolve now gives us a critical opportunity to achieve those arms-reduction goals that have eluded mankind for far too long. In this regard, I must tell you frankly that cancellation of key programs such as MX, or reductions in the defense budget, will prolong negotiations, not facilitate them, and will reduce our ability to achieve arms reductions and take away Soviet incentives to agree to reductions.

*Before Senate Foreign Relations Committee,
Washington, Jan. 31/The New York Times, 2-1:4.*

6

[On whether there are too many U.S. troops stationed abroad]: No. I don't think we have too many deployed abroad . . . From a military point of view, it would weaken us substantially to

WHAT THEY SAID IN 1985

(CASPAR W. WEINBERGER)

bring home or reduce the number of forward-deployed forces. In this kind of a world where you may have to respond very quickly, having forward-deployed forces can save you hours, days, weeks that you can never regain.

Before Senate Foreign Relations Committee, Washington, Jan. 31/U.S. News & World Report, 2-18:45.

1

The keystone of our military strategy since World War II has been deterrence. Deterrence provides security by convincing potential adversaries that the risks and costs of aggression will exceed any conceivable gains . . . Credible and prudent deterrence requires strong military capability. Mere threats are not enough.

Before Senate Foreign Relations Committee, Washington, Jan. 31/U.S. News & World Report, 2-18:45.

2

[Supporting President Reagan's proposed space defense system]: An effective defense—even if it were not a perfect defense, although we would always strive to make it perfect—could substantially raise the costs and enhance the uncertainty of aggression. It would especially reduce the advantage of pre-emptive attack, and thus promote stability. Finally, it would provide insurance against a world in which the Soviets—and the Soviets alone—could brandish their sword from behind the protective shield they are continuing to develop . . . The question we face is whether we are willing, in the 1980s, to preclude the possibility of developing, in the 1980s and beyond—with wholly new technologies unknown to people who drafted the ABM treaty—an effective defense against ballistic missiles. Are we truly such hostages of the past that we can never even consider a better way, a way to keep the peace that offers hope in place of one based always on balancing terror?

Written remarks to meeting of NATO defense officials, Munich, Feb. 10/The New York Times, 2-11:3.

3

Weapons systems are not put into a museum to look at. They are to look at. They are to use. And, as a result,

you've got to look at what the other side has. And if the other side is getting nice, unsophisticated, cheap, easy to maintain, basically some-what inaccurate kinds of things, then what you need is something a little better than that. If the other side is getting very accurate, very sophisticated things, in which they don't give much of a damn about the cost because of the system they have, it is not a very good idea to make something you know is inferior to that. Now, all through the 1970's, if we had to go to war, we would have had to send men out in tanks that we knew were inferior to the Soviets'. Now we have a tank that's better than theirs.

Interview/Newsweek, 2-11:22.

4

[Presenting evidence he says shows that the Soviets are working on a defense project similar to the proposed U.S. space defense system]: All of this emphasizes . . . the very extensive work and resources the Soviets are devoting to the very defensive systems that they propose and say are so very dangerous if *we* pursue them. They are not only doing it themselves; they clearly want a monopoly in this field. If the Soviets should get a kind of defensive system that we are doing research on now . . . you'd have a very much more dangerous world in which stability would not be one of the factors that you'd be permitted to talk about any longer.

News conference, Washington, April 2/Los Angeles Times, 4-3:(I)16.

5

In Congress at the moment there are more people interested in getting the deficit down than people worried about the fact that military budget cuts increase the risk. A great many people are trying to freeze the defense budget to almost 1990. I do not think that is possible. You cannot allow these [deficit] considerations to be determinative. The defense budget has to be determined by the size of the threat. And the size of the threat is going up; it has not diminished at all. I think we have made a very substantial improvement in U.S. readiness. The problem is that it is very easy to lose the effects of that if you give up or do not do nearly enough.

Interview/Time, 10-14:29.

(CASPAR W. WEINBERGER)

[Arguing against proposals to alter or abolish the Joint Chiefs of Staff]: . . I simply do not agree with the assumption behind the recommendations for fundamental changes in the Joint Chiefs of Staff organization. That assumption is that each chief is too parochial and is solely concerned with protecting his own power at the expense of national interests. This is simply not the case with the chiefs with whom I have worked. I have found their advice to be consistently timely, accurate, competent and innovative.

Before Senate Armed Services Committee, Washington,
Nov. 14/The New York Times, 11-15:14.

2

The Soviets, in working on an arms proposal, can say right now in 1985 that, by 1991, they want to reduce to *x* thousand numbers of warheads. What they may have in mind is that they want to modernize and make these warheads even more accurate than they are now. They know perfectly well that they can accomplish that, step by step, down to the last comma in 1991, or whatever. On the other hand, *we* have a similar agreement, and we haven't the faintest idea what we can have tomorrow or the next day or 1988 or '90 or '91. We've been debating the MX missile for 12 years now, but we still haven't deployed it. So this is a major difference. They [the Soviets] know what they want, and they know they can get it. We often don't have an agreed idea of what we actually want, and even if we did, we have no ability to guarantee that we can come up with it.

Interview/U.S. News & World Report, 11-25:34.

Seymour Weiss
Former Director, Bureau of Political
and Military Affairs, Department of
State of the United States

3

While the Soviets have been impressed with the fortitude of the current [U.S. Reagan] Ad-

ministration and its success in getting large defense budgets, they have no reason to be impressed by U.S. constancy in defense matters. They must perceive what has struck me—that is, that historically arms-control negotiations tend to have a kind of tranquilizing effect upon the American public, whether or not there are any results. Negotiations of the sort that we're talking about are bound to stretch out over a period of years. It would be my prediction that during these protracted negotiations, voices will soon be raised in our own councils that will say that we should not proceed with "Star Wars" [space defense system], MX, anti-satellite capabilities or the Midgetman missile, or other such programs, because that may prejudice the outcome of ongoing negotiations. The Soviets do not have that problem. And this is where the asymmetry of the two societies comes into play. I prefer our society to theirs, but in this case it happens to work against us. They can and do sit at the table and say *"Nyet"* and hold to their position, whereas the dynamics in our own society creates pressure to get an agreement, to make concessions while our own defense programs are brought to a halt. Therefore, the Soviets may well calculate they can gain concessions from the U.S. without giving up very much.

Interview/
U.S. News & World Report,
1-21:34.

Pete Wilson
United States Senator, R-California

4

When you vote for a strong defense, you're also voting for the employment of literally hundreds of thousands of Californians, a fact to which I am not indifferent. What it means is, our national-security interest coincides with our self-interest.

Interview, Washington/
Los Angeles Times,
5-12:(I)24.

Henry J. Aaron
Economist, Brookings Institution

If there is one thing the United States economy does not need—in fact cannot stand—it is yet another tax cut which would make the deficit still worse, the dollar still stronger and the international competitiveness of U.S. industries still weaker.

Before House Ways and Means Committee,
Washington, June 11/
The New York Times, 6-12:33.

1

Adolf Ahnefeld
Economist, Kiel Institute (West Germany)

[On the large U.S. Federal budget deficit]: Budget deficits are not all that important, in our view. What counts is the policy behind them. America's deficits stem primarily from tax relief to spur private initiative and raise productivity. That makes all the difference. [U.S. President] Reagan's policy would be even more convincing if spending, too, had been trimmed. But the tax cuts are a major step in the right direction.

U.S. News & World Report,
4-29:40.

2

John F. Akers
Chairman,
International Business Machines Corporation

[Saying his company has revised downwards its forecast for U.S. economic growth]: This disappointing performance does not result from a lackluster domestic demand, which I believe would support an annual [gross national product] rate of perhaps 4 per cent. It results primarily from the fact that too much of that demand is being met by imports—massive increases in U.S. imports, fueled by the strong dollar.

June 12/The Washington Post,
6-13:(E)4.

3

Bill Alexander
United States Representative,
D-Arkansas

[On a conversation he had with President Reagan]: . . . I said, "By the way, Mr. President, I've heard you speak of the need for a balanced budget. The question eating at me—and I've been wanting to ask you—if you are for a balanced budget, why don't you submit one?" There was a long pause, and then he acted enraged—or angry—and used profanity. He said, "This is the most hypocritical question that's ever been asked." And I said, "That's the most reasonable question that the American people want to ask. Why don't you submit a balanced budget?" He said, "You can't do it in one year." And I said, "You've got four years, and when you leave Washington and return to California by 1988, by your own figures you will leave the American people with a $185-billion deficit." The President finally said, "I haven't got all day to argue with you, goodbye," and hung up.

Interview, Washington, March 29/
Los Angeles Times, 3-30:(I)4.

4

Lamar Alexander
Governor of Tennessee (R)

Just think about this: The amount of money the [Federal] deficit will go up this year equals the amount of money that all the states will collect in taxes for the year. If we governors proposed doubling our taxes, we'd probably be shot. But that's exactly what Congress is doing and deferring payment until later. Somehow this is okay in Washington, but it is unthinkable in state governments.

Interview/U.S. News & World Report, 3-11:49.

5

James A. Baker III
Secretary of the Treasury of the United States

We want a tax [reform] program that's economically neutral to the extent it can be. But it can't be totally economically neutral. The Presi-

6

(JAMES A. BAKER III)

dent's call for saving the home-mortgage-interest deduction is a good example of why not. But the argument is being made that some of the changes in the tax code proposed by the Treasury will significantly impair capital formation, entrepreneurship and small businesses. We don't want to kill the goose that lays the golden egg, and neither do the Congressional authors of tax reform nor the tax-writing-committee chairmen. Yes, there are some differences among us, but there are more issues that link us than there are that separate us.

Interview/U.S. News & World Report, 4-8:27.

Malcolm Baldrige
Secretary of Commerce of the United States

1

Last year, the U.S. gross national product grew about 6.8 per cent after adjustment for inflation. The Europeans' grew about 1.8 per cent. Just by throwing a dart at the U.S. stock board, investors could do better than they could have in Europe or Japan because our growth rate was so much higher. That is part of the reason for the excessive strength of the dollar that the Europeans are complaining about. If the Europeans can stimulate their economies somewhat without risking inflation, they can grow this year at 3 per cent or more. The U.S. growth rate is slowing down to 4 per cent or less this year. When those growth rates converge, it means there's a lot more opportunity to invest in places other than the United States. That's not going to cause a run from the dollar, but it will have a downward effect on the dollar. And that's what we would like to see.

Interview/U.S. News & World Report, 5-13:49.

Robert Bandeen
Chairman, Crown Life (Canada)

2

I agree with [the late British Prime Minister] Winston Churchill, who once said that there are three ways to look at free enterprise. One is to see it as a tiger, ready to devour everything in sight. Another is to see it as a cow, as something to be milked. The third, to which I subscribe, is to see it as a horse, which pulls the heavy load of our economy.

Interview/Maclean's, 5-6:41.

Anthony C. Beilenson
United States Representative, D-California

3

Democrats feel it's the President's [Reagan] fault that we have these [Federal budget] deficits and that we shouldn't take the heat for them. But one of these days we have to take the responsibility for doing something about this problem. For political reasons, the [Democratic Party] leadership just doesn't want us to get out front on an issue like the deficit. [But] I still believe doing the right thing is the best politics.

The New York Times, 11-20:10.

Robert Bellah
Professor of sociology and comparative studies, University of California, Berkeley

4

[Many] individuals would like to live in and contribute to society and to work in a job they could really believe in—but don't know how to. They view their jobs strictly as instruments for giving them the wherewithal to live a certain life. Their commitment to work is often marginal and cynical. That doesn't mean they don't work hard. I know of people at large law firms who work extraordinarily long hours yet are quite alienated from what they do. They enjoy what the money they make buys, but it doesn't seem a terribly happy resolution to feel that your work has little intrinsic meaning. What we need to do is reappropriate the old notion of vocation as a calling. A career should not be just something in which you reach for ever higher stages of glory and fame but something that allows us to contribute to the good of all.

Interview/U.S. News & World Report, 5-27:73.

Barry Bluestone
Professor of Economics, Boston College

5

Contrary to received doctrine, a rising tide does not necessarily lift all ships. The U.S. eco-

(BARRY BLUESTONE)

nomic tide may be rising today, but it is bringing with it greater income inequality, greater regional differences in unemployment, and large increases in structural unemployment. Why is this happening? First, the new jobs that our economy is creating are usually in very different industries, and require very different skills, from the jobs that are being eliminated in heavy industry. Second, the new jobs are often located in different parts of the country. That is why the most obvious consequences of deindustrialization is rising structural unemployment . . . I think it's obvious that we are witnessing an enormous change in the employment structure of our country, a kind of occupational "skidding." Large numbers of workers are losing their jobs in basic industries and slipping down the occupational hierarchy. So when people say not to worry, that these laid-off workers are being "reabsorbed" into the economy, they are employing what I consider a rather disingenuous definition of that word.

Panel discussion, Harvard University/
Harper's, February:38,39.

1

Fernand Braudel
French historian

Economics not only shapes people; it also manipulates them. It functions in an unconscious, almost Freudian, way. It sheds light on everything. It occupies every level of activity. Thus, capitalism is the superstructure of the economic life that has always existed. It is, above all, in the realm of economic activity, the tip of the social pyramid. No governments—no handfuls of people—are the real masters of economic life.

Interview/World Press Review, March:31.

2

Roger Brinner
Senior economist, Data Resources, Inc.

[On the trade deficit]: Imports now capture 50 per cent of the growth in spending over the past year, and, as you look ahead, it seems the import problem will become big enough for

102

spending to be hurt, too. The average American householder may like the low [import] prices the strong dollar gives him, but in time he's going to find himself working shorter hours and learn that his neighbor has been laid off. Eventually, the money to spend on those low prices won't be there.

Los Angeles Times, 6-29:(I)12.

3

William E. Brock
Secretary of Labor of the United States

Our unions are playing an increasingly constructive role in addressing the problems of new technology and job displacement. And they've championed our many freedoms, not only here but around the globe as well. The split between labor and management should clearly be a thing of the past. Companies with progressive labor policies are showing their competitive strength through increased productivity and better labor-management relations. That means a better product at a better price. That means a sound future.

Before National Press Club, Washington,
April 30/The Washington Post, 5-1:(F)3.

4

[On the Reagan Administration's proposal for a lower minimum wage for teen-agers to induce employers to hire more young people]: Labor leaders have told me they are concerned it may become on effort to roll back the [general] minimum wage and, secondly, they have fair questions about the effect this might have in displacing older workers. These are concerns I share. We have no intention of rolling back the [general] minimum wage. It's no good to institute government policy that would give some one incentive to employers replacing one individual with another just because one happened to be young.

Interview/The Washington Post, 5-7:(A)3.

5

[Supporting the idea of a sub-minimum wage for teen-agers as a way of encouraging employment for young people]: The youth wage isn't *the*

(WILLIAM E. BROCK)

solution to 43 per cent unemployment among black teen-agers. It isn't *the* answer to 24 per cent unemployment among our Hispanic youngsters . . . Sure, these kids need training and remediation, too. But they also need to break this vicious Catch 22: no experience—no job, no job—no experience.

Before National Urban League, Washington/
The Christian Science Monitor, 7-26:4.

1

I think it's important that we have organized labor in this country. I think it's important that they continue to contribute to the process of social change, as they have in the past. And if you look at what labor's doing now, I think the prospects look pretty good. We have the strongest, most free-enterprise, pro-freedom labor movement of any country in the world. They are adjusting, they are making changes to adapt to a much more competitive world environment. They're being very introspective in looking at themselves and changing what may have been inappropriate habits a few years ago. And you've got a much healthier labor-management relationship in this country than you do in most other countries of the world. I think it's going to be much healthier for all of us.

Broadcast interview/"Meet the Press," NBC-TV, 9-1.

2

The problems this country faces in trade are not problems in Japan or Brazil or France or Peru; they're problems in Washington, D.C. We've got a $200-billion Federal deficit. The Federal government is borrowing that money here at home and overseas in order to keep spending $200-billion a year more than it's taking in. That's pushing our interest rates up. That's making us less competitive. That means we save less money in this country, so we have less money to invest in new plants, new equipment, new technology, research and development to improve our productivity. And we're going to continue to have a trade problem as long as the Congress seems unwilling or incapable of getting our Federal budget under control.

Interview/USA Today, 10-28:(A)15.

3

[On labor-management relations]: Management must reconsider the wisdom of clinging tenaciously to what it has long regarded as its inherent rights. And labor must reconsider the wisdom of demanding the perpetuation of work rules and jurisdictional boundaries between jobs that no longer make sense and on abandoning the last vestige of any belief that productivity, competitiveness and profitability are exclusively a management concern.

At AFL-CIO convention, Anaheim, Calif.,
Oct. 30/Los Angeles Times, 10-31:(I)30.

John H. Bryan, Jr.
Chairman, Sara Lee Corporation

4

If we can get rid of these tax shelters and special breaks for corporations and pull those [tax] rates down, it could be the most powerful stimulant for economic growth we could ever have. For the first time in 30 or 40 years, we would have some genuine reform by taking it out of the hands of these people here in Washington, who use the tax codes to help special interests . . . What they have done is fashion internal tax shelters, primarily in the leasing and credit business. For example, General Electric's number one profit center is not light bulbs or airplane engines, but financial services. They'll lease you anything; they will play every game under the sun. And it's a private tax shelter when General Electric isn't paying taxes at all—legally— and they make billions of dollars. That's what our government did in the name of jobs and growth. It's absurd.

Interview, Washington/
USA Today, 5-28:(A)9.

Robert C. Byrd
United States Senator, D-West Virginia

5

[Criticizing President Reagan's proposed Federal budget]: It is simply not fair, not right, that Social Security recipients are asked to sacrifice, and middle-income families are asked to sacrifice . . . and yet the largest, richest and most powerful corporations in American are permitted to get a free ride. But we will not

WHAT THEY SAID IN 1985

(ROBERT C. BYRD)

shortchange America's future by abandoning our investments in education, in research, in soil conservation, in medicine . . . and those are areas that represent the economic foundation of our future . . . . Let's look where the Reagan budget ax falls: It falls on Social Security, Medicare and life-support systems for the elderly. It falls on the nation's farmers, the backbone of the greatest food-production system in the world. It falls on families trying to finance college education for their sons and daughters. It falls on nutrition programs for infants and children.

Broadcast address to the nation, Washington,
April 24/The Washington Post, 4-25:(A)6.

William J. Byron
President, Catholic University of America

1

This is not the time in our national economic life for revenue-neutral tax reform. Revenues must be raised, so therefore taxes must be raised. Most observers say this simply is not going to happen over the next few years. Both the dilemma and the debate will continue. In the debate about tax reform, the voice of Catholic Charities should be heard . . . as it challenges the middle-income taxpayer to accept a higher levy and the high-income taxpayer to shoulder a relatively heavy but fair share of the income-tax burden. The voice of Catholic Charities, like the voice of the American bishops [recently], should call for reforms in the U.S. tax system that reduce the burden on the poor . . . . Recall the words of the U.S. bishops in stating their norm for the moral measurement of our economy: "Will this decision or policy help the poor and deprived members of the human community and enable them to become more active participants in economic life?"

At National Conference of Catholic Charities,
Oct. 27/The Washington Post, 10-31:(4)18.

Alec Cairncross
British economist

2

Often, economists have little to contribute to policy; their elaborate chains of reasoning are of

Interview/World Press Review, August 25.

little relevance to the actual problems and aims of decision makers . . . Just as economic events and policies may have their biggest impact outside the functioning of the economy—as world depression cleared the way for Hitler—so the most effective levers of economic policy sometimes bypass the market and operate on confidence and opinion, expectations and attitudes.

Before American Economic Association, Dallas/
U.S. News & World Report, 2-4:55;
The New York Times, 1-2:22.

Patrick Campbell
President,
United Brotherhood of Carpenters

3

We [unions] have strayed away from the basics and become deeply involved in politics. I'm not suggesting that we discontinue that involvement. But we must return to our basics, to the bread-and-butter issues. We must organize, organize, organize.

At AFL-CIO conference, Bal Harbour, Fla./
U.S. News & World Report, 3-4:96.

Fidel Castro
President of Cuba

4

[U.S.] President Reagan's idea—that saving the U.S. economy will save the world economy—is not only a fantasy, but also an elegant lie. The fantasy is his belief that he is the author of a Roosevelt-style economic recovery plan that will save the U.S. from a crisis more profound than that of the 1930s. He expects the American economy to grow by more than 6 per cent per year while inflation stays at 4 per cent. Increased production and stable prices are any administrator's dream, but that dream is as unreal as the mirage of an oasis in the desert. America's recovery is a facade because the difference between what Washington takes in and what it spends is massive. The public debt, expressed in treasury notes sold to finance this debt, is headed for the $2-trillion mark. This sum is beyond imagination; it sounds like science fiction.

Lawton Chiles
United States Senator, D-Florida

1

The [Reagan] Administration's budget is a wall without windows. It tells us what we're up against, but affords no vision . . . This budget's principal vision of the future is a chain of $170-billion deficits running for the next five years.

Feb. 4/The Washington Post, 2-5:(A)6.

Thad Cochran
United States Senator, R-Mississippi

3

[On the need to reduce government spending to cope with the budget deficit]: It's a little depressing when you realize the votes we'll have to cast to reduce spending. That's the reverse of what politicians like to do. They like to curry favor with their constituents, and we'll really be irritating a lot of people by cutting popular programs.

*Washington, Jan. 3/
The New York Times, 1-4:10.*

Barber B. Conable,
*Fellow, American Enterprise Institute;
Former United States Representative,
R-New York*

4

[Criticizing Reagan Administration proposals to cut tax deductions for charitable contributions]: In all four corners of America there are volunteers involved in some aspect of non-profit activity, be they United Way workers, volunteer firemen, members of church or social-welfare groups. As far as politicians are concerned, these groups represent opinion-setters; they set

the tone of the country. The politician ignores such groups at peril.

The New York Times, 1-24:9.

5

[Criticizing President Reagan's tax-simplification proposal]: Our present tax system reflects a history of responding to a complex national economy. We started with simplicity, but responses to demands for equity produced what we have today. Equity is the enemy of simplicity. It's an illusion to believe that you can have a simple tax system that will apply fairly across a complex economy . . . The perception is that the tax code is unfair—partly because the press focuses on that wealthy handful who pay little or no taxes. Reality is that the top 10 per cent are producing 50 per cent of income-tax revenue. Reality is that most top-bracket individuals are *not* heavily into sheltering income . . . The new tax plan does not achieve simplicity, benefit Federalism, advance the role of the private sector through charity, encourage savings and investment, promote populism, or aid the family. Yet the perception is that everybody good and virtuous is going to benefit.

Interview/USA Today, 5-30:(A)12.

Bettino Craxi
Prime Minister of Italy

6

What [U.S. President] Reagan has achieved [in the American economy] is the creation of a great number of jobs, and this should make not only Italy but the whole of Europe think. Now the anti-Americans say they are bad jobs with little value. But it's always better to have a bad job than no job at all, while we in Europe have too great an unemployment rate.

*Interview, Rome, Feb. 25/
The New York Times, 2-28:3.*

Mario M. Cuomo
Governor of New York (D)

7

[Criticizing President Reagan's tax-reform proposal which would eliminate the Federal deduction for state and local tax payments]: It would hit New York and other high-tax states

In the past several years, the [Federal] budget has become an instrument of national retrenchment rather than an investment in our future. The budget today is now used almost exclusively to cut spending without a real connection to the kind of country we want to build and without a sense of the role the Federal government should play in that effort.

The Washington Post, 4-26:(A)5.

(MARIO M. CUOMO)

disproportionately hard. To punish for having high taxes is to ignore the fact that we have them in part because of the Federal government's failure to deal with its responsibilities: drug trafficking, undocumented aliens and welfare as a national problem. It is a sneaky way for the Reagan Administration to raise about $30-billion to reduce its horrendous deficits without being perceived as increasing taxes, which the President promised in the election campaign he wouldn't do.

Interview/U.S. News & World Report, 6-3:71.

Mitchell E. Daniels, Jr.
Director,
Federal Office of Intergovernmental Affairs

1

[Supporting President Reagan's tax-reform proposal which has drawn criticism from states and cities because it would end the Federal tax deduction for state and local taxes]: Greater fairness and simplicity in the tax system will produce social cohesion and public confidence, and nowhere would those developments be more important than in our largest cities . . . Lower rates, double exemptions, special relief for the poor, greater fairness, economic growth—none of these goals can be reached without the revenue, some $30-billion of it, recaptured by repeal of deductibility.

At United States Conference of Mayors,
Anchorage, Alaska, June 17/
The Washington Post, 6-18:(A)4.

George Deukmejian (R)
Governor of California

2

[Supporting President Reagan's budget-cutting policies]: The people just about 100 days ago [in the Presidential election] made a choice, and they voted for the candidate [Reagan] who said he was going to address the deficit situation by cutting expenditures. He also said he wasn't going to go for tax increases. And finally, he indicated that we are to have a defense capability in this country that is second to none. I found that the provisions that are in the resolution passed by the [state governors, altering the

106

[Supporting President Reagan's tax-reform proposal which has drawn criticism from states and cities because it would end the Federal tax deduction for state and local taxes]: Greater fairness and simplicity in the tax system will produce social cohesion and public confidence, and nowhere would those developments be more important than in our largest cities . . . Lower

Reagan budget priorities], in effect, change those priorities and, in my view, we should give great deference to the vote of the people.

To reporters, Washington,
Feb. 26/Los Angeles Times, 2-27:(I)3.

Robert J. Dole
United States Senator, R-Kansas

3

[Saying cutting the Federal budget should be the first order of business in 1985]: If we in Washington can do the right thing on both ends of Pennsylvania Avenue and in a certain five-sided building across the river [the Pentagon], the people will really have something to celebrate next New Year's Eve: Sustained economic expansion.

U.S. News & World Report, 1-14:10.

4

[President] Ronald Reagan is committed to do all he can to bring the [Federal] deficit down sharply before he leaves office. He doesn't want to leave with a big, big deficit. I think you're going to see the President get into the fray with both feet. He already has told us very frankly that he's going to be out there helping us. Moreover, I think he's not going to rush out to help some Republican Senator who doesn't vote in the right way. It's known as hardball. We can't have it both ways in Congress—posture and talk about how bad the deficit is and then vote against a debt-reduction package. We've got to be tough, and I think the President's prepared to be just as tough.

Interview/U.S. News & World Report, 3-4:26.

Pete V. Domenici
United States Senator, R-New Mexico

5

[Saying there is resistance to cutting military and social expenditures in the effort to trim the Federal budget deficit]: You can't get there without including defense and Social Security for some kind of additional contributions, in equity and symmetry and to hold things together. We are at a crossroads. We might even be at gridlock.

Before National Press Club, Washington,
Feb. 7/The New York Times, 2-8:9.

Thomas Donahue
Secretary-treasurer, American Federation of Labor-Congress of Industrial Organizations

1

The Labor Department's efforts in industrial relations are all blue smoke and mirrors. What it should be is a think tank—the central focus of the government on what this country's industrial-relations policies ought to be. I defy you to go to the Labor Department and find anybody who could begin to answer that question. All they'll say is, "Labor and management need to get along." That's not enough.

U.S. News & World Report, 5-27:54.

Donald L. Dotson
Chairman, National Labor Relations Board of the United States

2

If you want to make a difference in the labor-relations area, you will run afoul of a three-ply defense designed to stop it. That defense is composed of three groups bound together by ties of interest and ideology. They are institutional labor, the working press and a large segment of the academic community.

Before North Carolina employers' group, May/The Washington Post, 7-17:(A)14.

David Durenberger
United States Senator, R-Minnesota

3

[On the Federal budget deficit]: In my more cynical moments, I think that the deficit is President of the United States. It, more than Ronald Reagan, has and will produce a revolution in the shape of the Federal government . . . And it is not just the programs we are cutting. The deficit has also kept us from doing anything new for a whole decade.

Speech, Minneapolis/ Los Angeles Times, 8-26:(I)10.

L. Wayne Farrell
Director of tax affairs, Reynolds Metals Company; President, Tax Executives Institute

4

[Opposing strict limits on tax deductions for business entertainment and meals]: Some of the best business relationships are nurtured through social contact. It's just another form of promotion and marketing that is required in order to do business . . . I favor the limits we already have. Current law, for example, does not allow deductions for lavish entertainment or meals. I think that can be judged by the taxpayer and the Internal Revenue Service . . . [President Reagan's proposal is] faulty in allowing a full deduction only for meals costing up to $25 a person when dealing with clients and business associates, with a deduction for only half the amount above $25. The latest plan also goes too far in disallowing all deductions for entertainment events . . . The fact remains that some of the best contacts are developed in a social atmosphere.

Interview/U.S. News & World Report, 7-29:66.

Thomas S. Foley
United States Representative, D-Washington

5

My view, shared widely by Republicans and Democrats, is that the only way to get a rational reduction of the [Federal] deficit, and eventually a balanced budget, is by reductions in spending and additions to revenues. If you can find serious people in the economic-business community who think you can close the deficit gap by cutting spending alone, without any revenues at all, they are in a minority. What Congress has been frustrated by is that the President [Reagan] went from a campaign promise of a tax increase only as a last resort—that's what he said—to no new taxes at all.

Interview/USA Today, 12-12:(A)11.

Douglas A. Fraser
Former president, United Automobile Workers of America

6

[On working life before unions]: The best way to describe it, to use an old-fashioned word, is that there was no *dignity*. You couldn't question any decisions and you couldn't dissent . . . Dignity was the great thing that came out of union organization. When you think of it, wages in the auto industry were not bad, and nobody had benefits of any kind. So you didn't realize

(DOUGLAS A. FRASER)

what you were missing. But what you gained from the union was the right to talk back, the right to question decisions, the right to dissent, and that's one hell of a feeling. They'll never take the democracy away from us, the right of the individual to speak up in dissent and file a grievance. That was a revolution.

Interview, Detroit/
American Heritage, February-March:58.

Richard A. Gephardt
United States Representative,
D-Missouri

1

Our tax code is a mess. First of all, it's unfair . . . Secondly, it's complicated . . . And last, it's bad economics to have people investing in things that make no sense just to get a tax break.

Reply to President's State of the Union address,
Feb. 6/U.S. News & World Report, 2-18:79.

Joseph Goffman
Attorney and tax lobbyist,
Public Citizen's Congress Watch

2

[Supporting putting limits on tax deductions for business entertainment and meals]: Taxpayers should not be asked to subsidize activities that are largely, or even exclusively, for personal pleasure rather than for business reasons. Taxpayers now are helping pay for meals at expensive restaurants and box seats at sporting events that only a few can enjoy, though most of us would like access to them . . . common sense suggests that at virtually every business meal or business-social event, the largest proportion of the benefit is personal. The average American rightly sees this as an example of the tax code supporting lots of fun for a few citizens. That just doesn't apply when you talk about clear-cut business costs . . . I can't believe that the conversations and transactions that go on over meals can't be done in somebody's office or over the phone.

Interview/U.S. News & World Report, 7-29:66.

Barry M. Goldwater
United States Senator, R-Arizona

3

We are beginning to see parochial interests that will prevent any effort at reducing the [Federal] deficit, balancing the budget or practicing fiscal sanity. When the chips are down, the question is, do we have the collective guts to do anything about this? Frankly, I don't think so.

U.S. News & World Report, 3-4-24.

W. Wilson Goode
Mayor of Philadelphia

4

The American dream is not a house in the suburbs with a white picket fence and two cars and someone driving into town every day to a $50,000-a-year job. The American dream is that if I am willing to work, then give me a job. Let me work and earn my keep and take care of my family . . . and maybe live in my row house in Philadelphia, in the Bronx, in Detroit, Chicago. Give me an opportunity to use my skills, to use my brain, to use my muscles.

Interview, Philadelphia/
The Christian Science Monitor, 4-29:4.

J. Peter Grace
Chief executive officer,
W. R. Grace & Company

5

[The Federal debt] builds up like a stone rolling down a hill and picking up mud. The interest this year is about $150-billion and is going to be one-and-a-half *trillion*, or 10 times that figure, in 15 years. You won't be able to afford to pay the interest . . . No kid being born today is going to have any future or any freedom if [the mounting deficit] is not turned around, because by the time that kid who's born today is 15 years old [we'll be] running with an annual deficit of 2 trillion.

Interview, Washington/The Washington Post, 2-28:(D)6.

David D. Hale
Chief economist, Kemper Financial Services

6

The problem with Japan is not that she exports too much or imports too little. It is that

(DAVID D. HALE)

Japanese domestic consumption has lagged far behind the rapid growth of the country's income and output. Should the U.S. . . . be exporting manufacturing jobs to an overcrowded chain of Asian islands where per-capita incomes now exceeds $11,000 per annum and half the homes are not yet connected to sewers, so that its citizens can generate a savings surplus which is then recycled back across the Pacific via the [U.S.] treasury debt market to subsidize the construction of more vacant office buildings in Houston and Los Angeles?

The Christian Science Monitor, 8-22:19.

Gary Hart
United States Senator, D-Colorado

1

This is the third straight year that I have served on the Budget Committee in which the majority party in the Senate [Republican], the President's [Reagan] own party, threw away the President's budget even before it got to the Hill, and began to try to fashion our own. And for those last three years it has been a bipartisan coalition in the Senate and the House that has fashioned a budget this country could live with. So it's almost as if the President isn't even a player, isn't even relevant to this process. Even if you accepted all of Ronald Reagan's proposed cuts, we'd still have a $180-billion deficit. So what we have, for the first time in a long time, under what has been called a strong President, is Congressional governing in this country, and it's very, very hard.

Broadcast interview, Washington/ "Meet the Press," NBC-TV, 3-10.

2

We will not achieve growth and opportunity merely by relying on the market, as this Republican Administration advocates. Markets can drive our economy, but they cannot calculate the national interest . . . *Aidez-faire,* not *laissez-faire*—to *make* change happen for the benefit of all, not to *let* things happen for the benefit of the few.

At American University, Washington, April 23/The Washington Post, 4-24:(A)3.

Walter W. Heller
Professor of economics, University of Minnesota; Former Chairman, Council of Economic Advisers to the President of the United States (John F. Kennedy)

3

To project that we can hold real growth and inflation growth at 3 per cent for the rest of the decade [as the Reagan Administration predicts] —that's really using rose-colored glasses. If you have a perfectly honest and executed policy, it is conceivable we could grow that long at those rates. But everything has to be perfectly modulated—no plunge of the dollar, no normal business cycle.

Los Angeles Times, 2-4:(I)6.

4

[On the Treasury Department's proposed tax reform plan]: Basically, it is a fine proposal, especially if there is any chance it is enacted en masse in its rather balanced fashion. It carries out the basics of what those who have labored in the tax vineyards have waited for for a long time. It does promote equity. It does provide simplification. It does elect market advantage over tax advantage.

The Christian Science Monitor, 2-7:22.

Walter D. Huddleston
Former United States Senator, D-Kentucky

5

Forty million Americans compete directly with illegal aliens for jobs. We could reduce unemployment in this country to below 4 per cent simply by regaining control of immigration.

The Christian Science Monitor, 2-20:1.

Thomas H. Kean
Governor of New Jersey (R)

6

Tax reform is a program whose time came long ago, because people have been so frustrated by all the complications and loopholes in the current system. Every time Congress has made a change, there were enough smart lawyers to figure out three new loopholes—and the richest people in the country wound up benefiting most from the tax code.

Interview/U.S. News & World Report, 3-11:50.

Howard H. Kehrl
Vice chairman,
General Motors Corporation

On the production side [of automobile manufacturing], competitive strength depends on moving away from labor-intensive models of the past. Modern technologies such as robotics, machining centers and flexible manufacturing cells are combining to change the rules of manufacturing competition. These technologies are dramatically reducing the labor content of traditional operations. And with fewer hours needed to make each product, it becomes less and less important to chase low labor costs around the globe.

At Worlddesign conference, Washington,
Aug. 21/The New York Times, 8-29:12.

1

Irwin L. Kellner
Chief economist,
Manufacturers Hanover Bank, New York

People often make the mistake of thinking the economy will simply run out of gas all by itself. But, in fact, it invariably takes a major shock to bring the economy to a halt, and as long as the Federal Reserve doesn't get too worried about the growing money supply, I don't think we're going to get such a shock soon.

Los Angeles Times, 4-20:(I)5.

2

Lane Kirkland
President, American Federation of
Labor-Congress of Industrial Organizations

[Criticizing President Reagan's tax-reform proposals]: In our view, the key test of a tax-reform proposal is the extent to which it diminishes unfairness toward people who work for their money and eliminates favoritism toward people whose money works for them. By that test, much of the President's program falls short.

Before House Ways and Means Committee, Washington,
June 12/The Washington Post, 6-13:(E)3.

3

[Criticizing President Reagan's tax-reform proposals]: In our view, the key test of a tax-reform proposal is the extent to which it diminishes unfairness toward people who work for their money and eliminates favoritism toward people whose money works for them. By that test, much of the President's program falls short.

Before House Ways and Means Committee, Washington,
June 12/The Washington Post, 6-13:(E)3.

4

[Criticizing U.S. companies that shift production to foreign countries, and calling for U.S. import restrictions]: Much of America has suffered devastation as a consequence of our surrender to the aggressive mercantilism of other nations, and vital sections of the [American] trade-union movement have suffered with their communities and their [country] . . . [Employees, unlike business, are] one with the communities in which they live . . . We cannot join capital in its flight to tax-free havens overseas. We cannot run up the Liberian flag [on U.S. ships]. We cannot heed the beckoning pimps and pursue the prostitution of other lands and people. Unlike the world of business and finance, in the world of labor, patriotism is not only our duty and belief, but our necessity.

At AFL-CIO convention, Anaheim, Calif.,
Oct. 28/Los Angeles Times, 10-29:(I)3.

5

For the first time, we have a young generation of Americans who do not expect to do as well as their parents. Their opportunities are shrinking, and so are their hopes. The steady erosion of America's industrial base is depriving millions of young workers of those stable, well-paying jobs that broadly sustain the American standard of living; and offer admission to the working middle class. Trapped in low-paying service jobs, they see the American dream fading fast.

At AFL-CIO convention, Anaheim, Calif.,
Oct. 28/The Washington Post, 10-29:(A)4.

6

The trade-union movement of America was not created by the National Labor Relations Board, and this yellow-dog board cannot stop the union movement. We are going to outlast the bastards, and sign up their undertakers on our way forward into the future.

At AFL-CIO convention, Anaheim, Calif.,
Oct. 28/The Washington Post, 10-29:(A)4.

7

Edward I. Koch
Mayor of New York

[Criticizing President Reagan's budget cuts]: I'm not sure who is responsible for all this. Some say it's [Treasury Secretary] Donald Regan. Some say it's Ronald Reagan. But whether

(EDWARD I. KOCH)

it's Regan or Reagan, Ronald or Donald, or Ronald McDonald, let's call the whole thing off.

State of the City address, New York,
Jan. 30/The New York Times, 1-31:14.

1

[On proposals to cut the business tax deduction for food and entertainment]: [If business spending] keeps restaurants and theatres going, then let's find out whether people won't go into restaurants and theatres if they have to pay for it themselves. Because it's a hell of a thing if the only thing that keeps restaurants and hotels and theatres going is because somebody else is paying your bill . . . I just happen to think there is something wrong with every day taxpayers' paying for the cost of rich taxpayers who use their credit cards to take off what everybody else has to pay for themselves.

To high-school students, New York,
June 3/The New York Times, 6-4:12.

Richard D. Lamm
Governor of Colorado (D)

2

[On the growing Federal budget deficit]: . . . this economy cannot be sustained for another 10 years under conditions where you borrow 20 cents out of every dollar you spend. I think we have been prodigal parents. History is not kind to civilizations that have heaped debt upon their children.

Interview, Denver/
The Christian Science Monitor, 11-6:3.

3

Christmas is a time when kids tell Santa Claus what they want and adults pay for it. [Budget] deficits are when adults tell the government what they want—and their kids pay for it.

U.S. News & World Report, 12-23:10.

Marvin Leath
United States Representative,
D-Texas

4

[On a Federal budget just approved by the House]: Only [a budget] we all hate can do the

---

Virginia Littlejohn
President,
Littlejohn Johnson, Inc., consultants

5

I see entrepreneurship as next to godliness. It's absolutely central to economic growth. Both political parties need to have entrepreneurship as the centerpiece of their thinking when formulating an economic-growth agenda that removes entrepreneurial barriers. We're not going to see the giant corporations generating millions of new jobs.

Interview/Nation's Business, January:55.

Ron Marlenee
United States Representative,
R-Montana

6

[On new, tougher IRS regulations on automobile business deductions]: When the IRS wrote the rules . . . they followed their usual practice of writing regulations that would make the Gestapo proud: assume everybody is guilty and then force them to prove their innocence.

Before House Ways and Means Committee,
Washington, March 5/USA Today, 3-6:(A)1.

Bill Marriott
President, Marriott Corporation

7

I think that we have too much government, that we pay too much tax. I think President Reagan has done a good job of beginning to whittle away at it, but he's trying to chop down the oak tree with a pocket knife.

Interview/Business Week, 1-21:75.

Robert T. Matsui
United States Representative,
D-California

8

[Saying he doesn't expect President Reagan's tax-reform proposals to pass without Congress

job. The President hates this budget. The Speaker hates this budget. That means it's probably a pretty good budget.

The Washington Post, 5-24:(A)7.

WHAT THEY SAID IN 1985

(ROBERT T. MATSU)

retaining many of the tax preferences the proposal wants to eliminate]: Most of our constituents aren't willing to give up any of their tax breaks simply for the promise of lower rates. The tax code is an expression of political reality, and that's why so many of these tax preferences for favored groups are going to remain practically untouched.

Los Angeles Times, 11-11:(I)1.

Mitch McConnell
United States Senator, R-Kentucky

1

As a county executive, I was the beneficiary of Federal revenue-sharing, community-development block grants and other grants. I'm acutely aware of the nice things that can happen as a result of these programs. Nevertheless, it's a fact that most state and local governments have a surplus, and the Federal government hasn't seen one in years. It seems nonsensical for a government that has over a trillion-dollar debt to be sending money to governments that by and large are in the black.

Interview/U.S. News & World Report, 4-15:37.

James L. Medoff
Labor economist, Harvard University

2

[On the decreasing number of big labor strikes]: The expected costs to a union of waging a strike are exceedingly high today. In many instances, management will use the opportunity to attempt to bust the union. And many unionists, at this point, are extremely insecure about their jobs. Hence, the membership is not eager for its leaders to gamble with these jobs.

The New York Times, 7-12:9.

James C. Miller III
Chairman, Federal Trade Commission

3

[The Federal budget] deficit is a symptom of other problems, not a disorder to be treated in isolation. [Thus, people] have refused to be stampeded into support for higher taxes

... Obviously, the deficit can be "explained" as a matter of inadequate tax revenues. But real economics reminds us that the challenge is not simply to enhance government revenues, but to do so in a manner that does not interfere with growth ... A growing economy will produce growing revenue for the government, while tax increases that hinder growth may ultimately prove counterproductive for the Treasury as well as disastrous for the public in general.

Before Association of Private Enterprise Education,
April 21/The Washington Post, 7-20:(4)8.

David S. Monson
United States Representative, R-Utah

4

As a CPA, I am shocked by the Federal government's budgeting practices. They ignore the most basic common-sense accounting principles. There is simply no correlation between how much money is taken in and how much is spent. I would be willing to bet that nearly every family in this country has better sense than the Federal government when it comes to watching pennies and balancing a budget. In fact, if a family followed Congress' example, their finances would be in the worst state of turmoil imaginable.

Before the House, Washington, Oct. 24/
The New York Times, 10-29:12.

Akio Morita
Chairman, Sony Corporation (Japan)

5

The American people fail to understand their [economic] problems. You [the U.S.] are losing your industrial base, while you are berating Japan [for unfair trade practices]. American industry is itself shifting production offshore and buying Japanese products. We are confused ... You have a basic invention by Americans, but the production technology is in Japan. So the Americans are buying Japanese products. Such a thing should be made by Americans. The inventor must get the benefit. It's a sad thing.

Interview, Los Angeles/
Los Angeles Times,
9-16:(IV)1,2.

112

Thomas P. O'Neill, Jr.
United States Representative,
D-Massachusetts

1

In 1981, when President Reagan took office, the national debt was just over $900-billion. Today it is $1.8-trillion, double what it was when he took office . . . The debt will be $3-trillion when he leaves office, triple what it was when the "Reagan revolution" began . . . Let us work hard to cut the deficit, Mr. President, but . . . do not point the finger at the distant past when you ... ... responsibility for these de...

Robert O...
Chief Eco...
Commerc...

In the ...
consume...
find for ...
buying A...
on the b...
the par...
America...
made, i...
industri...
more in...

Ron P...
Assista...
Depar...
of the ...

Th...
think...
boar...
ated ...
perc...
bles...
basi...

Donald E. Petersen
Chairman, Ford Motor Company

4

The whole concept of employee involvement—participation in management, team effort as opposed to individual effort—has many elements that are still quite fragile. This is because we come from a past in American industry that has been so fraught with bull-of-the-woods, top-down, don't-think-just-do-what-I-ask-you-to-do-type thinking. It is going to take time for everyone to become accustomed to participating together.

Interview/USA Today, 2-5:(A)7.

Thomas E. Petri
United States Representative,
R-Wisconsin

5

This government is only days away from borrowing our second trillionth dollar. Two trillion dollars in debt? Now, the word "trillion" doesn't seem to mean anything to anybody. Trillion sounds like billion, which sounds like million. We've been talking in illions around here for so long that everybody has developed illion immunity.

Before the House, Washington,
Sept. 17/The New York Times, 9-19:12.

Ronald Reagan
President of the United States

6

[On the Federal budget deficit]: . . . if I go out of office with having this budget for the first time in 50 years on the declining deficit pattern to where we can target the day certain the budget will be balanced—[then] that's the end of deficit spending. You have to realize how much this has been built in. This [deficit] increase is not anything we [this Administration] created. From 1965 to 1980, when the war on poverty and the Great Society really got under way, in those 15 years the budget increased almost five times what it was 15 years before, but the deficit increased to 38 times what it was before. From 1974 on up to past 1980, we're more than $500-billion in deficits. The pattern was set.

Interview, Washington,
Jan. 17/USA Today, 1-18:(A)13.

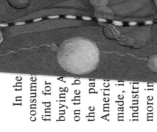

FUNtastic Reading

(RONALD REAGAN)

1

This is the first [economic] recovery in eight recessions, since World War II, that has been a real recovery. Unemployment has come down; at the same time inflation has come down; at the same time the interest rates have come down. Before we got here, we had double-digit inflation—the last four years, inflation is down to the four-percent range. The prime rate was 21 per cent; it's now 10.5 per cent—and I think we're going to see it go lower. There are close to 108 million people working, more people employed than ever in the history of our country. These solid gains show that what we came into office to do has been accomplished—except that it takes time. We'll have to keep at it.

Interview, Washington,
Jan. 17/USA Today, 1-18:(A)13.

2

The Constitution doesn't give the President the right to spend a nickel. That's up there on the Hill [in Congress]. And every budget that we have submitted since I've been here has been smaller than the one the Congress would finally agree to. So in fixing the blame for why we haven't done more than we've done in reducing spending seems to be pretty evident.

Interview, Jan. 26/
The Washington Post,
1-29:(A)1.

3

There will be substantial political resistance to every deficit-reduction measure proposed in this [Federal] budget. Every dollar of current Federal spending benefits someone, and that person has a vested self-interest in seeing those benefits perpetuated and expanded. Prior to my Administration, such interests had been dominant and their expectations and demands had been met, time and time again. At some point, however, the question must be raised: "Where is the political logrolling going to stop?" . . . The single most difficult word for a politician is a simple, flat "No."

The Washington Post,
2-4:(A)4.

4

We can't wait a moment longer to get our Federal budget under control. If we lose the budget battle, if we allow all the lessons of all the decades of unchecked government spending to go unheeded, we consign ourselves and our children to the tyranny of a government that respects no boundaries and knows no limits.

Briefing for Congressional leaders, Washington,
Feb. 4/The Washington Post, 2-5:(A)6.

5

The problems of excessive [Federal] spending and deficits are not new. In the absence of fundamental reform, they may recur again and again in the future. I therefore support two important measures: one to authorize the President to veto individual line items in comprehensive spending bills and another to constrain the Federal authority to borrow or to increase spending in the absence of broad Congressional support. These structural changes are not substitutes for the hard fiscal choices that will be necessary in 1985 and beyond, nor for the need to simplify our tax system to stimulate greater growth, but they are important to provide the mechanisms and discipline for longer-term fiscal health.

Written economic report to Congress,
Feb. 5/The New York Times, 2-6:34.

6

The primary economic responsibility of the Federal government is not to make choices for people but to provide an environment in which people can make their own choices.

Written economic report to Congress,
Feb. 5/The New York Times, 2-6:34.

7

We have cut tax rates by almost 25 per cent, yet the tax system remains unfair and limits our potential for growth. Exclusions and exemptions cause similar incomes to be taxed at different levels. Low-income families face steep tax barriers that make hard lives harder. The Treasury Department has produced an excellent reform plan whose principles will guide the final proposal we will ask you to enact. One thing that tax

(RONALD REAGAN)

reform will not be is a tax increase in disguise . . . Together, we can pass, this year, a tax bill for fairness, simplicity and growth, making this economy the engine of our dreams and America the investment capital of the world.

State of the Union address, Washington,
Feb. 6/The New York Times, 2-7:13.

1

The best way to reduce deficits is through economic growth. More businesses will be started, more investments made, more jobs created and more people will be on payrolls paying taxes. The best way to reduce government spending is to reduce the need for spending by increasing prosperity.

State of the Union address, Washington,
Feb. 6/The New York Times, 2-7:13.

2

[On critics of the large Federal budget deficits that have occurred during his Presidency]: Remember, with all their moaning and crying, the national debt was a trillion dollars when I came into office. And the first of those major big deficit increases occurred after I was in office. However, it was not my responsibility because your first eight months in office, you're on the other fellow's budget. I don't come into office and declare how much we can spend. The budget is there until the following October. In fact, when the bottom fell out of the economy in July of '81, not one facet of my economic program had been passed as yet. So it couldn't have had anything to do with that deficit. But what is happening now indicates the danger that over the 50 years, the situation keeps getting worse . . . So you've got a built-in, structural deficit . . . And, of course, it's multiplied and it's gotten worse. And a large part of this had to do with the great fall into recession that occurred in '81 and through '82. There's no question that we're going to be better off . . . if we get government back to where 43 states or so have it, and that is that you can't spend more than government takes in.

Interview/The Wall Street Journal, 2-8:8.

3

[Arguing against a value-added tax]: . . . it's hidden in the price of a product and that tax can quietly be increased and all the people know is that the price went up and they don't know whether the price went up because somebody got a raise or whether the company wanted to increase profits, or whether it was government. And I just am not enthused about it. I think I've said before, taxes should hurt in the sense that people should be able to see them and know what they're paying.

News conference, Washington,
Feb. 21/The New York Times, 2-22:10.

4

[Defending his cuts in Federal aid to cities and states]: There's simply no justification . . . for the Federal government, which is running a deficit, to be borrowing money to be spent by state and local governments, some of which are now running surpluses. I know the states still have their problems. But it's also true that many of your states are in better fiscal shape today because of the courage that you showed and the hard decisions you made during the recent recession. I hope that you can understand that these tough calls have to be made now at the Federal level.

Before National Governors' Association, Washington,
Feb. 25/The Washington Post, 2-26:(A)1.

5

I believe our tax system currently acts as the biggest single threat to stronger enterprise and lasting economic expansion. Many of our citizens are required to pay more than their fair share of the tax bill, while others are permitted to pay far less. Today's tax code drives money needed for investment and future growth into unproductive tax shelters. And hundreds of millions of dollars are wasted in needless paperwork.

Before National Association of Counties,
Washington, March 4/The New York Times, 3-5:29.

6

[Saying he is vetoing a farm-aid bill because it would be a budget-buster]: I asked for help [on the budget]. I asked Congress, which just days

WHAT THEY SAID IN 1985

(RONALD REAGAN)

ago was bemoaning the size of deficits, to demonstrate courage, hold the line and match rhetoric with deeds. Congress failed. In the first major bill since convening in January, a majority proved itself incapable of resisting the very tax-and-spend philosophy that brought America to its knees and wrecked our economy . . . The bottom line is that someone in Washington must be responsible. Someone must be willing to stand up for those who pay America's bills, and someone must stand up to those who say here's the key, there's the Treasury, just take as many of those hard-earned tax dollars as you want . . . I hope that Congress will get the message and work with me to reduce spending in a responsible way that does not threaten our national security. If it doesn't, then I'll do what must be done. I will veto again and again until spending is brought under control.

Statement upon vetoing bill, Washington,
March 6/The New York Times, 3-7-12.

The scene in the Senate Budget Committee this past week was a disappointing one for the American people. They [Senators] seem to be in full-scale retreat from spending cuts and are talking about raising people's taxes again. When push comes to shove, I guess it's always easier to let the taxpayer take the fall. Well, let them be forewarned: No matter how well intentioned they might be, no matter what their illusions might be, I have my veto pen drawn and ready for any tax increase that Congress might even think of sending up. And I have only one thing to say to the tax increasers: "Go ahead, make my day."

Before business executives, Washington,
March 13/Los Angeles Times, 3-14-(I)1,18.

1

One of the first rules of economics is, if you tax something, you get less of it. High tax rates discourage work, risk-taking, initiative and imagination. And they're really a tax on hope, optimism and our faith in the future.

Before business executives, Washington,
March 13/Los Angeles Times, 3-14-(I)18.

2

I believe we have to tear down our present tax structure and build a new one. We will propose a tax simplification plan. Tax simplification will make the rate structure simpler and more fair, it will limit deductions and it will lower tax rates further. With a simplified tax system, we would have a top rate far lower than the current top personal tax rate of 50 per cent. A side benefit of this is that it will move us away from the whole strange world of unproductive tax shelters. For once, all Americans will know that their neighbors, as well as they, are paying their fair share and not hiding behind loopholes and shelters. We want to make the tax system simpler and more fair, and we want to push tax rates down still further. This is economic justice; it is economic sense and the key to America's economic future.

At St. John's University, New York,
March 28/The New York Times, 3-29-12.

3

The American economy is like a racehorse that's begun to gallop out in front of the field. Other nations, hobbled by high tax rates and weighed down by oversized government spending, have been slow to catch up. And this has caused some painful dislocations, especially for America's exporting industries. But the answer is hardly to hamstring the American economy to make it drop back with the others. The solution is for our trading partners to throw off the dead weight of government—cut their own tax rates, spending and over-regulation and join us in opening up their markets to foreign competition so they can catch up with us in our race to the future.

At New York Stock Exchange, New York,
March 28/Los Angeles Times, 3-29-(I)26.

4

For the sake of fairness, simplicity and growth, we must radically change the structure of a tax system that still treats our earnings as the personal property of the IRS; radically change a system that still treats people earning similar incomes much differently regarding the tax they pay; and, yes, radically change a system

5

(RONALD REAGAN)

2

Many of you, I'm sure, have already had your first job, which means that you've had your first experience with the incredible shrinking paycheck. You have to see it to believe it. There is one box, it tells you your gross pay, and then you have all the little boxes with the taxes taken out: Federal tax, state tax, Social Security tax—the list seems endless. And at the end of it all is the figure for your net income. You may have wondered at that point whether you were working for yourself or the government, and that's a good question. The way our tax system is structured, the harder you work and the more you earn, the less you get to keep. One of the first priorities of our tax overhaul is to make sure that more of your hard-earned dollars will end up where they belong—in your wallets, not in Uncle Sam's wallets.

At North Carolina State University,
Sept. 5/The New York Times, 9-6:31.

that still causes some to invest their money, not to make a better mousetrap, but simply to avoid a tax trap. Over the course of the century our tax system has been modified dozens of times and in hundreds of ways. Yet most of those changes didn't improve the system; they made it more like Washington itself: complicated, unfair, cluttered with gobbledygook and loopholes . . . Will our proposal help you? You bet it will. We call it America's tax plan because it will reduce tax burdens on the working people of this country, close loopholes that benefit a privileged few, simplify a code so complex even Albert Einstein reportedly needed help on his 1040 form, and lead us into a future of greater growth and opportunity for all . . . My fellow citizens, let's not let this magnificent moment slip away. Tax relief is in sight. Let's make it a reality. Let's not let prisoners of mediocrity wear us down. Let's not let the special-interest raids of the few rob us all of our dreams.

Broadcast address to the nation, Washington,
May 28/The New York Times,
5-29:12.

Donald T. Regan

Chief of Staff to the President of the
United States; Former Secretary of the
Treasury of the United States

1

Seventy-two years after its inception, what is our Federal tax system? It is a system that yields great amounts of revenues, yes, but even greater amounts of discontent, disorder and disobedience . . . It is, finally, a system whose most serious sin may be its most subtle. For it seems so rigged, so unfair, that it corrupts otherwise honest people by encouraging them to cheat. Thirty and forty years ago, you didn't hear people brag at social get-togethers about how they got their tax bill down by exploiting this loophole and engineering that credit. But now they do, and it's not considered bad behavior. After all, goes this thinking, what's immoral about cheating a system that is itself a cheat? That isn't a sin, it's a duty . . . Our Federal tax system is, in short, utterly impossible, utterly unjust and completely counter-productive. It's earned a rebellion and it's time we rebelled.

At rally, Williamsburg, Va.,
May 30/The New York Times,
5-31:41.

3

[On the possibility of a flat-tax income tax policy]: No one likes to have their taxes raised, but there is no way you can cut rates and still have the same amount without having a broadened base. Take anything. Take a pile of sand and squish it and it flattens out—and that is what is called a flat tax. I think when people understand the trade-offs, that some of the industries now paying a higher tax will pay a lot lower and some industries that are now paying little or *no* taxes will pay some taxes, I think the majority of the people will be convinced it's for good.

Interview, Washington/
The Washington Post, 2-13:(B)13.

4

[On the inability of Congress to agree on a Federal budget]: Every municipality in this country . . . has a budget. Every state of the Union has a budget. The Federal government, the world's largest economy, the strength of the

117

(DONALD T. REGAN)

free world, is about to go into its new fiscal year without a budget. How ridiculous can you be?

Before U.S. Chamber of Commerce, Washington, July 18/The Washington Post, 7-19:(A)9.

John M. Richman
Chief executive officer,
Dart & Kraft, Inc.

[Supporting President Reagan's tax-revision proposal]: I am here today to tell you that the mainstream of American business is on your side. We, too, want tax reform . . . We are now, unfortunately, at the point where tax considerations not only outweigh but may even override economic considerations in business decisions. Every time a businessman makes a tax-motivated decision, the economy is weakened a little bit more.

Before House Ways and Means Committee, Washington, June 4/
The New York Times, 6-5:31.

1

Donald W. Riegle, Jr.
United States Senator, D-Michigan

. . . we are accumulating an increasing [national] debt of a dimension that we've not dealt with in contemporary history . . . The consumer debt is running at a rate of 72 per cent of personal income and in fact is rising. We've got the massive buildup of internal domestic debt coming off the fiscal deficit which we are all alarmed about. And now we've got this situation where we've just become a debtor nation in terms of our international balance sheet last month; and within 12 months, if we stay on these trend lines, we are going to surpass Mexico and Brazil and become the number 1 debtor nation in the world. I don't know any contemporary parallel to this. We haven't been a debtor nation since 1914.

At Senate Banking Committee hearing, Washington, July 18/The New York Times, 8-7:10.

2

Jerome Rosow
President, Work in America Institute;
Former Assistant Secretary of
Labor of the United States

The new workers of this decade are qualitatively superior to anything we've had in the past, and companies are coming to recognize that. These workers want to participate in decision-making that affects their work; they're more open to new technology than they've ever been; they have a keen desire to learn and grow. Their hidden potential is tremendous.

U.S. News & World Report, 9-2:47.

3

Dan Rostenkowski
United States Representative,
D-Illinois

Tax reform ought to be done. Tax reform can be done. All it takes is a lot of education, a lot of pushing and a lot of negotiating—all against the clock . . . Too often I talk to heads of business who declare their support for reform—only to be attacked by their Washington lobby pursuing the firm's special interest with a vengeance. Too often, the falconer never talks to his falcon. The cost? Confusion, ill will and delay . . . To those who are preparing to stand against change, I have warning. Don't underestimate the public demand for reform. Not just in think tanks and among liberal tax lawyers, but in the great belt of middle-income earners whose taxes are automatically withheld and sent off to Washington.

Before New York Economics Club, Feb. 25/The Washington Post, 2-26:(D)3.

4

[On proposals for a minimum tax on corporations]: The substitution of a minimum tax for comprehensive [tax] reform is a cop-out. Even though toughening the existing minimum tax would weaken the impact on preferences, it would not erase them. The weeds would be topped, but the roots would remain.

Chicago, April/Los Angeles Times, 5-6:(I)8.

5

(DAN ROSTENKOWSKI)

1

[On President Reagan's tax-reform proposal]: Every year, politicians get up and promise to make the tax code fairer and simpler—but every year we seem to slip further behind. Now, most of us pay taxes with bitterness and frustration. Working families file their tax forms with the nagging feeling that they're the country's biggest chumps. Their taxes are withheld at work—while the elite have enormous freedom to move their money from one tax shelter to another. Their bitterness and frustration is about to boil over. And it's time it did. But this time there's a difference in the push for tax reform. This time, it's a Republican President who's bucking his party's tradition as protector of big business and the wealthy. His words and feelings go back to Roosevelt and Truman and Kennedy. But the commitment comes from Ronald Reagan. And that's so important and so welcome. Because, if the President's plan is everything he says it is, he'll have a great deal of Democratic support. That's the real difference this time. A Republican President has joined the Democrats in Congress to try to redeem this longstanding commitment to a tax system that's simple and fair. If we work together with good faith and determination, this time the people may win. This time, I really think we can get tax reform.

Broadcast address to the nation, Washington,
May 28/The Washington Post,
5-29:(A)15.

Charles L. Schultze
Senior fellow, Brookings Institution;
Former Chairman, Council of Economic
Advisers to the President of the
United States (Jimmy Carter)

3

The general point of all industrial-policy advocates is this: Major economic change, without new interventionist government policies, inevitably means workers lose their jobs, which causes hardship. Well, that is certainly true. But proponents of industrial policy also claim that this is a particularly serious problem now—and I think that is highly debatable. Between the early 1950s and the late 1960s, for example, eight important industries that employed 40 per cent of America's manufacturing production workers lost, on average, 14 per cent of their work forces. That is, one in seven jobs were lost. In a dynamic economy, old factories close and new ones open, workers are laid off and then rehired. This process is always going on.

Panel discussion, Harvard University/
Harper's, February:37.

4

When you dig deep down, economists are scared to death of being sociologists. The one great thing we have going for us is the premise that individuals act rationally in trying to satisfy their preferences. That is an incredibly powerful tool, because you can model it.

The Atlantic Monthly, February:76.

Daniel A. Schwitter
Senior vice president,
Union Bank of Switzerland

5

I guess I'm probably like a lot of Swiss: I believe in a free market really, but with some kind of [central-bank] intervention necessary at times. I don't like it, but it's realistic. What I believe in is a combination of the two. But there's no doubt that it has been proven that intervention may work for some temporary help, but it hurts more than it helps in the long term. You have to have the right fundamental economic policies in place, too.

Interview, New York/
The New York Times, 11-5.26.

2

. . . any [tax] reform is better than present law. I'll take any measure of fairness I can get. People are not as conscious of what their tax rate is as they are conscious of what some people are gaming the system. That's what gets you, and it gets me, too. When I look at my kids' tax returns and I figure that they're paying nearly a third of what they're earning and I drive down the street and look at some of the big high-rises and I know that some of those people aren't paying a dime [in taxes] and living very comfortably, I think that's unfair.

Interview/
U.S. News & World Report, 6-17:28.

Leonard Silk
Journalist, Economist

There is such a thing as the economy. But *people* make decisions. Once bakers bake a pie, the pie exists. If decision-makers bake a poison pie, it'll kill you. The economy is like that. Once it exists, things flow from it. We have to look at Presidents, Federal Reserve Chairmen, business people and investors to see why things happen.

Interview/Forbes, 1-28-42.

1

Alan K. Simpson
United States Senator, R-Wyoming

I think the Civil Service pension is an outrage. I think the U.S. Congress retirement system is an outrage . . . They all have to be on the [spending-reduction] table. They all have to be looked at without crippling groups and without breaking our commitment to America. But we can't afford to let people retire at the end of 20 years in the military, can't afford to let civil servants retire at the age of 50, while we pay the bucks and have an unfunded liability of billions of dollars.

Broadcast interview, Washington/
"Meet the Press," Washington, 2-10.

2

Van P. Smith
Chairman, Ontario Corporation;
Chairman, Chamber of Commerce
of the United States

We want to see government maintain reasonable spending levels and minimum taxation levels, moderate the regulatory burden and hold to a stable monetary policy. If government would dedicate itself to doing those things, it's amazing what the American small-business community would do for government and for this country.

Interview/Nation's Business, January:55.

3

Beryl W. Sprinkel
Chairman, Council of Economic Advisers to
the President of the United States

This has bugged me all my life: It turns out that good economic policies that bring you better

To reporters, Washington, Feb. 13/
The Christian Science Monitor, 2-14.5.

4

growth, better employment, lower inflation and higher levels of prosperity usually have a short-run cost. You go through the pain first and get the goodies later. If I could change something, I would certainly get the goodies up front because it would solve a lot of political problems.

Interview/The New York Times, 8-9.8.

David A. Stockman
Director, Federal Office of
Management and Budget

[On preparing the Federal budget]: Making choices is the hardest part. It's hard in the sense that the budget is so big and the political system—the Administration, the leadership, the major elements in Congress—are just like so many blind men circling around an elephant, all grabbing at a different part, thinking that's where the solution lies and having a total lack of knowledge or comprehension about the remaining anatomy.

Interview, Washington/
The New York Times,
2-4.8.

5

We now have a budget that is a trillion dollars in its dimension, that is a blooming, buzzing mass of programs, projects, commitments and purposes responsive to the needs of our society . . . It is bolstered with a mountain of claims and counterclaims of every kind that are most difficult to sort out.

Before Senate Budget Committee, Washington,
Feb. 5/The New York Times, 2-6.1.

6

[On his accomplishments as head of OMB]: . . . if you look at the texture and content of the fiscal debate in the country today, I think we have brought fundamental change. Nobody is suggesting major new programs; nobody is trying to liberalize entitlements; nobody is suggesting we ought to be entirely preoccupied with the short run.

7

(DAVID A. STOCKMAN)

1

. . . we are violating badly, even wantonly, the cardinal rule of sound public finance: governments must extract from the people in taxes what they dispense in benefits, services and protections. Perhaps not every year, but certainly over any intermediate period of time . . . As the security crisis has worsened and the political conflict intensified, we have increasingly resorted to squaring the circle with accounting gimmicks, evasions, half-truths and downright dishonesty in our budget numbers, debate and advocacy. Indeed, if the SEC had jurisdiction over the Executive and Legislative branches, many of us would be in jail. So it is incumbent on both sides to come clean with the numbers, and thereby the true choices.

Before board of New York Stock Exchange,
June 5/The New York Times, 6-29:21.

David A. Stockman
Former Director, Federal Office
of Management and Budget

2

The [economic] joy ride is over. We just can't live with these massive [Federal budget] deficits without traumatic economic dislocations. We're beginning to see them in the panic on trade, the balance-of-payments deficit, this effort to try to tinker with the world currency market to bring down the dollar . . . If we're going to get out of this situation and restore any semblance of national solvency and fiscal discipline, it's going to take a very major tax increase, larger than we've ever had or contemplated before . . . I think the idea of a revenue-neutral tax reform is preposterous. The loopholes that we close, the revenues ought to be put in the Treasury to pay our bills, not to give further tax cuts. We can't afford the ones we have already.

Broadcast interview/
"This Week with David Brinkley," ABC-TV, 9-29.

Dick Thornburgh
Governor of Pennsylvania (R)

3

[Favoring President Reagan's tax-reform proposal which would eliminate the Federal deduc-

tion for state and local tax payments]: To the extent that the elimination of the deductibility of state and local taxes will contribute to the reduction of marginal Federal tax rates for all taxpayers, I think it's preferable to keeping the present system. The present system primarily benefits upper-bracket taxpayers in high-tax states with steeply accelerated rates . . . It is the present system that is unfair: Taxpayers in low-tax states are actually subsidizing taxpayers in high-tax states. The effect of the proposed reform would be to redress that imbalance and provide an across-the-board cut in marginal Federal rates for taxpayers equally in each of the 50 states.

Interview/U.S. News & World Report, 6-3:71.

Richard Trumka
President, United Mine Workers

4

Over a period of years, ethics has gone downhill on both sides of the [labor-management] bargaining table. If management starts telling untruths, labor will do the same to combat them. That's very, very sad. I'd like to see a return to the days when people were able to shake hands and live by their word.

U.S. News & World Report, 12-9:62.

George Voinovich
Mayor of Cleveland;
President, National League of Cities

5

Politicians are always looking for issues that will appeal to everyone. Well, I don't care whether you're an urban dweller or a farmer—the [Federal budget] deficit is the enemy. And if we don't do something about it, the impact will be more severe than anything any external enemy can do to us.

Interview, Cleveland/
The Christian Science Monitor, 8-27:6.

Paul A. Volcker
Chairman, Federal Reserve Board

6

The Federal Reserve can theoretically run the modern equivalent of the printing press—we can create more money. But more money is not the

WHAT THEY SAID IN 1985

(PAUL A. VOLCKER)

same as correcting the gross imbalance between our ability to generate real savings and the demands for those savings posed by housing, by investment and by the Federal deficit. To create money beyond that needed to sustain orderly growth would be to invite renewed inflation—damaging incentives to save in the process.

Before Senate Banking,
Housing and Urban Affairs Committee,
Washington, Feb. 20/The New York Times, 2-21:29.

1

We are dealing with a situation marked by gross [economic] imbalances that can neither be sustained indefinitely nor dealt with successfully by monetary policy alone, however conducted. We are borrowing, as a nation, far more than we are willing to save internally. We are buying abroad much more than we are able to sell. We reconcile borrowing more than we save and buying more than we sell by piling up debts abroad in amounts unparalleled in our history. Our key trading partners, directly or indirectly, have been relying on our markets to support their growth and, even so, most of them remain mired in historically high levels of unemployment.

Meanwhile, our high levels of consumption and employment are not being matched by the expansion in the industrial base we will need as we restore external balance and service our growing external debt. And after 2½ years of economic expansion, too many borrowers at home and abroad remain under strain or over-extended.

Before House subcommittee, Washington,
July 17/The Washington Post, 7-18:(E)1.

Clayton K. Yeutter

Trade Representative for the
President of the United States

2

. . . we have to recognize that what really made this country great was our capitalist system, and that's a system that has both winners and losers. If we attempt to alter that system in such a way that we try to insure that everyone is a winner, then in the long term nobody is going to be a winner. We will then be preserving industries and firms and jobs that really do not merit preservation under the competitive aspects of a capitalistic system. We will be much better off as a nation if we reward the winners—the most productive and efficient segments of our society—and phase out the losers, whoever they may be.

Interview, Washington/USA Today, 11-7-(A)12.

Education

John Agresto
*Acting Chairman, National Endowment
for the Humanities of the United States*

1

[Lamenting the lack of interest in history courses in high schools today]: The high schools are teaching consumerism, photojournalism, weight-watching. The more people think that schools are for the propagation of social niceties, the more history and literature will suffer. Why take Roman history when you can take bachelor living? . . . The defense of history has been incredibly poor in this country. If all you can say is that it's interesting and that you need it to get into college, then you have not defended it. We need to make people understand they won't know their way around this world unless they know history. Without a knowledge of history, you have no idea who you are, or why you are, or how to criticize your government, unless you know why it's like it is. If you want to understand what is happening, and to argue about it, you must understand what it was at the start.

The Christian Science Monitor, 11-29:33.

Gregory Anrig
*President,
Educational Testing Service*

2

[On the increase in testing of both teachers and students]: There is an old army adage: "If it moves, salute it: if it stands still, paint it!" Today that can mean for some [education] reformers, "If it moves, test it."

The Christian Science Monitor, 8-23:(B)3.

Alexander Astin
*President,
Higher Education Research Institute,
University of California, Los Angeles*

3

This idea that you need a little Chaucer and a few other things thrown in, and then you're "humanized," is patently not true. It's critical thinking and the ability to listen—the most neglected skill in academia—and to speak and write which

are important. The bottom line is learning. Higher education is going to be in trouble as long as it pretends educational objectives can be met through course requirements.

*Interview, Chicago/
The Christian Science Monitor,
3-20:4.*

Robert Bandeen
Chairman, Crown Life (Canada)

4

In the recent past, university education has been oversold and valued for the wrong reasons. People have been sold on a cash-register approach, equating levels of schooling to annual income. Pressure for increased specialization has been coming from within the universities as some of them market themselves in order to attract large numbers of young people and offer courses that will lead to specific positions in industry or the professions. These institutions are selling themselves and their students short. The undergraduate years constitute the only period when there is the time and enthusiasm to explore the intellectual heritage of civilization. There is a need to become exposed to a wide range of thought and human achievement in order that the young person can develop as an individual and gain a full perspective of life.

*Interview/
Maclean's, 5-6:41.*

Paul Bator
Professor of law, Harvard University

5

[On his leaving Harvard to become a law professor at the University of Chicago]: The Harvard Law School is the only educational institution I know where it is considered a symptom of right-wing extremism to be in favor of rigorous standards of scholarly excellence. Serious and productive non-left scholars do not want to be at an institution devoted to guerrilla warfare.

*The Washington Post,
12-21:(A)3.*

Terrel H. Bell
Former Secretary of Education
of the United States

1

The condition of the teaching profession is at an all-time low. We're getting tomorrow's teacher from the bottom of the spectrum of human ability.

USA Today, 5-2:(A)8.

2

Aside from curriculum changes such as a greater stress on languages, I would hope we [in the U.S.] could establish the respect for teachers that permeates Japanese society. I also recommend that state legislatures follow the Japanese lead in boosting teacher salaries. This means taxpayers would have to be willing to come up with the money for it. The salary structure of the Japanese teacher is set by law in the upper one fourth of the income level of the Japanese people. A Japanese teacher gets 30 per cent more than a career civil servant. The result is that a higher-caliber person is attracted to teaching in Japan. There, some of the most talented college graduates are competing to become teachers—just the opposite of what is happening in the United States.

Interview/U.S. News & World Report, 9-2:43.

William J. Bennett
Secretary of Education of the United States

3

[Supporting proposed Reagan Administration cuts in loan guarantees for college students, saying that for some students it would mean only cutting of some luxuries]: [It would be] divestiture of certain sorts: stereo divestiture, automobile divestiture, three-weeks-at-the-beach divestiture. I do not mean to suggest this will be the case in all circumstances, but it will, like the rain, fall on the just and unjust alike.

News conference, Washington,
Feb. 11/Los Angeles Times, 2-12:(I)8.

4

[Supporting moves to give parents more control of what their children are taught in school]:

124

It's not hard, if one looks at the last 15 years of education, to understand why parents are distressed. If I were a parent with a child in school . . . I would take a very close look at what my son was being asked to study, because there are a lot of things in schools that in my judgment don't belong there.

News conference, Feb. 11/
The Washington Post,
2-13:(A)4.

5

We are now running a student financial-aid system with government support in which we support many students who are at the very upper limits of American income—$80-, $90-, $100,000. This is not a sensible way to run a system. It's our belief that we must do what we can to provide access to the neediest. I don't wish to suggest that [student-aid] budget reductions won't have serious impacts, and obviously some people are going to have to tighten their belts in very serious ways . . . We understand that's difficult for some people who want to go to expensive schools. But the tradeoff is, given limited dollars, do you use those dollars to provide money for someone to go to college, any college, a college, or do you take the money and say, let's use it for those who want to go to the most expensive colleges? We realize that this is going to have some tough consequences, but we have a terrible budget problem. I think everyone knows that. There are terrible abuses in the loan and grant program.

Broadcast interview, Washington/
"Meet the Press," NBC-TV, 2-17.

6

[Accusing graduate schools of being obsessed with trivial]: Moving from undergraduate to graduate study should be like moving from being a college athlete to being a professional athlete. Instead, it is frequently like being transformed from a college athlete into a sports statistician.

Interview/Los Angeles Times, 3-3:(I)25.

7

Some colleges are worth it, and some are not. Quality can even vary within an institution from

(WILLIAM J. BENNETT)

department to department. We need to determine why university costs have gone up so much. We hear the phrase, "hospital-cost containment"; we do not hear the phrase, "university-cost containment." With 52 per cent of Americans graduating from high school and going on to college, that's an issue we should address. The most important question is: What are we getting for our money? In many cases, not enough. A college education should make a student knowledgeable about his or her civilization, not just teach job skills.

Interview/U.S. News & World Report, 3-4:81.

1

[I agree with former Supreme Court Justice Felix Frankfurter that] the "deposit left in the minds of men from teachers is something that works its way through a life." And although it may not make the front page, it will continue to inform the direction of a life in ways that are more subtle and more substantial.

Interview, Washington/
The Christian Science Monitor, 3-12:3.

2

Surely one of our highest charges in teaching is to teach what we ourselves have loved: *The Call of the Wild, Beautiful Joe, Treasure Island, Swiss Family Robinson, Huckleberry Finn.* If we remove this kind of content from our courses, we take away the very things that make students love to be students, and which lead to the improvement of skills. We should want every student to know how mountains are made, and that for most actions there is an equal and opposite reaction. They should know who said, "I am the state," and who said, "I have a dream." They should know about subjects and predicates, about isosceles triangles and ellipses. They should know where the Amazon flows, and what the First Amendment means. They should know about the Donner Party and slavery, and Shylock, Hercules and Abigail Adams, where Ethiopia is, and why there is a Berlin Wall. They should know a little about how a poem works, how a plant works and what "if wishes were horses, beggars would ride" means. They should know the place of the Milky Way and DNA in the unfolding of the universe. They should know something about the Convention of 1787 and about the conventions of good behavior. They should know a little of what the Sistine Chapel looks like and what great music sounds like. In certain places in America, there is a great zeal to remove certain things from study. Let us match that zeal for exclusion with a zeal for inclusion. As we decide what to teach our children, let us remember the advice of Wordsworth: "What we have loved, others will love, and we will teach them how."

Before National Press Club, Washington,
March 27/The New York Times, 4-9:10.

3

[On teaching children to read]: Parents play roles of inestimable importance in laying the foundation. Parent reading to child. Parent having books around the house. Parent encouraging child to read. Inestimable importance. I've said over and over again: Parents are the indispensable teacher. If parents don't encourage that early interest in reading, we're running behind the eight ball here . . . As with parents, so with teachers. Parents and teachers are allies. There's no substitute for a teacher who reads children good stories, tells children good stories. It whets the appetite of children for reading. This practice should continue throughout the grades, but in many places it doesn't . . . Reading is the fundamental skill. Reading ability is still strongly correlated with success in math and science. The ability to read successfully is the key to advancement, jobs, knowledge, pleasure. If you had to pick one thing, it would be reading.

Interview/
USA Today, 5-13:(A)9.

4

We have a public now that's in a large part better educated than the teachers have been in their schools. And they're bound to be critical. I think the American public is prepared to show honor and regard and respect for teachers, but they're not going to do it by just saying we have to honor and regard and respect *all* teachers. Thus the popular support for something like merit pay. People will support increased taxes

126

(WILLIAM J. BENNETT)

for teachers' salaries if they can give the money to the people who they think are the best.

Interview/USA Today, 5-13:(A)9.

1

We have to pay more attention to elementary schools . . . because they are arguably the most important in terms of what they do or what they fail to do in shaping attitudes.

Interview/The Washington Post, 7-29:(A)14.

2

[Saying efforts at bilingual education should be altered in favor of stressing English as the primary language]: To be a citizen is to share in something common—in common principles, common memories, and a common language in which to discuss our common affairs. Our common language is, of course, English. And our common task is to ensure that our non-English-speaking children learn this common language . . . We in the United States cherish our diversity, and local schools should be free—and more should be encouraged—to foster the study of the languages and heritages of their students in the courses they offer. But the responsibility of the Federal government must be to help ensure that local schools succeed in teaching non-English-speaking students English, so that every American enjoys access to the opportunities of American society.

Before Association for a Better New York, Sept. 26/ The New York Times, 9-26:16.

3

Ernest L. Boyer
President, Carnegie Foundation for the Advancement of Teaching; Former Commissioner of Education of the United States

[Saying education and training by business and industry has grown to be a major supplement to inadequate schools and colleges]: The danger is that in a bid for survival, higher education will imitate its [corporate] rivals, that careerism will dominate the campus . . . If that happens, higher education may discover that, having abandoned its own special mission, it will find itself in a contest it cannot win . . . Such nontraditional education has an essential place in our society. [But corporate classrooms] are unlikely to achieve the kind of insight and understanding that can result . . . from collegiate education at its best [whose goal] is to show how skills can be given meaning.

The Washington Post, 1-28:(A)4.

4

[Criticizing Reagan Administration education policy]: There are disturbing signs that education policies are controlled by political and ideological considerations and ignore basic commitments we've made to equity and social justice . . . There is a disturbing degree of partisanship and an inclination, on the one hand, to have government withdraw from the commitment to support and strengthen the public schools in terms of financing and equity; and on the other hand, to engage the government more completely in the philosophy and content of education.

Interview/The New York Times, 5-8:15.

5

It is possible for teen-agers to finish high school, yet never be asked to participate responsibly in life, never be encouraged to spend time with older people who are lonely, never help a child who hasn't learned to read, or even to help clean up litter on the street. We propose a service requirement for all students: . . . that during their four high-school years, students do volunteer work in or out of school. A service term for all students, whether at the school or college level, would uniquely bind the nation's youth together, helping them see connections between the classroom and the needs of people.

At Drury College commencement/ U.S. News & World Report, 6-3:66.

6

Teachers are expected to do what our homes and churches have not been able to accomplish. They are called upon not only to teach the basics, but also to monitor the playground, police

(ERNEST L. BOYER)

for drugs, reduce teen-age pregnancy, teach students how to drive, and eliminate graffiti. And, if teachers fall short anywhere along the line, we condemn them for not meeting our idealized expectations . . . Today [at this commencement] we honor not just the students getting their diplomas but also the great teachers—the university professors and first-grade teachers—who have made possible this day of celebration. I suspect that everyone in the audience today—the graduates, the parents, the children—can remember at least one great teacher you have had, perhaps two or three, who changed your life forever. And if this were a Quaker meeting, I'd suggest a moment of silence quietly to recall the outstanding teachers we have known.

At Bradford (Mass.) College commencement/
The Christian Science Monitor, 6-19:16.

1

Overall, you can't have students more outstanding than the quality of teachers. No [educational] reforms can stand unless anchored in quality teaching.

The Christian Science Monitor, 8-26:32.

Cleanth Brooks
Author, Critic;
Professor emeritus of rhetoric, Yale University

2

Neither reading nor writing flourishes in our blessed United States . . . In important respects, we are an illiterate nation.

U.S. News & World Report, 5-20:16.

Joy Brown
Director, The Richardson Study, a national investigation of the status of gifted students

3

Overall, what happens to gifted students who are not challenged [in the schools] is that there is a fairly high percentage of dropouts. And some who are bored become behavior problems. For most, it's a matter of drifting through the education program without being challenged.

USA Today, 1-21:(D)1.

Dennis Brutus
Poet; Professor, Northwestern University

4

It is customary to make dire predictions at this point to the [college] graduates in order to prepare them for what is referred to as "the real world." I decline to do so. Not that I could not make dire predictions, but because I think it is artificial to separate the campus from the community. The pressures are no less real here. Perhaps a principal difference is that, away from the university, idealism is less acceptable and compromise becomes commonplace.

At University of Massachusetts commencement,
Amherst/Time, 6-17:68.

Guido Calabresi
Dean-designate, Yale Law School

5

A friend once said that to me there are two ways of being creative: One can sing or dance, or one can create an atmosphere in which great singers and dancers can flourish. The job of a dean is to create that kind of atmosphere for students and teachers.

New Haven, Conn., Jan. 30/
The New York Times, 1-31:13.

Bill Clinton
Governor of Arkansas (D)

6

[Saying current teachers should have to pass a competency test]: It certainly won't measure someone's ability to maintain order, inspire students or communicate effectively. A person could achieve a perfect score and still not be a good teacher. But anyone who makes that argument as a reason for opposing the test should get an F in logic, because it does not follow that someone can be a good teacher and fail this test. A teacher must be competent in reading, writing and basic math to be effective.

Interview/U.S. News & World Report, 5-6:49.

Jon C. Dalton
Assistant vice president for student affairs,
Northern Illinois University

7

[College] rules and regulations are not very effective in promoting ethical development [in

(JON C. DALTON)

students]. Although it seems a simple solution, rules do not promote values; rules promote conformity . . . We know that what does promote moral development are role models. Studies show that students are influenced enormously by faculty and staff that they come to know . . . Studies show that students who frequently discuss moral issues tend to develop more sophisticated and more complex levels of thinking. The question is where do students find the opportunity today to talk about these issues. Bull sessions, including with faculty, used to be effective. These obviously still happen, but much less frequently because students are under more pressure to get good grades and faculty are concerned with tenure and publishing . . . For anyone who's responsible in education, there's this dilemma of how do you serve the marketplace without selling your soul.

At University of Redlands (Calif.)/
Los Angeles Times, 2-15:(V)24.

John R. Dellenback

President,
Christian College Coalition

[On religious-based colleges]: What difference does it make that you are teaching or learning at this kind of college? It depends on the subject. In a subject like history or English, it can make a great deal of difference. It does not make a difference in the atomic table in physics. Yet it makes some difference in all disciplines.

Los Angeles Times, 7-1:(I)21.

1

Harry Edwards

Professor of sociology,
University of California, Berkeley

The athletic departments of our major universities have become separate empires. They are completely autonomous. College presidents are so cowed by boards of trustees and alumni that they have abdicated their supervisory responsibilities. Of course, you always hear that the profits from athletics will be used to build chemistry buildings and to endow chairs in the En-

2

glish department. At most campuses this is utter nonsense. That money goes to pay for stadiums and so forth. The athletics tail has truly begun to wag the educational dog.

Panel discussion/"Harper's," September:53.

Chester Finn

Professor of education and public policy,
Vanderbilt University

A child can learn algebra or French without his parents knowing any of that. But it is hard to teach good character to a child if he starts with none at home.

U.S. News & World Report, 5-13:51.

3

Chester Finn

Assistant Secretary of Education
of the United States

If the problem of teacher quantity and quality is not solved, it could turn out to be the iceberg that sinks the whole school-reform ocean liner before it sails even halfway across the sea.

U.S. News & World Report, 12-30:111.

4

Edward Fiske

Education editor,
"The New York Times"

There's a polarization that's occurring between good [educational] institutions and lesser institutions in both the public and private sectors. Institutions that are not real good quality are not going to survive. Those in the middle are doing everything they can to intensify their programs . . . there are dozens of schools in this country where you can get a four-year education that will cost at least $20,000 and $25,000 less than you'd pay at comparable institutions . . . if you're willing to forgo the tunnel vision that often exists in choosing name colleges and settle for less prestige or less readily identifiable places . . . I'm not putting down going to a good school if you can afford it. My hunch is that people will continue to kill to get into the top of the Ivy League and to pay its costs. But in the long run, the most important thing about an education

5

(EDWARD FISKE)

is what you learn, and that you have professors who care about you. I'm saying that if you are prepared to attain less recognition for $25,000 lower in price, that now is an option for you.

The Washington Post, 12-6:(C)5.

Peter T. Flawn
President,
University of Texas, Austin

I've been a university president for 11 years. It's an extremely demanding job because there is always something else you can do. If I stay home one night, I am thinking about what group I might be meeting with. There is no time when you do not feel the pressure to keep things going. It consumes you. I can tell I do not have the same energy as I did 10 years ago.

Interview, Austin, Texas/
The New York Times, 7-16:18.

Mary H. Futrell
President,
National Education Association

We have to say to the children, "You will have to meet the [school] standards. And we, the parents, the teachers and the community are here to help you do that. And if you fail, it won't be because we didn't help you, but because you didn't try hard enough." There are too many children who can make it and don't. And a lot of them don't because they don't want to. Now, let's face the fact. I've seen kids with a lot of ability give in to peer pressure: It's not "in" to be smart; it's not "in" to get a passing grade. You hear all the kids say, "Man, you know, you're one of those bookworms." It's amazing how they give in . . . Sometimes I think we're too easy and don't give them enough credit or support. Parents should say to them all the way through, "This is the situation we face: I've got to go to work at eight o'clock in the morning; you've got to get up and go to school. You're going to have to assume some responsibilities, and I will assume certain responsibilities. We have to support each other." But are we now making life so easy

[1]

for kids—are we now taking away so much of the responsibility—that we don't let them be what they can be?

Interview/Ms., January:105.

[2]

According to all the information I have seen, private and/or parochial schools have not acquired any more support than they have had all along, which is about 10, maybe 11, per cent of the student population. As a matter of fact, back in the late '60s, I believe it was up to about 13 to 15 per cent. There will always be parents who send their children to private schools regardless of the condition of public schools. But I think those parents who do this on the assumption that all public schools are bad are often basing their decision on what they have seen, read or heard second- or third-hand. That is not to say the [public] schools are perfect; but I believe we are turning the public schools around. I think they are better than they have ever been because of the efforts of a large group of people . . . I think a lot of Americans fail to realize that when the educational system started in this country, it started as a private school system. And to a large degree, that school system was a religious one. Yet the general public moved away from private to public education to insure that each and every child in this country could, in fact, get an education. The public schools have to open their doors to everyone. We cannot turn away any child. If there is competition, it's between public schools in the same system.

Interview/
Christianity Today,
3-15:32.

[3]

[Calling for tests for new teachers]: Let us tell America that just as no law graduate can practice law without passing the bar exam, no teaching graduate should be allowed to instruct American children without first passing a valid exam that tests mastery of subject matter and professional skills . . . I've heard some say that pre-testing may hurt women and minorities. As a black woman, I don't buy that. As a matter of fact, I resent it. If we set clear and demanding expectations and then help all potential teachers

[4]

reach those expectations, we can have both quality and equality.

(MARY H. FUTRELL.)

At meeting of National Education Association, Washington, June 30/The New York Times, 7-1:15.

A. Bartlett Giamatti
President, Yale University

1

The university is our culture's assertion that what is made by the mind has value and can convey values. Universities are not here to be mediums for the coercion of other people; they're here to be mediums for the free exchange of ideas. Americans have been remarkably devoted to the capacity for belief, to idealism. That's why we get into trouble all the time. We're always viewed as naive.

Interview, Yale University/
The Christian Science Monitor, 6-21:32.

Bernard R. Gifford
Dean, Graduate School of Education, University of California, Berkeley

2

I don't think minorities are working up to their [educational] capacity, in many cases. There are a lot of faculty members who won't demand from black students what they are capable of generating, and the students adjust their sights downward. Some aren't aware of how poorly they are performing because their teachers aren't expecting much from them. And others are cynically taking advantage of well-meaning liberalism that overlooks poor performance on the part of minorities.

Interview/The Washington Post, 1-30:(A)19.

Patricia Albjerg Graham
Dean, School of Education, Harvard University

3

In the 1970s, there was a strong feeling in the schools of education that there were more important issues than schooling. Most often they got rid of the name "school of education" and became "centers of resource management," or

130

---

they got into psychology, or interested in the effects of television on children.

The Washington Post, 7-30:(A)10.

Mary Gray
Professor of mathematics, American University

4

There is a strong sense among faculty that too much money is being spent on administration [at the college]. In the sense it's become more businesslike, that's all to the good. But there is a danger of decision-making getting . . . out of the hands of faculty and to the administrators . . . There's a professional class of managers, and there's too many of them.

The Washington Post, 11-25:(A)10.

Gilbert M. Grosvenor
President, National Geographic Society

5

We know about malnutrition but we know very little of *where* millions are dying of famine. How can we help Africa when we don't know where Africa is? When geography was folded into the social sciences, it kind of got lost in the shuffle. To me, to graduate a kid from college when he barely knows how to drive home is a darn shame. I'm suggesting that ignorance kills, and I'm suggesting that if you are ignorant, you aren't going to go very far in the world.

Before Economic Club of Detroit/
Los Angeles Times, 4-23:(I)2.

Martin Guggenheim
Authority on rights of juveniles, New York University Law School

6

[On the recent Supreme Court ruling allowing searches and seizures of students and their property when there is reasonable suspicion of violation of law or school rules]: The decision is apparently written in good faith, but where it is wrong and disappointing is in the trust it places in school officials. What it really means is that school officials have a license to do as they wish.

The New York Times, 1-21:11.

Fred Hargadon
Senior vice president,
College Board

1

[On students who use outside counseling and coaching during the college admission process]: It's hard to argue against them putting their best foot forward . . . but if it's an unrealistic foot, there can be problems . . You're really looking for a representative example of the student's work . . . the *student's* work. When you read an application, you want to get some sense both of the student's abilities and his limitations, because you're going to have to put up with his limitations. When you get into class, you're not going to be doing five drafts with somebody over your shoulder.

Los Angeles Times,
2-25:(I)12.

Bill Honig
California State Superintendent
of Public Instruction

2

The intellectual leaders in this country have dropped the ball. Common civic goals—like helping public schools—don't interest them. We make something as boring as soap appealing in TV commercials, and we make something as inherently interesting as history—with its drama and characters—very boring in the classroom. That's got to change.

The Christian Science Monitor,
10-10:1.

3

If someone in the elementary grades is to teach English, history, literature, fine arts, science and mathematics, he or she has to know those subjects in enough detail to know how to present them and make them work for a variety of students. You can't do that if you haven't studied children's literature or don't know American history or world history. Much of the reliance on textbooks comes because teachers haven't had that preparation. Teachers need to become cultural ambassadors.

Interview/
U.S. News & World Report,
11-18:82.

Alice Ilchman
President, Sarah Lawrence College

4

It can be misleading to think [course] requirements, which are technical things, meet the purpose of education. I'm not a "great books" person. I don't think the common curriculum is as important as the process of inquiry—learning how to ask a question and how to sustain an argument . . . And I think the students' interest is as important as what we think they should learn. Students learn what they want to learn.

Interview, Chicago/
The Christian Science Monitor, 3-20:4.

Thomas H. Kean
Governor of New Jersey (R)

5

I have a terribly strong feeling that we have to find some way of rewarding great teachers. It is not right to have a profession where you don't get paid one cent more for being better. Getting teachers up to $50,000 or $60,000 a year, which I would like to see, isn't going to happen by raising everybody to that level.

Interview/
The New York Times,
8-20:20.

6

[Approving the current increase in testing of students]: We've got to be ready to go out there and explain very loudly to the public what we're doing and why, and the fact that these are standards which are important if a grade and a test score are going to mean something. And these are standards which any good school ought to be able to get their kids up to if they're doing the job. I worry about these kinds of measurements, though, because they can be misinterpreted by the public. We know that the failure rate is going to be higher, at least for the initial years. What does that say to the public? Does the public say that we've got a worse situation than we had? Is that their interpretation? If it is, of course it's a wrong interpretation, but it's one we've got to be aware of that might occur.

The Christian Science Monitor,
8-23:(B)3.

(THOMAS H. KEAN)

1

[In formulating education policy,] we have been doing too much talking and too little listening to teachers. I'm just not sure how much further the governors and state boards . . . ought to, or should, go without the classroom teacher. I don't see how much more productive they can get. If we want to build on what we've created and move on to new areas of creativity, it's got to be in conjunction with the classroom teacher.

Before Education Commission of the States, Philadelphia/The Christian Science Monitor, 9-9:27.

Eamon Kelly
President, Tulane University

2

[On his stopping Tulane's basketball program after indictments for bribery, conspiracy and drugs involving the team]: The focus of big money, the media pressure, drugs, gambling and betting are all part now of our national culture and intercollegiate athletics. That's when I thought it was time to say "no more, we've had enough" . . . I don't believe it's a harsh action. We have to reassert that our primary values are academics and that academic integrity is vital to university life. Our *raison d'etre* is teaching, it's learning, it's research. It's time for university presidents across the country to gain control of their institutions.

Broadcast interview/
"Face the Nation,"
CBS-TV, 4-7.

Paul G. Kumpel
Director of undergraduate mathematics,
State University of New York, Stony Brook

3

[Comparing small classes with large classes]: You really can't have much interaction between instructor and student in a large class and, as a consequence, what you do is lecture and just hope that the students are getting it. In smaller classes, not only is there a chance for lots of questions, but the students also become more attentive and are less likely to be absent.

The New York Times,
2-26:18.

Arthur Laffer
Economist;
Former professor of business economics,
University of Southern California

4

Can you imagine if all of a sudden you could get out of the ghetto by studying [in school] instead of by playing basketball? If you play basketball 16 hours a day, you become a great basketball player. If we could get these kids to study 16 hours a day, they'd become great students.

Los Angeles Times, 3-22:(I)28.

Gerald Lefcourt
Civil-rights lawyer

5

[On the recent Supreme Court ruling allowing searches and seizures of students and their property when there is reasonable suspicion of violation of law or school rules]: "Reasonable suspicion" in the courts is no more than a hunch, and I don't think this is an appropriate standard when student rights are involved. If school officials take an aggressive approach, students' privacy rights will almost evaporate.

The New York Times, 1-21:11.

Joan Lipsitz
Director,
Center for Early Adolescence

6

The junior high has been a school that basically tells kids, "Hold your breath and you'll grow out of it." It's been a transitional school for kids we hoped would get through the transition. But that's hardly the right message to be sending a group for which the here and now is particularly important.

Interview/The Christian Science Monitor, 1-25:(B)2.

John Maguire
President, Claremont (Calif.)
University Center and Graduate School

7

A great university brings its resources to bear on the problems of the community. In no way can you be isolationist or go it alone in the lofty

(JOHN MAGUIRE)

area of pure research if the world around you is going to hell in a hand basket. The university has a debt to society and it discharges it by doing what it does best [educate], generated by an awareness of the concerns of the society it finds itself in.

Interview/Los Angeles Times, 6-20:(V)30.

Joan M. May
Assistant dean of students, Cornell Medical College; Head, Graduate and Professional Financial Aid Council
1

[Criticizing proposed Reagan Administration cuts in student aid]: We're going to face the kind of pre-war educational system that we had and we thought was well behind us that had an elitist private sector with a token number of scholarship students. To return to that system after we have developed the most diverse and heterogeneous and rich system of education in the world is unbelievable.

Feb. 12/The New York Times, 2-13:8.

Robert McCabe
President, Miami-Dade (Fla.) Community College
2

Equipping someone [in college] just for an occupation may be crippling. They have to be able to grow and change. [At Miami-Dade,] we hope we produce people who will have strong information skills and who will be strong learners—people who will be able to live in the information age, change occupations if necessary and upgrade themselves as necessary.

Interview/The Washington Post, 12-16:(A)10.

Jack McCarthy
President, Center for Business Innovation, University of Missouri, Kansas City
3

Urban universities are the wave of the future. Most corporations now want a first-class university in the city where they locate so their people can continue their education. And I think most

professors, particularly in the science and business disciplines, really appreciate working with business people. It adds a degree of realism to their programs.

Kansas City/The Christian Science Monitor, 1-4:5.

Richard McCormick
Professor of Christian ethics, Georgetown University
4

College students now are heavily programmed to go out and get money. If that's the soil from which their other judgments grow, then no wonder they act the way they do.

U.S. News & World Report, 12-9:52.

Al McGuire
Sports commentator, NBC-TV; Former athletic director, Marquette University
5

[On college presidents who say they can't run their schools' athletic departments and control the cheating and gambling that goes on]: The presidents are full of baloney. They're academic people who don't want to come out of their shell. They view sports as below them. They still think that anyone who took physical education or spends time in a building that has a sweat odor is a peasant. They think: "We got to put up with guys walking around with no necks." But they can't shake and bake too much because the alumni like it.

Interview/ U.S. News & World Report, 7-1:65.

David T. McLaughlin
President, Dartmouth College
6

The college presidency is more time-demanding and more emotionally demanding than anything I experienced in the corporate world. It's not just the pluralism of lots of constituencies. It's almost a preoccupation with the process of decision-making, as opposed to the decision itself.

The New York Times, 4-24:14.

Julia M. McNamara
President, Albertus Magnus College

1

[On the increase in college business courses]: I suppose in an ideal world everyone could major in the liberal arts, but in a less than ideal world you also have to look at what the market wants.

The New York Times, 3-26:17.

James A. Michener
Author

2

I've been academically trained, and I believe in getting an education. I should point out that I don't think a person's time is wasted if he simply absorbs and lives. But I suggest college—at least a couple of years—while a person is finding his direction.

Interview, Austin, Texas/
The Saturday Evening Post, September:32.

Richard Moll
Dean of admissions,
University of California, Santa Cruz

3

Public higher education has been in the back seat in terms of public regard and public prestige for dozens and dozens of years in this country. But public universities have come of age. It [is] time for somebody to say that there [are] at least eight public universities out there that seem to be every bit as good in every way as the eight Ivys [Ivy League private colleges]. And by the way, they only cost about half of what it costs to go to the privates.

The Washington Post, 12-6:(C)5.

Walter F. Mondale
Former United States Senator, D-Minnesota;
1984 Democratic Presidential nominee

4

[Criticizing Reagan Administration cuts in aid to education]: There's a whole generation of my age that are doctors and lawyers and dentists and business leaders and nurses—every conceivable skill—that came from families who had no money . . . To say we're going to chisel on that, and cheat this next generation, I think is wrong as can be.

Interview/USA Today, 2-28:(A)2.

Gregory T. Moore
President,
United States Student Association

5

[Criticizing Reagan Administration proposals for cuts in student aid]: The proposals would affect nearly two million out of 5.3 million current student-aid recipients through a combination of caps, limits and new eligibility guidelines. This was a budget composed in the Office of Management and Budget with only one aim: to reduce the dollar figures without any regard to the students it affects. [If the cuts go through, they] would spell disaster for millions of students who would be forced to end their college career.

News conference, Washington,
Feb. 12/The New York Times,
2-13:8.

Ralph Mosher
Professor of education,
Boston University

6

[Saying schools cannot teach students personal morality]: You just can't take a big rubber stamp and stamp the Ten Commandments on a child's forehead and expect a child to understand what those Commandments mean. Children can memorize and they can parrot, but until they have constructed for themselves a moral framework, it is as meaningless as memorizing a chemical formula.

Los Angeles Times, 12-1:(I)28.

Frank Newman
President,
Education Commission of the States

7

There's this idea that higher education is short in producing technical manpower. That's wrong; the problems of this country are not caused by a lack of technical manpower. What's lacking? The skill of our college graduates in being creative, taking risks, being innovative, hav-

(FRANK NEWMAN)

ing the capacity to be entrepreneurial and see new solutions to problems.

Before American Association for Higher Education, Chicago, March 19/USA Today, 3-20:(D)6.

Dale Parnell
President, American Association of Community and Junior Colleges

1

What land grants did for agriculture, community colleges are doing for technology. I see a similar thing happening with community colleges with a different part of the economy. Training is our business. We have succeeded beyond our dreams. There are whole industries that depend on us now. Where would hospitals be [if community colleges didn't offer] the associate degree in nursing?

Interview/The Washington Post, 12-16:(A)10.

Nathan Quinones
Chancellor, New York City Schools

2

Do you know what it's like to be a teacher? There are probably not enough books. Public announcements may interrupt the lesson. The principal, other supervisors and fellow teachers seldom visit the class. The teacher probably monitors the halls, checks restrooms, supervises the lunchrooms.

Before New York State Senate Education Committee, Albany, Jan. 15/The New York Times, 1-16:37.

Diane Ravitch
Professor of history and education, Teachers College, Columbia University

3

Indifference to literacy has permeated the lower schools. The civilizing function of the schools—their mission as mass agencies of literacy—has been diluted, eroded and compromised by vocationalism. The pursuit of excellence, it seems, is to be found in honest form only on the athletic field, where indolence wins no rewards.

At Reed College commencement/ U.S. News & World Report, 6-3:66.

4

A liberal education is founded on the premise that knowldege is power and that ideas move the world. Or, this idea is expressed in what is known as the Law of Selective Advancement . . .: "The person who knows 'how' will always have a job. The person who knows 'why' will always be his boss."

At Reed College commencement/Time, 6-17:68.

5

[On high-school history courses]: History is first a story. If you can't tell it as a story, complete with heroes and devils, then you lose the drama. If you replace it with a dry social-science approach, then you lose the students.

The Christian Science Monitor, 11-29:33.

Ronald Reagan
President of the United States

6

In the area of education, we're returning to excellence; and again, the heroes are our people, not the government. We're stressing basics of discipline, rigorous testing and homework while helping children become computer-smart as well. For 20 years, Scholastic Aptitude Test scores of our high-school students went down. But now they have gone up two of the last three years. We must go forward in our commitment to the new basics, giving parents greater authority and making sure good teachers are rewarded for hard work and achievement through merit pay.

State of the Union address, Washington, Feb. 6/The New York Times, 2-7:13.

7

[Although] America boasts thousands of fine teachers, in too many cases teaching has become a resting place for the unmotivated and unqualified. We must give our teachers greater honor and respect. We must sweep away laws and regulations such as unduly restrictive certification requirements. And we must pay and promote our teachers according to merit. Hard-earned tax dollars have no business rewarding mediocrity. They must be used to encourage excellence.

Before National Association of Independent Schools, Washington, Feb. 28/Los Angeles Times, 2-28:(I)6.

WHAT THEY SAID IN 1985

(RONALD REAGAN)

[On his plan to cut student loans]: As things stand now, our nation provides some aid to college students from the highest-income families—some to students who come from families with incomes higher than $100,000. This defies common sense, insults simple justice and must stop. Government has no right to force the least affluent to subsidize the sons and daughters of the wealthy.

Before National Association of Independent Schools, Washington, Feb. 28/Los Angeles Times, 3-1:(I)6.

1

. . . I know that some of you are concerned about our proposed limits on financial aid for students. Well, we're trying to ensure an aid system that helps all those who need it. Now, you know that [Federal] spending on higher education is still more than $7-billion—as much as it was in 1982 and 1983, and more than double what it was 10 years ago. As Education Secretary Bill Bennett has pointed out, our student-aid program is big, and our commitment to it will continue. And its primary purpose will be to provide the vital assistance to those who couldn't get an education without it.

At St. John's University, New York, March 28/The New York Times, 3-29:12.

2

Illiteracy has been called America's hidden problem. Some estimates put the number of functionally illiterate persons in America as high as 23 million. Two out of five minority children are thought to be functionally illiterate. Inability to read well is at the core of just about every educational problem in our country . . . The question affects all of us: How much do we care about our future, our freedoms, the kind of life our children will lead? If we care deeply, we will make reading and learning to read a basic priority for the nation and use the methods of teaching reading that research and practice have proven to be most effective.

Dec. 9*/The New York Times, 12-30:10.

3

William Bradford Reynolds
*Assistant Attorney General,
Civil Rights Division, Department of
Justice of the United States*

[Criticizing schools that lower their standards for minority students who would not otherwise graduate]: It is doing nobody any favors to say to minorities in our educational system that we're going to let you sit in the classroom, or we're going to run you through a lower-grade kind of an education program, we're going to give you high grades so it makes the school look good . . . we give you a diploma . . . and you can't even meet basic requirements of reading, writing and arithmetic. It is the worst kind of discrimination to . . . give them a meaningless diploma.

The Washington Post, 11-5:(A)3.

4

Frank H. T. Rhodes
President, Cornell University

I still think [being a college president is] the best job in the world. It's tremendously varied. One minute you are talking to students, the next moment to the representative of a major corporation, and the next to a Congressman. It's a privilege to move in such an interesting range of circles.

The New York Times, 4-24:14.

5

Picking the "best" [college] is more like identifying a future spouse than picking a stock for investment. When you encounter the one for you, you'll know it.

U.S. News & World Report, 11-25:46.

6

Benno C. Schmidt
President-designate, Yale University

Competition [among students] . . . is corrupting to the highest possibilities of university education. To take the measure of oneself by reference to one's colleagues leads to envy or complacency rather than constructive self-examination.

Accepting the presidency of Yale, New Haven, Dec. 10/The Christian Science Monitor, 12-12:27.

7

Donna Shalala
President, Hunter College

1

Those who determine priorities in New York—the so-called power structure—have no real stake in the [educational] system. We either don't have children or don't send them to public schools. The parents of the children in the public school system are not seen as a constituency to be reckoned with. I believe that we need and can get from this city and state a substantially stronger financial and political commitment to education than we now have. I also believe that the unions, the business and civic interests as well as the school community are ready for change. But only if we have a comprehensive program, a direction, a fearless vision—and only if we make the case that education is the best economic-development strategy this city and state can undertake.

The New York Times, 2-12:27.

Albert Shanker
President,
American Federation of Teachers

2

[Arguing against requiring competency tests for current teachers]: We should test people *before* they become teachers, not after they have been in the classroom for years. It's dirty pool to hire teachers under one set of standards, let them teach 20 years as if they are doing a good job, and then say: "You could lose your job if you don't pass this test." We ought to begin a new program with people who are coming in, not those hired earlier. Perhaps professionals should be tested periodically to see that they know their stuff, but we don't test members of any other profession in this fashion. Until we do, we shouldn't single out teachers.

Interview/U.S. News & World Report, 5-6:49.

3

The country is going toward testing [of current teachers], and it's going because there is ample evidence that states—through past hiring practices—have hired people who are illiterate. If a person has been teaching for 20 years and they are illiterate, then they ought not to be teaching.

Interview, Washington, July 10/
The Washington Post, 7-11:(A)22.

4

[Criticizing the lowering of education standards]: When children have to work hard to achieve something, that carries meaning. When children are taught they can get something [grades] for nothing, they are introduced to bad morals—it's corruptive, corrosive.

At Christian Congress for Excellence
in Public Education, Kansas City/
The Christian Science Monitor, 8-9:21.

5

[On school drop-outs]: We didn't used to think of these kids as drop-outs; it was just that a lot of kids didn't keep going to school. Then along came then-President Kennedy and the civil-rights revolution, and everybody said, "Let's bring them back in," and we encouraged many more students to remain in school. Now they are much more visible as drop-outs than they were before. Before that, when they dropped out, there were jobs waiting for them, too. So it's a much more serious issue now . . . It's not such a long time ago that if a kid dropped out, we just said, "Well, he's a stupid kid" or "He's a bad boy." The parents and teachers would just assume that school is a sort of measure of virtue of each child, and that was it. It seems to me we've gone a long way now, that we've made very optimistic assumptions that everyone can be educated. In a sense, we blame ourselves where we used to blame the child or the child's family. I don't know that we should inflict that blame on ourselves, but it's a good attitude to keep trying to do better.

Interview/The New York Times, 12-31:14.

John Shattuck
Vice president for government, community
and public affairs, Harvard University

6

[Saying students and their universities are becoming active in local community affairs]: It's a different type of activism [from that of the 1960s]. In the '60s and early '70s, they were taking on global issues. Now the activism is community-based . . . The universities have given a little, but the state and local governments have also given some. The states that have a lot of universities now recognize that there is a link

(JOHN SHATTUCK)

between academics and high technology [which every state is trying to attract].

The Washington Post, 7-30:(A)10.

Dwight Smith
Chancellor, University of Denver

1

[Saying he has cut down the number of courses offered by his school]: We had lost focus, lost direction. We were trying to be a "people's college" by coming up with a program to meet every student desire. Other colleges are looking at the same problem . . . The way [the University of Denver] was, a freshman could choose from 300 courses . . . [But] students prefer to see a program that has a purpose and a small number of subjects that will hit that program.

*Interview, Denver/
The Christian Science Monitor, 3-8:6.*

Graham S. Spanier
*Vice provost for undergraduate studies,
State University of New York, Stony Brook*

2

[Comparing small classes with large classes]: There is something different about a class that is small enough for the professor to know the students' names, and circumstances under which the professor and the students can really make eye contact. You can't overlook the effect on a student when he feels that someone is actually following his progress.

The New York Times, 2-26:18.

Michael Timpane
*President,
Teachers College, Columbia University*

3

At the very time we are talking about raising the quality of [the teaching profession], we face a [teacher] shortage. There is a real conflict of interest out there that will test our mettle . . . There is a temptation to lower standards to get sufficient numbers of teachers. It's a great dilemma.

The Christian Science Monitor, 8-26:1.

Stephen Trachtenberg
President, University of Hartford

4

We want to reaffirm the centrality of the civilizing portion of our curriculum, the part that goes to the heart and soul as well as the mind.

*The Christian Science Monitor,
2-25:19.*

James D. Tschechtelin
*Executive director,
Maryland State Board for Community Colleges*

5

Community colleges are moving toward course work that might have been considered non-traditional at one time. There are more courses that are customized for business and industry . . . Many people who come for occupational purposes are very pragmatic. They are not coming for a degree. They are students who are coming for what they want—technical subjects—and they're gone . . . The community college is always going to be judged by its social utility. People are always going to use us in ways that are appropriate to their lives.

Interview/The Washington Post, 12-16:(A)10.

Lowell P. Weicker, Jr.
United States Senator, R-Connecticut

6

In Washington today, we have an Executive Branch which, by its actions, has mounted an all-out attack on public education. "No need for a Department of Education," they say. "No need for helping special populations like the economically disadvantaged, the non-English-speaking, the racially segregated or the physically or mentally disabled." "Let's bring America back," they say. "Back" indeed! Back to the days when the ability to pay instead of the ability to learn dictated educational opportunity. Back to the days when the religious right could dictate school prayer. Back to the days when minorities of all kinds were ignored and their human potential left unrecognized and unused. Well, Mr. President [Reagan] and Mr. [Education] Secretary Bennett, we friends of education have news for you. We're not going back. We're going forward, and your attempts to destroy public education through budget cuts, block grants, vouchers

(LOWELL P. WEICKER, JR.)

and tuition-tax credits are going to be rejected as has been your fiscal-year 1986 education budget. They're gone and so, too, will be your continued attempts to substitute ideology for substance in deciding the future of public education.

Before Connecticut Education Association, Hartford, May 17/The Washington Post, 5-24:(A)26.

Laval S. Wilson
Superintendent of Schools of Boston

1

[On high-school student drop-outs]: There are a lot of reasons. All young people don't have the same goals. They don't all have the same role models. Can we expect them all to be motivated? Can we expect them all to be well stimulated? Can we expect them all to have the desire to learn? Most parents can't even do that on the *weekends*. To prevent students from dropping out, we have to identify which youngsters have the *potential* for dropping out . . . Educators may need to require the students who are substantially below level and who will drop out unless their skills are improved to stay in school an extra few hours or even on the weekend. A longer school year is a possibility. But unless these kids spend more hours trying to improve themselves, they won't have the skills to get jobs. And if they drop out, society will be the loser.

Interview/USA Today, 9-9:(A)13.

2

I strongly support competency tests [for teachers]. I recall when I was a young teacher in Chicago, we had to take written exams. If you passed the written exam, you had to take an oral exam. The written exam gives some indication of your ability to think logically and to demonstrate at least a minimal level of competency in a teacher's area of expertise. Oral exams give some indication of a teacher's verbal skills and how well he or she can communicate with students. Competency exams will ensure that new teachers

coming into the profession are of a skill level that can be helpful to the youth we are responsible for.

Interview/USA Today, 9-9:(A)13.

Joe B. Wyatt
Chancellor, Vanderbilt University

3

I believe very strongly that education provides the "value added" more than anything else for the economic viability of this country. It has particularly in the recent past, and I think it will be even more so in the future, as we get to knowledge-based industry and value-added services as major parts of the economy. There's a direct linkage between the value added by education and the economic contribution of individuals and companies . . . I believe we need to prepare people very broadly, because the only thing that seems certain in our future is that change is going to increase. Those broadly educated people who are adaptable, have a good understanding of the basics—arts, humanities, sciences—are going to be able to deal with these changes better than people who are very narrowly trained.

Interview/ USA Today, 7-18:(A)7.

Thomas H. Wyman
Chairman, CBS, Inc.

4

My own education was in the liberal arts, and I have been convinced for a long time that it is the best way to start life. I hope . . . we can convince young people that they will not limit their futures by studying the liberal arts. For most of business, the need to find people who really know how to read and write and talk and think exceeds by a wide margin any other need. A person who writes a thesis on Yeats ought to feel comfortable going to IBM or Citibank or CBS. It should be recognized that such people have a head start in having their minds opened wider than others and in learning how to express themselves.

The New York Times, 3-26:20.

The Environment • Energy

Warren M. Anderson,
Chairman,
Union Carbide Corporation

1

[On the chemical leak at a Union Carbide plant in Bhopal, India, last year which killed 2,000 people]: You can be sure that when most people believe that all of this is over, it won't be over for us or the chemical industry. We're learning the lessons of Bhopal, and will be doing so for a long time to come. The Bhopal tragedy has raised a number of very important issues, prompting public concern in many areas: hazardous materials transportation; community awareness, preparedness and right to know; disaster planning; clean air and toxic regulations; Third World questions, such as the whole relationship between multinationals and developing countries . . . The standard of living we enjoy would not be possible without chemical products and technologies. Our industry's contribution may not be widely understood, but it's substantial and continues to grow. But growth is not enough. All of us in the chemical industry must work harder to gain public acceptance and understanding. And conversely, the public and government sectors cannot close their eyes to the needs of a viable and competitive U.S. chemical industry. In the final analysis, we're all going to live with chemicals because we can't live without them.

News conference, Danbury, Conn.,
March 20/The New York Times, 3-21:48.

David Attenborough
Naturalist

2

The real problem is not the loss of a particular species but the loss of particular kinds of environments. When you lose a big, dramatic species like the whooping crane, you don't notice that you are also losing other plants and animals. We are only putting Band-Aids on until we recognize we need to be protecting environments, not just endangered species.

Interview, Washington, March 13/
The New York Times, 3-14:15.

Bruce Babbitt
Governor of Arizona (D)

3

[On ground-water pollution]: When you live on the surface of the land, you are really living on the surface of a lake. It's like sitting in a rowboat in the middle of a lake. When you pour your junk over the side of the boat, it goes into the water. If you pour a half-empty can of pesticides out on your lawn, it's headed for the ground water. It may take a year or two—or 10, 20 or 30—but all that junk that was dumped and abandoned 20 years ago is now hitting and exploding outward. And we're pumping it back up . . . Half of all the people who drink water out of a glass in their homes are drinking from a well which is tapping ground water—often unregulated, often with no standards. The pollution problem is pervasive, difficult and poorly understood.

Interview/USA Today, 2-12:(4)9.

Ralph E. Bailey,
Chairman, Conoco, Inc.;
Chairman, National Petroleum Council

4

We're in an age where oil exploration has become more difficult, and countries that want to attract oil drilling are going to have to adjust their fiscal terms. Britain reduced taxes on oil companies in 1983 and was rewarded last year with a record number of exploration and appraisal wells. The current Canadian government has made it very attractive to explore in Canada. Even China has reduced some taxes in order to spur drilling in its offshore areas. Ironically, Washington seems to be going in the opposite direction at present. But I think that will change as the pace of drilling and reserve replacement in the U.S. slows.

Interview/The New York Times, 12-3:26.

5

We see astonishing television interviews with film stars campaigning to "save our beaches" from the oil companies. They describe how there would be oil derricks all over the place. I can think of no oil company, in this day and age, that would put oil rigs on resort beaches—even if

(RALPH E. BAILEY)

it were legally possible . . . Thanks to scientific and technological advances, including infrared satellite photography, and computer modeling utilizing an extensive data base built up over the years, oil companies know where they want to explore for petroleum in this country. They also have a pretty good idea of where petroleum is *not* likely to be found in commercial quantities. It is a fact that in many cases the areas of greatest environmental interest and concern are of the least with regard to their petroleum potential. So why argue about those? I can tell you that Conoco would have no interest in bidding on 90 per cent of the 6,460 California tracts, under current economic conditions, and the same probably would hold true in other areas. In all too many cases, people are getting hot under the collar for no good reason.

Before Town Hall, Los Angeles,
Nov. 19/The Wall Street Journal, 12-11:30.

Richard Benedick
United States delegate
to conference sponsored by
United Nations Environment Program

1

[On the increasingly harmful effects of chlorofluorocarbons released into the atmosphere]: One thing appears clear . . . If CFC use continues to grow over time, some depletion of the ozone layer is likely to occur. The margin of error between complacency and catastrophe is too small for comfort.

Geneva/The Christian Science Monitor, 1-31:14.

John F. Bookout
President, Shell Oil Company

2

We've [the U.S.] made considerable gains in energy security over the past decade. To keep that momentum we must continue to develop our own resource base. That, in turn, requires an understanding of the oil business—which in various debates about energy policy sometimes seems to be lacking. It sometimes seems people either don't realize or don't think it's important that the oil industry needs a long lead time from the time energy resource programs are begun

until they provide some addition to the overall supply . . . It took the industry almost 10 years from the 1973 oil embargo to begin to arrest the country's decline in oil production. We're now at about the pre-embargo level after having declined markedly below that during the late 1970s. That's the result of a very intense production investment program that began right after the embargo hit and reached the industry-wide spending level of as much as $55-billion in one calendar year. It's fallen back now to about $30-billion because of various factors including declining oil prices and the uncertainties in the tax and policy arenas.

Interview/The New York Times, 8-6:30.

William Y. Brown
Director of marine affairs,
Waste Management, Inc.

3

[Advocating increased incineration at sea of hazardous wastes]: Failure to develop this would create a huge and rapidly growing reservoir of toxic chemicals on land. These chemicals will leak and be dumped, contaminating our ground water, lakes, streams, rivers and the sea . . . I know that, philosophically, the EPA agrees that waste reduction at the source is the best thing to do. If you don't create it you don't have to worry about it. But the realities of life are that over the next three to five years we have a heck of a lot of waste to get rid of.

At Environmental Protection Agency hearing,
San Francisco/Los Angeles Times, 6-20:(I)30,31.

Anne McGill Burford
Former Administrator, Environmental Protection
Agency of the United States

4

[President Reagan is] the best this country could have in terms of his overall domestic and foreign policies. [But] the uncomfortable conclusion that I arrived at was that he really does not have a commitment to the environment. We don't have an environmental policy in this Administration, and I'm not at all comfortable with that . . . I think it's a question of benign neglect.

Broadcast interview/"Today" show, NBC-TV, 12-5.

WHAT THEY SAID IN 1985

(ANNE McGILL BURFORD)

1

This is a question the press always asks me: "How do you feel about the environment?" The first time, I thought, I'm going to gag myself with a spoon! I said, "I *feel* about my husband. I *feel* about my children. I *think* about the environment." That's not good enough for the liberal Eastern establishment press. [For them,] you've got to be an absolute tree-hugger and emote about the birds, which I did not. I'm a manager.

Interview/USA Today, 12-16:(A)11.

Barry Commoner
Director, Center for the Biology of Natural Systems, Queens (N.Y.) College

2

What happened in 1970 [at the first Earth Day observance] was a kind of inchoate outburst of people's feelings that the environment is important and had been neglected. There was damned little organization at first; everybody was sounding off in one direction or another. What really held it together was the very simple moral statement that future generations depend on the environment and we have been blind as to what's been happening to it. It was not structured. It didn't have a theory, an ideology. What's happened since then is pretty fascinating. The fundamental moral energy generated in 1970 has been piped off into various ideological and political channels, none of which, by and large, come close to relating to the basic issue, which is social governance of the means of production. [That means] you have to ask what's wrong with the way in which we produce cars or the way in which we produce plastics . . . the only sensible way to deal with the problems is to transform the technology of production to make it compatible with the environment.

*Interview, New York/
Los Angeles Times, 6-6:(V)1.*

Jacques Cousteau
Explorer, Environmentalist

3

A majority of ecologists have been accused—sometimes rightly so—of having a negative influence on progress. Every time there is a

project to build a dam or a generating plant, they say: "No, no, no, no. You are going to pollute." Instead of simply being negative, they need to offer constructive counterproposals. That may sometimes add to costs, but it is feasible. It requires a lot of imagination, but it contributes to the protection and improvement of life in a constructive manner. Within this framework, there are a lot of things I am concerned about. I want to contribute to avoiding the eradication of species. Each time we eradicate a species—and we are eradicating several hundred each day—we impoverish the planet for millions of years. Every time we suppress an animal forever, we lower the level of what we can teach our children. Everything goes slowly down, and we want to stop it.

Interview/U.S. News & World Report, 6-24:68.

Tam David-West
Minister of Oil of Nigeria

4

[On OPEC'S difficulties with maintaining oil-price standards]: There is a psychological need to have a standard that is fixed, but reality is something different. If you are planning a national economy, you don't go for sentiment, you go to reality.

*Interview/
Los Angeles Times, 1-27:(V)2.*

David Durenberger
United States Senator, R-Minnesota

5

Our nation is in a water crisis right now. We have problems with the need for water, with water quality and with who is going to pay for it . . . The land of plenty has created an insatiable demand for water where there isn't any, and a health crisis in terms of clean drinking water where there's a lot of it. Everybody's going to compete with each other to swing 51 per cent of a vote on the floor of the Senate to put money into ports, or to take that same amount of money and put it into eliminating toxic-waste contamination of ground water. The battle lines are drawn.

U.S. News & World Report, 3-18:67.

Charles Ebinger
Director, Energy and Strategic Resources
Program, Center for Strategic and
International Studies, Georgetown University

1

Clearly, OPEC will be back in the driver's seat in the 1990s. Since most oil that can be produced by non-OPEC countries already is being produced, each additional barrel of oil needed to meet rising world demand will come from OPEC. The cartel is likely to increase its share of the world oil market from 27 per cent today to about 55 per cent. And we will be confronting a new, truncated OPEC in the 1990s. By then, at least five of the 13 members—Ecuador, Gabon, possibly Algeria, Nigeria and Indonesia—will need all the oil they produce for their own consumption. The locus of power in OPEC will switch back to the Persian Gulf states, principally Saudi Arabia, Iran, Iraq and, to a lesser extent, Kuwait and the United Arab Emirates. Not enough attention has been given to the implications of this.

Interview/U.S. News & World Report, 5-27:37.

Nicholas Freudenberg
Professor of public health,
City University of New York

2

[On judging the risks in deciding whether or not to regulate an environmental pollutant]: It's an inexact science at best, and all too often it's used as a rationale for not regulating. The fact is that there is a tremendous amount of uncertainty, and if you need certainty, even from animal tests, you're not going to have it for decades.

The Washington Post, 1-3:(A)6.

August Heckscher
Environmentalist; Former Parks
Commissioner of New York City

3

The fear is that we will get a wall of 34-story buildings on East 96th Street [in New York] when we need low-rise development and relief from the sense of tension you get from these towers. We need "air parks"—big squares of air in the sky so you can breathe and see the moon and feel you are alive.

The New York Times, 7-23:27.

John S. Herrington
Secretary of Energy-designate
of the United States

4

[Saying he believes in the value of conservation]: [We] sat in the gas lines with the rest of America [in the 1970s]. We added insulation to our attic and we wrapped our water heater in an insulation blanket . . . I learned about "R-factors" and I watched my utility bills climb . . . Like the rest of America, I learned that we would never again be able to take our use of energy for granted . . . The country made a start toward the end of energy dependence.

At his confirmation hearing before
Senate Energy and Natural Resources Committee,
Washington, Jan. 31/Los Angeles Times, 2-1:(I)14.

John S. Herrington
Secretary of Energy
of the United States

5

[On his agency's expenditures in the energy field]: These are dollars-and-sense decisions, business decisions. The way I approach this is that when you put money into projects, you are taking it from the people. Do you take $2.5-billion out for the Portsmouth gas centrifuge plant when you know it's unneeded and uncompetitive? Do you pull out another couple of billion for Great Plains [coal gasification plant]? My answer is no.

Interview, Washington/
The New York Times, 8-26:10.

Jim Hightower
Commissioner of Agriculture of Texas

6

[On the recent pesticide food-poisoning found in California watermelons]: The same thing can happen in Texas or Nebraska. We in agriculture can no longer afford the luxury of saying, "That's just an isolated case out in California." What this teaches us is the same thing that we're learning in other unfortunate instances: These poisons are indeed very dangerous, and they are substances that we don't have an adequate system for dealing with in terms of ultimate consumer protection . . . This is not the farmer's

143

(JIM HIGHTOWER)

fault. It won't do to say, "You guys are to blame and we're taking all your poisons away." Larger forces than farmers have created this. We've allowed science to say this is the answer and it turns out not to be the answer.

July 8/USA Today, 7-9:(A)2.

Donald P. Hodel
Secretary of the Interior
of the United States

[Parks and wilderness areas] clearly would be areas that ought to be protected from development. The same thing for recreation areas, refuges and wetlands. And we also have land that is clearly multiple-use land, some of it suitable for grazing, some for off-road vehicle recreation, some of it suitable for skiing and camping and timber harvesting and mineral exploration. What I submit we ought to do is say that exploration for minerals ought to begin on the least sensitive lands and work from the least sensitive upward. You should not leap, as has happened, from the least sensitive to those that are adjacent to parks or in prospective wilderness areas.

Interview, Washington, March 5/
The New York Times, 3-12:11.

1

Edward G. Jefferson
Chairman, E. I. du Pont de
Nemours and Company

The Canadians are prepared to commit $30-million a year to controlling acid rain in Canada. We're [the U.S.] spending more than that on *research*, on top of the $150-billion we've already spent under the Clean Air Act. Some people feel it isn't fast enough. But if I went to the doctor and he said, "I'm not sure why you have this problem, but it might be fixed if we amputated your leg," I think I'd want to know more than that before I'd go along with radical surgery.

Interview/U.S. News & World Report, 4-15:61.

2

[On proposals for an oil import fee as a way to encourage oil-use conservation]: While ap-

pealing at first glance, a tax on imported crude oil would seriously impair the world-wide cost competitiveness of many domestic industries by forcing them to use energy and petroleum-based raw materials at prices above world levels. The advantages seen in energy taxes might well be realized, however, through an increased tax on gasoline at the pump. This would not have a negative impact on our industrial competitiveness since, unlike a tax on crude oil, it would be borne directly by the consumer.

February/The Washington Post, 7-26:(B)2.

William J. Levitt
Home-builder

[On environmentalists who criticize his use of land to build large numbers of low-cost, high-density single-family homes]: There are a great many human beings in this world. You just can't take these human beings and throw them out on the street. They've got to live some place. Environmentalists are right, up to a point. But can they put roofs over the heads of people without building any houses? If they can, fine. I'll be the first to adopt it.

Interview/USA Today, 1-28:(A)11.

4

Robert W. Lundeen
Chairman, Dow Chemical Company

Now, what are the facts on hazardous wastes? First, there are some genuine problems stemming from past industry waste-disposal practices that must be corrected. Second, exposure to problem disposal sites is usually low; therefore, the risk to public health is quite limited. Third, modern chemical waste-disposal practices can reduce the exposure hazard to workers and to the public to the no-effect level . . .[But] at the risk of sounding alarmist, I believe that if our industry simply waves the banner of scientific knowledge and ignores existing public perceptions, we will shortly face some very unpleasant economic realities. In the case of hazardous waste, reality might include higher waste taxes or the elimination of some disposal alternatives or an inability to open new plant sites due to public fears.

Before Societe de Chimie Industrielle,
Paris/The Washington Post, 1-31:(A)20.

5

3

Richard J. Mahoney
President, Monsanto Co.

1

[On concern about the safety of chemical plants following a poison-gas leak at a Union Carbide facility in Bhopal, India, which killed over 2,000 people]: People are tremendously more interested than they were before, and to tell them, "We're doing everything, don't worry," just isn't enough. I'd like to explain what we do and what our safeguards are. I think they're entitled to know that . . . If my neighbors said to me, "What are you making in there anyway?" how could I say anything but, "Come in and I'll show you"?

Interview/The Washington Post, 1-23:(A)7.

Paul N. McCloskey
Former United States Representative, D-California

2

[Saying that, from an aesthetic standpoint, farms should be preserved rather than paved over by developers]: How do we pay that guy for maintaining that farm? He can't make money selling artichokes any more. I'm always trying to devise a means by which we can say okay, that farmer is the caretaker of a park for us. Shouldn't we give that guy maybe $10,000 a year to keep this farm instead of turning it into a trailer park?

Los Angeles Times, 5-23:(V)32.

William Penn Mott, Jr.
Director-designate, National Park Service of the United States

3

There has to be more long-range research to really understand how to manage the resources [of national parks]. For example, let's take Sequoia National Park. Do we know enough to know that we are properly managing the big trees so that they'll be here 1,000 years from now? . . . The condors are the same thing. We're down to one nesting pair of condors and we're probably going to lose the condors. But 25 years ago we should have started the research and not wait until it's a crisis. Now it's too late. And I suppose people will say, "Well, so what?"

But if we don't have the capacity to maintain the condor, maybe we don't have the capacity to maintain human life on this earth.

*Interview, Oakland, Calif./
The Christian Science Monitor, 5-9:4.*

William Penn Mott, Jr.
Director, National Park Service of the United States

4

I believe in parks. I believe that parks are the most important element in government for the health and welfare and productivity of this country. I'll tell you what the value is. Why the hell don't we just not plant any more flowers, let the damn grass dry up, don't pick up any litter and see what happens?

Interview/The Washington Post, 6-28:(D)1.

5

We're getting more and more people living in the cities. That's the reason we're going to make a major effort to educate the city folks as to what their responsibilities are when they're out of doors, so they understand the [natural] resource and why we're trying to protect it. This is going to take a major educational effort on our part. Some of these recreational areas are really universities to train and teach the urban dwellers on what it's like in the out-of-doors and how they can enjoy it, respect it and understand it.

Interview/USA Today, 8-29:(A)9.

Daniel Moynihan
United States Senator, D-New York

6

On the floor of the Senate, I once said that you can live without oil and you can even live without love, but you cannot live without water. Deplete the Ogallala acquifer, and in 30 years' time you're not exporting wheat. Run down the acquifers under the Southwest, and in 50 years' time, no Phoenix. Sorry, friend, the water is gone. That's a real—and irreversible—crisis . . . Reversing this trend is going to involve, among other things, finding someone in the Executive Branch who will pay attention to the problem. I must confess I haven't found them. In

145

WHAT THEY SAID IN 1985

(DANIEL MOYNIHAN)

the [Jimmy] Carter Administration, it was deferred by concerns about waste and environmental desecration. Under the [current] Reagan Administration, the excuse is that it's money we can't afford. And both are tremendously short-sighted views.

U.S. News & World Report, 3-18-68.

Peter C. Myers
Chief, United States Forest Service

1

I feel very strongly that the Lord put the [natural] resources on this earth for man to use—to manage wisely, but to use. We're charged by law with the multiple use of the national forests, and that includes recreation, that includes wildlife, that includes soil and water, and that includes timber.

Interview, Washington/
The Christian Science Monitor, 6-18-5.

Yasuhiro Nakasone
Prime Minister of Japan

2

We believe that all living things—humans, animals, trees, grasses—are essentially brothers and sisters. Our generation is recklessly destroying the natural environment which has evolved over the course of millions of years and is essential for our survival. This folly can only be called suicidal.

At United Nations, New York,
Oct. 24/Los Angeles Times, 10-24:(I)14.

Roger Tory Peterson
Ornithologist

3

Many people go through life as though they are wearing blinders or are sleepwalking. Their eyes are open, yet they may see nothing of their wild associates on this planet. Their ears, attuned to motor cars and traffic, seldom catch the music of nature—the singing of birds, frogs or crickets—or the wind. These people are *biologically illiterate—environmentally illiterate*—and yet they may fancy themselves well informed,

146

Ronald Reagan
President of the United States

4

[Saying offshore oil platforms are not eyesores, as some critics have charged]: You know, I think this is really reaching to say that some structure out there, that far out in the ocean, when you've got that whole expanse of ocean . . . It isn't as if you were looking at the ocean through a little frame and now somebody put something in the way . . . Why don't we bring down some [mothballed World War II Liberty ships] and anchor them between the shore and the oil derrick? And then the people would see a ship and they wouldn't find anything wrong with that at all. They don't mind seeing piers that go out a half or a quarter mile into the ocean.

Interview, Santa Barbara, Calif./
Los Angeles Times, 2-18:(I)4.

William D. Ruckelshaus
Administrator, Environmental Protection
Agency of the United States

5

[On a meeting he attended between rubber-products-plant workers and the plant manager about cancer-causing vinyl chloride and new rules to limit exposure to it]: He [the manager] went on at some length explaining the risks, and how safety rules would change, and health monitoring. At the end of the presentation, he asked if there were any questions, and there was a long silence. And I thought, boy, are they going to storm the stage, or what? Finally, one worker piped up. He said, "When are you gonna get this damn cigarette machine fixed?"

The Washington Post,
1-3:(A)6.

perhaps sophisticated. They may know business trends or politics, yet haven't the faintest idea of what makes the natural world tick. We have biologists, of course, and biochemists. But we really need more bio-engineers, bio-lawyers and bio-politicians.

At Bloomsburg (Pa.) University commencement/
Time, 6-17:69.

Foreign Affairs

Bernard Aaronson
Former policy director,
Democratic National Committee

1

Democratic [Party] success in foreign policy was often defined as keeping America from being involved in another tragedy. But that is only half of foreign policy. The other challenge is to define how and where and according to what values we *should* be involved.

Newsweek,
6-24:46.

Raul Alfonsin
President of Argentina

2

[Saying countries cannot be expected to fight for another nation's freedom if they themselves do not have democracy]: To achieve security it is necessary that one have the desire to defend something that he already has. But what meaning can there be for the majority of a population in defending a freedom it does not enjoy or a prosperity it does not have?

New York, March 21/
The New York Times,
3-22:6.

Richard V. Allen
Former Assistant to the President
of the United States (Ronald Reagan)
for National Security Affairs

3

Platitudinous appeals for "good will on both sides" to resolve fundamental differences [between the U.S. and the Soviet Union] will net us very little in concrete terms; the differences are so stark, so fundamental that they cannot be bridged. Those who doubt this should remember that any occupant of a Soviet gulag could easily demonstrate the difference between the two systems.

Before Senate Foreign Relations Committee,
Washington/U.S. News & World Report, 2-18:47.

Richard L. Armitage
Assistant Secretary of Defense
of the United States

4

If a group is fighting a repressive regime and shares our values and our goals, then we have very little choice but to support them. For us, the issue is not whether freedom fighters deserve our support; the real question is what support should be offered.

Los Angeles Times,
6-16:(I)1.

Les Aspin
United States Representative,
D-Wisconsin

5

My view [after Vietnam] is that certain things are doable and other things are doable only at greater cost than it makes sense to pay for what you get in return, in terms of your real national security interests. Before you go in, you had better make sure whether the costs are worth it. In retrospect, Vietnam was an easy case in these terms. The tougher case is Central America.

The Wall Street Journal,
1-17:24.

George W. Ball
Former Under Secretary of State
of the United States

6

[I'm not] sure we've learned the lesson [of Vietnam] when I hear what comes out of the White House these days. We mine harbors in neighboring countries [Nicaragua]. We conduct a Brezhnev policy in the Caribbean and Central America. We turn our back on the World Court. We attack the United Nations because it doesn't always do our will. All of these things, I think, represent a deterioration of American principle which I think is extremely serious.

Newsweek,
4-15:67.

147

Zbigniew Brzezinski
Professor of government, Columbia University;
Former Assistant to the President
of the United States (Jimmy Carter)
for National Security Affairs

1

[On the forthcoming summit meeting between U.S. President Reagan and Soviet leader Mikhail Gorbachev]: I see three dangers in the summit. The first is that the Soviets will make Reagan look too rigid in Europe and America. The second is the opposite: The summit could generate such deceptive atmospherics—[the leaders' wives] Nancy Reagan and Raisa Gorbachev hand in hand—that we will be left with the impression that the U.S.-Soviet relationship has suddenly become one of friendship. Then there's the danger that the U.S. will be put on the defensive and accept a Soviet arms-control proposal that looks good to the public but produces more insecurity than existed before the proposal.

Interview/U.S. News & World Report, 11-18:37.

George Bush
Vice President
of the United States

2

[On the 40th anniversary of the end of World War II]: Many brave Americans paid dearly for the folly of those who stuck their heads in the sand instead of facing the realities of an increasingly dangerous world and the rising power of aggressive, totalitarian regimes. Let us on this day of remembrance pledge that we as a nation will never fall prey to complacency and unpreparedness again.

On carrier U.S.S. "Enterprise," San Francisco,
Aug. 14/Los Angeles Times, 8-15:(I)4.

3

[On his Administration]: We tried to do too much, too fast . . . particularly in foreign policy. We were sometimes simultaneously working on Middle East peace, Panama Canal treaties, normalizing relations with China, SALT II treaty, our new policy toward Rhodesia. . . . It was al-

Jimmy Carter
Former President
of the United States

6

[Criticizing President Reagan's public denunciations of terrorism]: Terrorism can be dealt with quietly and effectively rather than with threats addressed to a world audience. That's a mistake for the leader of a great nation like ours.

News conference, Corfu, Greece,
July 14/The New York Times, 7-15:3.

5

Our own [U.S.] leaders have stated that the Soviet people comprise an evil kingdom, are doomed to wind up on the ash heap of history, prefer war to peace and never negotiate in good faith, and do not honor agreements once reached. With these kind of presumptions, it is easy to see why little progress is being made in trying to rid the world of some of its nuclear armaments. The Christian community must not adopt these attitudes toward the Soviet people.

At Baptist World Congress, Los Angeles/
The Washington Post, 7-13:(C)12.

4

[On U.S. negotiating with adversary nations]: If you think you're all right and the other guy is all wrong, if you think you're a child of God and the other person is a child of the devil, if you think you're superior and the other person is inferior, if you think the other party will not carry out the terms of the agreement once reached— any of those beliefs will hurt negotiations . . . I think, in general, President Reagan looks upon matters in a black-and-white spectrum: "I'm right; they're wrong. We're good; they're bad. We'll keep the terms of an agreement; they will not. We will negotiate in faith; they have never done so." I think that's been one of the stumbling blocks that's kept Reagan from resorting to diplomacy and negotiation in his first four years.

Interview/USA Today, 4-4:(A)11.

ways a turmoil there . . . But even if I had it to do over again, I don't think I could change my basic character. You know, it's my nature to analyze the problems that I see, and to try to approach them all as rapidly as I can.

To reporters, Washington, April 2/
The Christian Science Monitor, 4-3:3.

148

George Carver
Senior fellow, Center for Strategic and International Studies, Georgetown University

1

[On the recent defection to the U.S. of Soviet KGB agent Vitaly Yurchenko and his subsequent decision to return to the Soviet Union]: In the Yurchenko case, the CIA conveyed an image of amateurish bumbling that will be a great deterrent to future defectors. Yurchenko had every right to be horrified when he saw what he had told us revealed on TV and in newspaper headlines. The handling of this case was about as sloppily unprofessional as anything I've seen by the CIA in a long time. I strongly suspect the Soviets made a point of reminding Yurchenko that his wife, son and the rest of his family were hostages to his transgressions, and it was that threat that induced him to make his decision to go back . . . We must learn, if we want more defectors, to keep our mouths shut about nuggets of information we gain from them. The U.S. government cut its own throat by crowing so much about what had been achieved—like children boasting in a schoolyard. The greatest danger has been done overseas, I'm afraid, because the KGB will now send out a clear message: "If you're even thinking about defecting, forget it, because the long arm of the motherland will bring you back. Don't be so foolish as to entrust your reputation—let alone your life—to those blabbermouth amateurs in the U.S."

Interview/U.S. News & World Report, 11-18:42.

William J. Casey
Director of Central Intelligence of the United States

2

[On Soviet recruitment of Americans for spying purposes]: Nobody ever said we were able to completely protect ourselves against this kind of activity. We do know the KGB has had a number of successes over the last 10 years—rather major ones, mostly gathering technical information about our weapons, our technology and our method of collecting intelligence. This is a big, wide-open country, and the KGB has large numbers of people at work. I think the FBI works very effectively in getting a picture of what

they're doing here, and CIA does, world-wide. But they've got a big intelligence-gathering apparatus. Each operation is done clandestinely, and it's tough to get all of them.

Interview/U.S. News & World Report, 6-17:23.

3

There is no one person, there is no one capital in the world that controls terrorism. There is an apparatus made up of about 50 major terrorist organizations. Some of them will be hired by one country to carry out a job, some by another. But these states also have their own apparatus: Iran has the Revolutionary Guards; Libya has its own gang of thugs. So the entire structure is very mixed up and highly complicated. It is very important that sanctions be imposed on these states, that they be economically squeezed and that their diplomatic apparatus be prevented from facilitating the movement, cover and support of terrorists. This is a war without borders, without clear enemies.

Interview/Time, 10-28:34.

Fidel Castro
President of Cuba

4

I wonder: Is there any Fascist regime in the past 40 years that has not been an ally of the United States? In Spain, the Franco regime; in Portugal, the Salazar regime; in South Korea, the Fascist military; in Central America, Somoza, the military dictatorships in Guatemala and El Salvador; and Stroessner, the military dictatorships in Argentina, Uruguay and Brazil, as well as the Duvalier regime. I don't know of any reactionary, Fascist state that has not been a close ally of the United States.

Interview, Havana/Playboy, August:177.

Dick Cheney
United States Representative, R-Wyoming

5

[On President Reagan's complaints of having to deal with Congress in his handling of foreign policy]: I think he's right on target. We [in Congress] tend to nitpick on foreign policy, and that

(DICK CHENEY)

should be the President's role. He's got to put up with every member of Congress with a Xerox machine and a credit card running around the world cutting deals with heads of state.

The New York Times, 5-29:10.

Lucie Cheng
Director of Asian-American studies,
University of California, Los Angeles

There cannot be a successful immigration policy. If you really want to do something about immigration, you improve the economies of the native countries. You can't build walls here.

Time, 7-8:65.

1

William S. Cohen
United States Senator, R-Maine

Whenever you step into the world of international intelligence, you descend into an infinitely long hall of mirrors. The multiplication of reflections makes it virtually impossible to distinguish image from reality. You walk down that hall, trying to touch something that looks like the way out, but it never is. There are layers upon layers of deceit built into the system. It is virtually impossible for anyone outside to discern what is true. Even on the inside, there are so many compartments, so many layers, one doesn't have access to.

Interview, Washington/USA Today, 11-6:(A)12.

2

Bettino Craxi
Prime Minister of Italy

I wouldn't do anything to bring Communism to one country in the world. But not everything is a matter of Communism versus anti-Communism. The Palestinians are not Communists; the coalitionists in Chile are not Communists. I think if you see it only in those terms, you run the risk of having a McCarthyite foreign policy.

Interview, Rome, Oct. 2/
The Washington Post, 10-17:(A)2.

3

Arnaud de Borchgrave
Author; Former editor,
"Newsweek" magazine

What was rejected by my editors as utter nonsense in 1978 has just been published by two people in a book called *Terrorism: The Soviet Connection.* Alexander Haig, when he first became [U.S.] Secretary of State, went public with the accusation that much of the terrorism today is aided, abetted and funded by the Soviets and their countries. He was laughed out of court by the mass media, which dismissed it as Cold War rhetoric. When [current U.S. Secretary of State] George Shultz repeated this recently, he was not laughed out of court. The evidence is now overwhelming and irrefutable. It's amazing that it takes years for these perceptions to penetrate in America when they have been penetrating in Europe for years.

Interview/USA Today, 1-16:(A)7.

4

Suppiah Dhanabalan
Foreign Minister of Singapore

I do not belong to the ranks of pessimists who claim that the days of the United Nations are numbered. I do believe, however, that the United Nations today is in some peril. There is clear danger that this organization may become irrelevant to issues of peace and security, the primary issues for which it was founded. To prevent this from happening, let each member of the United Nations ask itself this question: Who gains if the United Nations fails?

At United Nations, New York,
Sept. 23/The New York Times, 9-24:7.

5

Elizabeth Hanford Dole
Secretary of Transportation
of the United States

[On the increase in international terrorism, including recent violence against passenger airliners]: This is a time for concerted effort and courage throughout the world. We must act with all the strength and unity we can draw together. We must send international terrorists and their sponsors a clear message that we will never ap-

6

(ELIZABETH HANFORD DOLE)

pease them. We must, in short, prevail, or else our children will inherit a world of infernal barbarism.

At meeting of International Civil Aviation Organization, Montreal, June 27/Los Angeles Times, 6-28:(I)13.

John F. Donnelly
Director, Counterintelligence and Investigation Programs, Department of Defense of the United States

1

[On Soviet recruitment of Americans for spying purposes]: The Russians trust an American dealing with them for money much more than they trust an American dealing with them for ideological reasons. They are convinced, and they teach in their intelligence schools, that Americans are by nature avaricious. Even if somebody does give them something for ideological reaons, or because of disgruntlement, they will attempt to pay him the second or third time they deal with him. They just feel more comfortable if they have a guy on the payroll.

Los Angeles Times, 6-7:(I)14.

Roland Dumas
Foreign Minister of France

2

We are faced with a new form of terrorism, which seems to be directed specifically against the countries of the Atlantic Alliance. Until now, this sort of terrorism seemed to be present primarily in West Germany, but now it is sprouting here and there. There seem to be common sources of supply for different terrorist groups, an underground trade in terrorism that targets us all. And when terrorist groups pick out victims in common, putting them in the same boat, it is time for the victims to get together to consider the fate that is being planned for them.

Interview, Washington, Feb. 3/ The Washington Post, 2-4:(A)16.

Lawrence S. Eagleburger
Former Under Secretary of State of the United States

3

[On terrorist attacks on U.S. targets]: First, I am totally convinced that our failure to strike back will encourage more and more attacks on us. Second, the U.S. owes its citizens—here or in any other part of the world—protection to the degree it can give it. Retaliation would make it clear to everybody that Americans traveling abroad are nobody's free targets. Third, we have an obligation to punish murder of American citizens in places where courts of law cannot reach. My conviction is that we will save a lot more lives in the long run by being tough and steady.

Interview/U.S. News & World Report, 7-1:22.

James Eberle
Director, Royal Institute of International Affairs (London)

4

It is always comforting to have friends who are rich, powerful and generous, and the Americans are certainly all three. But when your friends become too rich and too powerful, they can be very difficult to live with and to like—especially when their need to feel appreciated requires constant reinforcement.

U.S. News & World Report, 7-15:30.

Anders Ferm
Swedish Ambassador/Permanent Representative to the United Nations

5

There was a time in the '50s when the UN was seen as dancing to the American tune [and] a time when, in the '70s, it leaned toward the left. But to say, as some do, that it is basically anti-West and pro-Soviet is preposterous and not borne out by the facts.

Interview, United Nations, New York/ The Christian Science Monitor, 10-17:19.

J. William Fulbright
Former United States Senator, D-Arkansas

6

[Calling for better relations between the U.S. and the Soviet Union]: This is not to suggest that

(J. WILLIAM FULBRIGHT)

we should give moral sanction to the totalitarian aspect of the Soviet system. That, I should think, would be quite impossible for people with our tradition of democracy and individual liberty. But I do think it is possible for us to think about the Russians as human beings like ourselves. We do not have to admire the Soviet system to allow of the possibility that the Soviet leaders, like our own, genuinely fear for their nation's security. Nor, it seems to me, is it wholly unreasonable to believe that the Russian people and government share the usual aspirations of other peoples for the good life, for good food and shelter, for all the amenities that make life interesting and fulfilling and that ensure a hopeful future for their children.

Upon receiving honorary degree from Georgetown University, November/
Los Angeles Herald Examiner, 12-1:(F)1.

Evan G. Galbraith
United States Ambassador to France

1

[Criticizing State Department Foreign Service professionals]: It's like the line about war being too important to leave up to the generals. Well, the Foreign Service officer is like a military person. To move up, he has to avoid trouble. He learns in time to have a horror of confrontation. The result is that the dominant operations are make-work "cover" operations that are not only useless but mislead people. It's just waves sloshing about without anybody really wanting to do something. There's something about the Foreign Service that takes the guts out of people. The tendency is to avoid confronting an issue.

Interview, Paris/
The New York Times,
2-13:12.

2

The traditional role of diplomacy . . . has changed vastly since the days of Benjamin Franklin, when he [as Ambassador to France in 1776] was off on his own, isolated for a long period of time . . . The best thing we can do as an

Ambassador is to engage yourself out in the open world and become an active advocate of your President's views and an active defender of them . . . I think it's important, especially in an allied country, to have somebody clearly identified with the President who can speak on his behalf with his heart in it. I don't care how adroit one is as an advocate; when you are taking someone else's case and arguing it [such as career diplomats do], you don't do it as convincingly as your own case. I think the President deserves to have somebody who can argue his case convincingly and with conviction.

Interview, Paris/
Los Angeles Times, 7-15:(I)10.

Rajiv Gandhi
Prime Minister of India

3

[On the UN]: We are conscious of the imperfections of the organization. [But] withdrawal into isolation will make for a more dangerous world where untrammeled acts by individual nations can threaten the peace. The UN and its specialized agencies have come to embody hope, change and man's concern for his fellow man. It has come to symbolize the inevitability of coexistence and interdependence for the solution of the problems that beset us all.

To countries supporting non-alignment, United Nations,
New York, Oct. 22/
The New York Times, 10-23:6.

John W. Gardner
Founder, Common Cause

4

I think the international conflict is a very grave problem, in a way rougher than the domestic problem because the final hazard there is an end to everything. I don't like us to be bellicose or belligerent. I think President Reagan started out that way, but he has toned that down. He's talking more now about trying to reach agreements. American people want a strong national defense. But they don't want bellicosity. They want talks, the effort to reach an agreement.

Interview, Washington/
The New York Times, 7-4:26.

Richard A. Gephardt
United States Representative,
D-Missouri

1

[On international terrorism]: Anybody who thinks terrorists aren't cunning or ruthless enough to pull off a nuclear attack has forgotten the Munich Olympics, the showdown at Entebbe and the shooting of the Pope. And anybody who thinks an outlaw country won't help terrorists "go nuclear" hasn't been to Teheran or Tripoli.

At Conference on International Terrorism,
July/The Washington Post, 8-27:(A)5.

John Glenn
United States Senator, D-Ohio

2

International publicity is the mother's milk of terrorism.

U.S. News & World Report, 7-8:14.

Henry B. Gonzalez
United States Representative, D-Texas

3

The flow of immigration [to the U.S.]—legal or illegal—is a sure index of desperation. Just as the Irish potato famine set off a wave of immigration, just as the Vietnam debacle threw the boat people to the sea, we have today a wave of immigrants fleeing from misery and desperation. The people we know as illegal immigrants do not want to become lawbreakers, but neither will they let mere laws stand between them and what may be their only chance to survive or attain some semblance of human dignity. Immigration reform is needed, but that will not stop illegal entry or even discourage it very much. The only way to solve the problem is to start alleviating the misery that creates it. Only when people see hope at home can they afford to stop looking for a chance somewhere else, like the United States.

News conference, Washington,
Aug. 1/The Washington Post, 8-7:(A)18.

Mikhail S. Gorbachev
General Secretary, Communist Party
of the Soviet Union

4

The Soviet Union has always supported the struggle of peoples for liberation from colonial oppression. And today our sympathies go out to the countries of Asia, Africa and Latin America which are following the road of consolidating independence and social renovation. For us they are friends and partners in the struggle for a durable peace, for better and just relations between peoples. As to relations with capitalist states, I would like to say the following: We will firmly follow the Leninist course of peace and peaceful coexistence. To good will the Soviet Union will always respond with good will, as it will respond with trust to trust. But everyone should know that we shall never waive the interests of our motherland and those of its allies.

Upon his assuming leadership,
before Soviet Communist Party Central Committee,
Moscow, March 11/The New York Times, 3-12:6.

5

The Soviet Union has never threatened anyone. But no one will ever be able to dictate his will to us. Socialism, as Lenin taught, will prove its advantages, but it will prove them not by force of arms but by force of example in all fields of society's life—economic, political and moral.

Eulogy for late Soviet leader Konstantin Chernenko,
Moscow, March 13/The New York Times, 3-14:6.

6

Confrontation is not an inborn defect of [U.S.-Soviet] relations. It is rather an anomaly. There is no inevitability at all of its continuation. We regard the improvement of Soviet-American relations not only as an extremely necessary but also as a possible matter.

Interview/The New York Times, 4-8:4.

7

The defeat in World War II of such a shark as was German imperialism, the defeat of militaristic Japan, the weakening of the once-powerful British and French competitors put American imperialism in the position of the leader of the capitalist world by all major indices—economic, financial and military. What seemed to promote the claims of the ruling class of the United States to world hegemony was also the fact that it actually found itself to be the only big country that had waxed fabulously rich on the war. Imperial-

WHAT THEY SAID IN 1985

(MIKHAIL S. GORBACHEV)

ist reaction, which found the social and international-political results of the war unsuitable to its interests, tried already during the early post-war years to take a kind of historical revenge and to press back the positions of socialism and other democratic forces. This strategy was spearheaded against the Soviet Union while the economic strength and the temporary monopoly of the United States in atomic weapons were used as levers. Atomic weapons were regarded by the ruling quarters of the United States as a means of military and political pressure on us and other countries of socialism, a means of intimidating all peoples.

Address celebrating World War II Victory Day, Moscow, May 8/The New York Times, 5-9:9.

1

The present-day world is complicated and unquiet, and there is no task more important today than . . . checking the slide into a nuclear abyss. Regardless of how acute and complex the problems of present-day world politics are, they can and must be resolved only by way of talks, a patient and constructive dialogue. It is this that our Party and our Soviet state are following and will continue to follow.

At reception after celebration of World War II Victory Day, Moscow, May 9/Los Angeles Times, 5-10:(I)12.

2

[On U.S.-Soviet relations]: We must not allow things to go so far as confrontation between our two countries. Surely God on high has not refused to give us enough wisdom to find ways to bring us an improvement in our relations, an improvement in relations between the two great nations on earth, nations on whom depends the very destiny of civilization . . . [But] all our attempts to somehow escape this present bad situation in Soviet-American relations, attempts to somehow lead matters toward ending the arms race—all these attempts come up against a negative position of the U.S. Administration. We keep hearing one and the same answer: "No, no, no. It's propaganda, propaganda, propaganda."

Interview, Moscow, Aug. 26/The New York Times, 8-27:3.

3

[On U.S.-Soviet relations]: The truth should be faced squarely. Despite the negotiations that have begun in Geneva and the agreement to hold a summit meeting, relations between our two countries are continuing to deteriorate, the arms race is intensifying; and the threat of war is not subsiding. What is the matter? Why is all this happening? My colleagues and I are quite exacting and self-critical when it comes to our own activities not only in this country but also outside of it, and we are asking ourselves again and again if [the decline in relations] is somehow connected with *our* actions. But what is there that we can reproach ourselves with in this context? In this critical situation, Moscow is trying to practice restraint in its pronouncements about the U.S.; it is not resorting to anti-American campaigns, nor is it fomenting hatred for your country. . . . I will not hide from you my disappointment and concern about what is happening now. We cannot be troubled by the approach that, as I see it, has begun to emerge in Washington. That is a scenario of pressure, of attempts to drive us into a corner, to ascribe to us, as so many times in the past, every mortal sin—from unleashing an arms race to "aggression" in the Middle East, from violations of human rights to some scheming or other, even in South Africa. This is not a state policy [for the U.S.], it is a feverish search for "forces of evil."

Interview, Washington/Time, 9-9:23.

4

We want to have good relations not only with Western Europe but also with the United States. Just as for that matter also with China, Japan and other countries. We are not pursuing a Metternich-like policy of "balance of forces," of setting one state against another, knocking together blocs and counterblocs creating "axes" and "triangles," but a policy of global detente, of strengthening world security and developing universal international cooperation.

To members of French National Assembly, Paris, Oct. 3/The New York Times, 10-4:7.

5

What moral right does the United States have [to lecture the Soviet Union on human rights]?

(MIKHAIL S. GORBACHEV)

There is lots wrong in the United States in this area. If the United States is so concerned . . . what about [apartheid in] South Africa and the [U.S.] attitude of "constructive engagement"? Thousands of black people have been killed. You do not mention [human-rights abuse in] Chile, so that apparently causes you no concern. This is a very interesting approach.

To visiting U.S. Senators, Moscow,
September/Newsweek, 11-25:37.

Albert Gore, Jr.
United States Representative, D-Tennessee;
Member, House Permanent Select
Committee on Intelligence

1

The CIA is a lot better and more capable than I believed when I went on the Committee. It's a new era. Those excesses of the past are extremely rare—the so-called "rogue elephant" syndrome.

Interview/The Washington Post, 1-2:(A)1.

Philip Habib
American diplomat

2

Our efforts and ability to bring about negotiations and peaceful solutions in critical situations set the United States apart in the world today. There is no other nation that can play this role as effectively.

At Washington University commencement/
U.S. News & World Report, 6-3:66.

Alexander M. Haig, Jr.
Former Secretary of State
of the United States

3

. . . inaction in the face of terrorist assaults is a far greater risk in the long run because it convinces assorted hit-men and fanatics and the calculating governments who help them that we are too confused or too fearful to resist. The gap between our resounding rhetoric and our demonstrated resolve may be the most dangerous imbalance of all.

Before Senate Foreign Relations Committee,
Washington, Feb. 7/The Washington Post, 2-8:(A)12.

4

As John Stuart Mill wrote: "Intervention to enforce non-intervention is always rightful, always moral, if not always prudent." Democratic values, not to speak of American security, can hardly survive in a world where the enemies of democracy feel free to intervene forcibly, but the friends of democracy are inhibited as a matter of principle from coming to their assistance.

Before Senate Foreign Relations Committee,
Washington, Feb. 8/The Washington Post, 2-12:(A)20.

Nizar Hamdoon
Minister,
Iraqi Interests Section, Washington

5

[On the imminent restoration of U.S.-Iraqi diplomatic relations, the resultant change to a full Iraqi Embassy in Washington and his elevation to Ambassador]: When you go to a Congressman and tell him you are head of an "interests section," you end up spending more time on a discussion of this matter of why we don't have normal relations than the subject you go to talk about. I have made some good contacts, but being an Ambassador will mean I can have a better dialogue and I will be able to arrange some Congressional visits to Iraq.

Interview, Washington/
The New York Times,
2-6:10.

Lee Hamilton
United States Representative,
D-Indiana

6

[Saying Congress' role in foreign affairs has increased]: Ambassadors today have become lobbyists; that's one of their roles. I have so many requests from ambassadors asking to come in and talk, that I can't meet them all . . . When I first came to Washington, a head of government would visit the President, the Secretary of State, the World Bank, and go home. Today, it's rare for a head of state to come to Washington without meeting members of Congress.

The New York Times, 5-29:10.

Norishige Hasegawa
Chairman,
United States-Japan Economic Council

1

There's nothing wrong at all in what the United States believes in and aims for in dealing with world affairs. But . . . Washington tends to impose unilaterally what Americans think right on other allies without giving due heed to their views.

U.S. News & World Report, 7-15:30.

William Haytor
Former British Ambassador
to the Soviet Union

2

[On negotiating with the Soviets]: The Russians are not to be persuaded by eloquence or convinced by reasoned arguments. They rely on . . . the calculation of forces. So no case, however skillfully deployed, however clearly demonstrated as irrefutable, will move them from doing what they have previously decided to do. The only way of changing their purpose is to demonstrate that they have no advantageous alternative, that what they want to do is not possible.

Los Angeles Times, 11-14:(I)29.

Richard M. Helms
Former Director of Central
Intelligence of the United States

3

[On international terrorism]: It is very important to keep these incidents in perspective and not get so incredibly worked up over them. Terrorism, of course, is a serious challenge, and we must do our best to deal with it. But to declare a "war on terrorism" is just to hype the problem, not solve it. The quiet, steady approach is better than bombast.

Interview/Time, 7-8:20.

4

[On revelations of Israeli spying in the U.S.]: We use all kinds of human agents in countries all over the world. The only sin is getting caught, and that friends spy on the United States surprises me not at all.

The Washington Post, 12-7:(4)12.

Stanley Hoffmann
Professor of international relations,
Harvard University)

5

Much of the ambivalence toward the U.S. stems from the contradiction between official U.S. ideology—the Declaration of Independence and the Bill of Rights—and American actions at home and around the world. Many see what the U.S. is doing and conclude it does not practice what it preaches.

U.S. News & World Report, 7-15:27.

Robert Hunter
Director of European Studies,
Center for Strategic and International
Studies, Georgetown University

6

Planning has indeed long been the *bete noir* of U.S. foreign policy—always recognized as valuable, always attempted, never particularly successful beyond the enunciation of general goals in documents like national-security decision directives.

The Christian Science Monitor, 1-31:12.

Henry J. Hyde
United States Representative,
R-Illinois

7

[On U.S. attitudes after recent terrorist attacks on Americans in various parts of the world]: A sense of national pride has been affronted. [There is a trend of] being less citizens of the world and more Americans. Our futile efforts to be loved globally perhaps are being supplanted by the realization that being respected [is more important].

The Christian Science Monitor, 7-15:3.

Brian Jenkins
Director,
research program on subnational conflict
and political violence, Rand Corporation

8

An act of terrorism is first of all a crime in the classic sense—murder, kidnapping. In many

(BRIAN JENKINS)

cases it would also be a violation of the rules of war, which prohibit the taking of hostages or violence against non-combatants. Second, it is carried out by a member of an organized group with political objectives. The real hallmark of terrorism is that it is intended to produce psychological effects beyond the immediate physical effects of the damage itself. Terrorism is intended to terrorize. It's aimed at the people watching.

Interview/USA Today, 3-13:(A)9.

1

[On international terrorism]: Terrorism functions as an avenue of political expression for extremists, whether they are motivated by ideology, ethnicity or religion. Increasingly, it is also becoming an instrument of state policy among certain governments. Indeed, one of the trends we see that makes it so difficult to deal with terrorism is the increasing participation of governments in adopting terrorist tactics, employing terrorist groups or exploiting terrorist incidents as surrogate warfare . . . If we do respond to state-sponsored terrorism with military force, we ought not to have any illusions about what we will achieve. We are not going to end terrorism, and indeed there may be more retaliatory actions against us. We also must recognize that although we may make moral distinctions between dropping bombs on a city from 20,000 feet and car bombs driven into embassies by suicidal terrorists, the world may not share that fine distinction. We can talk about containing terrorism, we can talk about trying to deal with incidents that do occur, but none of that implies that there is a final solution. Combatting terrorism is going to be an enduring task.

Interview/U.S. News & World Report, 7-1:31.

2

[On international terrorism]: The problem is that terrorists can attack anything, anywhere, anytime. The government cannot protect everything, everywhere, all the time. We protect airlines, they seize ships. We protect government officials, they seize tourists. We can do a lot, but we can't alter that fundamental equation.

The Christian Science Monitor, 10-15:7.

3

Terrorism will persist as a mode of political expression and surrogate warfare. In this country, we are inclined toward rhetoric that implies an ultimate victory. We're out to defeat terrorism. But if terrorism is a chronic condition, you can't do that. You try to contain it, but, like poverty, crime and other longstanding afflictions of mankind, you have to learn to live with it. And that's bad news.

Interview/U.S. News & World Report, 10-21:27.

4

Paul Johnson
British journalist and author

America is the richest, the most powerful country in the world. People in the West know in their hearts they're very dependent on America and are, in their rational moods, grateful. But if you're dependent on someone, you tend to resent them. So when America gets into a bit of difficulty, as over the [recent] hostage crisis in Lebanon, there's a certain quiet glee . . . The worst thing is to go around asking to be loved. That invites contempt. The best thing Americans can do is do what they believe right, do it firmly and above all do it quietly without a lot of shouting and arguing. The hate element doesn't come to the surface when America is acting strongly. It comes up when America appears to be weak and indecisive.

Interview/U.S. News & World Report, 7-15:33.

5

Max M. Kampelman
*Chief United States negotiator
at U.S.-Soviet arms-control talks*

If you want to negotiate with the Soviets, you have to be prepared to stay one day longer than they. If you are impatient to end it, you're at a disadvantage. They are not eager to end it. If you're impatient, the tendency is to say, "The hell with it, it's not important, let's give it to them." If they come to feel you might give, they will not. When they reach the point either where they must come to a decision or they are convinced you have come to your point, you can succeed. It's the easiest thing in the world at that point. But the pattern the West tends to follow,

(MAX M. KAMPELMAN)

which I think is disadvantageous, is to be reasonable. Not that we should ever be unreasonable. They are very serious people, capable, well-trained people. But if you give at the start, you are losing out. This is important: Don't look to show good-will by making a concession, because it is interpreted not as good-will but as a lack of will.

Interview, Washington/
The Washington Post, 1-23:(D)13.

1

We cannot wish [the Soviet Union] away. It is here and it is militarily powerful. We share the same globe. We must try to find a formula under which we can live together in dignity. We must engage in that pursuit of peace without illusion but with persistence, regardless of provocation.

Before Senate Foreign Relations Committee,
Washington, Feb. 26/The New York Times, 2-27:3.

2

[Advocating U.S. unity in foreign-policy matters]: I operate on the assumption that we have only one President at a time and, when he is President, he is my President and he is your President. I think it is essential that we do what we can to communicate to the world and, particularly, to the other negotiating partner, that he speaks for a united country.

Washington, March 25/
Los Angeles Times, 3-26:(I)5.

3

Stanley Karnow
Journalist

Thirty years ago, we [the U.S.] thought we could do anything. The concept of the American century—which Henry Luce promoted at the beginning of World War II—began to fall apart in Vietnam, but also we began to see that the Japanese can make better cars than we can, that the Swedes have a better health-care system, that the Arabs can cut off our oil. We realized that we're not a nation of John Waynes, that we can't dominate or influence everybody. I think that is a sign of maturity.

Interview/USA Today, 4-16:(4)9.

Jack Kemp
United States Representative,
R-New York

I don't see [Communists] under every bed. But, I think, as [the late Senator] Henry Jackson once said, they're like burglars in a hotel corridor, looking for open doors, and they're going to exploit doors that aren't locked. So we've got to make sure the doors are locked.

Los Angeles Times, 5-16:(I)15.

4

Donald Kerr
Director,
Los Alamos National Laboratory

Technology has advanced. But the issues are the same as in the late 1960s: missile defense and modernization of strategic forces. The level of understanding of Congress and the political leadership is no greater than it was 20 years ago. What is missing is a view of the role the U.S. should play on the world stage, how our economic, political, military life, which support our national posture, are to be woven together. We act as though military planning, arms control, trade were each an end in itself. We don't deal with the fundamental issues that cause us to deploy these arms, which require an integrated view. We address technology problems, like cruise missiles. But we don't ask why they are there at all. That's frustrating . . . What I've learned is that the issues which are really at the core of this confrontation aren't amenable to technical fixes. Science provides new opportunities, but it doesn't get to the heart of the political and social issues.

Interview, Los Alamos, N.M./
The New York Times, 10-1:27.

5

Jeane J. Kirkpatrick
United States Ambassador/Permanent
Representative to the United Nations

[On her image as a "hawk"]: Nobody ever quotes anything I've ever written or said when they try to paint me as an advocate of the use of force. And the reason is I've never written or said any such thing. I suppose it is my consistent

6

(JEANE J. KIRKPATRICK)

perception of Communist regimes as a serious problem that is the foundation of the charges. And because I talk about strength; I think it's very important that we maintain economic and military strength adequate to our own defense and that of our closest allies. But I really believe in the use of force only as a very last resort. I am not reluctant to use American power in its other aspects: economic, political, diplomatic. But force must only be used in extreme cases. If you happen to be the mother of three "war age" sons, then you think a lot about it. I do believe that having sons affects the way one thinks about war, or concretizes it.

Interview/Newsweek, 1-14:32.

1

[On her decision to leave the UN and return to teaching]: In private life—perhaps even more than in public life—I can speak out clearly on behalf of such shared foreign-policy objectives as restoring and preserving American strength, supporting democracy and independence in the Hemisphere, defending our friends, our principles and our interests in the Middle East and elsewhere . . . It has been an extraordinary honor to speak for freedom in that world forum. I believe that both the United States and the United Nations are stronger today and I am proud of my contribution to that end.

To reporters, Washington, Jan. 30/
The New York Times, 1-31:4.

2

I believe very deeply that the most important, most critical issues of our time are foreign policy and defense issues. I believe that our answers to foreign policy and defense problems will determine our security and that of our friends in Western Europe, Israel and elsewhere. That sounds melodramatic, but I think we live in one of those periods when the questions are ultimate and the risks are terrible . . . To an unusual extent, the world is balanced on a razor's edge. On one side, whole continents can fall to tyranny, and on the other side is national independence, self-determination and democracy. I think the policies of the next five years can to a very important extent determine whether whole continents fall apart and how safe or unsafe we, the democracies, become. So many countries could go either way.

Interview, New York/
Los Angeles Times, 3-31:(VII)1.

3

Jeane J. Kirkpatrick
Former United States Ambassador/Permanent Representative to the United Nations

The Soviet assault on liberal democratic legitimacy involves a demonstration of the failure of Western democracies to meet their own standards [accompanied by] assertions of Soviet loyalty to basic Western values. Our flaws are exaggerated; theirs are simply denied.

At seminar sponsored by Shavano Institute for National Leadership and the U.S. State Department, Washington/Time, 5-13:27.

4

Some people like to suggest that because there is so much difference among us all, there is, in fact, no kind of value system that anyone can agree on. That is, for example, [if] we cannot agree about who is a terrorist and who is a freedom fighter and who is an aggressor and who is a liberator, then maybe pure relativism is the only answer. What one sees often in the United Nations is not pure relativism, but relativism becoming cynicism, and cynicism becoming nihilism, and a kind of sickly pall settles over all of the discussion, really rendering the most eloquent kind of talk meaningless. We know a lot more than we think we do about what is right and wrong.

At Loyola College commencement,
Baltimore/USA Today, 6-3:(A)11.

5

As long as countries would rather fight than talk and there is no inclination to compromise their differences, then no organization [such as the UN] can resolve these problems. A mediator has to be above the conflict, and the conflict-resolution machinery at the United Nations is not above politics; it is part of world politics. And it is not realistic to believe that any reform of the UN structure is possible to make it an ef-

(JEANE J. KIRKPATRICK)

fective instrument of conflict resolution. There is a terrible disjunction in the United Nations between responsibility and power. This is what is at the root of the problems in the UN administration and budget, which are very serious, in my opinion.

Interview/Newsweek, 10-28:52.

Henry A. Kissinger
Former Secretary of State of the United States

1

What we absolutely need is some kind of consensus of what is a vital interest. If an interest is vital, we have to be able and willing to defend it. We have to be willing to face the fact that the challenge is almost certain to be ambiguous; if you could prove that the danger to us is over-whelming, everybody would agree; but by the time the danger is overwhelming in the modern period, it is too late to do something about it.

Interview/Los Angeles Times, 4-28:(IV)2.

2

How to combine peace and justice and how to relate the absence of war to the survival of freedom: This is the overwhelming problem of our period. Our national-security requirements cannot be traded off as part of a domestic deal between various constituencies. The world in which you will be in the position to make decisions will be affected by the ability of this generation to prevent both war and the erosion of freedom. These issues are capable of resolution by American action. There's no other nation in the world that can make this claim.

At University of South Carolina commencement, Spartanburg/USA Today, 6-3:(A)11.

3

We hear very often, with the advent of the new Soviet General Secretary, calls for a meeting between our President and the General Secretary of the Soviet Union. This reflects a profound American temptation to believe that foreign policy is a subdivision of psychiatry and

that relations among nations are like relations among people. But the problem is not so simple. Tensions that have persisted for 40 years must have some objective causes, and unless we can remove those causes, no personal relationship can possibly deal with it. We are doing neither ourselves or the Soviets a favor by reducing the issues to a contest of personalities.

At University of South Carolina commencement, Spartanburg/Time, 6-17:68.

4

It is, of course, true when you confront the Soviet Union, or when you even consider confronting the Soviet Union, you have to recognize that the nuclear threat increases. And, in fact, you cannot act as if you exclude the nuclear threat or, paradoxically, you encourage it. Diplomacy in the modern age is conducted against the backdrop of nuclear weapons. Even day-to-day-diplomacy.

Interview/Los Angeles Times, 8-11:(IV)6.

5

[Saying he does not want the U.S. government to negotiate for his release should he be captured by terrorists]: I feel so strongly about this that I have deposited a letter with every national-security adviser that if I should ever be captured, I want no negotiation, and if I should request a negotiation from captivity, they should consider that as a sign of duress.

Sept. 24/USA Today, 9-25:(A)6.

6

[On summit meetings, such as the forthcoming one between U.S. President Reagan and Soviet leader Mikhail Gorbachev]: The real success of a summit can only be that neither side wins. Because, in a world of sovereign states, you can't have any permanent victories short of military victory. There are no permanent victories in diplomacy without some kind of compromise of benefit to both sides.

The New York Times, 11-13:27.

Tommy T. B. Koh
Ambassador from Singapore
to the United States

1

Public esteem for the UN around the world is at an all-time low. It is perceived as an organization drowning in a sea of words and suffocating under an avalanche of paper. The General Assembly is seen less and less as a forum expressing the decent opinion of mankind and more and more as a forum whose pronouncements are partisan, intemperate and unhelpful . . . The primary burden for revitalizing the United Nations lies with the developing countries. If they could act impartially between the superpowers and exercise their majoritarian power with wisdom, they would make a significant contribution. The West should play a more active role, with an agenda which it is prepared to negotiate. The Soviet bloc must stop using the United Nations for propaganda purposes and to exploit the weaknesses of the West.

Interview/Newsweek, 10-28:52.

Natarajan Krishnan
Indian Ambassador/Permanent
Representative to the United Nations

2

At the UN everybody wins a few, loses a few, settles for half a loaf. No one, not the U.S., not the U.S.S.R., not Japan, not China, not India can get away with playing the Big Bully or the Lone Ranger.

Interview, United Nations, New York/
The Christian Science Monitor, 10-17:19.

Irving Kristol
Co-editor, "Public Interest" magazine

3

[Saying U.S. foreign policy is not forceful enough]: We [conservatives] feel the State Department and its legalistic view of the world still dominates foreign policy. They're always thinking in terms of world opinion, how our allies will react, how the UN will react, what our obligations are under various treaties. They don't act in a vigorous way, which one anticipated [President] Ronald Reagan would do.

Interview/The New York Times, 7-12:10.

We are not going to achieve any stability in this world or reach any level of satisfaction, or attainment, in American foreign policy until the Soviet Union has been pushed into an ideological reformation—that is to say, until the Soviet Union ceases being a political regime with an established religion called Marxist-Leninism imposed on the Soviet people. To achieve such a reformation is the goal of American foreign policy because this regime, this established religion, is legitimated at the moment only by its successes in foreign policy.

At conference sponsored by Committee
for the Free World, Washington/
The New York Times, 11-25:8.

Robert Kupperman
Senior adviser, Center for Strategic and
International Studies, Georgetown University

[On the current hijacking of an American airliner by Shiite Moslems and the holding hostage of the passengers in Beirut]: A simple-minded policy of retaliation [against the terrorists] would invite equally simple-minded counter-retaliation . . . The main goal is to get our people out of there. If we simply lash out, we'll likely find ourselves with very deep domestic problems. There are organizations that exist in the U.S.—for example, the pro-Khomeini Iranian groups. They are not only apparently willing to engage in terrorism overseas but against U.S. interests here as well. If we lash out blindly, the terror we see overseas will almost surely migrate to the U.S. . . . We know our society is vulnerable. To assume the dangers don't exist is nonsense. The issue is prudence in the face of a substantial chance that we'll end up in trouble. Our infrastructure—the electricity grid, natural-gas lines, communications, water—is extraordinarily vulnerable. We could have several key facilities hit and the Northeast [U.S.] would be without electricity for weeks. If we go berserk over a tragic but comparatively small incident such as the Beirut matter, what are we going to do if we get hit hard here?

Interview/
U.S. News & World Report,
7-1:22.

Spyros Kyprianou
President of Cyprus

[The UN] has already degenerated into a complaints bureau and an international registry for the mere recording of international political problems.

At United Nations, New York,
Oct.15/The New York Times, 10-16:11.

1

Richard D. Lamm
Governor of Colorado

Just like every house needs a door, every nation needs a border. *We should decide who comes here, not* [Cuban President] Fidel Castro or some smuggler from Mexico. I believe the U.S. does have room for additional people but that illegal immigration is cheating our own people. William Raspberry, the columnist, says this so well: "What about our own huddled masses?" I do not think the United States can take all the surplus population from Mexico and still do justice to its own unemployment.

Interview/USA Today, 10-23:(A)11.

2

Tom Lantos
United States Representative,
D-California

[Citing linkage between arms-control negotiations and the human-rights situation in the Soviet Union]: We did not come here to have phony euphoria or get the key to the Kremlin. This [human-rights] issue will not go away. The [negotiating] climate will be poisoned if their human-rights record is as bad as it is now. There's some feeling the Soviet Union is ready to move toward detente without a human face, and we don't think we have to buy improvement in the overall situation at the expense of human rights.

News conference, Moscow, Jan. 16/
Los Angeles Times, 1-17:(I)7.

3

Patrick J. Leahy
United States Senator, D-Vermont

[On Vitaly Yurchenko, a top Soviet KGB agent, who defected to the U.S. and then, to the

162

dismay of U.S. officials, decided to return to the U.S.S.R.]: You either have got a defector who was allowed to just walk away under circumstances that I still cannot accept, and cause a significant embarrassment to the United States; or you have a double agent who was planted on the United States—and then you have far more than a significant embarrassment—you have an out-and-out calamity. No matter what, something is wrong.

Washington, Nov. 5/
The New York Times, 11-6:1.

4

Michael Ledeen
Center for Strategic and International
Studies, Georgetown University

[On revelations of Israeli espionage in the U.S.]: If any ally hires Americans to betray their country, then that is wrong—and I don't care who the ally is. We give our allies tens of millions of dollars in information. If we find that any of them are spying on us, I suspect there is going to be a reaction which may bring restrictions on such information. That doesn't help them, and it doesn't help us.

Interview/U.S. News & World Report, 12-9:27.

5

[Saying the U.S. should work to overthrow the leader Muammar Qaddafi, who is alleged to be involved in international terrorism]: When you have a serious challenge—in this case, the phenomenon of state-sponsored terrorism—you must deal with the state sponsoring it. Qaddafi has made his desire to destroy the Western world quite explicit. He supports all kinds of terror to that end. It would be much easier to have a restrained attitude if he were the only one doing this and if the [recent] attacks at the airports in Rome and Vienna were isolated incidents. But they're part of a growing pattern of attacks against American and Western interests . . . If indeed the only alternatives in a place like Libya were Qaddafi or something worse, then the option I'm talking about would not exist. But Libya is in shambles internally, with Qaddafi surrounded by East German bodyguards. There must be a certain number of Libyans who would

6

operating against this country, and particularly against the military services. It's remarkable that we are as effective as we are, given the scale of the effort against us.

Interview/USA Today, 10-30:(A)9.

(MICHAEL LEDEEN)

rather have a civilized country in which wealth is spent for the citizenry rather than for murder.

Interview/
U.S. News & World Report, 1-20:79.

1

To a certain kind of intellectual, it seems legitimate to call for the overthrow of the governments of South Africa or the Philippines, whereas it is not legitimate to call for the overthrow of our enemies. Indeed, one must be careful that our means aren't as barbaric as those of our enemies. I am not talking about assassination, for example, or intervention by U.S. forces. But what we need to do is give our friends the means to fight their own battles.

Interview/U.S. News & World Report, 1-20:79.

John F. Lehman, Jr.
Secretary of the Navy of the United States

2

[On the plea bargain agreement in the trial of a retired U.S. Navy seaman who committed espionage for the Soviet Union]: We in the Navy are disappointed at the plea bargain . . . It continues a tradition in the Justice Department of treating espionage as just another white-collar crime; and we think that it should be in a very different category . . . Here's a guy at the age of consent who was out on an aircraft carrier with 5,500 other kids risking their lives, and he was prepared to compromise all of his shipmates, not to mention his whole country. Here he was turning over documents knowingly to the Soviet Union. One can have a human sympathy for his family situation and . . . his father leading him astray, but nevertheless a human being is responsible for his acts, and the acts were traitorous acts and ought to be treated differently than insider trading [in the stock market].

Interview, Washington, Oct. 29/
The Washington Post, 10-30:(A)6.

3

[On Soviet espionage against the U.S.]: I don't think we're hemorrhaging national secrets. We have a security system that essentially works. We just have a tremendous effort by the Soviet Union, and its other Warsaw Pact allies,

Jacques Leprette
Former French Ambassador to the United Nations

4

[The UN] has been a useful stock exchange of ideas and formulas. Diplomats from every part of the world, from every ideology, have come into contact here, have exchanged their points of view, have learned from others. I myself have witnessed how diplomats moved beyond their previous righteousness, looked at things through new angles after having talked to people from other countries.

Interview, United Nations, New York/
The Christian Science Monitor, 10-17:19.

Stephen Lewis
Canadian Ambassador/Permanent Representative to the United Nations

5

The sense that the place [the UN] works by rigid divisions of blocs of votes is not borne out. People conjure up bloc voting as if some specter. It is true that groups of countries often demonstrate a community of interest on given subjects. But from time to time, often enough to give the place value, the blocs split up.

The New York Times, 10-23:6.

Vladimir B. Lomeiko
Chief, press department,
Foreign Ministry of the Soviet Union

6

[On Western critics of human rights in the Soviet Union]: Those gentlemen in Western countries who are prepared in any convenient situation to hold forth on so-called human-rights violations in socialist countries are very often modern slave traders. They take part in big-capital networks of houses of prostitution where on their free time from the business of speaking out against socialist countries they go to amuse themselves on the weekend. They travel to debauch young girls of developing countries, and

(VLADIMIR B. LOMEIKO)

after that put on their fancy suits and make speeches and try to teach other countries to live by their standards. That is Phariseeism, hypocrisy and unparalleled demagoguery.

News conference, Moscow, July 19/The New York Times, 7-20:4.

Edward C. Luck
President, United Nations Association

[On bloc voting at the UN]: You can see a trend emerging in which blocs are beginning to crumble. As early as the late 1970s, you began to see fissures, which are now turning into gulfs. Countries are increasingly voting for national interest.

The New York Times, 10-23:6.

1

Richard G. Lugar
United States Senator, R-Indiana

[As a result of the Vietnam war,] the United States has been and continues to be uncertain about the use of force in the conduct of American foreign policy. [Before Vietnam,] some widely shared assumptions were held about the national interest and potential threats to it. Some consensus was apparent on appropriate remedies to our problems. One of the costs of Vietnam was the breakup of this consensus . . . In poll after poll, Americans express their concern about hostile governments which imperil our interests in Latin America and elsewhere. But in these same polls, Americans display an equal and overwhelming opposition to any course of action which might actually frustrate governments which are harmful to us. It is important to restore a greater degree of consensus about our interests and commitments around the world and about our willingness to defend them. Do we really have vital interests all around the globe? Do we have the economic and military capabilities and the political will to support these interests with a safe margin of risk? Do we have a long-term, substantial and correct view of the Soviet Union? Do we have an appropriate understanding of the economic, political and spiritual forces that move nations?

Before National Press Club, Washington, Jan. 23/The New York Times, 1-24:1.

2

Charles Malik
Former Foreign Minister of Lebanon; A signer of original United Nations Charter

We were euphoric 40 years ago [upon the founding of the UN]. Today we know that the United Nations can't prevent people from fighting each other, or hating each other, or intriguing against each other.

Interview, San Francisco, June/The New York Times, 9-23:10.

3

Reis Malile
Foreign Minister of Albania

It is hard to find any region in the world today which is not encountering the interference of one or the other superpower [the U.S. and the Soviet Union], or both. True, the superpowers have up to now avoided a direct conflict between them. This has come about not because they wish to spare the people, but because they fear the catastrophic consequences which such a conflict might bring, in the first place, to them.

At United Nations, New York, Sept. 20/The New York Times, 10-1:9.

4

Ferdinand E. Marcos
President of the Philippines

You Americans have the habit of preaching not only to the Philippines but to the world. You are the original evangelists and proselytizers. You are so taken up with your system that you very often forget the world is composed of nations that have problems different from those your Founding Fathers had when they adopted your Constitution and Bill of Rights. There are nations now facing crises which cannot be met with classic solutions of political freedom, independence, and this American obsession with political rights ahead of economic rights.

Interview, Manila, Nov. 16/USA Today, 11-18:(4)11.

5

Robert C. McFarlane
Assistant to the President of the United States for National Security Affairs

[On U.S. response to terrorist attacks on its people and interests]: If we do not use our forces where their use is clearly justified, we get neither the direct benefit nor the deterrent value of having such forces in the first place. We need that deterrent; we cannot proceed in such a way that terrorist groups or their sponsors feel they can make free, unopposed use of violence against us. That deterrent cannot really be made to work unless we demonstrate our will to meet a terrorist challenge with a measured dose of force, occasionally. We have never used force casually or indifferently. This places us at a very marked disadvantage, I think, in responding to those who declare themselves to be our adversaries.

Washington, March 25/
Los Angeles Times,
3-26:(I)22.

Francois Mitterrand
President of France

[On economic and political meetings of world leaders]: These summits never produce what they should, but they always produce more than what would have existed had they not occurred.

At economic conference with other world leaders,
Bonn, West Germany/Newsweek, 5-13:31.

Langhorne A. Motley
Former Assistant Secretary for Inter-American Affairs, Department of State of the United States

[On why he resigned his State Department post]: Running the Latin American bureau in the State Department is like being given 1,000 pounds of canaries and a box that will only hold 500 pounds. Right away, you begin banging on the sides of the box, trying to keep enough canaries in the air so that the box won't burst open. After a while, your arms get tired.

The New York Times, 5-10:14.

Daniel Moynihan
United States Senator, D-New York; Former United States Ambassador to the United Nations

The notion of [nations] being independent and democratic is the same, [but] that hasn't worked out, and in that context the working majority of the [UN] General Assembly and the blocking majority of the Security Council simply do not subscribe as governments to the principles which the [UN] Charter assumes to be shared. The clearest example you have is the Soviet Union has invaded Afghanistan, and neither a majority in the General Assembly or a working majority in the Security Council desires to do anything about that.

USA Today, 9-25:(A)5.

Paul H. Nitze
Special Adviser to the President of the United States for Arms-Control Negotiations

Can the Russians be trusted? I'm not going to get into that kind of a question, about whether the Russians can be *trusted*. It's important to get to know these people, and get to know them in various different contexts, not just the context of the negotiations. It helps to understand . . . You learn something about a person by the character of his wit, for instance . . . And one also learns something from their wives and their children.

Interview, Washington/
The Washington Post, 1-4:(D)1.

Richard M. Nixon
Former President of the United States

I have been relieved about what seems to be a change of view within the [Reagan] Administration on the wisdom of a full-blown [U.S.-Soviet] quickie summit [meeting]. I have always thought that a get-acquainted, atmospheric summit, with all the trappings, would be much more in the Soviets' interests than in ours. It would be a public-relations blockbuster, and the Europeans would say, "Thank God the Americans and the Russians are getting together." But if nothing came of it, there would be a lot of disillusionment, and it would be directed against us. That is one rea-

(RICHARD M. NIXON)

son why I favor annual summits. That way, you can keep the pressure on. Annual summits will inhibit the Soviet Union. Nations tend to behave better when they have big meetings coming up between their leaders. A summit must not labor and bring forth a mouse. Mickey Mouse things, like fishing rights and a new consulate in Kiev and commercial agreements, are fine. We had them at the first Moscow summit in 1972. They're the froth. But you've also got to have some good stout beer.

Interview/Time, 4-22:14.

1

[On new Soviet leader Mikhail Gorbachev]: It is a testament to Gorbachev's brilliance as a politician that he could preside over four years of failure in agriculture and still come out smelling like a rose. He has the confidence of the Soviet bureaucracy because they believe he is a true believer. He isn't going to change the system. He is going to try to make it work better. Does that mean we can't do business with him? Of course not. But it will be like doing business with the American robber barons of the 19th century. Gorbachev is not going to be a fastball pitcher. He'll throw curves, knuckleballs and spitters if he can get away with them. Of course, [U.S. President] Reagan has played a pitcher too, in that movie *The Winning Team*, and he's also a very shrewd political leader. So you've got two pretty good pitchers going against each other. The question is, which side can hit?

Interview/Time, 4-22:14.

2

I didn't really begin to realize the significance of the [atomic] bomb until I was a candidate for Congress and came to Washington in 1947. Even then, my sense of how the bomb changed the geopolitical balance of the world grew rather gradually . . . Suddenly the U.S. was the most powerful nation in the world. From that time forward, whether we wanted to or not, we would have to play a major role on the world's stage. And I would say that we did *not* want to play that role. World power is something very much opposed to the ingrained American attitude. Basically, Americans are idealists. We go into war for pragmatic reasons, but we have to be appealed to on idealistic terms. We are very impatient about being in a world where balance of power may make a difference, where one must sometimes recognize that you win without getting total victory. The fact that the bomb made us a world power meant that we had to learn how to be one, and it has been very difficult.

Interview, New York/Time, 7-29:49.

Conor Cruise O'Brien
Irish diplomat; Former assistant to the Secretary General of the United Nations

3

[On the UN]: I think the idealism and the hopes founded on idealism were deceptive, and that . . . from the beginning, the superpowers were largely in an antagonistic relationship. And the body could not fulfill the hopes that were centered on it in 1945 except with superpower concensus, which has seldom prevailed . . . [But] it is a place and a set of techniques to which powers can resort when they find themselves getting into trouble, when people are on the brink of a confrontation which maybe both sides don't really want . . . The UN, in those conditions, provides first of all a place where people can let off steam. That's to say, where you make a strong verbal reaction which releases you from the necessity of doing very much.

*Interview, Hanover, N.H./
The Christian Science Monitor, 3-14:21.*

Thomas P. O'Neill, Jr.
*United States Representative,
D-Massachusets*

4

[On his meeting with new Soviet leader Mikhail Gorbachev]: He appeared to be the type of man who would be an excellent trial lawyer, an outstanding attorney in New York, had he lived there. There is no question that he is a master of words and a master in the art of politics and diplomacy. Was he hard? Was he tough? Yes, he is hard, he is tough . . . People can disagree in policy and disagree in philosophy and in the art of running governments, but they can still speak to each other; and if you can do that, you can get to the basis of all problems.

*News conference, Moscow,
April 10/The New York Times, 4-11:6.*

(THOMAS P. O'NEILL, JR.)

1

The strongest opponent to democratic values [the Soviet Union] is also our most formidable adversary in the world. What we have in common is not a habit of friendship, but an experience of competition. This competition is both philosophical and military. It is a competition that we dare not fall behind in and one that, without a doubt, we do not wish to resolve by a test of nuclear strength.

Washington, Nov. 13/
The Washington Post, 11-15:(A)26.

Claiborne Pell
United States Senator,
D-Rhode Island

2

I think the [U.S. Reagan] Administration has looked on the UN more as a nuisance center, a sounding board for those who don't like us, rather than as a center for the resolution of problems. This gradual drift away from a strong belief in the UN began during the Vietnam era and is not unique with this Administration. It has become a field for propaganda.

The New York Times, 9-17:1.

Javier Perez de Cuellar
Secretary General of the United Nations

3

Prior to the existence of the United Nations, the world community was nothing more than a concept. With the establishment of the world organization it has become a reality. A giant step has thus been taken in humanity's political evolution. But its full significance can be realized only when states no longer resort to the threat or use of force in their relations with one another, when a just and rational code of conduct compels their unswerving allegiance, when the human race is released from the fear of nuclear annihilation, and when large parts of the world are no longer consigned to the despair of poverty and ignorance. This is a gigantic vision, but what was a vision and a dream in former times has now become a necessity if ordered human society is to survive.

On 40th anniversary of signing of United Nations Charter/The Washington Post, 6-25:(A)14.

4

The system of collective security has malfunctioned because the five permanent members of the [UN] Security Council have . . . at different times stopped the UN Charter from being implemented through using their veto. Other UN member states have also refused to use UN mechanisms to settle their disputes. They all profess to love the UN and to be law-abiding countries, but when their interests are at stake they trample these noble principles and return to the law of the jungle where might means right.

The Christian Science Monitor, 10-17:18.

Richard Pipes
Professor of history, Harvard University;
Former Director, Soviet and East
European Affairs, National Security
Council of the United States

5

Our differences with the Soviet Union are very profound, to put it mildly. These are not family quarrels that can be resolved just by sitting down and "talking them out." But the sense that things could be better if only the two leaders meet personally is powerful among our people, and U.S. political leaders have to be responsive to that mood. The dangers should be obvious: The Chamberlain-Hitler summit at Munich led directly to World War II. The Kennedy-Khrushchev summit in Vienna led to the Cuban missile crisis. Summits arouse expectations on the part of the U.S. and Western European public and they allow the Soviet side to make all kinds of promises that we cannot reciprocate.

Interview/USA Today, 4-9:(A)10.

Timothy Raison
Overseas Aid Minister
of the United Kingdom

6

[On Britain's decision to withdraw from UNESCO]: There has been some reform [in the inefficiency and politicization], but the degree of reform is not sufficient. It is sad that an organization which began with such high hopes, and to which this country has contributed so much in the past, should have gone so wrong. But we

(TIMOTHY RAISON)

have to deal with what the organization has become. [The decision to leave] is in no way aimed at the United Nations system as a whole. But we are determined that our support for the UN should be seen as support for effective and efficient organizations. Unfortunately, UNESCO is not such a body.

Before House of Commons, London,
Dec. 5/The New York Times, 12-6:7.

Shridath Ramphal
Secretary General,
(British) Commonwealth of Nations

1

[On the Commonwealth today]: I think it has become more useful and more relevant as it has devolved from the British Commonwealth to the Commonwealth, because that meant a shift from an Anglo-centric Commonwealth to a more realistic community of countries. What has emerged is a grouping of [49] countries so diverse that their very variety is a source of strength. It is the fact that a group of different countries can work together in a habitual and broadly harmonious manner that makes it unique. There is almost no process of harmonization taking place at the international level. [But] in the Commonwealth we have a facility that allows a big sample of the international community a better chance of harmonizing views. It is true that the Commonwealth cannot negotiate for the world; but it can help the world to negotiate. That is our primary responsibility now. We [also] have special obligations and responsibilities regarding cooperation among Commonwealth countries.

Interview, London/
The Christian Science Monitor, 9-4:18.

Ronald Reagan
President of the United States

2

We cannot play innocents abroad in a world that is not innocent. Nor can we be passive when freedom is under siege. Without resources, diplomacy cannot succeed. Our security-assistance programs help friendly governments defend themselves, and give them confidence to work for peace. Congress should understand that, dollar for dollar, security assistance contributes as much to global security as our own defense budget.

State of the Union address, Washington,
Feb. 6/The New York Times, 2-7:13.

3

We must remember that the Soviet record of compliance with past agreements has been poor. The Soviet Union signed the Yalta accord pledging free elections, then proceeded to dominate Eastern Europe. They signed the Geneva convention banning use of chemical weapons, and the ABM treaty, but are now violating all three. And they signed the Helsinki accord, solemnly pledging respect for human rights, but then jailed the individuals trying to monitor it in the U.S.S.R.

At luncheon, Quebec City, Canada,
March 18/
The New York Times, 3-19:4.

4

[On the killing of a U.S. Army Major by a Soviet soldier in East Germany and whether it will affect a proposed summit meeting between Reagan and new Soviet leader Gorbachev]: This was a murder, a coldblooded murder, and it reflects on the difference between the two societies: one that has no regard for human life and one like our own that thinks it's the most important thing. And, yes, I want a meeting [with Gorbachev] even more so, to sit down and look someone in the eye and talk to him about what we could do to make sure nothing of this kind happens again.

Interview, Washington, April 1/
Los Angeles Times, 4-2:(I)1.

5

The United Nations is an important body and one that deserves our most serious attention. At the same time . . . it is generally recognized that the United Nations as it now functions does not fulfill many of the aspirations of its founders. [The question] is whether the United Nations can be made a more effective institution for

(RONALD REAGAN)

the solution of international conflicts, for the promotion of national independence, democracy and economic and social development—in short, whether the United Nations can renew its dedication to the ideals enshrined 40 years ago in its Charter. I share Secretary General Javier Perez de Cuellar's desire to make the United Nations a positive force in the maintenance of world peace.

Written report to Congress, Washington,
April 26/The Washington Post, 4-27:(A)7.

1

Understanding the true nature of totalitarianism will be worth as much to us as any weapons system in preserving peace. Realism is the beginning of wisdom, and where there is wisdom and courage, there will be safety and security.

Before German students, Hambach, West Germany,
May 6/The New York Times, 5-7:4.

2

[Criticizing the influence of Congress on the President's power over foreign affairs]: We've got to get where we can run a foreign policy without a committee of 535 telling us what to do.

To Republican Congressional leaders, Washington,
May 21/The Washington Post, 5-22:(A)22.

3

[Criticizing Communist nations for not contributing enough humanitarian aid to needy countries]: It seems with all their sloganeering, about the only things Communist countries produce in quantity are misery, weapons, and aggression. The record of humanitarian assistance provided by the Soviet bloc governments, even to their own allies, is a disgrace; and the world, especially the developing world, should know about it. Of course, Communist countries have trouble producing even enough food for their own populations.

Before Lions Club International, Dallas,
June 21/
The New York Times,
6-22:4.

. . . Iran, Libya, North Korea, Cuba, Nicaragua—continents away, tens of thousands of miles apart—but the same goals and objectives. I submit to you that the growth in terrorism in recent years results from the increasing involvement of these states in terrorism in every region of the world. This is terrorism that is part of a pattern—the work of a confederation of terrorist states. Most of the terrorists who are kidnapping and murdering American citizens and attacking American installations are being trained, financed and directly or indirectly controlled by a core group of radical and totalitarian governments, a new, international version of Murder Incorporated. And all of these states are united by one simple, criminal phenomenon: their fanatical hatred of the United States, our people, our way of life, our international stature. And the strategic purpose behind the terrorism sponsored by these outlaw states is clear: to disrupt or alter our foreign policy, to sow discord between ourselves and our allies, to frighten friendly Third World nations working with us for peaceful settlements of regional conflicts and, finally, to remove American influence from those areas of the world where we are working to bring stable and democratic government. In short, to cause us to retreat, retrench, to become "Fortress America." Yes, their real goal is to expel America from the world . . . The American people are not—I repeat, not—going to tolerate intimidation, terror and outright acts of war against this nation and its people. And we are especially not going to tolerate these attacks from outlaw states run by the strangest collection of misfits, Looney Tunes and squalid criminals since the advent of the Third Reich.

Before American Bar Association, Washington,
July 8/The New York Times,
7-9:8.

5

[On international terrorism]: This terrorism . . . is the most frustrating thing to deal with. You want to say "retaliate" [against the terrorists] when this is done, "get even." But then, what do you say when you find out that you're not quite sure that a retaliation would hit the people who were responsible for the terror and

WHAT THEY SAID IN 1985

(RONALD REAGAN)

you might be killing innocent people? So you swallow your gorge and you don't do it.

To high-school students, Chicago,
Oct. 10/Los Angeles Times, 10-12:(I)2.

1

[On the interception in mid-air and capture by U.S. warplanes of terrorists who recently hijacked an American cruise ship in the Mediterranean and killed an American passenger]: . . . I am proud to be the Commander-in-Chief of the soldiers, sailors, airmen and Marines who deployed, supported and played the crucial role in the delivery of these terrorists to Italian authorities. They, and the men and women of our foreign service and intelligence community, performed flawlessly in this most difficult and delicate operation. They have my gratitude and, I'm sure, the gratitude of all of their countrymen. These young Americans sent a message to terrorists everywhere. The message: You can run but you can't hide.

News conference, Washington, Oct. 11/
Los Angeles Times, 10-12:(I)2.

2

We have noted with great interest . . . expressions of peaceful intent by leaders of the Soviet Union. I am not here to challenge the good faith of what they say. But isn't it important for us to weigh the record, as well? In Afghanistan, there are 118,000 Soviet troops prosecuting war against the Afghan people. In Cambodia, 140,000 Soviet-backed Vietnamese soldiers wage a war of occupation. In Ethiopia, 1,700 Soviet advisers are involved in military planning and support operations along with 2,500 Cuban combat troops. In Angola, 1,200 Soviet military advisers [are] involved in planning and supervising combat operations, along with 35,000 Cuban troops. In Nicaragua, [there are] some 8,000 Soviet-bloc and Cuban personnel, including about 3,500 military and secret police personnel. All of these conflicts, some of them underway for a decade, originate in local disputes but they share a common characteristic: They are the consequences of an ideology imposed from without, dividing nations and creating regimes that are, almost from the day they take power, at war with their own people. And, in each case, Marxism-Leninism's war with the people becomes war with their neighbors.

At United Nations, New York,
Oct. 24/The New York Times,
10-25:9.

3

[On his forthcoming summit meeting with Soviet leader Mikhail Gorbachev]: I don't think this is just a get-acquainted meeting, important though that may be. I think there are many areas for agreement here. And, as I say, I am not pessimistic about them. I think we will sit and face each other and lay our cards on the table as to the fact that they don't like us or our system and we don't like theirs. And they better not try to change ours. But we have to live in the world together. And we are the only two countries that probably could start World War III. We are also the two countries that could prevent World War III from happening.

Interview, Washington, Nov. 12/
The Washington Post, 11-13:8.

4

[On his forthcoming summit meeting in Geneva with Soviet leader Mikhail Gorbachev]: The history of American-Soviet relations . . . does not auger well for euphoria. Eight of my predecessors—each in his own way in his own time—sought to achieve a more stable and peaceful relationship with the Soviet Union. None fully succeeded. So I don't underestimate the difficulty of the task ahead. But these sad chapters do not relieve me of the obligation to try to make this a safer, better world. For our children, our grandchildren, for all mankind—I intend to make the effort.

Broadcast address to the nation, Washington,
Nov. 14/The New York Times, 11-15:8.

5

The United States is not an aggressor nation. One can look back to the years following World War II, when we were the only major nation in

(RONALD REAGAN)

the world that had not had its industry pounded to rubble by bombings. Our military strength was at its very height, even though we had grievous losses in the war. And we had the ultimate weapon—a monopoly on that weapon. In all those years, we not only did not take advantage of that strength when we could have dictated to the world, but we tried to introduce measures that would place nuclear power in international hands so there wouldn't be any country with a monopoly on it. Contrast that with the Soviet Union's vast military buildup—which is basically offensive, not a defensive buildup. Contrast it with their aggression in Afghanistan, Ethiopia, South Yemen and here in our own hemisphere. If there's anyone that has a right to believe they're threatened, it is the West to believe it is threatened by the Soviet Union.

Interview/
U.S. News & World Report,
11-18:31.

Loret M. Ruppe
Director,
United States Peace Corps

1

Peace Corps volunteers are in a people-to-people program. They are helpers at the grass-roots level. They learn languages; they are willing to go to the remote areas. Right from the beginning, volunteers were accorded none of the special privileges and courtesies generally expected by diplomats or others working overseas . . . In January, I made an appeal for 10,000 Americans with agricultural skills—to inquire about Peace Corps service to volunteer to help [in Africa]. We were besieged with calls from all over the country. We asked for 10,000. I am proud to report that 20,000 responded. People are still willing to give two years of their lives—two years away from their homes, families and comforts of living in the most prosperous nation in the world—to prove that America is willing to give more than from its pocketbook.

To Hubert Humphrey North-South Fellows Program,
Minneapolis/
The Washington Post,
7-16:(A)14.

Sadruddin Aga Khan
Former United Nations
High Commissioner for Refugees

2

I feel strongly about the role that the middle powers can play at the United Nations; they are the raft on which the UN needs to be refloated. A consensus for action can be developed by using the middle powers, who don't have the same preoccupations and concerns as the superpowers. They can prevent the tearing apart of the UN. They can bridge the polarized elements and with imaginative thinking can strengthen the international organization. I would include countries from Asia with large populations, such as India, the Nordic nations, countries like Australia and New Zealand which have a strong geographical position, and socialist countries like Yugoslavia. These countries, some 20 or so, will not suddenly find common cause politically. But they have in common important international interests, and they all favor a strong United Nations.

Interview/Newsweek, 10-28:52.

Richard Schifter
Head of United States delegation
to international human-rights
conference in Ottawa, Canada

3

[Accusing the Soviet Union of human-rights violations against its own citizens in contravention of the Helsinki human-rights agreement it signed]: The government of the United States has made clear to the government of the Soviet Union our interest in improvement of our bilateral relations, our interest in concluding a genuine arms-control agreement. But . . . we believe that performance in the field of human rights is inextricably linked to all aspects of improved bilateral relations. If we failed to make that point clear at a meeting of this kind, we would be sending a false signal . . . Our people have a right to wonder whether a country that fails to keep its word in matters unrelated to considerations of its security will do so when its security is at stake.

At international human-rights conference,
Ottawa, Canada, May 15/
The New York Times, 5-16:7.

WHAT THEY SAID IN 1985

James R. Schlesinger
Former Secretary of Defense
of the United States

1

The United States has lost its pre-eminence. While it remains the leading nation on the international scene, its power, which earlier was scarcely disputable, is now very much disputable. Simultaneously—and not simply by coincidence—national unity has been fractured—both in terms of the national consensus and in terms of the agreement between the Executive and Legislative branches. In short, these changes imply that the costs and risks of sustaining our international position have risen.

Before Senate Foreign Relations Committee,
Washington, Feb. 6/
The New York Times, 2-7:6.

2

[On the domino theory]: I think that in the original form, it probably is outmoded. The original form suggested that there was something inevitable, that one domino would knock down the other dominoes. The domino theory is really a psychological theory. The effect of a fall of one government is likely to infect its neighbors. But in some cases the neighbors get more firm in resistance, so it depends upon the psychological reaction to the takeover of a country.

Broadcast interview/
"Meet the Press," NBC-TV, 4-28.

3

[On how to respond to international terrorism]: More important than any particular mechanism is for us to establish a pattern of behavior on which other nations will base their expectations. It is important for others to have a high level of expectation that the perpetrators of terrorist acts will be punished. The character of the punishment matters a hell of a lot less than the certainty that they will be punished. That means establishing a pattern over a period of years. It means avoiding sending conflicting signals. It means not issuing threats and then backing off. If you make a threat [to retaliate against terrorism] and then don't deliver, that raises morale and whets the appetite on the other side.

Interview/Time, 7-8:21.

Eduard A. Shevardnadze
Foreign Minister of the Soviet Union

4

It is our conviction that detente of the 1970s was not an accidental development which has since sunk into oblivion. This is valuable experience which strengthens the belief that constructive dialogue and mutually beneficial cooperation constitute a natural state of international relations which is in line with common interests.

To foreign ministers commemorating 10th anniversary
of signing of Helsinki human-rights accords, Helsinki,
Finland, July 30/Los Angeles Times, 7-31:(I)14.

Arkady N. Shevchenko
Former Soviet diplomat
(defected to the United States)

5

... the fundamental long-range aspiration of the U.S.S.R. is the idea of expanding Soviet power to the point of world domination. Whether through ideology, diplomacy, force or economics, Moscow believes that eventually it will be supreme—not necessarily in this century but certainly in the next.

Interview/Los Angeles Times, 3-10:(Book Review)1.

R. Sargent Shriver
Former Director,
United States Peace Corps

6

[On the Peace Corps]: The greatest advertisement of the United States is not a gigantic Coca-Cola sign up on the hills around Caracas [Venezuela]. The best advertisement of the United States is a free, erect, intelligent, dedicated human being ... who has come to give themselves in service for a minimum of two years.

At celebration of 25th anniversary of Peace Corps,
Ann Arbor, Mich., Oct. 7/USA Today, 10-8:(A)2.

George P. Shultz
Secretary of State
of the United States

7

[Soviet Foreign Minister Andrei Gromyko is] the living embodiment of the Soviet Union's

(GEORGE P. SHULTZ)

great advantages—continuity, patience, the ability to fashion a long-term strategy and to stick with it. The democracies, in contrast, have long had difficulty maintaining the same consistency, coherence, discipline and sense of strategy . . . Our ways of thinking have tended too often to focus either on increasing our strength or on pursuing negotiations, [rather than take] clearly the most sensible course [of doing both simultaneously].

Before Senate Foreign Relations Committee,
Washington, Jan. 31/The Washington Post, 2-1:(A)10.

1

A decade or so ago, when the United States was beset by economic difficulties, neglecting its defenses and hesitant about its role of leadership, the Soviets exploited these conditions. They had reason for confidence that what they called the "global correlation of forces" was shifting in their favor. Today, the West is more united than ever before. The United States is restoring its military strength and economic vigor and has regained its self-assurance. We have a President with a fresh mandate from the people for an active role of leadership. The Soviets, in contrast, face profound structural economic difficulties, a continuing succession problem and restless allies. Their diplomacy and their clients are on the defensive in many parts of the world. We have reason to be confident that the "correlation of forces" is shifting back in our favor.

Before Senate Foreign Relations Committee,
Washington, Jan. 31/
Los Angeles Times,
2-1:(I)1.

2

The Soviets can be counted upon periodically to do something somewhere that is abhorrent or inimical to our interests. The question is how the West can respond in a way that could help discipline Soviet international behavior but does not leave our own strategy vulnerable to periodic disruption by such external shocks. We must never let ourselves be so wedded to improving relations with the Soviets that we turn a blind eye

to actions that undermine the very foundation of stable relations.

Before Senate Foreign Relations
Committee, Washington, Jan. 31/
U.S. News & World Report, 2-18:44.

3

[On international terrorism]: We must summon all our resources, all our knowledge and all our will to find ways to protect ourselves, our installations and the people, both in government and in the private sector, who represent America abroad. When terrorist intimidation succeeds in changing our policies, when it forces businesses to close down overseas, we hand them a victory. This only opens the door to more terrorism. It shows that terrorism works, it emboldens those who resort to it and it encourages others to join their ranks . . . Experience has taught us over the years that one of the best deterrents to terrorism is the certainty that swift and sure measures will be taken against those who engage in it. Sanctions, when exercised in concert with other nations, can help to isolate, weaken or punish states that sponsor terrorism against us. Too often, countries are inhibited by fear of losing commercial opportunities or fear of provoking the bully. Some countries are clearly more vulnerable to extortion than others—but surely this is an argument for banding together in mutual support, not an argument for appeasement.

Before American Society for Industrial Security,
Arlington, Va., Feb. 4/
Los Angeles Times, 2-5:(I)8.

4

I believe very strongly that we in the democracies simply cannot put up with a [Soviet] "Brezhnev doctrine." As you know, the Brezhnev doctrine, in effect, states that once a country has been taken into the socialist camp, it never can leave. Or, to put it more colloquially, under the Brezhnev doctrine, what's mine is mine, what's yours is up for grabs. I don't see any reason why we should put up with that.

Before House Foreign Affairs Committee,
Washington, Feb. 19/
The New York Times,
2-20:6.

WHAT THEY SAID IN 1985

(GEORGE P. SHULTZ)

So long as Communist dictatorships feel free to aid and abet insurgencies in the name of socialist internationalism, why must the democracies, the target of this threat, be inhibited from defending their own interests and the cause of democracy itself?

San Francisco/Newsweek, 3-4:16.

1

[Americans] will always be reluctant to use force. It is the mark of our decency. [But] a great power cannot free itself so easily from the burden of choice. It must bear responsibility for the consequences of its inaction as well as for the consequences of its action.

Time, 4-15:45.

2

A principal Soviet aim throughout the post-war period has been to divide the [Western] alliance. Instead of pursuing arms negotiations seriously in the quest for an equal and stable strategic balance, the Soviets have often tried to develop and exploit differences among the allies, leaving us to negotiate among ourselves while they [the Soviets] sit back and wait for unilateral concessions that they need not reciprocate.

At East-West Center, University of Hawaii, July 17/The New York Times, 7-18:4.

3

The reality of the democratic revolution [around the world] is demonstrated by the rise of national-liberation movements against Communist colonialism. Unlike the old European empires that came to accept the post-war reality of self-determination and national independence, the new [Communist] colonialists are swimming against the tide of history. They are doomed to fail.

At United Nations, New York, Sept. 23/ Los Angeles Times, 9-24:(I)8.

4

We cannot send American troops to every region of the world threatened by Soviet-backed

174

Communist insurgents, though there may be times when that is the right choice and the only choice, as in Grenada. The wide range of challenges we face requires that we choose from an equally wide range of responses, from economic and security assistance to aid for freedom fighters to direct military action when necessary.

Before National Committee on American Foreign Policy, New York, Oct. 2/Los Angeles Times, 10-3:(I)1.

5

Our national interests require us to be on the side of freedom and democratic change everywhere, and no less in such areas as Central America, South Africa, the Philippines and South Korea [U.S. friends that are not democracies] . . . If we use our power to push our non-democratic allies too far and too fast, we may, in fact, destroy the hope for greater freedom; and we may also find that the regimes we inadvertently help bring into power are the worst of both worlds. They may be both hostile to our interests and more repressive and dictatorial than those we sought to change.

Before National Committee on American Foreign Policy, New York, Oct. 2/ Los Angeles Times, 10-3:(I)36.

6

Terrorism is the war we're fighting right now. We must take action. If free peoples do not move against the terrorists, no one will stop them. We must have the courage to act, without violence if possible, but recognizing that sometimes violence cannot be avoided. If our dedication to that principle paralyzes us, all our principles will be in jeopardy. They [terrorists] seek to instill fear—the fear that anyone who captures and brings to justice the terrorists becomes a target to the terrorists. We must stand for the rule of law, but we must not let fear turn it into a key to the jailhouse door. When we get our hands on terrorists, we have to prosecute them. We shouldn't hesitate about that.

At meeting of North Atlantic Assembly, San Francisco, Oct. 14/ Los Angeles Times, 10-15:(I)1.

7

(GEORGE P. SHULTZ)

1

If we use our power to push our non-democratic allies too far and too fast, we may, in fact, destroy the hope for greater freedom.
The Christian Science Monitor, 10-25:16.

Julian L. Simon
Professor of business and social science, University of Maryland

2

Immigrants don't just take jobs; they also purchase goods and services, thereby enlarging the market, while adding to the national productivity, and they also bring their brains and their creativity. Immigration helps rather than hurts the economy . . . All the evidence shows that immigration at present levels is beneficial [to the U.S. economy]. And it has been beneficial at all levels previously known, including the period when it was six times what it is now. The present level is beneficial. Doubling it would be better. It's like putting fertilizer on your lawn. Some fertilizer helps, more can help more, but there is a level at which you burn up your lawn. Maybe something like that could be theoretically true with immigration; we just don't know.
Interview/The Washington Post, 7-5:(A)17.

Joseph Sisco
Former Under Secretary of State of the United States

3

I'm struck that too many people, especially the younger generation, are saying, "We've got to know where we're going [in foreign policy]; we have to define the national interest; the American people have to be informed; Congress has to support the Executive." This epitomizes a search for guarantees in a dangerous nuclear world that is impossible. The logic of it is a prescription for paralysis.
The Christian Science Monitor, 5-7:40.

Helmut Sonnenfeldt
Former Counsellor, Department of State of the United States

4

[On the forthcoming summit meeting between U.S. President Reagan and Soviet leader Mikhail Gorbachev]: . . . over time, dealings with Soviet leaders, who are often thought to be very rigid and controlled, can become more relaxed. Yet, in the end, the great differences in culture and ideology between the U.S. and the Soviet Union still weigh very heavily. Thus, the relationship between an American President and a Soviet leader ultimately contains an element of reservation, doubt and question. One can develop the human relationship, as [former President] Nixon did with [the late Soviet leader Leonid] Brezhnev, but you can't mistake personal rapport for a rapport of interests. That is the big booby trap in this summit exercise.
Interview/U.S. News & World Report, 11-18:36.

Larry Speakes
Principal Deputy Press Secretary to the President of the United States

5

[On the recent increase in terrorist attacks on Americans, such as the previous night's killing of Americans in El Salvador and the current hijacking of an American airliner and the holding hostage of its passengers in Lebanon]: As for the President [Reagan], he believes that our actions must be appropriate and proportionate to the criminal acts which have been taken against our citizens. Those who are responsible for such lawlessness and those who support it must know the consequences of their actions will never be capitulation to terrorist demands. We are both a nation of peace and a people of justice. By our very nature, we are slow to anger and magnanimous in helping those in less fortunate circumstances. But we also have our limits. And our limits have been reached. We cannot allow our people to be placed at risk simply because they are blessed in being citizens of this great republic.
Washington, June 20/
The New York Times,
6-21:7.

6

[On Soviet leader Mikhail Gorbachev's recent interview with an American news magazine]: This is something that is relatively new, the Soviet access to the United States media . . . He's expressed his views; he's had

(LARRY SPEAKES)

open access to our media, as do Soviets every day, virtually. There's a new Soviet face on our television virtually once a week. Yet, the access to the Soviet media, as far as United States individuals, is severely limited, if not nonexistent. And furthermore, we have made a serious proposal months ago to the Soviets to allow [U.S.] President Reagan to appear on Soviet television. The request has gone not only unanswered but unacknowledged . . . We are pleased that Mr. Gorbachev was able to present his views to the American public. The interview is a prime example of the openness of the American system, and the access the Soviets enjoy to the American media. If President Reagan had a comparable opportunity to present his views to the Soviet people, through the Soviet media, this would doubtless improve our dialogue and indicate Soviet willingness to accept a degree of reciprocity in an important aspect of improving our relations.

Washington, Sept. 3/
The New York Times, 9-4-8.

1

[On U.S. policy toward international terrorism]: . . . if you can find terrorists, seek them out and hit those responsible for it, go at it. [But] we are firmly opposed to a cycle of violence which contains the seed of broader and more devastating hostilities. In that context, we have urged, and will continue to urge, restraint by all states—restraint for action that would feed that cycle. But, at the same time, it remains our firm policy that terrorism cannot go unanswered. We have always retained the right to respond to terrorist acts in an appropriate measured and focused way. In one case, we want to avoid a widening conflict of hostilities and the dangers they pose. On the other hand, terrorists should know that we have the option of responding in a direct manner to their barbaric acts.

Palm Springs, Calif., Dec. 30/
The New York Times, 12-31:4.

2

Margaret Thatcher
Prime Minister of the United Kingdom

Both [the U.S. and Britain] have suffered at the hands of terrorists. We have lost some of our best young lives. And I have lost some close and dear friends. Free, strong, democratic societies will not be driven by gunmen to abandon freedom and democracy. The problems of the Middle East will not be solved by the cold-blooded murder of American servicemen in Lebanon or by the murder of American civilians on a hijacked aircraft. Nor will the problems of Northern Ireland be solved by the assassin's gun or bomb.

Before joint session of U.S. Congress,
Washington, Feb. 20/
The New York Times, 2-21:6.

3

Hope is such a precious commodity in the world today that some are tempted to buy it at too high a price. We shall have to resist the muddled arguments of those who have been induced to believe that Russia's intentions are benign and that ours are suspect, or who would have us simply give up our defenses in the hope that where we led, others would follow. As we learned cruelly in the 1930s, from good intentions come tragic results.

Before joint session of U.S. Congress, Washington,
Feb. 20/
The Washington Post, 2-21:(A)9.

4

The Russians judge the West too much by old stereotypes. These stereotypes have taken deep roots in their minds because they have so little chance to familiarize themselves with the outer world. It is, therefore, vitally important that we communicate with them. I believe in the usefulness of exchanges with the Soviets, because they simply do not understand how a free, democratic society works and how deeply the West, including the United States, is committed to peace.

Interview/USA Today, 4-10:(A).

5

[On the UN]: It has acted as a court of world opinion, and now no government can afford to neglect or ignore its views . . . the United Nations has shown that it is a reality, not a sham; it is a force for action . . .; it is a temple of peace, not just a tower of Babel. For all its dangers, the world is safer and more orderly, thanks to the

(MARGARET THATCHER)

United Nations . . . The United Nations is only a mirror held up to our own uneven, untidy and divided world. If we do not like what we see, there's no point in cursing the mirror. We had better start by reforming ourselves.

At United Nations,
New York, Oct. 24/
Los Angeles Times,
10-25:(I)26.

Henry Trofimenko
Head, U.S. foreign-policy section,
Institute of American and Canadian
Studies, Soviet Academy of Sciences

1

[The U.S. and Soviet Union] don't have to remake each other's society to avoid nuclear war. During the Cold War, you tried to force the Soviet Union to change its internal system, and only if we changed our internal system would you deal in peace with us. Detente meant trying to change both sides' international behavior, thereby creating security for both without going into the other's business. Live and let live. That's a good American slogan under which a lot of things could be done.

Interview,
Middlebury College/
Los Angeles Times, 1-13:(IV)2.

Stansfield Turner
Former Director of Central
Intelligence of the United States

2

The revelation of recent efforts by the CIA to recruit [foreign] nationals that resulted in a truck bombing that killed civilians [in Lebanon]—things like that dirty our skirts and prevent us from claiming we're free from conducting terrorism . . . I'm sure the CIA did not authorize that group to go out and put a truck bomb into an apartment building that killed 80 innocent people. But the fact that we were associated in any way with that group makes us look like we're willing to stoop to the Soviets' level.

Interview/USA Today, 6-20:(A)9.

Brian E. Urquhart
Under Secretary General
of the United Nations for
Special Political Affairs

3

There are moments when I feel that only an invasion from outer space will re-introduce into the [UN] Security Council that unanimity and spirit which the founders of the Charter were talking about.

The New York Times, 9-23:10.

William L. Ury
Director, Nuclear Negotiation
Project, Harvard University

4

[Comparing U.S. and Soviet negotiating styles]: We're [the U.S.] a bargaining culture where, after some give and take, you split the difference to reach agreement. But the Soviets see negotiation as a dialectic in which, after an argument, the right side wins. That's their side, of course . . . As a nation, we are at the extreme impatient end of the patient/impatient spectrum. The Soviets—and the Japanese—are at the patient end. They outwait us. Our way to deal with conflict is to avoid it. If a marriage doesn't work, get a divorce; if a neighborhood is bad, move.

Interview/Los Angeles Times,
11-14:(I)1, 29.

Cyrus R. Vance
Former Secretary of State
of the United States

5

[The 1973 War Powers Act] needs to be strengthened . . . to make it clear that consultation [between the President and Congress] means consultation. Most Presidents haven't truly consulted with Congress before dispatching troops [to overseas hotspots]—they have made the decision and then simply informed the Congressional leadership. When you look at the record, it's a pretty sorry one.

Before Senate Foreign Relations Committee,
Washington, Feb. 4/
Los Angeles Times, 2-5:(I)1.

178

William von Raab
Commissioner,
United States Customs Service

1

[On illegal transfers of U.S. technology secrets to the Soviet Union]: I don't think the problem will ever go away. The Russians are dependent on U.S. technology to feed their ravenous war machine. The Soviet military has a voracious appetite. It's always hungry and always in need of nourishment. Our high-technology items are the vitamins in its diet. Without them, the military gets sick. It's got to continue to consume all this high technology or it will wither away. So as we raise the ante, they raise the ante. We cannot become complacent. I cannot sit back and say: "We're in great shape; we'll just stay with our program and rock along." We have to raise the ante. It's a race with no finish line. Our job is to stay ahead of them on the track.

Interview/
U.S. News & World Report, 8-12:39.

Vernon A. Walters
United States Ambassador/
Permanent Representative-designate
to the United Nations

2

Ever since the signature of the North Atlantic treaty alliance, the prime objective of Soviet foreign policy has been to divide the United States from its allies by telling the allies that the United States was not a reliable protector . . . When we did not [destroy the Soviet missiles in Cuba during the Cuban missile crisis, French President Charles] de Gaulle said it [the U.S.] was weak. "If they are not going to fight for Cuba 90 miles from the United States, why should I believe they are going to fight for France 3,500 miles from the United States? And if they are not, I must draw the consequences." And the consequences were his own nuclear efforts. Do we want to live in a world where 35 nations will develop nuclear weapons in order to protect themselves because they do not trust the United States? That is why the credibility of the United States is so important . . . If it is now true that the United States is incapable of preventing the establishment [in Nicaragua] of an outpost of Communist Soviet power in the heart of the

Americas, will the allies not wonder whether the time has not come for accommodation with the Soviet Union?

Before American Newspaper Publishers Association,
Miami Beach, May 8/
Los Angeles Times,
5-9:(I)20.

Vernon A. Walters
United States Ambassador/
Permanent Representative
to the United Nations

3

[On U.S. foreign policy]: If one seeks only to be loved, one cannot do the difficult things that must be done to pursue human freedom. I think, on balance, I would prefer that the world respect, more than merely like us. If we could have both, it would be even better.

U.S. News & World Report, 7-15:33.

4

I would say [the UN] has been a measured disappointment. One of the disappointing things is that the United Nations has drifted away from its role as an institution for the resolution of conflict. I think that only the very naive believed that we would get a truly effective organization that would resolve all the conflicts that arose after World War II. But the less naive hoped the UN would do more than it has in the way of conflict resolution. Let me emphasize that I think the United Nations is important to the world. First, because people all over the world think it is important, and second, because it is a forum in which every nation, no matter how small, can make its voice heard. But basically, it has drifted away from resolution of conflicts because of what I call a little bit of kidnapping of the non-aligned countries by the radicals in that group for their own political propaganda . . . [But] it would be irresponsible just to say we don't care, that the UN means nothing to us. I believe it is important to maintain our membership and to maintain our efforts to bring the UN back to the original purpose for which it was created.

Interview/
U.S. News & World Report,
9-23:29.

William H. Webster
Director,
Federal Bureau of Investigation

1

[On Soviet recruitment of Americans for espionage in the U.S.]: One consistent pattern I have observed over the last seven years is that we are not encountering ideology, which suggests that the Marxist-Leninist political side is not really selling in this country . . . What we're seeing now in substantial doses is an effort to achieve military and economic superiority through other efforts, such as the acquisition of American high technology and military information . . . These kinds of intelligence activities necessarily involve on their part efforts to recruit American citizens . . . They're not doing it by ideological conversion. They're doing it by resorting to what appears to be our greatest vulnerability—individual greed.

Interview/Newsweek, 6-17:28.

Caspar W. Weinberger
Secretary of Defense
of the United States

2

Our [U.S.] ability to influence foreign events may be somewhat limited in a world torn by religious and social upheaval. Violence in many parts of the world is endemic. This does not signal a slackening of our global responsibilities, because isolationism never was and never will be a practical model for American foreign policy. We do not, nor will we ever, have a strategy of global interventionism, but we do, and should, have a strategy of global assistance to our friends and allies.

Before Comstock Club, Sacramento, Calif.,
July 19/The Washington Post, 7-20:(A)4.

3

[On those in the West who criticized U.S. President Reagan two years ago for calling the Soviet Union an "evil empire"]: What does it say about the current state of political culture in the West that so many in intellectual circles should deem such a remark inappropriate or perhaps a gaffe of some sort? It's not that the critics really argue that the characterization is untrue;

I've heard very little of that. But it is that spotlighting the inherent evil of the coercive and tyrannical system of our Communist adversaries is done so seldom that it strikes some people as being crass or even provocative.

Before International Democrat Union, Washington,
July 25/The Washington Post, 7-26:(A)22.

4

I've always tried to take the position that we certainly do not want to do anything to perpetuate conditions that we abhor [such as the apartheid system in South Africa]. But we do have to look at alternatives. And I always keep going back to Iran, where some people a few years ago thought the Shah was a very repressive ruler and had a very repressive regime, and paid no attention whatever to the alternatives that would flow from not supporting him. And as a result, [following the overthrow of the Shah] we have the most repressive government since the Middle Ages [in Iran], and that could have been avoided, in my opinion.

Interview/The Washington Post, 8-2:(A)28.

5

[Saying the U.S. should reduce the number of Soviet representatives permitted to live in the U.S.]: We have to bear in mind, and it's only prudent to do so, that the Soviets don't send people to countries like the United States unless they are fully equipped, fully trained and they're part of the KGB.

News conference, Washington, Sept. 19/
The Washington Post, 9-20:(A)12.

Seymour Weiss
Former Director, Bureau of Political
and Military Affairs, Department of
State of the United States

6

Basically, U.S. and Soviet national objectives are sharply juxtaposed. In the case of the Soviets, military power—including nuclear power—is the single most important factor underlying what the Soviets call the "correlation of forces," which they believe must be in their favor if they are to pursue successfully their objective of a

(SEYMOUR WEISS)

world pliant to Moscow's preferences. As they perceive it, they need this favorable correlation of forces for several purposes: to support revolution, which they call "wars of national liberation" in Third World areas; to invade neighbors, as is currently the case with regard to Afghanistan; or to attempt political intimidation of Western Europe, which most recently we witnessed in the controversy over the deployment of American Pershing 2 and cruise missiles in Europe. Therefore, it is impossible to imagine that in negotiations with us they are going to bargain away the military advantage which they see as essential to pursue their aggressive policies and that they have developed at enormous sacrifice. The Soviets simply do not give away in negotiations advantages which they do not believe they can be forced to give up in the ongoing political contest between the superpowers or, should it come to that, in a contest of arms.

Interview/U.S. News & World Report, 1-21:33.

Charles Z. Wick

Director,
United States Information Agency

1

Through the explosion of global satellite communications, a technological "genie" has been unleashed which will change forever the way that governments communicate ideas and information abroad. Because of the expansion of technology, foreign policy is no longer the exclusive domain of elites. Diplomats of one nation will continue to conduct business with diplomats of another, as they always have—privately. But there is now a new dimension—the dimension of public diplomacy. Telecommunications has now made it possible for governments to speak directly to people in other countries. The impact is unparalleled in the world's history.

At George Washington University School of Public
and International Affairs commencement, May 5/
The New York Times, 5-7:10.

2

We're confronted with a vast amount of Soviet disinformation and absolute untruths about our

---

[U.S.] system and what we're trying to do. They outspend us in the war of ideas—and the war is being fought only outside the Soviet Union. The Soviets can and do get interviews in our press and on our TV networks whenever they want. They can take an ad in [*The New York Times*] to advocate their positions; yet [they] wouldn't accept an [American] ad in *Pravda* . . . [But] despite considerable Soviet efforts, we are winning the hearts and minds of people around the world. Nobody tries to climb the Berlin Wall going the other way! People yearn to be governed by consent and to be free to pursue their own way of life. To the extent that they perceive our system as affording that freedom while the other one does not, we will always win.

Interview/U.S. News & World Report, 10-7:38.

Paul Wilkinson

Authority on terrorism,
University of Aberdeen (Scotland)

3

I do not accept that there is nothing we can do [about terrorism]. The rule-of-law approach; firm political will, no concessions or deals with terrorists; professionalism in policing and intelligence work; skillful and precise use of legal measures—these are the methods we should continue to use . . . In practically every case of a protracted terrorist campaign in Europe, you find some country that has taken an ambivalent attitude: being unhelpful, at worst, being positively supportive to terrorists . . . We have to galvanize the political will of the community of democratic states behind the idea that one democracy's terrorist is another democracy's terrorist.

Interview, Aberdeen, Scotland/
The Christian Science Monitor,
1-31:10.

Howard Wolpe

United States Representative,
D-Michigan

4

When someone claims to be anti-Communist, we assume he's a good guy, and that Marxists are hostile to American interests. Reality is far more complicated than that. We end up being manipulated by labels, and make the mistake of inter-

(HOWARD WOLPE)

preting everything that happens in Africa and the Third World in East-West terms.

The New York Times, 12-3:24.

Leonid Zamyatin
*Chief foreign-policy spokesman
for the Soviet Union*   1

Since 1980, relations between the U.S. and the Soviet Union have been worsening with every month. They have been reduced to such a state that practically all our previous agreements have been practically torn in two, and only a few remain. Those remaining few represent the brakes that prevent relations from deteriorating completely. **Relations have never been worse, except perhaps for those years prior to 1933 when we had no diplomatic relations.**

*Interview/
Newsweek,
10-28:50.*

Government

Gary L. Ackerman
United States Representative,
D-New York

[Arguing against privatization of many government services]: The [Reagan] Administration wants to turn the whole government over to the private sector, on the pretext that they're going to save money, but they've yet to substantiate that claim. Dollars have been taken out of the paychecks of government workers and put into the hands of private contractors . . . They're [the Administration] not shrinking the size of anything. They're just processing the checks themselves, through their own corporate friends. We're creating jobs for private industry. We're just shifting the weight from one foot to another . . . The people who are championing this cause are waving the flag of the free-enterprise system, but they're living off the government.

The New York Times, 11-11:14.

1

Mark Andrews
United States Senator,
R-North Dakota

Ego [in a politician] can be a weakness, but leadership without ego may not be worth a damn.

The Washington Post, 1-28:(A)3.

2

Bruce Babbitt
Governor of Arizona (D)

I was upset at the recent and astounding decision by the Supreme Court requiring state and local governments to meet Federal wage-and-hour standards with our employees. The Federal judiciary is supposed to be the referee in disputes between Washington and the states. This time a majority of the Court was saying: "We're retiring from the field. We're hanging up our striped shirt and heading for the showers. We will no longer be here to judge the balance between the Federal and state government because

182

that balance is up to Congress." With the referee off the field, the Federal team ultimately may reduce the states to administrative arms of the Federal government.

Interview/U.S. News & World Report, 3-11:50.

1

Howard H. Baker, Jr.
Former United States Senator,
R-Tennessee

[Advocating TV coverage of Senate proceedings]: It would have a remarkable disciplining effect. It would create a permanent historical record of the real Senate . . . and that would help improve the quality of legislation.

USA Today, 9-18:(A)10.

4

James A. Baker III
Secretary of the Treasury of the
United States; Former Chief of
Staff to President of the
United States Ronald Reagan

[On holding a powerful position in the Federal government]: A lot of people think that it's glamour and glory, and it isn't. It's 14-hour days, it's keeping your eye on the ball and, frankly, it's being able, to some degree, to be careful not to seek too high a profile. There's a saying around this town: The higher the monkey climbs the more you can see of his behind. The higher you climb, the more people you have shooting at you.

Interview, Washington/
The Washington Post, 4-30:(C)2.

5

What surprised me most about the exercise of power in the White House was the speed with which issues moved and required resolution. You're hitting everything right at the very top. You really don't have a chance to get into things in the depth I was used to in the private sector. The job is really not unlike running a campaign. Decisive movement is important. You've got to be able to make decisions.

Interview/U.S. News & World Report, 5-20.65.

6

Charles E. Bennett
United States Representative,
D-Florida

1

[On being 74 years old and passed by for the Chairmanship of the House Armed Services Committee after a 36-year House career]: I'm a guy 74 years of age, in good health, and my peers turned me down. I have the appearance of being a very old man. I think a lot of people think that age is looking at yesterday only . . . And since it's my career, just like being a doctor, it's not nice to fail at it, particularly at age 74. There are not many chances to recoup. But 10 or 15 years from now, I'll be knocking at the pearly gates and St. Peter won't ask me if I was ever Chairman of the House Armed Services Committee.

Washington, Jan. 4/
Los Angeles Times, 1-6:(I)17.

Kenneth T. Blaylock
President, American Federation
of Government Employees

2

[Criticizing a new Federal policy of hiring more temporary workers in government]: The whole intent of the merit system, when it was established 100 years ago, was to build a long-term career work force that would maintain continuity when government changes at the top. With temporary employees, you get people who are just floating, who are between jobs or not looking for solid work. Are those the kind of people we want inspecting meat, treating veterans and writing Social Security checks?

The New York Times, 1-2:6.

Sherwood L. Boehlert
United States Representative,
R-New York

3

[On the House of Representatives]: There was mutual respect back then [in 1962]. Sure, Democrats and Republicans would battle it out on the floor over the Great Society issues, but later they would get together in some club to drink a beer and talk about baseball. [But now] the mood of the House these days is one of feeling that people

are out to cheat each other, to do one another in. I see it in both parties, and it bothers me greatly. Twenty-one years ago, in April, 1964, I came to this institution as a young staff member. There was a magic about the House, a real luster. But there has been a change. Somehow, the magic is slowly evaporating. The luster is gradually tarnishing right before our own eyes. There is a dark cloud hanging over this chamber. The tolerance level is going down, down and down. Motives are being questioned. Integrity is being challenged. Name-calling is rampant. Emotionalism is at a fever pitch, with all too frequently nasty results. Mr. Speaker, it is time for all of us to do a little soul searching. Clearly, and sadly, the House is out of order.

Before the House, Washington/
The New York Times, 5-3:14.

Bill Bradley
United States Senator, D-New Jersey;
Former basketball player, New York "Knicks"

4

I was here a couple of months when I was in the Democratic cloakroom in the Senate. It was one or two a.m. I looked around and there was a Senator pacing back and forth, another quietly reading, another telling a joke; and my reaction was, You know, this isn't a lot different from the *Knicks* locker room.

Interview, Washington/Cosmopolitan, August:66.

5

[On being a Senator]: There are always more things I want to know. That's why this job is so great. I think human personality and human interaction, as well as government institutions and the functioning of an economy, are infinitely various and challenging. As long as you realize that it's a constant learning process, then life becomes exciting.

Interview, Washington/
Cosmopolitan, August:83.

Fernand Braudel
French historian

6

I do not believe in the convenient distinction between civil and political society. Political so-

WHAT THEY SAID IN 1985

(FERNAND BRAUDEL)

ciety is the state, which in past centuries comprised a small group of men. But the state has expanded. Today it encompasses everything. It is a superstructure that spans the masses. At the summit, however, there are never more than a few.

Interview/World Press Review, March 31.

William J. Brennan, Jr.
Associate Justice, Supreme Court of the United States

We current [Supreme Court] Justices read the Constitution the only way that we can: as 20th-century Americans. The genius of the Constitution rests not in any static meaning it might have had in a world that is dead and gone, but in the adaptability of its great principles to cope with current problems.

USA Today, 10-17:(A)14.

1

Zbigniew Brzezinski
Professor of government, Columbia University; Former Assistant to the President of the United States (Jimmy Carter) for National Security Affairs

To succeed at the top in government you need strong nerves and a thick skin. Public officials today are so exposed that they're subjected to continuous criticism from within the government and outside it—and a lot of it tends to be ad hominem—so a thick skin is an absolute prerequisite . . . Beyond that, it's crucial to come into government with a larger perspective of what you wish to accomplish, with clear priorities, because once in office, you tend to be so overwhelmed by events that it is very easy to lose perspective and get absorbed in specifics. You can become increasingly responsive to situations rather than using your power to shape situations and to define outcomes . . . In the final analysis, my years in government probably have made me more tolerant. You begin to realize how important it is to accommodate on issues and not just have your own way, as intellectuals are inclined to do. In politics, even when you have a

184

---

great deal of power—as you do when you're very close to the President—ultimately it is the sharing of some of that power that's the key to moving forward on issues.

Interview/U.S. News & World Report, 5-20:65.

McGeorge Bundy
Professor of government, New York University; Former Assistant to the President of the United States (John F. Kennedy and Lyndon B. Johnson) for National Security Affairs

One problem is the apparent lack of a unified stand by the Reagan Administration. The President tolerates a level of explicit conflict in his Administration that is truly astonishing to me. It's really not possible for me to imagine President Kennedy allowing the Department of Defense to present its case, as DOD now does, in repeated, very strong-minded speeches from the Secretary, as well as leaks to journalists. At the same time, the Secretary of State is having to intervene when something in his view is dangerously wrong, but becomes—at least temporarily—Administration policy. This is very sloppy work, and it results from Presidential inattention and Presidential tolerance of deeply different positions.

Interview/U.S. News & World Report, 11-18:36.

3

George Bush
Vice President of the United States

In Washington, in our time, public men and public women, most of whom get more than their share of attention and honors and most of whom are important and celebrated, often find it difficult to keep their eye on the most important things, the enduring things, the things that really count. One can find oneself being a public hero and a private failure, giving less and less attention to the family and the children and the life that goes on in the home.

At services for late U.S. Supreme Court Justice Potter Stewart, Washington, Dec. 11/The New York Times, 12-12:56.

4

Stuart Butler
Authority on privatization,
Heritage Foundation

1

[On the trend toward privatization of certain government functions]: The reason that privatization . . . has aroused such interest recently is that it seems to offer a solution to the problem that confronts many politicians seeking to reduce government spending. The anger of someone denied a government service is always greater than the gratitude of a taxpayer when savings are made. By providing the option of a similar, or even superior, service from the private sector at less cost to the taxpayer, privatization allows the legislator the chance of satisfying both constituencies at once.

Nation's Business, August:18.

Robert C. Byrd
United States Senator,
D-West Virginia

2

I do not know what there is about the Presidency, when it comes to a [phone] call from that august and lofty position. I just cannot understand what it is that is so awesome about it. There is something that likens it to lockjaw. Some individuals [in Congress], when they receive a call from the President, apparently do not know how to say "no."

Before the Senate, Washington/
The New York Times, 7-26:8.

Alec Cairncross
British economist

3

Government is not a simple optimizing activity that can be reduced to a second differential in a mathematical equation. It is more likely to be a collection of bald-headed and somewhat bewildered men sitting around a table, harassed and short of time, full of doubts and dogmatism, with all the strengths and failings of successful politicians.

Before American Economic Association,
Dallas/The New York Times, 1-2:22.

John Carlin
Governor of Kansas (D);
Chairman, National Governors' Association

4

I would say [being a governor is] a good training ground [for potential Presidents]. But the fact that the last two Presidents have been governors—they were not successful because they were governors, as much as because they were the right personality at the right time. Certainly they needed some foundation, some place to come from. I suppose you might argue that the governorship contributed because they [Jimmy Carter and Ronald Reagan] both ran on an anti-Washington theme, and it's kind of hard to do that if you're a U.S. Senator. But I don't think it necessarily is a trend.

Interview/
USA Today,
2-27:(A)9.

Clark Clifford
Presidential adviser;
Former Secretary of Defense
of the United States

5

We went through a period, from late Nixon on, with the growing feeling that there had been a diminution of the Presidency and that the legislative was superseding it. Reagan has quieted that and, while I don't approve of his major domestic and foreign policies, I think that's good for the country.

Interview/
The Washington Post,
1-21:(G)8.

Bill Clinton
Governor of Arkansas (D)

6

Our critics have said we [Democrats] want too much government, while they want government off our backs. Well, we want the government off our backs, too; but we need it by our side.

Reply to President's State of the Union address,
Feb. 6/The Washington Post, 2-7:(A)17.

185

Barber B. Conable, Jr.
Fellow, American Enterprise Institute;
Former United States Representative,
R-New York

I find I am in great demand as a speaker. The minute you leave Congress, they think of you as a statesman.

The New York Times, 1-25:8.

1

Mario M. Cuomo
Governor of New York (D)

[Addressing graduating students]: Unless people like you give us a new generation, willing to take on the challenge of self-government, willing to accept its responsibilities, to reform it, to change it, to make it fairer and more responsive—unless you do, the very rich will get richer, the poor will become fired in their desperation, violence will increase and here, as in so many places around the world, the purpose of government will be reduced basically to a matter of maintaining order instead of improving conditions . . . Much of the talent here, much of your enormous potential, will go into the world of business, of science, of law or academics, and in the process bring new strengths, new improvements to our society. But there will probably be no similar commitment to our political process—even if just at the level of voting or advocating. And I'm afraid we'll pay a price for this. In fact, I think that disinterest in politics is already affecting us negatively and pervasively.

At University of Rochester (N.Y.) commencement,
May 12/The New York Times, 5-13:13.

2

Mitchell E. Daniels, Jr.
Director, Federal Office of
Intergovernmental Affairs

Only a few years ago, local government was thought to be the preserve of hidebound conservatives, bigots and incompetents who were rural-dominated and anti-humanitarian. Today, state and local offices are worth aspiring to.

The New York Times, 7-3:12.

3

Thomas A. Daschle
United States Representative,
D-South Dakota

When you try to create a campaign to pass a bill, it's more than just a debate on the House floor. You have to create national attention to change the climate. We [in Congress] don't have the platform by which the President can draw attention to an issue simply by walking through the door. Congress is a firehouse. If it's a one-alarm fire, you'll be ignored . . . The success you have in getting Congress to address an issue is directly related to how many bells you can ring.

The New York Times, 3-22:14.

4

Alan Dershowitz
Professor of law,
Harvard University

[Criticizing President Reagan's appointment of Attorney General Edwin Meese as a policymaker for his Administration]: Where the problem starts and ends is having a political intimate of the President in charge of seeing that the President complies with the law. The Meese case is an institutional change that reflects a practical change in the Attorney General's role that is several decades old.

The New York Times, 4-22:15.

5

Robert J. Dole
United States Senator, R-Kansas

If you're hanging around with nothing to do and the zoo is closed, come over to the Senate. You'll get the same kind of feeling and you won't have to pay. You watch all these speeches being made and nothing going on at all and you think, "Where am I? I can't believe this." But don't worry about it. If there are not many people there, you're lucky because you can't do business without a quorum. As long as there are only three to four people on the floor, the country is in good hands. It's only when you have 50 to 60 in the Senate that you want to be concerned.

To local New York officials,
May 7/The New York Times, 5-9:14.

6

Pete V. Domenici
United States Senator,
R-New Mexico

1

I have believed for the last three years that the processes of Congress—including the budget process—ought to be reformed. A two-year, instead of a one-year, cycle for appropriations bills and the budget ought to be looked at. The budget process itself should be streamlined—made easier and stronger, not weaker. But none of those kinds of things is magic. Our kind of government is going to be complicated. None of the processes in Congress, including the budget process, is going to work well unless there is a will to make it work well. This process is phenomenally flexible and will do almost anything we set out to do. It's just that we never can get enough people to agree.

Interview/U.S. News & World Report, 8-12:20.

Thomas F. Eagleton
United States Senator, D-Missouri

2

The [Senate] filibuster, once used by and large as an occasional exercise in civil-rights matters, has now become a routine frolic in almost all matters. Whereas our rules were devised to guarantee full and free debate, they now guarantee unbridled chaos . . . We, the great deliberators, are deliberating ourselves into national ridicule and embarrassment. As I depart [the Senate] for a more sensible life, I urge that the next majority leader in 1987 make as a top priority item the restructuring of our rules, not to stifle legitimate speech but to avert incipient legislative anarchy, and to avoid the continued degradation of the United States Senate as an institution of competence, capacity and trust.

Before the Senate, Washington,
Nov. 23/The New York Times, 11-27:14.

Stuart Eizenstat
Former Assistant to the President
of the United States (Jimmy Carter)
for Domestic Policy

3

The single most important decision a President has to make is beyond who is Secretary of State or Secretary of Treasury or Director of OMB, but who is [White House] Chief of Staff. It is absolutely the single most important position. The White House cannot function properly without a strong and effective Chief of Staff. And if the White House cannot function properly, then the Executive Branch can't.

Interview/The New York Times, 1-22:12.

John W. Gardner
Founder, Common Cause

4

When the nation was founded, we had a population of about three million. We fielded at least 6 world-class leaders: Washington, Jefferson, Adams, Madison, Franklin and Hamilton. You could name others. We now have 80 times the population, so you could argue we ought to have 480 Jeffersons, and so forth. Now, they are out there, but hearing no call to leadership and probably quite unconscious of the possibilities within them. And it's just interesting to ask yourself what you could do with that talent if you could put it to work in the service of the community and the nation . . . I am worried about the real long-term public servants. I think it is infinitely harder for them to come in and stay in. The whole trend of the past 15 years has been away from a self-respecting public service and toward the subordination of such people by political loyalists who have no interest in public service as a career and no particular interest in the subject matter. They come in as political loyalists, committed to an individual or an ideology, and that's it.

Interview, Washington/
The New York Times, 7-4:26.

Barry M. Goldwater
United States Senator, R-Arizona

5

The outgoing Congress was probably the worst I've ever seen, and I'm really worried about it. When I came here, there were older, highly respected men of great stature in Congress. Today the minute a man or woman gets elected to the House or the Senate, he or she starts running for the next election. I don't think the election of a certain Senator is all that impor-

(BARRY M. GOLDWATER)

tant. We've had 1,758 Senators in the history of the Senate. Three weeks after you lose your job, nobody ever heard of you.

Interview/Los Angeles Herald Examiner, 1-13:(4)15.

1

If the U.S. does not see a more courageous Congress, this country will go bankrupt in 10 years maximum. Congress has to show guts, leadership and to defend the Constitution. To hell with defending farmers, railroads or anything else!

Interview/U.S. News & World Report, 12-30:130.

Charles E. Grassley
United States Senator, R-Iowa

[On criticism that members of Congress are inconsistent in their voting]: I think you'd be a nervous wreck if you tried to be consistent on all issues. It would blind you to the needs of your constituents and to changing times. I don't think there's a particular merit to consistency as long as you don't compromise your basic principles.

Interview, Washington/The New York Times, 12-5:14.

2

William H. Gray III
United States Representative,
D-Pennsylvania

[On his being black and the head of a House committee]: There is no title here called "Black America Budget Chairman." There is no title here called "Black Caucus Budget Chairman." It's called House Budget Committee Chairman. I happen to be black and there is no conflict in that . . . It's been proven over the years that blacks can provide leadership in Congress.

Interview, Washington/
The Washington Post, 5-24:(B)4.

3

Alexander M. Haig, Jr.
Former Secretary of State
of the United States

I'm not one who believes that the press is the culprit in the host of unauthorized [government]

188

leaks over the years I've been involved in government. Precisely the opposite. The press is doing its job, essentially. It is the public official, and usually it is a fellow at a very, very high level who thinks he has to protect the President from himself, has to, somehow, self-aggrandize himself as a man in the know. Or perhaps he doesn't believe in the policies. So my program is, first, to apply some discipline within my Executive Branch. And I would clean house when it came to high-level leaks—generally, they're either from the White House or from the Cabinet. They're not from the underlings.

Seminar, Princeton, N.J./
Harper's, November:51.

Bennett Harrison
Professor of political economy
and planning, Massachusetts
Institute of Technology

Industrial policy doesn't have to be solely the province of some bureaucracy in Washington. It can be a lot of different things: a community-development corporation in the neighborhood; a city council trying to find a way to deliver health care to a depressed community; a state-funded economic revitalization program that allocates tax revenues to start new businesses, retool older ones, or repair deteriorated roads and bridges. And in fact, such programs are already under way, in states and cities around the country. "Public" doesn't have to mean the big Federal bureaucracy. It means us. We're the public.

Panel discussion, Harvard University/
Harper's, February:47.

5

Gary Hart
United States Senator,
D-Colorado

The Democratic Party must govern well, but it must not be the party of government. Democrats must understand that government exists to serve the people and not the people to serve the government.

To his supporters, Boston, Feb. 4/
The Washington Post, 2-5:(A)7.

6

Barbara Jordan
Professor of public values and ethics,
University of Texas, Austin; Former
United States Representative, D-Texas

1

[As a member of Congress,] I would hope that I could vote on a plane higher than politics. My problem is that it's politics that keeps us reluctant to do the things we could boldly do. It is politics that keeps us from making recommendations that we feel will not be marketable to the public. If no one was going to be re-elected to Congress, I think we could have one whale of a program that would be in the interest of people—in the public interest. So, if I were in Congress today, I would probably engage in the kinds of marginal adjustment, which is so often the case.

Interview/Ms., April:75.

Jack Kemp
United States Representative,
R-New York

2

. . millions of Americans look to government as a lifeline. I have never felt personally that the idea of beating up on government was good politics. It's true that government is best which governs least. But it's equally true that government is best which does the most for people, and you need a balance between what government does for people and what people should be able to do for themselves.

Interview/Los Angeles Times, 6-2:(I)12.

Edward M. Kennedy
United States Senator,
D-Massachusetts

3

We [Democrats] cannot and should not depend on higher tax revenues to roll in and redeem very costly [Federal] programs. Rather, those of us who care about domestic programs must do more with less—and, in fact, some of the measures we should take will save money instead of spending it . . . The mere existence of a program is no excuse for its perpetuation—whether it is a welfare plan or a weapons system.

At Hofstra University, March 29/
Los Angeles Times, 3-30:(I).

Paul G. Kirk, Jr.
Chairman,
Democratic National Committee

4

If [President] Ronald Reagan were left to his own devices, there'd be no Federal government. He'd just sit in the White House and, except for military affairs, just say, "Good luck, governors." But he reigns over the government and then kicks it around—strips education, cuts energy. Democrats believe that government should at least be the final arbiter of fairness in our society.

Interview/U.S. News & World Report, 3-18:52.

Madeleine Kunin
Governor of Vermont (D)

5

[On rural America]: We don't want Washington to assume that simply because fewer people are affected by something such as a nuclear power plant or a toxic-waste site, that makes it more acceptable to locate it there, or diminishes the problems created by such a location. The people in Washington must not discriminate against people on the basis of where they happen to live; they must realize that rural Americans need the same treatment as urban Americans. Also in the allocation of funds, the Federal government needs to recognize that you don't always have the economies of scale in rural areas, that it is more expensive to provide services to a rural state. It's more expensive to provide telephone service, power and electricity, for example. I think a sensitivity to those needs is important.

Interview/USA Today, 1-8:(A)9.

Arthur Laffer
Economist;
Former professor of business economics,
University of Southern California

6

If you look at Congressmen and Senators, you see a group who invariably prefer complex error over simple truth. If you ever saw what those guys actually did for a living, you'd recognize their banality and you'd throw them out of office.

Los Angeles Times, 3-22:(I)28.

WHAT THEY SAID IN 1985

Richard D. Lamm
Governor of Colorado (D)

1

I go back and I ask myself in history: When was there ever a democracy that reformed itself from its excesses? I can't find one. I can find [action] when Pearl Harbor hits, when Dunkirk hits. I am not at all sure that democracy doesn't need a crisis to act.

Interview, Denver/
The Christian Science Monitor, 11-6-5.

Thelma Zeno Lavine
Professor of philosophy,
George Washington University

2

There's no sense of a philosophic presence in Washington. It's probably not a good city for philosophy . . . I wouldn't think that there will ever be a Secretary of Philosophy. The philosopher can be useful, however. Because if he's trained at all, he can *think*. He can make distinctions; he can see inconsistencies. He can see a single line of thought developing. He can see the nature of dialogue and the opposing positions and the possibilities. Any graduate student, in principle, could take any political theory and shoot it full of holes.

Interview, Washington Post, 2-22:(E)1.

Rex E. Lee
Solicitor General
of the United States

3

[On a Supreme Court ruling that Congress has broad power over state and local governments]: Those of us who feel strongly about states' rights . . . can only hope that Congress will take very seriously what is implicit in this opinion—that the bulwark of protection for state interests has shifted to Congress itself.

Feb. 19/The Washington Post, 2-20:(4)6.

John V. Lindsay
Former Mayor of New York

4

The spirit or tone of a national Administration finds expression in our daily lives, just as it does in America's relationship with the world beyond our borders. The proper exercise of political power in a democracy demands a sensitivity to all groups, and the ability to build coalitions between different factions to pursue the common interest. In the past, this kind of bipartisan coalition-building has been the genius of our democratic system. As one who participated in, helped form and led several such coalitions both as Congressman and mayor, I can assure you that we would not have sweeping civil-rights legislation or revenue-sharing today had Republicans and Democrats representing all sorts of constituencies not pulled together for the sake of improving people's lives. Nor in earlier times would we have created the Marshall Plan, formed Pacific Basin alliances or built the Tennessee Valley Authority. America is not being led that way today. Instead, the political process is based on the clever use of polarizing code words—often cast in media-appealing one-liners. This technique is not only accepted, but admired for its effectiveness. That's part of the tone set at the top, too. The vast majority quietly falls in line, if not to be with the "winners," then to dissociate themselves from the "losers" . . . The tone America's leadership sets—the values it communicates—is felt acutely around the globe. But the polarization produced by a doctrine-ridden Administration that divides the world into categories of friends and enemies, winners and losers, has also infected our national spirit.

At Lehman College, September/
The Washington Post, 10-17:(A)22.

Scott M. Matheson
Former Governor of Utah (D)

5

[On being Governor]: It is a job description whose final paragraph, I think, will never be written. It evolves from the needs of the people, and one of its first rules is that the Governor must keep in touch with those needs.

At swearing-in of his successor, Salt Lake City,
Jan. 7/The New York Times, 1-8:7.

Charles McC. Mathias, Jr.
United States Senator, R-Maryland

6

[Criticizing the increasing use by Senators of their free mail privileges to make mass mailings

(CHARLES McC. MATHIAS, JR.)

to their constituents]: I know of no other areas of public expenditure where an individual can just put his foot on the pedal and run up a bill of $3.8-million in a year and never have anyone know about it. Mass mailings are like a snowfall, gently falling all over the country. You don't hear much, but it does begin to pile up.

U.S. News & World Report, 12-23:22.

Mitch McConnell
United States Senator, R-Kentucky

1

[On the Senate]: This is a place that—with all due respect to those who run it—doesn't function terribly well. The slow pace at the start of a session is exasperating. In the first five weeks we had, I think, three roll-call votes on such highly controversial matters as Cabinet secretaries. I know what's going to happen later in the year: We're going to be up all night long.

Interview/U.S. News & World Report, 4-15:37.

Edwin Meese III
*Attorney General
of the United States*

2

We have far too much classified information in the Federal government. A lot of things which shouldn't be classified are, and therefore there is kind of a ho-hum attitude toward the protection of national-security information. [There should be a] tightening up [on classification] so that only material that really has to be kept secret in the interests of national defense or national security is classified, and then that the news media as well as government officials work together to make sure that that information is not improperly disclosed. I think that ultimately is the solution to this whole problem.

*Before Washington Press Club,
March 20/The New York Times, 3-21:10.*

3

[Saying the President should have the power to remove officials of independent Federal agencies]: Power granted to Congress should be properly understood as power granted to the Executive. It should be up to the President to enforce the law . . . Federal agencies performing Executive functions are themselves properly agents of the Executive. They are not "quasi" this or "independent" that. In the tripartite scheme of government, a body with enforcement powers is part of the Executive Branch of government.

*Speech, Sept. 13/
The New York Times, 11-6:12.*

Barbara A. Mikulski
*United States Representative,
D-Maryland*

4

Out of every lemon comes lemonade, and in the post-Watergate era legislative branches took a strong look at themselves. Before, there were informal codes and informal ways of monitoring behavior; now, legislative bodies have established ethics committees and mandatory requirements, such as financial disclosure.

U.S. News & World Report, 12-9:62.

Walter F. Mondale
*Former United States Senator, D-Minnesota;
1984 Democratic Presidential nominee*

5

Having seen the inner workings of our defense system, there is no one who believes more than I that there is information which must remain absolutely secret. We have espionage and treason laws to handle such situations. But I also believe that journalists, academics, public servants and whistle-blowers have just as much right to free speech as do the high officials who call reporters into their offices and leak classified information in support of Administration policy. The danger isn't just in censorship. It's in the threat of censorship. Those in power are not the ones who will be prosecuted under an official secrets act. The defendants will be those who have challenged them to explain themselves, to reconsider their policies, and to tell the truth.

*At University of Minnesota Law School
commencement, Minneapolis/Time, 6-17:69.*

Bill Moyers
Journalist

If you would go forth from here to serve democracy well, you must first save the language. Save it from the jargon of insiders, who talk of the current budget debate in Washington as "megapolicy choices between freeze-feasible base lines"—sounds more like a baseball game played in the Arctic Circle. Save it from the smokescreen artists, who speak of "revenue enhancement" and "tax-base erosion control" when they really mean a tax increase . . . Save it from the partisan deniers of reality—who now refer to the physically handicapped as "differently abled"—and from the official revisionists of reality, who say that the United States did not withdraw our troops from Lebanon, we merely "backloaded our augmentation personnel."

At Lyndon B. Johnson School of Public Affairs commencement, University of Texas, Austin/ Time, 6-17:68.

1

Ralph Nader
Lawyer;
Consumer-rights advocate

[On the U.S. Presidency]: The country is too dependent upon it for embarking on new objectives, too dependent on it for defining the direction of the country. The Presidency has become a symbolic media hotbed from which signals emerge that set the tone and feeling and priority in the country. You just can't have a country of our size depend on the White House to that extent.

*Interview, Washington/
The New York Times, 11-23:8.*

2

John Naisbitt
Author;
Authority on national trends

[On the trend toward privatization of certain government functions]: Privatization is part of the process of rethinking the welfare state. Society is searching for new ways of delivering services because of our collective sense of efficiency. The entrepreneur, not the bureaucrat, is

the hero of society. While we can't be sure how it will all turn out, privatization will be part of the emerging post-welfare state.

Nation's Business, August:18.

3

Thomas P. O'Neill, Jr.
United States Representative,
D-Massachusetts

Whenever I meet with a group of successful business people, someone always stands up and says we would be better off without government. For such persons, I have a very simple question: Who paid for your college education? Was it a state government that helped pay for a state university? Or was it a community college or a city university? Or was it the GI Bill that financed your education—or a government-sponsored loan? Then, I have another question for them: If they, the "success stories" of this country, needed a helping hand up the ladder of success, why should we not try to give the ladder of success, those young people who are trying to get ahead today? If government could offer opportunities to young people back in the 1950s and 1960s, why should we deny that same help to young people in the 1980s? I believe it is wrong for someone who has found his way up the economic and social ladder to pull that ladder up behind him, to deny those at the bottom the chance to pull themselves up. No society can exist on a public philosophy of "I got mine; forget the others" . . . America has worked, America has progressed, because we have combined our enterprise, both public and private, for the good of all. That is how we pulled our nation from the Great Depression, won the Second World War, released the power of the atom and put Americans on the moon. That is how we built the fairest, freest, most progressive society in the world.

*Alfred M. Landon Lecture, Kansas State University,
April 22/The Washington Post, 4-25:(A)22.*

4

I am an insider kind of fellow. I'm the last of an old bloc. I do more behind the scenes without it ever getting into the news than the average fellow does in a lifetime. I've put billions of dollars

5

(THOMAS P. O'NEILL, JR.)

into the budget. I have the ability and the knack to handle people and get things done.

Interview/The New York Times, 8-19:(I)13.

1

Every President wants a line-item veto. [Senator] Ted Kennedy came up to me the other day and he said, "You know, my brother [the late President John Kennedy] always said we ought to have a line-item veto." But there's never been any enthusiasm for the line-item veto in the House. [President] Reagan's argument to me is that with nearly every [state] governor doing it, why can't the President? My answer to him is that the Founding Fathers intended equality in our government.

Interview/U.S. News & World Report, 9-16:25.

2

Thomas Paine was the first critic of Congress, and we've had them ever since. Now there is a bunch of columnists who don't know chicken soup from chow mein, but they like to bear on Congress. Well, they make the image, so the image of Congress has always been low. But the individual Congressman in his local area, he is seen as good. Congress has always been the whipping boy of the American public and, under our democracy, that's the way it will always be.

Interview/U.S. News & World Report, 9-16:25.

Norman J. Ornstein
Resident scholar,
American Enterprise Institute

3

There's no truth to the idea that the office [of President] is too big for one individual, and [President] Reagan has very nicely put that lie to rest. He has an instinctive feel for the job. The truth is it was impossible even 100 years ago for a President to get into every detail of government. A President's role is to make the big decisions, to project an image of leadership and to set national priorities. That's what a President should do, that's what a President can do and that's what a good President will do.

Interview/U.S. News & World Report, 1-28:53.

4

When I saw [President] Ronald Reagan give a televised address on the budget the same night the House was voting on aid to the [Nicaraguan] contras and right before he took off for the [European] summit, I said, here is the cardinal sin of politics. You do not let your own momentum trip all over itself. That was [former President] Jimmy Carter's classic failing. He never understood that what you do today affects what you do tomorrow.

The Washington Post, 5-23:(A)6.

5

The extraordinary thing about Congress is that it really works. This is a good institution, operating well . . . It goes against the grain of American culture to say that Congress is effective and decent—and most members of Congress are decent. Television's natural emphasis on scandal has amplified our natural, cultural American view of politicians as sex-starved thieves . . . In the final analysis, I'm a defender of Congress. If [James] Madison were here today and looked at Congress, he'd say, "This is what we envisioned."

Interview, Washington/
The New York Times, 7-15:10.

William Proxmire
United States Senator, D-Wisconsin

6

[Arguing against TV coverage of Senate proceedings]: Television thrives on the dramatic. Any additional incentives to confrontation [in the Senate] can only mean more argument—and probably worse legislation.

USA Today, 9-18:(A)10.

Ronald Reagan
President of the United States

7

[On criticism that he is manipulated by his aides as a result of his "board-of-directors" approach to running government]: I'm too old and too stubborn to put up with that. [There is] this picture that's being created that I sit at the desk and wait to see who's going to grab this arm and

WHAT THEY SAID IN 1985

(RONALD REAGAN)

pull me this way, or grab this one and pull me that way. I make up my own mind. The only difference between them [the Cabinet] and a board of directors is that we don't take a vote. When I've heard on all sides the discussion and debate, I make a decision. No vote.

Interview, Washington,
Jan. 17/USA Today,
1-18:(A)1.

1

If you really look at the whole tone of government today and what was being debated in government up until four years ago—then it was about programs and let's spend money over here. Now, the whole debate now has turned around to how much should the rate of cutting be and what should we cut. No one is talking about new programs and spending more money by government. No one is talking about more authority in the Federal government.

Interview, Washington,
Jan. 17/USA Today,
1-18:(A)13.

2

The Vice President shouldn't be just someone standing by waiting to be called off the bench. He should be like an executive vice president in a corporation or a business. You use him.

Interview, Washington, Feb. 11/
The New York Times,
2-12:6.

3

[On his periodic trips to his California ranch]: I find, and I guess every President before me has found . . . there's something that you need. And I look at it another way: At my age, how many more years do I have to go to the ranch and enjoy the ranch? You give up an awful lot of privacy and so forth [by being President], and I think you're entitled.

Interview, Santa Barbara, Calif./
Los Angeles Times,
2-18:(I)4.

4

Perhaps the biggest mistake mankind has made in this century is to think that the big answer is . . . the State—that's their idea, the State with a capital S. Well, the political edifice that man has built to govern himself—some have said that this is the thing from which all blessings come. But if we've discovered anything these past few decades, it is that our salvation is not in the State—our salvation is in ourselves and what we do with our lives and the choices that we make. It is in the things that we choose to worship. If we've learned anything, it is that government that is big enough to give you everything you want is more likely to simply take everything you've got. And that's not freedom, that's not servitude. That isn't the way Americans were meant to live.

At St. John's University, New York,
March 28/The New York Times, 3-29:12.

5

[On being President]: . . . I have come to understand very much why Abraham Lincoln once said that he had been driven to his knees many times because there was no place else to go. And he said if he didn't believe that he could call on someone who was stronger and wiser than all others, he couldn't meet the responsibilities of his position for a single day. All you can do is try to do the best of your ability and with all the input and knowledge you get, then hope that the decisions you make are based on what is morally right.

At Fallston (Md.) High School,
Dec. 4/The New York Times, 12-5:14.

George E. Reedy

Professor of journalism, Marquette University; Former Press Secretary to the President of the United States (Lyndon B. Johnson)

6

This country lacks the consensus that brings about strong leadership. Congress can play little other than a harassing role until that consensus is brought about.

U.S. News & World Report, 5-20:60.

Donald T. Regan
Secretary of the Treasury of the United States; Chief of Staff-designate to the President of the United States

1

[During World War II,] at age 25, I had 900 men under me in battle. If you don't think that seasons you for combat in Washington later in your life, you're crazy.

Interview, Washington, Jan. 18/Time, 1-21:20.

2

[On his forthcoming switching of jobs with White House Chief of Staff James Baker]: [Some time ago, Baker] was grousing about something that had happened to him [and] I was grousing about something that happened to me. We're two fellow Marines, and we can communicate—not necessarily in language that a family publication can print. I said, "Baker, you know what the hell we ought to do? Swap jobs." He said, "You're kidding," I said, "I'm not. That would get both of us rid of these frustrations." He said, "You're damn right." And we dropped it. But he didn't forget it, and neither did I.

Newsweek, 1-21:18.

3

[Saying it was difficult to adjust to the slow pace of the government bureaucracy after coming from the world of private business]: When I was chief executive and I said, "Jump," people said, "How high?" As Secretary of the Treasury, I say, "Jump," and people say, "Well, do you have an environmental impact statement? What do you mean, jump?"

U.S. News & World Report, 1-21:23.

Donald T. Regan
Chief of Staff to the President of the United States

4

[White House] policy is not set by one [staff] person dictating it. Policy will be set by discussions among a lot of us, finally the President

[Reagan] deciding on the policy and then going from there. When you accept the King's shilling, you sign aboard.

News conference, Washington, Feb. 5/The New York Times, 2-7:10.

Charles Robb
Governor of Virginia (D)

5

Government simply can't . . . continue to try to do everything and to try to fund everything and at the same time be compassionate.

Reply to President's State of the Union address, Feb. 6/U.S. News & World Report, 2-18:79.

John D. Rockefeller IV
United States Senator, D-West Virginia; Former Governor of West Virginia (D)

6

[Comparing being a Senator with being a governor]: The linear authority you have as governor is greater. You say "do this" and the next day it's done. As Senator, you're passing laws, putting into effect what one is lobbying about as governor. The implications are enormous, and it's a much broader scope.

Interview/Cosmopolitan, September:262.

Edward J. Rollins
Assistant to the President of the United States for Political and Governmental Affairs

7

[On his decision to leave his White House position to return to private business]: The truth of the matter is, coming back here [to the White House] after running the campaign [for President Reagan's re-election], where I made the decisions, where I had my own fiefdom, was a little like a one-star general who ran a base coming back to the Pentagon. There's a lot of one-star generals in the Pentagon. And the two-star, three-star and four-star generals are the ones with clout. Financially, it's been a bit of a struggle; I'd like to earn some more money. Equally important, I want to get away from the phone calls in the middle of the night. I want to have

(EDWARD J. ROLLINS)

the freedom of speaking out, having an opinion again. I need to get back into an environment that I'm comfortable with. I have a reputation for being candid. I wasn't trained to be a diplomat . . . I'll miss some things, but not everything. People always say, "Don't you feel powerful here?" Powerful! I've never felt anything other than tired in the White House.

Interview, Washington/
The New York Times, 9-30:12.

Louis Rukeyser
Host, "Wall Street Week,"
PBS-TV

1

[T]he worst deficit in Washington is above the neck and down the spine.

TV broadcast/
"Wall Street Week," PBS-TV, 7-26.

Daniel Schorr
Former senior correspondent,
Cable News Network

2

I [as a journalist] will not yield patriotism to the government. I will not yield a monopoly on patriotism to those who happen to be elected or appointed officials. Our experience in the press has been—in the Pentagon Papers case, the representation was made that irreparable damage would be done by the publication of those papers, and the judge didn't find that to be true. I've seen classified information used. The President of the United States goes on television and says, "Here are pictures which were previously secret, but which I will now show you in order to show what the Cubans are up to down there in Central America." I will not accept the idea that we [the press] are less patriotic than those in government who play their games for their own purposes and then come and say, "This is national security". . . The fact of the matter is, the worst leaks, the ones that really hurt the country, have nothing to do with the press at all. They come from shoddy, inefficient management by our government. And the government likes to pick on the press because it is such an easy target. There was a question about "who elected the press." All these people [in government] are elected, they are entrusted with all these secrets, and who are we [in the press] to decide? The fact is that the First Amendment was written, and some of those who wrote it said so, in order to provide a means for exposing the secrets of government. Our government was founded by people who didn't trust government unchecked, unhindered and unrestrained, and who wrote the First Amendment with the precise idea that things kept secret tend to fester inside the government, and are not very good for the country. While excessive disclosure has on occasion hurt this country, I would submit that excessive secrecy has been much more harmful.

Seminar, Princeton, N.J./
Harper's, November: 51,52.

Georgiana H. Sheldon
Former Commissioner, Federal
Energy Regulatory Commission

3

I find that, looking at the business of government in general . . . the last few Administrations have not really understood how government operates. There is a cadre of professional people in the government which makes government work. And I believe it is the political appointee's responsibility—indeed, his mandate—to take your professional people, let them know what you want to do, and they'll help you do it. It's when you arrive in the city of Washington with an idea that you're going to change the government, that it's all bad, of course there's going to be resistance.

Interview/The Washington Post, 7-24:(4)17.

Mike Sherwin
Former Managing Director,
Civil Aeronautics Board of
the United States

4

In government you have a lot more masters to serve than you would in private industry—all of them with different agendas. Congress is always looking over your shoulder. So is the public. And the laws also are staring you in the face.

(MIKE SHERWIN)

There are a whole lot of people to be accountable to. It's frustrating to many of us. It can be a very wrenching experience.

Interview/U.S. News & World Report, 1-28:52.

George P. Shultz
Secretary of State
of the United States

1

Congress is a very changeable operation. They're in favor of something one time, then things happen and they change their mind, and all of a sudden you've got a program that's derailed . . . That's very disruptive.

Kuala Lumpur, Malaysia, July 10/
Los Angeles Times, 7-11:(I)4.

2

[On the Reagan Administration's proposed use of lie detectors for government employees as a way to trace information leaks, and whether he would be subject to those tests]: The minute in this government I am told that I'm not trusted, is the day that I leave . . . Personally, I have grave reservations about so-called lie-detector tests because the experience with them that I have read about—I don't claim to be an expert—it's hardly a scientific instrument. It tends to identify quite a few people who are innocent as guilty, and it misses at least some fraction of people who are guilty of lying; and it is, I think, pretty well demonstrated that a professional, let us say, a professional spy or a professional leaker, can probably train himself or herself not to be caught by the test. So the use of it as a broad-gauged condition of employment, you might say, seems to me to be questionable.

News conference, Washington,
Dec. 19/The New York Times, 12-20:13.

Arlen Specter
United States Senator,
R-Pennsylvania

3

[On being a Senator]: This is a fascinating job, challenging, demanding, a great opportunity to serve. Every problem in the world comes to the U.S. government, and every problem in the government comes to the U.S. Senate.

Interview/The Washington Post, 7-6:(A)4.

David A. Stockman
Director, Federal Office of
Management and Budget

4

Idealism [of people in government] ultimately is based on a certain presumption, even arrogance, that you are possessed with a doctrine, a blueprint, that will fundamentally reorganize the structures of a complicated society and millions of people will be better if your doctrine is imposed. But the longer you're in the daily meshing of the political gears of this society, the more you realize that nobody's doctrine should be turned loose on the system. Besides that, the forces of status quo and continuity far overwhelm any doctrine that might mobilize, energize.

Interview, Washington/
The New York Times, 2-4:8.

Law • The Judiciary

Floyd Abrams
Lawyer

1

[Criticizing the trend of public figures and organizations suing outspoken individuals for libel or slander]: If we see a further increase in the amount of these lawsuits, then individuals, even more than newspapers and broadcasters, will have to think twice before they speak out critically about public officials and immediately subject themselves to crippling libel or slander suits.

The New York Times,
2-14:12.

Joseph J. Balliro
Lawyer

2

[On criticism of lawyers who are actively engaged in criminal defense]: I don't know of any society in the world that went down the drain because of defense lawyers standing up for their clients. Every one of them went down the drain because of the corruption of government power.

At symposium sponsored by President's Commission
on Organized Crime, Washington, March 11/
The New York Times,
3-12:10.

Paul Bator
Professor of law,
Harvard University

3

Congress and the courts have been partners in promiscuity by encouraging a system in which too many economic and social decisions are made through litigation. Many judges use a make-it-up-as-you-go-along version of the Constitution to remake social policy. We are beginning to have powerful voices in the courts for the view that judges do not have unrestrained power to impose their policy preferences on society.

U.S. News & World Report,
10-14:65.

Harry A. Blackmun
Associate Justice,
Supreme Court of the United States

4

This [current Supreme] Court is not a great Court, but I think it is not the worst Court that we have had in history. [Being a Supreme Court Justice is] a battle, it's not a picnic and it's plain hard work. If I had any sense, I think I'd step down.

To Federal judges, Little Rock, Ark.,
August/The Washington Post, 9-20:(A)25.

Derek C. Bok
President,
Harvard University

5

Access to the courts may be open in principle. In practice, however, most people find their legal rights severely compromised by the cost of legal services, the baffling complications of existing rules and procedures, and the long, frustrating delays involved in bringing proceedings to a conclusion.

Report to Harvard's Board of Overseers/
Los Angeles Times, 9-6:(II)5.

Robert H. Bork
Judge, United States Court of
Appeals for the District of Columbia

6

In a constitutional democracy the moral content of law must be given by the morality of the framer or the legislator, never by the morality of the judge. The sole task of the latter—and it is a task quite large enough for anyone's wisdom, skill and virtue—is to translate the framer's or the legislator's morality into a rule to govern unforeseen circumstances. That abstinence from giving his own desires free play, that continuing and self-conscious renunciation of power—that is the morality of the jurist.

Francis Boyer Lecture sponsored
by American Enterprise Institute/
The New York Times, 1-4:8.

William J. Brennan, Jr.
Associate Justice,
Supreme Court of the United States

1

We current Justices read the Constitution in the only way that we can, as 20th-century Americans. We look to the history of the time of framing and to the intervening history of interpretation. But the ultimate question must be, what do the words of the text mean in our time.

At Georgetown University, Oct. 12/
The Washington Post, 10-28:(A)7.

Warren E. Burger
Chief Justice of the United States

2

[Calling for a new panel of judges to handle many cases now decided by the Supreme Court]: Why is it so difficult to grasp the reality that just as we need more police and more courts to deal with automobile traffic than we did 75 years ago . . . we need something more to deal with the avalanche of cases coming to the Supreme Court?

Before American Bar Association, Detroit,
Feb. 17/Los Angeles Times, 2-18:(I)5.

3

[Saying the Supreme Court is overburdened and cannot review all the lower-court rulings it should]: Unless some relief is given, it is not unreasonable to think that there may be some judges in some courts who will exploit the reality that, since the chance of being reviewed by the Supreme Court is swiftly diminishing, they need not pay very much attention to what the Supreme Court decides. Some careful, responsible observers think this is already happening.

Before American Newspaper Publishers Association,
Miami, May 7/Los Angeles Times, 5-8:(I)5.

4

[Opposing advertising by lawyers]: My advice to the public is never, never, never, under any circumstances, engage the services of a lawyer who advertises. I am not ready to say that publicly yet, but someday I will. I'd go out and dig ditches before [advertising] . . . Any idea we

need the kind of advertising I am addressing . . . the kind that I call sheer shysterism, is nonsense.

Before closed meeting
of an American Bar Association commission,
Washington, July 7/Los Angeles Times, 7-8:(I)9.

5

In recent years, people have expressed concern about the attacks on the Supreme Court and on the Constitution. There is nothing new about such attacks, and there is nothing inherently bad in most of them. When free people challenge their servants—The Executive, the Congress, and the courts—temperately and with reasoned debate, we have nothing to fear. [Such criticism is] what an open society is all about.

Before American Bar Association, London,
July 19/The Christian Science Monitor, 7-19:2.

6

[Calling for arbitration and mediation of some cases to reduce the load on courts]: A host of new kinds of cases have flooded the courts: students seeking to litigate a failing mark, professors litigating denial of academic tenure, and another great load on the courts, welfare recipients. [Appellate judges learn] very quickly that a larger part of all the litigation in the courts is an exercise in futility and frustration. These protracted cases not only deny parties the benefits of a speedy resolution of their conflicts, but also enlarge the costs, tensions and delays facing all other litigants waiting in line . . . Sometimes I've thought there is some form of mass neurosis developing in the country that leads people to think courts were created to solve all the problems of society. We must learn from the experience of labor and management that courts are not the best places to resolve certain kinds of claims. In terms of cost, time and human wear and tear, arbitration is better by far. We must now call on the inventiveness, the ingenuity and the resourcefulness of American businessmen and the American lawyers, the Yankee Trader innovativeness, to shape new tools to meet new needs.

Before American Arbitration Association,
St. Paul, Minn., Aug. 21/The New York Times, 8-22:14.

(WARREN E. BURGER)

[Saying TV cameras should not be allowed in courtrooms]: Television cameras make show business out of the most serious business in the world—namely, the trial of a case . . . I recall a discussion of this with some television news moguls. They wanted to cover a trial. I said, "Of course, you will put on the whole arguments from beginning to end." And they said, "Oh, no, we can't do that; that would be too expensive" . . . It is difficult enough for nine Justices, having studied the particular case, to understand and grasp the nuances of what's going on in an oral argument. For someone to come in on the 7 o'clock news and show a snippet of two minutes—that's not constructive . . . If television would put on the whole argument, and make their case, I think that would be a different story. But, even then, I am not sure how educational it would be.

Interview/
USA Today, 12-12:(4)11.

1

[Criticizing attorneys for bringing frivolous lawsuits to court]: No one wishes to suppress hard-fought advocacy. But a line needs to be drawn between fair blows and fouls; zealous representation is our ideal, not dilatory and abusive gamesmanship. The time has come to penalize those few lawyers and litigants who treat the judicial system as an arena for a sporting contest . . .

Annual report on the judiciary,
Dec. 29*/Los Angeles Times, 12-30:(I)7.

2

Mario M. Cuomo
Governor of New York (D)

There is less respect for the law in this country than ever before . . . Stand at a street corner late at night and see how many people disregard red lights—just drive through them as if they weren't there. Look at the numbers of people who, despite all the warnings and pleadings and threats, continue to drive while drunk and to kill other human beings in the process. Consider that some communities have begun walling themselves off from the outside world, as the villages and towns of Western Europe did at the onset of the Dark Ages . . . Sometimes all of us become impatient with the law and feel it stands in the way of real justice. But remember—that's God's judgment to make. We lesser beings must live by the laws of our own human society.

At New York State Police graduation ceremony,
Albany, March 8/The New York Times, 3-9:9.

4

Alan Dershowitz
Professor of law,
Harvard University

The Reagan Justice Department is hazardous to our Constitutional health. [Attorney General] Ed Meese is smart and he has surrounded himself with brilliant, nice men with a radical mission to roll back our most fundamental Constitutional protections, without looking reflectively at Constitutionally embedded traditions.

U.S. News & World Report, 10-14:65.

5

Clark Durant
Chairman, Legal Services
Corporation of the United States

I believe the provision of legal services is too important to be just another Federal program. It

7

Alan Cranston
United States Senator,
D-California

[Criticizing the Senate confirmation process for Federal judges]: All too often, the Senate deals with nominations in a very cursory way. We've drifted into a situation where almost anyone who can pass the bar is acceptable, unless he's been behind bars.

The New York Times, 11-26:10.

3

I think we have too many lawyers trying to save too much money for too many rich people—and too few lawyers trying to protect the liberty of everyone.

To law students/
U.S. News & World Report, 10-21:12.

6

(CLARK DURANT)

is an essential and integral part of our system of justice. Almost everyone needs legal representation at one time or another, and we have an obligation to make sure that even the poorest of the poor have places to turn to with their legal problems.

Before House subcommittee, Washington/
The Christian Science Monitor, 4-30:23.

Charles Fried
Solicitor General
of the United States

1

The very notion that somehow judges' notions of enlightened morality should be the source of their decisions is one which I strongly reject. After all, judges exercise power; they exercise power over other people and, most dramatically, over the democratic process, to limit—in the Constitutional area—what the democratic process can accomplish. Now, that power surely should only be exercised on the basis of some warrant, some authority. And the only warrant for a judge exercising that rather dramatic form of power is the authority which the Constitution itself, as a written document, gives the judge. I disagree with the notion judges have some special competence to discern enlightened morality. They are no more competent than you or I, or than legislators are. Their special competence relates to the interpretation of law.

Interview, Washington/
The New York Times, 12-28:9.

Ira Glasser
Executive director,
American Civil Liberties Union

2

[Criticizing the trend of public figures and organizations suing outspoken individuals for libel or slander]: I've been seeing these kinds of cases in recent years, whereas I never saw them before. Public officials and others are telling themselves, "Hey, this is a way we can put a price on dissent that our tormentors won't be able to meet."

The New York Times, 2-14:12.

Harold H. Greene
Judge, United States District
Court for the District of Columbia

3

There is . . . in this country a strain of violence and vigilantism apart from the law, which stems from the civilizing of the wilderness not long ago, as historical time is measured. If all these strains are to be contained, if centrifugal forces are not to tear the nation apart, there must be centers of gravity apart from the shifting political majorities. The law, represented by its guardians, the judges and lawyers, is one such fixed star.

At George Washington University
Law Center commencement/Time, 6-17:69.

Elizabeth Holtzman
District Attorney,
Brooklyn, N.Y.

4

[On being District Attorney]: You can't just look at the prosecution of each individual case. You also have to be an advocate for the improvement of the system, to be imaginative, experimental. Yet you also can't be like Emerson, looking through the puddles and paying attention to the sky.

Interview/The New York Times, 3-13:14.

Irving R. Kaufman
Chief Judge,
United States Court of Appeals
for the Second Circuit

5

Problems of legal ethics have increased dramatically in recent years, and this increase is, in my view, attributable to a disturbing trend within the profession. Growing specialization and stratification within the bar has fostered a professional ethos in which some lawyers think of themselves as tradesmen whose duty is to simply carry out clients' directives, rather than as professionals who advise and counsel their clients on the propriety, as well as the legality, of the client's conduct.

At symposium sponsored by President's Commission
on Organized Crime, Washington, March 11/
The New York Times, 3-12:10.

William Kunstler
Civil-rights lawyer

I surprise judges now because they expect me to be a roaring maniac. I'm not one who roars; but when I'm right and I feel I'm right, I will stick.

Interview, New York/
USA Today, 3-1:(A)2.

1

Rex E. Lee
Solicitor General
of the United States

The principle responsibility of the Solicitor General is to win cases in the Supreme Court and to maintain the stature of the office. Where that can be done, consistent with the broader principles the incumbent President may hold, that's fine. But my audience in the final analysis is not millions, not thousands or even hundreds, but nine [the Supreme Court Justices].

Interview, Washington, April 30/
The New York Times, 5-1:15.

2

Thurgood Marshall
Associate Justice,
Supreme Court of the United States

We recognized long ago that mere access to the courthouse does not by itself assure a proper functioning of the adversary process, and that a criminal trial is fundamentally unfair if the state proceeds against an indigent defendant without making certain that he has access to the raw material integral to the building of an effective defense. To implement this principle, we have focused on identifying the "basic tools of an adequate defense or appeal," and we have required that such tools be provided to those defendants who cannot afford to pay for them.

Written Court decision, Washington,
Feb. 26/The New York Times, 2-27:10.

3

Edwin Meese III
Attorney General of the United States

Too many of the [U.S. Supreme] Court's opinions, on the whole, have been more policy

202

4

choices than articulations of long-term Constitutional principle. The [Court's] voting blocs, the arguments, all reveal a greater allegiance to what the Court thinks constitutes sound public policy than a deference to what the Constitution—its text and intention—may demand.

Before American Bar Association, Washington,
July 9/Los Angeles Times, 7-10:(I)1.

5

[Saying Supreme Court Justices should not rule according to their own personal opinions but should follow the Constitution]: Where the language of the Constitution is specific, it must be obeyed. Where there is a demonstrable consensus among the framers and ratifiers as to a principle stated or implied by the Constitution, it should be followed. Where there is ambiguity as to the precise meaning or reach of a Constitutional provision, it should be interpreted and applied in a manner so as to at least not contradict the text of the Constitution itself.

Before lawyers' division, Federalist Society,
Washington, Nov. 15/Los Angeles Times, 11-16:(I)4.

6

Mario Merola
District Attorney,
Bronx, N.Y.

The bottom line is, give me a good judge and the worst [court] system and he'll make it better. You give me a lousy judge and the best [court] system and he'll find out how to mess it up.

The New York Times, 4-22:15.

7

Newton N. Minow
Lawyer; Former Chairman,
Federal Communications Commission

After 35 years, I have finished a comprehensive study of European comparative law. After careful study of four legal systems, here are my conclusions: In Germany, under the law, everything is prohibited except that which is permitted. In France, under the law, everything is permitted, except that which is prohibited. In the Soviet Union, under the law, everything is prohibited, *including* that which is permitted. And

(NEWTON N. MINOW)

in Italy, under the law, everything is permitted, *especially* that which is prohibited. Now, there may be some of you who ask, What about the United States? I suggest that is why there are American law schools and law professors. We ask American law professors that you teach us not only what is prohibited and what is permitted, but also *why*—and we also ask you to reflect on what *should* be prohibited and what *should* be permitted.

Before Association of American Law Schools,
Washington/The Wall Street Journal,
2-4:20.

Norman J. Ornstein
Resident scholar,
American Enterprise Institute

1

[On whether there is a need for another level of appellate courts to reduce the burden on the Supreme Court]: I'm skeptical about the need for another level of courts. What tends to happen is that after you create a new level, the workload expands, and in another 10 years people are clamoring for still another level. It would make more sense to find a different way of allocating responsibilities among the appellate courts and the Supreme Court. It would help, too, for the Supreme Court to take on fewer cases by exercising a little more internal discipline.

Interview/
U.S. News & World Report, 1-28:54.

2

I have great problems with the judiciary right now, but you can spread the fault around. In the last 15 to 20 years, both Congress and the President have found it convenient to avoid making tough decisions. It's easier to pass the buck to the judiciary or to regulatory agencies. Judges—conservatives as well as liberals—have eagerly grasped the responsibility and been more than willing to move in and make the decisions.

Interview/
U.S. News & World Report,
1-28:54.

Richard A. Posner
Judge, United States Court of
Appeals for the Seventh Circuit

3

The level of uncertainty in American law is remarkable. At some point, the great amount of litigation just seems to have blown things apart. Now there's not much predictability.

The Wall Street Journal, 3-15:22.

4

Federal courts are experiencing a case-load crisis that is endangering the quality of justice: There is less time to focus on a case. Also, there has been a tremendous increase in the number of law clerks, magistrates and other aides, which makes for a less-efficient system. The judiciary used to be unique in government because it consisted of a small body of people who did their own work and were accountable in a very direct way for their actions. Now the judge is in danger of disappearing in a growing bureaucracy. Adding judges creates more room for disagreement among them; it is much harder to maintain coherent law. Enlarging the bench also speeds up litigation, which means more cases are filed. That's what's really frightening: The growth seems to feed on itself.

Interview/U.S. News & World Report, 4-15:72.

Ronald Reagan
President of the United States

5

The independence of the courts from improper political influence is a sacred principle. It must always be guarded. And let me assure you it will always be guarded while this Administration is in office. But, as you know, the Founding Fathers knew that, like any other part of the government, the power of the judiciary could be abused. They never intended, for example, that the courts pre-empt legislative prerogatives or become vehicles for political action or social experimentation, or for coercing the populace into adopting anyone's personal view of utopia.

To U.S. Attorneys, Washington,
Oct. 21/The New York Times, 10-22:1,9.

(RONALD REAGAN)

Over recent years, we have had [Supreme] Courts that tended to legislate rather than interpret the Constitution. Their ruling against prayer in schools is kind of strange in a body that opens with prayer and that has over its doorway, "In God We Trust."

Interview/
U.S. News & World Report, 11-18:32.

1

William H. Rehnquist
Associate Justice, Supreme
Court of the United States

Why did the species of lawyer-statesmen virtually disappear in the century following the Civil War? I think it was in part because the 19th-century legal training and experience taught skills that were transferable in their entirety to the stump speeches and printed tracts by which political campaigns and debates were carried on in those days. One suspects that Alexander Hamilton, Abraham Lincoln and William H. Seward, successful lawyers all, did not worry to the same extent as their present-day counterparts about the number of hours they had billed. Law is surely a more profitable profession for those who practice it now than it was then, but one cannot help doubting whether its contribution to the political life of the nation has not been sadly diminished in the process.

Before Federalist Society, University of Chicago,
May 6/The Washington Post,
5-7:(A)7.

2

Herman Schwartz
Professor of law,
American University

[President] Reagan is trying to win in court what he cannot win in Congress. All this talk about judicial restraint is hogwash. Presidents appoint judges who will rule in their favor. Few Presidents have tried to make the courts so ideologically rigid as Reagan has.

U.S. News & World Report, 10-14:65.

3

John H. Shenefield
Lawyer; Former Assistant Attorney
General of the United States

I believe that lawyers, as well as members of other professions, should be subject like any other American citizen to the antitrust and consumer-protection laws of the United States. Recent efforts by some bar associations, led by the Texas and American Bar Associations, to diminish Federal Trade Commission jurisdiction over lawyers and other professionals are an unabashed attempt to create special-interest treatment for professionals. Those seeking special status for professionals argue that professionals are most appropriately regulated by members of their own profession. Any system in which the regulated are the sole regulators is fraught with inherent conflicts of interest. It is above all unseemly for lawyers to seek special treatment under the law. The legal profession needs now more than ever to demonstrate that it operates efficiently, honestly and responsively in the interests of those who need and hire lawyers and who pay them so well. It would seem prudent for the profession to invite special scrutiny and go out of its way to reassure all Americans that it respects the law by being subject to it.

Before House Commerce, Transportation
and Tourism Subcommittee, Washington,
April 17/The New York Times, 4-23:12.

4

Paul Simon
United States Senator, D-Illinois

[Criticizing the caliber of nominees for Federal judgeships coming to the Senate for confirmation]: We're just getting too many nominees who just barely get by the bar association. When you're talking about a Federal judge, he ought to be someone of really sterling character and qualifications.

The New York Times, 11-26:10.

5

William Reece Smith
Former president,
American Bar Association

[President] Reagan cutbacks in the Legal Services Corporation have harmed the government's

6

(WILLIAM REECE SMITH)

ability to meet the legal needs of the poor. The Administration continues to oppose the program even though Congress has acted to prevent improprieties. The agency has had defects, but it continues to be one of the most effective social programs that our country has.

U.S. News & World Report, 10-14:65.

John Paul Stevens
Associate Justice, Supreme
Court of the United States

1

If a randomly selected group of average citizens were asked whether Supreme Court proceedings should be televised, I am sure most would answer "Yes," or perhaps "Why not?" If, however, instead of responding to an abstract question, they were given the opportunity to view four hours of oral argument on live television on a daily basis, I feel sure they would exhibit a rather decided preference for soap operas, grade B movies or even sumo wrestling. For the most part, what happens in our courtroom is not high drama for the average viewer. We do provide a spectacle that usually holds the interest of a group of tourists for a span of 5 or 10 minutes; but plenty of seats are almost always available, and, even though admission is free of charge, I think we have only one or two Court watchers who would even consider subscribing for season tickets. If live attendance is any barometer of the probable value of the television market for our arguments, the public demand is almost always in the "ho-hum" bracket.

At Florida State University/
The New York Times, 2-26:8.

Laurence H. Tribe
Professor of law,
Harvard University

2

When we put people with life tenure on our Federal courts, and especially the Supreme Court, we are not simply awarding certificates for prizes to the best and the brightest; we are entrusting our Constitutional future to a series of fallible human beings with marked opinions about the direction in which the Constitution should move. Just as we would never dream of giving the President the single-handed power to amend the Constitution, so we should not give the President the power to single-handedly change the Constitution's direction by allowing the President to nominate to the Federal courts virtually anyone he wants, as long as that person has a sufficiently impressive legal resume and no skeletons in the closet.

Interview/USA Today,
10-7:(A)7.

Sol Wachtler
Chief Judge,
New York State court system

3

The courts have become a nice, easy target to blame for all of society's ills. Even if the courts could operate at maximum efficiency, they would still have little impact on crime. Courts don't cause crime. Courts don't stop crime. And courts are not quiet extensions of the prosecutor's office. If that were recognized, it would also be recognized that we're doing an admirable job.

News conference, New York,
Jan. 31/The New York Times, 2-1:13.

Politics

Bill Alexander
United States Representative,
D-Arkansas

1

[On Congressional votes in which Democrats split on various issues]: It's the way the Democratic Party is. We are a diverse party that divides up on issues and rarely marches in lockstep.

Washington, March 26/
The New York Times,
3-27:11.

Lamar Alexander
Governor of Tennessee (R)

2

[On why Republicans have fared poorly in gubernatorial elections recently but did well in the Presidential races]: Republicans, particularly those in the South, are fascinated with Washington issues. If you give them a chance, they'll run for mayor and argue about the gold standard. They'll attack the Federal deficit when they ought to be talking about potholes, prisons and garbage. The national Democratic Party has no message that a majority of people will support, but many of their local and statewide candidates do understand the need to concentrate on gut issues like good roads and quality schools.

Interview/
U.S. News & World Report, 3-11:50.

Les Aspin
United States Representative,
D-Wisconsin

3

In this business, if somebody isn't unhappy with you, then you're not doing your job.

Newsweek, 4-1:31.

Bruce Babbitt
Governor of Arizona (D)

4

A lot of people are starting to understand that the problem of the Democratic Party is not the

lack of a messenger but the incoherence of our message. Some of us said that same thing after the 1980 election—that we needed an integral debate to produce ideas with an edge, and not another pot of mush. But we were ignored. Now I think Democrats understand it would be a great mistake to trot out a new set of candidates for a cattle show, only to lead them all to slaughter.

Interview/
The Washington Post National Weekly, 1-7:5.

5

The Democratic Party has become a cathedral of orthodoxy in which true believers endlessly reiterate sacred scripts with no admissible debate. But a lot of people in the back benches of the cathedral are not listening to the sermons.

At meeting of Democrats,
Los Angeles/
Los Angeles Times,
4-9:(I)14.

Birch Bayh
Former United States Senator,
D-Indiana

6

Political action committees make it possible to spend too much money in politics. The amounts of money being raised in campaigns now are almost debilitating to the process. A candidate spends more of his time figuring out how to stay on TV than he spends figuring out his positions and what he will do when elected. I know the importance of the First Amendment. But I wonder if the Founding Fathers, when they conceived of the First Amendment, meant to give millionaires the right to buy ads and donate money to put something on TV that is misrepresentation and character assassination. The farmer, or auto worker, or grocer can only afford to make a $1 or $5 contribution. The First Amendment should give us all an equal voice. A millionaire should not get a $1-million voice.

Interview, Indianapolis/
USA Today,
6-25:(A)10.

Hyman Berman
Professor of history,
University of Minnesota

1

[On Walter Mondale's losing the 1984 Presidential election, and the liberal Democratic policies he represented]: Walter Mondale was a second-generation personification of these impulses, and his failure came because he exercised them when the rest of the nation wanted either to forget them or reject them. The spirit of progressivism and reform is not alive and well in the nation, and even in [Mondale's home state of] Minnesota it is in a kind of terminal state, an advanced state of cancerous decay.

The Wall Street Journal, 1-2:30.

Larry Berman
Professor,
University of California, Davis

2

[President] Ronald Reagan is the most successful and most underestimated political leader since Franklin Delano Roosevelt. Ronald Reagan has clearly reshaped the dialogue on the national agenda. We're looking at a fundamental alteration in domestic priorities.

Panel discussion sponsored
by American Political Science Association,
New Orleans, Aug. 29/The New York Times, 9-2:11.

Joseph R. Biden, Jr.
United States Senator, D-Delaware

3

Our [Democratic] Party went astray by failing to remember what got us this far: moral indignation, decent instincts, a sense of shared sacrifice and mutual responsibility, and a set of national priorities that emphasized what we had in common.

U.S. News & World Report, 7-8:38.

Bill Bradley
United States Senator,
D-New Jersey

4

If you look at the way people think in Congress, they tend to think in terms of a legislator.

They define that as balancing this group against that group, pleasing the plumbers, not making the realtors too mad, keeping the truckers at arm's length, making sure of the farmers—just make sure not too many people are mad at you . . . Then they come to re-election, and they've got to forget all that skill, all the effort they have been investing in keeping everybody happy, and devise a clear message to the broadest number of people. My point is that if you start from the premise that the politician's first objective is to get re-elected, and if you then say that the way he gets re-elected is by devising a message that's clear to the broadest number of people, if you've decided what that message is—economic growth, lower rates, a fairer system—that liberates you from all the shuffling and pulling and tugging that the legislative process has demanded.

Interview/USA Today, 4-9:(A)11.

George Bush
Vice President of the United States

5

[Saying he will not make himself more publicly visible during his second term]: I want to support the President, support our policies—I have a hand in formulating them and shaping them. If that means foregoing a fast "Hey, Mom, I'm on TV," I'll forgo it from time to time.

Broadcast interview/
"Face the Nation,"
CBS-TV, 1-20.

6

I think Republicans have learned from the Democrats. The Democrats used to slug it out with each other in the trenches and the Republicans would be sitting on the sidelines, rubbing our hands in glee, saying that this is going to spell the end of Senator X or candidate Y. But the Democrats would have a miraculous way of getting together. Now I think we are better at that than we used to be, and maybe the Democrats are less good than they used to be, at least in the last election. I hope it is a lesson we have learned, because it is an important one.

Interview, Washington, April 25/
The New York Times, 4-26:9.

Patrick Caddell
Democratic Party public-opinion analyst

[President Reagan is] not the omnipotent, beloved person people in Washington think he is. Ronald Reagan's strength is that he's an ideologue. He does believe in something. He believes in what he says at a time when no one thinks any politician believes in anything.

Interview/The Washington Post, 1-21:(G)6.

1

Joseph A. Califano, Jr.
Former Secretary of Health, Education and Welfare of the United States

[On the possibility that Chrysler Corp. chairman Lee Iacocca will run for President]: His life is the stuff of American legend. He was born in a log cabin in Allentown, Pennsylvania; as a youth, he threw a silver dollar across the Lehigh River; and today some see the jaunty tilt of the cigar clenched in his teeth and find themselves recalling the inevitable cigarette holder tilted at precisely the same angle many years ago—they ask themselves: "Could this man be the next F.D.R.?" And the answer comes: It's too soon to tell; we don't even know whether he is a Democrat. Does Lee Iacocca have what it takes to be President of the United States? I've studied the Presidency, I've written about it, I've worked in the White House, I've served two Presidents at close hand and I can tell you that Lee does have what it takes. When he reads cue cards, you cannot see his eyes moving.

At fund-raising affair for restoration of Statue of Liberty, Washington/The New York Times, 10-2:14.

2

Dick Cheney
United States Representative, R-Wyoming

[On Ronald Reagan's victory over Jimmy Carter in the 1980 Presidential election]: Two things were critical to our success. One is Ronald Reagan. The other is Jimmy Carter. You sort of had to have Carter to have Reagan happen.

Interview/The Washington Post, 1-21:(G)6.

208

Shirley Chisholm
Professor, Mount Holyoke College; Former United States Representative, D-New York

I don't think anyone could have beaten Ronald Reagan [in the 1984 Presidential election]. He really was able to worm his way into the hearts of the American people. People would tell you in one breath about the deleterious impact his policies had on their lives, then in the next breath they'd say they were going to vote for him anyway, that they liked the old cowboy. Such contradictions I've never heard politically in terms of electing a President.

Interview/Ms., February:66.

4

Bill Clinton
Governor of Arkansas (D)

[On how to get the Democratic Party out of the doldrums]: Show that the Party is interested in promoting an economic and national-defense and social program which is more than simply redistribution of income for specific governmental programs. And I do not believe that we need, in order to do that, to become more like the Republicans. I do not believe that we need to abandon our commitment to equal opportunity without regard to race. I do not believe that we need to abandon all of our social programs. But I think we do need to say that we are willing to take responsibility for holding ourselves accountable for the money we spend in social programs.

Interview, Atlanta/ The Christian Science Monitor, 7-15:8.

5

Tony Coelho
United States Representative, D-California

[On the Democratic Party]: As far as the Federal government is concerned, we're the minority party. Out in the country, at the state and local level, we're the majority party.

The Washington Post, 1-21:(G)6.

6

to figure out how to make it work. We cannot become the majority party without black support.

Before National Urban League, Washington,
July 22/The Christian Science Monitor, 7-23:4.

Edwin B. Edwards
Governor of Louisiana (D)

[On the many government investigations of him for corruption]: [The government probes are the result of] overzealous Republican prosecutors . . . a vicious, cynical and heartless group of people. The Republican Party today is in the hands of neo-Nazis and arch-conservatives. [By going after a liberal Democrat such as himself,] Republicans hope to shed the image of Watergate—*the* major political-corruption scandal in America, next to the *other* major Republican scandal, Teapot Dome.

Los Angeles Times, 8-14:(I)1.

Frank J. Fahrenkopf, Jr.
Chairman,
Republican National Committee

The Republican Party today is riding on the crest of a rising demographic wave. However, this victory is not yet complete because of one last statistic. [President] Ronald Reagan and [Vice President] George Bush received only 8 to 11 per cent of the black vote [in the 1984 election] . . . Blacks alone, among all demographic groups, cast their votes almost exclusively for the Democratic ticket—a ticket that was not just rejected but was repudiated by [a margin of] more than 16 million voters, 49 states and 525 electoral votes.

At NAACP convention, Dallas,
June 26/The Washington Post,
6-27:(A)3.

Geraldine A. Ferraro
Former United States Representative,
D-New York; 1984 Democratic
Vice Presidential nominee

We have some women in the House who are biologically female, but Attila the Hun would be

Kent Cooper
Director, Public Records Section,
Federal Election Commission

Money shouldn't be a factor in deciding to run for public office. [But] now candidates mortgage their homes, hit up their relatives, and still have to raise hundreds of thousands of dollars. Fund-raising has become a never-ending activity. There has to be a better way.

Interview, Washington/
The New York Times,
12-17:10.

Alan Cranston
United States Senator, D-California

[Saying that, when raising funds for his political campaigns, he doesn't spend much time talking with people who can't contribute the legal maximum of $1,000]: Some people are able to give the maximum amount; they're accustomed to it. But people who can only afford $100 may have to think twice about it. It's not worth my time to raise it in $100 amounts. I have to concentrate on the people who can max out.

Interview/Los Angeles Times, 2-10:(I)29.

Mario M. Cuomo
Governor of New York (D)

[Saying he does not plan to run for President in 1988]: I don't think I have what it takes. I don't think I have the persona.

To reporters, Washington, Feb. 26/
The Washington Post,
2-27:(A)7.

Robert J. Dole
United States Senator, R-Kansas

Many blacks say Republicans have turned their backs on them. I assure you very few Republicans take pride in the lack of Party votes from black people. I want to see more black delegates at the Republican convention. I helped organize the Black Council of the National Republican Committee in 1971. We're still trying

WHAT THEY SAID IN 1985

(GERALDINE A. FERRARO)

closer to their philosophy. . . Who would I want to elect to office? Give me a feminist.

*New Orleans, Aug. 5/
USA Today, 8-6:(A)12.*

Thomas S. Foley
*United States Representative,
D-Washington*

. . . the Democratic Party is still the majority party, and we have more mayors and more city councilmen, more Congressmen and state legislators, almost as many Senators. We have one fewer President than the Republicans. But the Democratic Party is not about to be eclipsed, and I think you're going to see a resurgence of the Democratic Party in the coming years. We have two great political parties, and, every once in a while, somebody predicts the death of one, as they predicted the death of the Republican Party in 1964.

*Broadcast interview, Washington/
"Meet the Press," NBC-TV, 2-10.*

1

Barney Frank
*United States Representative,
D-Massachusetts*

. . . principled and thoughtful and responsible liberalism is not only morally correct, but politically correct as well. There is an internal pendulum in American politics, a self-correcting mechanism. When you go too far in one direction you have to go back the other way. It is at least arguable that the [conservative] peak has past.

*Before New American Agenda/
The Washington Post, 6-10:(A)7.*

2

J. William Fulbright
*Former United States Senator,
D-Arkansas*

The democratic system requires the existence of a loyal opposition. It's unrealistic to expect people to submerge their views in some ideal of

210

3

bipartisanship . . . You don't really want a bunch of zombies over there who just support the President, come what may. People who disagree shouldn't be made to feel like skunks at a picnic.

Los Angeles Times, 2-1:(I)10.

Newt Gingrich
*United States Representative,
R-Georgia*

[On his publicly criticizing his fellow Republicans]: Democrats have been in the majority for almost 60 years, cheerfully fighting in public. Majorities worry about gathering the energy of conflict in order to dominate.

The Washington Post, 1-3:(B)2.

4

John Glenn
United States Senator, D-Ohio

Some have argued that the adoption of a National [Presidential] Primary Day would clearly favor well-known and well-financed candidates while reducing the prospects for so-called "dark horse" candidates . . . I believe that any candidate who has failed to win a national record and reputation . . . probably has no business on the ballot in the first place.

*Before Committee on National Elections,
Washington, June 18/The Washington Post, 6-19:(A)7.*

5

Barry M. Goldwater
United States Senator, R-Arizona

What we have today is a government mostly of special interests. This town [Washington] is filled with them. They don't give a damn about the whole government. They just want their little baby taken care of, whether it's franchises on beer, bowling balls or airplanes—and they're damn hard to beat.

Interview/Los Angeles Herald Examiner, 1-13:(4)15.

6

[Lamenting the high cost of Presidential election campaigns and the proliferation of political

7

(BARRY M. GOLDWATER)

action committees]: We must prove that the Oval Office is not a prize to be auctioned off to the highest bidder. Our task is to restore control over elections to candidates and the people, and to take power away from the political merchants who are enriching themselves with booty collected from special interests and wealthy donors seeking to control the country's political agenda.

Before Commission on National Elections,
Washington, Sept. 17/The Washington Post,
9-18:(A)6.

Charles E. Grassley
United States Senator, R-Iowa

Since the beginning of his [President Reagan's] Administration, they never really tried to have a social relationship and a friendly relationship with members of Congress. When they wanted us, they called. When we wanted them, they were generally too busy. And that's been the case over the last five years. The inability of the President himself, and more particularly his staff, to build up a personal and professional relationship with people on the Hill has made it impossible for his legislative goals to be accomplished. And the fact that he's a lame duck makes the situation worse.

The New York Times, 12-17:11.

William H. Gray III
United States Representative,
D-Pennsylvania

[President Reagan is] like the Baptist preacher. He may be a lousy administrator, a terrible pastor, but the question is, "Can he preach at 11 o'clock on a Sunday morning?" And, if he can preach for that 20 minutes, people withstand a whole lot of garbage on the rest of the issues. Why? Because in the Baptist Church, the emphasis is on the proclaimed word, the preached word. Now, this President has that ability to do it at 11 o'clock on Sunday morning. He does preach the word. The word is the values of America, things that all of us can agree to, whether you're Democrat or Republican. . .

We need symbols. You need them. I need them. Look back over the last few years. You had [Richard] Nixon, who almost stole the country, went out in disgrace. You had [Gerald] Ford, kind man, played golf. You had Jimmy Carter, who was not able to excite the American people, communicate. And all of a sudden you have this guy [Ronald Reagan] who's been reading those lines excellently for years. What you get is the impression and the symbol that this guy is speaking from the heart, an articulate President who knows the issues. And, boom! If you've been living over the last 15 years and looking at what's been in the White House, you say: "Praise the Lord! Finally we've got a preacher who can preach."

To reporters, June 27/
The New York Times,
7-4:26.

1

Fred I. Greenstein
Professor of politics,
Princeton University

Some people say [President] Reagan's mind is full of rigidities. But throughout his public life he's shown he can play the game of politics in a standard way and move away from public ideological positions when he thought it served a practical purpose . . . On a psychological level, what this says to me is, as much as I realize he's someone who could cut a deal when he wanted to, I've underestimated him. Beneath the rhetoric, this is a guy who can operate in a way that a [late Chicago Mayor Richard] Daley or Bismarck could operate.

The New York Times, 3-27:12.

3

I am struck by the surface similarity between [President] Ronald Reagan and the person for whom he cast his first vote: F. D. R. The Reagan operation seems to have a striking professionalism. They both had a capacity for impressive dramatics. On economics, both men were similarly ignorant.

Panel discussion sponsored
by American Political Science Association,
New Orleans, Aug. 29/The New York Times, 9-2:11.

4

Tom Harkin
United States Senator, D-Iowa

We Democrats have to quit defending ourselves and start attacking. And we must adopt a real populist agenda. I don't believe Ronald Reagan ever got to be President because he defined some great vision for America that people rallied around. What Ronald Reagan understands is you only win if you attack. Americans like a fighter. We should attack the Republicans' basic premise of laissez-faire capitalism. Our rallying cry as Democrats should be, "Capitalism with a conscience."

Interview/U.S. News & World Report, 4-15:38.

1

Gary Hart
United States Senator, D-Colorado

[Since the early 1970s,] in terms of both themes and substance, and ideas, [the Democratic] Party has been out of steam. I think we permitted a vacuum to form which [President] Ronald Reagan has partly filled. I think the real question is what happens after Reagan . . . The Democratic challenge is to recapture the initiative—symbolically, thematically and substantively.

Interview/The Washington Post, 1-21:(G)6.

2

[On the Democratic Party]: Traditional liberalism protected and preserved our national values for more than 50 years. Now to advance those same values, we must accept change. Our past achievements are not a cathedral in which to worship but a firm foundation upon which to build a new vision . . . The party of change must change.

To his supporters, Boston, Feb. 4/
The Washington Post,
2-5:(A)7.

3

John Heinz III
United States Senator,
R-Pennsylvania

[Saying he has no current plans to run for President]: Any of us in public office, because

4

we have some kind of competitive spirit, can't help measuring ourselves against people in the highest office—but only if you're willing to take partial leave of your senses.

Interview/Cosmopolitan, September:261.

Charlton Heston
Actor

[On actors being involved in politics]: Actors are on the one hand perceived by society as basically irresponsible airheads, with some justification. On the other hand, they are or should be more effective communicators than, say, lawyers or professors or even most elected politicians. They come with a built-in advantage as candidates—a pre-established public identity and an ability to communicate.

Interview/
USA Today, 12-6:(A)13.

5

Jim Hightower
Commissioner of Agriculture of Texas

Pundits tell us the Democrats have to attract yuppies if they are going to win, Democrats got to put on little happy faces like [Republican President] Ronnie Reagan does, put on a new suit of Republican clothes. Well, that's like trying to put socks on a rooster. It just ain't going to work.

Los Angeles, 12-19:(V)41.

6

Jesse L. Jackson
Civil-rights leader;
President, Operation PUSH
(People United to Save Humanity)

[On the Democratic Party's loss in the 1984 Presidential election]: I have not heard from the Party one rational analysis of why the Party lost. [The Party lost] because it was an election between one candidate who was popular [Republican Ronald Reagan] and one who was not [Democrat Walter Mondale]. One candidate [Mondale] said he would raise taxes if he won, an idea so unpopular he couldn't coerce some Democratic leaders to get on the stage with him.

7

(JESSE L. JACKSON)

Democratic candidates were running for office and saying, "I am not a Mondale Democrat."

Interview, Washington, Feb. 10/
The Washington Post, 2-11:(A)13.

1

The Democratic Party is really becoming more exclusive, as opposed to inclusive—it's contracting rather than expanding. All this talk [within the Party] of "new patriotism," "new center," "anti-caucus" . . . is trying to gain in the jet stream of [Republican President] Reagan . . . I think our Party is misreading the broader public. It has to reach out and seize the issues that impact upon people's lives.

Interview, Chicago/
The Christian Science Monitor, 6-5:40.

2

The shadow of [Republican President] Ronald Reagan hovers over the Democratic Party. He has intimidated the Democrats [into joining the Republicans in a] radical shift to the right.

Before National Black Caucus of State Legislators,
Philadelphia, Dec. 6/The Washington Post, 12-7:(A)15.

Marvin Kalb
Correspondent, NBC News

3

Whenever I talk to or see Senator [Barry] Goldwater, my mind immediately goes back to the convention in 1964 when the Republicans nominated him to be their Presidential candidate. Of course he didn't win, but at that time, too, there was Ronald Reagan, that first major speech that he gave, and that was almost the beginning of the rebirth of the modern conservative movement in the United States. Either they both were way ahead of the country, or the country belatedly has caught up with them. But conservatism, as expressed by this Senator, as expressed by this President, is very much, it seems, the dominant strain in American politics today.

TV broadcast, Washington/
"Meet the Press," NBC-TV, 1-27.

4

It is one of the wonders of American democracy that the candidate who loses a Presidential election does not show up the next day at the White House with the 1st Cavalry Division demanding a recount, or worse still, demanding political power at the point of a bayonet. The defeated candidate may be angry and frustrated, but he accepts the decision of the electorate. One day he's surrounded by the Secret Service and a few hundred reporters. Then one day he's standing on line waiting for the shuttle, just like everyone else. It's democracy, American style. It's not fun if you lose, but it works.

TV broadcast, Washington/
"Meet the Press,"
NBC-TV, 4-7.

Jack Kemp
United States Senator,
R-New York

5

I'm not for the status quo, which is Latin for "a mess." I believe in change in a free and liberal society. If I'd lived in the 18th century, I'd have been a Jeffersonian classical liberal—free, open and generous . . . I'm not interested in just being a Congressman. I'd like to change the course of human events.

Interview/
Cosmopolitan,
September:260.

Edward M. Kennedy
United States Senator,
D-Massachusetts

6

As Democrats, we must understand that there is a difference between being a party that cares about labor—and being a labor party. There is a difference between being a party that cares about women—and being the women's party. And we can and we must be a party that cares about minorities without becoming a minority party. We are citizens first and constituencies second.

At John F. Kennedy Presidential Conference,
Hofstra University, March 29/
The Washington Post,
3-30:(A)11.

Bob Kerrey
Governor of Nebraska (D)

1

I've always avoided the word "liberal" for two reasons: It's political suicide, and I don't know what it means . . . I don't follow old voters, let alone new voters. But there is a change in people's interests. They're more interested in business than they were 25 years ago; there's an increased interest on the part of women in becoming entrepreneurs, an increased interest in capitalism.

Interview/
Esquire, November:121.

Paul G. Kirk, Jr.
Chairman,
Democratic National Committee

2

[Saying he is opposed to the Democratic Party's special-interest caucus system]: We've operated now for too long on the politics of separation by defining ourselves in different special categories. This party's diversity should be its strength and not its weakness . . . I think the caucus system . . . is political nonsense, in my view. And I think, during the course of the next year or so, you'll find that the caucuses . . . will fall of their own weight because people will have a greater voice in the party.

Broadcast interview/
"Meet the Press,"
NBC-TV, 2-3.

3

We [Democrats] have been portrayed, rightly or wrongly, as sort of a status quo party, kind of trapped in the past and not fighting to get up with the country as it goes through transition. [Republican President] Reagan comes in after really 25 years of difficulties in the country. Whether it's assassination, civil-rights riots, social upheaval, Watergate, Vietnam, energy crisis, hostages, the luck lines ran right for him. He got a lucky turn on the economy after the recession and he plays it very well. And I think he hit the mood on an upbeat and was able to say, "Look, we are the party of opportunity." I don't see that as something that's permanently lost to our

party. We can reclaim that and do it with justification.

Interview, Washington, Feb. 14/
The New York Times, 2-15:10.

4

In my view, the trade-union movement can strengthen the [Democratic] Party's [Presidential] nominee by refraining from an early endorsement. Let the candidates use the primary process to develop and to demonstrate their own broad political appeal and their own strong political base before giving [one] your full and united backing.

Before Communications Workers of America,
Washington, March 25/The Washington Post, 3-26:(A)1.

5

Many pragmatic Republicans are coming to realize that the policies of their party have set this country on a collision course with the future and have jeopardized their own political future as well. Small wonder that Republican candidates of 1986, struggling for their own political survival, are distancing themselves from the policies of their own party.

At Kennedy School of Government,
Harvard University,
Oct. 3/
The Washington Post,
10-4:(A)4.

Lane Kirkland
President, American Federation of
Labor-Congress of Industrial Organizations

6

We supported [unsuccessful] 1984 Democratic Presidential nominee] Fritz Mondale because we agreed with what he stood for, and we knew that he was a man who wouldn't run away from those things just because it wasn't politically profitable. We like winning. We've tried both and winning is better. But winning isn't really everything. It's more important to stand for something. If you don't stand for something, what do you win? I'm not interested in a candidate who's charming and appealing but is empty of principles or positions that, in our view, re-

(LANE KIRKLAND)

flect the hopes and aspirations of working people.

News conference, Bal Harbour, Fla.
Feb. 18/The New York Times,
2-19:6.

1

The most successful political operators, people who have functioned as heads of party operations in recent years, have been Ray Bliss for the Republicans and Bill Brock [also for the Republicans]. They're identified with their capacity to put into being a highly efficient, highly effective infrastructure; creating a party throughout the country, rebuilding it, strengthening it as a delivery system. I think that is the primary shortcoming of the Democratic Party today . . . Someone once said that it's like men and women. If there were a third viable sex, neither of the others would have a chance. But we have a two-party system and that's the way it is. It's fruitless to deplore it or to attack it. The job is to try and make it more effective.

Interview, Washington, March 19/
The New York Times,
3-21:13.

2

Some who aspire to leadership in the Democratic Party are proposing that the Party further distance itself from its natural constituency. Their formula for electoral success is to take out a piece of the conservative field and call it the center. In other words, take all the [U.S. President] Reagan formulas and say "me, too." Elbow out of the Democratic Party the very groups who produced the most [in the Presidential election] last year. Without labor, both parties would be controlled by the most narrow and selfish special interests—the bankers, the oil barons, the lawyers and lobbyists of corporate greed, not to mention that self-absorbed new class, the "yuppies" of America.

Before local union leaders,
Providence, R.I.,
April 28/
The New York Times, 4-29:11.

Jeane J. Kirkpatrick
United States Ambassador/Permanent Representative to the United Nations

3

[Saying ideological rivalries are not involved in the many recent high-level personnel changes in the Reagan Administration]: [Such assumptions are] media melodrama. It's not over-simplification—just fiction. There have been differences in personality, some differences in views. Interests clash, ambitions clash . . . But none of those differences fit anything that could reasonably be called a struggle of conservatives versus moderates.

Interview/
Newsweek, 1-14:30.

4

[Saying some Reagan Administration officials have misunderstood and distorted her views]: I was a woman in a man's world. I was a Democrat in a Republican Administration. I was an intellectual in a world of bureaucrats. I talked differently. This may have made me a bit like an ink spot. People projected around me . . . A lot of people said things about me that were not true. There was a very large distortion of my views. Initially, it may have come from the State Department.

Interview, Jan. 31/
The New York Times, 2-1:1.

5

I can best sum up myself by saying I am in the [Henry] "Scoop" Jackson tradition. It is a noble tradition of caring in domestic affairs, of understanding there is a legitimate role for government providing minimum standards of well-being on the one hand, and being deeply persuaded of the legitimacy and success of American society and the failure and tyranny of Communist societies on the other hand.

Time, 2-11:35.

6

I'm becoming a Republican, because finally I began to feel a couple of years ago it was perfectly clear that I was no longer a Democrat. I wasn't thinking like a Democrat. I wasn't acting like a Democrat. I didn't feel like a Democrat any more. The people with whom I found I could work most closely on issues I cared about were almost always Republicans. I had really ceased being a Democrat. I don't agree with everything about the Republican Party, but I realize there are more people called Republicans working toward ends that are important to me than people called Democrats.

Interview, New York/ Los Angeles Times, 3-31:(VII)1.

Richard M. Koster
Member,
Democratic National Committee

1

This body [the Democratic Party] is morally, spiritually and intellectually dead. It's just lying here like a piece of hamburger on the griddle...

June 26/The Washington Post, 6-27:(A)3.

Madeleine Kunin
Governor of Vermont (D)

2

[On whether being a woman made a difference in her campaign for Governor in 1984]: I don't think so. I've always campaigned as myself. I think what I had to do in the campaign was to get people to look beyond the gender question and look at my qualifications and where I stood on the issues. I think Vermonters did that. I think you have to get over that hurdle so that they're not simply discussing the fact that you're a woman, but where you stand on the issues and whether you can do the job. The fact that I had run before helped because it became less of a phenomenon that a woman was running for Governor.

Interview/USA Today, 1-8:(A)9.

Richard D. Lamm
Governor of Colorado (D)

3

[Saying he is not interested in running for Senator]: I consider six years in Washington not to be a term, but to be a sentence.

Denver, Jan. 3/The Washington Post, 1-5:(A)3.

4

[On his being somewhat of a maverick politician]: . . . history teaches us that all great truths begin as heresies, and that there is always a Copernicus or a Darwin out there somewhere who is saying something that is at first upsetting and then is generally recognized as truth. But almost everybody, except politicians, are saying these things. I'm really not a lonely voice. I am a political voice saying what every banker, businessman and economist will tell you.

Interview/U.S. News & World Report, 12-16:60.

Paul Laxalt
United States Senator, R-Nevada

5

[On President Reagan's second term]: Post-election, the political scars are so deep, [with Democrats wanting to] teach Reagan a lesson. The Democrats, at least on the Senate side, have done a marvelously good job of mounting a loyal opposition. The aura of the original [Presidential] mandate wears off. The magic of a Presidential telephone call is still strong, but not electric.

The Washington Post, 5-23:(4)6.

Carl Levin
United States Senator, D-Michigan

6

The New Hampshire "first-in-the-nation [Presidential] primary" and the "snowswept Iowa caucus" have assumed a mythical role in American politics. And I certainly do not think that we ought to be making changes just for the sake of making changes. However, because those first primaries have an undisputed and disproportionate impact on the outcome of the nomination process, we really have to look at them closely. Fairness means that we want Democratic voters in Iowa and New Hampshire to have a voice and a vote. But their voice ought not to be any louder than anyone else's, and their vote ought not to count for any more than that of any other Democrat's. That isn't the way the system works now.

Before Democratic National Committee Fairness Commission, Lansing, Mich., Aug. 10/The New York Times, 8-13:10.

Thomas E. Mann
Executive director,
American Political Science Association

1

[President Reagan] plays the game very well—the game of changing rhetoric in response to specific needs and different situations. But there's a key difference between Reagan and other Presidents. Reagan never changes his mind about the fundamentals, about what he wants to accomplish. He conveys a very consistent set of goals and does not lead people to think he's changing direction. With [former President] Jimmy Carter, say, there were confusing signals about what he was trying to accomplish. With Reagan, there really isn't any confusion. It's that constancy on fundamentals that permits him to alter his rhetoric, tailoring it to specific situations and not be accused of being indecisive or contradictory.

The New York Times, 3-27:12.

John McCain
United States Representative, R-Arizona

2

[On the prospects for the Republican Party after President Reagan leaves office]: Our biggest problem is the failure to understand that the glue holding this whole thing together is a 74-year-old guy named Ronald Reagan.

U.S. News & World Report,
4-22:26.

Walter F. Mondale
Former Vice President
of the United States;
1984 Democratic Presidential nominee

3

[On the period after his loss in the 1984 Presidential election]: For the first month or so, I'd wake up at 3 in the morning still debating, still getting ready for the next speech, and so on . . . One of the phenomena of American political life . . . [is] that it all stops one day. One day you've got 200 reporters and cameras and everybody is hanging on you. And three days later, you're alone. And it's quite a transition. And I knew it would be. I've been around a long time. Some handle it well; others don't . . . I think I handled it just right. I was very careful not to crowd myself.

Interview/
USA Today, 2-28:(A)2.

4

[On his losing campaign in the 1984 Presidential race]: I was essentially correct on the fundamental issues . . . [But] the fact of the matter is, President Reagan's ability to communicate—even things that I think are demonstrably not accurate—verges on genius. I don't think anybody accused me of the same capability.

Broadcast interview/
"Meet the Press,"
NBC-TV, 4-7.

Eleanor Holmes Norton
Professor of law,
Georgetown University

5

I think that women and minorities alike may have all learned that it does not pay to go around saying that women are going to elect the next President, blacks are going to elect the next President, Hispanics are going to elect the next President, or anybody is going to elect the next President. It turns out that American politics is a coalition affair. Historically, it has been the case that only broad-based political parties succeed in America.

Interview/Ms., February:66.

Sam Nunn
United States Senator, D-Georgia

6

[Saying conservative Southern Democratic voters are turning increasingly to the Republican Party]: Those of us in the [political] middle of the Democratic Party are caught . . . like the little boy who didn't know quite what to do because he got kicked out of the parochial school for cussing, and he got kicked out of the public school for praying.

At Democratic Leadership Council meeting,
Gainesville, Fla./
The Christian Science Monitor, 5-23:4.

Lawrence F. O'Brien

Former Special Assistant to the President of the United States (John F. Kennedy and Lyndon B. Johnson); Former chairman, Democratic National Committee

[Arguing against a six-year, one-term Presidency]: We're fortunate in our democracy to have a broad-based public decision every four years on the stewardship of our national government. For nearly two centuries, this system has served the nation well. I see no reason to inhibit the American voters' range of choice in this system . . . And I'm inclined to think that [the 22nd] Amendment [limiting a President to two terms] wasn't such a great idea, because it has put a barrier across the Presidential decision-making process of the future . . . Denying a President the right to seek re-election could sharply limit his leadership ability by limiting his political clout both within his own party and within the country at large. But, more critically, this proposal is one more potential barrier on the prerogatives of the American voter. And I'm not convinced that limitations on those prerogatives are any plus for democracy.

Interview, New York/
USA Today,
1-21:(A)12.

1

Thomas P. O'Neill, Jr.

United States Representative,
D-Massachusetts

[Saying the Democrats in the House will permit a vote on President Reagan's domestic policies, rather than blocking it]: I said to him, "We can read. You got 59 per cent of the votes [in last November's Presidential election], and there's no question in my 50 years of public life, I've never seen a man more popular than you are with the American people, and in view of that I want you to know that everything is on the table." When I say everything, I mean everything. We will give him a vote on the economic and domestic policies that he is interested in. There's a mandate out there demanding these things.

Washington, Jan. 22/
The New York Times,
1-23:8.

2

You have to analyze the last election [in which President Reagan won almost every state]. The President won by 59 per cent to 41 per cent, a landslide margin of 16 million votes. But of the 81 million who voted in Congressional elections, Democrats won by 5 million votes. While the voters liked the President, they wanted to make sure there was a "Tip," O'Neill and a Democratic Party to watch and protect them.

Interview/U.S. News & World Report, 9-16:25.

3

Norman J. Ornstein

Resident scholar,
American Enterprise Institute

I do not see PACs or the campaign-finance system as the root evil of this country. I think candidates for Congress have to raise too much money from too many individual sources, and PACs have become the easiest place to turn. Sure, money influences campaigns. But, still, we probably have a cleaner system today than we've ever had in history.

Interview/U.S. News & World Report, 1-28:54.

4

James E. Pappas

Nebraska State Senator (D)

[On why he switched from the Republican Party to the Democrats]: A lot of people don't think there's room in the Republican Party for moderates and liberals. You have to be conservative, hard-line, pro-business, pro-wealthy and against social programs. The Party doesn't cater to the mainstream and I don't like the slowness in reducing the big [Federal budget] deficits. The only ones who benefit from them are the rich, people with money who draw interest.

The Washington Post, 4-20:(A)3.

5

Norman Podhoretz

Editor, "Commentary" magazine

[Saying some now call him a neo-conservative]: I'd be happier with the term neo-nationalist. Being an American nationalist, especially on the left, was not exactly popular for a long time. I remember being on a talk show

6

(NORMAN PODHORETZ)

and they were all talking about [liberal Senator] Gary Hart and "new ideas." I had to laugh. I said for most young Americans the idea of praising America was a new idea. They hadn't heard much of that in their young lives.

Interview, New York/
The Washington Post, 1-30:(C)9.

Nancy Reagan
Wife of President of the
United States Ronald Reagan

2

[Criticizing those who say President Reagan is not in charge in Washington]: Poor Ronald Reagan is going to be doing [in the next four years] exactly what poor Ronald Reagan has been doing for the last four years—and that's run the government.

U.S. News & World Report,
1-28:16.

Ronald Reagan
President of the United States

3

[On whether he thinks of his place in history when he makes Presidential decisions]: Actually, I get that question an awful lot, as if you sit over here and that's all you think about. The truth of the matter is, I don't think about it at all. I think about trying to get the job done.

Interview, Washington,
Jan. 17/USA Today, 1-18:(A)13.

4

There's an understandable tendency when a second [Presidential] term begins to think that all of our great work is behind us, that the big battles have been fought and all the rest is anti-climax. Well, that's not true. What has gone before is prologue. Our greatest battles lie ahead. All is newness now, [presenting] the possibility of great and fundamental change. We can change America forever. That's some great and beautiful music we've been playing the past four years—but the way I see it, from here on it's shake, rattle and roll.

Before 3,000 of his appointees, Washington,
Jan. 25/Los Angeles Times, 1-26:(I)6.

5

[On suggestions that he might not strongly back for re-election those Republican Congressmen who do not support certain of his policies]: I suppose this comes from the suggestion that I am supposed to penalize some members in the coming campaign. No, I've never done that. I'm a charter member of the California-born 11th

William Proxmire
United States Senator, D-Wisconsin

1

[On the possible candidates in the forthcoming 1988 Presidential election]: Our [Democrats'] advantage in '88, of course, is that [current Republican President] Reagan won't be on the ticket. I'm very impressed by [Gary] Hart, just as a person. He's an articulate, eloquent Senator, more than most I've served with over the past 30 years. And I'm also impressed by [New York Governor Mario] Cuomo—we've got a lot of talent in our Party. Edward Kennedy? I like Ted very much. He's basically a very good Senator, but he has so much baggage to carry, so many negatives. People just won't forget Chappaquiddick [when Kennedy was involved in an auto accident in which a woman companion was killed]. Actually, I think the best Senator of the three Kennedys is Ted Kennedy. He's a good man, but he's unlikely to be nominated and very unlikely to be elected. [On the Republican side, Vice President] George Bush? Bush is just an absolute, ideal Yale Eli. You couldn't have made a better caricature of an Ivy Leaguer; a great athlete, and he's a very admirable person, but he is about as preppy as you can get. That will probably hurt him. [Representative] Jack Kemp? I just can't understand how anybody can take Jack Kemp seriously. He's got all kinds of energy, and he can talk very fast and smoothly. But he's just so identified with supply-side economics, and it's just so utterly ridiculous. [Senator] Robert Dole? Dole I admire and respect. He'd be their [Republicans'] strongest candidate. He's got all kinds of things going for him. He's a serious man.

Interview, Washington/
The New York Times,
11-12:8.

219

WHAT THEY SAID IN 1985

(RONALD REAGAN)

Commandment: Thou shalt not speak ill of another Republican. And therefore I'm dedicated to doing my best to see if we can't maintain the majority we have in the Senate and someday get ourselves a majority in the House, which we haven't had for more than 26 years. So, no, I'm not going to hold a grudge on anyone.

News conference, Washington,
March 21/The New York Times, 3-22:10.

We Republicans have been blessed with grass-roots supporters who are committed to the ideals of individual freedom, family values, free enterprise and a strong America. While the [Democratic] Party has tried to build a coalition by segmenting America into warring factions—over the years pitting white against black, women against men, young against old—we've taken a more positive path. The Republican Party has sought to unite our citizens by building on those fundamental beliefs that made America the great land that she is. We don't promise quota systems and giveaway programs. We promise to do what's right for America.

At Republican fund-raising dinner, Miami,
May 27/Los Angeles Times, 5-28:(I).

1

A few moments back I mentioned Americans' skepticism about politicians. When I did, I have a hunch you said to yourself, "Look who's talking." It's true I've been in public office for more than a dozen years now, with roughly three years and four months to go, the Lord willing. Since the Constitution limits a President to only two terms, there are no more elections for me, and, therefore, no need for political considerations in any decision I'm called on to make. Like you, I'll be living with everything we do in these next few years there in Washington.

Labor Day address, Independence, Mo.,
Sept. 2/The New York Times, 9-3:14.

2

[On how he made his decision to run for President]: I've always said that you don't decide, the people tell you. The truth is, I never sought or thought I ever would seek public office. I, as a performer [a professional actor], as an entertainer, I always thought that you kind of pay your way. So I supported causes and candidates that I approved of. And, being an entertainer, I could attract an audience, and so forth, and therefore be useful at a fund-raiser—things of that kind. Never did [I] ever dream in my wildest time that I would ever want to be in public life. [Then] there was a group that came to me. And my first reply was a refusal. This group that came wanted me to seek the governorship [of California]. And finally, they convinced me I had an obligation I should do it and that I could win, and so I ran. I had thought that I was giving up a career, which I did love, in the other business, and that I'd find this [government] very dull. I found out it wasn't at all. And then, subsequent to eight years in the Governor's office, there were people that came, and on that basis said that I should try for this [the Presidency]. So I did.

Interview/The New York Times, 10-15:10.

3

Dorothy S. Ridings
President,
League of Women Voters

[On criticism that her organization has become politicized]: The very first president of the League of Women Voters once said that "To be political without being partisan in a country where the two words are nearly synonymous has always been a delicate undertaking." And you know, she was right. A lot of people confuse being political, which we surely are, with being partisan, which we surely are not.

Interview, Washington/
The New York Times, 3-12:24.

4

Charles Robb
Governor of Virginia (D)

[Saying pressure groups exert too much influence on the Democratic Party]: That's the thing many of us find most troubling. Not that any particular candidate would get blown away [by special-interest pressure], but that the Party ac-

5

(CHARLES ROBB)

tivists have, for the most part, dominated. [Yet] Party activists don't really represent the mainstream of the Party. It's not that they shouldn't be part of the process. It's that they exert disproportionate influence at the critical nominating time. And, of course, they frequently exert a disproportionate influence in constructing the Party's [national] platform.

Interview, Washington/
The Christian Science Monitor, 2-1:4.

Joe Robbie
Owner, Miami "Dolphins" football team;
Former politician

1

Politics are every bit as tough as pro football. The main difference is that, in politics, they use *you* for the football.

Interview, Oakland, Calif./
Los Angeles Times, 1-20:(III)3.

Pat Robertson
Evangelist;
President, Christian Broadcasting Network

2

Over the last nine years, members of the evangelical community have become politically activated in a way I would never have dreamed possible. The reason they have been activated is because they perceive continuous assaults by government agencies, and by the courts, against their deeply held beliefs. They were told 10 years ago that politics was sinful and evil. Now they're being told that it's sinful and evil *not* to get involved in politics. There's a complete reversal. The evangelical movement, in fact, is getting to be one of the most powerful forces in American politics.

Interview/U.S. News & World Report, 11-4:71.

Edward J. Rollins
Assistant to the President
of the United States for
Political and Governmental Affairs

3

The [Republican] Party is in a position of its greatest strength in modern history—it is totally

identified with [President] Ronald Reagan; he is able to bring all factions under a single tent. He's attracted Democrats, independents, young people, non-traditional voting blocs. Will the Party be big enough for all? One of the things about young people is they're basically libertarian. If this becomes a Party totally dominated by social issues, we're going to lose that base. At the same time, if you don't have any concern at all for social issues, you lose some of that other constituency. It's a balance. Neither party is a majority party. It's important we are able to attract independents.

Interview, Washington/
The New York Times, 9-30:12.

Richard M. Scammon
Political analyst

4

The great dilemma nationally of the Democratic Party is that it is trying to be a party and a cause at the same time. And a party, by definition . . . is a middle-of-the-road, compromising, let-me-make-you-a-deal-you-can't-refuse type of organization. It has to be. Otherwise, you can't get the 50 million votes you need to elect a President.

Interview/The Christian Science Monitor, 3-5:4.

William Sheffield
Governor of Alaska (D)

5

I was not a professional politician when I became Governor 2 1/2 years ago, and I'm still not. But I've learned a lot about politics in that time. Frankly, a lot of what I learned disgusts me.

U.S. News & World Report, 8-19:10.

Mark A. Siegel
Member of the board,
Coalition for a Democratic Majority

6

[Saying the Democratic Party should push for a more moderate image]: What we're saying is that the Party has always been a coalition of groups, but the moderates and conservatives had not actively participated in the debate and there-

(MARK A. SIEGEL)

fore had let the left define the Democratic agenda, and that agenda has been rejected by the Democratic rank and file. Let's forget the Republican rank and file. We're talking about Democratic voters. They have not felt at home with the Party as they saw it in San Francisco [during the 1984 Party convention], or as it has emerged in the national committee.

Washington, Jan. 29/
The New York Times,
1-30:9.

Alan K. Simpson
United States Senator, R-Wyoming

[Saying Senators who are up for re-election may not get the full backing of President Reagan if they don't support his programs]: There are 22 of those chaps, and I [as majority whip] haven't the slightest desire to do a number on any of them. Hellfire, a guy who supported the President for six years—I'm not about to swab the deck with him. That's crazy. However, there are one or two who constantly get a perverse kick out of doing something which does not meet the President's requirements or the leadership's desire. With those one or two, we have to slap them along the head with a piece of stove wood. Let them know there's a bigger picture than just plain selfishness.

The New York Times, 3-15:13.

1

Larry Speakes
Principal Deputy Press Secretary to the President of the United States

[President Reagan] enjoys an unprecedented post-war second-term popularity. Historically, all five second-term Presidents since World War II have gone down [in the polls] an average of 18 points. On the other hand, President Reagan has increased. [And] when the President's numbers go up, so do the numbers of those who are seeking election or re-election on the Republican ticket.

Los Angeles Times,
9-9:(I)9.

2

Allan Swift
United States Representative,
D-Washington

3

[On uniform poll-closing time suggestions as a way to combat early election-result predictions before everyone has voted]: We have felt that changes in our election laws, such as uniform poll-closing time, to recognize the fact that this is a big country spanning several time zones, were potentially part of a solution. However, as long as the [broadcast] networks declined to provide a firm commitment not to short-circuit such a change in the law with their exit-polling data, we felt it was useless to pursue any such possibilities. But now the networks have given their word that they will not short-circuit a uniform poll-closing time.

News conference, Washington,
Jan. 17/The New York Times,
1-18:5.

Sander Vanocur
Correspondent,
ABC News

4

[On broadcast debates between Presidential candidates]: In a way, debates are very useful, but they become almost too dominating . . . When 1980 came along, everything in the Reagan-Carter campaign came down to that one debate in Cleveland. That meant the campaign was in a state of suspended animation to almost the end . . . [In future debates,] I am all for [leaving reporters out of the questioning] because [that would make it] a classic debate with participants and a moderator. I say that as a reporter. As a person who has been on a panel, as a person who has moderated debates, I think this is especially true of us in television—we become too much a part of the campaign anyhow . . . [Debates] should be much earlier in the campaigns. They should start right around Labor Day—maybe get them over by the first week in October. But the more you put them toward the end of the campaign, the more they take on the status of being the determinant force in the campaign.

Interview/USA Today,
9-25:(A)11.

James G. Watt
Former Secretary of the
Interior of the United States

1

The Establishment is dominated by liberal philosophy and liberal leaders in every area, including big business and labor, the media, education, entertainment, churches and government. We conservatives are the outsiders, and it's therefore our responsibility to confront, convince and convert American thought if we are to bring needed changes . . . If the Republican Party doesn't become the conservative movement, it'll die—and it ought to die. There's nothing sacred about the Republican Party.

Interview/U.S. News & World Report, 11-11:79.

Stephen Jay Wayne
Professor of political science
and public affairs,
George Washington University

2

I think history will not view the Reagan Presidency in the same glow that it is viewed today. How can a person so inattentive to details, ignorant of facts and personally disengaged be viewed as a strong leader? Where is the idealism of the '60s? Where is the leadership one looks to to extend basic American values: individual dignity, equal rights, sensitivity for the less-fortunate?

Panel discussion sponsored
by American Political Science Association,
New Orleans, Aug. 29/The New York Times, 9-2:11.

Vin Weber
United States Representative,
R-Minnesota

3

The central question for the Republican Party now is how do we cement the loyalty of voters under 40 years old. The big division in the Republican Party today is not between left and right, it's between people who want to make the Republican Party a majority party and people who are locked into a minority-party mindset.

The New York Times, 2-4:9.

4

[On the effect on Jewish voters of President Reagan's planned visit to a German cemetery where Nazi soldiers and SS officers are buried]: We [Republicans] have had a tremendous chance to move the Jewish community. The Jews had provided most of the talent, brainpower and money for the Democratic Party. Many Jews were prepared to vote for Reagan . . . But the Democrats succeeded [in 1984] in making [evangelist] Jerry Falwell and the religious right a centerpiece issue. A lot of Jewish voters got the uneasy feeling that there is a growing anti-Semitic force within the Republican Party. I don't believe that's true, but I understand that concern. I thought that was a one-time problem. Then comes Bitburg [cemetery], many candle-power greater than the Falwell issue.

Interview/The Washington Post, 5-1:(A)13.

Timothy E. Wirth
United States Representative,
D-Colorado

5

The present Democratic leadership in Congress grew up with World War II; I grew up with Vietnam. They grew up with black-and-white print; I grew up with television. They grew up with Franklin Roosevelt; I grew up with John F. Kennedy. They grew up with the Depression; I grew up in the '60s. It's a dramatic difference.

U.S. News & World Report, 2-25:46.

Robert Wussler
Executive vice president,
Turner Broadcasting System

6

When the [broadcast] networks project elections results based on their own computer manipulation of exit-polling data they have collected, they cross the line of responsible journalism, in our opinion. They are reporting on information of their own manufacture . . . There is a significant risk that their actions may influence the electoral process itself.

Before House Elections Subcommittee,
Washington, May 9/Los Angeles Times, 5-10:(VI)1.

Social Welfare

T. Berry Brazelton
Associate professor of pediatrics,
Harvard University Medical School

Representative Patricia Schroeder has introduced a bill that would give mothers four months of protected maternity leave. "Protected" leave means a guarantee that they would have a job when they returned and wouldn't lose seniority. A month's leave for fathers would be good, too. We [the U.S.] are the last industrialized country to establish these kinds of policies. Every European country has child-care programs. So have Israel, Russia, Japan and China. In Sweden, the mother takes the first six months, and she and the father can divide up another six months between them. With more mothers working in the U.S. each year, we are going to have to establish more family-oriented policies that will be good for parents and their children, so that people can better balance a career with a home life.

Interview/U.S. News & World Report, 10-21:71.

1

Cyril F. Brickfield
Executive director, American
Association of Retired Persons

Social Security has become a substitute for the old "hands-on" approach of two or three generations in the same household. We have to tell the younger people that Social Security is not a fight between generations—it's a family affair.

Newsweek, 5-13:38.

2

Joseph A. Califano, Jr.
Former Secretary of Health, Education
and Welfare of the United States

All I can really do is pose the questions: Where would this country be if it hadn't been for the Great Society [programs]? How many kids would not have been able to go to college? How many more people would have died or been incapacitated for lack of proper health care? Where would our elderly go if the government didn't

pay for nursing homes? What would our air be like? Our water? I don't know all the answers, but I do know we as a country would be much worse off.

The New York Times, 4-17:9.

3

Mario M. Cuomo
Governor of New York (D)

We are agreed that the maintenance of our systems of public education, public health, public schools, public transit, public safety—our courts and schools and roads and police—are all the proper responsibilities of government. We know that what gives government the resources to do these things is the free-enterprise system. We believe, therefore, that government must accommodate the producers of wealth; indeed, that it must encourage as many people as possible to pursue the honest rewards of imagination, ambition and hard work. But we recognize that, even at its best, the free-enterprise system won't be able to include everyone, that there'll always be those left out, the frail, the poor, the old; those without skills or hope, sometimes without even a roof over their heads. We are confident that government can act progressively and pragmatically to help care for those who simply can't care for themselves.

Chubb Fellowship lecture, Yale University,
Feb. 15/The New York Times, 2-16:9.

4

We have more single-parent families than ever before. More women in poverty. More teen-age mothers without a proper education or the prospect of a job. We have increasing numbers of children whose mental and physical development have already been stunted by poor nutrition and inadequate medical care . . . At the same time, we've heard [from the Reagan Administration] a symphony of noble words about the sanctity of the family and the dignity of motherhood and reverence for life, we've seen savage cuts in the programs that help mothers and fathers sustain their children, that educate the young, that

5

(MARIO M. CUOMO)

prevent birth defects and infant diseases, that give parents the chance to earn their own bread.

At Children's Defense Fund conference,
Washington, Feb. 27/The New York Times, 3-1:21.

Ernest N. Dutch
Mayor of New Orleans;
President, United States
Conference of Mayors

1

The economic recovery has been selective in terms of the people benefiting from it. Over all, conditions for the poor have not improved, and in many cases have worsened. Any solution to this nation's economic problems must include a solution to the problems of poverty, joblessness, hunger and homelessness, problems faced by a continuously growing number of Americans.

At meeting of United States Conference of Mayors,
Washington, Jan. 17/
The New York Times, 1-18:5.

Don Edwards
United States Representative,
D-California

2

Mr. President [Reagan], yesterday the Republican Senate, at your request, voted to reduce Social Security payments by 6 billions of dollars. That is why virtually every Democratic Senator voted No. The Senate Republican budget would mean an additional 500,000 of America's senior citizens would be below the official poverty level. Most of these poor older Americans will be women, Mr. President, and many thousands will be mothers. Mr. President, on Mother's Day have you forgotten about the grandmothers of America? . . . What hurts, Mr. President, is that the Republican Senate at your request cut Social Security pensions and in the same vote gave the military a 10 to 12 billion-dollar increase . . . It is simply not fair that you are asking Social Security pensioners to take less . . .

Broadcast address to the nation/
The Washington Post,
5-17:(A)22.

Harold E. Ford
United States Representative,
D-Tennessee

3

This [Reagan] Administration has said loud and clear that we have a recovery in this country, but [a] Congressional study showed that even during periods of economic growth, poverty still grew at a rapid pace. This is because of the real inequities involved in the distribution of economic growth in this country. Single females raising children—and there are so many—simply are not in a position to participate in the economic growth without real support services, like day care, education and job training.

Interview/USA Today, 6-5:(A)9.

Barry M. Goldwater
United States Senator, R-Arizona

4

What I'd like to see is a national vote on Social Security, whether or not it would be voluntary or compulsory. My hunch is that young people would rather have it voluntary, because if they invested the same money they put into Social Security, they would receive almost four times more in benefits when they retire. Let those who want compulsory Social Security continue to pay for it.

Interview/Los Angeles Herald Examiner, 1-13:(A)15.

5

I believe completely in the statement of Abraham Lincoln that it is the duty of the Federal government to take care of those people who cannot take care of themselves; but we have gone past that point. The wage earner, the wealthy, the middle class, the retired people living on the wages of others have to know that everyone is going to have to make a change in life. It is not easy to tell someone to lower their sights and lower their way of living. But if we don't, then we had better pray that the American people with their eternal courage will say, "Let's do what we have to do and not get this country into more trouble." The time for speeches has passed and it is now time for some courageous action.

Speech, Jan. 24/
The New York Times, 1-30:8.

WHAT THEY SAID IN 1985

Paula Hawkins
United States Senator, R-Florida

[On her proposal to limit social benefits dispensed by the government to illegal aliens]: A person who has violated the immigration law and entered this country illegally should not have access to government benefits paid for by United States taxpayers. We in this body [the Senate] have an obligation first to the people of the United States, the people we were elected to represent. We have an obligation to Americans first.

Before the Senate, Washington,
Sep. 13/The New York Times, 9-14-1.

1

Margaret M. Heckler
Secretary of Health and Human Services of the United States

. . . not only is the mind a terrible thing to waste, but so is the body. Now is the time to say, "It is simply not right that white Americans should be healthier than blacks." Now is the time to say, "It's not right that black infants should weigh less than white infants." It's not right that black adults should be far more susceptible to serious disease than white adults. And it's not right that black seniors should expect to live fewer years than white seniors in the United States of America.

Before National Urban League, Washington, July 23/
The Washington Post, 7-24-(A)8.

2

John Heinz III
United States Senator,
R-Pennsylvania

As a nation with an increasingly aging population, early retirement schemes are creating serious problems. As we live longer and work shorter, there is an increasing burden on retirement-income programs like Social Security and private pensions. With longer life expectancy, we should be encouraging longer periods of employment rather than discouraging them. I do have sympathy for employers, however. Most employers offer these [retirement] incentives with the most humane intentions in mind. Unfortunately, the results can be disastrous for the older worker who jumps at the chance to retire early without careful thought about how he or she will survive down the road.

Los Angeles Times, 6-7-(I)27.

3

Tom Joe
Director, Center for the Study of Social Policy

[Poverty is] the most scary thing we ought to be concerned about, because we're locking in people in growing numbers and you see an increasing disparity between the upper and lower quintiles of society. We seem to have no massive initiative to create jobs. There is a split society on the horizon, and that's a very serious problem.

The Christian Science Monitor, 1-23-5.

4

Barbara Jordan
Professor of public values and ethics, University of Texas, Austin; Former United States Representative, D-Texas

[On the late President Lyndon Johnson's Great Society programs]: The legacy of Lyndon Johnson continues to enrich our lives. He saw the enemy and the enemy was not government. The enemy was ignorance, poverty, disease, ugliness, injustice, discrimination. He believed it was the duty of government to defeat the enemy . . . The Great Society was larger than number-crunching or charts and graphs. It was a commitment of mind and spirit.

At Great Society symposium, University of Texas,
Austin, April 18/The Washington Post, 4-19-(A)4.

5

Jack Kemp
United States Representative,
R-New York

I don't see people in terms of cultural differences as much as some of our elitist friends, who think when you're poor, you'll be poor perpetually and all that government can do is take care of you ad infinitum . . . [and] that potential for human growth resides only in the suburbs,

6

(JACK KEMP)

but not in the inner city among the blacks and Hispanics. Poor people don't want redistribution of wealth. They just want an opportunity to get some of it. The tax system shouldn't be structured to make the rich poor, but the poor rich.

Interview/U.S. News & World Report, 12-16:60.

Sar A. Levitan
Director, Center for Social Policy Studies, and professor of economics, George Washington University

4

Viewed in the context of the goals first articulated half a century ago, the welfare system has nearly achieved its fundamental objectives. Most of the destitute have been assured at least a meager stipend to meet basic needs, and the percentage of Americans living in poverty declined dramatically during the three decades following World War II. Social Security and Medicare have removed the greatest threats to solvency in old age. Workers forced into idleness have gained temporary support through unemployment-compensation programs, and disabled workers are protected by insurance that provides medical care and basic income . . . [But the conservative viewpoint is that] the poor are not trying hard enough; welfare encourages indolence, and Federal intervention is therefore counterproductive . . . [President] Ronald Reagan is living in a dream world, where jobs are plentiful and one need only read the "help wanted" columns and apply. He has an idealized view of the past.

Interview, Washington/ The New York Times, 7-31:8.

William J. Levitt
Home-builder

5

I was an early advocate who believed that local and Federal government should build public housing only in that bracket that private housing could not handle. If private housing can satisfy a multitude, yes, privately we should do it. If, on the other hand, there's a huge segment of people who cannot find housing built by private builders, I'm very much in favor of not only subsidized housing, but government housing.

Interview/USA Today, 1-28:(A)11.

Grace Kilbane
Deputy Administrator, Bureau of Unemployment Services of Ohio

1

[On Federal cutbacks in unemployment aid]: Congress has been lulled into a sense of feeling better about things because unemployment has dropped across the country. The mood at the national level is, "We have to attack the [Federal budget] deficit." The deficit is a huge factor, but if we don't believe our people are the best resources in the country, then we're making a big mistake.

Los Angeles Times, 3-30:(I)24.

Edward I. Koch
Mayor of New York

2

One of the greatest offenses of humankind is to be uncaring about the elderly. One of the most important good deeds should be what you're doing in life to make the lot of the elderly better than what it might be. They deserve much more than society provides.

At dedication of subsidized housing for elderly and disabled, Bronx, N.Y., Sept. 22/The New York Times, 9-23:18.

Richard D. Lamm
Governor of Colorado (D)

3

As a Democrat, I've always defended social programs. But you look at some of these problems, and you say, "What's a happy outcome?" Eighty-nine per cent of the teen-age births in [New York's] Harlem are illegitimate—children having children. Give me a happy outcome when you've got a 16-year-old mother with an 8th-grade education. I am worried that, after 30

Roger M. Mahony
Roman Catholic Archbishop of Los Angeles

1

The common good demands justice for all. And the obligation to provide justice for all means that the poor have the single most urgent claim on the conscience of the nation. The investment of wealth, talent and human energy should be specially directed to benefit those who are poor or economically insecure.

Interview, Los Angeles/
Los Angeles Times Magazine, 11-17:18.

Gerald McEntee
President, American Federation of State,
County and Municipal Employees

2

[Saying work-for-welfare programs are having a detrimental effect on public employees]: Workfare has been a disaster for public employees. Thus far, the record has been one of substituting [welfare recipients] for public employees, and it has been devastating for morale and it encourages layoffs.

Interview, Washington, Sept. 24/
The Washington Post, 9-25:(A)7.

Jim Moody
United States Representative,
D-Wisconsin

3

The time has come to recognize that, for future generations, a modified Social Security system is preferable to no Social Security system at all. But declaring all aspects of the current Social Security system as absolutely undiscussable and unchangeable, we are in effect reducing the money available to others in need.

Los Angeles Times, 5-5:(I)9.

Charles Murray
Senior research fellow,
Manhattan Institute for Policy Research

4

It's called Social Security. We insist on pretending that Social Security is an insurance program and that if you're 78 years old and have been getting Social Security for 13 years, you're

still getting what you're owed from it. That's not true. It has never been an insurance program in that sense. There are huge sums of money that are going to members of this society who are getting back far more than they ever paid into it and whose incomes are quite substantial. Until we are ready to deal with that, it's very hard to put together much of a rationale for dealing with this.

Interview/
USA Today, 1-29:(4)9.

Thomas P. O'Neill, Jr.
United States Representative,
D-Massachusetts

5

I began my public life in 1936 on a slogan of "work and wages." I remain convinced that our greatest goal is to give the average family the opportunity to earn an income, to own a home, to educate their children and to have some security in their later years. That is still the American dream and it is still worth fighting for. Today there are those who argue that the way to achieve this dream is to go it alone, to forget about those less fortunate. This new morality says that the young should forget about the old, the healthy should ignore the sick, the wealthy should forget the poor. This is an alien philosophy to our country. We Americans believe in hard work, in getting ahead, but we also believe in looking out for the other guy.

Alfred M. Landon Lecture on Public Issues,
Kansas State University, April 22/
The New York Times, 5-3:14.

Claude Pepper
United States Representative,
D-Florida

6

[On the Social Security system]: I don't know of any other government program that has meant so much to so many. It has helped bring a better life for millions of Americans. Social Security is not a handout; it has become a sacred, hallowed American right.

Los Angeles Times,
8-12:(I)15.

Samuel R. Pierce, Jr.
Secretary of Housing and Urban
Development of the United States

1

I'm proud to say we're helping to house more needy people than ever have been housed before. This [Reagan] Administration is directing our assistance to *people*—not bricks and mortar. We're doing this while *reducing* the nation's assisted-housing debt. We switched emphasis from new construction programs to those which utilized existing housing stock. As part of that effort, we developed the rental rehabilitation initiative and the voucher program, which provides housing assistance to eligible families at about one third the cost of new construction . . . We have a commitment to provide decent, safe and affordable housing for those who are needy. With these changes and new programs, we can honor that commitment quicker and at a lower cost in the future.

Before House subcommittee,
Washington/USA Today,
3-26:(A)8.

Ronald Reagan
President of the United States

2

Social Security as a part of the [Federal budget] deficit is nothing but a bookkeeping gimmick. Social Security runs a surplus. By incorporating it in the budget, you then add to the budget the outgo and the income. But with that surplus, this apparently reduces the size of the deficit. But the Social Security payroll tax goes into a trust fund and cannot be used for anything else. Not one penny of it can be used to reduce the deficit in the overall management of government. To continue to say that this could somehow reduce the deficit by reducing Social Security benefits is a snare and a delusion. And that's why I believe that we shouldn't even wait till 1992 when it is slated to be taken out of the budget and made a separate program. It originally was and it was during the [Lyndon] Johnson years that Social Security was incorporated into the budget for the very purpose of making the deficit then look smaller than it was.

News conference, Washington,
Aug. 5/The New York Times, 8-6:10.

3

I've been accused—oh boy, have I been accused—of wanting to tamper with Social Security more times than I've had birthdays, and that's getting to be a pretty big number. As long ago as the 1976 campaign, I was saying that correcting the problems of Social Security must be done without reducing the benefits for those receiving them. I want you to know that nothing in our tax plan would affect your Social Security checks in any way—period.

To senior citizens, Tampa, Fla.,
Sept. 12/The Washington Post, 9-13:(A)2.

Charles R. Richey
Judge, United States District Court
for the District of Columbia

4

[On the problem of the homeless in the U.S.]: No more delay can be tolerated in the face of this human misery. No less than the President of the United States should treat this as a national emergency in order that the full impact of the nation's resources can be brought to bear to eliminate this national disgrace.

Washington, Aug. 19/The New York Times, 8-20:9.

Edward R. Roybal
United States Representative,
D-California

5

Since three out of four baby-boomers will marry and have children, Social Security provides them and their families with protection against risks which no savings or investment plan could ever adequately protect and for which private insurance would be prohibitively expensive.

Los Angeles Times, 8-12:(I)15.

Alan K. Simpson
United States Senator, R-Wyoming

6

[On poverty among elderly Americans]: How did we get to the point in America where somehow everybody over 65 is eating out of a garbage can?

To reporters, Washington, Jan. 16/
The Christian Science Monitor, 1-17:3.

David A. Stockman
Director, Federal Office of Management and Budget

The elderly of this country depend on Medicare and Social Security for their living standard. We can't continue to support that system as huge as it is, more than $250-billion a year, unless we have a strong economy and a lot of people working to pay the taxes to support it. So, as we look at our overall economic situation and as we look at the commitments and promises that we have made, we have to find ways to balance both, and I think that we have done this in a very fair way. And I think most of the elderly people in this country recognize that the day of reckoning has come and everybody is going to have to give up a little bit of something if we're to get our fiscal house in order.

Broadcast interview/"Meet the Press," NBC-TV, 4-14.

1

Franklin A. Thomas
President, Ford Foundation

The growth in social spending over the past two decades has produced what many analysts are calling the crisis of the welfare state. The problem is not unique to the United States; nearly all the industrialized democracies are straining to pay for the social protection and welfare needs of their people . . . Many social policy experts argue that given slower rates of economic growth, aging populations and other social changes, democracies can no longer bear the increasing burden of social programs. They argue for reductions, but too often focus primarily, or only, on programs for the poor that have limited political constituencies. A more thorough examination of social policy would need to look not only at safety-net programs for the needy but also programs that provide entitlements to citizens with incomes well above those of the poor.

New York, Jan. 24/Los Angeles Times, 1-25:(I)5.

2

James Harold Thompson
Speaker of the Florida House of Representatives (D)

The difference, in my opinion, between a conservative Democrat and a Republican is we

3

[Democrats] care more about the people as individuals. We got that through our parents and grandparents because they survived the Depression that the Democrats brought us out of. The Republicans would be willing in a situation like that to let the system work, to let free enterprise work; and my dad wouldn't have been able to go to the CCC camps and work. And the WPA wouldn't have been available to my grandfather. That's the big difference.

Interview/The Christian Science Monitor, 5-23:4.

James G. Watt
Former Secretary of the Interior of the United States

By concentrating power in government institutions, liberals chisel at the three pillars of society: the family unit, work ethic and faith. That's not good for America. Take Aid to Families with Dependent Children. Is there a need to help parents in poverty? Absolutely. But the Federal government has become the provider for that family with certain strings—that there not be a man in the house. We need to see that if there's poverty, there is assistance given to supplement what the parents can do instead of tearing the family unit apart.

Interview/U.S. News & World Report, 11-11:79.

4

Leonore Weitzman
Sociologist; Associate professor, Stanford University

Laws are redefining the nature of marriage and changing our expectations of husbands and wives. If a court awards alimony to a woman who has spent 20 years as a homemaker and mother, it is saying it values her role and is rewarding these activities. But if a court says, "You are not entitled to any alimony; you should go out and support yourself," it suggests we do not value what she has done. The only thing that matters is her ability to support herself. The underlying message—for both men and women—is clear: We should not invest in our family, and we should not invest in our children; the only security in this world is one's own career. That clearly undermines the whole notion of a marital

5

(LEONORE WEITZMAN)

partnership and penalizes those who care about children. The ultimate question is which set of values we, as a society, want to foster.

Interview/U.S. News & World Report, 11-4:63.

Robert Woodson
Director, Council for a Black Economic Agenda; President, National Center for Neighborhood Enterprise

1

Right now, government has about 1,000 grant-in-aid agencies that distribute about $350-billion annually. You have thousands and thousands of professionals who make their living off poverty. The people experiencing the problems live in one section and are characterized by certain economic situations; the people serving them are middle-class and tend to be white. So you have a whole service industry of social workers who make their living based upon the existence of poverty and an underclass. Our current system of aid to the poor has evolved into a system that has a perverse incentive to maintain poor people in their current state of dependency.

*Interview/
USA Today, 1-24:(A)7.*

Coleman A. Young
Mayor of Detroit

2

Young kids today are frustrated. They look at television, at all the glamour and glitter and affluence on the screen, and then they reflect upon their own poverty. Not only in Detroit today, but throughout the United States, there is a permanent and growing underclass—people without hope. I know three and four generations of people who have never had a job, whose mothers and grandmothers depended totally on government assistance. That's frightening. This tragedy has got to be the concern of the whole nation. President Reagan and the Federal government cannot wash their hands of this responsibility; and if they do, it's going to come back to haunt the whole nation.

Interview/USA Today, 1-31:(A)9.

Transportation

Philip Caldwell
Chairman,
Ford Motor Company

1

An important part of our business is simplifying the product. The Taurus and Sable [new car models] have some 1,700 fewer parts than their predecessors. One reason is that we're offering fewer decisions for consumers to make because we're collecting that information ourselves. Henry Ford's idea—give them any color as long as it's black—was another way of saying simplification. That was carried to an extreme, perhaps, and gave rise to General Motors. But somewhere in-between those two is the balance we are looking for.

Interview/Fortune, 3-4-'84.

David Cole
Director, Office for the
Study of Automotive Transportation,
University of Michigan

2

[On General Motors' plan for a new automobile, the Saturn, and a new division to build it]: [GM chairman] Roger Smith and his people have decided to throw away the rule book and the gospel according to conventional wisdom. They have seen that past experience isn't going to do the job . . . Look at the way [GM] cars are made now and how expensive that is. You start with engine blocks [made] in Saginaw; they're shipped to Lansing for machining and then on to Detroit for assembly—and then the finished car sits around awhile. [But with Saturn,] we're going to see vertical integration of manufacturing right on the site of the plant; engine built right there and stamping done right there; raw materials coming in one end of the manufacturing complex and finished cars coming out the other.

Newsweek, 1-21-56.

Edwin I. Colodny
Chairman, USAir

3

[On the increasing age of many airliners in use today]: We have older aircraft flying longer.

232

They are flying longer because that is the way you get into the business. Buy an older airplane, fly it and hope that you don't have a problem before it gets to its next check. [There is] an inherent conflict between competition and safety improvements, [and the public should understand that safety has] got to come out of the ticket price.

At air-safety conference sponsored
by Flight Safety Foundation/
Los Angeles Times, 2-4-:(l)4.

Mario M. Cuomo
Governor of New York (D)

4

[On his state's new law requiring the use of automobile seat belts]: A law requiring the use of seat belts is no more intrusive on individual rights than the laws requiring us to stop at red lights or to drive within the speed limit. All of them are there to protect not only the individual but society at large . . . That couple of seconds that it takes to reach around and snap shut your seat belt is a vivid reminder that you're in an auto, that safety is a concern, that other human beings are out there, your family you're obliged to—whether your personal family, the family of New York, or the nation, or the family of man. It says something quickly and clearly about obligation and responsibility.

Interview, Albany, N.Y./
USA Today, 2-1:(A)6.

John C. Danforth
United States Senator, R-Missouri

5

[Calling for Federal driver's licenses for interstate truck and bus drivers]: Most drivers are responsible professionals; most operators keep their vehicles in safe condition. But some do not. Impaired drivers should be found, punished and taken off the road. The public expects from motor-carrier employees no less than it expects from airline and rail employees—sober and unimpaired performance on the job.

The New York Times, 12-16-18.

James J. Howard
United States Representative,
D-New Jersey

1

[Arguing against doing away with the 55-miles-per-hour national speed limit]: Do the proponents of increasing the speed limits really believe those lives [saved by the 55 limit] and those serious injuries [prevented by the 55 limit] are less important than the time that would be saved by driving at 70 miles per hour rather than 55 m.p.h.? There should be no mistake about those speed limits. If the law is changed to 65 m.p.h., then the average speed on the interstate highways will be closer to 70 m.p.h . . . It may be unfashionable these days to believe that the Federal government should enforce social policy that saves lives. But I believe it is even more unfashionable to risk all those lives to save a few minutes traveling time.

The New York Times, 7-2:12.

George A. Keyworth II
Director, White House Office
of Science and Technology Policy

2

[Urging new research into producing U.S. supersonic commercial aircraft]: Potential advances in technology could make virtually all of today's operational civil and military aircraft obsolete before the end of the century . . . Although this Administration has made no commitment to a supersonic transport, we are laying the groundwork . . . in the fundamental technologies essential for any future efforts in supersonic flight . . . In light of the growing foreign competition in aviation, as well as the very real constraints on resources available for research and development, we have to make certain that our research objectives are visionary and reach out to long-range, high-payoff areas.

Washington, April 1/
Los Angeles Times, 4-2:(I)5.

Bill Moyers
Journalist

3

Deregulation of the [trucking] industry has increased competition, but more trucks are haul-

ing less freight over long distances and earning less money. To cut costs in the face of cutthroat competition, some drivers are spending more time behind the wheel without sleep or rest and are cutting corners on safety. Truck driving has become one of the most dangerous jobs in America. And yet these truckers have a problem: They're in it for a living; their profit margin is small. It's kind of Catch-22. It seemed a good idea at the time to deregulate trucking and increase economic competition—let the market do it. But some things the market can't or won't do, and its failure has to be reckoned now in human life and injury. The price is rising steadily for the drivers of big rigs and for all of us who share the road with them.

Commentary/"Evening News," CBS-TV, 12-16.

Ralph Nader
Lawyer;
Consumer-rights advocate

4

[On Secretary of Transportation Elizabeth Dole]: I would call her a weak, ineffectual Secretary of Transportation with good, basic instincts that would require a progressive President to nurture . . . She does not like conflict or confrontations. When you're dealing with ideologues, you either have to go head-on or they roll over you.

The Washington Post, 7-23:(A)1.

Brian O'Neill
Executive director,
Insurance Institute for Highway Safety

5

[Arguing against raising the 55-miles-per-hour speed limit]: . . . most of the time saved [by drivers exceeding the limit], in fact the vast bulk of it, are savings of three to four minutes per person per trip. And there is good evidence that those sorts of savings are basically considered trivial by the persons involved . . . It's the old problem of dealing with time. Sixty people saving one minute each is not the same as one person saving an hour . . . People understand that the 55-miles-an-hour speed limit does not mean that everyone is going below 55 miles per hour. It means everyone is driving just below 65

(BRIAN O'NEILL)

miles per hour. But a 65-miles-per-hour speed limit would mean that the bulk of the people would be driving just below 75 miles per hour.

The New York Times, 2-6:9.

Donald E. Petersen
Chairman,
Ford Motor Company

1

Overall, the world auto industry has a problem of chronic excess capacity. This has led to the fact today that only in America does anybody make any money. The Europeans can't make money in Europe; the Japanese can't make money in Japan. They all look to [the U.S.] market for their profit. So there is just extraordinary competition in the American market—and you see it in its most dynamic form in the bottom half of the market—smaller cars—where price gets to be very important.

Interview/USA Today, 2-5:(4)7.

Ronald Reagan
President of the United States

2

Every time a passenger boards an Amtrak train, the American taxpayer pays about $35. But on the New York-to-Chicago train, it's much higher. In fact, on that run, it would cost the taxpayer less for the government to pass out free tickets. The mass-transit Federal subsidy is another head shaker. In Miami, the $1-billion subsidy helped build a system that serves less than 10,000 daily riders. That comes to $100,000 a passenger. It would have been a lot cheaper to buy everyone a limousine.

Before National Association of Counties,
Washington, March 4/The New York Times, 3-5:33.

Steven G. Rothmeier
President,
Northwest Airlines

3

[On whether the recent increase in airline ac- quisitions by other airlines will result in oligopo- lies and higher fares]: In the international

marketplace, yes. In the domestic [U.S.] marketplace, I don't think so. If you look at the first six years of deregulation in the [U.S.] airline industry, there are a number of carriers that have emerged that are low cost and low priced—People Express, Continental, America West and Midway. I think if there was consolidation in the domestic marketplace, these carriers would continue to impact the over-all pricing structure. They will just continue to create competitive fares, which means low-cost trips for the public. It is different on the international level. If a carrier like United were to get access to the greater part of the Pacific, with the other barriers to entry, and with it essentially competing with a dominant foreign-flag carrier, there is less incentive for low pricing.

Interview/The New York Times, 7-2:32.

Ted Schwinden
Governor of Montana (D)

4

[On laws that require the use of automobile seat belts]: Mandatory seat-belt laws cross the tenuous line between protection of the motoring public and interference with the rights of individuals to set their own standards of conduct.

USA Today, 2-1:(4)6.

Ralph L. Stanley
Administrator, Urban Mass Transportation
Administration of the United States

5

The issue for the nation is that the Federal government cannot afford to pay the share of mass-transit costs it has carried in the past. We can't underwrite it all, and there are going to be winners and losers . . . Now we are setting up objective criteria to find out if the localities have the financial resources to provide for the continued operation of a [mass-transit] system. I'm not going to any more ribbon cuttings at the opening of a transit system and tell people we don't have to worry about the future. When the ribbon cuttings are over, the cities must understand they have to pay their own way for a transit system.

Interview, Washington, March 28/
The New York Times, 3-29:8.

David A. Stockman
Director, Federal Office of Management and Budget

1

There are few programs I can think of that rank lower than Amtrak in terms of the good they do, the purpose they serve and the national need they respond to. If we don't have the courage, the foresight, the comprehension of our problem that is sufficient enough to get rid of Amtrak, I don't think we're going to shave much off the [Federal] budget at all. Amtrak is the litmus indicator . . . Without total subsidy termination and the opportunities offered through liquidation of Amtrak's assets, the Federal government will continue to pour billions of dollars more into the Amtrak mobile money-burning machine.

Before Senate Surface Transportation Subcommittee, Washington, April 29/The New York Times, 4-30:1, 9.

Steven D. Symms
United States Senator, R-Idaho

2

[Saying states should be allowed to raise their highway speed limits above 55 and not be penal-

ized by the Federal government]: Enactment of the uniform speed limit had two positive effects: It saved fuel, and it saved lives. Enactment of the uniform speed limit had another important effect. The National Research Council has estimated that reduced speeds cost the nation an extra one billion hours of driving time per year. That lost time has an economic value. I do not contend that saving lives and fuel is unimportant. I'm only saying there is nothing magical about 55. To argue that extra travel time is worth the cost of lives leads one to conclude that we probably should stop driving cars altogether.

The New York Times, 7-2:12.

James R. Thompson
Governor of Illinois (R)

3

[Acknowledging the criticism of opponents of a new law, which he just signed, requiring the use of automobile seat belts]: Since politicians regularly promise people to get government off their backs, it my seem strange to impose it around their waists.

USA Today, 1-9:(A)5.

Urban Affairs

Alan Beals
Executive director,
National League of Cities

1

Austerity and budget restraint have been the order of business during four hard years for cities, but local economic recovery finally seems to be broadly under way. Now, after two years of recovery and low inflation, increased public demands are apparent for services and for restoration of recession-forced budget cuts . . . [The last few years have resulted in a] pent-up demand for services that are going to be a key problem for them in balancing their budgets.

News conference, Washington,
Jan. 2/The Washington Post, 1-3:(A)4.

2

[Criticizing Reagan Administration budget cuts affecting local government]: It amounts to a declaration that our national government should ignore its role in helping to deal with problems that exist in our cities and towns, and occur there simply because that's where most people live, particularly people in need. State and local government have been in the front lines in the effort to fight inflation, recession and record Federal deficits. We have made the sacrifices. We have absorbed severe cuts. We have shored up our own finances to maintain essential services. The loss of general revenue-sharing, job-training, transit, housing and economic-development assistance cannot be made up from local revenue sources that are already stretching their limits. It is unrealistic for anyone to pretend that states and local governments could do something other than make unthinkable cuts or once again seek new taxes.

The Washington Post, 2-15:(A)24.

Pat Choate
Author;
Authority on urban affairs

3

The encouraging thing I see [in cities] is almost philosophical. Cities are realizing they've

got to pull up their own socks and do something. One of the things that was always amazing [to me] in the 1970s was the extent to which communities would delay projects—waiting to get a Federal grant. Now, all of a sudden, they realize they're on their own.

The Christian Science Monitor,
6-7:7.

Raymond Flynn
Mayor of Boston

4

[On President Reagan's proposed cuts in Federal aid to cities]: If the proposed Federal budget were enacted this afternoon, all of us [cities] could hang the "Going Out of Business" sign tonight.

Newsweek, 2-25:26.

John Fowles
Author

5

Cities are neurotic. I think people who live in the country, the provinces, are lucky. If people were economically free to move, I somehow think there would be an enormous exodus from places like Chicago or New York or London.

Interview, New York/
The Washington Post,
9-12:(C)8.

Edward I. Koch
Mayor of New York

6

In running a major city, it is important to exercise leadership. That means if you think what you're doing is right, do it. If you make a mistake and it becomes evident to you that you have, correct it. Don't hesitate to admit error. And don't take polls before you do something to decide whether it will be popular, though there's nothing wrong with polling later to find out whether what you did satisfied those who elected

(EDWARD I. KOCH)

you. Having a sense of self-confidence—knowing that out of all of those who offered themselves for the position you hold, the people decided you were best—is essential to doing the job.

Interview/
U.S. News & World Report, 5-20:68.

Ernest N. Morial
Mayor of New Orleans; President,
United States Conference of Mayors

[Criticizing President Reagan's budget proposal to reduce Federal grants to local governments]: In the name of deficit reduction, this budget proposes to cut or eliminate nearly every Federal investment of benefit to the cities. Viewed another way, it spells the beginning of the end of the historical Federal-city partnership that has contributed so much in so many ways to our economic development and vitality . . . We are deeply concerned about the Federal deficit and the effect it is having on the economy. But we do not believe that destroying the Federal-urban partnership and ending vitally needed programs—including those aiding low-income people—is in the best interests of our nation.

News conference, Washington,
Feb. 7/The Washington Post, 2-8:(A)5.

William Proxmire
United States Senator, D-Wisconsin

[On New York City's recovery from a fiscal crisis in the 1970s]: That New York City saga should carry a vivid message for this [U.S.] Congress. If New York City, with its long tradition of permissive, easygoing government and its notorious lack of discipline, can embrace austerity and succeed, why can't this Congress? . . . Here was profligacy personified. A city without a disciplined bone in its flabby, fun-loving body. Like so many good-time Charlies, it fell into deep financial trouble. So deep that it came to the Federal government for a bail-out . . . Most

of us who were here in the Senate at the time only remember that New York City officials engineered a highly professional lobbying and public-relations campaign. They won their bail-out . . . [But] the Congress didn't really do much for the city. It provided a $1.5-billion guarantee. But it tied a guarantee fee into the settlement. There was no Federal cost. In fact, the Federal government made a $30-million profit on the deal. So the New York City recovery from the shadow of bankruptcy was strictly an achievement of New York City itself. How were its elected officials able to impose this reign of responsible but very painful austerity on the good-time capital of America? They made painful, obviously unpopular, decisions, because they had to.

Interview, Washington, Nov. 19/
The New York Times, 11-20:16.

Ronald Reagan
President of the United States

[On his plans to cut Federal aid to state and local governments]: There's simply no justification . . . for the Federal government, which is running a deficit, to be borrowing money to be spent by state and local governments, some of which are now running surpluses.

At meeting with state governors, Washington,
Feb. 25/The New York Times, 1-26:1.

Stephen R. Reed
Mayor of Harrisburg, Pa.

Because of the Reagan Administration, we have certainly seen a shift in Federal policy regarding urban communities, but it is fair to say that a number of American cities had become in an unhealthy way too dependent on direct cash grants from the Federal level. What cities must learn to do—as we are teaching Harrisburg to do—is to be creative in marketing, financing and development. You can frequently accomplish that without Federal cash grants.

Interview/
USA Today, 6-18:(A)9.

Harold Washington
Mayor of Chicago

1

[Criticizing proposed cutbacks in Federal aid to cities]: [Cities] are the repositories of civilization, culture, art, infrastructure, fine cuisine . . . To reduce us to special pleaders . . . is to put cities down.

At rally, Washington, March 26/
The Washington Post, 3-27:(A)6.

Walter E. Washington
Former Mayor of Washington, D.C.

2

[On being Mayor]: You look at it like college presidents. Some are good foundation men and some are good builders . . . When I was going through it, I felt rightfully that everything I was doing was to build a foundation for the future of this city.

The Washington Post, 1-1:(A)12.

PART TWO

International Affairs

Africa

Herbert Beukes
South African Ambassador-designate to the United States

1

[Criticizing foreign economic sanctions against his country to protest South Africa's apartheid system]: You cannot influence someone if you antagonize them . . . I don't believe a government is going, if it were not willing to do so and had not realized the need to do so of its own accord, to make fundamental departures from a whole ideology . . . on the basis of bank loans not being available to the government or that krugerrands [South Africa's gold coins] might not be sold here [in the U.S.].

To editors and reporters, Washington,
Sept. 12/The Washington Post,
9-13:(A)20.

Dawid Bezuidenhout
Chairman,
transitional government of Namibia

2

[On his new government, just established in Namibia by South Africa]: The people of Namibia are tired of this armed struggle waged about them. They are tired of having their children abducted into Angola. They are tired of the death and destruction sown by land mines, bombs and fragmentation grenades. They have no interest in foreign ideologies or the struggles forced upon them by those with imperialist designs on southern Africa. Our people, the people of this country, have now stood up and said, "Leave us alone. Let us determine our future."

Inaugural address, Windhoek, Namibia,
June 17/Los Angeles Times,
6-18:(I)10.

Allan Boesak
South African clergyman; President,
World Alliance of Reformed Churches

3

At no time in my lifetime has the opinion of blacks [in South Africa] of the United States been so low as now. [Blacks in South Africa]

perceive the United States [government] to be on the side of the [white] minority rule [in South Africa]. We perceive the United States to be racist. We perceive the United States Administration to be concerned only with the white power structure.

Interview, Washington/
The Washington Post, 2-2:(G)11.

Alex Boraine
Chairman, Progressive Federal Party of South Africa

4

[On South African President Pieter Botha and that country's apartheid system]: I have no doubt that Mr. Botha has attempted to act within a moral framework, and in this he is unique among his predecessors. Regrettably superimposed over this moral framework, however, is the straitjacket that has been fashioned of a narrow sectionalism and race consciousness [that has left him] temperamentally and historically incapable of introducing the very reforms his moral framework implies and demands.

Los Angeles Times,
8-26:(I)14.

Pieter W. Botha
President of South Africa

5

We are committed to cooperative coexistence [among the races in South Africa], and we believe that this ideal can be achieved only if the diversity of our society is recognized and it is accepted that the composition of our country's population need not be an obstacle in our way. But this is possible only within a system in which there is no domination of one population group over another, which in turn requires self-determination for each group over its own affairs and joint responsibility for and cooperation on common interests . . . The government has been engaged for some years now in a program of fundamental reform in every sphere of life. Reform, and specifically Constitutional reform, is a continuing process. The government is resolved to

241

WHAT THEY SAID IN 1985

(PIETER W. BOTHA)

pursue peaceful and democratic solutions that satisfy the requirements of fairness and justice.

Before Parliament, Cape Town,
Jan. 25/USA Today, 2-27:(A)8.

1

[Criticizing demonstrations against South Africa's apartheid system]: It saddens me that certain people, under the guise of moral and religious conviction, should take the lead in fomenting disobedience, violence and destruction. They want to see the country go up in flames . . . They want to bring South Africa to its knees . . . I want to state clearly and categorically that they will not succeed. Their schemes are transparent for all of us to see. Responsible South Africans reject revolutionary activities and outside interference in our internal affairs . . . It is ironic that now, at exactly the time that we have taken new initiatives that encompass cooperation on so many levels and in so many spheres, people of ill intent instigate demonstrations and marches that result in arson, violence and death.

Before Parliament, Cape Town, March 27/
Los Angeles Times,
3-28:(I)18.

2

[On his country's establishment of an autonomous local government in Namibia, despite continuing international efforts aimed at gaining full independence for that area]: [South Africa is committed to] an internationally acceptable independence [for Namibia] as long as there is a possibility that recent international negotiations hold any realistic prospect of bringing about the genuine withdrawal of Cuban forces from Angola . . . [But] we have a message for the world, for Soviet strategists shifting their pieces on the international chessboard, for Western diplomats anxious to remove, at any cost, this vexatious question from the international agenda, for terrorists of the South-West Africa People's Organization lurking in their lairs in Angola: We are not a people who shirk our responsibilities . . . South Africa has clear-cut regional inter-

ests in southern Africa that it is not prepared to relinquish.

Before Namibia's new Cabinet and National Assembly,
Windhoek, Namibia, June 17/
Los Angeles Times, 6-18:(I)10.

3

[On those in the U.S. who are calling for sanctions against South Africa to protest that country's apartheid system]: If there are elements in Washington who think that South Africa is going to be run by the United States, then it must be made quite clear that those elements are heading for a confrontation with the South African government and people. [The call for sanctions raises] the basic principle that no self-respecting nation can allow any other country, large or small, to dictate to it how it should be governed . . . I do not believe in an artificial, unitary state on the basis of one-man, one-vote. I do not believe in a system in which minority groups can be dominated . . . I do not believe in a path in which stability and Christian and civilized values are thrown on the rubbish heap . . . We regard a unitary, melting-pot system as unsuitable and unacceptable for South Africa.

Before South African Parliament, Cape Town,
June 19/Los Angeles Times,
6-20:(I)24.

4

[On the current anti-apartheid pressure on his government]: Let me state explicitly that I believe in participation of all the South African communities on matters of common concern. I believe there should exist structures to reach this goal of co-responsibility and participation. I firmly believe that the granting and acceptance of independence by various black peoples within the context of their own statehood represent a material part of the solution . . . [But] I am not prepared to lead white South Africans and other minority groups on a road to abdication and suicide. Listen, my friends, listen. Destroy white South Africa and our influence in this subcontinent of southern Africa, and this country will drift into factions, strife, chaos and poverty . . . The alternative is bloodshed; the alternative is murder; the alternative is gunpowder; the alternative is a thief who wants to get

(PIETER W. BOTHA)

control of power in South Africa so he can ruin our country and way of life . . . Any future constitutional dispensation providing for participation by all South African citizens should be negotiated. The overriding common denominator [in those talks] is our mutual interest in each other's freedom and well-being. Our peace and prosperity are indivisible. The only way forward is through cooperation and co-responsibility.

At opening of Natal Provincial Congress,
Durban, South Africa, Aug. 15/The New York Times,
8-16:4; Los Angeles Times, 8-16:(I)20.

1

[On the racial situation in South Africa]: We have many peoples and many communities. No single community can be the only winner. We must be winners together, or we shall all be losers . . . There is no more place for hatred and fear. There is no more time for suspicion and conflict. We must obey the word of God. We must live our lives in the spirit of Christ. We must carry out our obligation to love one another and do what is just and good . . . We must jointly strive to find out what our problems are, and then we must jointly strive to find solutions. There is no hatred we cannot heal with love. There is no fear we cannot change to understanding. We must make a new beginning.

At church gathering of blacks/
Los Angeles Times, 8-26:(I)15.

2

[Criticizing U.S. President Reagan's announcement of sanctions against South Africa to protest that country's apartheid system]: Sanctions cannot solve our problems. South Africa's decisions will be made by South Africa's leaders. The leaders of South Africa will themselves decide what is in our interests. Our objective is peaceful reform. Reform can only be retarded by outside attempts to interfere . . . We see understanding of the fact that even limited sanctions destroy jobs and progress. Punitive sanctions—however selective—do not select their victims. The welfare of blacks and whites is indivisible. [It is ironic that] this punitive campaign is continuing at the very time [when South Africa has rejected] political domination by any one community of another; the exclusion of any community from the political decision-making process; injustice or inequality in the opportunities available for any community; racial discrimination and the impairment of human dignity . . . Despite outside pressure, the South African government will actively pursue its program of reform. We remain committed to negotiation with all leaders who renounce violence.

Pretoria, Sept. 9/
The New York Times, 9-10:4.

3

[On anti-apartheid unrest in his country]: Because we remain committed to peace, South Africa will not be surrendered to control by fire-raising, stone-throwing mobs. Freedom is not to be found along this road. Action by the government to maintain law and order and to ensure the safety of all members of our society must therefore be judged in terms of the government's irrevocable commitment to reform. I wish to emphasize that security action does not oppose reform . . . [and] does not occur for purposes of oppression and maintaining the status quo. We recognize the right to protest, but the right to protest may not lead to violation of the law.

At National Party conference, Port Elizabeth,
South Africa, Sept. 30/
Los Angeles Times,
10-1:(I)5.

Roelof F. Botha
Foreign Minister of South Africa

4

I believe the present [U.S.] Administration is doing what it does in southern Africa first and foremost in the interests of the United States of America. In some areas our interests may coincide. In others they don't. We have no illusions that should the United States in its global views consider it necessary to take actions to the detriment of my country that you [the U.S.] will not hesitate to do so.

Interview, Cape Town, Jan. 28/
The Washington Post, 1-29:(A)8.

243

(ROELOF F. BOTHA)

The South African government is committed to change or to repeal laws and practices which discriminate in a negative, inhumane or humiliating way against people on account of the color of their skin. Yes, South Africa is changing. But it is changing at a pace which we believe the white voters can absorb . . . My government cannot be a party to a change which will [destroy] not only the well-being of the whites, but also that of our black friends.

Interview, Pretoria/Newsweek, 3-11:32.

1

We cannot achieve majority rule on the basis of one man, one vote—not only because the whites are against it, but because all moderates [of any race] are against it. If you could remove all the whites tomorrow from the face of South Africa, you would be no nearer to a political solution, because there is no way you are going to force the various black peoples into a unitary system . . . [Majority rule would] force the strongest group to the top, which would then discriminate against and dominate all the other groups.

Interview, Pretoria/Newsweek, 3-11:32.

2

Apartheid is no longer the policy of this government. Reform is our policy. Apartheid is the social reality, but our commitment is to the abolition of apartheid.

At meeting with U.S. evangelist Jerry Falwell, Aug. 18/The Christian Science Monitor, 8-20:2.

3

Lester Brown
President, Worldwatch Institute

Three forces are acting in concert to put Africa on the skids in terms of food supplies. First, Africa now is experiencing the fastest population growth of any continent at any time in human history. Second, the continent is undergoing widespread soil erosion from Mediterranean countries in the north all the way to the Cape of Good Hope in the south. Third, African governments have neglected agriculture, giving it low priority in public investment and following food-

244

price policies that placate urban consumers, thus discouraging farmers. All three of these forces are now converging in a truly devastating fashion. What we are seeing is a situation that's been in the making for many years but has only now been brought into sharp focus by a severe drought.

Interview/U.S. News & World Report, 2-25:71.

George Bush
Vice President of the United States

[On the famine in Ethiopia]: From our point of view, the most serious abuse of human rights has been the [Ethiopian] government's refusal to allow relief agencies safe passage to take food into areas of Eritrea and Tigre not under its control. Famine has been so devastating in Ethiopia in part because the government has used it as an instrument of war [against anti-government rebels] in Eritrea and Tigre.

Before National Press Club, Washington, Feb. 25/The Washington Post, 2-26:(A)13.

5

[On U.S. aid to combat the famine in Africa]: Africans seek our help not because they want to depend on us, but because other models have failed and they want to get back on their own feet. We donors have a responsibility to our own citizens and to Africa alike to give both relief and forms of aid that do not perpetuate dependency . . . People said [in the 1930s] that [U.S. Dust Bowl] land would never produce crops again. Today, an important part of the food America ships to Africa comes from what was once the Dust Bowl. With more research, Africa, too, will reclaim its once productive land.

At United Nations conference on famine relief, Geneva, March 11/The Washington Post, 3-12:(A)12.

6

Gatsha Buthelezi
Chief Minister of KwaZulu (black South African homeland); Leader, South African Zulu people

[Criticizing U.S. economic sanctions against South Africa to protest that country's apartheid

7

(GATSHA BUTHELEZI)

system]: I challenge anyone to go to a meeting—say in [the black township of] Soweto or in any other township—and talk that language [of sanctions], that people should lose jobs and that their dire straits, in which they find themselves, should get worse . . . In general, black people do not support sanctions . . . I think the South African [white] regime needs to have a country that is as powerful as the United States breathing down its neck . . . And I think that if you are going to remove the only leverage which you have in the United States of having your corporations operating in South Africa, then you will remove the only leverage which you can apply as far as economic justice for my people is concerned.

Broadcast interview, London/
"Meet the Press," NBC-TV, 8-4.

1

[Saying he is against armed rebellion as a way for blacks to end South Africa's apartheid system]: One man, one vote is a cherished ideal of all black leaders. I am saying let's make a start where it is possible to make a start on that journey toward the ideal. [South Africa] is a completely different kettle of fish from other places where the armed struggle has worked, such as Zimbabwe. We don't have settlers. We have an indigenous white population which is as indigenous as Americans in America. They have got nowhere else to go, and if you put them up against the wall they will scorch the earth . . . If you ask me, black disunity is the biggest problem. Most of the deaths happening now [in the current black unrest], the burning of people that we have seen, is not being done by the government, but by black people to other black people. You have got an incipient civil war going on already. My brothers and sisters in the UDF state that they would like to make the country "ungovernable" and they synchronize their moves with the ANC. I think it is nonsensical to regard the killing of blacks by blacks as a liberation struggle.

Interview, Jerusalem, Israel,
Aug. 13/The New York Times,
8-14:3.

2

[Saying Americans should send money and education supplies to help South African blacks, rather than supporting economic sanctions against that country to protest the apartheid system]: Our children are educated in shells. Our schools need libraries. We need books . . . I wish Americans would send their books and dollars instead of supporting sanctions, if they really want to help the black people here . . . I speak to tens of thousands of black people and they always tell me they want [foreign] investments because investments produce jobs . . . If Americans want to come here to help us, we welcome them—teachers, doctors, anyone. There is no limit to what Americans can do for us. Change [in apartheid] will come about nonviolently, I'm assured of that. But we need to educate our people.

Ulundi, South Africa/
The Christian Science Monitor, 11-29:25.

3

[On the apartheid system in South Africa]: Even in the government itself, they're not very proud of apartheid any more. I definitely see an end of it. The recent by-elections, in which the President [Pieter] Botha lost only one of four seats, shows that whites are not challenging his program of reform. Mr. Botha could move more boldly, and I think it's tragic that this man, who could get South Africa out of this quagmire, lacks the courage to do so.

Interview/U.S. News & World Report, 12-2:40.

4

Fidel Castro
President of Cuba

Until [UN] Resolution 435 [providing for independence of Namibia] is carried out, or at least until concrete steps in this direction are taken, not one single Cuban soldier will be withdrawn from Angola. And if more soldiers are needed, we will send more soldiers.

At secondary school, Isle of Youth, Cuba,
May 29/The Washington Post, 5-30:(A)23.

5

[South Africa's] apartheid is the most shameful, traumatizing and inconceivable crime that

(FIDEL CASTRO)

exists in the contemporary world. I don't know of anything else as serious—from the moral and human standpoint—as apartheid. Particularly after the struggle against Nazi Fascism, after the independence of all the former colonies, the survival of apartheid is a disgrace for humanity. The major industrialized countries, however—the United States included—have made heavy investments in and have collaborated economically, technologically and through the supply of weapons with the apartheid regime. In fact, South Africa is an ally of the West's, and it is the West that has actually made it possible for that system to endure.

Interview, Havana/Playboy, August:177.

Arthur Chaskalson
*Director, Legal Resources
Center (South Africa)*

1

[On South Africa's apartheid system]: I think it is probably easier for someone who has grown up outside the Afrikaner establishment to look upon the structure which the Afrikaners have erected to gain power and protect their position far more critically than they would do themselves. Just about everybody who looks at South Africa accepts that the system is not going to last; it's just a question of when it will go. Twenty years ago I wouldn't have believed that the system would still be as firmly in place as it is now. So I've stopped thinking in terms of time.

Interview/The New York Times, 3-25:4.

Joe Clark
Minister of External Affairs of Canada

2

[On Canada's decision to impose sanctions against South Africa to protest that country's apartheid system]: The fundamental changes in South Africa we had hoped for during the past quarter-century have not come about. One tragic incident follows another, and almost 400 South Africans have lost their lives in the past year. In these circumstances, the persistence . . . of institutionalized racism can only cause a widening

gulf between our two countries. We regret that, but the time has come for a basic change, for the repudiation of apartheid as a concept and a policy.

*To reporters, Ottawa, July 6/
Los Angeles Times, 7-8:(I)7.*

Jack F. Clarke
*Managing director,
IBM South Africa*

3

[On South Africa's apartheid system]: The laws affecting the right of a person to sell his labor must be abolished . . . Laws which force a person working in a first-world environment at the office to return to the deprivations of a Third World climate at night must be changed.

The New York Times, 3-27:25.

Chester A. Crocker
*Assistant Secretary for African Affairs,
Department of State of the United States*

4

Most African governments have strangulated private initiative. There needs to be more incentive in more countries to enable people to make a profitable return. There's a strong tendency to subsidize people who live in the urban areas where the political power base is. That's understandable politically, but it's led to a situation that's produced distortions in the agricultural economy of many African states.

The Christian Science Monitor, 3-5:36.

5

[On South Africa's apartheid system]: It isn't a question of Afrikaner or governmental intentions. If there is not constructive change, there's going to be chaos, there's going to be anarchy, there's going to be a blow-up. And that's the key pressure for change inside that country. The white minority cannot run it with guns. They cannot run it on the basis of a labor force that is overwhelmingly black unless there is a basis of consent and dialogue and some shared values.

*Broadcast interview/
"This Week With David Brinkley,"
ABC-TV, 3-24.*

(CHESTER A. CROCKER)

1

[Criticizing proposals for U.S. economic sanctions against South Africa as a protest against that country's apartheid system]: We Americans are builders, not destroyers. Clearly, our goal must be a more hopeful, just and prosperous South Africa with expanded opportunities for all its people. Irrespective of how South Africa will be run or by whom, damaging its economy now will not only stunt economic growth, it will stunt the lives of this and coming generations.

At Commonwealth Club, San Francisco, Aug. 16/The New York Times, 8-17:5.

2

[Arguing against U.S. economic sanctions to protest apartheid in South Africa]: We don't believe that the cause of justice in ending apartheid will be advanced by economic measures that would, in fact, hurt those we're trying to help . . . We must keep in mind the effect on the majority of the people, their government and neighboring countries . . . Our message is one of dissociation from racism and making clear that we want to see apartheid ended now . . . The policy is not one of soft talk—that's a distortion—but of using our influence in a way likely to work. In some cases, we speak out very clearly in public in strong terms; in others, we rely on diplomatic channels. We must recognize that the key factors for change are internal to South Africa. We have limited influence.

Interview/U.S. News & World Report, 9-9:35.

Jose Eduardo dos Santos
President of Angola

3

The Soviet Union, with its material, moral, political and diplomatic support, continues to be the dependable rearguard for all people who struggle for freedom and independence. Cuba's sons have irrigated our sacred soil with their blood and have supported, shoulder-to-shoulder with their Angolan brothers, the defense of the conquest of the revolution against external aggressions.

At Marxist-Leninist Movement for the Liberation of Angola-Workers Party conference, Luanda, Angola, Dec. 9/The New York Times, 12-16:4.

Sheena Duncan
President, Black Sash
(South African anti-apartheid organization)

4

[On the apartheid system in South Africa]: You Americans must understand that in South Africa the issue is not civil rights. People in the [U.S.] equate apartheid with the kind of race discrimination you had [in the U.S.]. That is a very wrong impression. There is a fundamental difference between your [U.S.] Constitution and ours. Your Constitution guarantees civil rights. In our country that is totally lacking. We have no bill of rights or constitutional protections. Rather, the purpose of apartheid—and it is built right into the Constitution—is to deny blacks political power.

At Church Center for the United Nations, New York/The Christian Science Monitor, 10-31:29.

Laurent Fabius
Premier of France

5

[On France's decision to suspend all new investment in South Africa as a protest against that country's apartheid system]: For all people who support justice and the rights of man, the apartheid regime in South Africa is inadmissible. It institutionalizes racial discrimination; it undermines the moral and political principles on which our society is based. Events of the last few days [the institution of a state of emergency by South Africa in response to racial violence there] have shown a grave and serious deterioration. By installing the state of emergency, and conferring full powers on the army and police, in multiplying arbitrary arrests, and in giving the order to fire on the population, the South African government has only reinforced its repression.

Paris, July 24/The New York Times, 7-25:7.

Bernardus G. Fourie
South African Ambassador to the United States

6

[Criticizing those who protest outside the South African Embassy about his country's apartheid policy]: South Africa has changed

(BERNARDUS G. FOURIE)

more during the last five years than in the previous 50, so we find the reaction against us perplexing . . . It seems to us the pure motive [of the protestors] can't be infringement of human rights. It's obvious . . . Certain groups that lost out in the [U.S.] election are looking for something to propel them back into the media, to the news of the day. I don't believe in standing in front of the South African Embassy two to three minutes, and when the cameras clicked and the TV people are gone, the afternoon show is over. That's not sincerity.

News conference, Los Angeles, March 13/Los Angeles Times, 3-14:(I)8.

1

David Gardner
President, University of California

[Arguing against the University divesting itself of stocks of companies associated with South Africa as a means of protesting apartheid in that country]: I am simply not persuaded that the selling of UC-held stocks and bonds of companies doing business in South Africa would accomplish much more than a change of ownership of the shares to be sold. It would surely not end apartheid, nor, in my opinion, improve the well-being of non-white South Africans.

Berkeley, Calif., June 21/ The Washington Post, 6-22:(A)17.

2

Jan Christiaan Heunis
Minister for Constitutional Development and Planning of South Africa

[On the South African government's attempts to modify the apartheid system]: It's difficult, damned difficult, to negotiate with leaders of black, Indian and Colored communities who are immediately branded as stooges [by anti-apartheid activists] for talking to [government representatives]. But it's impossible, flatly impossible, to develop new political structures—let alone to write a Constitution that will be accepted and will work—except through negotiations . . . We have committed ourselves to one country, one citizenship, one Constitution. We have accepted the permanency of the black urban population, property rights for them, the need for political entities for them, their representation at the highest levels of government, and for these political structures to be negotiated. I won't say this was unthinkable three years ago, but it certainly was not government policy then.

Interview, Pretoria/Los Angeles Times, 12-20:(I-A)1,2.

3

Jesse L. Jackson
American civil-rights leader; President, Operation PUSH (People United to Save Humanity)

[Criticizing outside support of South Africa's apartheid system]: [South Africa is] the economic prostitute of the Western world. Some of our churches, our universities and our government jump into bed with South Africa and make cheap love, cheap profits off slave labor.

At Harvard University, April 4/The New York Times, 4-5:2.

4

John Kane-Berman
Director, South African Institute of Race Relations

[On South Africa's apartheid system]: Given his track record, my impression is that President [Pieter] Botha will continue with the kind of ad hoc reform program he has pursued since 1979. The real danger is not that the reform process will stop but that it will retain its present temporizing, patchy nature and not get to grips with the fundamental issues. There's no sense of real urgency or decisive leadership here. Indeed, more and more this government gives the impression of fiddling while Rome burns. One of the reasons is that it is trying to hang on to as much of traditional political apartheid as it can. This is simply no longer acceptable to any black leader.

Interview, Johannesburg/ U.S. News & World Report, 8-5:32.

5

Kenneth Kaunda
President of Zambia

[Supporting the use of foreign economic sanctions against South Africa to protest that

(KENNETH KAUNDA)

country's apartheid system]: We have been told several times that it is we [black Africans] who will suffer most if sanctions are imposed. Nobody knows that better than I do, nobody. I've gone through it, my people and I, as a result of the British-imposed sanctions at the United Nations [against Rhodesia in the 1960s]. But an explosion is about to take place in South Africa and, when it does, it will destroy everything in its wake. So whether there is explosion or whether there are sanctions, we are involved. As a matter of both principle and self-interest, we want to do everything possible to avert that explosion. Final arrangements can only be determined by the South Africans themselves. But we might give a hint: It's always dangerous giving too little too late. I told [South African President Pieter] Botha in my border meeting with him in 1982: "You and the moderate whites in commerce, the moderate blacks in commerce form a very substantial middle group. You should together form a new structure for the country, politically, economically and socially. Once you do that, South Africa will be home free. Fail, and disaster." How to do this is their concern, but speed is of the essence.

Interview, Lusaka, Zambia/Time, 9-16:44.

Edward M. Kennedy
United States Senator,
D-Massachusetts

1

[On migrant-worker hostels in South Africa for blacks who must leave their families behind when they go to work in the cities]: This camp is one of the most distressing and despairing visits that I have made to any facility in my lifetime. Here, individuals are caught between trying to provide for their families or living with their families. I don't really know of any other place in the world where that kind of cruel, harsh, difficult choice must be made by any people who believe in family life . . . This is alien to every kind of tradition in the Judeo-Christian ethic, and I find it appalling.

Soweto, South Africa, Jan. 6/
Los Angeles Times,
1-7:(I)10.

2

[Criticizing South Africa's system of apartheid]: The decisive issue is full and equal citizenship [for blacks], not within the space of generations but in a reasonable span of years . . . Some in business may say that [apartheid] is not your [businessmen's] policy, but unless it is changed, it surely will shape your destiny. Does anyone really believe . . . that peace and order can be permanently founded on a system that represents so fundamental a disorder in human relations and human aspirations? . . . It is disheartening to hear it said so often, and with such confidence, that progress is being made in this country—only to learn that the basic question of political participation for black South Africans is hardly ever raised, and never really taken seriously, in the dominant precincts of white power. Even the talk of reform seems to stop before it touches the ballot box.

To South African businessmen, Johannesburg,
Jan. 8/Los Angeles Times, 1-9:(I)4.

3

[Criticizing South Africa's apartheid system]: My nation will not long continue a policy of so-called "constructive engagement" with a social order so entirely destructive of human rights. Only a very few extremists in my country still defend the government of South Africa. Patience is running out across the [American] political spectrum. Not only Democrats, but Republicans and [U.S.] President Reagan even, are speaking out against apartheid.

At multiracial rally, Cape Town,
Jan. 11/Los Angeles Times, 1-12:(I)22.

4

South Africa is eventually going to be free [of apartheid]. A continuation of existing [U.S.] policies will place the United States among the last allies of the basically white supremacist regime there and alienate a whole new generation of leaders. It is an awesome prospect.

Interview/The Washington Post, 2-7:(A)33.

5

[On his recent visit to South Africa]: Apartheid is a kind of a condition that you can read

249

(EDWARD M. KENNEDY)

about and you can talk to people who've experienced it, but until you feel it with your hands, till you see it with your eyes, until you touch the people who are seared by that extraordinary experience of absolute discrimination solely on the basis of the pigmentation of one's skin, it's difficult to really understand the full dimensions of the horror of apartheid.

Interview/USA Today, 2-8:(A)13.

Jeane J. Kirkpatrick
Former United States Ambassador/Permanent Representative to the United Nations

1

[On whether the U.S. policy of constructive engagement with South Africa to change that country's apartheid system, rather than trade sanctions, is damaging to U.S. relations with Third World countries who want stronger anti-apartheid policy from the U.S.]: Oh, no, I don't think so. First of all, it's important always to distinguish between nations when you're talking about the Third World. And it's very important to be clear that the United States does not have any sort of unique relationship with South Africa. We don't have a relationship with South Africa that's any different from that of other Western nations. With regard to trade, we do not have a different relationship with South Africa than the European Economic Community or Scandinavian nations or the Soviet bloc. In fact, in terms of trade, we don't have a different relationship with South Africa than the other African states. These states are deeply involved in and dependent on trade with South Africa. So that to suggest that our trade relations with South Africa are somehow uniquely damaging to U.S. relations with the Third World is just simply not true.

Interview/U.S. News & World Report, 9-9:47.

Jim Leach
United States Representative, R-Iowa

2

[Advocating U.S. economic sanctions against South Africa to protest that country's apartheid system]: When white rule is finally doomed [in South Africa], we [the U.S.] don't want to go down as the one government that held the coattails of the remaining vestiges of colonialism and racism in Africa. The strategic argument is thus for an immediate shift of U.S. policy away from anything that appears to legitimize the government in power.

The Christian Science Monitor, 8-2:32.

Patrick Lekota
Publicity secretary, United Democratic Front of South Africa

3

The question is how to oppose apartheid, and that means we must first answer how we understand the nature of the problem. Is the problem white people, or is it the policy of this minority regime [the South African government], which is largely made up of white-skinned people? We in the United Democratic Front see the problem not as white people but as an unjust policy. For AZAPO [Azanian People's Organization], the problem is white people, and the solution is black people.

Los Angeles Times, 2-3:(I)6.

Mickey Leland
United states Representative, D-Texas

4

The [U.S.] Congressional Black Caucus has expressed to the Senate and the House of Representatives our strongest opposition to any covert or direct [U.S.] assistance to the pro-South Africa UNITA forces [trying to overthrow the government] in Angola. It is our unequivocal position that any aid, whether military or under the guise of humanitarian assistance, would establish the United States government as an ally of the Pretoria regime. To aid in the war against the people of Angola and Namibia would compromise our policy of pressuring South Africa to end apartheid and its illegal occupation of Namibia.

*Washington, Nov. 14/
The Washington Post, 11-15:(A)35.*

Willie Lubbe
Professor of classics,
University of South Africa

1

[Supporting South Africa's apartheid system]: If it was God's will that all people should have the same colored skin, He would have created us that way. Why do you think there are differences? Because He wanted them. Why don't animals integrate? Because it is not natural. Yet people are to be forced to live together. Why? . . . There is no other way for us now than partition. You will never create real peace in South Africa and stability and happiness amongst its people if you don't partition them. We are going to get our own country for the white man—never mind the cost—because that is the only future for us. I've got nothing against black people; they are my neighbors. But if blacks take over, we will see bloody battles. The black man wants power; he wants absolute power. And he doesn't want anybody next to him. The Afrikaner is white. He has his own history, his own traditions, his own culture, lifestyle and language, which are very dear to him. So our only hope is partition. Racial integration cannot work here. Differences are too great.

Interview/
U.S. News & World Report,
10-14:33.

Magnus Malan
Minister of Defense
of South Africa

2

[On his country's support of the UNITA guerrillas in Angola]: As far as Angola is concerned, we have reached a watershed. Through our connections with UNITA, we maintain the interests of the free world on our subcontinent. Supporting UNITA in Angola concerns stopping foreign intervention by Cubans and other Communist soldiers. It concerns stopping Marxist infiltration and expansionism. We will break our links with UNITA only on the condition that all foreign forces are withdrawn from Angola.

To reporters, Pretoria,
Sept. 20/
Los Angeles Times,
9-21:(I)16.

Nelson Mandela
South African black civil-rights leader;
Leader, African National Congress

3

[Saying he will not renounce violence as a condition for his being released from prison]: Let [South African President Pieter] Botha renounce violence. Let him say that he will dismantle apartheid. Let him unban the people's organization, the African National Congress. Let him free all who have been imprisoned, banished or exiled for their opposition to apartheid. Let him guarantee free political activity so that the people may decide who will govern them . . . What freedom am I being offered whilst the organization of the people remains banned? What freedom am I being offered when I may be arrested on a pass offense? What freedom am I being offered to live my life as a family man with my dear wife, who remains in banishment in Brandfort?

Written statement read to rally,
Soweto, South Africa, Feb. 10/
The New York Times, 2-11:1.

Johannes Maree
Director, Barlow Rand, Ltd.
(South Africa)

4

[Criticizing Americans who call for U.S. disinvestment in South African industry as a way to fight that country's apartheid system]: We have to get Americans to understand that the faster the South African economy has grown, the faster the blacks in [South Africa] have advanced.

Newsweek, 5-6:44.

Peter McPherson
Administrator, Agency for International
Development of the United States

5

[On the current famine in some African countries such as Ethiopia]: It's my personal view that countries in Africa can have a good future, but they've got to do the right thing. Economic policies are a critical component of whether a country is going to be able to pull itself out over the long term. Yet I don't really think that Ethiopia is going to change its policies of collectivized

(PETER McPHERSON)

farming. They're not going to change their policies next year or the year after. The current regime is locked into an ideological position, even though it is very counter-productive.

Interview/U.S. News & World Report, 5-13:38.

Mobutu Sese Seko
President of Zaire

1

If there exist on this planet men who profoundly know their country and their people, I can say without any pretense that I am one of them.

The Washington Post, 5-23:(A)29.

Robert Mugabe
Prime Minister of Zimbabwe

2

[Criticizing white voters in Zimbabwe for re-electing former white Prime Minister Ian Smith to Parliament]: What came out is that the enemy of yesterday is still today's enemy . . . The vote cast by the majority of the white electorate has shown us that the trust we laid in the whites and our belief that they would reconcile to the reality of a new political order was a trust and belief that was not deserved. They did not deserve that trust. We were, therefore, deceived into believing that those who had waged an unjust fight against the people of Zimbabwe, those who had spilled the innocent blood of many thousands of our people, had repented. In fact, the vote has proved that they have not repented in any way, that they still cling to their past, that they still support the very man who caused the country numerous problems, the man who planned the murders, assassinations that resulted in mass graves, the man who erected in this country an illegal regime and created a series of horrors against the African people . . . We cannot accept that [the Constitution provides for 20 Parliamentary seats for whites] in the new Zimbabwe. That dirty piece of paper will be cleansed. I can assure we will not live with indignity and insult for very much longer.

*At rally, Harare, Zimbabwe,
June 30/The New York Times, 7-1:3.*

3

We of the young Republic of Zimbabwe look to the Soviet Union and other socialist countries for, example, inspiration and indeed guidance.

*At banquet in his honor, Moscow/
Los Angeles Times, 12-5:(I)6.*

Willie Muzurwa
*Editor,
"Sunday Mail" (Zimbabwe)*

4

[On Zimbabwe's forthcoming national elections]: These elections will be a political watershed for us in many ways. They are, of course, the first elections we have run ourselves, and the importance of that in the country's political development should not be minimized. Moreover, the government that is elected will be the one that works out our long-term economic development, drafts a new constitution and creates Zimbabwe's own form of socialism. And, finally, we hope that this election will put behind us the most divisive aspects of the rivalry between ZANU and ZAPU because, if they are not, some people fear that they could fester into a civil war and an attempt at secession in Matabeleland.

Los Angeles Times, 5-23:(I)16.

Beyers Naudé
*General Secretary,
South African Council of Churches*

5

[Saying he supports the banned African National Congress]: The majority of the people in South Africa support the ANC, seeing it as the legitimate movement of liberation [from apartheid]. Surveys have confirmed that between 75 per cent and 80 per cent of all blacks support the ANC—not its violence, but certainly its goals and aspirations. A second reason I support it is because the ANC has clearly stated its wishes to see a non-racial, democratic government set up [in South Africa]. The ANC is not calling for black majority rule, but democratic rule for all. That's important.

Interview/USA Today, 11-25:(4)11.

6

[On the apartheid system in South Africa]: The government can only go in its reforms as far

(BEYERS NAUDE)

as its own white electorate will allow it to go. And that white electorate will not allow [President] P. W. Botha to take any steps they believe will jeopardize their dominance of political and economic power. The black community of South Africa rightly demands a full sharing in political rights and in the economic wealth of the country. So you have these two immutable forces, the one against the other ... We in the South African Council of Churches have called for no further [foreign] investment in South Africa until apartheid ends. I believe that is a very meaningful, peaceful, nonviolent step to force the government to change its policies much more rapidly than they're doing at present ... I say this not only for the sake of the blacks. I am an Afrikaner. My people are the people in power. I'm saying it for their sakes, because they are either so afraid, or they're so blind, that they don't realize not only what they're doing to others but they do not realize what they are doing to themselves.

Interview/U.S. News & World Report, 12-2:40.

Louis Nel
Deputy Foreign Minister of South Africa

1

[On foreign economic sanctions against South Africa to protest that country's apartheid system]: Let us be frank; our neighboring states will suffer before we do. Those measures will have an impact on the whole of southern Africa, and South Africa will be better able to absorb them than its neighbors. The choice is between sanctions on the one hand and political, social and economic progress on the other.

News conference, Pretoria, Sept. 5/
The Washington Post, 9-6:(A)29.

2

[On the current anti-apartheid unrest in South Africa]: We [the government] are the reformers, and some other people are the revolutionaries. We want to bring about change through negotiation, [and] they want to bring about change through violence and the overthrow of the South African government. It is not really possible for a reformist and a revolutionary to sit down and negotiate [until] the revolutionary has undergone a change of attitude and approach. There are some people you have to confront and other people you have to negotiate with.

Interview/The Washington Post,
9-17:(A)18.

Herman W. Nickel
United States Ambassador to South Africa

3

[On apartheid in South Africa]: The plain fact is that racism is incompatible with both the ethic and the practical requirements of a free economy. Indeed, I would submit that perhaps the most significant single catalyst for change in this country has been the realization that a growing industrial society cannot function in the political straitjacket of an essentially pre-industrial political ideology. That is why measures whose effect it would be to retard this dynamic and to reduce the economic leverage of blacks, both as producers and consumers, strike me as a singularly wrong-headed way to fight apartheid.

Before South African and American business community, Johannesburg, Jan. 8/
The Washington Post, 2-8:(A)18.

John L. Nkomo
Administrative secretary, Zimbabwe African People's Union

4

The [Zimbabwe] economy has been bungled, badly bungled, for the past five years, in the government's mad pursuit of socialism. The drought had an undeniable impact over the last three years, but our problems are not really in agriculture. Factories have closed by the dozens, industrial production has been scaled back, thousands of workers have been retrenched, new investment is simply zero. This contraction of the economy is as much due to the government's policies in spending money we did not have, in letting inflation rise to 15 per cent, 20 per cent and even 25 per cent in some years, and in scaring investors with talk of nationalization and all sorts of regulations that mean they cannot get a fair profit. This government has pushed too hard and

(JOHN L. NKOMO)

for socialism without thinking its policies through.

Interview/Los Angeles Times, 4-1:(I)10.

1

[Criticizing the government of Prime Minister Robert Mugabe]: What has happened to all those bright hopes we had five years ago? This Mugabe government has failed to fulfill any of them, and it is repeating many of the mistakes we have seen our neighbors make. No wonder some people are so disillusioned that they say they were better off under [former white Prime Minister] Ian Smith.

Los Angeles Times, 5-26:(I)29.

Maurice Nyagumbo
Minister for Political
Affairs of Zimbabwe

3

[On the government of Zimbabwean Prime Minister Robert Mugabe]: If you want to see what this government has done, you should go to one of those remote places where nothing had ever been built . . . either by the old colonial administration or even by the missionaries. Today, you will see children going to school, people getting medical care, farmers able to irrigate some of their fields and get their crops to market. We have done all this on a big scale. It is not enough, but it is a start.

Los Angeles Times, 4-15:(I)16.

us in certain directions . . . Naturally, there is a backlash.

Los Angeles Times, 4-15:(I)16.

Carl Noffke
Director, American Studies Institute,
Rand Afrikaans University (South Africa)

2

[On calls for U.S. disinvestment in South Africa to protest that country's apartheid policy]: South Africans like American products, and their lives would be unimaginable without them. They get up in the morning and brush their teeth with Colgate toothpaste and wash with Palmolive soap. They have Kellogg cereals for breakfast. They ride to work in cars with Goodyear and Firestone tires. They use IBM typewriters and Xerox copiers at the office. They drink Pepsi and Coke at lunch . . . If all these products disappeared suddenly, the impact would be tremendous. It is not that there are not other cereals or toothpastes or typewriters, but some of the comforts and certainties of life would have been abruptly changed, and it would bring a feeling of isolation . . . I doubt very much, however, whether it would speed the [apartheid] reform process. It would almost certainly retard it and could well kill it as whites retreat in self-defense. At a time when we are trying to create good-will among all our people, divestment and other sanctions generate ill will. At a time when we are trying to find a solution to our problems that will bring progress for all [racial] groups and satisfy all, this kind of pressure tries to force

Peter Onu
Interim secretary general,
Organization of African Unity

4

[Criticizing Western press coverage of events in Africa]: The power that the industrialized nations and their monopolies wield with respect to information and disinformation has real influence over political, economic and social events in the Third World. Africa, which has suffered only too much from imperialist domination not only at the political and economic levels but also at the cultural and information level, is determined to correct its distorted image as well as the negative and biased news disseminated by the five major Western news agencies.

At meeting of African information ministers,
Addas Ababa, Ethiopia, March 29/
The New York Times, 3-30:2.

Shimon Peres
Prime Minister of Israel

5

[Saying Israel condemns South Africa's apartheid system]: [Apartheid is] completely contrary to the very foundations on which Jewish life is based. We can't be expedient in that

(SHIMON PERES)

matter. We are serious, we are definite, we are determined not to accept the policy of discrimination under any circumstances.

Jerusalem, Aug. 10/
The Washington Post, 8-12:(A)9.

Muammar el-Qaddafi
Chief of State of Libya

1

I am a terrorist if the matter involves the pride and honor of this Arab nation. The Americans say anything which is Palestinian is a sin, taboo. I swear by God that everything which is American is a sin for us—their cars, goods and even their friendship.

Interview/USA Today, 3-21:(A)7.

2

We plant roses, we breed chickens and we eat candy—but before we eat candy we must eat the kidneys of our enemies.

U.S. News & World Report, 9-16:14.

Ronald Reagan
President of the United States

3

[Criticizing proposed U.S. economic sanctions against South Africa to protest that country's apartheid system]: I believe the results that we've had in this [current policy of] constructive engagement with South Africa justifies our continuing on that score. Obviously, and as we've made very plain, we all feel that apartheid is repugnant . . . But if you look at the gains that have been made so far by our so-called constructive engagement, the increase in complete biracial education, the fact that American businesses there have, over the last several years, contributed more than a hundred million dollars to black education and housing, the fact that the ban on mixed marriages no longer exists, that some I think 40-odd business districts have been opened to black-owned businesses, labor-union participation by blacks has come into being, and there's been a great desegregation of hotels and restaurants and parks and sport activities and sports centers and so forth . . . I can't list them all here, but all these have been coming about as they've continued to work toward what is the final answer [to apartheid].

News conference, Washington,
Aug. 5/The New York Times, 8-6:10.

4

[On his recent statement that apartheid has been eased in South Africa]: I'm sorry that I carelessly gave the impression that I believe it had been totally eliminated. There are areas where it hasn't . . . [But] I was not nearly as ill-informed as many of you have made it out that I was. I may have been careless in my language in that one thing, but I was talking about improvements that actually do exist there and have been made. But as I say, I know that segregation has not been eliminated totally, and in some areas there has been no improvement. But there has been a great improvement over what has ever existed before.

News conference, Washington,
Sept. 6/The New York Times, 9-7:9.

5

The system of apartheid [in South Africa] means deliberate systematic, institutionalized racial discrimination, denying the black majority their God-given rights. America's view of apartheid is simple and straightforward: We believe it's wrong. We condemn it, and we are united in hoping for the day when apartheid will be no more. Our influence over South African society is limited, but we do have some influence and the question is how to use it. Many people of good-will in this country have different views. In my view, we must work for peaceful evolution and reform. Our aim is not to punish South Africa with economic sanctions that would injure the very people we are trying to help. I believe we must help all those who peacefully oppose apartheid, and we must recognize that the opponents of apartheid, using terrorism and violence, will bring not freedom and salvation, but greater suffering and more opportunities for expanded Soviet influence within South Africa and within the entire region. What we see in South Africa is a beginning of a process of change. The changes in policy so far are inadequate—but ironically

(RONALD REAGAN)

they have been enough to raise expectations and stimulate demands for more far-reaching, immediate change. It is the growing economic power of the black majority that has put them in a position to insist on political change . . . I am signing today an Executive order that will put in place a set of measures [sanctions] designed and aimed against the machinery of apartheid, without indiscriminately punishing the people who are victims of that system—measures that will disassociate the United States from apartheid but associate us positively with peaceful change.

News conference, Washington,
Sept. 9/Los Angeles Times, 9-10:(I)17.

1

[On his decision to meet and deal with Marxist President Samora Machel of Mozambique]: All I know is that for some time now there has been an indication that he, who had gone so far over to the other [Soviet] camp, was having second thoughts. We just think it's worthwhile to show him another side of the coin, and we think it's worth a try to let him see what our system is and see that he might be welcome in the Western world, and that's why I'm meeting with him [in Washington].

News conference, Washington,
Sept. 17/The New York Times, 9-18:14.

Charles E. Redman
Spokesman for the Department
of State of the United States

[Criticizing the South African government's tactics during the current anti-apartheid demonstrations in South Africa]: Banning individuals and organizations from political activities is one of the most odious practices of the South African government. It offends the democratic values of free speech and assembly and accentuates the anger and frustration felt by all the opponents of apartheid. The South African government's contention that it upholds Western values is belied by such actions. A society can never effectively come to terms with its problems by repressing dissent. We call on the South African govern-

2

ment to honor its commitment to democratic values and to show respect for those who have legitimate grievances against the system of apartheid.

Washington, Aug. 28/
The New York Times, 8-29:9.

C.R.E. Rencken
Member of South African Parliament;
Chief information officer, National
Party of South Africa

[On South Africa's apartheid system]: The basic political reality of South Africa is that the National Party holds power, the ability to carry out far-reaching change lies with it, and the initiative must come from it. The National Party accepts this responsibility, and it is now the main agent for change, not only in the white electorate but within the country as a whole. But we have to persuade people to accept change, and that takes a great deal of political education and a lot of time. It is simply not possible for this government to declare it will abolish apartheid all at once. It has to introduce reforms step by step to gain psychological acceptance for them and so that it can remain in power to carry out the whole program of reform . . . Most whites' real fear is, quite frankly, a black government. They have watched what has happened in the rest of Africa, and they feel that they would have to leave if a black government of that sort came to power here. But they don't want to. This is their country, and there is nowhere else for them to go. And that means we have to solve our problems in such a way that whites accept the changes and are reassured.

Interview/Los Angeles Times, 9-24:(I)16,17.

Annon Rubenstein
Minister of Communications of Israel

[On the pressure on Israel to stop trading with South Africa as a protest against that country's apartheid system]: Israel is in a state where beggars cannot be choosers. We are boycotted by so many countries in the world that where we have trade we cannot afford to give it up . . . If the world community of nations decides to stop all

3

4

(AMNON RUBENSTEIN)

the trade with South Africa, this is a different story. [But] it would be hypocrisy to pick up on Israel and say, "You alone of all nations stop your rather small trade with South Africa."

Jerusalem, Aug. 11/
The Washington Post, 8-12:(A)9.

1

Lawrence Schlemmer
South African social scientist

[On the attitude of black South Africa toward the U.S. vis-a-vis South Africa's apartheid system]: It's actually one of the weaknesses in internal black politics here that people still have too much faith in what the external world can do. There's still an intense, even naive, hope that the United States will come along and solve problems. It may be true that the black intellectual is disenchanted, but for the average black person America remains the land of Coke, Kennedy, Superman and all manner of wonderful things.

Johannesburg/The Washington Post, 9-25:(A)28.

2

George P. Shultz
Secretary of State
of the United States

[On the apartheid system in South Africa]: . . . as far as [U.S. President Reagan] is concerned and our Administration policy, apartheid is a horror. We have nothing but opposition to it. We seek to work with South Africa, to do everything we can [to] bring it to an end. In the meantime, I think American investment and businesses in South Africa are providing jobs for blacks, as many of the blacks have pointed out . . . and it would be a great mistake to look at a problem and say, it's horrible, and then just walk away from it. You've got to engage yourself and try to help on it, and help in the turmoil and conflict in southern Africa generally, which our diplomacy has been doing, and gradually moving away from military to diplomatic means of dealing with those issues.

Broadcast interview/
"Meet the Press," NBC-TV, 1-13.

3

Apartheid [in South Africa] must go, but the only course consistent with American values is to engage ourselves as a force for constructive, peaceful change while there is still a chance. It cannot be our choice to cheer on, from the sidelines, the forces of polarization that could erupt in a race war; it is not our job to exacerbate hardship, which could lead to the same result.

Before Senate Foreign Relations Committee,
Washington, Jan. 31/The New York Times, 2-1:4.

4

[On criticism of U.S. political and economic support for South Africa despite that country's apartheid system]: There has been more [racial] reform in South Africa in the past four years than in the previous 30. We choose to focus on getting results. We can't have it both ways. We cannot have influence with people if we treat them as moral lepers, especially when they are themselves beginning to address the agenda of change . . . If we recognize that white opinion holds vital keys to change, then we must also recognize that change must originate in shifts in white politics. In this regard, in the past three years the white government has crossed a historical divide: It has been willing to accept major defections from its own ranks in order to begin to offer a better political, economic and social deal to the nation's black majority . . . [As for foreign economic sanctions against South Africa that have been suggested by some,] I do not understand why it is good for American investors to create jobs for black workers in Zimbabwe or Zaire, but not in South Africa. And I suspect that tens of thousands who have flocked to the squatters' camps outside Cape Town in a desperate search for work do not understand either.

Before National Press Club, Washington,
April 16/Los Angeles Times, 4-17:(I)1.

5

[On South Africa's apartheid system]: Change is inevitable. The issue is not whether apartheid is to be dismantled, but how and when. And then, what replaces it: race war, bloodbath and new forms of injustice? Or politi-

(GEORGE P. SHULTZ)

cal accommodation and racial coexistence in a just society? . . . This much is clear: There must be negotiation among South Africans of all races on constitutional reform. True peace will come only when the government negotiates with—rather than locks up—representative black leaders. The [racial] violence will end only when all parties begin a mutual search for a just system of governance.

At United Nations, New York,
Sept. 23/The New York Times, 9-24:6.

1

Apartheid [in South Africa] is through. It is not only wrong in our view, but at least in my judgment it is over. It can't last. I think that there comes a time when people stop arguing about whether something is a good idea or not and accept the fact that that's irrelevant. It doesn't matter whether you think apartheid is a good idea or not, it's going to disappear. Now, the question is how do you manage the transition. That's the problem psychologically we would like the South Africans to address because if they address it even now, there is a real chance of doing so through a process of discussion and negotiation. If it isn't addressed, we can have a cycle of continued violence and at least one can readily imagine this blowing up into a really violent upheaval.

Interview, New York, Oct. 31/
The New York Times, 10-4:1.

Ian Smith
Member of Zimbabwean Parliament;
Former Prime Minister of
Rhodesia (Zimbabwe)

2

[On the government of Zimbabwean Prime Minister Robert Mugabe]: If we go on like this, drifting toward Communism, we are heading for bankruptcy. I hope we can get the government to recant Communism. It is insane—it robs the industrious and the intelligent to subsidize the lazy and the poor. If we can restore some sanity, whites will stop leaving, and return. That is my goal now.

Los Angeles Times, 5-24:(I)16.

Roger Smith
Chairman, General Motors Corporation

3

[On the apartheid system in South Africa]: One of the worst things I can think of is for apartheid to end in such a way that they've got an economic disaster on their hands. What good is the end of apartheid to a black guy if it just gives him the right to starve to death? So we're trying to keep the business systems and the commerce and industry of that country intact. When they get done with all this, they're going to have an enormous problem of feeding all those people still.

Interview/
USA Today, 10-31:
(4)11.

Stephen J. Solarz
United States Representative,
D-New York

4

[Advocating U.S. economic sanctions against South Africa to protest that country's apartheid system]: Without pressure on South Africa to abolish apartheid, the incentive to eliminate institutionalized racism would be virtually nil. The white minority leads a very good life and benefits from exploitation of the black majority. Also, the U.S. has a fundamental interest in preventing the spread of Soviet influence throughout southern Africa—and Communism's prospects increase the longer apartheid exists . . . These sanctions by themselves are not going to bring fundamental change any more than gentle persuasion. In the absence of progress, we will have to ratchet the sanctions up, hopefully in cooperation with other countries, to make it clear South Africa cannot conduct business as usual with the West unless it is willing to move away from apartheid . . . Serious sanctions with an impact will hurt blacks as well as whites. But man lives by more than bread alone. The black people of South Africa want more than anything else the sense of dignity which comes from being able to participate in determining their own destiny.

Interview/
U.S. News & World Report, 9-9:35.

Larry Speakes
Principal Deputy Press Secretary to the President of the United States

1

[On the current racial violence in South Africa]: We call on the government of South Africa to act with the greatest restraint at this tense time. It is essential that the government in Pretoria respect the fundamental rights of all South Africans. The world is watching how that government and the South African police conduct themselves. The real cause of violence in South Africa is apartheid. A lasting peace will take hold in the [black] townships and throughout the country only when apartheid is dismantled. We are deeply concerned whenever civil liberties are suspended anywhere in the world. This is certainly the case in South Africa, where violence and repression will not solve the country's problems.

To reporters, Washington,
July 26/The New York Times, 7-27:1.

Leon Sullivan
American Baptist minister

2

[On the code of principles, called the Sullivan Principles, which he developed for U.S. firms doing business in South Africa as standards for dealing fairly with black people living under that country's apartheid system]: My aim is not to keep American companies there [in South Africa]. They can leave. But the companies must become part of the fiber of the liberation movement. If you can use the American companies, like a crowbar, to move a great big rock, you have to . . . It's not a solution [to apartheid]. It's a part of a process to bring about fundamental change. When I started with the idea, I thought I'd build. I thought the more I got companies on my wagon, the further I'd push my wagon. I thought I could move them in a direction they, maybe, didn't know they were going.

Interview, Philadelphia/The New York Times, 9-9:6.

Helen Suzman
Member of South African Parliament

3

[Criticizing foreign economic sanctions against South Africa to protest that country's

apartheid policies]: My main opposition to any steps that inhibit economic expansion is that such action blunts the only weapon that blacks have or are in the process of acquiring—the economic muscle that accompanies upward mobility on the economic ladder by virtue of greater skills and increased consumer power. Too slowly, but nevertheless surely, blacks are obtaining the leverage with which to demand redress in the imbalances in power and wealth and privilege in South Africa. It is totally counterproductive to put obstacles in the way of the economic forces that so far have led to changes that are more than cosmetic—trade unionism, skilled job opportunities, urbanization. And it is counterproductive to drive whites, who are in growing numbers increasingly disillusioned with apartheid and who have begun to accept power-sharing, back into the laager. I have to admit I resent the way in which people living many thousands of miles away from South Africa totally ignore the hundreds of thousands of white South Africans who abhor race discrimination and who have been fighting apartheid for years.

Luxembourg, July 10/
The Washington Post, 7-24:(A)19.

4

[On the South African government's release from prison of five anti-apartheid activists]: The release of these men is not going to count for much in the outside world or in the lives of the people themselves. What we want is that people be free to protest lawfully against government policy. The line between lawful protest and what the government regards as subversion is becoming thinner and thinner in this country.

Los Angeles Times, 11-14:(I)22.

Abdel Rahman Swaraddahab
Chief of State of Sudan

5

[On U.S. concern about his new government's contacts with Libya and Ethiopia]: I am keen to see friendly relations with the United States continue. We would like to thank the people and government of the U.S. for all its aid . . . Our relations with Ethiopia and Libya will never be at the expense of relations with the U.S. and other friendly countries . . . We have

(ABDEL RAHMAN SWARADDAHAB)

the question of the [rebels in the] south [of Sudan]. Libya and Ethiopia have much to do with this question. Unless we come to terms with Ethiopia and Libya, solving this question will be quite difficult.

Interview, Khartoum/
The Christian Science Monitor, 5-10:14.

Oliver Tambo
President, banned African
National Congress (South Africa)

1

The persistence of apartheid [in South Africa] leaves us no alternative but to escalate the violence. And we are not talking about anything like equal degrees of violence. The violence associated with the ANC is minimal, infinitesimal next to the violence of the apartheid regime . . . Our target is not negotiations, it is the end of the apartheid system. There can be no compromise about that. At some stage, negotiations will become a factor. The first sign that the regime is ready to talk would be the release of Nelson Mandela and other political prisoners . . . We [the ANC] have no intention to nationalize everything. We will have private property, private businesses and so on. We will trade with everybody. There will even be foreign investment now because we want to end the apartheid system . . . We see a South Africa that is enriched by the various racial origins of its population, a South Africa that in spite of our history has become integrated. We all belong to South Africa, and South Africa belongs to us all.

Interview, Dar es Salaam,
Tanzania/The New York Times, 9-7:4.

2

[On Soviet support of his organization in its fight against the white government of South Africa]: The Soviet Union will give us what the West does not want to give us, namely, weapons. We cannot boycott the Soviet Union. It is willing to help. A liberation group does not have the luxury of selecting.

Interview/ Lusaka, Zambia,
Sept. 8/The Washington Post, 9-9:(A)18.

3

[Saying South Africa's apartheid system must be eliminated now, rather than gradually]: I think we would be less than natural to demand anything less than to be free now. Nobody wants to endure pain for a moment longer than they have to. There is no question of a gradual transition to majority [black] rule; to make it gradual would be to make the crime continue. The only negotiations we would see would be about the mechanisms for an immediate change to majority rule.

Interview, Lusaka, Zambia/Newsweek, 9-16:27.

Hassan Turabi
Leader,
Muslim Brotherhood of Sudan

4

Frankly, I am not absolutely confident democracy can work [in Sudan] unless the people, particularly the leaders, have really learned a lesson from the past. We've seen the pattern before: There is division, strife, conflict, and the country adopts democracy, because everything else has failed. A vacuum develops, but not stability. People feel uneasy and someone exploits the frustration and steps in. He can't hold things together because Sudan is so diverse. Pressure builds and the regime falls. The cycle starts again.

Los Angeles Times, 5-4:(I)24.

Desmond M. Tutu
Anglican Bishop of Johannesburg;
Winner, 1984 Nobel Peace Prize

5

Despite whatever anybody says, I have not yet campaigned for disinvestment [in South Africa by foreigners as a way to combat apartheid]. I have called up to now for political, diplomatic, but above all economic pressure as our last chance to avert the blood bath . . . For goodness sake, will people realize just how desperate I am to avert that ghastly alternative. When a pile of cups is tottering on the edge of the table and you warn that they will crash to the ground, in South Africa you are blamed when that happens, when your warning was meant to cause people to move the cups to the center of the table, away from di-

(DESMOND M. TUTU)

saster. For goodness sake, will they hear, will white people hear what we are trying to say? Please, all we are asking you to do is to recognize that we [blacks] are humans, too. When you scratch us, we bleed. When you tickle us, we laugh.

News conference,
Johannesburg, Jan. 2/
The New York Times, 1-3:3.

1

If apartheid were to be removed today, South Africa would be amazed at how eagerly the world wants to embrace it. And we would be such a tremendous country, a country that would be helpful in developing the rest of Africa. We have the potential to be the breadbasket of Africa. Technologically, we are in advance of many parts of this continent, and yet we are spending so much of our energies trying to defend the indefensible [apartheid].

Interview, Johannesburg/
Newsweek, 3-11:33.

2

[Criticizing the apartheid system in South Africa]: God did not create us [blacks] for slavery. God did not create us to have our noses rubbed in the dirt every day. God did not create us so that we could be doormats . . . God created us to be able to stand upright and hold our heads high. And we thank you [Americans who are protesting against apartheid], sisters and brothers, that you have reminded the world that, yes, we belong together and that we can be human only together.

Los Angeles, May 9/
Los Angeles Times, 5-10:(I)28.

3

[On South Africa's apartheid system]: In South Africa, a beautiful and richly endowed country, we are seeing played out a human tragedy that could be of catastrophic proportions. One group has decided to exalt a biological, eth-

nic attribute—skin color, race—to be the determinant of access to the good things that abound in that land . . . Apartheid is a threat to world peace, for it leaves South Africa destabilized and with neighbors who might be tempted to call in others to help them against the might of South Africa, as happened with Angola and the Cubans. Apartheid is the best recruiter for Communism, and your government [the U.S.] aligns itself with these oppressors in its policies of "constructive engagement" . . . My vision is of a South Africa where all people, black and white, will walk tall knowing they count, not because of a biological irrelevance, but because all, black and white, are created in the image of God. We will have a new kind of society—nonracial, democratic, just. Black and white will know we belong to one family, the human family, God's family: interdependent, caring, compassionate and sharing.

At University of Kentucky,
May 11/USA Today, 5-20:(A)10.

4

[Calling on the U.S. to help in the elimination of apartheid in South Africa]: Please. Please, for goodness sake, help us . . . Help us, for we don't want to spill blood in our land. Help us, please, avoid Armageddon. Of course, if racial war breaks out in South Africa, you [the U.S.] won't be able to stay on the sidelines . . . Whether you like it or not, what the United States does is of monumental significance in the world . . . What you do has an impact that is incalculable . . . The moral imperative is for you to take action so that tomorrow, when we are free, we will know that you were our friends. And we will remember those who helped us in the process of becoming free, and we would like to be your friend because you will have taken the type of action that will have avoided Armageddon in our land.

Before California State Legislature, Sacramento,
May 13/Los Angeles Times, 5-14:(I)1,3.

5

[On the current state of emergency declared by South Africa in response to racial violence there]: I think we have a government that really

(DESMOND M. TUTU)

doesn't know where it's going—and, for that reason, it's like a dangerous animal. They have never known how to deal with dissent. The only response they know is the mailed fist. Declaring a state of emergency is a typical reaction. It doesn't really change much; it just removes the last vestiges of our [blacks'] rights, and it means that whatever they do to us now, they can do with more impunity.

Interview, Johannesburg/Newsweek, 7-29:25.

/
1

[Saying U.S. President Reagan's announced sanctions against South Africa to protest that country's apartheid system are too mild]: Reagan is bending over backwards to save the South African government from the consequences of its actions. This government is generally acknowledged as vicious, immoral and evil, and yet we get all this wonderful sophistry [from Reagan] about "constructive engagement" turning into "active engagement." I can only say that if you are supporting a system that is racist, what does that make you? If Reagan is supporting a racist policy, doesn't that make him a racist? . . . If he were my President, I would be very ashamed of him.

*Johannesburg, Sept. 9/
Los Angeles Times, 9-10:(I)1,18.*

2

[On the apartheid system in South Africa and the civil unrest it is causing]: What we are getting [from the government] are piecemeal reforms, really talk of reforms, when what we need is the rapid and complete dismantling of apartheid. If this unrest is to stop, people must be given hope to replace the despair that now fills them. If the violence is to stop, then people must see that non-violence works, that it can bring real change . . . I preach non-violence, I counsel patience, I urge reconciliation, I pray for peace . . . and these [black] kids look at me and say, "Hey, man, what an old fool! He prays for peace, and [President] P. W. Botha sends him the army. He preaches non-violence, and the police just beat us up. He says be patient, and the state President says we will reform this or that,

but not too fast." What, they ask, have I to show for non-violence? At best, a few crumbs.

Los Angeles Times, 9-30:(I)12.

Cyrus R. Vance
*Former Secretary of State
of the United States*

3

. . . all of us, no matter what our political parties may be, share an abhorrence of the evils of apartheid [in South Africa] . . . What can we do to try and change that situation? I think we have to make it very clear where we stand in this matter and to use our diplomatic efforts with their government to urge them to begin to dismantle the Bantu system, a system of pass laws and all of the other elements of it which are so reprehensible . . . On disinvestment, I would be opposed to disinvestment at this time. I think we should hang in there for the time being and see if we cannot use our influence, coupled with the influence of the leaders of the business community in South Africa who are calling for change, to bring about a striking down of the pass laws, of forced repatriation, of depriving the blacks of citizenship, and all of those other reprehensible elements of the Bantu system.

*Before Senate Foreign Relations Committee,
Washington/U.S. News & World Report, 2-18:46.*

Robert S. Walker
*United States Representative,
R-Pennsylvania*

4

[On U.S. attitudes toward South Africa's apartheid system]: There is a split in the conservative community [in the U.S.]. You have a long-standing position among American conservatives in support of South Africa, nearly a carte-blanche attitude that says, "Whatever they do is acceptable because it is a nation that is friendly to the West and has great strategic value to us." However, there is now a substantial, growing number of conservatives who say, "Yes, South Africa is important to us strategically, but the danger of losing her strategically is greater if we support a government that is intransigent to change, which is almost inevitable in that society."

*Interview, East Petersburg, Pa.,
Aug. 20/The New York Times, 8-21:3.*

Vernon A. Walters
United States Ambassador/Permanent
Representative to the United Nations

1

[Criticizing foreign economic sanctions against South Africa to protest that country's apartheid system]: There are those who say we have not done enough to pressure the South African government, and no significant change can be effected without totally isolating Pretoria,

economically and politically. The United States firmly believes, however, that such isolation will lead to more bloodshed, to increased autarky of the South African economy, a curtailment of external influence to effect change and, in the end, to greater suffering for the very people we are all trying to help. [Current] U.S. policy has teeth. We believe our actions have had an effect.

At United Nations, New York, July 25/
The Washington Post, 7-26:(A)32.

Elliott Abrams
Assistant Secretary for Inter-American Affairs, Department of the United States

1

There's been tremendous progress [for democracy in Honduras and Guatemala]: In the case of Honduras, a military dictatorship ruled from 1974 to '82. Now you have one democratically elected President replacing another. That is a key test. It's not just having one election. It's having a series of elections and having one democratic President succeed another. That is about to happen in Honduras. That indicates they're moving along. They are not yet at that stage in Guatemala, because this [recently] was their first election. But it was an excellent election in every mechanical sense—votes fairly counted, no intimidation, people able to vote, polls open the right hours. In addition, there was a wide choice of candidates from the extreme right to fairly far left. So voters had a wide choice. And that's a major achievement for Guatemala.

Interview/U.S. News & World Report, 12-16:44.

Manuel Acosta Bonilla
Former Minister of Finance of Honduras

2

Honduras allowed the United States to put the contras [Nicaraguan anti-government rebels] here, to put the training center here, and toed the [U.S.] Reagan Administration line. Now people call Honduras the vassal, the puppet, of the United States. We have lost the respect of Central American countries because we do not even have our own foreign policy.

The Christian Science Monitor, 1-24:8.

Ricardo Alarcon
Deputy Foreign Minister of Cuba

3

. . . if the U.S. ends its politics of hostility toward Cuba . . . Cuba would be willing to negotiate with the United States any theme that would affect the bilateral relations between them. The conclusion is obvious. Both regimes, both countries with different regimes, contrary even in their philosophies and concepts, must find the means of coexisting in a neighborhood that neither of the two can modify. Now, this neighborhood presents realities of Cuban families that are divided . . . It is in the interest of the Cubans that there be a normal situation. On the other hand, to have normal relations with a neighbor country must have consequences in commerce, in cultural exchanges, in sports exchanges, areas in which there are many points of mutual interest.

Interview/
The Christian Science Monitor, 1-29:15.

Bill Alexander
United States Representative,
D-Arkansas

4

In Nicaragua [U.S.] President Reagan is supporting guerrilla groups [the contras] intent on the violent overthrow of the [Sandinista] government there. While we may not like their government, unilateral intervention violates U.S. law that respects the sovereignty of other nations and the right of self-determination . . . Mr. Reagan supports the guerrillas he calls "freedom fighters." Many of these men were officers of the corrupt dictator [Anastasio] Somoza who was ousted by the people of Nicaragua. To support the guerrillas is to return to the past, which the people of Nicaragua will never agree to do . . . Mr. Reagan's alliance with violence in Nicaragua is against the American way. It is contrary to the principles of our Founding Fathers. The real enemies in Central America are poverty, ignorance, hunger, social injustice and political corruption. The voices of the people are crying out for food, for shelter, for peace and for justice. The effect of Mr. Reagan's reign of terror in Nicaragua actually strengthens the Sandinista government he wants to overthrow.

Broadcast address to the nation,
March 31/The Washington Post,
4-4:(A)16.

Raul Alfonsin
President of Argentina

1

We are convinced we have inaugurated an era of real democracy in Argentina. We don't think of it so much as a system of government as a philosophy of life. Of course, there are still those who are nostalgic for the old days. In the end, they will be defeated because people realize that social justice is found only in a democracy. But it is also necessary to understand that while we are encouraging this new wave of democracy sweeping through Latin America, there is still great risk, which is caused by the heavy foreign debt burdening many of these countries. They are underdeveloped; they are poor. Thus the debt is not just a financial but a political problem. To enjoy liberty, you must have a minimal level of subsistence.

Interview, New York/Time, 4-1:50.

2

[On his country's dispute with Britain about sovereignty over the Falkland Islands]: The problem? [British Prime Minister Margaret] Thatcher. We are ready to solve this question peacefully. We have asked for a dialogue with an open agenda, but the British government does not want to discuss sovereignty. I did not agree with the war Argentina waged [against Britain in 1982] over the Malvinas [Falklands], but you can understand that people get tired. Anybody who has studied the subject will tell you that Argentina is right in the dispute. Now we are facing an additional problem, the fortification of the islands. That is a tremendous danger, not only for Argentina but for the whole area. Next month the British will complete construction of an airfield in the islands that will allow them to bring in all manner of war supplies, including nuclear weapons. It is necessary to stop this.

Interview, New York/Time, 4-1:50.

3

[Announcing new efforts to shore up the Argentinian economy]: I come to you now to present the battle plan so that together we will be able to definitely cancel the chapter of national decay. We do not have any option; we have to reconstruct Argentina . . . No one, particularly any worker, can feel minimally calm with an inflation that erodes his salary. With this level of inflation it is impossible to think of gradual methods. We are therefore imposing a drastic, definitive policy, and so we have decided to freeze prices, tariffs, and salaries. I don't doubt the capacity of Argentina to support this plan. I don't doubt the decision to fight. But I am aware that all of our efforts must have clear goals.

Broadcast address to the nation, Buenos Aires,
June 14/The New York Times, 6-15:1.

Bayardo Arce
Coordinator of party affairs,
Sandinista National Liberation
Front of Nicaragua

4

What is Sandinismo today? It is a synthesis of all of this here in Nicaragua. So I guess you could say that Sandinismo is Marxist-Leninism applied in Nicaragua. But I would also say that Sandinismo is Christianity applied in Nicaragua. And I can also tell you that it is liberalism applied in Nicaragua . . . [U.S. President] Reagan says we are Marxist-Leninists because with that he means to scare everybody. I have asked people who are afraid of that if they know what Marxist-Leninism is. And I have come to realize that usually they don't know. All that they know is that it must be something quite awful, something you would not want on your skin. It is a little bit difficult to explain to people who don't even know what Marxist-Leninism is, anyway. So I ask them, do you think we're going to be like the Soviets? . . . We will not be . . . We aren't going to be like the Cubans or the Czechoslovakians or the Vietnamese. Nor like the U.S. citizens or the French or the Spanish. Nor even the Mexicans. We are going to be what we are, learning from everything. For example, I would like to include the methods of the U.S. electoral system the next time we have elections. It's a good system.

Interview/Mother Jones, Aug.-Sept.:23.

Bruce Babbitt
Governor of Arizona (D)

5

In the city of Guadalajara [Mexico], a [U.S.] Drug Enforcement Administration agent was

(BRUCE BABBITT)

kidnapped and murdered. In Washington, the President of the United States responded to that tragedy not by doing the normal thing, which would be picking up the telephone, calling the President of the Republic of Mexico and saying we had better get a handle on these problems and make certain that it doesn't happen again. How did the President of the United States react? He reacted by closing down the border between our countries, punishing millions of innocent Americans and Mexicans on the flimsiest of pretexts about rumors of possible trouble along the border; in the process humiliating the Mexican government, forcing the Mexican government in front of its own people to react under that kind of irrational pressure. A month later, an American military officer was murdered in East Germany by a Russian soldier in uniform. And the Secretary of State in Washington responded by saying we know they didn't mean it, it was an unfortunate incident. And I suggest in Mexico City that government leaders must be asking who does America consider to be its friend and who does it treat as an enemy?

At National Hispanic Media Conference, Tucson, Ariz./ The Wall Street Journal, 7-8:10.

Michael D. Barnes
United States Representative, D-Maryland

1

[Criticizing President Reagan's imposition of a U.S. trade embargo against Nicaragua]: This act of economic warfare once again tells the Sandinistas that we are not interested in reaching an agreement with them. It once again confirms the position of the hard-liners in Managua: that peace with the United States is not possible so long as the revolution survives, so they may as well complete the process of gaining control over their society and aligning themselves with the Soviet Union.

At House subcommittee hearing, Washington, May 7/Los Angeles Times, 5-8:(I)17.

Belisario Betancur
President of Colombia

2

[On his idea of getting the Colombian armed opposition into the political process]: I am convinced that there are democratic answers . . . to subversive tendencies that don't involve giving in to Marxism-Leninism and that don't involve resorting to military repression . . . It is a model based on the philosophic belief that the essence of democracy consists in admitting with humility that he who disagrees with my point of view may be partially right, may be half right, and that if he wins in a free election, society does not fall apart. So those who disagree with my belief in law, those who think armed struggle is necessary, may be partly right. And I don't think that. After all, an enduring peace cannot be a military peace, for if it is to last, it must arise from within.

To foreign editors/ Los Angeles Times, 11-27:(II)5.

Herbert Blaize
Prime Minister of Grenada

3

[On whether Grenadian Marxists will try to destabilize the country now that American troops are leaving]: Troublemakers are always looking for opportunities to make trouble. If they make trouble, we'll be ready to deal with them . . . The Americans are a symbol of security and, to some people, the symbol is more important than the fact. The fact that the Americans are leaving does not mean that we are being abandoned.

Interview/Los Angeles Times, 6-12:(I)16.

Tomas Borge
Minister of the Interior of Nicaragua

4

[On the guerrilla war against the Sandinista government of Nicaragua]: This is not a war starring John Wayne, shooting blank bullets. It is not a "Rambo" war. It is a war that is turning this country into a riddled, impoverished nation in a constant state of alert.

Oct. 17/Los Angeles Times, 10-18:(I)25.

Wilson Braga
Governor of Sergipe state, Brazil

1

We have two countries here [in Brazil] under one flag. One part of Brazil is in the 20th century, with high-technology computers and satellite launchers. And, beside that, we have another country where people are eating lizards to survive.

Los Angeles Times, 3-15:(I)1.

McGeorge Bundy
Professor of history, New York University; Former Assistant to the President of the United States (John F. Kennedy and Lyndon B. Johnson) for National Security Affairs

2

[Criticizing U.S. aid to the contras, rebels fighting the Sandinista government of Nicaragua]: This covert [aid], by itself, is doomed to failure. It will not bring the Sandinistas to [U.S.] President Reagan's feet, and it will not overthrow them. It will confirm and not undermine their Marxist-Leninist leanings. It will not fulfill the hopes of the democrats among the contras. It will shed blood on all sides, and it will intensify the existing polarization among Nicaraguans. It will bring discredit on our government among millions of our own citizens and more millions of our friends abroad. It will make constructive change in Nicaragua less likely, and regional support for any necessary stronger course much harder to obtain. It will do great harm along the way, and it simply will not work.

Before House Foreign Affairs subcommittee, Washington/The New York Times, 6-10:21.

George Bush
Vice President of the United States

3

[On Nicaragua's new peace plan offered to the U.S.]: On the face of it, offering to remove about 1 per cent of the Cuban presence or to pause in their imports of arms, which they acknowledge could not be absorbed at this time, do not appear to represent significant moves. But it is relevant to ask why they bother. Is it because Nicaraguan young men are refusing to serve in

the army out of revulsion at their government's policies and are joining the [U.S.-backed] resistance? Is it because of the outrage being expressed by the [Roman Catholic] church in Nicaragua? Is it because of the collapse of their economy under the weight of Sandinista militarism and corruption? Is it because their people see what is going on in neighboring countries and want it for themselves? . . . All we are asking is that the Sandinistas commit themselves to specific, concrete actions that would show their good-faith interest in peace . . . stop exporting subversion to their neighbors, reduce their bloated military to restore regional balance, sever military ties with Cuba and the Soviet bloc and begin to honor their promises to the Organization of American States to create a democratic, pluralistic system.

Before Austin (Tex.) Council on Foreign Affairs, Feb. 28/Los Angeles Times, 3-1:(I)23.

Adolfo Calero
President, national directorate, Nicaraguan Democratic Force

4

[On the contras, rebels fighting the Sandinista government of Nicaragua]: We have been called [U.S. President] Reagan's army, the CIA's army, every army but our own. The fact that we continue to exist and operate successfully means that we are here of our own free will. We are no one's creation.

Interview/The New York Times, 3-18:6.

Jimmy Carter
Former President of the United States

5

[Criticizing U.S. President Reagan's imposition of a trade embargo against Nicaragua]: An economic blockage against Nicaragua won't work because it actually accomplishes the reverse. It pushes the population away from you and toward your adversary because the average citizen [of Nicaragua] is so hurt by it. I don't think we can call Nicaragua a Communist regime. Certainly some of the [ruling] Sandinistas are Marxist-Leninist, but it is hardly Cuba. Did you know that, percentagewise, there is more

(JIMMY CARTER)

private ownership of property and business in Nicaragua than there is in Great Britain?

On "Talk to America" show, Voice of America/
USA Today, 5-13:(D)2.

William J. Casey
Director of Central Intelligence
of the United States

1

Our analysts have studied [the] blueprint for taking over a government and consolidating a totalitarian regime as it has been exemplified in seven totalitarian regimes . . . They have identified 46 indicators of the consolidation of power by a Marxist-Leninist regime. These indicators measure the movement toward one-party government, control of the military, of the security services, of the media, of education, of the economy, the forming or takeover of labor or other mass organizations, exerting social and population control, curbing religious influence, and alignment with the Soviet bloc. Of the 46 indicators, Nicaragua in five and one-half years has accomplished 33. They have established control of the media, taken over radio and TV, censored the broadcasts of Sunday sermons of the Archbishop of Managua, and subjected the only free newspaper, *La Prensa*, to a brutal daily censorship. They have taken control of the education system. Nicaraguan textbooks now teach Marxism. They attack the tenets of Western democracy. They attack traditional religious teachings and encourage children to maintain revolutionary vigilance by watching for signs of ideological impurities in their neighbors, friends and relatives. The Sandinistas have taken control of the military. They have taken control of the internal secret police and have established a Directorate of State Security. That directorate, according to our reports, has hundreds of Cuban, Soviet, East German and Bulgarian advisers. There are Soviet advisers at every level of the secret police. In fact, it is safe to say that it is controlled by the Soviet Union and its surrogates. Block committees have been established to watch and control the people. The church has been persecuted. Witness the campaign mounted by the Directorate of State Security to harass and embarrass Pope John Paul II during his 1983 visit to Nicaragua. They have used political mobs—similar to the Red Guards of Soviet and Chinese revolutionary history—to attack democratic politicians, union members and religious leaders. And finally . . . following Hitler and Khrushchev, the Sandinistas have told the world that they would spread the example of Nicaragua beyond El Salvador to Honduras, Guatemala and the entire region.

At Metropolitan Club, New York,
May 1/The Wall Street Journal, 8-16:18.

Fidel Castro
President of Cuba

2

Nicaragua is arming itself, but against whom? Not against Costa Rica or Honduras, but against the source of so many aggressions: the greatest imperialist country in the world [the U.S.]. What does the United States want, that we should disarm and drop to our knees?

Malacatoya, Nicaragua,
Jan. 11/The New York Times, 1-14:5.

3

[Saying he is not in a hurry to re-establish relations with the U.S.]: The United States benefits [from relations] more than us. No one should think that we are anxious or impatient to negotiate. [I will not] change a single one of my principles for a thousand countries like the United States.

Broadcast interview/
"MacNeil-Lehrer News Hour," PBS-TV, 2-11.

4

The political, economic and social situation of Latin America is such that it can't hold up under any more restrictions and sacrifices . . . If a solution isn't found for the economic crisis—and above all for the crisis of the [foreign] debt—South America is going to explode . . . The solution will be for the industrialized countries to take over the debts owed to private banks if bankruptcy of the financial system is to be prevented . . . The banks would recover the capital they had invested, U.S. export companies would

(FIDEL CASTRO)

increase their exports, and U.S. investors would increase their profits . . . I am not saying this because I have become a conservative. But I feel that the banking system cannot be permitted to go broke. If problems of development cannot be solved, a revolution by itself will not solve them . . . We want to avert revolutions—because explosions will help no one . . . I am happy to be friendly with conservatives. If a boat is sinking, it is not a question of progressive or conservative, socialist or capitalist, Catholic or Protestant, Moslem or Hindu—for we are all in the same boat. Better a calm and resolute conservative than a frightened progressive if you want to save the boat.

Interview, May 29/
The Wall Street Journal, 6-12:28.

1

[On U.S. President Reagan]: How can you take this man seriously? Perhaps even he doesn't know what he is talking about . . . He is the biggest liar of all the American Presidents . . . the worst terrorist in the history of mankind.

News conference, Havana, July 9/
The Washington Post, 7-10:(A)16.

2

There is . . . a tendency in the West to see the leader of any Third World country as a chieftain; there's a certain stereotype: Leader equals chieftain. From that, there is a tendency to magnify the role of the individual. I can see it myself in what you [in the West] say about us: Castro's Cuba, Castro did this, Castro undid that. Almost everything in this country is attributed to Castro—Castro's goings, Castro's perversities. That type of mentality abounds in the West . . . I don't make decisions totally on my own. I play my role as a leader within a team. In our country, we don't have any institution similar to the Presidency of the United States. Here, all basic decisions—all the important decisions—are analyzed, discussed and adopted collectively. I don't appoint ministers or ambassadors; I don't appoint even the lowliest public servant in the country, because there exists a system for select-

ing, analyzing, nominating and appointing those officials. I do, in fact, have some authority; I have influence. But my only real prerogative is to speak before the Central Committee, before the National Assembly, before public opinion. That's the main power I have, and I don't aspire to any other. I don't want or need any other. Those are the conditions in which a political leader in our country must work. I don't think any of these mesh with the idea of a dictator, which comes from the verb "to dictate"—one who is always dictating orders of all kinds. I don't act that way, nor am I empowered to. I don't give orders; I reason. I don't govern by decree, nor can I.

Interview, Havana/
Playboy, August:
59,62.

3

I think U.S. and Cuban conceptions of liberty are very different. For example, there are more than 1,000,000 children who have disappeared in the U.S. Next to your millionaires, you have beggars. We have neither abandoned children nor beggars without homes. You [in the U.S.] always speak of freedoms. Since your Declaration of Independence, you have spoken of freedoms. We, too, consider it self-evident that all men are born equal. But when George Washington and the others created U.S. independence, they did not free the slaves; not long ago, a U.S. black athlete could not play baseball in the major leagues. And yet you called yours the freest country in the world . . . If you are a Communist in the U.S., where are your freedoms? Can you work in the State Department, in any form of government employment? Can you speak openly on TV? In what papers can you write? We may be criticized in Cuba, but at least we are cleaner than you. Our system is cleaner because we're not pretending to be the best of liberty . . . When I see a Communist writing in *The New York Times* or *The Washington Post,* or speaking on CBS, I promise you I will open the doors so all the counter-revolutionaries will be able to write in our newspapers! But you set the example first.

Interview, Havana/
Playboy, August:64,65.

(FIDEL CASTRO)

1

When I look at the Presidents of the United States in their relations with Latin America, it is impossible not to sense their contempt, their underestimation of these Latin-American peoples—this strange mixture of proud Spaniards, black Africans and backward Indians; an uncommon and strange mixture of people who deserve no [U.S.] consideration or respect whatsoever. I think that some day, that policy—the policy of intervening in all countries of Latin America, setting guidelines, saying what type of government should be elected, the social changes that can or cannot be performed—will give out and result in a crisis; and I really believe that that moment is drawing nearer. The United States has been lucky in that, up to now; these problems have come up in small, isolated countries like Cuba or Grenada or Nicaragua, in Central America. It can still afford to speak of invasions, acts of intervention and solutions based on force, as had already been the practice in 1965 against another small Caribbean country, the Dominican Republic. But when it is faced with these problems everywhere in the Southern Hemisphere, in any one of the large or medium-sized countries in South America, it won't be able to solve them through intervention, dirty wars or invasions; that would be catastrophic.

Interview, Havana/Playboy, August:67.

Vinicio Cerezo
President-elect of Guatemala

2

[On his being elected the first civilian President of Guatemala in over 30 years]: If we fail, democracy will be finished, and there will be war. If we are triumphant, we will have democracy, and it will be consolidated. I say "We," because it is not Vinicio Cerezo. It is a team of people who have been dedicated for a long time. I was just the one lucky enough to become famous only because I survived three of their [his enemies] attempts to kill me.

Los Angeles Times, 12-10:(I)16.

3

[On his being recently elected President in a democratic election]: [It will not be easy] to

---

Pedro Joaquin Chamorro
Former editor,
"La Prensa" (Nicaragua)

4

La Prensa has a very special significance for Nicaraguans because it is the only independent communication and news medium that provides news and commentaries on a daily basis. For the past three years, *La Prensa* has been subjected to prior censorship. There have been very difficult moments which made it impossible for us to publish a paper . . . The pretext is that the [ruling] Sandinistas want to eliminate any information with military content because, so they say, it could endanger the security of the state. But the experience of the past few years has shown us that most of the censored news items have nothing at all to do with military issues. In fact, they mostly have to do with political issues, with human rights and even ideology.

Interview, Los Angeles/
USA Today, 1-10:(A)9.

5

[On whether the recent Nicaraguan election was honest]: No. An election where one party [the ruling Sandinistas] has all the means of the state at its disposal does not allow equal competition by other parties. And you cannot have an honest election without a free press. You cannot have an honest election when the people have not

---

build democracy in a country where you have suffered and lived for 20 years under some kind of dictatorship. I am asking for comprehension in this attempt. We are only beginning to build democracy, and we could succeed if we had the benefit of the doubt, the benefit of comprehension that the political situation in Guatemala is very complex. We have to deal with the Army of Guatemala to be able to establish a real civilian government. We have to deal with a society that is not accustomed to sharing its wealth and opportunities. And we have to deal with the confrontation inside the country, where many people are fighting and dying. Give me time. We are going to work hard.

News conference, Washington,
Dec. 17/The New York Times, 12-18:8.

(PEDRO JOAQUIN CHAMORRO)

been made part of the institution. The vote count was honest, but the number of people who voted was far smaller than the number who registered. According to the Sandinistas, we have more than 1.5 million registered voters; fewer than a million votes were cast.

Interview/World Press Review, February:33.

1

[Saying Nicaragua's Sandinista government censored *La Prensa*]: One of the first things that a Marxist-led revolution does when it comes to power is impose press control. Some examples in our region are Cuba, Grenada and—most recently—Nicaragua. In August, 1979, the Sandinista junta passed its first censorship laws, which say that all criticism of public authorities should express a concern for the success of the revolution and not be instruments of opposition. For political reasons the Sandinistas need *La Prensa* alive at the moment. But they censor it because they cannot tolerate a free press.

Interview/World Press Review, February:33.

2

Joe Clark
Minister of External Affairs of Canada

[On the occasions Canada's foreign policy opposes that of the U.S.]: We are a country of the West. We will disagree with the United States on Policy A or Policy Q from time to time, but we agree with the alphabet. We do not want to take actions that would lead the Soviet Union to think it was possible to drive a wedge into the West.

To reporters, Ottawa, May 20/
Los Angeles Times, 5-21:(I)9.

3

Arturo Cruz
Opposition leader against
Nicaragua's Sandinista government

[Arguing against a cut-off of U.S. aid to anti-Sandinista rebels]: A unilateral withdrawal of U.S. aid will not get the withdrawal of the Soviet Union, Cuba and other Soviet-bloc countries from Nicaragua . . . The political alternatives are narrowing in my country . . . We must be realistic, and those who have chosen the military option have a point.

News conference, Washington,
Jan. 3/USA Today, 1-4:(A)4.

4

Thomas P. d'Aquino
President, Business Council
on National Issues (Canada)

In the past, Canada never had to worry about its future. We always said we had our vast natural resources to see us through. The circumstances of the past lent themselves more to government intervention, but the circumstances of the present are different. Canadians now realize they must be more self-reliant. It is getting tougher to compete and natural resources are not enough; political leadership alone is not enough. These are the messages that are beginning to penetrate in Canada.

Fortune, 6-10:94.

5

Miguel de la Madrid
President of Mexico

[Calling for austerity measures in Mexico, such as the government's recent increase in the cost of gasoline and electricity]: We are a country of 77 or 78 million people, growing at a rate of 2 million per year, and without these steps we would reduce our income and thus further undermine our standard of living . . . It is true that the past two years have been hard and difficult, and we have had to conscientiously swallow some bitter pills, but this is necessary because we know that a great country can only be forged through effort and perseverance.

Televised New Year's message, Mexico City,
Jan. 6/Los Angeles Times, 1-8:(IV)2.

6

Mexico holds regular elections. Mexico maintains a climate of freedom. Mexico has a legal system by which citizens can defend themselves from arbitrary actions by government . . . I cannot deny that there are isolated cases of

(MIGUEL DE LA MADRID)

abuse of authority. But I do not think it is fair to judge Mexico as a country where human rights are systematically violated.

Interview/Newsweek, 8-12:47.

1

I am not claiming that we [in Mexico] have a perfect laboratory of democracy. I know there are errors, many of which even stem from the social and cultural level of the people. But I deny that the Mexican political system is based on electoral fraud, and I know that there are problems in all countries and that you [the U.S.] are aware of some in your own.

Interview/The Wall Street Journal, 9-10:32.

Miguel d'Escoto
Foreign Minister of Nicaragua

2

[On U.S. support of the contras, rebels fighting the Sandinista government of Nicaragua]: There is a war on that is being declared, directed and financed by [U.S. President] Reagan. We want to put an end to it . . . and we're saying to Reagan, "Please come to your senses. Come and talk. You have no right to the systematic murder of our people." It makes no sense to talk to the hirelings [the rebels]. So why talk to them? They can't decide anything. It's Reagan's war. He can stop it. Theoretically, I have no problem with a government, even our government, at some point in time entering into a dialogue with people who have taken up arms . . . if you are really talking about an indigenous group. But this is a totally artificially created group of people at the service of the CIA, and in fact they are soul brothers of the President [Reagan]. They see the interests of the President as their own interests. But those are not the interests nor the dispositions of the infinite majority of the Nicaraguans.

Interview, Managua, April 5/
The Washington Post, 4-6:(A)1.

3

[The U.S. Reagan Administration should] do what we always wanted to do with the United

States: sit down as responsible people in bilateral negotiations to iron out our differences. We admittedly have been standing for, demanding if you want, a new type of relationship with the United States. It is irrational and unrealistic to try to maintain antiquated modes of relations with countries that have been treated in a certain and very real sense as colonies. We don't want to be colonies; we are independent nations.

Managua, June 6/The New York Times, 6-8:5.

Christopher J. Dodd
United States Senator,
D-Connecticut

4

[Criticizing the U.S. Reagan Administration's policy toward the Sandinista government of Nicaragua]: . . . we are not so bankrupt as a nation that the only tool we have remaining to us to deal with this problem is a military one. We think we have other options available to us. The Contadora process is one, an historic opportunity which has never presented itself before in this part of the world, where Latins, particularly the Mexicans and Venezuelans, have agreed to take the leadership position in trying to resolve this problem. I, for one, and I know others feel as I do, that we should never eliminate the military option, at all. I would never tell the Sandinistas, or anyone else for that matter, that we would never exercise that option. But I cannot believe, sitting here in this day and age, that with all the power that we have available to us and the allies we have in this hemisphere, that . . . a financing of counter-guerrilla operations in Nicaragua is the only way in which we can deal with the Sandinistas. That's the mistake.

Broadcast interview, Washington/
"Meet the Press," NBC-TV, 3-3.

Jose Napoleon Duarte
President of El Salvador

5

[On the political assassinations in his country]: This is a product of the culture of terror. There is in people's minds a permanent hatred, a spirit of terrorism, of death. They believe they can reach solutions simply by assassinating and killing.

The Washington Post, 1-21:(A)10.

(JOSE NAPOLEON DUARTE)

1

[Saying his government will engage in peace talks with Salvadoran guerrillas when they show a sign of good faith and not present preconditions his government can't agree to]: I don't want to fool around with the hopes of the people. The answer is simple. They only have to come out and say, "We don't believe that violence is the way to seize power" . . . They want this government to eliminate itself, to depart from the Constitution, to destroy the efforts at democracy and to polarize [Salvadoran political forces]. And you see, what they're asking me is for me to eliminate myself; and if I eliminate myself, with whom are they going to negotiate?

Interview, San Salvador, Jan. 21/
The Washington Post, 1-23:(A)1,18.

2

The people of the extreme right and the people of the political right thought that even if I took office, it was a matter of weeks and they would destabilize the government. And they were expecting to count on the armed forces to overthrow the government. They were basing their conduct on the idea that when I started to act in the direction of controlling the armed forces and exercising authority, there was going to be confrontation, and that these confrontations were going to weaken me and my position. They were talking about 15 days, then two months, then Christmas. But things are different.

Interview, San Salvador/
The Washington Post, 1-30:(A)12.

3

If you analyze the [anti-government] guerrillas in proportion, they are from 2 to 10 per cent of our population. Just imagine what would happen [in the U.S.] if you had that percentage of the population involved in Communist tactics. How many people do you have [in the U.S.]? . . . 236 million. How about having two million Communists with arms inside your country, and not just pistols. I'm talking about machine guns, sophisticated arms, missiles and all that. And they attack Chicago or New York and kidnap a

mayor of Cleveland or of San Francisco. Imagine what this means for any country. That's what we have [in El Salvador].

Interview/
USA Today, 5-18:(A)11.

4

[On whether the contras, rebels fighting the Sandinista government of Nicaragua, are "freedom fighters"]: No, I wouldn't use that term. I'll give you the difference. The political parties are against, the unions are against and the churches are against the Sandinistas. This is the democratic action inside [Nicaragua], fighting for democracy. But then there are people who have had to leave the country because they just couldn't live there. They were threatened with death and all that. They were frustrated and also radicalizers. They went out and started organizing armies. Some of them were [deposed dictator Anastasio] Somoza's army officers in the guerrillas. This is why they are called the contra revolutionaries, because they were against the Sandinista revolution . . . These people are trying to look for a violent solution to the problem because they think there is no other way. This is what they call "freedom fighters." To me, the most important freedom fighters are the ones who are *inside* the country, like we did in our country. We're presenting a democratic solution, a democratic revolution to solve the problem.

Interview, May 18/
USA Today, 5-21:(A)11.

5

I think that our whole society has been dehumanized and that this is the root of the abuses of authority. This is the root of the violence. This is the root of the hate in the hearts of the people . . . You have to understand that our society, until this moment, is absolutely with no order. So I had to put order back into the society. There was a time when people were killed and nobody knew about it. All the systems were broken. So we are now restoring control, and we are reducing violence. Before, we had a lot of people being killed because of the abuses of authority . . . In the past 10 months, you have not had any abuses of authority, of killing people.

(JOSE NAPOLEON DUARTE)

There have been a few killed that I have been investigating. Every case that is presented, I personally investigate it as a symbolic action that I have to control this.

Interview, May 18/
USA Today, 5-21:(A)1.

[On a terrorist attack at a restaurant in San Salvador which killed 13 people, including 6 Americans]: There are people in the world who have lost all reason. The doctrine of terrorism and the religion of death have been created in which life is not important. We in El Salvador have lived, during all these years, moments of great crisis, but even in the midst of so many deaths there has never been an act so savage [as this].

At ceremony for those slain, Ilopango, El Salvador,
June 21/The New York Times, 6-22:3.

1

[On the kidnapping of his daughter by terrorists]: Not even in the most troubled times have I felt such suffering as I do now that one of my daughters is not with us, victim of the injustice, the cruelty and the barbarity of those who have kidnapped her. I tell you sincerely, I have never felt such sorrow . . . So I say especially to those who have crushed the most sacred part of my being, fatherly love, the love of my children, that they have no moral reason to harm me, that it is not possible to put forward any causes or motives that would make me deserve this cruel affront, that there is no right in the name of which the banners of infamy and hate can be raised. If those who carried out this terrible deed of the kidnapping of my daughter sought to torment a father who at the same time is President of the republic, then of course they have succeeded. But they also have provoked the anguish of a mother, the desperate tears of small children, the sorrow of a people and the astonishment of civilized nations.

At Independence Day ceremony, San Salvador,
Sept. 15/The Washington Post,
9-16:(A)12.

2

In Central America, in my own country, countless persons from all walks of life, and in the case of my family, my daughter, Ines Guadalupe [who was recently kidnaped and subsequently released by terrorists], would not have been victims of the merciless violence of the terrorists if terrorists did not have the support, direction, approval and timely protection of the terrorist dictatorship in Nicaragua. Nicaragua is the Central American source for terrorists, and is the sanctuary for totalitarianism and violence, and is the sanctuary for terrorists.

Before National Press Club, Washington,
Oct. 31/The New York Times, 11-1:3.

3

David Durenberger
United States Senator,
R-Minnesota

Nicaragua is an important part of a brand-new United States relationship with Central America, on which we will base our policy toward Latin America for the next couple of generations. In the past, our policy has been, "our friends, right or wrong." So we've landed Marines, we've supported mining and/or banana industries. Today, in Central America, our policy is democratic revolution. We have helped it in [El] Salvador, and we are helping it in Guatemala, and we ought to help it in Nicaragua. But I don't think anybody thinks that is our policy in Nicaragua . . . At various times, it has appeared our policy is to stop Spanish-speaking refugees from invading our country and to keep Russian missiles from being based in the hemisphere—to keep Eastern bloc and other Communist infiltration from destroying the Americas . . . If everyone would agree to the policy of democratic revolution, you could then work quite a variety of programs, perhaps including some kind of covert activity. But it has to be genuinely covert. Otherwise you'll never sell the American public on the value of supporting democratic revolution.

Interview/USA Today, 2-26:(A)1.

4

[On U.S. policy in Nicaragua]: Our government appears to be reacting to events, rather

5

(DAVID DURENBERGER)

than carrying out a strategy with specific goals. What we need is a comprehensive policy which can provide a road map for the future. Thus far, the [Reagan] Administration has failed to provide such a road map . . . It is not clear why covert aid [to rebels fighting against the Sandinista government of Nicaragua] is the critical action on which our policy must stand or fall. Thus far, our rhetoric has far exceeded our actions. If we oppose the regime in Managua, why do we buy Nicaraguan beef and bananas when Honduras could use our trade? And if we truly feel that the Sandinistas have lost their legitimacy . . . why do we continue diplomatic relations?

Before National Press Club, Washington, March 26/Los Angeles Times, 3-27:(I)14.

Jean-Claude Duvalier
President of Haiti

1

[Criticizing the U.S. Congress for placing human-rights requirements on its foreign aid to Haiti]: We are grateful to [U.S.] President Reagan . . . He understands that foreign aid must not be tied to the political. It's easy [for Congress] to be liberal about Haiti; it doesn't cost them anything . . . But their attitude isn't healthy for development of this country; it's not helping to improve education, public health, transportation, growth, and to create jobs. It only hurts the poor people of Haiti . . . We want people to try to understand our history. We are weak, we are poor; it has been the same since independence. We hope the American public will at least give us some credit for trying to build a new system, because we need investments here to create more jobs. Our efforts must be doubled in every sector. Within the next 15 years, we must invest $500-million in the energy sector alone. That is just an example of our problems. So, far from being reduced, or even kept at present levels, foreign aid *must* be increased . . . The foreign press never reports our achievements, the progress we are making . . . only the negatives, the sensational. Haiti is good merchandise; it sells newspapers. But I hope

history will judge me based on what my government is trying to do today—not on the past.

Interview, Port-au-Prince, Haiti/ Los Angeles Times, 12-17:(I)18.

Lucio Garcia del Solar
Argentinian Ambassador to the United States

2

Our [Latin American countries] are still choking on debt. That is a greater danger to the security interests of the United States than guerrilla wars in Central America, because if the situation is not alleviated, the democratic presidents emerging in the biggest, most pivotal countries will be unable to counter the political consequences of debt. They will be vulnerable to surges of populism pushing them toward the extreme right or left. In some countries, it could mean a return to military dictatorship. In some, it could lead to resurgent leftist terrorism that will draw them into the East-West conflict. In the Andean countries like Colombia, Peru and Bolivia, there literally is a danger of the narcotics traffic becoming so important a source of national revenues that entire governments will be corrupted and come under the control of local drug mafias.

The Washington Post, 6-8:(A)13.

Alan Garcia Perez
President of Peru

3

[Saying his country will limit its foreign-debt payments to a percentage of its export earnings]: Alan Garcia has been elected by 20 million Peruvians and not by international bank officials. Peru has one overwhelming creditor: It is our own people.

Inaugural address, Lima, July 28/The New York Times, 7-29:1.

4

[Saying he is reducing the high-living privileges of Peru's Ambassadors to other countries]: There cannot be Ambassadors who earn $7,000 [a year]. When you are an Ambassador of Peru,

WHAT THEY SAID IN 1985

(ALAN GARCIA PEREZ)

you are an Ambassador of a country that is suffering a crisis of poverty and you should be an Ambassador accustomed to poverty.

Interview, Lima,
The Washington Post,
8-10:(A)16.

I am a Marxist, and Peru is going to follow a hard, anti-imperialist line. But we also must be realistic . . . Imperialism was imported, imperialism that stole our resources and kept us in bondage. We were forced to import wheat from North America, a food alien to our culture of corn and potatoes. Private property, another alien concept, was forced upon us by the imperialists.

Interview, Lima/
The Wall Street Journal, 8-30-13.

John Gavin
United States Ambassador to Mexico

[On Mexicans who cross the border and work illegally in the U.S.]: Traditionally, the flow of Mexican workers to the United States has been a safety valve for Mexico. The fact is, however, that it is obviously a symbiotic situation. Although there are complaints about the strains that illegal aliens put on hospitals, schools and other services, many businesses in the U.S.—both in industry and agriculture—say they desperately need these workers. Now, with the Mexican economy suffering, there are increased pressures for people to go north to get jobs. Only 600,000 new jobs are created each year in Mexico, while 900,000 new people come into the labor market. And while the rate of population growth has declined somewhat, estimates are that there will easily be 150 million Mexicans by the middle of the next century—up from 78 million now. There is already considerable unemployment and even greater underemployment. What Mexico needs to do is to create wealth in order to create jobs.

Interview/U.S. News & World Report, 8-19:42.

Alan Greenspan
Former Chairman, Council of Economic
Advisers to the President of the
United States (Gerald R. Ford)

[On Latin American nations which are finding it difficult to pay their foreign debt]: Clearly, the Argentine situation is deteriorating. It is having difficulty in complying with the International Monetary Fund's terms. Mexico, which had been doing exceptionally well, now is doing less well. Brazil finds itself in the same circumstance. Debt rescheduling, by itself, is not going to resolve the deep-seated economic problems in the region. Our major accomplishment there has been that no country has chosen to repudiate its debt. Repudiation would have caused a real crisis. But the Latin Americans realized that they would be hurt as much as we. The learning of that lesson is the most important but un-talked-about event in international financial affairs.

Interview/U.S. News & World Report, 6-3:27.

Ramiro G:rdian
President, Union of
Agricultural Producers (Nicaragua)

There is no private sector in Nicaragua today. One sector of the economy is state owned; the other is state controlled. The government tells you what to produce, how much to pay labor and the selling price. The businessman only manages his property for the state. No one trusts the government. Everyone is convinced they will eventually have their lands confiscated. So no one makes improvements in coffee or cotton production. No new tractors. No new factories. You just keep going.

U.S. News & World Report, 12-2:42.

Tom Harkin
United States Senator, D-Iowa

. . . the contras [rebels] fighting the Sandinistas [the Nicaraguan government] were really created by the U.S. with the sole purpose of overthrowing the democratically elected government of Nicaragua. The Sandinistas are not all pure and clean by any standard, but the U.S. and

276

(TOM HARKIN)

neighboring countries continue to recognize them as the legitimate government . . . The Sandinistas do get military assistance from [Cuba and the Soviet Union]. After the revolution against [Anastasio] Somoza, we [the U.S.] grudgingly gave help—a little help—to Nicaragua. But under the Reagan Administration's policy of hatred and overthrow of the Sandinistas, the Sandinistas had nowhere to go for support but to Cuba and the Soviet Union. Like it or not, they have a right to defend themselves. As for the threat to neighboring countries, since 1981 there has not been one piece of credible evidence of any gunrunning from Nicaragua to El Salvador or any other country.

Interview/U.S. News & World Report, 4-1:33.

Silva Herzog
Minister of Finance of Mexico

1

I am convinced that the possible way Mexico can obtain reasonable rates of [economic growth]—meaning one that will provide a modest increase in the standard of living of the population—would be through a more export-oriented economy, making Mexico more productive, more efficient, making Mexico in a position to take more advantage of our geography [the proximity to the U.S.]. Sometimes you are really surprised to see a good number of products that could be produced in Mexico and sold in the U.S.—and when you see the tag, they are coming from countries 7,000 miles away.

Interview, Mexico City/
The Christian Science Monitor, 8-29:8.

Fred C. Ikle
Under Secretary for Policy,
Department of Defense
of the United States

2

[On the Sandinista government of Nicaragua]: Both the [military] equipment and their strategic objective at this time is to destroy the armed opposition; they want to get control of their own country. What they have now, and even what they may have a year hence, is not an inva-

sion force to attack El Salvador and Guatemala. That's nonsense. We shouldn't be saying that; I hope we haven't been saying that . . . They will try to change the regime in Costa Rica and Honduras and eventually in El Salvador—not by conventional invasion but by feeding an insurgency.

Los Angeles Times, 4-21:(I)1.

Helio Jaguaribe
Brazilian political scientist

3

Brazil is a Western Latin American society in the Third World. This duality between that of a Western nation and that of a Third World nation constitutes . . . the most basic characteristic of Brazil.

The Christian Science Monitor, 3-13:18.

John Paul II
Pope

4

[Addressing rebels fighting the government of Peru, telling them to lay down their arms]: Evil is never the road to good. You cannot destroy the life of your brothers. You cannot continue sowing panic among mothers, wives and daughters. You cannot continue intimidating the elderly. The cruel logic of violence leads nowhere. No good is obtained by contributing to its growth. If your objective is a more just and fraternal Peru, seek the roads of dialogue and not those of violence. Don't let your potential for generosity and altruism be exploited. Violence is not a medium of construction. It offends God, those who suffer and those who practice it.

Speech, Ayacucho, Peru,
Feb. 3/The New York Times, 2-4:4.

Salvador Jorge Blanco
President of the Dominican Republic

5

[On the foreign debt of many Latin American countries]: Those who see the foreign debt crisis as a problem between bankers, as a matter of balance sheets and exchange projections, suffer from intellectual blindness. What we need is a political solution. This implies that the industrial [lender] countries should provide financial

(SALVADOR JORGE BLANCO)

resources which the private [lender] banks cannot supply alone. It also means that these countries should improve access to their markets for our exports, particularly of agricultural origin.

At Latin American debt conference, Santo Domingo, Dominican Republic, Feb. 7/Los Angeles Times, 2-8:(IV)1.

Bernard Kalb
Spokesman for the Department of State of the United States

1

It is unfair and inaccurate to charge that our strategy in El Salvador is overwhelmingly military. Our program includes support for democratic institutions, a revitalization of the economy in an equitable manner, an increased security from extremist violence and support for dialogue . . . Certainly, if the United States provides food, shelter and medical care for refugees, it helps the government deal with the results of the conflict, but we reject the claim that aid to refugees therefore becomes something other than humanitarian assistance.

To reporters, Washington, Feb. 12/ The Washington Post, 2-13:(A)19.

John Kerry
United States Senator, D-Massachusetts

2

One of the greatest errors of [U.S. involvement in the war in] Vietnam was our inability to read history. We were unwilling to look at the long-term process that was playing itself out between North and South and among Vietnam, Cambodia, Laos and other areas. Today, in the same way, we are not looking at the history of American involvement in Central America as well as the aspirations of the indigenous population. Were we to do so, we might come up with a different set of goals . . . In Nicaragua, for example, we are simply picking one group—the contras [rebels fighting the Sandinista government there]—and looking at them as the salvation, building them into something that they're not. It's fraught with dangers.

Interview/U.S. News & World Report, 4-15:37.

3

[Criticizing U.S. President Reagan's support for the contras, rebels fighting the Sandinista government of Nicaragua]: I have no illusions about the Sandinistas. [However,] we are still trying to overthrow the politics of another country in contravention of international law, against the Organization of American States charter. We negotiated with North Vietnam. Why can we not negotiate with a country smaller than North Carolina and with half the population of Massachusetts? It's beyond me. And the reason is that they just want to get rid of them [the Sandinistas]; they want to throw them out; they don't want to talk to them.

Interview/The Christian Science Monitor, 7-18:32.

Jeane J. Kirkpatrick
United States Ambassador/Permanent Representative to the United Nations

4

[On U.S. policy in Central America]: The Contadora process should be supported and left to try to solve the problems of the region. I believe very deeply in the importance of our respecting the independence and sovereignty of those countries whose fates are being shaped by these agreements. But as long as the [Nicaraguan] Sandinistas sustain themselves not with the consent of the governed and not with indigenous force, but with a massive importation of foreign arms and personnel, then it seems to me not only legitimate but morally necessary for the United States to help those Nicaraguans [the rebel contras] who seek to provide to their country the democracy the Sandinistas promised and have denied.

Interview/Newsweek, 1-14:32.

Henry A. Kissinger
Former Secretary of State of the United States

5

We have to make a fundamental decision with respect to Nicaragua. First, what is it we actually want to achieve? Do we want a reduction of their military and intelligence capability and elimination of the Cuban forces? Or do we want a transformation of the government? If we want a

(HENRY A. KISSINGER)

transformation of the government, is it enough for us that the Sandinistas maintaining power permit some democratic opposition, or do we actually want the Sandinistas to be overthrown? We have to make sure that we know what our objective is and that we then select the means that are appropriate to that objective . . . [The U.S. Reagan Administration] has to make up its mind because if it does not, it may wind up with the worst of all worlds, with neither resolution of the military nor resolution of the political issues.

Interview, New York/Los Angeles Times, 5-19:(IV)2.

Robert E. Lamb
Assistant Secretary for Administration and Security, Department of State of the United States

1

[On a terrorist attack at a restaurant in El Salvador, which killed 13 people, including 6 Americans]: Terrorism of this type represents ideological bankruptcy. It's the last desperate act of men and women who think their cause has no future. It's a perverse tribute to the fine work that's being done here in El Salvador to achieve your [Salvadoran President Jose Napoleon Duarte's] goals. This new warfare is waged by cowards who stalk the innocent and prey on the weak. It is a war without frontiers, a war that is not easy to win. But it is a war we cannot lose.

San Salvador, June 21/The New York Times, 6-22:3.

Patrick J. Leahy
United States Senator, D-Vermont

2

[On atrocity charges against the U.S.-supported contras, rebels fighting against the Sandinista government of Nicaragua]: There is a growing body of evidence that the contras have committed widespread violence against the civilian population. I am concerned that money from our government goes to an organization that commits atrocities. I have been given affidavits by victims of atrocities, terrible photographs.

At Senate Appropriations Subcommittee on Foreign Operations hearing, Washington, March 7/Los Angeles Times, 3-8:(I)24.

J. B. Lemos
Editor, "Jornal do Brasil," Rio de Janeiro

3

Brazil has no desire to form blocs or cartels—neither a debtors' cartel nor a Latin American region aligned against the North. Even Brazil's foreign ministry, which has a shade of Third World orientation, wants to continue on its independent path, drawing on its resources to resolve problems—without losing the spirit of solidarity with its brother nations . . . Brazil's diplomacy traditionally is not aggressive, but . . . there will be a change in foreign policy. The next government will be more assertive. Brazil must adopt a diplomatic line similar to that of other countries, in which the Ambassador is a negotiator—a seller as well as a buyer for his country.

Interview/World Press Review, January:32.

Rene Levesque
Premier of Quebec, Canada

4

[Saying Canadian law should recognize the predominantly French residents of Quebec as a distinct people]: If for 400 years we have formed a people, that people has to be recognized. All Quebec governments have demanded this and once and for all it has to be recognized.

The Christian Science Monitor, 5-30:10.

Abraham F. Lowenthal
Professor of international relations, University of Southern California

5

The decline of U.S. influence in the Western Hemisphere will surely accelerate unless the United States sustains a major effort to help Latin American [countries] overcome the financial bind that ties their prospects to those of the United States. Otherwise, whatever his intentions and his efforts, [U.S. President] Ronald Reagan could go down in history as the President who lost Latin America.

The Washington Post, 6-8:(A)13.

Richard G. Lugar
United States Senator, R-Indiana

1

[On U.S. aid to the contras, rebels fighting the Sandinista government of Nicaragua]: The covert aid situation, I suspect, is not a viable proposition because it is no longer covert . . . [And] you verge very close to a declaration of war if you go [the overt] route. We did not want to declare war on Nicaragua, and the American people may still not want to declare war on Nicaragua . . . The problem remains how to keep some leverage going so there are some talks [between the U.S. and Nicaragua]. I think we are on the threshold of having to formulate a new situation in which we are able to maintain leverage on the Sandinista government, so that genuine negotiations can proceed with that government toward the end that it will not be a menace to its neighbors, destabilizing their activities, and will not be a base for the Soviet Union in our hemisphere.

To reporters, Washington,
Jan. 23/Los Angeles Times, 1-24:(I)6.

Pablo Emilio Madero
Chairman,
National Action Party of Mexico

2

[Charging vote fraud by Mexico's ruling Institutional Revolutionary Party]: We do not recommend violence as a route [for protest] because the government has more repressive capacity than anyone—they can retaliate. [But we cannot control] the reaction of a people when civilized routes are closed.

Interview/The New York Times, 1-21:5.

Robert C. McFarlane
Assistant to the President of the
United States for National Security Affairs

3

There is solid evidence throughout Nicaragua that the Sandinista regime enjoys very little popular support. At the same time, there is growing evidence that the opposition, civilian and military, is garnering massive support. It seems likely to me that the expression—politically, economically and militarily—of that opposition can prevail, and without U.S. troop involvement, I think 1985 will provide the answer to whether I'm right or wrong.

U.S. News & World Report, 4-1:29.

Robert H. Michel
United States Representative,
R-Illinois

4

[Calling for continued U.S. aid to the contras, rebels fighting the Sandinista government of Nicaragua]: If we abandon the democratic force in Nicaragua, we will guarantee a clash of arms between Americans and totalitarians in this hemisphere. It may not come next week, or next month, or next year. But it will come.

Before the House, Washington,
April 23/The New York Times, 4-24:8.

Alfredo Montealegre
President,
Nicaraguan Chamber of Industries

5

[Criticizing the announced U.S. trade embargo against Nicaragua]: This is what the United States tried to do to Cuba. It didn't do any good. All it did was give [Cuban President Fidel] Castro excuses for everything he did in Cuba. That's what will happen here with the [ruling] Sandinistas. This will give them the excuse to repress the private sector, to get rid of us.

The Washington Post, 5-2:(A)34.

Langhorne A. Motley
Assistant Secretary for Inter-American Affairs,
Department of State of the United States

6

From my perspective, I think that Chile has faced challenges and come a long way and, I think, still has a way to go. But the important thing, I think, for me to take back to the leaders of my government is that the destiny of Chile is in Chilean hands—and by that I mean all Chileans: people in the government, people that want to participate in the political process, people in the economic and social arena. And the impression that I take back to the leaders of my government is that this destiny of Chile, in Chilean hands, is in good hands.

Santiago, Feb. 21/The New York Times, 2-28:2.

Adroaldo Moura da Silva
Professor of economics,
University of Sao Paulo (Brazil)

1

[When they were in power in Brazil,] the military wanted to develop a modern state, and they knew how to . . . build highways and power dams and put settlers on the frontier. But they never learned how to supply health services or schools or community development. They didn't see these as part of national security.

Los Angeles Times, 3-15:(I)22.

Brian Mulroney
Prime Minister of Canada

2

[On charges that he "has put Canada up for sale" by trying to attract foreign investment in Canadian industries]: Who wants to buy it? What is there so compellingly attractive about Canada that causes us to think that anybody is going to rush in simply because somebody says, "I'd like to do business with you"? We do not have a very good track record. Our products have not been of the highest quality. Our deliveries have been lacking in reliability. Our expertise has been in large measure borrowed. Our technology has been purchased. What the hell makes us so special? If somebody wants to buy some oil, somebody wants to buy some wheat, hell, we're in the business. That's what it's all about. Forest products, mining—God, we'd love it if somebody wanted to joint-venture with us in mining, taking our products at competitive prices. Damn right we would.

Interview, January/Fortune, 3-4:116.

3

[On how U.S. President Reagan should view Canada]: He should get up in the morning and say to himself, "Thank God for Canada. What can I do for Canada today?" Canada is the best friend and neighbor that the United States of America can ever conceive of having around the world . . . This great trading partner, friend. Reliable, honorable, decent people. He's got to be saying to himself, "By Jesus, did I get lucky when I had these guys as neighbors. I better do something for them."

Interview, January/Fortune, 3-4:116.

4

[Repeating what he said to a foreign leader who criticized the U.S.]: What the hell do you mean "imperialist nation"? We have a 5,000-mile border with them, and for 172 years there hasn't been a shot fired in anger.

U.S. News & World Report, 11-4:12.

5

Our system of social programs, our commitment as Canadians to fight regional disparities, our unique cultural identity, our special linguistic character—these are the essence of Canada. You [in the U.S.] will have to understand that what we call cultural sovereignty is as vital to our national life as political sovereignty.

At "Time" magazine's Distinguished Speakers Program,
University of Chicago/Time, 12-16:41.

Tancredo de Almeida Neves
President-elect of Brazil

6

[Saying he will not pay off Brazil's foreign debt at the expense of the country's economy]: We owe money, and money you pay with money—not with hunger, misery and unemployment.

News conference/Newsweek, 1-28:36.

7

[On why he made no promises during his election campaign]: The people would not forgive me if I proferred impossible miracles, if I opted for a demagogy that would bring illusory success but would eventually destroy the enormous credibility that public opinion has conferred in me.

Newsweek, 1-28:37.

David R. Obey
United States Representative,
D-Wisconsin

8

The [Nicaragua-ruling] Sandinistas haven't done anything recently that would increase anybody's confidence in them. There is something to be said for keeping the Sandinistas under pressure or in doubt as to our [U.S.] intentions. . . , but our involvement with the contras [anti-Sandinista rebels] tends to make the gringos [Americans] the point at issue, rather than the shortcomings of the Sandinistas.

The Washington Post, 1-28:(A)14.

Thomas P. O'Neill, Jr.
United States Representative,
D-Massachusets

[Criticizing U.S. President Reagan's policy of aiding the rebels who are fighting the Sandinista government of Nicaragua]: He is telling the world that our country will keep aiding the rebels in Nicaragua until the government of that country cries "uncle," until it agrees to the kinds of internal reforms Reagan demands. The United States has played "uncle" in Latin America for far too long. It is time to play brother.

Washington, Feb. 26/The New York Times, 2-27:4.

1

Last Wednesday, the Nicaraguan government asked for a resumption of direct talks with the United States. We should take them up on that offer—now. In any negotiations, our fundamental goal should be to make sure the [ruling] Sandinistas do not intervene in the internal affairs of their neighbors, and their goal no doubt will be to make sure that the United States does not intervene in Nicaragua . . . It is time we eased our covert efforts to make war in Central America and instead engaged in overt efforts to make peace there. And it is time that we realized that the greatest enemies of democracy in our hemisphere are poverty, disease and illiteracy.

At Tufts University commencement,
May 19/The Washington Post, 5-20:(A)16.

2

[Criticizing U.S. President Reagan's hostile policy toward the Sandinista government of Nicaragua]: If we can sit down with the Russians, the most formidable of our adversaries, then I don't see why we can't sit down with the most feeble of our adversaries. I just feel the President is determined, because of a Class-B movie attitude, to get our [fighting] boys down there.

Interview, Washington/The Washington Post, 6-5:(A)29.

3

[Criticizing President Reagan's policy against the Sandinista government of Nicaragua]: [Reagan] is not going to be happy until he has our Marines and our Rangers down there for a complete victory. He can see himself leading a contingent down Broadway with paper flying out the windows, with a big smile on his face like a kind of Grade-B motion-picture actor coming home the conquering hero.

News conference, Washington,
June 12/The Washington Post, 6-13:(A)20.

4

Richard M. Nixon
Former President of the United States

The most clear-cut case where we are justified in supporting rebels is Nicaragua. The Sandinista government represses its own people. That gives us a moral right to support the contras [rebels fighting Nicaragua's Sandinista government], but is it enough? No. However, there is a second factor, which is that the Nicaraguan government is expansionist and aggressive; it is attempting to export its revolution. Moreover, Nicaragua is close to us. Also, it is a potential Soviet military base in the Americas. Put all these factors together, and you have a strong case for support of the contras.

Interview/Time, 4-22:15.

5

Humberto Ortega
Minister of Defense of Nicaragua

Nicaragua will continue to be friends, brothers, with the Cuban people. We are not turning back a single millimeter, we are not turning back a single instant in the content of our just, noble, revolutionary, exemplary relations between the people of Cuba and Nicaragua, between the governments of Nicaragua and Cuba.

Farewell message to 100 Cuban advisers returning
to Cuba, Managua, May 2/Los Angeles Times, 5-3:22.

6

Daniel Ortega
President of Nicaragua

1

[Criticizing U.S. policy against his government]: A truly dramatic situation has been imposed on the Nicaraguan people by the military, political and economic war that U.S. leaders are promoting. Today they are demanding an added budget from the American people to continue the orgy of blood in Nicaragua . . . Despite this situation, Nicaragua is not an enemy of the United States and defends its right to normalize relations with that nation, whose leaders—without consulting with its people—have been carrying out a policy of genocide against the people of Nicaragua.

Inaugural address, Managua,
Jan. 10/Los Angeles Times, 1-11:(I)10.

2

[Nicaragua is facing] the same ghosts and the same horrors that have been launched against Nicaragua since the last century, and that have placed in office regimes that oppress people and are supported by foreign power. Nightmares continue coming to Nicaragua sent by the leaders of the United States . . . If there was revolution in Nicaragua, it is a consequence of bad American policy. If there is struggle and if there are demands for justice in Central America, that is only the just response of the people to this policy.

Inaugural address, Managua,
Jan. 10/The New York Times,
1-11:(A)3.

3

[On the recent election that installed him as President]: When there is an economic crisis, there is discontent. It is a given. But I would ask, what government can go to an election in a situation like that of Nicaragua and still win? We went to an election in the midst of profound crises and won with 67 per cent of the public's vote. If any other Latin American government had gone to elections in the situation we have lived through, it would lose.

Interview, Managua/
The Christian Science Monitor, 1-28:32.

4

Nicaragua does not form part of any bloc, and it does not have military alliances with anyone . . . Nicaragua is not and never will be an aggressor country . . . In the face of the pretexts and unscrupulous manifestations of all types alleged by the U.S. government in respect to its security, Nicaragua reaffirms again that it is not and never will become a military base of any foreign country or power.

To reporters and diplomats, Managua,
Feb. 27/The Washington Post, 2-28:(A)26.

5

[On U.S. criticism of his recent trip to Europe which included visits to several Communist countries]: Our country is a sovereign country. We are not a satellite of the United States. We are not obligated to ask the permission of the American President or the American Congress . . . to go to Moscow, Montevideo, Brasilia, Paris or Rome.

Managua, May 20/The New York Times, 5-21:6.

6

[On the U.S. Reagan Administration's hostile attitude toward his government]: We had good relations and good communications with [former U.S. President Jimmy] Carter's Administration. The problem is that Reagan has always had a very closed position on Latin America. When Carter was trying to solve the Panama Canal problem, Reagan was opposed. Reagan represents a U.S. position that goes against the grain of history. What is at stake is relations, not between the U.S. and Nicaragua, but between the U.S. and Latin America.

Interview, Madrid/Newsweek, 5-27:41.

7

[Saying U.S.-supported Nicaraguan rebels engage in terrorism, not his government]: Nicaragua has neither practiced nor supported terrorism, nor has it been involved in any terrorist act . . . Who blew up the oil tanks in Corinto? Who mined Nicaraguan ports? Who bombed Sandino Airport? Who published the CIA crime manual? So who are the terrorists?

At celebration of sixth anniversary
of Sandinista government, Managua,
July 19/The New York Times, 7-20:3.

(DANIEL ORTEGA)

The rulers of the U.S. have backed regimes of injustice and terror in Central America. Since 1981, the government of the United States of America has attempted to destroy Nicaragua's democratic process and has tried to deny the existence of a non-aligned Nicaragua in the Central American region. In the last four years, 11 U.S. military maneuvers have been carried out, openly threatening Nicaragua's sovereignty, as part of the military preparations of the U.S. government to launch a direct military invasion against my country . . . no solution or document will be effective in Central America until U.S. rulers totally cease to attack the people of Nicaragua, directly or indirectly, in a covert manner or by any other means.

At United Nations, New York,
Oct. 21/The New York Times, 10-22:5.

1

[On the deteriorating Nicaraguan economy]: What is at stake here is the future of the Nicaraguan economy. We are looking for a way to survive. Despite the aggression [by anti-government rebels], despite the blockade [of Nicaraguan ports by the U.S.], despite all the damage that the U.S. is doing to Nicaragua, we want to survive. And to do that, we have to go through some serious difficulties. What other road is open to us?

To Nicaraguan factory workers/
U.S. News & World Report, 12-2:42.

2

Enrique Parejo Gonzalez
Minister of Justice of Colombia

[On Colombia's role in the international drug trade]: There is hardly an area of political activity or institutional life [in Colombia] that in some way has not been affected by drug corruption.

Newsweek, 2-25:15.

3

Victor Paz Estenssoro
President-elect of Bolivia

One doesn't go through life without changing. I have changed. I still believe in reform, but

284

---

sometimes one has to put aside some of the things you believe in because the times require other policies. Moderation is called for today.

Interview/The Christian Science Monitor, 8-6:13.

4

Augusto Pinochet
President of Chile

This country is under active threat from the Communist conspiracy led by Moscow, which does not forget that the Chilean armed forces freed this country from the threat of a Communist takeover. Now [since a new government decree suspending many civil liberties] it's up to the political parties in this country are not able to maintain the defenses against Communism, and only the military institutions can perform this national task.

To his Cabinet, March/
Los Angeles Times, 4-24:(I)16.

5

Carlos Ramirez
Editor, "La Prensa" (Nicaragua)

[Saying the government of Nicaragua censors his newspaper]: Over the last year, between 20 and 40 per cent of our material has been cut by censorship. Now [since a new government decree suspending many civil liberties] it's up to 80 per cent and more. This week, we are a paper that says nothing about Nicaragua.

The New York Times, 10-24:1.

6

Sergio Ramirez
Vice President of Nicaragua

[On press censorship in his country]: We do have press censorship, and I consider it a disgrace for the country that we have such censorship. The problem is how not to have censorship. It must not be forgotten that we are in a situation of war [with anti-government rebels]. Press censorship is not the only consequence. We have other, worse consequences . . . We suffer all the consequences: the killing, the disruption, the shortages of goods, everything—and the censorship of the press. Imagine this war being fought in U.S. territory, and you had thousands of counter-revolutionaries on your borders—except the 10,000 counter-revolu-

7

(SERGIO RAMIREZ)

tionaries we have here would be half a million for [the U.S.]. If some papers in the United States were every day printing opinion in favor of the invaders, I am not sure that the Congress of the United States would permit it.

Interview, Managua/USA Today, 1-10:(A)9.

1

One part of the [U.S. Reagan] Administration wants to invade us today. The other part wants to invade us tomorrow. I don't see how we are not going to have tension if there is a Reagan Administration in Washington and a revolutionary government here.

USA Today, 2-20:(A)8.

2

[Criticizing the U.S. rejection of Nicaragua's peace proposal]: For those who simply want our heads, there is no proposal that will be sufficient. The only sufficient proposal will be our heads in a basket. We defy other Central American countries involved in this conflict and the government of the United States to make this type of "empty" proposal. A good kind of empty proposal would be that the [U.S.] Reagan Administration cease its financial support of the counter-revolutionaries.

Interview, Managua, Feb. 28/
The Washington Post, 3-1:(A)16.

3

I think we would need few pretexts to say, "All right, the United States mines our ports, the United States supports terrorists, the United States imposes an embargo on Nicaragua and declares an economic boycott; the United States finances the counter-revolution, the United States maintains a counter-revolutionary army in Honduras, and therefore there are no other possibilities here except a socialist, Marxist-Leninist state [in Nicaragua]" —the pretexts are there. [But] we do not aspire to a political-economic system of that kind. The fact that here the Marxist ideology is not a persecuted ideology—and Marxists can be found in the government or in

the Sandinista Front—that does not mean that our political project is to take the country toward a one-party regime, abolition of private property and a Leninist framework of power. The Constitution has totally different lines—of pluralism.

Interview, Managua/Los Angeles Times, 11-14:(I)14.

Ronald Reagan
President of the United States

4

The transition to democracy, especially in Central America, has been accompanied by a concerted and well-financed effort by the Soviet bloc and Cuba to undermine democratic institutions and to seize power from those who believe in democracy. The subversion we're talking about violates international law. The Organization of American States, in the past, has enacted sanctions against Cuba for such aggression. The Sandinistas [of Nicaragua] have been attacking their neighbors through armed subversion since August of 1979.

At Western Hemisphere Legislative Leaders Forum,
Washington, Jan. 24/The Washington Post, 1-25:(A)14.

5

The Sandinista dictatorship of Nicaragua, with full Cuban Soviet-bloc support, not only persecutes its people, the church, and denies a free press, but arms and provides bases for Communist terrorists attacking neighboring states. Support for freedom fighters is self-defense, and totally consistent with the OAS and UN Charters. It is essential that the Congress continue all facets of our assistance to Central America.

State of the Union address, Washington,
Feb. 6/The New York Times, 2-7:13.

6

[On U.S. support for the "contras," rebels fighting the Sandinista government of Nicaragua]: The purpose of aiding them is to aid the people of Nicaragua, who are striving to get the government that the revolution promised them. If you'll recall, during the revolution, the revolutionary forces appealed to the Organization of American States for help. And they asked the

285

(RONALD REAGAN)

Organization if they would try to persuade [then-head-of-state Anastasio] Somoza to step down and thus end the bloodshed. And in return for this, they gave the Organization of American States the declaration of principles of what it was they were seeking in the revolution. And this was pure democracy. This was all the civil rights and human rights, freedom of speech, freedom of labor unions, freedom of religion, and all of these things. Now, what happened we saw happen once before with Castro's coming to power in Cuba. He had other allies that wanted a democracy and he never admitted to his true leanings until that revolution was over. Well, what happened [in Nicaragua] was the faction known as the Sandinistas took over. They ousted a number of other revolutionary leaders. Some of them were exiled, some, I think, were done away with, some imprisoned. But they have set up a totalitarian government. They've made it plain, their allies are Cuba, the Soviet Union, the Communist bloc, even [Libya's Muammar] Qaddafi, and now Iran is getting into the picture. But they've set up a totalitarian government. They have betrayed the principles that the people of Nicaragua were fighting for. And what we think is that we should be on the side of those people who actually are only asking for the democracy that they'd fought a revolution to get.

Interview/The Wall Street Journal, 2-8:8.

1

The [ruling] Sandinistas [of Nicaragua] aren't democrats but Communists, not lovers of freedom but of power, not builders of a peaceful nation but creators of a fortress Nicaragua that intends to export Communism beyond its borders. The true heroes of the Nicaraguan struggle, non-Communist, democracy-loving revolutionaries, saw their revolution betrayed and took up arms against the betrayer. These men and women are today the democratic resistance fighters some call the "contras." We should call them "freedom fighters" . . . America may never have been born without the help and support of the freedom-loving people of Europe—of Lafayette and Von Steuben and Kosciusko. And now the free people of El Salvador, Honduras and, yes, of Nicaragua,

ask for *our* help. They are our brothers. How can we ignore them? How can we refuse them assistance when we know that ultimately their fight is our fight?

Radio address to the nation, Santa Barbara, Calif., Feb. 16/USA Today, 2-20:(A)8.

2

[Supporting the contras, rebels fighting the Sandinista government of Nicaragua]: I am against sending [U.S.] troops to Central America; they are simply not needed. Given a chance and the resources, the people of the area can fight their own fight. They have the men and women, they are capable of doing it, they have need is our support . . . All they need is proof that we care as much about the fight for freedom the people of their country behind them. All they 700 miles from our shores as the Soviets care about the fight *against* freedom 5,000 miles from theirs. And they need to know that the U.S. supports them with more than just pretty words and good wishes.

At Conservative Political Action Conference, Washington, March 1/The New York Times, 3-2:4.

3

[On U.S. relations with Canada]: We are more than friends and neighbors and allies. We are kin who together have built the most productive relationship between any two countries in the world today. For the United States, there is no more important relationship than our tie to Canada.

Airport statement on his arrival in Quebec City, March 17/The New York Times, 3-18:4.

4

[Saying the U.S. provided $119-million in aid to the Sandinistas in Nicaragua when they came to power in 1979]: How did they respond to America's outstretched hand of friendship, trust and generosity? Well, the Sandinistas became, as they always planned, eager puppets of the Soviets and Cubans. They created their own Karl Marx postage stamps. They sang an anthem that called the United States the enemy of mankind. They brought in East Germans to organize their

(RONALD REAGAN)

state security. They became a rubber stamp for the Communist bloc in the UN, voting against democracies on virtually every crucial issue, from refusing to condemn Vietnam's invasion of Cambodia to not accepting Israel's credentials. While the United States was offering friendship and providing unprecedented sums of aid, the Sandinistas were building up an army that dwarfed and bullied their neighbors . . . And yet, because we are such a trusting people, anxious to believe others and believe that they share our hopes and our dreams, some still find it hard to look reality in the eye, or to rouse themselves even when our most vital interests are threatened.

Before Central American business and civic leaders, Washington, March 25/The New York Times, 3-26:6.

1

The Soviet Union has its own plan for Central America, a plan designed to crush self-determination of free people and crush democracy in Costa Rica, Honduras, El Salvador, Guatemala and Panama. It's a plan to turn Central America into a Soviet beachhead of aggression that could spread terror and instability north and south, disrupt our vital sea lanes . . . and send tens of millions of refugees in a human tidal wave across all our borders.

Before Central American business and civic leaders, Washington, March 25/USA Today, 3-26:(A)5.

2

. . . great numbers of Nicaraguans are demanding change and taking up arms to fight [the Sandinista government] for the stolen promise of freedom and democracy. Over 15,000 farmers, small merchants, whites, blacks and Miskito Indians have united to struggle for a true democracy. . . We believe that democracy deserves as much support in Nicaragua as it has received in El Salvador . . . Democracy and freedom are winning in El Salvador. President Duarte is pulling his country together and enjoys wide support from the people. And all of this with America's help kept strictly limited. The formula that worked in El Salvador—support for democracy, self-defense, economic development and dialogue—will work for the entire region.

News conference, Washington, April 4/The New York Times, 4-5:4.

3

The truth is, there are atrocities going on in Nicaragua. But they are largely the work of the institutionalized cruelty of the Sandinista government—cruelty that is the natural expression of a Communist government, a cruelty that flows naturally from the heart of totalitarianism. The truth is [the late overthrown dictator Anastasio] Somoza was bad, but so many of the people of Nicaragua know the Sandinistas are infinitely worse. Some people say this isn't America's problem. Why should we care if Nicaragua is a democracy or not? Well, we should care for a whole host of reasons. Democracy has its own moral imperatives, as you well know, but it also has advantages that are profoundly practical. Democratic states do not attack their neighbors and destabilize regions; democratic states do not find it easy to declare and carry out war. Democratic states are not by their nature militaristic; democracies are traditionally reluctant to spend a great deal of money on arms. Democratic states have built-in controls on aggressive, expansionist behavior, because democratic states must first marshal wide popular support before they move. None of these characteristics applies to totalitarian states, however. And so totalitarian Nicaragua poses a threat to us all.

Broadcast address to the nation, Washington, April 15/The New York Times, 4-16:4.

4

[Calling for continued U.S. support for the contras, rebels fighting the Sandinista government of Nicaragua]: I truly believe—the history of this century forces me to believe—that to do nothing in Central America is to give the first Communist stronghold on the North American continent a green light to spread its poison throughout this free and increasingly democratic hemisphere. I truly believe that this not only imperils the United States and its allies, but a vote against [continued aid to the contras] is literally a vote against peace, because it invites the condi-

WHAT THEY SAID IN 1985

(RONALD REAGAN)

tions that will lead to more fighting, new wars and new bloodshed. We cannot have the United States walk away from one of the greatest moral challenges in post-war history. I pledge to you that we will do everything we can to win this great struggle.

Broadcast address to the nation, Washington,
April 15/The New York Times, 4-16:4.

1

Those who question our efforts in Central America should take note of the heartwarming progress that President [Jose Napoleon] Duarte [of El Salvador] has made . . . The people of El Salvador had another free election in March, economic reforms are continuing, Communist guerrillas are losing ground. And none of this would have been possible without the economic assistance and military training and equipment that we provided. If there's to be peace and democracy in the region, if our neighbors are to be spared the tragedy that comes from every Communist dictatorship, we must have the courage to help all our friends in Central America.

After meeting with Duarte, Washington,
May 16/The New York Times, 5-17:1.

2

[The late Cuban independence leader] Jose Marti once wrote that a nation is not established the way a military encampment is run. Today, the most prominent achievements of [Cuban President] Fidel Castro's regime are the militarization of Cuban society and the propagation of malice and hatred.

Taped statement to banquet celebrating
Cuban independence, Miami, May 18/
The Washington Post, 5-20:(A)21.

3

[Criticizing the Sandinista government of Nicaragua]: The little dictator [Nicaraguan President Daniel Ortega] who went to Moscow in his green fatigues to receive a bear hug did not forsake the doctrine of Lenin when he returned to the West in a two-piece suit. He made his choice long ago . . . Soon, the United States

288

Congress must make a crucial choice for our future [whether or not to provide aid to the contras, anti-Sandinista rebels]. We had better hope that this time they choose wisely. It was a dark day for freedom when, after the Soviet Union spent $500-million to impose Communism in Nicaragua, the United States could not support a meager $14-million for freedom fighters in Nicaragua. We failed them once. We dare not fail them again.

At Republican fund-raising luncheon, Oklahoma City,
June 5/The Washington Post, 6-6:(A)37.

Alan Romberg
Spokesman,
Department of State of the United States

4

[On the U.S. decision not to accept the World Court's jurisdiction on U.S. policy regarding Nicaragua]: [The Nicaraguan case] presents political questions that are not susceptible to resolution by any court and that under the United Nations Charter are specifically not intended for the World Court. The broad political, economic, social and security problems of Central America will be solved only by political and diplomatic means—not through a judicial tribunal. When the United States accepted the Court's compulsory jurisdiction in 1946, it certainly never conceived of a role for the Court in the case of ongoing armed conflicts . . . [The U.S. has been] one of the foremost supporters [of the World Court and] will remain so where the Court acts within its competence.

Washington, Jan. 18/Los Angeles Times, 1-20:(I)23.

Adalberto Rosas
National Action Party candidate
for Governor of Sonora, Mexico

5

[On his attempt to become the first governor in Mexico not to be a member of the Institutional Revolutionary Party]: What is at stake in this election is whether Mexico is ready to define itself once and for all: Is this a dictatorship or a democracy? You can't have a one-party state and call it a democracy—not here, not in China, not anywhere.

Interview, Hermosillo, Mexico/
Los Angeles Times, 6-17:(I)1.

Julio Sanguinetti
President of Uruguay

1

[On his being the first elected President of Uruguay after 12 years of military rule]: I can assure that the armed forces are going to be conducted within the guidelines of the Constitution. I will assume supreme command of the armed forces . . . and carry out that responsibility with a sense of dignity for military institutions. The dignity will be based in the lofty duty of the soldier, which is the defense of sovereignty and the defense of the Constitution.

Inaugural address, Montevideo,
March 1/Los Angeles Times, 3-3:(I)1.

2

Democracy is our political system. It is our reason for being. It is our philosophy of life. It is our reason to feel in our fight that we can overcome.

Inaugural address, Montevideo,
March 1/The Washington Post, 3-2:(A)15.

Jose Sarney
Acting President of Brazil

3

[On his country's large foreign debt]: We have a social debt that is much larger than the foreign debt. We cannot accept a demand for a commitment that we cannot meet. The foreign debt has created impassible barriers. There are limits of health, of hunger, of education. They are the limits of survival. If we do not take these into consideration, our [economic] plan will collapse. The success or failure of our government will depend on our ability to renegotiate the debt. After 20 years of military rule, we are mindful that we cannot fail.

Interview, Brasilia/The Washington Post, 3-27:(A)26.

Jose Sarney
President of Brazil

4

Brazil has almost limitless resources. It is like a milllionaire who happens to be sitting in a restaurant with no available cash in his pocket. Still he is solvent.

Interview, Brasilia/
The Christian Science Monitor, 8-12:32.

Edward Seaga
Prime Minister of Jamaica

5

We [Jamaica] are not a country that has large-scale capital resources that can indulge in a totally free economy. We never have been and I doubt that we ever can be.

Interview/The Washington Post, 1-29:(A)9.

George P. Shultz
Secretary of State
of the United States

6

. . . almost 95 per cent of the population of Latin America and the Caribbean today live under governments that are either democratic or clearly on the road to democracy—in contrast to only one third in 1979. Over the last five years, popularly elected leaders have replaced military rulers or dictators in Argentina, Bolivia, Ecuador, El Salvador, Honduras, Panama, Peru and Grenada. Brazil and Uruguay will inaugurate new civilian presidents in March. Guatemala is in transition to democracy. After a long twilight of dictatorship, the trend toward free elections and popular sovereignty in this hemisphere is something to cheer about.

Before Senate Foreign Relations
Committee, Washington, Jan.31/
U.S. News & World Report, 2-18:44.

7

I think what we have in Nicaragua is a government that is bad news. How can that be changed? We'd like to see them see the error of their ways, [but] they don't seem to be disposed to do that. A Communist totalitarian regime any place is bad news for the people concerned, is bad news for the [countries in the] neighborhood and is bad news for our own security interests—particularly if it is nearby.

Before House Foreign Affairs Committee,
Washington, Feb. 19/Los Angeles Times, 2-20:(I)5.

8

In Nicaragua, in 1979, the Sandinista leaders pledged to the Organization of American States, and to their own people, to bring freedom to

(GEORGE P. SHULTZ)

their country after decades of tyranny under [the overthrown dictator Anastasio] Somoza. The Sandinistas have betrayed these pledges and the hopes of the Nicaraguan people; instead, they have a new and brutal tyranny that respects no frontiers. Basing themselves on strong military ties to Cuba and the Soviet Union, the Sandinistas are attempting, as rapidly as they can, to force Nicaragua into a totalitarian mold whose pattern is all too familiar. They are suppressing internal dissent, clamping down on the press, persecuting the church, linking up with the terrorists of Iran, Libya and the PLO, and seeking to undermine the legitimate and increasingly democratic governments of their neighbors. This betrayal has forced many Nicaraguans who supported the anti-Somoza revolution back into opposition. And while many resist peacefully, thousands now see no choice but to take up arms again, to risk everything so that their hopes for freedom and democracy will not once again be denied.

Before Commonwealth Club, San Francisco, Feb. 22/The New York Times, 2-23:4.

1

[Saying the U.S. must support anti-Sandinista forces in Nicaragua or else what happened in Cuba and Indochina will repeat itself in Central America]: Those who assure us that these dire consequences are not in prospect are some of those who assured us of the same in Indochina before 1975. The litany of apology for Communists, and condemnation for America and our friends, is beginning again. Can we afford to be naive again about the consequences when we pull back, about the special ruthlessness of Communist rule? Do the American people really accept the notion that we, and our friends, are the representatives of evil?... The ordeal of Indochina in the past decade, as well as the oppressions endured by the people of Cuba, and every other country where Communists have seized power, should teach us something. The experience of Iran since the fall of the Shah is also instructive. Do we want another Cuba in this hemisphere? How many times must we learn the same lesson?... Broken promises. Com-

290

munist dictatorship. Refugees. Widened Soviet influence, this time near our very borders. Here is your parallel between Vietnam and Central America... Just as the Vietnamese Communists used progressive and nationalist slogans to conceal their intentions, the Nicaraguan Communists employ slogans of social reform, nationalism and democracy to obscure their totalitarian goals.

To State Department employees, Washington, April 25/The New York Times, 4-26:6.

2

There are some in this country who would deny that America has a strategic stake in the outcome of the ideological struggle under way in Nicaragua today. Can we not, they ask, accept the existence of this [Sandinista] regime in our hemisphere even if we find its ideology abhorrent? Must we oppose it simply because it is Communist? The answer is we must oppose the Nicaraguan dictators not simply because they are Communists, but because they are Communists who serve the interests of the Soviet Union and its Cuban client, and who threaten peace in this hemisphere. Had the Communists adopted even a neutral international posture after their revolution; had they not threatened their neighbors, our friends and allies in the region, with subversion and aggression; had they not lent logistical and material support to the Marxist-Leninist guerrillas in El Salvador—in short, had they not become instruments of Soviet global strategy, the United States would have had a less clear strategic interest in opposing them.

Before National Committee on American Foreign Policy, New York, Oct. 2/The Washington Post, 10-3:(4)5.

Larry Speakes
Principal Deputy Press Secretary to the President of the United States

3

Recently we have been successful in discussing with the Cubans the matter of immigration, and our lines of communication, for our part, remain open. [But] we do have fundamental disagreements. They include their subversive activities in Central America and South America... large deployment of Cuban troops

(LARRY SPEAKES)

in Africa . . . close allegiance to the Soviet Union, and their . . . violation of human rights in Cuba. On those four points we disagree . . . We want to see actions from the Cubans . . . we have seen only words.

Interview/The Washington Post, 2-5:(A)10.

Gerry E. Studds
United States Representative,
D-Massachusetts

1

[Arguing against U.S. aid to the contras, rebels fighting the Sandinista government of Nicaragua]: Hasn't the President [Reagan] got any more to ask of us than that we support a mixed group of mercenaries and thugs and democrats who are trying to overthrow the government of a wretched country that has known nothing [in its history] but repression? Aid to the contras is dead.

At House Foreign Affairs Committee hearing, Washington, Feb. 19/Los Angeles Times, 2-20:(I)5.

Guillermo Ungo
President,
Revolutionary Democratic Front of El Salvador

2

[On the stalled peace talks between his rebel group and the government of El Salvador]: We believe that [Salvadoran] President [Jose Napoleon] Duarte has little capacity to impose his will to have a dialogue with us—if, in fact, that is his will—because the real power is held by the military and by the [U.S.] Reagan Administration. We know that the military has told Duarte that it is all right to talk with us as long as there is no real negotiation and they can pursue their military aims on the battlefield. We don't see the point of talking just for the sake of talking.

News conference, Mexico City, Feb. 7/Los Angeles Times, 2-8:(I)21.

Carlos Eugenio Vides Casanova
Minister of Defense of El Salvador

3

[Saying El Salvador now needs economic backing in the pursuit of its war against left-ist rebels]: Structural, moral and economic strength is as important as military strength . . . Friendly countries should understand that, having gained a step in the orderly democratic process of the country, what is needed is sufficient economic backing . . . to guarantee our productivity and our capacity to generate jobs. If at this point we are denied the right that we have to receive this aid, because we have sacrificed our lives and spilled our blood for Western democracy, the last five years . . would be useless.

At Day of the Soldier ceremony, San Salvador, May 7/Los Angeles Times, 5-8:(I)17.

Joaquin Villalobos
Salvadoran guerrilla leader

4

[On the guerrilla war against the government of El Salvador]: We don't think the prolongation of this war is against us. We have the capacity to resist [the government]. In the next year we expect to have spread the war throughout all the territory, to all the roads, to all the cities. The [U.S.] Reagan Administration can send all the weapons it wants [to the government]. It could never replace the [Salvadoran] Army's casualties, the fallen troops. It cannot solve the morale problem . . . Everyone knows that the economy, in any way, is a military target. Therefore, we are committed to a policy of attacking basic business branches and electrical power, paralyzing traffic on roads, sabotaging telephone communications and destroying the crops that produce foreign exchange . . . The fundamental point in the process of a negotiated solution is the end of North American intervention. [But] under no conditions will we lay down our arms. We will *never* lay down our arms.

To reporters/Newsweek, 7-15:35.

Ted Weiss
United States Representative,
D-New York

5

[Addressing and criticizing U.S. Secretary of State George Shultz on his testimony defending Reagan Administration policy toward Nicaragua]: Nothing more clearly illustrates the ap-

(TED WEISS)

proach the Administration takes than the response you just gave . . . regarding the narcotics problem, when you gratuitously drew in by the heel Cuba and Nicaragua to a situation where you know that whatever role they are playing—and I am not ready to defend their role—is miniscule compared to the role that has been played in narcotics importation to the United States from countries which are the allies of the United States. It reminds me of the Army-McCarthy hearings in 1954 when [then-Senator] Joe McCarthy decided to attack a young, recent law graduate as one way of getting back at the Army, and then attorney Welch said at long last, "Mr. McCarthy, have you no decency?" It seems to me that the Administration policy toward Nicaragua has been an exercise in twisting facts, in distorting facts, in misstating facts.

At House International Operations Subcommittee hearing, Washington, Feb. 27/ The New York Times, 2-28:6.

Michael Wilson
Minister of Finance of Canada

1

For the past 100 years, Canada lived on its resources. For the last 10 years, it has lived on credit. Now it must live on its wits and intelligence.

Fortune, 6-10:94.

John Yochelson
Director, international economics programs, Center for Strategic and International Studies, Georgetown University

2

[On President Reagan's imposition of a U.S. trade embargo against Nicaragua]: For something like this to succeed, you almost have to have multilateral participation, but I can't see the Europeans and the Latin Americans joining us. And it's hard for me to imagine the Soviets letting the Sandinistas [in Nicaragua] go down the tube. But you also have to consider the kind of message this sends to the Soviets. If we don't do this, right in our backyard, what kind of resolve do we have? And we are upping the ante to the Soviet Union in terms of what it costs them to support Nicaragua.

Los Angeles Times, 5-1:(I)15.

Ruben Zamora
Political leader, Revolutionary Democratic Front of El Salvador

3

We believe that, in the end, a dialogue will come about [between the Salvadoran government and his rebels fighting to take over the country] because that is the only way to end the war. But we can't say when, because it is not up to us but to the government. Meanwhile, people continue to die, and our country proceeds on the path to destruction.

News conference, Mexico City, Jan. 22/Los Angeles Times, 1-23:(I)6.

Asia and the Pacific

Elliott Abrams
Assistant Secretary for Human Rights,
Department of State of the United States

1

[Comparing the recent South Korean election in which government opponents gained impressively with the return to that country of South Korean dissident Kim Dae Jung, who was hustled away from the airport in a scuffle with government security officers]: [The opposition election gain was] a pretty rare event in the Third World. How many Third World countries are there in the entire globe that have this kind of vigorous campaign and an election campaign where the opposition is allowed to fight freely and get a lot of seats in Parliament? . . . [The Kim Dae Jung airport scuffle was] a trivial incident. If you're talking about the development of democracy in Korea, the return home and not the jailing of Kim Dae Jung is important. These elections in which there was a tremendous showing for the opposition after a vigorous campaign—that's important. Shoving and scuffling at the airport is just not a very important incident in the political history of South Korea.

Broadcast interview/
"Face the Nation,"
CBS-TV, 2-17.

Corazon Aquino
Candidate for the Presidency
of the Philippines

2

[On the forthcoming Presidential election in the Philippines]: I am very different from [current President Ferdinand] Marcos. I'm not a politician. I don't know how to tell a lie or take advantage of others. I'm not a dictator. I thank God I'm really very different from him, because if we really want to save the country, we need a leader very different from Marcos.

At campaign rally,
Manila, Dec. 15/
The Washington Post,
12-16:(A)17.

Malcolm Baldrige
Secretary of Commerce
of the United States

3

If you took China by itself . . . you're looking at a quarter of the world's population and you're looking at a country that has to supply work for over 30,000 net new job entrants every day. That puts a strain on their economy that has to be met by overhauling and renovating and modernizing their industrial base as well as some of their farming techniques. To do that, they're going to have to turn to either the Western world or the Soviet Union for technology transfer . . . It's an opportunity we [in the U.S.] can lose if we don't handle it right.

To reporters, Washington, May 30/
The Washington Post, 5-31:(D)3.

Ricardo J. Bordallo
Governor of Guam (D)

4

[Saying the U.S. government has not given enough attention to Guam]: There's been a tremendous neglect. We see the economies of the [World War II] enemy—Japan and Germany—restored and in robust health. Yet we are part of the American family, and there's never been a plan, never a program for our people. When V-J came, they forgot all about us and packed up and went home. Much of our infrastructure is still what was left by the military in World War II . . . Very few people know about our history. We're stuck in a time warp, a World War II image. Everyone remembers us as the place where the Marines landed and the bombers flew off to bomb the Japanese.

Interview/The Washington Post, 5-10:(E)4.

John Bruk
Founder,
Asia Pacific Foundation (Canada)

5

If we [Canadians] do not quickly establish ourselves as a major economic and political force within the Asian community, we will face

(JOHN BRUK)

diminishing world stature and a declining standard of living. The focus of global economic vigor has shifted from Europe to Asia, and as a Pacific nation we have a natural opportunity to share in the region's dynamism. But to do so will require a concerted national effort. . . In my dealings with Asian peoples, I find that they understand very well the subtle differences between Canada and the United States, but are puzzled at our lack of appreciation of their wants. The Japanese, for example, are successful because they know precisely what our needs are. They don't try to sell us their kimonos or chopsticks but hire Italian designers to fashion the goods that will attract non-Asian customers. We should not be surprised that they are so successful. They have simply put the necessary effort into it.

Interview/Maclean's, 1-21:43.

Fidel Castro
President of Cuba

1

[On the Soviet invasion of Afghanistan]: Afghanistan is one of the most backward countries in the world, where a feudal regime had existed until April, 1978. It had an illiteracy rate of 90 per cent and an infant mortality rate of 235 for every 1,000 live births—one of the highest in the world. Two thousand families owned 70 per cent of the land, and the population consisted of around 1,500 tribes. I believe that Afghanistan was one of the places in the world where a revolution was becoming more and more indispensable. . . I sincerely believe that the Afghan Revolution was just and necessary, and we could support nothing that would jeopardize it. We sympathize with and support the Afghan Revolution; I say this frankly. But I think Afghanistan could be a non-aligned country—but one in which the revolutionary regime was maintained. If a solution is sought that is based on the idea that Afghanistan should go back to the old regime and sacrifice the Revolution, then, unfortunately, I don't think there will be peace there for a long time. I think it's in the interest of all the neighboring countries, including the Soviet Union, to find a solution. And I believe that observance of the principle of respect for Afghanistan's sovereignty and for its right to make social changes, build the political system it deems best and correct and have a non-aligned government—as a Third World country—should serve as the basis of a solution for the problems there.

Interview, Havana/Playboy, August:174,177.

Chang King-Yuh
Director General,
Government Information Office of
the Republic of China (Taiwan)

2

[On dealing with the Communist government of mainland China]: Our fundamental stand has not changed. We will not negotiate with them, we will not make direct contact with them, and we will not compromise our stand . . . In our view, Communism cannot be made to work in China. What we have been doing here on Taiwan is to provide an alternative to the Communist government on the mainland. Eventually, our way of life will be chosen by the people on the mainland, though it's very difficult to fix a timetable for this.

Interview, Taipei/
The Christian Science Monitor, 12-2:22.

Chen Yun
Senior economic planner,
Communist Party of China

3

[On the recent experimentation in China with free-market economics]: The planned economy's primacy and the subordinate role of market regulation are still necessary. Market regulation involves no planning, blindly allowing supply and demand to determine production. We are Communists. Our goal is to build socialism . . . There are now some people, including some Party members, who have forsaken the socialist and Communist ideal and turned their backs on serving the people. In pursuit of their own selfish gain, they "put money above all else," regardless of the state's and people's interests . . . Some of them have become rich by unlawful means, such as speculation and swindling, graft and the acceptance of bribes.

At Chinese Communist Party conference,
Peking, Sept. 23/The Washington Post, 9-24:(A)26.

Chiang Ching-kuo
President,
Republic of China (Taiwan)

1

[On the possibility of reunification of Taiwan and mainland China]: With the implementation of constitutional democracy in the Taiwan area, our people enjoy a free, peaceful, happy and prosperous life. This greatly disturbs the Chinese Communist leaders [on the mainland]. Therefore, they spare no effort in using all kinds of plots trying to confuse the China question with a so-called Taiwan question. And early reunification of China is the common wish of all Chinese. However, we shall never, just for the sake of reunification, deprive the people on the mainland of their hope to strive for a free and democratic life. Our position is unequivocal: As long as the Chinese Communists impose the Communist system on our people in the mainland, there is no possibility for the two sides to negotiate.

Interview/Time, 9-16:46.

Alan Cranston
United States Senator, D-California

2

[Saying the Philippines should begin to enact political reforms, such as free elections, or else risk a Communist takeover]: [In the Philippines are] all the makings for the United States of another Vietnam, another Iran, another Nicaragua. I believe the best friend Communists have in Manila today is [Philippine President] Ferdinand Marcos. Every day Marcos continues to monopolize all the levers of power brings closer the day the Communists will rule in Manila.

At Senate Foreign Relations Committee hearing,
Washington, Oct. 30/Los Angeles Times, 10-31:(I)23.

F. Rawdon Dalrymple
Australian Ambassador
to the United States

3

[Criticizing U.S. failure to pressure France to stop its nuclear testing in the South Pacific]: If you want the South Pacific to become an area where the Soviet Union, Cuba and others of that stripe can find fertile ground for anti-United

States, anti-West propaganda, and in which they can develop activities directly prejudicial to our interest, then continue with a policy of indifference to what the French are doing there . . . Continued French use of Mururoa Atoll [a French possession] for nuclear testing is absolutely certain to prejudice the South Pacific people against the West, against the United States and Australian interests in a way that will quite possibly prove very costly.

Before Asia Society, Washington,
Sept. 24/The Washington Post, 9-25:(A)26.

Deng Xiaoping
Vice Chairman,
Communist Party of China

4

[On current government efforts to foster some private enterprise in China and increase the country's economic involvement with the rest of the world]: The basic things will still be state-owned, publicly owned . . . [But] we cannot fail to open up; the open-door policy cannot harm us. I think some old comrades fear that after they fought all their lives for socialism, for Communism, suddenly capitalism is coming back. They can't bear it; they are afraid. [But] if we don't open and we return to a closed self-reliance, then we will never catch up with the level of the developed countries within 50 years. It is impossible . . . No country can now develop by closing its door. We suffered from this, and our forefathers suffered from this. Isolation landed China in poverty, backwardness and ignorance.

Before Chinese Communist Party Central
Advisory Commission/Los Angeles Times, 1-2:(I)10;
The New York Times, 1-2:1.

5

In our propaganda, we must firmly oppose bourgeois liberalism, that is, publicity that favors taking the capitalist road. We exert ourselves for socialism not only because socialism provides conditions for faster development of the forces of production than capitalism, but also because only socialism can eliminate the greed, corruption and injustice that are inherent in capitalism.

At Chinese Communist Party conference,
Peking/Time, 10-7:46.

(DENG XIAOPING)

1

I think we should uphold two things [in China]. First, public ownership should always play the dominant role in our economy. Second, we should try to avoid polarization [of rich and poor] and always try to keep to the road of prosperity. Our policy of opening to the outside world, and the new approach introduced at home to stimulate the economy and to take more flexible measures, will not lead to polarization. As long as public ownership plays a dominant role in our country, I think the polarization can be avoided. There will be differences when the different regions and peoples become prosperous. Some people will become prosperous first, and others later. The regions that have become prosperous will help the regions that have not. That's what I mean by common prosperity.

Interview, Peking/Time, 11-4:39.

2

Soviet strength in Asia has grown; that's true. Their naval strength in the Pacific is the same as their strength in the Atlantic. One-third of [their] strategic missiles are directed against the Asian Pacific region, and that includes China, of course. They have one million troops with modern equipment on the Sino-Soviet border. We hope to normalize Sino-Soviet relations. But there are three obstacles that must be removed. First, Soviet support for the Vietnamese invasion of Kampuchea [Cambodia]. Second, [the Soviet military involvement in] Afghanistan. Third, reduction of missiles and troops on the Sino-Soviet border. These three obstacles threaten not only China but also all of Asia. We bring this up at every meeting with the Soviets, and we realize that removing all three at the same time ''might be difficult.'' [So now we say] one at a time. So far, we have had no positive response.

Interview, Peking/Time, 11-4:40.

Patricia Derian
Former Assistant Secretary for Human Rights, Department of State of the United States

3

[On the seizing of South Korean opposition leader Kim Dae Jung by government security personnel upon his return after living in the U.S.]: [The South Korean government] is a military dictatorship trying to pass itself off as a democracy. And they seem to have sold that bill of goods to the [U.S.] Department of State . . . By the miscalculation and stupidity of the President of South Korea, all the world now knows the state of human rights in South Korea. God knows what happens to the ordinary citizen of South Korea who steps out of line.

Washington, Feb. 11/ Los Angeles Times, 2-12:(I)16.

Pham Van Dong
Premier of Vietnam

4

Vietnam has left tragic wounds on the U.S. But the U.S. half-destroyed Vietnam [during the Vietnam war in the 1960s and '70s]. The Americans came to this land when they were not invited. The Americans did here something that cannot be tolerated by people of conscience. That is why I would say that the Americans are morally and materially responsible for Vietnam. People of conscience are always responsible. But it is we who moved first to heal the wounds, and the U.S. should do something to that end, too. Trade, investment and education are all areas we are interested in. There may be others as well. We consider national economic development our prime task today. We are prepared to develop economic relations with all the countries of the world. The door is open. Why don't you come in?

Interview, Hanoi/Time, 11-11:42.

Laurent Fabius
Premier of France

5

[On the French government's involvement in the sinking of an environmentalist ship in New Zealand]: Agents of the DGSE [French secret services] sank this boat. They acted on orders. The truth about this affair is cruel. But it is essential that it be clearly and thoroughly established . . . The people who merely carried out the act must of course be exempted from blame, as it would be unacceptable to expose members of the military who only obeyed orders and who,

(LAURENT FABIUS)

in the past, sometimes have carried out very dangerous missions on behalf of our country.

News conference, Paris, Sept. 22/
The Washington Post, 9-23:(A)1,21.

1

[On the French government's involvement in the sinking of an environmentalist ship in New Zealand]: In a democracy like ours, the responsibility for a decision of this kind lies with the political authority, the minister [in this case, Defense Minister Charles Hernu and head of French intelligence Pierre Lacoste] . . . My conviction is that, in acting, both of them were animated by the idea that they had the interest of the country [the environmentalist ship might have interfered with French nuclear testing in the South Pacific]. My conviction is that responsibility is situated at their level. But the decision was bad, its execution unfortunate, and it entailed serious circumstances and consequences . . . I was never informed by the Minister of Defense about the preparation of this project. When the attack took place, the response to my questions "Were French services involved?" was always "No."

Broadcast interview, Paris,
Sept. 25/The New York Times, 9-26:10.

Rajiv Gandhi
Prime Minister of India

2

[On his country's relations with Pakistan]: Our real problem is not with [Pakistani] President Zia but with some of the more junior officers around him. If what President Zia says could filter down to his officials, we would have no problem at all . . . We're not happy, of course, with the weapons that are being supplied to Pakistan—not because we want to keep Pakistan disarmed. We are not interested in a conflict with Pakistan at all, but the new supply of weapons to Pakistan has started an arms race on the subcontinent we would very much have liked to avoid . . . We would also like them to end their nuclear-weapons program. I know they say they are not making nuclear weapons, but we have reason to believe they are.

Interview, New Delhi/Newsweek, 1-14:40.

3

[On U.S. concern that India is "tilting" toward the Soviet Union]: I think it's a misunderstanding. We don't have such a tilt. We like to look at issues on merit, and we would like to continue doing that. What the United States must understand is that we are not against the United States or any other country. Where we find that we are not in agreement with U.S. policies, we would like to have the option of speaking out—and we will speak out. But as far as friendship is concerned, I think we have a very good relationship with the United States, a relationship that we would like to improve.

Interview, New Delhi/Newsweek, 1-14:40.

4

There are lots of [internal] dangers [in India]. If you look at the castes, the religious groups, the various regional linguistic groupings, each is a prospective danger. But the real danger is economic stagnation. Whenever we have had a problem with minorities, it has been when there has been an economic problem. The [recent] elections have shown that the country stands united. I don't think there is a problem [of internal differences] as long as we politicians don't try to build on them.

Interview, New Delhi/Time, 1-14:42.

5

. . . at the moment, I don't see a situation arising where we would start up again making the [nuclear] bomb. Just the fact that Pakistan made a bomb would not make us change our policies. We don't want to become the same as the others. That would only make the situation worse, not better. It would make us no different than the others who are making a bomb, whom we are trying to talk out of making a bomb. We have been a very good example to the world. Firstly, because we can make a nuclear bomb, and have not done so; secondly, because we will not be drawn into a race.

Interview, New Delhi/
Los Angeles Times, 2-21:(I)10.

6

In the U.S., you have always felt that we have tilted toward the Soviet Union. We ourselves

(RAJIV GANDHI)

don't feel that. On many issues we do side with the Soviet Union, but so do 100-odd other countries. On many issues we disagree with them. And we would like to keep that option open. That is why we are non-aligned. The Soviet Union has been a very old friend of India's for over 30 years. They have helped us in our development; they helped us militarily with equipment when we needed it.

Interview, New Delhi/Newsweek, 6-3:42.

1

[On his economic philosophy]: It's pro-Indian. It's not capitalism or socialism. It has to be a mix of the two. It has to progress as we progress, as our base develops . . . We don't fear a debt problem, but we do feel that the U.S. is blocking our getting aid from some [international] institutions. I will make our case based on our performance in development, in agriculture. We could have been an Africa. We've had two-three major droughts in the last five years, but we're still self-sufficient in food.

To reporters, New Delhi, June 4/
The Christian Science Monitor, 6-5:10.

2

We think the Indian Ocean should be a nuclear-free zone, a zone of peace. We would like our area to be kept out of tension. We don't want South Asia to become a Middle East. The United States, like any third country, coming in with large defense commitments, does affect the balance, and exacerbates the tension.

To reporters, New Delhi, June 4/
The Christian Science Monitor, 6-5:10.

Goh Chok Tong
First Deputy Prime Minister of Singapore

3

The democratic system of government does not have a stabilizer to steady the ship against waves of popular demands that want to be satisfied immediately. That is why many governments elsewhere roll from left to right and right to left every now and then. The absence of a stabilizer is a design fault of the democratic system . . . I think a stable system is one where there is a mainstream political party representing a broad range of the population. Then you can have a few other parties on the periphery, very serious-minded parties. They are unable to have wider views but they nevertheless represent sectional interests. And the mainstream is re-turned all the time. I think that's good. And I would not apologize if we ended up in that situation in Singapore.

At National University, Singapore/
The New York Times, 8-14:8.

Alexander M. Haig, Jr.
Former Secretary of State of the United States

4

A major industry has grown up devoted to the manufacturing and distribution of "lessons" supposedly derived from the Vietnam war . . . Events after the American departure from Vietnam amply confirm that whatever the indigenous problems of South Vietnam, the war became in the end a conquest of the south by the north, aided by the U.S.S.R. Our trouble was not in the morality of the approach.

Before Senate Foreign Relations Committee, Washington, Feb. 8/The Washington Post, 2-12:(A)20.

Selig S. Harrison
Senior associate, Carnegie Endowment for International Peace

5

At best, the [U.S.] Reagan Administration's resumption of military aid to [Pakistan] is seen in India as evidence of a growing divergence of geopolitical and strategic interests between Washington and New Delhi; at worst, it is seen as revealing deliberate malevolence. An atmosphere of xenophobic resentment is building up among many key military and political figures who could have a major voice in shaping New Delhi's regional military role in the decades ahead.

Before House Asian and Pacific Affairs Subcommittee, Washington, Feb. 27/The Washington Post, 3-15:(A)20.

Bob Hawke
Prime Minister of Australia

1

[Criticizing France's nuclear tests in the South Pacific and French President Mitterrand's invitation to Pacific heads of state to visit the test site]: He is saying to the countries of the region "come and see how absolutely safe it is." I have one message and one message alone for President Mitterrand: . . . Take his tests back to France and have those "absolutely safe" tests in metropolitan France.

At celebration of 10th anniversary of independence of Papua New Guinea, Port Moresby, Sept. 16/The Washington Post, 9-17:(A)16.

Deane R. Hinton
United States Ambassador to Pakistan

2

[On Pakistan's recent election]: Pakistan is a country with little political experience and with a reputation for volatility and taking to the streets in violence. With a population overwhelmingly illiterate, will democracy work under such circumstances? We think it can, but we are aware of the risks. Nobody can predict . . . I think [President] Zia came to the conclusion [to hold the election] all by himself. I think he understands pretty well you need a broader base—what they call an Islamic consensus—than just the military and the bureaucracy.

Interview, Islamabad, Feb. 26/ Los Angeles Times, 2-27:(I)8.

3

You shouldn't judge Pakistan by the standards of Jeffersonian democracy or Westminster democracy. It is a country that for 37½ years hasn't worked very well.

Interview, Islamabad, Feb. 26/ The Washington Post, 2-27:(A)14.

Takashi Hosomi
Head, Overseas Economic Cooperation Fund of Japan

4

[On South Korea's cool relations toward Japan because of Japanese occupation earlier in

the century]: It is not a happy situation to have a neighbor of ours cling forever to a defiant attitude . . . I won't say there is no guilty conscience [on the part of Japanese government leaders. But] ordinary Japanese don't have a guilty conscience [about the colonial rule of Korea]. It's a matter they don't concern themselves with. But we have now come to understand that with the great gap in perception [between Japanese and Koreans], we cannot get along with South Korea. No victimizer ever perceives [himself as] having been a victimizer; but all victims always perceive having been victimized . . . The strong never understand the suffering of the weak . . . We are teaching ourselves now that we were probably the victimizer. The Japanese people now are digesting [that idea] intellectually, but they do not have an emotional feeling that it was bad.

Los Angeles Times, 8-8:(I)14.

Arthur W. Hummel, Jr.
United States Ambassador to China

5

. . . we no longer need to plan for the possibility of war with China. Our [U.S.-China] official relations are characterized by more candor, and less confrontation. I think Chinese and Americans get along well, partly because we're an up-front kind of people and the Chinese can be, too, when there's a reasonable amount of trust . . . The combination of the very strong desire of the Chinese for modernization, and their almost equally strong desire to have the United States involved in that modernization because of our leading edge in technology and managerial skills, has produced an amazing web of relationships.

Interview, Peking/ The Washington Post, 9-21:(A)24.

Mushahid Hussain
Editor, "Muslim" (Pakistan)

6

[On the recent Pakistani elections]: These elections were credible elections, honest and fair, and there are some good people coming to Parliament. It won't be a rubber stamp. I think [President Zia will] have to come to an arrange-

(MUSHAHID HUSSAIN)

ment with Parliament on the lifting of martial law. He now has the confidence behind him of a large voter turnout, and even though it wasn't quite what the generals wanted, with nearly the entire government going down to defeat, I suspect they'll go ahead, following the Turkish model. There was definitely a significant message in this vote. The people have solidly repudiated Islamic fundamentalism and a government of martial law.

The Christian Science Monitor, 2-27:28.

Fred C. Ikle
Under Secretary for Policy,
Department of Defense of
the United States

[By the end of this century, India] could be a power that contributes to world stability the way the U.S. will see it and want to shape it—a power we can work together with, much as we try to work together with other major powers now to enhance our long-term national-security aims. It has certain parallels with our changing relationship with China. Our concern with China in the '50s was its wanting to spread all over Asia, wanting to take on Vietnam, pieces of India and Korea and Japan. Now we have a different attitude toward China. We have a common strategic interest and a feeling in the West that China is not now pushing to take over neighboring countries.

Interview, New Delhi, May 3/
Los Angeles Times, 5-4:(I)22.

1

Gulam Mustafa Jatoi
Leader, Pakistan People's Party

[On why his party is not taking part in the Pakistani national elections]: I could give you endless reasons why we are not participating in the elections. They are not being held under the [suspended] 1973 Constitution. [President] Zia has said he's going to amend the Constitution, but he hasn't said how. Therefore, no one knows what powers will be awarded to the President, to Parliament, or to the Premier. He's going to in-

2

stitutionalize the role of the Army, but we don't know how . . . Even if we had agreed in principle to participate in partyless elections, under martial law, this would have been an extraordinary concession, and if General Zia is so secure, why was he not prepared to make similar concessions? . . . Mark my words, another general is about to come along.

Interview/The Christian Science Monitor, 2-21:11.

J. R. Jayewardene
President of Sri Lanka

We consider Sri Lanka as one land belonging to all citizens, consisting of 75 per cent Sinhalese and 25 per cent of other races. As such, we will settle Sri Lankans in this proportion throughout the island on state land . . . We will not accept the theory that certain parts of the island are the traditional homeland of the Tamils or any other race.

At public meeting, Anamaduwa, Sri Lanka,
Jan. 21/The New York Times,
1-22:2.

3

[On the Tamil separatist movement]: I do not intend to invite or have discussions with any party that advocates separatism in the future. I will not talk to them even if I am dragged to them by an elephant.

Los Angeles Times, 2-14:(I)6.

4

Mohammad Khan Junejo
Prime Minister of Pakistan

[On the Soviet Union's involvement in the war in Afghanistan]: These people came into Afghanistan expecting everyone to bow before them. They found the local people would not bow to that almighty authority. They wouldn't have come in if they'd know they'd be there six years, but now they can't just walk away from it. They're a superpower, so it's become a question of prestige.

Interview/Newsweek, 6-24:50.

5

Bernard Kalb
Spokesman for the Department of State of the United States

1

[On New Zealand's decision not to allow U.S. ships carrying nuclear weapons into its ports]: We believe that alliances require interaction of military forces and equitable burden-sharing. Some Western countries have anti-nuclear and other movements which seek to diminish defense cooperation among the allied states. We would hope that our response to New Zealand would signal that the course these movements advocate would not be cost-free in terms of security relationships with the United States.

Feb. 5/The New York Times, 2-6:6.

James A. Kelly
Deputy Assistant Secretary of Defense of the United States

2

[Criticizing New Zealand's decision not to allow U.S. ships carrying nuclear weapons into its ports]: Whatever the real or perceived risks of alliance defense cooperation, those risks are minimal compared to the dangers associated with a decay in the perceived will of Western nations to support one another.

Before House Asian and Pacific Affairs Subcommittee, Washington, March 18/The Washington Post, 3-19:(A)13.

Kim Dae Jung
A leader of opposition to government of South Korea

3

There is a growing number of radicals among the young men [of South Korea]. But I believe they are not pro-Communist or anti-American; they are only dissatisfied with the present dictatorial rule and American support of the dictatorship. I want to meet with them to comfort and persuade them not to be radical, not to be violent . . . Such radicalism only gives benefit to military dictators.

Interview/ USA Today, 1-30:(A)7.

4

If the government [of South Korea] is really supported, why should they fear my return [from exile]? If a government can't allow freedom of speech, it must be afraid of public opinion. If a government does not allow free elections, it clearly shows it will not be supported by the people . . . Most of our people, I think, are supporting my cause for democracy, especially intellectuals, farmers, laborers, small businessmen. Some people say I am not supported by the military. This is not true. At present, if there is freedom of expression among generals, most of them would support democracy and human rights.

Interview/The Christian Science Monitor, 1-30:15.

5

[On the recent South Korean election in which his supporters gained a large percentage of the votes]: For 13 years, the government has continuously labeled me a "revolutionary," a "demagogue," a "pro-Communist." The people are no longer listening. That the propaganda has no effect was shown by the support received by the candidates who used my name in campaigning in this election . . . [President] Chun [Doo Hwan] labeled us as dangerous and put a lid on us for five years, but this election showed the people didn't agree . . . It is necessary for the United States to show our people that it supports democracy . . . Quiet diplomacy is no good. The United States should try to make the Korean mass media publish its comments fully and, if that fails, should use the Voice of America, [Stars and Stripes] and the Armed Forces Korea Network to get its message across in South Korea. The Korean mass media doesn't report; U.S. agencies don't report. So the South Korean people wind up listening to North Korean broadcasts, and then they find out that what the North Koreans report is true. But in the midst of such reports is Communist propaganda. This situation is fearful.

Interview, Seoul, Feb. 14/ Los Angeles Times, 2-15:(I)22.

6

American forces are here for the security of South Korea. The greatest damage that can occur to security is for the [Korean] military to

(KIM DAE JUNG)

participate in politics. Therefore, for the sake of security, not for the sake of Korean politics, the U.S. commander must continually insist that the military not participate in politics. [Whether the commander does this] will be the key to whether the Korean people will return once more to friendship with the United States or become eternal enemies of the United States. I repeatedly urge my American friends—please don't force us to be anti-American; please don't force us to become another Vietnam.

Interview, Seoul/Los Angeles Times, 9-5:(I)14.

Kim Young Sam
A leader of opposition to
government of South Korea

1

This [South Korean] regime is extremely good at managing its public relations by lying to the people and to the international community. International opinion has been cultivated with these lies . . . Our country has never had a dictator who admitted on his own that he had taken away the people's freedom and that he should give it back as a favor. Democracy is something that has to be fought for and won. If you don't fight for democracy, you can never have it.

Interview, Seoul/
The Christian Science Monitor, 2-8:38.

Jeane J. Kirkpatrick
United States Ambassador/Permanent
Representative to the United Nations

2

[On the Soviet intervention in Afghanistan]: The Afghan people have been gassed, bombed, buried, driven from their homes and now they may be starved [as a result of Soviet action]. It seems likely that the Soviet goal in Afghanistan is incorporation of Afghanistan [into the Soviet Union] and achievement of a warm-water port and geopolitical access to the Afghan nation to Iran and Pakistan. The resistance of the Afghan nation to incorporation, its struggle to survive, is a challenge to the carefully cultivated image of Soviet invincibility. But Soviet triumph in Afghanistan is not inevitable. Defeat of the [Afghan rebels fighting the Sovi-

ets] is not inevitable. The expansion of Soviet power in the region is not inevitable.

Before Congressional Task Force on Afghanistan,
Washington, March 11/The Washington Post, 3-12:(A)6.

Henry A. Kissinger
Former Secretary of State
of the United States

3

[On the recent improvement in Chinese-Soviet relations]: I think we should be relaxed. China broke with the Soviet Union not as a favor to us; in fact, we didn't even understand it was going on. They did it for their own reasons. As long as they are concerned about their independence and their territorial integrity, they will not get so close to the Soviet Union as to lose American or, for that matter, Japanese interests in their future. Short of this, it is entirely up to them what they do. They, after all, have a tradition of 3,000 years of conducting their own affairs, and I'm perfectly relaxed. I think we should express no opinion, we should show no concern and we should let them do what they think is appropriate, because there are limits that geography, history and the national interest impose. They do not need our advice on that.

Interview/Los Angeles Times, 3-24:(IV)2.

Ernst Kux
Swiss political scientist;
Foreign editor,
"Neue Zürcher Zeitung," Zurich

4

[Chinese leader] Deng Xiaoping is replacing the rigid Stalinist model by a so-called socialism with Chinese characteristics that combines central planning with market regulation, movement on the inside with opening to the outside world. The aim is to catch up with the new technical revolution on a global scale and to bring China into the forefront of the developed industrial societies . . . According to my observations in China, a great movement has begun and reached a point of no return. Deng's policy has now broad support—so much so that I don't believe any of Deng's successors will be able to go back to the old radical Maoist approach. If they tried it now, it would produce tensions, or even uprisings.

Interview, Zurich/U.S. News & World Report, 2-4:43.

David Lange
Prime Minister of New Zealand

1

[On his decision not to allow U.S. ships carrying nuclear weapons into New Zealand ports]: Our policy is against nuclear weapons, not against the United States, not against the alliance, not against ANZUS . . . I have very few really burning convictions in political life, and being opposed to nuclear armaments escalation and their existence is one of them.

News conference/
The Christian Science Monitor, 2-6:14.

2

[On New Zealand's refusal to allow U.S. ships carrying nuclear weapons into its ports and the effect that decision will have on his country's defense posture]: This government is committed to an alliance with the United States. We have no intention of withdrawing from it. There need be no comfort given to the Soviet Union in thinking we have withdrawn. We have not. The United States is our mate. The Soviet Union is not; it is a respectful acquaintance, not a mate . . . I think that the response from the United States and Australia to a situation of aggression against New Zealand would be there irrespective of AN-ZUS or not. Now, that is not to say that we don't value ANZUS. But the response would be based on an assessment of our security interests and the security interests of Australia and the United States. They would not rush off and consult the text of the ANZUS treaty.

Interview, Wellington,
Feb. 11/The New York Times, 2-12:7.

3

[On his decision not to allow U.S. ships carrying nuclear weapons to enter his country's ports, and the subsequent U.S. retaliation of cutting back on intelligence-sharing and military exercises with New Zealand]: I regret these [U.S.] moves. They are serious, and they will be, to a degree, damaging. They are not, in my view, the kind of actions which a great power should take against a small, loyal ally which has stood by it, through thick and thin, in peace and war.

Written statement, Wellington,
Feb. 26/The New York Times, 2-27:7.

4

[Criticizing France's nuclear testing in the South Pacific, its alleged involvement against nuclear protestors in New Zealand, and its President Francois Mitterrand's recent visit to the testing site at Mururoa Atoll]: New Zealand did not buy into this fight. France put agents into New Zealand, France put spies into New Zealand, France lets bombs off in the Pacific, France puts its President in the Pacific to crow about it.

Los Angeles Times, 9-16:(I)12.

5

[Criticizing the French government's involvement in the sinking of an environmentalist ship in New Zealand and France's refusal to release the names of its agents who carried out the sinking, saying they were only obeying orders]: This is not a war. The defense of acting under orders is clearly inappropriate. The idea that acting under the order of a foreign power gives anyone license to execute criminal acts in another country with immunity, and remain inviolate from prosecution or sanction, is, of course, quite absurd. If that became the state of affairs that governed international relations, that would be sheer anarchy.

To reporters, Sept. 23/The New York Times, 9-23:12.

6

[On his country's refusal to allow U.S. ships carrying nuclear weapons into its ports]: If the ANZUS treaty requires us to accept nuclear weapons, then it is the treaty which is the obstacle to the maintenance of good relations between New Zealand and the United States . . . The United States sees the ANZUS alliance in the context of its global strategies of deterrence. That is why the United States places so much importance on its wish to have unquestioned access to New Zealand ports for vessels which may carry nuclear weapons. It is not that New Zealand has much strategic significance to the United States. Our importance lies in the fact that New Zealand has to some extent been part of the global projection of American nuclear power which underpins the deterrence strategy. If the ANZUS alliance is merely a nuclear deterrent and New Zealand's contribution to ANZUS

WHAT THEY SAID IN 1985

(DAVID LANGE)

in the form of the presence of nuclear weapons is the price we pay for that deterrent, then the price is too high.

Before New Zealand Labor Party's regional council, Christchurch, Sept. 27/ The Washington Post, 9-28:(A)16.

1

[On his refusal to permit U.S. ships carrying nuclear weapons to enter New Zealand ports]: Our anti-nuclear policy is not an anti-American policy. It is impossible to be anti-American in New Zealand and be a political survivor.

Interview, New York, Oct. 23/ The Washington Post, 10-24:(A)1.

Salvador Laurel
*Leader, UNIDO
(coalition of parties opposed to Philippine President Ferdinand Marcos)*

[On President Marcos' call for elections in the Philippines next year]: I am confident that in a free and fair election we [the opposition] cannot lose. [But Marcos] may hold a very dishonest election. I am asking for a [reformed election commission] that's able to count ballots correctly, free access to media, a neutral military and a reasonable campaign period of 90 days. Unless these things are granted, the elections will be dirty, and being dirty they will be bloody. People are going to protect the ballots with their lives. They are going to go to the polls armed with anything they can get their hands on. The Communists will exploit the situation and use it to say it's pointless to participate in elections. If Marcos wins in a free and fair election, we salute. [But] if we [the opposition] lose, and it was dirty, it may be the last election in our country.

Interview/Newsweek, 11-18:60.

3

[On Philippine President Marcos' call for elections next year]: The first objective of the opposition [parties] is to dismantle the [Marcos] dictatorship and restore democracy. If we win

304

the election, that will have been achieved. Then we will attack the peace-and-order problem. We believe that, given a democratic system and a credible leadership, if we issue a general amnesty to all political offenders, 90 per cent will lay down their arms because we believe 90 per cent of the people who have joined the [Communist] New People's Army are not Communists. They are just disgusted with the Marcos regime. We will offer the remaining 10 per cent a plural society. If they disavow the use of force and violence, if they forswear the use of guns and agree to disband the NPA, there is no reason why they shouldn't be allowed to join the political mainstream. If they resist, they will have declared themselves as public enemies, but they will be easier to subdue.

Interview, New York/Time, 11-18:54.

Lee Kuan Yew
Prime Minister of Singapore

4

[On the difference in social outlook between his country and the West: If you compare us to Western societies—America or western Europe —we are a different society. We have a different background. It's more the *right* of society—and the *obligation* of the individual. We're not so well off as not to worry about the survival of society. . . . If we were so secure as America or Britain or France or West Germany, people could become more demanding of freedoms; but all around us we see manifestations of poverty. It behooves us to see our material well-being is not jeopardized.

Interview, Raleigh, N.C./USA Today, 10-15:(A)11.

Li Peng
Vice Premier of China

5

While we [in China] are introducing some advanced things into the country, we should not allow in the capitalist concept of value and decadent way of life, because they conflict with our socialist system. Any attempt to follow the capitalist road will not succeed in China. Bourgeois liberalism would only make a mess of Chinese affairs and would not be tolerated.

To university students, Peking, Dec. 8/Los Angeles Times, 12-9:(I)7.

Li Xiannian
President of China

1

We will never enter into an alliance or strategic relations with any big power. It is China's policy to open up to the whole world, with no discrimination against any country.

Before National Council for U.S.-China Trade,
Washington, July 24/The Washington Post, 7-25:(A)4.

Richard G. Lugar
United States Senator, R-Indiana

2

[Saying he is skeptical that Philippine President Ferdinand Marcos intends to conduct a fair election next year as he has announced]: We are not convinced there really is a will here. My own suspicion is that to a certain extent [Marcos] is humoring us. He feels a little bit of pressure here and there, a little feint and jab . . . but in terms of commitment to democracy, that we haven't seen.

At Senate Foreign Relations Committee hearing,
Washington, Dec. 18/USA Today, 12-19:(A)4.

Raul S. Manglapus
Former Foreign Minister
of the Philippines

3

[On Philippine President Ferdinand Marcos' call for Presidential elections in early 1986 to counter criticism that he runs a dictatorship]: I am finishing a study at Harvard of countries all over the world that have returned to democracy from dictatorship peacefully in the last 10 years. In all of them, the dictatorship had to be terminated first—and then democratic elections were held. In the Philippines we are [now] allowing ourselves to be maneuvered by Marcos into trying to do the reverse—accepting elections in which the dictator himself is to be a candidate, as he retains all his absolute power and his control of the army, the Commission on Elections, the secret police, all national media, and all significant public and private funds.

Speech, Washington/
The Washington Post, 10-29:(A)20.

Mike Mansfield
United States Ambassador to Japan

4

[On the U.S. security treaty with Japan]: It's a good treaty. It works both ways. Under the treaty—we had a big hand in writing it—we've agreed to come to the defense of Japan if it's attacked. And we will. But we're not out here just to defend Japan. We're out here in our own defense as well. Bases in Japan are stable, secure and rent-free. With the [U.S.] bases in the Philippines—quite expensive, located in a country which is undergoing tremendous political and economic difficulties—they form the outermost line of our defense. And if we didn't have these bases in Japan especially, but in the Philippines as well, we'd have to ask ourselves a couple of questions: How far back would we have to withdraw? How many tens of billions of dollars would it cost us to build a new line, and how effective would the new line be? So if there ever was a security treaty that was in the mutual interest of each country, this is it.

Interview, Tokyo/
U.S. News & World Report, 10-28:33.

Ferdinand E. Marcos
President of the Philippines

5

[On comparisons between his rule in the Philippines and the rule of the Shah of Iran, who was toppled from power]: The Shah of Iran was so far above reality that the people really did not know him. The big difference is, all the reforms that we conducted were approved by the people. They supported them. Being above reality is a danger for any leader. There are people who want to polish up the apple with you and curry favors. But a *cordon sanitaire*, no. I have a telephone. I can get in touch with any governor, mayor or battalion commander, if necessary, and I do. When I receive a report and it sounds funny, it's too good, I immediately have it checked. I check it myself.

Interview, Manila, Oct. 31/
The New York Times, 11-1:6.

6

[On whether the Philippines is a dictatorship]: It is not true that I dictate what should be done. There is a dialogue. Now, you say that the

WHAT THEY SAID IN 1985

(FERDINAND E. MARCOS)

situation is rigged up in my favor. Well, probably if they [the opposition] spend more time organizing in the provinces instead of quarreling here in Manila, then they can improve the situation.

Interview, Manila/Time, 11-11:4.

1

[On which is more serious in the Philippines—the Communist insurgency or the growing economic problems]: You cannot abandon your counter-insurgency efforts as you are seeking economic recovery. Insurgency and criminality increase with the crisis. You have laborers who are not paid, who are going hungry perhaps, and who are, therefore, available to the blandishments of the Communists. So while you are fighting Communists, you have to solve the economic problems.

*Interview, Manila, Nov. 16/
USA Today, 11-18:(A)11.*

2

[Saying U.S. military bases should remain in the Philippines]: I am for the maintenance of a balance of power in Asia. Otherwise, there will be war in Asia. And that balance of power can be maintained only if those military bases are kept by the United States.

*Interview, Manila, Nov. 28/
The Washington Post,
11-29:(A)37.*

3

A country makes all kinds of contingency plans, and this is one scenario: that America might suddenly decide to abandon us, just as you [Americans] abandoned [South] Vietnam and your allies in Africa, notwithstanding the commitments made by your Executive Department. What is the saying of Cervantes? "Don't cry like a woman over the kingdom you lost, because you did not defend it like a man." That is one of my favorite quotes. In short, the [South] Vietnamese should have defended their own land and not depended on the Americans to do it for them.

Interview, Manila/Time, 12-16:28.

4

[Saying he is thinking of the future of the Philippines after he leaves office]: I want out. You cannot be President for 20 years and not be tired of it. Let's admit it. I'm tired. All the burden has always been on me. All the critical decisions have been made by me. I want somebody who will pick up the burden. Probably I can advise him from behind or from the side . . . I think I'll live another 20 years, but I would devote much of my time to training successors.

Interview, Manila/Newsweek, 12-30:26.

Imelda Marcos
Wife of President of the Philippines—Ferdinand Marcos

5

[On criticism that she is too extravagant and indulges in frivolity and opulence]: People say I'm extravagant because I want to be surrounded by beauty. But tell me, who wants to be surrounded by garbage?

Interview/The Washington Post, 7-22:(4)17.

6

[On U.S. pressure on the Marcos government for political reforms]: We can't really understand why America keeps on thrashing away [at us], while the Soviets don't. The Soviet leaders did not press us at all [during her trip to the Soviet Union]. "Tell us what you need," they said, "and we will give it to you." [U.S.] President Reagan is no problem; he is very enlightened about us. It's the [U.S.] system . . . While America is immersed in high technology and hardware, Russia is building relationships—and when it's people you are cultivating, you can hardly go wrong. America had better watch out. The moment [the Marcoses] are no longer here, the Russians will take over. Stupid America!

Interview, Manila/Time, 11-25:73.

John McCain
*United States Representative,
R-Arizona*

7

[On how Vietnam has handled the issue of U.S. servicemen still missing in action after the

(JOHN McCAIN)

Vietnam war]: It's my belief that for 10 years Vietnam has used the MIA's in the most cynical fashion. They give back a few bodies every number of months to some visitors. Some of those bodies were of men we know were shot down, captured and photographed. To give these bodies back 10 or so years later is the most cynical thing possible . . . I think our government has made a very plain commitment. The President [Reagan] has said if we can get hard evidence of someone alive, he will take whatever action is necessary. I don't think he can state his commitment any better. The next move is up to the Vietnamese, and how much they want to cooperate is the key to the resolution of this issue.

Interview/U.S. News & World Report, 3-11:33.

Robert C. McFarlane
Assistant to the President
of the United States for
National Security Affairs

1

[On the Soviet invasion of Afghanistan and the anti-Soviet guerrilla war in that country]: Today, 120,000 Soviet soldiers there are waging the most brutal war now under way on the face of the earth. For what? It's not so easy to say. Soviet officials say that they need a friendly Afghanistan on their borders. But how is friendship to be built? Our proposition to the Soviet leadership is that their present policy is only increasing the Afghan people's hatred.

Before Channel City Club
and Channel City Women's Forum,
Santa Barbara, Calif., Aug. 19/
The New York Times, 8-20:6.

Francois Mitterrand
President of France

2

[On criticism by South Pacific nations of his country's nuclear testing in that area]: France, which is present in the Pacific, intends to exercise its sovereignty in deciding on matters that affect its national interest there. I invite the chiefs of state of the governments of the Pacific Forum to go to the [testing] site at Mururoa

[Atoll]. France has no enemies in the South Pacific. It intends only to make sure that its rights are respected . . . Not a single one of these tests has failed. The environment is tested: 3,000 people, Polynesians and Europeans, live on the site where they devote faith, dedication and competence to the task. None of them, since the beginning, suffers or has suffered from health problems due to radioactivity.

Broadcast address to the nation, Paris,
Sept. 15/The New York Times, 9-16:3.

Mochtar Kusumaatmadja
Foreign Minister of Indonesia

3

[On the Vietnam-Cambodia conflict]: Basically the Cambodian problem is at least four, maybe five, problems rolled into one. [First, it is a conflict between the Vietnamese and Cambodians as people. Second,] it is an attempt on the part of the Vietnamese Communist Party to be the party of the whole of Indochina. Third, it is a problem between Vietnam and Cambodia for hegemony in that part of southeast Asia. And then you have the fourth problem, and this is how it is dealt with at the United Nations: as the Socialist Republic of Vietnam attacking an independent country. If you add a big-power dimension to it, you have five big problems. These problems will have to be solved one by one.

Interview, Jakarta/The New York Times, 2-14:6.

Yasuhiro Nakasone
Prime Minister of Japan

4

[On foreign criticism of Japan's international economic policies]: There is nothing as shameful as being called unfair in international society . . . In international relations, if we do not maintain manners of fair play, we have failed as internationalists. I am trying to implant that consciousness in Japanese minds . . . We have become an [economic] presence which has a great impact on the world whether we desire it or not. We are the country that received the greatest benefits of free trade in becoming a great economic power. That . . . means that we must exercise responsibility in line with that

(YASUHIRO NAKASONE)

power and return the [favor of] the benefits we received to poor countries that are now in a developing stage.

Interview, Tokyo, Aug. 1/
Los Angeles Times, 8-2:(I)1,8.

1

[Saying Japan takes peace and security too much for granted]: We used to think security was free, like air or water. Now we know neither air nor water is free, and neither is security.

The Christian Science Monitor, 8-14:1.

2

Since the end of [World War II], Japan has profoundly regretted the ultra-nationalism and militarism it unleashed [during that war], and the untold suffering the war inflicted upon peoples around the world and, indeed, upon its own people. Having suffered the scourge of war and the atomic bomb, the Japanese people will never again permit the revival of militarism on their soil.

At University of International Business and Economics,
Peking, Sept. 4/The New York Times, 9-5:8.

Richard M. Nixon
Former President of the United States

3

[On China's experiment with capitalist economic techniques]: It is not for me, or for others in America, to tell China what its economic system should be. What the people of China want will not be in all respects the same as what the people of the United States would want. But in some respects it will be the same. The bottom-line test of any economic system, as you know better than I, is whether it works.

At United Nations, New York,
Oct. 23/Los Angeles Times, 10-24:(I)14.

308

---

stroy the very core of the international free trading system. None of us wants to see protectionist trade wars, but if it comes to that, the United States is one of the few nations with the natural resources and the domestic economic strength to go it alone. Japan is not in such a position.

Before Executive Managers' Association of Japan,
Tokyo, Jan. 21/Los Angeles Times, 1-22:(IV)1.

Ronald Reagan
President of the United States

5

The Philippines—the United States certainly has a close relationship and alliance over the years, and we've got a good relationship with President Marcos. Now, we realize there is an opposition party that we believe is also pledged to democracy. We also are aware that there is another element in the Philippines that has Communist support and backing. What we are hopeful of is that the democratic processes will take place, and even if there is a change of party there it would be that opposition faction which is still democratic in its principles. I think it would be a disaster for all of us if, out of the friction between those two parties, the third element, the Communist element, should get in, because we know that their result is always totalitarian.

Interview, Washington,
Feb. 11/The New York Times, 2-12:6.

William Piez
Minister-Counselor for Economic Affairs,
United States Embassy, Tokyo

4

The huge trade imbalance between our two countries [the U.S. and Japan] threatens to de-

6

Today the Vietnamese Communists can celebrate the transformation of their nation into one of the poorest countries on earth. They can celebrate the creation of new Vietnamese gulags, 10 years of torture and forced relocations and the flight of nearly a million refugees and boat people. After a prolonged season in hell, the memory of freedom still survives. The young children may have known only the darkness of Communist tyranny, but even they have parents and older relatives who tell them of South Vietnam before the fall and bring a ray of hope into their lives. And 10 years later, the people for whom our brave American soldiers fought and died and sacrificed are still profoundly grateful.

At Republican fund-raising luncheon, Birmingham, Ala.,
June 6/The New York Times, 6-7:3.

(RONALD REAGAN)

1

[On the Soviet military intervention in Afghanistan]: It is clear that the Afghan spirit of independence cannot be crushed, that continued war will only mean more bloodshed, and that only a political solution is possible. The Soviets claim that they, too, believe in a negotiated settlement. I will be asking [Soviet] General Secretary [Mikhail] Gorbachev in Geneva whether, if that is so, he is willing to address the crucial issue: withdrawal of the more than 100,000 Soviet troops in Afghanistan and the restoration of that country's independence and non-alignment. The way to solve regional problems is through dialogue and negotiations, not invasion and occupation.

Interview, Oct. 21/
The New York Times, 10-24:8.

Jovito S. Salonga
A leader of opposition to
Philippine President Ferdinand Marcos

2

[U.S.] President Reagan has got to change his view of Marcos. He thinks the only alternative to Marcos is the Communists, and I am not a Communist. Marcos is in no position to do anything any more for the Philippines.

Honolulu, Jan. 17/
Los Angeles Times, 1-18:(I)10.

3

I am a moderate. I have put out a Liberal Party program of government which seeks the establishment of a just, truly democratic and pluralist society in the Philippines. I'm not in favor of the predominance of any one ideology, but I believe in the need to lift up the masses since 80 per cent of our people are now living below the poverty level . . . Only 81 families control the wealth of the nation. So from the economic point of view, I may be considered a little left of center . . . The Communist threat is important only because of the military abuses, the abuse of power, the excesses and the abuses of the Marcos regime. If the underlying social and economic causes are attended to by a democratic government, the Communist threat will subside.

Interview, Honolulu, Jan. 17/
The Christian Science Monitor, 1-21:12,13.

4

[On the gain in strength of the Communist New People's Army in the Philippines]: Social injustice, corruption and abuse of power is what it's about. Eighty-five per cent of all Philippine children suffer some sort of malnutrition. The rich-poor gap is so huge that about 80 families control most of the country's wealth. To the peasant who can't go any lower, the NPA seems a good alternative.

U.S. News & World Report, 4-15:33.

George P. Shultz
Secretary of State
of the United States

5

[On the Soviet armed intervention in Afghanistan]: We do sympathize with the freedom fighters [against the Soviets] in Afghanistan, and we provide humanitarian aid. We're very much in support of that—the kind of resistance they're putting up. The point is, there is a potential solution to Afghanistan, and it is that the Soviet Union withdraw its forces, that a government get established there that represents the people of Afghanistan, and that provisions be made so that the large number of refugees come back without prejudice to their condition.

Broadcast interview/
"Meet the Press," NBC-TV, 1-13.

6

[On New Zealand's decision not to allow U.S. ships carrying nuclear weapons into its ports]: New Zealand made a decision. We are sorry about that. We have great affection for the people of New Zealand, but we also remind them that those who value freedom have to be willing and prepared to defend it.

To reporters, Washington,
Feb. 6/The New York Times, 2-7:4.

7

A sense of Pacific community is emerging. There is an expanding practice of regional consultation, and a developing sense of common interest in regional security. In this sense, a

WHAT THEY SAID IN 1985

(GEORGE P. SHULTZ)

decade after [the war in] Vietnam, the United States has more than restored its position in Asia.

Before Senate Foreign Relations Committee,
Washington/Los Angeles Times, 4-29:(I)7.

1

[Criticizing New Zealand's decision not to allow U.S. ships carrying nuclear weapons into its ports]: If New Zealand's objective was to enhance specific security and reduce the nuclear danger, it has acted against its own interests. By adding a new element of risk and uncertainty, New Zealand has weakened regional stability, one of the most important links in the effort to prevent nuclear war. And the erosion of Western unity only weakens the Western position and the chances for success in arms control . . . We cannot allow the enemies of our way of life [such as the Soviet Union] to attack each ally one by one in the hope that we will be divided and thus incapable of a coordinated response. Our differences with New Zealand are specific and immediate. Yet they raise the most basic questions about alliances and about alliance responsibilities in the modern world . . . If one partner is unwilling to make these sacrifices, others will wonder why they should carry their share of the burden. The result may be the gradual erosion of popular commitment to the common cause.

At East-West Center, University of Hawaii,
July 17/The New York Times, 7-18:4.

Norodom Sihanouk
Former Chief of State of Cambodia

2

[On his fight against Vietnamese occupation of Cambodia]: We have courageous soldiers, but they cannot win. My allies in the coalition are unrealistic when they talk about defeating the Vietnamese. That does not mean I am ready to give up the resistance; it is our duty to fight. The U.S. House Foreign Affairs Committee has decided to give us $5-million, but it's too late. The Soviets spend the equivalent of $4-million to $5-million a day to help the Vietnamese. I see the

future of my country as very bleak, very black . . . The only thing the Vietnamese want now is to get me in Phnom Penh to cooperate with them like a kind of Marshal Petain. But I am not a quisling. I will not serve them. My people are proud people. They want Cambodia to be Cambodia—not to be Chinese, not to be Vietnamese, not to be Thai, not to be Soviet or American, but to be Cambodia, Cambodge, le Cambodge.

Interview, Peking/
Newsweek, 4-22:37.

3

[On why he is working with the Cambodian Communist Khmer Rouge]: I love my people and I love my country. But I have to be realistic; I cannot be blind to facts. As a Buddhist, I must get rid of hatred and vengeance. By staying with the Khmer Rouge, I try to persuade them not to create more sufferings for my people. If I decide to fight them or denounce them, I can have no influence, no opportunity to persuade them to deal reasonably with the Cambodian people.

Interview, Pyongyang, North Korea,
June 10/The New York Times,
6-11:3.

Hiroshi Takeuchi
Research director,
Long-Term Credit Bank of Japan

4

Japan is very isolated in Asia in ethics. Asians say Japanese are like a banana: Their face is yellow but their heart is white. An Indonesian complained to me that when the NHK Philharmonic [of Japan] came to Indonesia and played Beethoven—yes, it did give the impression that standards are high in Japan. But he told me that when Indonesians want to hear Beethoven, they will invite an orchestra from the Netherlands. "If the NHK Philharmonic visits, naturally it would play Japanese, Korean or Chinese music, we think," he said. "But you Japanese are white at heart" . . . They think we are siding with the United States and Europe and neglecting Asia.

Los Angeles Times, 8-8:(I)14.

Margaret Thatcher
Prime Minister of the United Kingdom

1

[Criticizing New Zealand's refusal to permit allied ships carrying nuclear weapons into its ports]: All of our ships are seconded to NATO. At any moment's notice they might be instructed to take up NATO positions, and therefore they must carry whatever is appropriate to their NATO task. And I have no intention whatsoever of revealing whether or not a nuclear armament is part of their weaponry aboard any particular ship. And, therefore, I hope they would not ask whether they are carrying them, [and] would accept, if they asked, that we would not say. I should be very disappointed if our naval ships cannot visit New Zealand.

News conference, Washington,
Feb. 21/The New York Times, 2-22:6.

Jean-Marie Tjibaou
Leader, Kanak Socialist National
Liberation Front of New Caledonia

2

[Calling for independence from France for New Caledonia]: [French President] Francois Mitterrand holds in his hand the ample flag of France. He is colonizing us. Our profound wish is for Mr. Mitterrand to take away the flag and to restore to us the legitimacy that we claim for ourselves.

News conference, Noumea, New Caledonia,
Jan. 18/The New York Times, 1-19:3.

John W. Vessey, Jr.
General, United States Army;
Chairman, Joint Chiefs of Staff

3

My visit [to China] has come at a time when our two nations are working to preserve and strengthen a peaceful environment [in Asia and the world]. In my talks with General Yang [Dezhi, Chief of the General Staff of the Chinese Forces], we found that there is much to agree on; as Defense Minister Zhang Aiping has said, our mutual goal is to make the Pacific region truly pacific, truly peaceful. It is important for all to

know that our military ties are designed to promote peace and understanding, and threaten no third party.

At banquet, Peking, Jan. 14/
The New York Times, 1-15:3.

Vernon A. Walters
United States Ambassador/Permanent
Representative to the United Nations

4

When American bombs were falling everywhere in Vietnam, when there was fighting in every village, when all the young men were drafted into the South Vietnamese Army, there were no boat people [Vietnamese fleeing the country on rickety boats]. It took the coming of a Communist government in Saigon to drive two million people to the sea in open boats.

Interview, United Nations, New York/
The New York Times, 5-31:6.

John C. Whitehead
Deputy Secretary of State
of the United States

5

[On Soviet intervention in Afghanistan]: Afghan school curricula have been revised to include Marxist-Leninist ideology. Revised history books written by Soviet scholars have been introduced. Afghan professors have been replaced with those from Communist countries. The intent is clear: Moscow seeks to obliterate Afghan cultural values from the minds of the country's youth and to substitute a made-in-Moscow view of the world.

Before Washington World Affairs Council,
Washington, Dec. 13/The New York Times, 12-14:6.

Heydn Williams
President,
Asia Foundation

6

The impact of China's trade is already being felt in the Pacific region. It is growing with the United States, Japan, Korea, Southeast Asia and Australia. It is also a potential major source of

(HEYDN WILLIAMS)

energy—coal and oil—and a market for foreign imports. If its current policy directions are maintained, it will inevitably become a major player in Pacific economic affairs... It would appear the Chinese experience with Marxism as an economic doctrine has been less than successful. China is now pursuing policies to encourage private initiatives and enterprise. It is opening free economic zones and inviting joint ventures with western capitalists. There is no sign, however, that Marxism as a political ideology is being abandoned.

Interview/
USA Today, 10-9:(A)11.

Paul D. Wolfowitz
Assistant Secretary
for East Asia and Pacific Affairs,
Department of State of the United States

1

[On the unrest in the Philippines]: While military reform is essential, the Communist insurgency cannot be combated effectively without also addressing the political and economic problems that the Communists exploit. The best antidote to Communism is democracy.

At National Defense University, Honolulu,
Feb. 22/The Washington Post, 2-23:(A)11.

2

[Criticizing New Zealand's decision not to allow U.S. ships carrying nuclear weapons to enter its ports]: The American public will not long support commitments and alliances that protect others, if those others will not uphold their own responsibilities. New Zealand's refusal to allow access to their ports for our ships confronts us with such a situation today. Ironically, the effect of New Zealand's action, small though it may be, is exactly opposite to its announced purpose of reducing the risk of nuclear war. Without access to ports and the surface-ship deployments that access supports, we cannot maintain the naval presence in the Pacific that helps to deter war and preserve the peace. And we can't go around advertising which of those ships has nuclear weapons on board, or when they do and when they don't. With words, New Zealand assures us that it remains committed to ANZUS. But by its deeds, New Zealand has effectively curtailed its operational role in ANZUS. A military alliance has little meaning without military cooperation. New Zealand can't have it both ways.

At National Defense University, Honolulu,
Feb. 22/The New York Times, 2-27:7.

Mohammed Zia ul-Haq
President of Pakistan

3

[On when he will lift martial law]: After a few months of the coming into being of both houses of Parliament, and when I, in consultation with the new government and the Prime Minister, feel that the government is strong and stable enough, steady enough, to throw away the crutches, and there will no longer [be the need] for the umbrella of martial law. It has to be a gradual process. It cannot be a switch-on, switch-off exercise. But we are very hopeful that, if all goes well and we're able to have this transition and change over from the military to the civilians in a smooth and steady manner, it will be lifted in a few months.

Interview, Rawalpindi/
The Christian Science Monitor, 3-1:1.

4

[Saying his country would agree to banning the spread of nuclear weapons if India does the same]: Let's have an even-handed policy from international agencies and also from countries like the United States to deal with India and Pakistan on the same plane. Pakistan's offer is that if India agrees to sign a nuclear non-proliferation treaty, we will be signing one minute before... Let's have mutual inspection of both nuclear installations, and if that is not acceptable, let's have a bilateral nuclear non-proliferation treaty, and if that is not acceptable, an international agreement. What's good for the goose is good for the gander. Why should Pakistan alone be put on the spot?

Interview, United Nations, New York,
Oct. 20/The New York Times, 10-21:6.

Gerry Adams
*Head of Sinn Fein party
(Northern Ireland)*

1

Ireland does not stop at a British border. No Irish institution, government or otherwise, has the right to sign any treaty with the British which encroaches on Irish sovereignty [in Northern Ireland]. Northern Protestants have as much right as any other section of the Irish people to shape or veto the shape of any future independent Irish society; but Unionists have absolutely no right to veto that society's right to national self-determination.

*At Sinn Fein party conference,
Dublin, Ireland,
Nov. 3/The New York Times,
11-4:5.*

Georgi A. Arbatov
*Director, Soviet Institute of
U.S.A. and Canadian Affairs*

2

[On changes coming in the Soviet Union]: If you read our [news] papers, there is much more discussion on all things, including criticism of very highly placed people, even members of the Cabinet. Our goal is to make everything much more controlled by the public. This is the beginning of a process which will go on and will be very important. One of our goals is what we call development of Socialist Democracy, but this is not to develop our society by your [Western] standards. Socialist Democracy will include wide discussions of the country's really vital problems, criticism, self-criticism, and much broader access of people at large to what is being done by the government on all levels . . . There will be very serious changes [in the economy]. In some respects maybe even revolutionary changes, a word used not by [Soviet leader Mikhail] Gorbachev but by some leading personalities in our Party. We won't return to private ownership, but we will make collective ownership work in a better way. We will make everybody—from a minister to a worker—more dependent on the quality and quantity of his

work for what he gets. It's a system of material incentives and also of punishments.

*Interview, San Francisco/
Los Angeles Times,
9-27:(I)24.*

John Ashworth
*Vice chancellor, University of Salford
(England); Member of committees advising
the British Prime Minister on technology*

3

. . . there's considerable enthusiasm at the moment among Common Market governments for an expanded European space program. As far as other kinds of technology are concerned, my impression is that there isn't much political will in Europe to do anything, even though it's becoming obvious even to the French—not to mention the British and Germans—that Europe's technological competitiveness is eroding at an alarming rate.

*Interview, Salford, England/
U.S. News & World Report,
5-27:47.*

Peter Barry
Foreign Minister of Ireland

4

[Criticizing Americans who support Noraid, an organization providing funds to Northern Ireland factions involved in violence in their effort to separate from England]: . . the Irish and British governments are engaged in a serious common effort to find a way which would create progress toward lasting peace, stability and reconciliation in Ireland . . . It is regrettable that we cannot say the same for that tiny minority of Noraid supporters whose visit here has provided a focus, not for peace or reconciliation, but only for hatred and destruction. I am certain that I can speak for the overwhelming majority of nationalists and unionists when I say: "The people have suffered too much; too many are dead, too many are maimed; too many young people are in jail. Do us all a favor and go home."

Aug. 9/The Washington Post, 8-13:(A)16.

Anthony Beaumont-Dark
Member of British Parliament

[Criticizing Prince Charles for commenting on racial problems in Britain]: If he wants to inherit a united kingdom, he should remember that politics is this side of the barrier—and royalty is on the other.

U.S. News & World Report, 11-4:12.

1

Seweryn Bialer
Authority on the Soviet Union,
Columbia University

[On new, and younger, Soviet leader Mikhail Gorbachev]: Even before Gorbachev was selected, there was already a cult of personality around him, the hope that he would be able to get the Soviet Union moving again and to keep it moving. In my opinion, that was as important a factor in his quick victory as the votes of loyalty he got from the Politburo. It was a question of the mood of the elite. They needed somebody like him, not another member of the Old Guard. At the same time, Gorbachev is a very good tactician. It was crucial to his success that a year ago, when [the late Soviet leader Konstantin] Chernenko was selected, Gorbachev became his close ally and never offended the others in the Old Guard.

Time, 3-25:22.

2

Alexandr Bovin
Member, Central Auditing Commission
of the Soviet Union

If you look at Western society, you see that the driving motor is private property: This is mine. This is yours. And I want mine to be greater. Not a bad motor, actually. But it seems to me as a Communist, as a Marxist, that this system of private property is disappearing. Adam Smith would probably roll over in his grave if he could see how capitalism has evolved. Even [U.S. President] Ronald Reagan's attempt to retreat to the 19th century to unregulated, laissez-faire capitalism is unlikely to succeed. The essence of our [Soviet] revolution was to break up this traditional motor of society and re-

place it with an entirely new motor that will, in the end, produce a more just society. This motor is communal property. Not yours. Not mine. But ours. A great achievement of our revolution was that it brought security of life to all the people. Here [in the Soviet Union] you'll never be cast out by society. You'll always have work. You'll always have a doctor. Your children will always be able to have an education. Here you find confidence in society and in the future.

Interview/U.S. News & World Report, 7-29:42.

Heinz Brahm
Director, Federal Institute for Eastern
and International Studies (West Germany)

[On Mikhail Gorbachev, new Soviet leader, who is younger than previous Soviet top men]: We can expect a new charm offensive toward Western Europe. We may find ourselves longing for the days of the old men who didn't talk very much.

Time, 3-25:18.

4

Willy Brandt
Chairman,
Social Democratic Party of West Germany;
Former Chancellor of West Germany

[Criticizing U.S. President Reagan's planned visit, at the invitation of Chancellor Helmut Kohl, to a German cemetery where Nazi SS officers are buried]: The reconciliation between peoples that were once enemies is a long, even long-endangered process which cannot be ordered on command or arranged, like a TV event . . . What has been done here through irresponsible, publicity-seeking and historically inappropriate planning of the visit is shattering. With [former Chancellor] Helmut Schmidt this would not have happened, nor with me, either.

News conference, April 29/
The New York Times, 4-30.5.

5

[On East and West Germany]: Both states, loyal to their alliances, which will exist for the foreseeable future, should see a common duty.

3

6

(WILLY BRANDT)

They should use the chances presented by their proximity [to each other] to make a contribution to replacing the present fruitless confrontation of those alliances by a partnership of security.

At luncheon in his honor, East Berlin,
Sept. 19/Los Angeles Times, 9-20:(I)4.

Fernand Braudel
French historian

1

I believe Europe is condemned, for a while anyway. The center of world strength is moving toward the countries that are not worn out by power. England is worn out. So is France, to a lesser degree. Europe would only have been able to pull itself together, to reinvigorate itself, if it had somehow been linked to the Eastern bloc. Europe was murdered by both the Soviet and U.S. economies. Its best chance for survival is to unite resources and territory into a single entity.

Interview/World Press Review, March:32.

Harold Brooks-Baker
Publishing director,
"Burke's Peerage"

2

[On the young members of the British Royal Family]: This is the first group of royals really to work, to study at university, to be people in their own right and not be overshadowed by their mothers and fathers. In the past, the brothers and sisters of whoever was on the throne, and their children, were never visible to the outside world. They tended not to be well educated and lived in a cloistered world. This is the first time in history that royals are becoming normal rich people, not locked away in the tower. They're leading an upper-class existence—working, having affairs, going skiing and surfing.

The Washington Post, 2-21:(D)4.

Zbigniew Bujak
Leader, Solidarity
(banned independent Polish trade union)

3

We [Solidarity] now have about 50,000 to 70,000 activists who participate in our work di-

rectly. Those who work with us from time to time number about 200,000 to 250,000. Poland never had more people engaged in conspiracy. . . . I am ready for a long struggle, a fight which may end up in anything, even jail. I expect it to last 10 to 15 years. We are living in a country in which there is no normal life, so insane gestures must be performed in order to win something. [But] something will certainly move. I am convinced I am going to see it.

Interview/Newsweek, 9-2:33.

Arthur F. Burns
United States Ambassador
to West Germany

4

I think there is a yearning in the German soul for reunification [of East and West Germany]—not often articulated clearly, but the yearning is there. In the U.S. we have always been a patriotic people, and there has been a strong revival of patriotism in America in recent years. This last summer, going back to my farm in Vermont, in a small village, there were more American flags flying than I have seen at any time in the past 50 years. Where are the flags flying from German homes? [There is] a certain loss of identity on the part of the German people. Well, that causes anguish to the soul.

Interview, Bonn/
The Christian Science Monitor, 3-19:13.

Fidel Castro
President of Cuba

5

After World War II, the Soviet Union was surrounded by dozens and dozens of nuclear bases—in Europe, the Middle East, Turkey, which lies on the Soviet border, the Indian Ocean, Japan and other Oriental countries—and by military fleets near its coasts in the Mediterranean, the Indian Ocean, the Pacific Ocean. No one can deny these facts. It was surrounded by nuclear bombers, nuclear submarines, military bases, spy bases, electronic installations—a country totally surrounded. How can the Soviet Union be accused of warmongering and aggressive attitudes in the face of these historical realities? How can we not explain the Soviet Union's

(FIDEL CASTRO)

highly sensitive reactions regarding anything that occurs near its territory? Who is historically responsible for this lack of trust on the part of the Soviets? How can international politics be explained so simplistically?

Interview, Havana/Playboy, August:177.

Juan Luis Cebrian
Editor, "El Pais" (Spain)

[On Spain's emergence over the past 10 years as a democracy after a long-time dictatorship]: It is very difficult to explain what it means for a country to lose its fears, not to be afraid to participate, to give opinions, to walk in the streets . . . All the Spanish people, even the Spaniards of the regime [of the dictatorship]—and I know, because my father was a man of the regime—all of us had fear of expressing ourselves for many, many years. The losing of fear is very, very strange to explain. You have to live under it to feel it.

Interview/Los Angeles Times, 11-8:(I)14.

1

Joe Clark
Minister of External Affairs of Canada

[Criticizing the Soviet Union for not adhering to provisions of the Helsinki human-rights agreements]: We simply do not believe that any government represented here is so weak and should feel so insecure that it must treat as criminals or traitors those individuals who believe that we all meant what we said in the Final Act [the rights accords]. We take this occasion to affirm that failure to implement provisions dealing with human rights is related directly to progress on other provisions.

*At meeting commemorating 10th anniversary
of Helsinki agreements, Helsinki, Finland, July 31/
Los Angeles Times, 8-1:(I)8.*

2

Michael Eaton
*Chief spokesman,
National Coal Board (Britain)*

[On the collapsing year-long British coal miners strike]: Our job is to run an effective

3

coal-mining industry, and that we shall do. Our men are frankly fed up with being in battle. They would like to return to work, to what they have to do, then go home and live a normal life. I don't think they will welcome the statements made by [coal union president Arthur] Scargill about the dispute continuing.

London, March 3/The New York Times, 3-4:8.

Laurent Fabius
Premier of France

Is there really a trend toward conservatism [in the world]? Or is there simply a trend against the people who happened to be in office during the economic crisis—between 1975 and 1982—and [who] were often socialists or social democrats? In Germany, for example, you had [Chancellor] Helmut Schmidt, and he was beaten. In periods of difficulty there is a feeling of selfishness. Maybe the traditional way the social democrats and socialists had of intervening, with its emphasis on the state, was a bit too heavy. Our ways of thinking about our problems had to be questioned. It is true in France and it is true across Western Europe. But I do not think it is going to be a permanent tendency.

Interview, Paris/Time, 3-25:51.

4

[Criticizing the efforts of the environmental group Greenpeace to hamper France's nuclear-weapons testing]: The question is to know whether Greenpeace is an organization known, as was the case four or five years ago, for its honorable struggle to protect baby seals, or is it an organization that claims to dictate a defense policy to France.

*Broadcast interview, Paris,
Sept. 4/The New York Times, 9-5:7.*

5

Lawrence Freedman
*Head of war studies,
King's College, University of London*

[On the European attitude toward U.S. President Reagan's proposed space defense system, which he claims could eliminate the usefulness

6

of nuclear weapons]: There's no doubt about his sincerity. That's what makes it so difficult. But the vision he offers is one that makes Europeans uncomfortable. We don't believe in it. The only way your country [the U.S.] can be hurt is with nuclear weapons. That's not true in Europe. If war came, the conventional side could dominate. And rightly or wrongly, nuclear weapons have been one of the ways that threat has been held back.

Interview/The New York Times, 5-13:6.

Evan G. Galbraith
United States Ambassador to France

1

[On his imminent departure as Ambassador]: I got along well with the [French] government here, people who know I don't approve of social-ism. If there were complaints about me saying negative things about the Communists while they were still in the government, well, I think I did the Communists a substantial disservice, and I'm glad.

Interview, Paris/The New York Times, 2-13:12.

Paolo Garimberti
Editor, "La Stampa," Rome

2

The [Italian] Communist [Party's] problem is simply that today Italian voters understand that there are alternatives to Communist and Chris-tian Democratic rule. That has left the Commu-nists isolated and alone. Until they can find a way of forging alliances with the Socialists, whom they now just attack, or some other natu-ral political ally, they will remain in the wilder-ness.

The Washington Post, 7-25:(A)28.

Hans-Dietrich Genscher
Foreign Minister of West Germany

3

[Criticizing the Soviet Union for not adhering to provisions of the Helsinki human-rights agreements]: We do not and shall not remain si-lent when human rights are infringed. We shall not look the other way when people, the name-

less as well as the well-known ones, have to suf-fer persecution and unfair treatment for invoking promises made in the Final Act [the rights ac-cords]. The flow of goods and services and en-ergy between countries has multiplied. In a few hours one can travel from one end of the Conti-nent to the other. But innumerable people are still unable to meet each other. It is technically possible to telephone all corners of the globe from one's living-room, and to receive television pictures from all continents. But the free flow of information between Europeans in West and East is still not guaranteed.

At meeting commemorating 10th anniversary of Helsinki agreements, Helsinki, Finland, July 31/ Los Angeles Times, 8-1:(I)8.

Jozef Cardinal Glemp
Roman Catholic Primate of Poland

4

[Criticizing the Polish government for being anti-religion]: How can one build the future when there are efforts to erase from it the values that are most important, those connected with belief in God? The believer who is to build the future of the atheistic homeland feels like some-body who is cutting the tree he is sitting on out from under him for the good of some branch that grows from the side.

Sermon, Czestochowa, Poland, Aug. 26/The Washington Post, 8-27:(A)10.

Barry M. Goldwater
United States Senator, R-Arizona

5

The Russians don't want to go to war with us. Russia has always been our ally, and we theirs. She will fight to the death for her homeland, but it is very rare that she wanders out. When she does, she gets in trouble—like the trouble she's in now with Afghanistan, Red China and Poland.

Interview/Los Angeles Herald Examiner, 1-13:(A)15.

Felipe Gonzalez
Prime Minister of Spain

6

[On Spain's entry into the Common Market]: It means the culmination of a struggle of mil-

(FELIPE GONZALEZ)

lions of Spaniards who have identified freedom and democracy with integration into Western Europe . . . Without doubt, the greatest benefit of Community membership will be the political transition, in the most noble sense, toward ending more than 150 years of isolation.

Interview/The New York Times, 7-8:5.

Mikhail S. Gorbachev
*General Secretary, Communist Party
of the Soviet Union*

1

Satisfying the growing requirements of the Soviet people, improving the conditions of their work and life, have always been and remain the major concerns of the Party and the state. The development of the initiative and creative endeavor of the masses, strict observance of law and order, consolidation of labor, state and Party discipline will continue to remain in the center of attention. We will support, encourage and elevate in all ways those who by deeds, practical results, rather than by words, show their honest and conscientious attitude toward civic duty. We shall fight any manifestations of showiness and idle talk, swagger and irresponsibility, everything that contradicts socialist norms of life.

Eulogy for late Soviet leader Konstantin Chernenko, Moscow, March 13/The New York Times, 3-14:6.

2

More than once we have expressed readiness to dissolve the Warsaw [Pact] treaty if NATO should agree to respond in kind. This principled stand continues to be fully valid.

At ceremony extending Warsaw Pact, Warsaw/Time, 5-6:35.

3

One cannot help seeing that difficulties in [Soviet] economic development began to be felt in the early 1970s. The main reason was that we did not display in time perseverance in reshaping the structural policy, management forms and methods, the very psychology of economic activity . . . One must admit that the quality, the

318

technical and economic standard of [Soviet] products remains a vulnerable element of the economy. All this inflicts serious social, economic, moral and political damage. Even products put in the highest quality class in the Soviet Union sometimes pale in comparison with the best world models.

At meeting on science and technology, Moscow, June 11/The New York Times, 6-12:10.

4

It is often asserted in the West that it would take the U.S.S.R. 50 to 100 years to restore all that had been destroyed as a result of the Fascist invasion [in World War II]. Having restored their national economy in the shortest possible time, the Soviet people did what would have seemed the impossible. But the fact remains that, after the [Russian] Revolution, we were forced to spend almost two decades, if not more, on wars and reconstruction. Under those arduous conditions, using our system's potential, we have succeeded in making the Soviet Union a major world power. This has attested to the strength and the immense capabilities of socialism. There are also difficulties of a different nature due to our own shortcomings and deficiencies. We make no secret of this. Sometimes we do not work well enough. We have not yet learned proper managerial skills as is required by a modern economy. The imperative of our time is to decisively improve the state of things.

Interview, Moscow/Time, 9-9:24.

5

We are planning in the next 15 years to create an economic potential approximately in equal scale to what had been accumulated throughout the previous [68] years of Soviet government and to increase almost two-fold the national income and industrial output. Labor productivity is to go up 130 per cent to 150 per cent [by the end of the century]. This will help double the volume of resources directed at meeting the requirements of the people . . . This is a program of struggle for peace and progress. It is aimed at transformations of a truly historical scale—the implementation of a new technical reconstruction of the economy . . . It is noteworthy that, in the new five-year plan period, [an] increase in the na-

(MIKHAIL S. GORBACHEV)

tional income and the output of all branches of material production will be achieved entirely, for the first time, by raising labor productivity. Comrades, however inspiring the drafted plans may be, the target set can be achieved only by strenuous and highly efficient work.

Before Soviet Communist Party Central Committee, Moscow, Oct. 15/Los Angeles Times, 10-16:(I)20.

and small, from close up and from a distance. They watch, just waiting for some sort of crack to appear in the Soviet leadership. The unanimous opinion of the Politburo is this: Once again, we, the Central Committee and the Politburo, will not give our political enemies satisfaction on that count.

Announcing the selection of Mikhail Gorbachev as new Soviet leader, before Soviet Communist Party Central Committee, Moscow, March 11/ The New York Times, 3-19:5.

1

[On foreign criticism of discrimination against Jews in the Soviet Union]: Jews are a part of the Soviet people. They are fine people. They contribute a lot to disarmament. They are very talented people and they are very valued in the Soviet Union. The problem—the so-called [discrimination] problem—in the Soviet Union does not exist. Perhaps this problem only exists with those who would like to mar the relations with us, who cast their doubts and aspersions.

To U.S. civil-rights leader Jesse Jackson, Geneva, Nov. 19/The Washington Post, 11-20:(A)1.

Lord Gowrie
Member, British House of Lords

2

[Britain's] national fortunes depend on getting on with the hard job of earning our living, winning back lost markets at home and abroad, and not paying ourselves more than we earn. And that's more a matter for industry of all kinds than for government. What the government can and must do is create the conditions in which industry and commerce can prosper. We must also do all we can to mitigate the social and personal costs of the overdue changes through which our economy is passing.

In House of Lords, London, Jan. 23/The New York Times, 1-24:4.

Andrei A. Gromyko
Foreign Minister of the Soviet Union

3

We live in a world in which, figuratively speaking, various telescopes are aimed at the Soviet Union, and they are not a few of them, big

Gary Hart
United States Senator, D-Colorado

4

In every NATO country but one, defense is a contentious issue, not only among politicians but also among the citizens. There is only one exception, one country where there is a broad political consensus behind defense. It is France. France is also the only NATO nation where defense is clearly seen as *national* defense, defense that is important to every Frenchman's security. Why is this so? In most NATO nations, defense is seen less in terms of national defense than in terms of doing what America wants. This is, in part, a legacy from the immediate post-war period, when the United States naturally emerged as the leader of the alliance. Today, we continue in that role to a larger degree than facts warrant. This contributes to the European perception that defense is to some degree a matter of "keeping Uncle Sam happy." This is something no citizenry can find very attractive. It suggests, at best, being patronized and having to live with it. The national feeling that should support a strong defense effort, as it does in France, instead works against it, because it sees defense as being foreign-controlled.

At University of Edinburgh, Scotland, Jan. 12/The Washington Post, 1-25:(A)22.

5

If our citizens believe the risk of war, especially nuclear war, is growing, and that NATO policies are contributing to that growth, they will begin to look for alternatives to NATO . . . Change is not a danger. The only danger is

(GARY HART)

freezing NATO in a rigid mold as the world changes around it.

At seminar of French Institute of Foreign Relations,
Paris, Jan. 15/Los Angeles Times 1-16:(I)5.

Arnold Horelick
Director, Rand/UCLA Center
for the Study of Soviet International Behavior

1

[On the death of Soviet leader Konstantin Chernenko and the installation of Mikhail Gorbachev, a younger and more personable man, as his successor]: The Soviets are becoming sensitive to the fact that all over the world the Soviet Union is perceived as a power in decline. The physical appearance of the leader seemed to reinforce this mood. Politically, it was extremely damaging both at home and abroad. I think Gorbachev will be very sensitive to that and will try to give the impression that the Soviet Union is on the move. Everyone is waiting for someone to appear on the Soviet side in whom you can invest some illusions.

Los Angeles Times, 3-12:(I)1.

John Hume
Leader, Social Democratic
and Labor Party of Northern Ireland

2

[On the Irish Republican Army's political wing, Sinn Fein]: As far as I am concerned, the differences between Sinn Fein and myself are very fundamental as long as they are wedded to a policy of violence—because their violence is mainly why the problem [of British control of Northern Ireland] is a lot worse.

Interview, Derry, Northern Ireland/
The Christian Science Monitor, 3-21:10.

Wojciech Jaruzelski
Prime Minister of Poland

3

[On Poland's worsening economy]: A grave, even brutal, dilemma is taking shape. We shall either get modernized, catch up with the times, improve the nation's material existence, and

320

strengthen our position in the socialist community, Europe and the world . . . or we shall remain behind, facing the threat of a degradation which, in social terms, would mean wretched pauperization.

At economic conference sponsored
by Polish Communist Party,
June/The Christian Science Monitor, 8-2:11.

4

[Calling for a large turnout in Polish national elections this fall]: It is no exaggeration to say that the whole world will again be watching Poland this October. Friends will do so with the hope that the voting will confirm the process of stabilization and consolidation of agreement among the Poles. They will not be disappointed. Foes will harbor opposite expectations. These will not materialize. We have demonstrated that Poland will not be a pawn in someone else's game. Once again we shall confirm this in the elections.

Before Central Committee, Polish Communist Party,
Warsaw/Los Angeles Times, 8-8:(I)10.

5

[Criticizing U.S. trade sanctions imposed on Poland to protest martial law there four years ago during labor unrest]: No matter what pressure is brought to bear on us, we shall never abandon our course. The right to judge is commonly usurped by those who in their own land want law and order to prevail, while in Poland they stake on anarchy and chaos.

At United Nations, New York,
Sept. 27/The New York Times,
9-28:5.

6

[On the Solidarity independent trade-union movement in Poland]: That chapter has been closed. The American public has been continuously misinformed about the real situation in Poland, including the origins of Solidarity and the destructive consequences for the stability of the nation. Solidarity was a very broad amalgamation, from Trotskyites to religious fanatics, who were joined by expediency and, temporarily, by their relationship to the state. This is why there

(WOJCIECH JARUZELSKI)

have been so many irresponsible actions that have threatened the nation's economy and brought it to the brink of destruction. National income dropped by close to 25 per cent. There was almost total ruin that had to be stopped.

Interview, New York/Time, 10-28:57.

Janos Kadar
First Secretary,
Communist Party of Hungary

1

There is a saying that a people lives in its language, and I believe that is particularly true of a country like Hungary. It owes much to it in its survival for 1,100 years. We must encourage our young people to use a human language and not just emulate those Western youngsters who can only chant "yeah, yeah!" I think we have had a little bit too much of that.

At Hungarian Communist Party Congress, Budapest,
March 25/The Christian Science Monitor, 3-26:12.

Yannis B. Kapsis
Foreign Minister of Greece

2

[Saying there is a Turkish menace to the Greek Aegean islands]: Do not hope for another fait accompli in the Aegean. Our message is very clear: If there is a military attempt [by Turkey], there will be a full-scale war. We prepare ourselves so that not an inch of our territory will fall to sudden attack to be put as a stake on the bargaining table [in Greece's dispute with Turkey over Cyprus].

Interview, Athens, Jan. 16/
The New York Times, 1-18:3.

George F. Kennan
Former United States Ambassador
to the Soviet Union

3

There is much about the Soviet Union that I don't like any more than anyone else does. It's a country in serious trouble, and it's not a proper model for any society. But I cannot go along with those who see the Soviet leadership as some monster devoid of all humanity. I get a little fed up being reminded that the Soviet leaders are not nice people. I think I know more about that than most people reminding me.

Interview/Esquire, January:73.

Edward M. Kennedy
United States Senator, D-Massachusetts

4

[Criticizing U.S. President Reagan's plan to visit a cemetery in Germany where Nazi SS officers are buried]: President Reagan made a mistake when he scheduled this visit and he will be making an even bigger mistake by refusing to cancel it. The trip to the Bitburg cemetery contradicts the important purpose of his visit [to Europe]. It opens old wounds at the expense of reconciliation.

Before the Senate, Washington,
April 27/Los Angeles Times, 4-28:(I)11.

Neil Kinnock
Leader, Labor Party of Britain

5

[On what he feels about Prime Minister Margaret Thatcher's government trying to limit the extent of the welfare state in Britain]: Anger. Occasionally enough to make me speechless. Because it's such a destructive act. It's immoral. And it's a real reduction in liberties. But it also is massively wasteful and inefficient. Margaret Thatcher wants to roll Britain back to the same place it was in during the 1930s; and there's no thought for the talent that will be lost, the unnecessary pain that will be inflicted, the preventable economic rundown that's bound to occur. . . Perhaps what's happening now is the fault of the previous generation. Perhaps they didn't tell enough people that those gains didn't fall out of the sky, that they had to be fought for, and that it requires all kinds of efforts to keep them intact. There's a dreadful historical lesson right now being taught the British people. They elected a government in complacency, thinking that no government would break the contract between the British people and the British government of sustaining certain standards of care and justice. But I always counsel myself: "Don't get mad—get even."

Interview, London/Mother Jones, January:24.

(NEIL KINNOCK)

1

The obligation foolishly accepted by the [British Prime Minister Margaret] Thatcher government of accommodating [U.S.] cruise [missiles] means that in the most basic question of life and death for my country, they have forsaken an essential residual independence. Every country must have some things which it keeps for itself. And I think the acceptance of the cruise, without any system of participation and control over its use, is a significant surrender of our basic independence. Now, I don't make that as a nationalistic argument. I make that as a democratic argument. Cruise raises the risks of nuclear war without increasing our security in any respect. It is a weapon that can only have first use, since the technology of "cruising" is utterly useless for retribution. So, thanks to Mrs. Thatcher's acquiescence, we now have this weapon on our soil whose only function is first use, and it is a weapon of continual threat and danger. It doesn't deter. But it *does* attract the possibility that southern England, where cruise is stationed, would be the target of pattern bombing, annihilatory bombing to be sure to take the missile [system] out.

Interview, London/Mother Jones, January:25.

2

[On new Soviet leader Mikhail Gorbachev]: [He is] sharp, straight, bright, and he enjoys an argument. That certainly was my experience in my 3 1/2 hours with him. What I liked is that he could take it as well as give it, and I think that bodes well for future developments, if we've got someone who's willing to put his cards on the table.

The Washington Post, 3-12:(A)20.

3

[Criticizing the British government's decision to join with the U.S. in developing a space defense system]: The project is deluded, destabilizing and dangerous. It is the British technologists that the United States wants, not British technology. Every day in her relations with [U.S.] President Reagan, Mrs. [Margaret] Thatcher makes herself less like the Prime Minister of Britain and more like the governor of the 51st state of the [U.S.] union.

Dec. 6/Los Angeles Times, 12-7:(I)18.

Jeane J. Kirkpatrick
Former United States Ambassador/
Permanent Representative to the United Nations

4

I believe that for the first time in the post-World War II period—probably the first time since Joseph Stalin consolidated power in the Soviet Union—there is a possibility that the Soviet political ruling elite will have somewhat different goals than they have had since the consolidation of Stalin's power. The reason is that there has been genuine generational change [with new, younger Soviet leader Mikhail Gorbachev]. In a closed society such as that in the Soviet Union, generational change offers one of the very few possibilities for authentic change in the society. That generational change is now taking place across a much broader swath of the Soviet elite than I think is often recognized. There is a possibility that we have today in the Soviet Union a leadership group with somewhat different goals than their predecessors. It's very important that we are sensitive to that possibility and that we keep open that question.

Interview/U.S. News & World Report, 9-9:46.

Henry A. Kissinger
Former Secretary of State of the United States

5

[Advising caution to those who predict a softer line from new Soviet leader Mikhail Gorbachev]: The first thing one has to remember is that you don't get to the head of the Politburo by being a choirboy.

U.S. News & World Report, 3-25:14.

Helmut Kohl
Chancellor of West Germany

6

Germany bears historical responsibility for the crimes of the Nazi tyranny. This responsibility is reflected not least in never-ending shame . . . We must not nor shall we ever forget the atrocities committed under the Hitler re-

(HELMUT KOHL)

gime, the mockery and destruction of all moral precepts, the systematic inhumanity of the Nazi dictatorship. A nation that abandons its history forsakes itself.

At ceremony on 40th anniversary of liberation of Bergen-Belsen concentration camp, Belsen, West Germany, April 21/Los Angeles Times, 4-22:(I)1.

1

It is not easy to explain everything [about the Nazi period] 40 years after the war, because two-thirds of the people now living in West Germany had not yet been born then. They have no personal experience and many speak about some of the events of that period as incomprehensible to them . . For too many, the reaction to the Nazi period is a big hole in our history. For many, the best way to react to the Nazi period is to deny history. You have to be able to take history's dark and its bright chapters. But I think our country has undergone a very great change. A new generation has grown up, most of whom are sensible, open-minded people.

Interview/USA Today, 4-23:(A)9.

2

We keep talking about the Japanese [economic] challenge. I don't think the Japanese are in any way brighter than we [in Europe] are. They only got used to getting up earlier in the last 10 years than we do, and they kept talking about the future while we talked about leisure. We must speak more about the future and get up earlier. What matters most is not our vacation, but how we can best safeguard our future. Then you will see that we have no reason to be afraid of the Japanese or the Americans.

Interview/USA Today, 4-23:(A)9.

3

[On criticism of U.S. President Reagan's planned visit to a Bitburg, West Germany, cemetery where Nazi soldiers and SS officers are buried]: I am grateful to the President of the United States for this noble gesture. I find it most regrettable that this great man, who is a friend of

the Germans, has encountered considerable domestic difficulties because of this envisaged noble gesture . . . Reconciliation is when we are capable of grieving over people without caring what nationality they are. We demonstrated that in Verdun, and we want to demonstrate that in Bitburg . . . Does it truly fall to us to judge people [those buried in that cemetery] who were involved in that [Nazi] injustice and lost their lives, while we respect the others who were perhaps no less involved but survived and have since then . . served the cause of freedom and our republic?

Before West German Parliament, Bonn, April 25/The Washington Post, 4-26:(A)30.

4

The picture of Germany today is like a picture taken with a flash camera. It is only the image of the moment. You cannot understand the Germans of the present if you do not see the Germans of the previous century: the Wilhelmian Germany, the First World War, the collapse of the empire, the first great attempt at establishing a republic . . . the confusion which resulted in [Adolf] Hitler's gaining power [and] the perversion of patriotism to nationalism. Our present situation as a divided country [also] puts us in an extremely unusual situation. The misery, the deaths and the suffering cannot be redeemed. What can be made good materially, we have tried to do. We will achieve more, in light of this history, if, to use a German expression, we each make sure our own steps are clean.

Interview/Los Angeles Times, 5-7:(I)12.

5

[On calls in the U.S. for removal of the American military presence in Europe]: There is indeed the facile question why 200 million Americans should protect 200 million Europeans against 200 million Russians. But . . . what Americans tend to forget is that their freedom, too, is being defended.

USA Today, 5-8:(A)8.

6

The political situation in Europe has never been better for America. Friends of [U.S.]

(HELMUT KOHL)

President Reagan hold power in London and in Bonn. President Francois Mitterrand of France is especially loyal on nuclear defense. The coalition ruling Italy is a reliable partner on all European affairs. The general position is optimal.

Interview, Bonn/Los Angeles Times, 11-10:(IV)2.

Jack Lang
Minister of Culture of France

[Blaming the policies of British Prime Minister Margaret Thatcher for the riot started by British fans at a soccer match in Brussels that resulted in many deaths and injuries]: If Britain's young hooligans are prone to such violence, it's because of the kind of economic system Thatcher has created that liquidates national companies and leaves thousands of young people with no hope.

TV broadcast, Paris, June 3/ Los Angeles Times, 6-5:(I)6.

1

[On the increase of foreign influence on European culture]: If there is a cultural invasion, it is not the United States or Japan or others who are responsible. It is the Europeans themselves and the French, above all. Do we or do we not have in ourselves the energy to create beautiful works, to invent beautiful things and to discover new scientific horizons?

Interview/The New York Times, 8-15:4.

2

Golo Mann
West German historian

I am not sure that the people of East Germany want to be governmentally unified with the Federal Republic [West Germany]. Their institutions are well established. The people might like to change a few things, but I believe that they would be happy if they could travel freely. Then they would probably keep their institutions as they are. We cannot go back. East Germany is now almost 40 years old. It is a functioning state, not a nest of unrest. It is not explosive like the Third Reich was.

Interview/World Press Review, November:34.

3

Martin McGuinness
Member, Northern Ireland Assembly

The primary cause of political instability, social injustice and violence [in Northern Ireland] is the British presence in our country. Settlements that ignore reality, that ignore history, that do not confront the real issue, are not solutions at all, but devices that enable Britain to refine its repression of republicans and its partition of Ireland.

At Sinn Fein party conference, Dublin, Ireland, Nov. 3/The New York Times, 11-4:5.

4

Roy Medvedev
Soviet dissident; Former member, Soviet Communist Party

There are major shortcomings in almost all aspects of Soviet life. But from my point of view, the most serious shortcoming is the lack of free expression here, even free expression of Communist ideas. This is an authoritarian system in which decisions adopted today are the only truth. If, for example, a decision is taken to remove a political leader, that's today's truth, and there is no possibility to protest against it . . . The Soviet Communist Party does not have to share power, but it must allow an opposition. There could be an opposition within the Party, or there could be opposing factions. There should be an open political battle. In almost 70 years, we have not developed personnel capable of working in such an environment, neither at the highest political levels nor at the lowest. The Party has turned into a bureaucratic organism. It cannot and does not want to live in an environment of free speech and democracy.

Interview/U.S. News & World Report, 7-29:42.

5

Melina Mercouri
Minister of Culture of Greece

[On the establishment of an annual European cultural festival sponsored by the Common Mar-

6

(MELINA MERCOURI)

ket]: . . . our peoples, having as their goal progress within societies of consumerism and economic success, were losing part of their soul. Looking for happiness, we are losing it. If there is something important today in this Europe, which is declining demographically and economically, it is the variety and uniqueness of its cultures. It is our history, and it has only one enemy, but a strong one. That enemy is forgetting.

News conference, Athens,
June 20/The New York Times, 6-21:19.

Alessandro Natta
First Secretary, Communist Party of Italy

1

We [the Italian Communist Party] do not demand a revolution of democratic ideals, and we won't automatically demand early Parliamentary elections if we pass the Christian Democrats [in local elections] again. That is a scarecrow that the Christian Democrats are waving. The *sorpasso* is nothing new, since we outpoll the Christian Democrats in so many cities already. People won't be scared if it happened. Nor would Italy be ruined if we were in power.

Los Angeles Times, 5-12:(I)22.

David Owen
Leader, Social Democratic Party of Britain

2

[On new Soviet leader Mikhail Gorbachev]: I think he is bright, technically able, able to absorb the new concepts of government and science. I think that's a great help to us because many of these issues are only susceptible to a pretty sharp intelligence. And if you are going to get some shift in position, particularly in arguing with the military in the Soviet Union, who are very powerfully entrenched, then the leader has got to be pretty capable, pretty effective.

The Washington Post, 3-12:(A)20.

Turgut Ozal
Prime Minister of Turkey

3

[Calling for a Greece-Turkey summit meeting to resolve differences between the two coun-

tries]: I propose here and now to the Greek leadership to proceed to comprehensive negotiations. We are ready to participate in such negotiations anywhere, any time and at any level they like . . . Was it not Plato, an eminent philosopher of ancient Greece, who argued the merits of dialogue in the search of truth?

To foreign correspondents, Ankara,
March 12/The Washington Post, 3-13:(A)14.

4

How can we be a threat to Greece when we are members of the same security pact—NATO? All this nonsense about a Turkish threat, I think, makes [Greek Premier Andreas] Papandreou's true motives clear: It is an election year in Greece, and he is using this propaganda in order to bring the Greek people around to his way of thinking. One of my government's first foreign-policy steps was to extend an olive branch— several, in fact—to Greece. We were rebuffed at every turn.

Interview, Ankara/
U.S. News & World Report,
4-1:44.

Andreas Papandreou
Prime Minister of Greece

5

In 1974, Turkey invaded Cyprus with NATO arms, and since then it has occupied 37 per cent of the island. Neither Turkey nor Greece has any business being in Cyprus. Cyprus is not Greek territory, but there are ethnic bonds of language, culture and history between Greece and Cyprus. What has NATO done to curb Turkish aggression? Turkish leaders have never accepted the legal status quo in the Aegean. They want either the partition of the Aegean or co-sovereignty over the region. They want half of the continental shelf in the eastern Aegean, and claim that Turkey, rather than Greece, has air-defense responsibility for an area that includes some of Greece's most important islands. It looks like the beginning of the dismemberment of Greece. Since all NATO exercises in the Aegean validate the Turkish viewpoint, we do not participate in them.

Interview/Time, 2-25:40.

(ANDREAS PAPANDREOU)

1

Let me stress that we are not threatened from the north. We have excellent relations with Yugoslavia and Albania, and also with Bulgaria. The chief danger comes from the east, from an ally, Turkey. It is paradoxical and perhaps unique in the history of mankind that one should be threatened by one's ally, but this is the case . . . The leadership of Turkey must decide to put an end to its demands for vital space. Remember *Lebensraum?* It goes back to the period of Hitler. If Turkey stops trying to acquire *Lebensraum* in the Aegean to the detriment of our continental shelf and our airspace, the problem will be dispelled.

News conference, April 2/
The New York Times, 4-4:3.

2

The voters [of Greece] have shown disinterest in the Common Market, NATO as issues; they are not greatly interested in foreign policy. The immediate issue is their daily lives. It's amazing—the two major parties do not make foreign policy into a major issue. The voters want responsible handling; they don't want adventures. This message I get from the people. The dimension of responsibility is important. It is as if these matters have become tiresome.

Interview, Ioannina, Greece,
May 27/The New York Times, 5-28:4.

3

[On the forthcoming Parliamentary elections in Cyprus]: We [Greece] do not intervene, but we must state clearly to the Cypriot people that if they accept a timetable of withdrawal—which would mean that the Turkish troops would never withdraw—we would consider that damaging to the Greek national interest. If the Turkish occupation of Cyprus is legalized, the threat to the Aegean will become more immediate and menacing. A decision to reach a solution while Turkish troops remain is nationally unacceptable to us. We, for our part, will not agree that there is a solution until the last Turkish occupation soldier leaves [Cyprus].

Before Parliament, Athens,
Dec. 6/The New York Times, 12-7:5.

Shimon Peres
Prime Minister of Israel

4

[Criticizing U.S. President Reagan's visit to a cemetery in Bitburg, West Germany, where Nazi soldiers and SS officers are buried, even though he then visited the site of a Nazi concentration camp]: Even death cannot obscure the difference between those who were buried as murderers [at the Bitburg cemetery] and those [at the concentration camp] who were buried as murder victims. Gravestones have not the power to obliterate the abyss that yawns between those who led to others' murders and those who were led. I believe that President Reagan is a true friend of the Jewish people and the state of Israel. It is precisely for this reason that we feel deep pain at the terrible error of his visit to Bitburg. There can be reconciliation between peoples. There is no reconciliation between times. There is no legitimation for what occurred.

Before the Knesset (Parliament), Jerusalem,
May 6/The New York Times, 5-7:5.

Charles Price
United States Ambassador
to the United Kingdom

5

The main fear of our [European] allies is not the shadow of the Russian bear. It is that they are being rapidly outdistanced by technological and economic advances of the United States and, more recently, Japan.

U.S. News & World Report, 5-27:45.

Ronald Reagan
President of the United States

6

[On the influence of new Soviet leader Mikhail Gorbachev]: [Soviet leadership is] a collective government [where the policy is] really determined by a dozen or so individuals in the Politburo. And while an individual, once chosen by them, can undoubtedly influence or persuade them to certain things that might be particular theories or policies of his, the government basically remains the same group of individuals.

At White House luncheon, Washington,
March 11/The Washington Post, 3-12:(A)20.

(RONALD REAGAN)

1

[On criticism of his planned visit to a German cemetery where Nazi SS officers are buried]: My purpose was, and remains, not to reemphasize the crimes of the Third Reich in 12 years of power, but to celebrate the tremendous accomplishments of the German people in 40 years of liberty, freedom, democracy and peace. It was to remind the world that, since the close of that terrible war, the United States and the Federal Republic [West Germany] have established an historic relationship, not of superpower to satellite, but of sister republics bonded together by common ideals and alliance and partnership.

At conference on religious liberty, Washington,
April 16/The Washington Post, 4-17:(A)27.

2

[On his just-concluded visit to a German cemetery where Nazi soldiers and SS officers are buried]: This visit has stirred many emotions in the American and German people, too. I have received many letters since first deciding to come to Bitburg cemetery, some supportive, others deeply concerned and questioning, others opposed. Some old wounds have been reopened, and this I regret very much, because this should be a time of healing. To the veterans and families of American servicemen who still carry the scars and feel the painful losses of that war, our gesture of reconciliation with the German people today in no way minimizes our love and honor for those who fought and died for our country. They gave their lives to rescue freedom in its darkest hour. The alliance of democratic nations that guards the freedom of millions in Europe and America today stands as living testimony that their noble sacrifice was not in vain . . . There are more than 2,000 [Nazi soldiers] buried in Bitburg cemetery. Among them are 48 members of the SS. The crimes of the SS must rank among the most heinous in human history. But others buried there were simply soldiers in the German Army. How many were fanatical followers of a dictator and willfully carried out his cruel orders? And how many were conscripts, forced into service during the death throes of the Nazi war machine? We do not know. Many, how-

ever, we know from the dates on their tombstones, were only teen-agers at the time. There is one boy buried there who died a week before his 16th birthday. There were thousands of such soldiers to whom Nazism meant no more than a brutal end to a short life. We do not believe in collective guilt. Only God can look into the human heart. All these men have now met the Supreme Judge, and they have been judged by Him, as we shall all be judged.

At U.S. Air Force Base,
Bitburg, West Germany, May 5/
The New York Times, 5-6:6.

3

[On the Bergen-Belsen concentration camp that operated during the Nazi era]: Here lie people—Jews—whose death was inflicted for no reason other than their very existence. Their pain was borne only because of who they were and because of the God in their prayers. Alongside them lie many Christians—Catholics and Protestants. For year after year, until that man [Adolf Hitler] and his evil were destroyed, hell yawned forth its awful contents. People were brought here for no other purpose but to suffer and die. To go unfed when hungry, uncared for when sick, tortured when the whim struck, and left to have misery consume them when all there was around them was misery . . . What we have felt and are expressing with words cannot convey the suffering that they endured. That is why history will forever brand what happened as the Holocaust. Here, death ruled. But we have learned something as well. Because of what happened, we found that death cannot rule forever. And that is why we are here today.

Address at site of Bergen-Belsen
concentration camp, Bergen, West Germany,
May 5/
The New York Times, 5-6:8.

4

No country in the world has been more creative then Germany. And no other can better help create our future. The experts expected it would be decades before Germany's economy regained its pre-war level. You did it in less than one. The experts said the Federal Republic [West Germany] could not absorb millions of refugees, es-

(RONALD REAGAN)

tablish a democracy on the ashes of Nazism and be reconciled with your neighbors. You did all three. Germany's success showed that our future must not depend on experts or on government plans, but on the treasures of the human mind and spirit—imagination, intellect, courage and faith.

Before German students,
Hambach, West Germany, May 6/
The New York Times, 5-7-4.

Donald T. Regan

Chief of Staff to the President
of the United States; Former Secretary
of the Treasury of the United States

1

We are told that [U.S. President Reagan] wants to tell our allies to get their own economies in order, yet the Germans are saying that they are not going to prime the pump with government money because they don't want to increase their deficits. How do you convince them to prime the pump? They don't have to. What they should do is cut taxes. That's what we tried back in the United States. It worked. We had a recovery as soon as we cut our taxes, and we've had the best recovery of any of these [European] nations. And we're advocating the same medicine to all of them. And as a matter of fact, their people and their industries will respond much more to a tax cut than they will to more government spending.

Interview, Bonn, May 2/
The Washington Post, 5-3-(4)33.

Menachem Z. Rosensaft

Chairman, International Network
of Children of Jewish Holocaust Survivors

2

[Criticizing U.S. President Reagan's decision to visit a German cemetery where Nazi soldiers and SS officers are buried]: The time for soft-spoken words and appeals is over. For the sake of history, we must prevent him from going to Bitburg . . . [When he visits the Nazi concentration camp at Bergen-Belsen.] President Reagan plans to stand beside the mass graves

where Anne Frank and tens of thousands of other Jews lie, buried anonymously . . . and probably intends to deliver a moving speech. How we wish that he would have decided to go to Belsen voluntarily. How we would then have valued his presence at the one place in contemporary history which symbolizes both the Holocaust and the rebirth of the Jewish people. Tragically, we must now reject his gesture as totally inadequate. Today, let us say to President Reagan clearly and unambiguously that if he insists on going to Bitburg we do not need him and we do not want him in Bergen-Belsen. [If he does visit the German cemetery,] let him pass in front of us [at Bergen-Belsen] and look into our faces, and perhaps then, at last, he will understand the enormity of the outrage which he is perpetrating. For heaven's sake, let him find another cemetery. There must be at least one in all of Germany which does not contain SS men.

At ceremony for Holocaust survivors,
Philadelphia, April 21/
The New York Times, 4-22:6.

Dean Rusk

Former Secretary of State
of the United States

3

[On the East-West division of Europe created by the 1945 Yalta conference]: There's no way to undo the division of Europe short of general war. You can reduce the importance of the boundaries with trade and cultural exchanges. But the boundaries are a fact of life, and that's not going to change.

The Christian Science Monitor, 2-4-3.

Gebhard Schweigler

Senior fellow, Carnegie
Endowment for International Peace

4

Even the [two] Germanys have written off the goal of reunification as achievable, except in the very long term as part of a general European reunification. [Reunification is not a] current practical policy goal. As both Germanys continue to develop a separate national identity, reunification will become harder, not easier.

The Christian Science Monitor, 2-4-5.

Arkady N. Shevchenko
Former Soviet diplomat
(defected to the United States)

1

[On his defection to the U.S.]: I had everything [in the Soviet Union] except a very small thing—my own personal freedom. I had to live in a country where everything, everybody, has to be hypocritical, even in the family. You cannot even openly talk with your own wife, with your friends. You live in a situation where you are forced to pretend all the time. That's why I consider this system pushed me out of the Soviet Union. I could just not stand it any more.

Broadcast interview/"60 Minutes," CBS-TV, 2-3.

George P. Shultz
Secretary of State of the United States

2

I do not envy [Soviet leader Mikhail] Gorbachev and the challenge he faces in trying to defy the laws of economics and squeeze more productivity out of a system of imposed discipline and bureaucracy. He must come to realize that he must loosen up.

Before Pilgrims Society, London,
Dec. 10/Los Angeles Times, 12-11:(I)5.

Mario Soares
Prime Minister of Portugal

3

It is true that there are people who live poorly here [in Portugal], on small salaries, in bad housing. But I have never met a person who comes here and says he can't eat. I heard there was hunger in Setubal, across the river from here. I started a program to feed the poor. No one came. They said they didn't want charity. If they were really hungry, they would have come, charity or not. The Communists have put out this idea that people are hungry. Then they go and march all the hungry people down the street—in good clothes.

Interview, Lisbon/
The Christian Science Monitor, 5-10:10.

Sergei L. Sokolov
Minister of Defense of the Soviet Union

4

[On Soviet contributions to the defeat of Nazi Germany in World War II]: Capitalist propa-

ganda is making strenuous efforts to falsify history . . . to belittle the role of the U.S.S.R. in the rout of the Fascist invaders. But the truth cannot be overturned. The whole world knows that it was the Soviet Union that made the decisive contribution. Victory cost us 20 million lives, and we will never forget it.

At celebration of World War II Victory Day,
Moscow, May 8/Time, 5-20:32.

David Steel
Leader, Liberal Party of Britain

5

[On new Soviet leader Mikhail Gorbachev]: Judging from my own meeting with Mr. Gorbachev, I think there is a greater sense of flexibility, of openness, of a willingness to argue and counter-argue, rather than simply the wooden presentation of the standard line which has been the case with the older leaders.

The Washington Post, 3-12:(A)20.

Lord Stockton
Member, British House of Lords

6

What have the Americans done? They have tackled the problem [of the economy]. They've been the protagonists in invention, in development and in exploitation of the new technology. They have done that on an immense scale, and what is interesting is that they have reduced at the same time unemployment by means of the new wealth created. We [British] must not be the slowest ship in the convoy. We must be leader of the convoy, or at any rate make an attempt to regain the leadership we have had so long.

In House of Lords, London,
Jan. 23/The New York Times, 1-24:4.

John Stokes
Member of British Parliament

7

[Arguing against TV coverage of Parliamentary proceedings]: However absurd or comical our proceedings may be sometimes, what we are generally about is the state of the nation—and that is not a form of entertainment.

U.S. News & World Report, 12-2:14.

Franz-Josef Strauss
Minister-President of Bavaria,
West Germany; Leader,
Christian-Social Union of West Germany

1

[On whether he is for reunification of East and West Germany]: I am without "yes" and "but," only "if" and "but." A fanatic adherent of freedom. I don't care for unity if the price is freedom. I want a democratic Germany, but not at the cost of the enterprise, of losing our freedom. I prefer a part of Germany free, instead of entire Germany being a part of the Soviet system, or a puppet and a lacky in the hands of Soviet policies.

Broadcast interview, Bonn, West Germany/
"Meet the Press," NBC-TV, 5-5.

Margaret Thatcher
Prime Minister of the United Kingdom

2

Today, out of the forces of the alliance in Europe, 95 per cent of the divisions, 85 per cent of the tanks, 80 per cent of the combat aircraft and 70 per cent of the fighting ships are provided, manned and paid for by the European allies. Europe has more than 3 million men under arms and more still in reserve. We have to. We are right in the front line.

Before joint session of U.S. Congress,
Washington, Feb. 20/
The Washington Post, 2-21:(A)9.

3

So long as a majority of the people of Northern Ireland wish to remain part of the United Kingdom, their wishes will be respected. If ever there were to be a majority in favor of change, then I believe that our Parliament would respond accordingly.

Before joint session of U.S. Congress,
Washington, Feb. 20/
The Washington Post, 2-21:(A)9.

4

It takes quite a long time to turn an economy from the kind of rather rigidly controlled society we had—to turn it into the kind of vigorous, enterprising society like the U.S. and Japan. However, we have done a great deal. A lot of the controls have gone. We have had the biggest de-

330

nationalization program ever. Inflation is down to about 4.6 per cent. Production and investment last year were all-time records. But we are not creating jobs fast enough yet. That is part of being a technological society. And the only answer to that is more goods, more small business, more new business.

Interview, London/Business Week, 2-25:42.

5

[On the almost-year-old coal miners strike in her country]: We have 80,000—or well over 40 per cent—of the miners working. The National Union of Mineworkers is split. The strikers have not had major support from a single trade union. As unions have begun to realize, other than the NUM, you don't get business if you strike. You have a very different attitude toward wages. What matters is not the wages you're paid but wages in relation to performance. That's the critical factor . . . It [the strike] has to end in a way which means that uneconomic pits must be able to be closed. They always have been in the past; they must be in the future. You never compromise with violence and intimidation, and you cannot compromise with the right of a board of an industry to manage that industry.

Interview, London/Business Week, 2-25:43.

6

[On her Administration]: In the 6½ years we have served the nation, much has been achieved. The nation's output, the nation's investment, the nation's standard of living are at an all-time high. Inflation is down . . . Personal ownership is growing. Our overseas assets have multiplied more than sixfold in six years.

At Conservative Party conference,
Blackpool, England, Oct. 11/
The Washington Post, 10-12:(A)16.

Malcolm Toon
Former United States Ambassador
to the Soviet Union

7

[On speculation in the West that possible future Soviet leaders such as Mikhail Gorbachev and Grigory Romanov may moderate that country's policies]: You can be sure that there will not be much of a change no matter who takes

(MALCOLM TOON)

over. I think it's a mistake to get too excited about Gorbachev taking over. Whether it's Gorbachev or a man a little bit older, like Romanov, you are talking about people who have been identified with the collective leadership for six years. Unless you have a radical change in the composition of the Politburo and a radical change in the [Soviet Communist Party] Central Committee, I don't think you will see a major change in policy.

Interview/Los Angeles Times, 2-10:(I)16.

1

[I don't] call [the Soviet Union] a superpower, because they are a superpower in only two respects—the tremendous military arsenal they control and the tremendous hunk of real estate they control. But in all other respects, I think that they are far less than a major power . . . Look at the way they treat their people, the way they treat their so-called friends—the Poles and the Afghans—and the way they have mismanaged their resources. Their economy is a mess, and they can't feed their own people, despite the tremendous terrain they control. In all these respects, the Soviet Union is far from being a superpower.

Interview/USA Today, 8-26:(A)9.

2

Paul E. Tsongas
Former United States Senator,
D-Massachusetts

My concern is that the [U.S.] Reagan Administration tilts toward Turkey [rather than toward Greece]. No question of that. It considers Turkey's strategic value to exceed that of Greece, and it does not perceive the Turkish threat to Greece to be real. Given that, it has always fallen to [the U.S.] Congress to add some balance.

Interview/The New York Times, 4-30:2.

Lech Walesa
Former chairman, now-banned Solidarity
(independent Polish trade union);
Winner, 1983 Nobel Peace Prize

3

I don't want to describe the situation in Poland in terms of winners and losers. For me, what is important is for Poland to be a winner. We are not satisfied with the current situation in this country, but I repeat: I don't want to see any losers in our country. I would rather have everyone love the government, have the government serve the people—but unfortunately this is not the case. Many people who have a different opinion are not allowed to express it on various subjects . . . I believe in our victory, which doesn't mean taking the power from the government. Above all, we want to create a more efficient system and a better, more interesting and more comfortable life. Victory means the realization of our program. One can say our behavior is bringing changes within the system. Even now, being objective, one must say that, thanks to our stubbornness, some things have been achieved.

Interview/USA Today, 3-7:(A)9.

Thomas J. Watson, Jr.
Former United States Ambassador
to the Soviet Union

4

[On new Soviet leader Mikhail Gorbachev]: I don't think the United States should expect any real change in the Soviet Union as a result. The government of the U.S.S.R. is a very solid, firmly-in-place, bureaucratic government. We like to think that everyone there would like to revolt, but that is simply not the fact. Most of the Soviet people are happy; they may be unhappy about some things, but they are not about to revolt. Occasionally, there are some freedom moves, but such activity is very minimal.

Interview, March 11/
The New York Times, 3-12:8.

Caspar W. Weinberger
Secretary of Defense of the United States

5

The real issue, you might argue, is whether Europeans will become hostages to the Soviet Union as the United States retreats to an illusory fortress across the ocean. There is no fortress, and there can be no retreat. America could not

(CASPAR W. WEINBERGER)

survive, nor live, in a world in which Europe was overrun and conquered.

Written remarks to meeting
of NATO defense officials, Munich,
Feb. 10/Los Angeles Times, 2-11:(I)7.

1

[On the recent killing of a U.S. military liaison official by a Soviet soldier in East Germany]: We don't plan to shoot every Russian sentry we see. That's what they do. It was a coldblooded murder and, worse than that . . . they accompanied it by preventing any kind of medical assistance from reaching him while he was dying on the ground. It was a totally reprehensible, barbaric type of act.

Before American soldiers, West Berlin,
May 21/Los Angeles Times, 5-22:(I)19.

2

[On the recent spy scandal in West Germany]: Espionage is a very unfortunate act wherever it occurs, and we'll do our best to guard against it. But we aren't going to say that because there has been espionage in Europe that we therefore can't trust Europe with anything.

To European reporters, Washington,
Sep. 9/The Washington Post, 9-10:(A)5.

3

[Asking U.S. President Reagan not to make a planned visit to a German cemetery where Nazi SS officers are buried]: So may I speak to you, Mr. President, with respect and admiration, of the events that happened? We have met four or five times. And each time I came away enriched, for I know of your commitment to humanity. And therefore I am convinced, as you have told us earlier when we spoke, that you were not aware of the presence of SS graves in the Bitburg cemetery. Of course you didn't know. But now we are all aware. May I, Mr. President, if it's possible at all, implore you to do something else, to find a way, to find another way, another site? That place, Mr. President, is not your place. Your place is with the victims of the SS.

Elie Wiesel
Author; Chairman,
United States Holocaust Memorial Council

Oh, we know there are political and strategic reasons [to visit that cemetery], but this issue, as all issues related to that awesome event, transcends politics and diplomacy. The issue here is not politics, but good and evil. And we must never confuse them. For I have seen the SS at work. And I have seen their victims.

Upon receiving Congressional Gold Medal
of Achievement, Washington, April 16/
The New York Times, 4-20:4.

Janusz Wodzinski
Director, Department of Prices,
Government of Poland

4

We have to deal with the expectations of the [Polish] consumers who naturally want the lowest possible price and who do not really understand the relationship between costs, productivity and availability. And we have to deal with the producers who want to obtain the highest return possible. Then there is a third set of expectations, that of the Administration, which wants prices to be such that the market will be in balance, stores will be full of goods, workers will have enough to buy and will be more productive, and conditions will exist for greater risk-taking and more flexibility . . . Sometimes [workers] understand that there is a connection between cost and supply, but often they feel that the government simply has an obligation to supply everything they need. I am afraid that our consumers have been spoiled by their very poor understanding of a very primitive socialism.

Interview, Warsaw/The New York Times, 8-5:4.

Yevgeny Yevtushenko
Soviet poet

5

[Calling for more freedom and less political censorship for writers in the Soviet Union]: Today's long-awaited striving for change for the better in our country gives us profound hopes that self-flattery will be forever rejected, and that non-concealment will become the norm of civic behavior. We, men of letters, will not be worth a penny if we simply report and laud the social transformations taking place independently of us.

At Congress of Russian writers,
Dec. 12/The New York Times, 12-18:1.

The Middle East

Hatem Abu Ghazaleh
Member, Palestine National Council

1

[Criticizing Israel's refusal to allow PLO Chairman Yasir Arafat to take part in proposed Arab-Israeli peace talks]: The Israelis should be demanding that Arafat join the negotiations, or otherwise they will go nowhere. Do you think a fourth-rate Palestinian can sign for peace with Israel? It will be null and void the minute the ink is dry. We have to demonstrate to the Israelis that Arafat is ready to negotiate with Israel, and that he is the one Palestinians in the West Bank support.

The Washington Post,
12-11:(A)34.

Ibrahim al-Amin
Chief spokesman,
Lebanese Shiite Moslem Hizbullah
(Party of God)

2

[On Moslem suicide bombers who killed hundreds of U.S. Marines and are involved in other anti-U.S. actions]: [The truck bombers] fought these people [the Marines] in the only way they could. These people [the Moslems] don't have the same strong quality of weapons as the enemy. They have only the willingness to die [to] become an example for all freedom seekers in the world. They are not terrorists. We have not gone to America; the Americans came to us. We haven't sent an army to America—not even a [battleship] *New Jersey.* We haven't bombed the American people—not even a car bomb . . . It's of no concern who blew up the Marines or who made those suicide operations against the Israelis or the American Embassy [in Beirut]. All that is of concern is that these are believers, the real martyrs, much bigger than any big organization, because they give their people the most valuable thing they have. The revolutionary Moslem is an example for the whole world.

Interview, Beirut/
Newsweek, 7-8:33.

Yasir Arafat
Chairman,
Palestine Liberation Organization

3

[Criticizing the U.S. for continuing to demand conditions for meeting with the PLO]: I am sorry to say that the American Administration is still looking from its narrow angle, from the Israeli narrow angle. They are still trying to hide the sun with their finger, neglecting reality and facts in this area.

News conference, Peking,
May 12/The New York Times,
5-13:4.

4

The PLO denounces and condemns all terrorist acts, whether those involving countries or by persons or groups, against unarmed innocent civilians in any place. The PLO as of today will take all punitive measures against violators . . . The PLO reiterates the right of the Palestinian people to fight against the Israeli occupation in all possible ways, with the aim of the withdrawal of the Israelis from these lands . . . [But] incidents have affirmed the PLO's conviction that terrorist acts committed outside have adverse effects on the Palestinian people's cause and disfigure their legal resistance for freedom.

Cairo, Nov. 7/
The New York Times, 11-8:3.

George W. Ball
Former Under Secretary
of State of the United States

5

[On the recent hijacking of an American airliner by Lebanese Shiite Moslems and the holding hostage of its passengers]: We shouldn't be talking about retaliation [against the hijackers]. It is not the business of the U.S. to be conducting blood feuds with people. We may be angry, but the Shiites have a sense of deep grievance and they associate the United States with it.

The Christian Science Monitor, 7-2:36.

Nabih Berri
Minister of Justice of Lebanon;
Leader, Shiite Moslem Amal movement

1

[On the current hijacking of an American airliner by Shiite Moslems, the holding hostage of the passengers in Beirut, and his being the spokesman and negotiator for the hijackers]: I am not a go-between. I am a party, and I and the Amal movement have adopted the demands of the hijackers [that Israel release hundreds of Shiite prisoners they are holding]. I gave guarantees to the hijackers that I will not release the [U.S.] hostages or the passengers without the release of the [Shiite] prisoners [in Israel]. If Israel does not release them, I would say to the kidnapers, "Now you take the [American hostages] and do what you want."

News conference, Beirut, June 17/
The Washington Post, 6-18:(A)1.

2

[On the kidnaping of Americans in Beirut by Moslem extremists]: We in the Amal movement do not believe in such methods, especially the kidnaping of ordinary people. On the other hand, we are well aware of how oppressive American policy is toward us, and we are opposed to American policies, which provide the material, moral, political and strategic coverage for all that Israel does. We are aware of the hostile American attitude, but we always distinguish between the American individual and American policies.

Interview/Los Angeles Times, 6-18:(I)1.

Kenneth J. Bialkin
President, Conference of Presidents
of Major American Jewish Organizations

3

[On revelations of Israeli espionage in the U.S.]: Israel is not a nation hostile to the United States, and there is no danger that the kind of information that was obtained in this particular regard will be circuited back to anti-U.S. countries. The need for Israel to obtain this kind of information stresses again Israel's circumstance in the world, namely, that there is no other nation whose neighbors exist in a declared

state of war with an intention to destroy it, and where the imperatives of obtaining information of the type that was obtained are so apparent. There ought to be an increase in impatience with the rejectionism of the Arab world that creates the sort [of] tensions that put pressure [on] relations between friends. The need for Israel to obtain this intelligence is there. Unfortunately, the techniques employed to obtain that intelligence went beyond the policies of the government of Israel, and I would say that you have to be naive in this world to believe that nations will not seek the maximum intelligence available. But in the case of the U.S. and Israel, that has to be done within the framework of the understanding that exists, and I'm not suggesting otherwise.

Interview, Jerusalem/The Washington Post, 12-3:(A)34.

Jimmy Carter
Former President of the United States

4

[Saying U.S. President Reagan should take a more active posture in formulating Arab-Israeli negotiations]: You have to acknowledge that there is a limit to what people like [Jordanian King] Hussein and [PLO chairman Yasir] Arafat and [Israeli Prime Minister Shimon] Peres can do on their own initiative and in public without a response from the other side. It's embarrassing to be rejected. You make yourself vulnerable to attacks at home. The militants are always in the wings waiting for any kind of mistake to be made. . . . We [in the Carter Administration] were always eager to take the slightest indication of accommodation and pursue it with the parties; that approach doesn't exist [under Reagan].

Interview, Washington, April 2/
Los Angeles Times, 4-3:(I)12.

5

I think there are some Israeli leaders who have characterized all Palestinians, at least all PLO members, as terrorists. This is an attitude that causes me some concern . . . I think it would be a serious mistake for anyone to characterize the Israelis as racists. But there is a stigma attached to Palestinians by many Israelis because they're equated with terrorists. There's a stigma attached to Jews by many Arabs because of the

(JIMMY CARTER)

same inclinations, to stigmatize an entire race. This is obviously one of the obstacles before us.

Interview/USA Today, 4-4:(A)11.

1

It is Israel that remains the key, the tiny vortex around which swirl the winds of hatred, intolerance and bloodshed . . The Arabs must recognize the reality that is Israel, just as the Israelis must acknowledge Palestinian claims to civic equality and their right to express themselves freely in a portion of their territorial homeland . . . I would like to have had a chance to follow up over a longer period of time on the Camp David accords and the peace treaty between Israel and Egypt, because I'm convinced that the people in that region genuinely want peace and that the obstacle is the leaders and their timidity. I think in the second term [of his Presidency] I would not have exhibited any timidity. I would have been an eager partner for any person, any leader, in the Middle East who wanted to take even a tentative small step toward peace.

Interview, Beverly Hills, Calif./
Los Angeles Times, 4-10:(V)1,6.

Mohamad Jawad Chirri
Director, Islamic Center of America

2

The Shiites [Moslems] see that the United States has identified itself with Israel. Israel to them is a usurper of their land, of Palestine. Israel is an invader of Lebanon, a killer of their women, children and men— a government that destroyed many buildings, even demolished cities and big apartment buildings. They killed them with one bomb. And with the other eye they see the United States, who they used to love very much, approving everything Israel does. So from the eyes of the Shiites, they do not see the difference between the United States and Israel . . . They would tell the United States that Israel has no place to stay in the Middle East because Israel occupied Palestine. Those people were uprooted, driven out of their homes. They were prevented even from returning to look in-

side their homes—the simplest human right. This was done by the Israelis, but it was supported, wholeheartedly, by the United States.

Interview/USA Today, 7-8:(A)11.

David Clayman
Jerusalem representative,
American Jewish Congress

3

[On revelations of Israeli espionage in the U.S.]: There is anger in American Jews that they've been betrayed by Israel. They will express anger to the Israeli establishment for having ruptured their confidence that there's a complete identity of interests between Israel and the United States. All of our efforts are aimed at gaining and keeping support for Israel in the United States. Suddenly, there is this tremendous erosion.

Jerusalem/The Christian Science Monitor, 12-2-8.

Anthony H. Cordesman
Authority on Middle East military affairs

4

The rate of military expansion in the Middle East has reached the point where the real problem the nations in the region face with "modernization" is not such cultural issues as "Westernization" but the practical threat of "militarization."

The Christian Science Monitor, 10-2:1.

Abba Eban
Member of Israeli Knesset (Parliament);
Former Foreign Minister of Israel

5

[On the recent Jordan-PLO negotiations and agreement]: It is not a negative development [for Israel]. It is very positive that they are agitating themselves about this question and believe that time is not on their side. But on the other hand, it is hard to expect Israelis to throw their hat in the air over this. My God, after 37 years, all they can come up with is implicit recognition of UN Resolution 242. We need explicit recognition of the state of Israel, and they offer implicit recognition of 242.

Interview/The New York Times, 2-25:4.

1

[On Israel's 1982 invasion of Lebanon]: I think the general line should be to get rid of any vestige that reminds us of the nightmare of the Lebanese war. We have got to banish the Lebanese war, wipe it out of our minds, banish it from our consciousness. It is by far the least successful enterprise in modern Jewish history; therefore, anything that reminds us of it should be liquidated as soon as possible.

The New York Times, 7-2:4.

2

[On Arab terrorism against Israel]: One of the difficulties is the individual nature of these attacks. Paradoxically, it is easier to deal with outrages that are performed by an organization, because an organization is a target. It is punishable. All you can do with an individual is to catch him and bring him to trial. So, the more individual these actions are the greater the problems they pose for the security authorities.

Interview/The Washington Post, 8-5:(A)8.

3

[On Israel's concern over Syria's moving medium-range missiles close to the Lebanese border, thus jeopardizing Israel's reconnaissance flights over that area]: We have to put up with the fact that other people have sovereign territory in which they can do what they like, and one cannot possibly have any influence on what sovereign countries do in their territory. I'm sure Syria would love to be able to tell us where to put our missiles in such a way so as not to have any influence on Syrian territory.

Radio broadcast, Jerusalem, Dec. 16/ The Washington Post, 12-17:(A)23.

Mohammed Hussein Fadlallah
Lebanese Shiite Moslem religious leader

4

[On the current hijacking of an American airliner by Lebanese Shiite Moslems and the holding hostage of its passengers in Beirut]: We urge America to study the matter objectively and on its merits and to understand what the issues are.

The New York Times, 5-22:1,8.

Does America ever ask itself what gives rise to what it calls terrorism? Is it due to external influence or insane fervor, or is it triggered by a genuine condition emanating from a context of reality. We believe violence breeds violence. If America tries to carry out its policies in the area through violence directly, or indirectly via Israel, then I don't believe it will come up against reasoned logic, but it will participate in the madness of the region. And when this area goes crazy, then naturally neither its rulers, those allied to America, or America, will be able to do anything.

Interview, Beirut, June 20/ The Washington Post, 6-21:(A)31.

Fahd ibn Abdel Aziz al-Saud
King of Saudi Arabia

5

The Palestinian question is the single problem that is of paramount concern to the whole Arab [world] and affects the relations of its peoples and countries with the outside world. It is the one problem that is the root cause of instability and turmoil in the region.

Addressing U.S. President Reagan, Washington, Feb. 11/Los Angeles Times, 2-12:(I)13.

Shlomo Gazit
Former Chief of Military Intelligence of Israel; Former military governor of Israeli-occupied West Bank

6

[Criticizing the Israeli-Arab agreement for an exchange of 1,150 Palestinian prisoners and terrorists held by Israel for 3 Israeli prisoners held by the Arabs]: I am disgusted. Never again will Israel be able to condemn any other country which will be blackmailed into freeing terrorists who have killed Jews, whether it is in France, Germany or England. We can't even say any more that we are at the forefront of fighting terrorism. That is all bunk... No one takes Soviet citizens hostage because they know you will not get a penny out of the Soviet Union if you do. Once you start making bargains, it only becomes a question of whether you give up 5 or 5,000.

The New York Times, 5-22:1,8.

(SHLOMO GAZIT)

1

[The original Israeli philosophy in administering the West Bank was], first, that we must wait for a political settlement [of Arab-Israeli hostilities] to determine the fate of these areas and that settlement will not be between Israel and the local inhabitants but between Israel and some outside power. Until that settlement comes, the two sides should find a way to live together with the minimum damage to both. Secondly, we Israelis argued that "We were as embarrassed at being a military government as much as you Arabs are suffering. Hence, if you behave yourself, you will not see us, you will not notice our patrols, you will not feel our presence" . . . Our original philosophy doesn't hold water any more. We have gone from a policy that subtly facilitates peace and quiet and keeping all political options open, to one that subtly facilitates the closing of political options [by making Israeli occupation more permanent]. This latest wave of anti-Israel violence [in the occupied areas] may calm down, but things cannot go on like this. I don't know whether it is going to be the summer of '86 or '87 or whenever, but if this situation continues there is going to be a real explosion.

The New York Times, 10-3:4.

Amin Gemayel
President of Lebanon

2

The struggle for our [Lebanon's] Arab identity has been one of the main causes of our problems. We have excellent relations with the Arab world, and Syria is our gateway. She is our big Arab neighbor with whom we must have special relations. We share the same democratic values as the Western world, but politically we are non-aligned . . . I know the outside world thinks that Lebanon is finished, that the world is tired of us. But from my position I see the crisis coming forcefully to an end. All the [rival political and religious] factions are exhausted. No one believes any longer that military solutions are possible. In my opinion, a political solution is much closer than before. There is now a consensus that we have one identity, and it is Arab. This is the main reason I believe we are nearing a solution.

Interview, Beirut/Time, 10-28:52.

Butros Ghali
*Minister of State
for Foreign Affairs of Egypt*

3

For Americans, the Middle East is no more a priority. They have the East-West problems and detente. They have Latin America. They have NATO and Europe—and the Middle East is only fifth on the list. This is problem number one for us: how we can play a role to bring it from category five to category one or two.

Interview/The Washington Post, 1-30:(A)14.

Barry M. Goldwater
United States Senator, R-Arizona

4

We stand a better chance of going to war in the Middle East because of promises we've made to Israel, without any treaties. It is hard for me to say this because I'm part Jewish: I don't like the way Israel has been playing around with our promises to come to her aid, almost regardless of reason . . . Frankly, I'd get [the U.S.] out of that part of the world. Except, perhaps, for Saudi Arabia, I'd close everything, including embassies, and say, "Fellows, you clean up your own back yard, and we'll come back."

Interview/Los Angeles Herald Examiner, 1-13:(A)15.

Mikhail S. Gorbachev
*General Secretary,
Communist Party of the Soviet Union*

5

[On the possibility of re-establishing Soviet-Israeli diplomatic relations]: The Israeli leadership is conducting a policy which is not farsighted. For one, it dissolves its policy with regard to separate agreements. Perhaps some temporary agreements can be reached, but naturally it would have to be an overall approach to improve the situation in the Middle East. I think the sooner things normalize in the Middle East, the sooner we'll be able to settle the question of normalizing relations. For us, there will be no objectives, there will be no obstacles. We realize that Israel has the right to exist, its sovereignty, and we understand its security concerns. But we have big differences about how we understand

WHAT THEY SAID IN 1985

(MIKHAIL S. GORBACHEV)

their security and how Israel understands security. We have to think about the process and taking it as the opportunity to give such advice. It's not an easy issue.

News conference, Paris,
Oct. 4/The New York Times, 10-5:4.

Alexander M. Haig, Jr.
Former Secretary of State
of the United States

1

[On the recent capture by U.S. fighter planes of Arab terrorists who hijacked an Italian cruise ship in Egypt and killed an American passenger]: In any decisive action, there are good and bad results. In this instance, the good outweighs the bad. It's clear that the U.S. could not afford, in light of its damaged credibility in the Mideast, to appear helpless again in the face of a terrorist outrage. The price we've paid in relations with Egypt and Italy is regrettable. But I think Americans spend too much time looking for failures in Presidential policy even when it's successful, as this was.

Interview/U.S. News & World Report, 10-28:22.

Mohammed Heikal
Egyptian writer and commentator

2

The whole area is in a mess. To my mind, an era in the Middle East has ended and another era is being born now. How is it going to come? Which way? We can see the signs—Moslem fundamentalism, the vulgarity which you see. The elements of contradiction are there and accelerating day by day. What's going to come at the end, I cannot tell you; but we are heading for trouble, all of us.

Mark A. Heller
Professor, Jaffe Center
for Strategic Studies,
Tel Aviv University (Israel)

3

[On the increase in attacks by Arabs on Israelis in the Israeli-occupied territories]: We are

338

witnessing a whole new phenomenon here: local residents willing to go after Israelis in the territories, not with stones and roadblocks, but with weapons fashioned at home or smuggled in . . . Those young [Arab] people turning 18 this year have no living memory of any other regime but the Israeli military occupation. They don't think they have much to hope for from the outside, either from Jordan or the PLO. They see themselves in a direct political conflict with Israel. It is not that they believe what they are doing will necessarily make a difference; it is rather that they don't have any faith in anyone else any more or any other methods.

Interview/The New York Times, 9-6:4.

Jerry F. Hough
Professor of political science,
Duke University; Soviet policy specialist,
Brookings Institution

4

[On recent Arab terrorist attacks against Soviet citizens in Lebanon as a way of getting the Soviet Union to influence Syrian actions]: Obviously, we [the U.S.] would like the Soviets to react in a drastic way [against the terrorists] that undercuts Soviet interests. If the Soviet Union reacts in some drastic way, Muslim fundamentalists may drive trucks loaded with explosives into Soviet embassies throughout the Middle East. This reminds us that when great powers try to introduce order into totally chaotic domestic situations in other countries, they find it is a tar baby. We've tried to do it often, using Israel as a proxy, and the Soviets have tried to use the Syrians. The terrorists just go one step back—they hold us responsible for what Israel does and they hold the Soviets responsible for what Syria does.

Los Angeles Times, 10-5:(I)5.

Hussein I
King of Jordan

5

The movement toward peace in the Middle East has never been at a more critical crossroads than it is today. For the first time since Israel invaded and captured the West Bank, including East Jerusalem, Gaza and the Golan Heights, 18 years ago, there exists an unprecedented oppor-

(HUSSEIN I)

tunity for the parties involved to reactivate the peace process, based on the return of territory in exchange for peace . . . I refer to the Jordanian-Palestinian accord concluded in February between the government of Jordan and the Palestine Liberation Organization, the sole legitimate representative of the Palestinian people recognized by the majority of nations . . . For the first time, we in Jordan, with our Palestinian brethren, have structured an initiative representing the pursuit of their goals of self-determination through peaceful means . . . If the PLO continues to be denied a part in the peace process and the creeping annexation of the West Bank continues, how long will it be before the Palestinians and Arabs conclude that peace in our time is unattainable and struggle is the only alternative?

Address, via satellite, to National Association of Arab Americans, Washington, May 4/ The Washington Post, 5-10:(A)24.

1

The Lebanese tragedy has caused both Israelis and Palestinians to reassess the validity of their previous policies. Each is considering the need for negotiated peace. Each is skeptical. The Palestinians need hope, the Israelis need trust. It is important for all of us to provide the hope and the trust they need.

Washington, May 31/The New York Times, 6-1:4.

2

The tragic war between Iraq and Iran has entered its sixth year, although the rationale behind the confrontation has all but disappeared. International attempts have all but failed to bring the war to a close or to persuade the Iranian leadership to heed the voice of reason and respond to Iraq's sincere and persistent call for peace.

At United Nations, New York, Sept. 27/The New York Times, 9-28:5.

3

Things have never been so close as they are now [for Arab-Israeli peace talks]. The Palestin-

ians are ready. You have a debate in Israel between people who like peace and people who have other ideas. On the American scene you have the first second-term President [in more than a decade]. There is the beginning of a U.S.-Soviet dialogue. It either happens now or the possibilities will deteriorate rapidly . . . It is the last chance for peace.

Interview, Amman/Newsweek, 9-30:45.

4

[Saying Israeli-control of Jerusalem will not last]: It will not be long before the day that the Arab flag will fly over Jerusalem and the voices [from the mosques] will cry "God is great," and the bells will ring from the churches there.

At Royal Military Academy, Amman, Nov. 10/Los Angeles Times, 11-11:(I)6.

Brian Jenkins
Director, research program on subnational conflict and political violence, Rand Corporation

5

[On the current hijacking of an American airliner by Shiite Moslems and the holding hostage of the passengers in Beirut]: With regard to the current situation in the Middle East, we must understand the deep suspicion and hatred with which Shiites view us [the U.S.]. They see every bullet fired at them as made in America. And they view many aspects of Western cultural influence as blasphemous. Shiite extremists, in addition to the TWA hostages, hold an American diplomat, an American journalist, an American librarian and a couple of American priests. The message is: "We don't want any American influence here. We want you guys out."

Interview/U.S. News & World Report, 7-1:31.

Walid Jumblatt
Leader of Lebanese Druze

6

[Saying Lebanese President Amin Gemayel will be overthrown]: Let him remember that his palace at Baabda is no protection. The Shah of Iran was a thousand times greater, and he fell when a hungry people revolted. The Lebanese

(WALID JUMBLATT)

people, with their groups and communities united, will do the same and break this despotic and hated regime.

Speech, Beirut, Feb. 17/
Los Angeles Times, 2-18:(I)6.

Meir Kahane
Member of Israeli Knesset (Parliament)

Western democracy as we know it is incompatible with Zionism. Zionism came into being to create a Jewish state. Zionism declares that there is going to be a Jewish state with a majority of Jews, come what may. Democracy says, "No, if the Arabs are the majority [such as in the West Bank and Gaza Strip] then they have the right to decide their own fate." So Zionism and democracy are at odds. I say clearly that I stand with Zionism. I want a Jewish state, not a Hebrew-speaking Portugal.

The New York Times, 8-5:4.

1

Edward M. Kennedy
United States Senator,
D-Massachusetts

[On the U.S. Senate's vote to postpone a large arms sale to Jordan unless that country begins direct peace negotiations with Israel]: There is no justification for any weapons sale to Jordan or any other Arab nation that might endanger the security of Israel. By our action delaying—and denying—the sale for now, we offer a clear, continuing and appropriate incentive to Jordan to make peace with Israel.

Washington, Oct. 24/
The Washington Post, 10-25:(A)9.

2

Mohammed Khatib
Minister of Information of Jordan

There have been statements made recently by American and Israeli officials suggesting that Jordan's stand with regard to direct negotiations with Israel have begun to change. We would like to affirm at this time in particular that Jordan categorically refuses to hold direct negotiations or to conclude partial or separate settlements with Israel. An international conference to be attended by all the parties concerned, including the PLO and the five permanent UN Security Council members . . . is the only way of achieving a just and comprehensive solution to the Palestinian problem.

Amman/The Washington Post, 10-28:(A)21.

3

Ruhollah Khomeini
Spiritual leader of Iran

[On the current Iran-Iraq war]: You all know what [Iraqi President] Saddam [Hussein] will do to us and to our country if he gets a chance. This is not a war between Iran and Iraq. This is a war which Saddam started to destroy Iran and Islam, and we will fight against him to the end and until he is defeated.

The Washington Post, 5-18:(A)15.

4

Jeane J. Kirkpatrick
United States Ambassador/
Permanent Representative
to the United Nations

I don't think anyone would say our [U.S.] Lebanon policy was very successful. I think once the Israelis had gone into Lebanon and the Syrians and PLO were on the run, we should not have discouraged the Israelis from running the Syrians out of the Bekaa [Valley] and the Palestinians out of Beirut. Our aversion to the use of force, which I share, nonetheless helped to create a situation where Lebanon remains torn by violence.

Interview, New York/Los Angeles Times, 3-31:(VII)2.

5

Henry A. Kissinger
Former Secretary of State
of the United States

[On the current hijacking of an American airliner by Shiite Moslems and the holding hostage of the passengers in Beirut]: If anybody in the world who thinks that injustice is being done to them can capture 50 Americans, kill one of

6

(HENRY A. KISSINGER)

them, beat up the others, humiliate and cause anguish to the families . . . [then] Americans are going to become the whipping boys for every crisis all over the world. Here, innocent Americans are being kidnaped for a situation in which America played absolutely no role. This is the issue.

Broadcast interview, "Today" show,
NBC-TV/Newsweek, 7-1:37.

Chedli Klibi
Secretary General, Arab League

1

Either the Arab peace efforts are met on the Israeli side and supported by Western Europe and the United States, [or] Israel can continue to reject all peace settlements and continue its policy of force . . . In this [latter] case I can only envision darkness, for Israel as well as for the Arabs. Lebanon has given us a taste of this darkness.

Los Angeles Times, 7-16:(I)1.

Tom Lantos
United States Representative, D-California

2

[Criticizing the U.S. decision to sell arms to Saudi Arabia and Jordan]: I will oppose it, and the majority of my colleagues will oppose it. The Saudis are in no need of arms sale; the Jordanians are in no need of an arms sale. I still very much hope that the good judgment of [U.S. Secretary of State] George Shultz in the final analysis will prevail against the professional Arabists in the State Department.

Interview, Sept. 5/Los Angeles Times, 9-6:(I)1.

Samuel W. Lewis
United States Ambassador to Israel

3

[The 1982 Israeli invasion of Lebanon] was a failure largely because of basic misconceptions from the start, and that failure was assured by a lot of mistakes along the way by all of the parties, including ourselves. The Lebanon war, the preoccupation with the Lebanon era, was a great

diversion and made it impossible for Israel, the United States or Jordan to seek a way to continue the peace process. I think we would have been able to renew the peace process in 1981 or 1982 had Lebanon not diverted diplomatic and psychological energies.

Interview, Tel Aviv, May 24/
The Washington Post, 5-25:(A)1.

Theodore Mann
President, American Jewish Congress

4

[On the suggestion by Egyptian President Hosni Mubarak and Jordanian King Hussein that the U.S. should agree to meet PLO Chairman Yasir Arafat to try to work out an Arab-Israeli peace settlement]: There is indeed a genuine desire on the part of both President Mubarak and King Hussein to move ahead with the peace process. This is not contrived; it is not part of some conspiracy; it is a genuine desire that they have because they understand that if progress is not made quickly, whatever possibilities exist may disappear . . . Everybody we talked to insisted that an element of the PLO, Yasir Arafat in particular, was becoming more moderate and held potential for becoming still more moderate and that they wanted to test that . . . I must say the PLO has had the opportunity to be tested for more years than I care to count. [However,] the judgment as to whether it would hinder the peace process or advance the peace process to let them be put to the test one more time is an exquisitely difficult judgment that governments ought to make, not people like myself.

News conference, Jerusalem,
Sept. 11/Los Angeles Times, 9-12:(I)1,12.

Yoel Marcus
Columnist, "Ha'aretz" (Israel)

5

Just as there has sprung up a new generation of Jews who have not known Israel without the [occupied] territories, so there has sprung up in the territories a new generation [of Arabs] that knows only hatred for the Israeli occupation. And with no breakthrough to a settlement based on dividing the land, the two peoples are on the way to a civil war.

U.S. News & World Report, 9-2:36.

Laurence Michalak
Vice chairman, Middle East Center,
University of California, Berkeley

1

I think Arabs are the most maligned ethnic group in the United States, and they're pretty much maligned with impunity. Americans are the most virulently anti-Arab people in the world.

The Christian Science Monitor, 10-21:3.

Yitzhak Modai
Minister of Finance of Israel

2

[On the severe austerity measures imposed on Israel by its government to bolster an ailing economy]: If you want to recover, sometimes you have to undergo surgery, and we have nobody to operate on except the people of Israel.

July 1/The Washington Post, 7-2:(A)12.

3

You can't control the economy forever by administrative measures. They tried it in the United States [in 1973], didn't they? [Then-U.S. Secretary of the Treasury George] Shultz himself thought that he could control prices forever. Ridiculous. He controlled it for six months and then ran away from it like it was fire. He had to hand it back. We [in Israel] took it upon ourselves to control [the economy] for a transition period. From then on, either the market forces have the muscle or not. If they don't have, then something is basically wrong with our economy or with our people.

Interview, Jerusalem/
The Washington Post, 8-29:(C)3.

Hosni Mubarak
President of Egypt

4

I am not an ambitious man at all. I didn't ask to be President. I just accepted it because it is in the interest of the country—not for the fame . . . or its luxurious life.

USA Today, 3-8:(4)2.

5

[Asking for a reduction of interest rates on his loans from the U.S.]: Just to maintain the infrastructure in so many parts of this country: railways, electricity, roads, houses, communications —I'm meeting all these needs—is fantastic. The level of interest in military [purchases] is putting me in a difficult situation. You're [the U.S.] giving me about $815-million in economic aid. Each year I'm giving you back, as interest on the military loans, about $500-million. The rest is only about $300-million. It's not helping me raise the standards of the people.

Interview, Cairo/Newsweek, 3-11:42.

6

I withdrew the [Egyptian] Ambassador [from Jerusalem] after the [Israeli] invasion of Lebanon and the massacre that took place—the minimum I could do. The Israelis are going to withdraw [from Lebanon]. Very good. [Now we need] a move on the Palestinian problem, then Taba. I don't think these are difficult questions. [But] I can't say publicly that I am ready to return the Ambassador. I would be a big liar in front of the Egyptian people. I can't do it. It would be explained as pressure from the U.S.

Interview, Cairo/Newsweek, 3-11:42.

7

Some have suggested that the United States should wait and see how things develop [in the Middle East]. In effect, the proponents of this view advocate inaction as a line of policy. I beg to differ. This is almost a defeatist approach based on a series of wrong premises. The argument goes that the responsibility for moving the peace process falls squarely and solely on the parties to the conflict. The inference here is that the United States can play only a secondary role, and even this secondary role cannot be played independently. [But] the role of a great country like the United States is not simply to endorse what was agreed upon.

Before National Press Club, Washington,
March 13/Los Angeles Times, 3-14:(I)1.

8

[Saying the PLO must be involved in an Arab-Israeli peace plan]: You in America can't under-

(HOSNI MUBARAK)

stand, really, what we mean. We mean comprehensive peace. Genuine peace. Not just any kind of solution where we can say we reached a solution but terrorism can continue. That's why I'm telling you the PLO is the sole representative of the Palestinians, whether we like it or not. I would like you in the United States to understand this perfectly well. The PLO are people everywhere. They are in the United States, in Europe, in Algiers, in Egypt, in Israel. They are everywhere. So solving the problem and at the same time trying to ignore the PLO, this will never lead to comprehensive peace.

Interview, Cairo, Dec. 8/
The Washington Post, 12-23:(A)18.

Abu Nidal
Leader,
Palestinian Revolutionary Council

1

My enemy is the Zionist occupation of my homeland, Palestine. My enemy is imperialism in all its forms. My enemies are the breakup of my Arabic nation into separate [states] and its disunity. My enemies are also the conventions and the chaotic circumstances in our Arabic society and the seduction of our youth . . . If there is anything absolute in this world, it is our enmity to American imperialism, for without American help the Zionist creation [Israel] would no longer exist . . . I can assure you of one thing: If we are given the chance to cause America even the most insignificant harm, we will not hesitate to do it. Between the Americans and us there exists a war to the death. In the coming months and years the Americans will be thinking about us . . . That the Zionists used force to grab for themselves a piece of my Arabic homeland is not in my eyes actually *the* crime. Rather, for me *the* crime would be if we were to allow that these Zionists could ever leave our homeland alive again. That is my philosophy. I, Abu Nidal, view myself as the answer to the misfortunes of the Arabs.

Interview, October/
Los Angeles Times, 1-1('86):(II)5.

Shimon Peres
Prime Minister of Israel

2

I would gladly go to Cairo to meet with [Egyptian] President Mubarak without prior conditions. I would gladly go to Amman without prior conditions to meet with [Jordanian] King Hussein. I am willing to speak to the leaders of both these countries without any advance promises from them. I believe that we have to show our people that peace is not just between two governments but also between the people. Peace is a purpose in itself. I genuinely believe that the Egyptian people are for peace. It is my hope that when President Mubarak and I do meet, we shall be able to solve all the problems standing in the way of peace in the Middle East.

Interview, Jerusalem/
U.S. News & World Report, 1-14:30.

3

[Criticizing a proposed "who is a Jew?" law in the Israeli Parliament]: Let not a law constitute an impediment to a Jew—even a Jew who has sinned—and let no legislation be an obstacle in the way of the in-gathering of all the dispersed, the bringing together of those from afar. Who is a Jew was already determined many generations ago. Our generation is charged with providing an answer as to how to preserve the Jewish people in the face of changing conditions and changing dangers, how to keep it together, with all its streams and ideas, both under conditions of sovereignty and throughout the Diaspora.

Before Knesset (Parliament),
Jan. 16/Los Angeles Times, 1-17:(I)13.

4

I sometimes feel like the rabbi who was praying on the top of a mountain so hard that he almost fell off—at which moment another mountain moved and closed the chasm. I am now praying for the same movement in our Cabinet. But so far, against all predictions, we've been able to take a lot of decisions and to accomplish a lot . . . My job is to serve the people on a day-to-day basis, and leave the rest to the historians. But one change which I did plan in advance was

343

WHAT THEY SAID IN 1985

(SHIMON PERES)

to close the deep divisions in this nation, and I believe that's been accomplished. I've avoided the temptation of recriminations and proclaiming my righteousness, and I've concentrated on the problems of today and of the future. This has changed the atmosphere in Israel, making it more united and optimistic.

Interview, Jerusalem/Newsweek, 2-18:40.

1

By its own reckoning, Egypt got back 99.99 per cent of its territory [which Israel had occupied after past wars]. What we'd expect is to get from Egypt 99.99 per cent of peace . . . At any rate, I don't expect our relations with the Arabs to be always symmetrical. My government has decided to seek peace between us and the Arabs, and we will stick with this policy whether their reaction is gratifying to us or not.

Interview, Jerusalem/Newsweek, 2-18:40.

2

For this last period of time, both Washington and we felt very strongly that the best way really to move ahead in the direction of peace was by the only way which exists, namely, negotiation between the Arabs and Israel. On the Arab side, there were many attempts to try and convince Washington to commit the United States on behalf of Israel and twist Israel's arm. May I say that Washington stood very firm: "You gentlemen go ahead and negotiate." Because, after all, the problem is not to make peace between Jordan and the United States. And it's complete folly to think that, even if Washington would theoretically agree, which it did not, that Washington can twist Israel's arm. Israel is an independent country.

Interview, Jerusalem, March 1/
The Washington Post, 3-2:(A)12.

3

We cannot accept that the PLO will become a party to the [Israel-Arab] negotiations. I have been asked, "Don't you have terrorists in Israel?" Yes, we have people who were terrorists.

4

We don't have people who *are* terrorists. If somebody is a terrorist, we put him in prison. The PLO is still engaged in terror. Shooting and talking don't go together . . . Peace is a must for us and a must for the Arabs. Whoever looks at modern technology and at the results of past wars should come to the only sane conclusion—which is to solve the problems diplomatically and peacefully. Even if someone tells me, "Look, your chances are very dim," I wouldn't change my convictions or my optimism. If you lose optimism, you're out of business.

Interview, Tel Aviv/
Time, 3-18:31.

5

I think we can say to our friends across the ocean, and to our neighbors across the [Jordan] river, that despite all the obstacles and difficulties on the road, Israel believes that it is possible to arrive at direct negotiations [with Jordan], that those negotiations are likely to bear fruit and that Israel is ready to contribute much to advance them as much as possible . . . If he [Jordan's King Hussein] wants peace, he must understand that he has to sit with Israel and not keep trying to place her in some darkened waiting room until everything is concluded without her.

Before the Knesset (Parliament),
Jerusalem, June 10/Los Angeles Times,
6-11:(I)10; The New York Times, 6-11:1.

[On the economic austerity measures he has instituted]: What would have happened if we hadn't done it? In my view, we would have remained without dollars, inflation would have skyrocketed, the first victims would have been the workers. I didn't do it with an easy heart . . . The first reason was to prevent an actual collapse. What does collapse mean? Our foreign currency was about to run out, so we would have had to move to a regime of rationing. We wouldn't have money for spare parts, for food—because under such inflation the dollars flee, foreign currency flees.

Broadcast interview/
The Washington Post, 7-4:(A)26.

(SHIMON PERES)

1

I think all the countries in the Middle East, because of the experience from past [Arab-Israeli] wars, and the terrible potential of modern military technology, are objectively closer to peace than ever before. Because the wars did not produce from the Arab point of view the desired results. For us, they were military victories but not political conclusions. For the future, the Middle East is full of missiles. I think responsible people must try to do their very best to prevent an additional war. And I'm working sincerely to achieve it. I can't trade images for strategies.

Interview, Jerusalem, July 11/
Los Angeles Times, 7-14:(IV)2.

2

If someone wants to have a Palestinian identity, he's entitled to do so. But if he has a gun in his pocket, it's a different story . . . I distinguish between aspirations and positions. To aspire, everybody's free. To shoot, nobody is free.

Interview, Jerusalem, July 11/
Los Angeles Times, 7-14:(IV)2.

3

Nobody brought more tragedy on the Palestinians than PLO terrorism. Our enemy is not a people, a race, a religion, or a community. Our enemy is belligerency, hatred and death. We know that there is a Palestinian problem. We recognize the need to solve it honorably. We are convinced that there is no solution but through diplomatic means. From this rostrum, I call upon the Palestinian people to put an end to rejectionism and belligerency. Let us talk. Come forth and recognize the reality of the State of Israel—our wish to live in peace and our need for security. Let us face each other as free men and women, across the negotiating table. Let us argue, but not fight. Let us arm ourselves with reason. Let us not reason with arms.

At United Nations, New York,
Oct. 21/The New York Times, 10-22:5.

4

[On revelations of Israeli espionage in the U.S.]: I object to certain hints in the media that a

community or a country was spying. In fact, it was a single spy, which did cause unpleasant occurrences in our midst and which was contrary to our policy, which is not to spy against the United States. This was not and is not a Jewish affair or a national affair. It is a case of a single person, and we will take steps to investigate what led to it and to see to it that justice is done.

Before Conference of Presidents
of Major American Jewish Organizations,
Dec. 2/Los Angeles Times, 12-3:(I)14.

5

[On the potential for Arab-Israeli peace]: There are occasions in history when you can meet the double requirement of a procedure that may lead to peace and of a coalition that can follow the procedure. I think both are potentially existent. I should regret it very much if it should be missed. [But] while there are changes in the policies of the Arab countries, there is unfortunately no change in the quarters of the Palestinian leadership. For the last 37 years since the creation of the state of Israel, I cannot recall a single occasion where the Palestinian leadership discovered a window open even when it was open.

Interview/The Washington Post, 12-23:(A)18.

William Quandt
Former staff member,
National Security Council
of the United States

6

[Saying the U.S. should take more initiative in trying to get Israel and the Arabs together]: If the Arabs and Israelis could make peace on their own, I would urge them on. But you have hesitant leaders on both sides who need to point to quick, tangible gains from any agreement, and they expect the U.S. to provide these gains. So [for the U.S.] to be so standoffish is not historical . . . without a third party [the U.S.], they made it [to the Camp David talks in 1978]. [Today, U.S. President] Reagan and [U.S. Secretary of State] Shultz want the burden to be on the Arabs. The trouble is that you can get so locked into a waiting game that you lose out.

The Christian Science Monitor, 3-20:32.

Yitzhak Rabin
Minister of Defense,
and former Prime Minister, of Israel

1

I believe that among the many surprises, and most of them not for the good, that came out of the war in Lebanon, the most dangerous is that the war let the Shiites out of the bottle. No one predicted that; I couldn't find it in any Israeli intelligence report. The Shiites, the largest community in Lebanon, were oppressed by the PLO. They didn't like the struggle against the PLO, and they received us in the beginning as liberators. But in the last year and a half, they looked at us the way they looked at the PLO, as a foreign occupation force. It's more than that. In trying to forge an identity, they had to have somebody to fight, and so they started a struggle against Israel. If, as a result of the war in Lebanon, we replace PLO terrorism in southern Lebanon with Shiite terrorism, we have done the worst [thing] in our struggle against terrorism.

Interview, New York/Time, 2-11:44.

2

[Supporting the controversial Israeli-Arab agreement for an exchange of 1,150 Palestinian prisoners and terrorists held by Israel for 3 Israeli prisoners held by the Arabs]: I don't believe that we have the right to say [to] our men, "Go to hell, end your life in a prison." And where? In the hands of terrorists! I don't believe that a government, or I as Minister of Defense, can say to the soldiers, the parents or my conscience, "Well, they were captured. They are held by terrorists in a place where I can't release them by force," and then I do nothing . . . I as Minister of Defense feel a commitment, a responsibility for every soldier whenever he is sent on a combat mission, to take care of whatever happens to him. Maybe the terrorists could have stayed in jail another two years. But out of the 879 we released from our jails, 526 had already served more than 10 years anyway . . . I believe that since 1968 we have pursued a policy that basically said: "Whenever you have got a military option to release most of the [Israeli] hostages or prisoners of war from the hands of terrorist organizations it should be preferred. But if the hostages or prisoners of war are being

held in places that are impossible to get at, I can't see not negotiating an exchange for terrorists."

Interview, Tel Aviv, May 23/
The New York Times, 5-24:4.

3

In the long run, fighting will be ended between some of the Arab countries—if not all—and Israel. We've believed that from the very beginning, but we assumed that, since the phenomenon of the Jewish people returning to the land of Israel and establishing an independent state is almost unprecedented in the history of mankind, it might take time. After having the historic breakthrough of the peace between Egypt and Israel, I believe it's possible, but it might take 10, 20 or 30 years. One has to bear in mind that not only political interests, but emotions, religious contradictions, are involved; therefore, it takes time.

Interview/USA Today, 6-12:(A)11.

4

[On the current hijacking of an American airliner and the holding hostage of its passengers by Lebanese Shiite Moslems demanding that Israel release hundreds of Lebanese Shiites it is holding]: Let's not play games. If there is a desire, if there is a request on the part of the United States that this has to be done in relation [to], or as a part of, a deal for the release of the [American] hostages, please, come out and say it. The problem is an American problem [not an Israeli problem]. The hostages are Americans. They were caught on board an airline which carries the United States flag. The United States government has to make up its mind: What do they want to do? It's first and foremost their decision. I've never tried to avoid responsibility. I've never shrugged off my shoulders the need to make a decision as Prime Minister and now as a Defense Minister, facing terror acts against Israelis. I expect the United States to do the same.

Broadcast interview/
"Nightline," ABC-TV, 6-19.

5

[On Israel's recent air attack against PLO offices in Tunisia]: We cannot tolerate . . . immu-

(YITZHAK RABIN)

nity for the PLO because they are located in countries which are not active against Israel. As long as PLO terror, or any other terror, acts against Israel, Israel will wage war against it. Israel will determine the method of warfare, the place of the strike, in accordance with *its* judgment and *its* judgment only . . . I repeat that no PLO terrorist target is immune, no matter where it is located, against attack by us. I don't want you to draw conclusions from this regarding if and when we will decide to attack such a target. I will add no more.

To reporters, Tel Aviv, Oct. 1/
Los Angeles Times, 10-2:(I)8.

1

[Jordan's] King Hussein has to make up his mind. Does he want peace with us? If he wants, [it must be] without [PLO chairman Yasir] Arafat. With Palestinian leaders, yes. Any one of the authentic leaders of the West Bankers, the Gazans, to join him would be fine with us. And I believe that they have to participate in the peace process, because their fate, their future, will be decided in these negotiations.

Before United Jewish Appeal, Jerusalem/
Los Angeles Times, 10-23:(I)22.

2

Ronald Reagan
President of the United States

We're not seeking to impose a settlement on anyone [in the Middle East]. But I feel that we have to make the moderate Arab states recognize that we can be their friend as well as the friend of Israel. And this could be helpful in our trying to be of help in peace negotiations. And part of this would be—they're under threat, there's a war going on just minutes away from them by air. The Soviet Union, with its invasion of Afghanistan, has made it evident that the Middle East can't rule out the possibility of expansionism on the part of the Soviets there. And we think that they're [the Arabs] entitled to some defense weapons also. At the same time, we have insured Israel that we will never see them lose their qualitative edge to the point that they're endangered by anything we do.

Interview, Washington, Feb. 11/
The New York Times, 2-12:6.

3

. . . will whoever represents the Palestinians be willing to say that they recognize the right of Israel to exist as a nation? This is a great sticking point. It's why we cannot enter into any negotiations with the Palestinians—the PLO—as long as they say that. How do you talk to a country and say to a country, "You should negotiate with these people," when "these people" say, "We don't recognize that country's right to exist"?

Interview, Washington, Feb. 11/
The New York Times, 2-12:6.

4

[Addressing visiting Egyptian President Hosni Mubarak]: One question that we must address forthrightly is how the Palestinians should be represented [in Middle East negotiations]. Mr. President, you have wisely stressed the need for practicality. In our quest for peace, we reaffirm with you that in all stages of the negotiating process there should be Palestinian participation. As we have said many times before, these Palestinians should include representatives from the [Israeli-occupied] West Bank and Gaza and other Palestinians as mutually agreed by the parties. These are wide parameters. They provide ample scope. They should be put to use.

At dinner honoring the Egyptian President, Washington, March 12/
Los Angeles Times, 3-13:(I)14.

5

[On U.S. involvement in Egyptian-Israeli negotiations]: Our proposal in the very beginning was that we did not want to participate in the negotiations—wouldn't be any of our business to do so—but that we'd do whatever we could to help bring the warring parties together—in effect you might say continue the Camp David process and continue trying to find more countries that would do as Egypt did and make peace. And we haven't been idle . . . We have been trying to build up a relationship with the Arab nations as well as the relationship that we have always had with Israel, and we discussed with [Egyptian] President Mubarak the things that he has proposed and the idea of the Palestinians. We did have to make it clear that we couldn't meet if it was the PLO. They still refuse to recognize the UN Resolutions 242 and 338, and they refuse to agree or admit that Israel has a right to exist as a nation. But we have said Palestinian representatives, yes. There's a large Palestinian community, and I'm sure that there are people that do not consider themselves represented by the PLO.

News conference, Washington, March 21/
The New York Times, 3-22:10.

1

[On the current hijacking of an American airliner by Shiite Moslems and the holding hostage of its passengers in Beirut]: Let me . . . make it plain to the assassins in Beirut and their accomplices, wherever they may be, that America will never make concessions to terrorists. To do so would only invite more terrorism. Nor will we ask nor pressure any other government to do so. Once we head down that path, there'll be no end to it. No end to the suffering of innocent people; no end to the bloody ransom all civilized nations must pay. This act of terrorism is a stain on Lebanon and particularly on those Lebanese in whose name it has been done. Those in Lebanon who commit these acts damage their country and their cause, and we hold them accountable. I call upon those holding our people to release them without condition. I call upon the leaders of Lebanon, political and religious, to meet their responsibilities and to do all that is necessary to end this crime now in the name of the God they worship. And I call on other governments to speak out and use their influence as well. This attack is an attack on all citizens of the world who seek to live free from the fear and scourge of terrorism.

News conference, Washington, June 18/
The New York Times, 6-19:11.

2

[On how to retaliate against those who hijacked an American airliner and are currently holding the passengers hostage in Beirut]: . . . the problem is, who is perpetuating these deeds, who their accomplices are, where they are located, because retaliation in some people's minds might just entail striking a blow in a general direction, and the result would be a terrorist act in itself and the killing and victimizing of innocent people . . . I'm as frustrated as anyone. I've pounded a few walls myself when I'm alone about this. It is frustrating. But as I say, you have to be able to pinpoint the enemy. You can't just start shooting without having someone in your gun sights.

News conference, Washington, June 18/
The New York Times, 6-19:11.

3

[On the current hijacking of an American airliner by Shiite Moslems and the holding hostage of the passengers in Beirut]: I don't think anything that attempts to get people back who have been kidnapped by thugs, murderers and barbarians is wrong to do. We're going to do everything we can to get all of the Americans back . . . When terrorism strikes, civilization itself is under attack. No nation is immune. There's no safety in silence or neutrality. If we permit terrorism to succeed anywhere, it will spread like a cancer, eating away at civilized societies and sowing fear and chaos everywhere. This barbarism is abhorrent. And all of those who support it, encourage it and profit from it are abhorrent. They are barbarians.

To residents and city leaders,
Chicago Heights, Ill., June 28/
The New York Times, 6-29:5.

4

[On the increase in international terrorism and the recent release of 39 Americans held hostage in Beirut after their airliner was hijacked]: The United States gives terrorists no rewards and no guarantees. We make no concessions. We make no deals. Nations that harbor terrorists undermine their own stability and endanger their own people. Terrorists be on notice: We will fight back against you in Lebanon and elsewhere. We will fight back against your cowardly attacks on American citizens and property.

Broadcast address to the nation, Washington,
June 30/The New York Times, 7-1:10.

(RONALD REAGAN)

1

[Addressing Americans who were recently held hostage by Lebanese Shiite Moslems after an American airliner was hijacked]: None of you were held prisoner because of any personal wrong that any of you had done to anyone. You were held simply because you were Americans. In the minds of your captors, you represented us. Well, whatever the presumed grievance or political motive that caused these actions, let there be no confusion: A crime was committed against you. Hijacking is a crime; kidnapping is a crime; murder is a crime; and holding our people prisoner is a crime. When cruelty is inflicted on innocent people, it discredits whatever cause in whose name it's done. And those who commit such deeds are enemies of peace, enemies of the peace.

At Andrews Air Force Base, Va.,
July 2/The New York Times, 7-3:8.

2

[On Arab terrorism against Jews in the Israeli-occupied West Bank]: Wherever there is a terror attack, normal life must not be allowed to go on. In a place where Jews cannot live, where Jews cannot come and go peacefully, there will be neither peace, nor quiet, nor security for non-Jews. They must know that they stand to lose from every murder and terror action.

Speech, Aug. 25/
The Christian Science Monitor,
8-27:32.

Victor Shemtov
Member, Israeli Knesset (Parliament)

3

[On the recent bomb attack in Lebanon that killed 2 Israeli soldiers]: It is obvious that so long as the Israeli Army occupies Lebanese land, it is a target for such ghastly attacks. We have become part of the Lebanese hell . . . There is no justification, militarily or politically, for remaining in Lebanon.

Jerusalem, March 11/
Los Angeles Times, 3-12:(I)22.

Samir S. Shihabi
Saudi Arabian Ambassador/
Permanent Representative to the United Nations

4

[Criticizing Israel's operations in Lebanon]: Hitler preceded them with his Nazi destructive machinery in the ways of brutality and murder, collectively and individually. And even though they [Israel] have surpassed them now, his end was inevitable and their end will be inevitable if the world does not stop them before it is too late.

At United Nations, New York, March 12/
The New York Times, 3-13:3.

Yousef Shirawi
Minister of Development of Bahrain

5

[On the decline in oil revenues being experienced by Middle East oil-exporting nations after years of boom]: We became the rich poor [during the boom years]; we had money but not skills. However, the Arabians are very honorable people. We accepted the influx of power that came with the petrodollars with humility, and we are accepting the shrinkage today with a lot of grace.

Los Angeles Times, 7-18:(I)12.

George P. Shultz
Secretary of State of the United States

6

[Saying some Arab policies against Israel have hurt Palestinians]: Now is the time for the Arabs to let negotiations proceed. Those who chased illusions of "armed struggle," those who engaged in terrorism, those who thought that Soviet support would intimidate the United States and Israel, have only brought death to innocents and prolonged the suffering of the Palestinian people. Such methods have achieved nothing constructive and never will . . . The way to find out what the answer is is to get the people immediately concerned to the bargaining table face to face and have them work it out. In a very deep sense the process is the substance. I don't mean to say that there isn't tremendously difficult substance to struggle with, but plans are a dime a dozen. Anyone can think up a plan. The problem is to get a process under way that is undertaken

349

WHAT THEY SAID IN 1985

(GEORGE P. SHULTZ)

in good faith and good spirit by serious people who understand the problems, understand their interests, who represent them strongly, but who are there and will try to work it out.

Before American Israel Public Affairs Committee, Washington, April 21/The New York Times, 4-22:5.

1

Israel is the true witness to the Holocaust and the truest symbol of the victory of good over evil. That is why Israel must endure, and that is why the American people are forever committed to Israel's security.

At Yad Vashem memorial, Jerusalem, May 10/The New York Times, 5-11:7.

2

[Criticizing U.S. Congressional attempts to block American arms sales to Jordan just after Jordan's King Hussein offered an Arab-Israeli peace plan]: King Hussein has taken some important initiatives that are positive and that move in the direction of peace and move in the direction of direct negotiations, that employ the word "non-belligerency." To greet those moves by the Senate sticking its finger in his eye doesn't seem to me to be a particularly good thing for the United States to do. So I'm unhappy about the broad, bipartisan effort to stick the Congress' finger in King Hussein's eye. However, [Congress is] a separate and more-than-equal branch of the government, so they do whatever they want to do.

To reporters, en route to Portugal, June 4/Los Angeles Times, 6-5:(I)9.

3

We differ from some of our European friends over the role of the PLO. To us, it seems obvious that the PLO excludes itself as a player [in the Arab-Israeli peace process] so long as it rejects UN Security Council Resolutions 242 and 338 and Israel's right to exist. Is the PLO becoming a more moderate organization? Will it renounce "armed struggle"? We shall see. Meanwhile, the PLO is not entitled to any payment in ad-

350

vance so long as it rejects what are, after all, the basic premises of the peace process. A country [Israel] cannot be expected to make concessions to those who resort to terrorism and who treat negotiation as only a way-station on the road to its ultimate destruction. If PLO policy changes, that factor will be acknowledged. We have always said this. Unlike some of our European friends, however, we feel that gestures toward the PLO, while it has not accepted 242 and 338, only mislead its leaders into thinking their present inadequate policy is gaining them international acceptance and stature.

Before Pilgrims Society, London, Oct. 10/The New York Times, 12-11:6.

Joseph Sisco
Former Under Secretary of State of the United States

4

[On the current hijacking of an American airliner and the holding hostage of its passengers in Beirut]: This incident illustrates the difficulties a major power [the U.S.] has applying force in a regional dispute. The Shiites who took over the TWA aircraft not only are aiming at the release of [Arab prisoners held by Israel], but their broader objective is to eliminate U.S. influence in the Middle East. These are anti-peace, anti-American, anti-Israeli, anti-moderate-Arab acts. The objective of the fanatical Shiites is the ultimate establishment of an Islamic fundamentalist state in Lebanon on the model of the Ayatollah Khomeini [in Iran].

Interview/USA Today, 6-19:(4)11.

Larry Speakes
Principal Deputy Press Secretary to the President of the United States

5

[On Israel's air attack against PLO offices in Tunisia]: While the resort to violence is deplorable, it is useful to recall the antecedents to this attack, which included repeated attempts to infiltrate terrorists into Israel, and the outrageous murder of three Israeli civilians at Larnaca [Cyprus]. The air strike, against this background, is understandable as an expression of self-defense. Our distress is especially acute, however, since

(LARRY SPEAKES)

one act of violence touches off another, and a pattern of escalation is established. Such acts of violence are contrary to our overall objective of a peaceful, stable Middle East and cannot be condoned.

Washington, Oct. 2/The New York Times, 10-3:1.

Mustafa Tlas
Minister of Defense of Syria

1

I am beginning to agree with the [late] French President [Charles] de Gaulle. He said the United States has no foreign policy, only foreign problems. Look at the United States in Lebanon. A total failure. How can we have respect for the United States when we see the biggest of countries coming and supporting the [Israeli] invasion of a tiny country like Lebanon? The cluster bombs dropped on Beirut by the Israelis in 1982 were only two months old, straight from California. They were the latest armaments and weaponry from the United States. And still [U.S.] President Reagan wonders why we don't love the United States in this region.

Interview, Damascus/
The Washington Post, 5-3:(A)28.

Ezer Weizman
Former Minister of Defense of Israel

2

[Saying Israel should be more forthcoming in seeking peace with the Arabs]: Three people risked their careers for the Israel-Egypt peace treaty. [Then-U.S. President] Jimmy Carter put his career on the line. [Then-Egyptian President Anwar] Sadat gave his life. And [then-Israeli Prime Minister Menachem] Begin now sits at home. I resigned from the Ministry of Defense because I thought in 1980 my government was wrong and not fulfilling the treaty. Sadat once said to me, "Ezer, I'm talking to you of big, big, big business." Peace is big, big business. I say to some of my colleagues in the Labor Party I hope history won't be so cynical as to judge that Menachem Begin brought peace and [current Israeli Prime Minister] Shimon Peres lost it. If Israel wants to become a strong established country, it has to come to a political decision and make peace with the Arabs.

Interview/
The Christian Science Monitor,
10-15:22.

Zhao Ziyang
Premier of China

3

The Israeli authorities and their supporters still refuse to recognize the legitimate rights of the Palestinian people, refuse to recognize the PLO and refuse to hand back the Arab lands they are occupying. Their mistaken stand is the greatest obstacle to a peaceful settlement of the Mideast problem. Only when they change this position can the Middle East move toward peace.

Peking, May 10/
The New York Times,
5-11:7.

War and Peace

William S. Cohen
United States Senator, R-Maine

1

I don't think this [Reagan] Administration or any other Administration could commit U.S. forces to war in the absence of a broad public consensus that we needed to fight. It doesn't mean we won't send our soldiers to fight *any-where*. It does mean that we won't send them to fight everywhere.

Newsweek, 4-15:37.

Mikhail S. Gorbachev
General Secretary,
Communist Party of the Soviet Union

2

The time has come when the threat of nuclear holocaust compels us to learn the great, difficult art of living together . . . For, despite all our differences, in perception and approach, we [the U.S. and the Soviet Union] have something in common—our understanding that nuclear war is inadmissible, that it cannot be waged and that there will be no winner in a nuclear war.

News conference, Geneva, Nov. 21/
Los Angeles Times, 11-22:(I)5.

George Jacobson
Former Special Assistant
to the United States Ambassador
to South Vietnam

3

[On the U.S. pullout from the war in Vietnam in 1975]: It's just the result of not obeying the "Jacobson rule," which has three elements. The first is never, ever, ever, ever become involved in a "limited war," because the other side may not have the same definition of that term as you do. We were fighting a limited war and the Communists weren't. The second is, the moment you learn your country is not 100 per cent behind you, get the hell out—no matter what the losses might be. The third element is censorship. I am convinced that without censorship—and with unlimited television—we would have lost World War II. There is nothing that looks quite like

352

blood on color television. You can't have scenes of American bodies, thrown into trucks like so much cordwood, served up with dinner night after night and expect the American people to support the situation. Those three elements of Jacobson's rules should help for future conflicts.

Newsweek, 4-15:68.

John Paul II
Pope

4

[Calling for success in East-West arms-control talks]: All will be fragile and precarious unless a new philosophy is accepted in international relations. [That means] renouncing egoistic and ideological interests that feed the tensions, hatreds, subversions. [Nations should dedicate] the energies and resources freed by disarmament to the great cause of our time—the struggle against hunger, of human rights and the welfare of people. If this happens, it will change not only the East-West relations but also the North-South relations. Is it a dream? No, it's my earnest appeal for all of you, the peoples of all continents, and to the youth of the world.

New Year's Day address, Vatican City,
Jan. 1/The New York Times, 1-2:4.

5

The men who put their faith in armed struggle . . . have allowed themselves to be tricked by false ideologies. Evil is never a road to good . . . Violence inexorably engenders new forms of oppression and slavery, ordinarily more grave than those which it pretends to liberate.

Ayacucho, Peru/Time, 2-18:70.

Henry A. Kissinger
Former Secretary of State
of the United States

6

If we commit ourselves [to military action], we must prevail. You cannot fight a war for a stalemate; you can only fight a war for a victory, and then you can be generous in the settlements.

(HENRY A. KISSINGER)

You may be able to make a compromise if you are on the way to victory. But if you proclaim stalemate as an objective, you're likely to lose or at any rate get into so protracted a conflict that the public will not sustain it.

Interview/Los Angeles Times, 4-28:(IV)2.

1

In the first 40 years [of the nuclear age], there were 20 years in which we [the U.S.] had a huge nuclear superiority, maybe even 30 years. Most of the crises were in areas where the United States and the Soviet Union controlled most of the decision-making . . . In the next 40 years many new centers of decision-making will emerge, and weapons will become increasingly complex . . . [There will be] other countries which acquire nuclear weapons, or other countries that can involve the nuclear powers through their alliances or their perceptions of the national interest . . . The danger we face is more a conflagration on the model of World War I than of World War II. Nuclear weapons make it unlikely that a superpower will deliberately aim for world conquest in one throw of the dice. But this does not exclude a gradual escalation or a creeping expansion.

Interview/Los Angeles Times, 8-11:(IV)6.

Jiddu Krishnamurti
Indian philosopher

2

I have been saying this for 60 years: We have had thousands of wars through the years, and we remain barbarians, barbarous; we are cruel to each other, we try to hurt each other physically and psychologically. So the problem is whether the world realizes what it is, whether humans realize what they are. It is a crisis in our consciousness. We cannot allow it to go on. Is it possible for human beings—always talking of peace and never having it, with our technology and wars—can we do anything radically to break from this pattern completely? I think it is possible if we had a mind to.

Interview, Washington/
The Washington Post, 4-18:(D)2.

Richard D. Lamm
Governor of Colorado (D)

3

I feel with an Old Testament certainty that we cannot continue indefinitely the way the world is now going, with the world's weapons set on a hair trigger and the doomsday clock at five minutes to noon . . . It has historically been one thing to die *for* your country. It is a different thing to die *with* your country.

At Christian Science Monitor's "Peace 2010"
contest award luncheon, Boston, April 22/
The Christian Science Monitor, 4-24:5.

Golo Mann
West German historian

4

War, the politicians' final arbiter, has disappeared and left them powerless. They must either work together or content themselves with little gains here and there in a game that can never be won. If we look at the past 40 years, there are no longer any reasons to go to war. If there had been reasons, we would have had another war long ago. A single incident like the shooting down of the Korean airliner [by the Soviets] two years ago would have been a reason. Wars no longer have any goal. There are neither declarations of war nor peace treaties. In Korea there is an armistice, and in Vietnam war was never declared. There are only agreements to suspend hostilities. There are now gigantic industries that depend on the arms race. But this simply means that there are no important differences between the U.S. and the Soviet Union—the interests are the same whether the capitalists or the marshals are in power. And in arms research, there is little difference between peaceful and military ends.

Interview/World Press Review, November:34.

Ronald Reagan
President of the United States

5

Think of it. You're sitting at that desk [in the Oval Office]. The word comes that they're [Soviet missiles] on their way. And you sit there knowing that there is no way, at present, of stopping them. So they're going to blow up how

353

(RONALD REAGAN)

...much of this country we can only guess at, and your only response can be to push the button before they get here so that even though you're all going to die, they're going to die, too... There's something so immoral about it... After World War I, all sorts of rules were made about war and the protection of civilians. And here we are, all these years later, and the principal weapon on both sides is a weapon that is designed mainly to kill millions of civilians with no discrimination—men, women and children. How do we think that we're more civilized today when our peacemaking policy is based on the threat that if they kill our people, we'll kill theirs?

Interview, Washington/Time, 1-28:29.

1

[On the Soviet statement that the U.S. use of the atomic bomb against Japan in World War II was "barbaric"]: Well, I always thought it was barbaric of Stalin to kill some 20 million people in his own country, of his own countrymen. But we dropped the bomb in an effort to end what had been the greatest war in man's history. The resistance of the enemy and the island campaigns leading up to an invasion of Japan was such that we knew we would be facing that kind of to-the-death resistance. The casualties were estimated at more than a million if we continued. And I think to second-guess now those who had to make that awesome decision is ridiculous. I think, horrible as it was, we have to say this too, that it did give the world a view of the threat of nuclear weapons and I think that should be an aid in one day now ridding ourselves of them. But I think we have to recognize that that and the presence of our nuclear weapons is a deterrent that kept us at peace for the longest stretch we've ever known, 40 years of peace.

News conference, Washington,
Aug. 5/The New York Times, 8-6:10.

2

Perhaps we can start by remembering this: that all those who died [in wars] for us and our country were, in one way or another, victims of a peace process that failed; victims of a decision to forget certain things; to forget, for instance, that the surest way to keep a peace going is to stay strong. Weakness, after all, is a temptation—it tempts the pugnacious to assert themselves. But strength is a declaration that cannot be misunderstood.

Veterans Day address,
Arlington National Cemetery, Va.,
Nov. 11/The New York Times,
11-12:10.

3

Freedom and democracy are the best guarantors of peace. History has shown that democratic nations do not start wars. The rights of the individual and the rule of law are as fundamental to peace as arms control. A government which does not respect its citizens' rights and its international commitments to protect those rights is not likely to respect its other international undertakings.

Broadcast address to the nation, Washington,
Nov. 14/The New York Times,
11-15:8.

Dean Rusk
Former Secretary of State
of the United States

4

[On how the U.S. handled its involvement in the Vietnam war]: Were we right in deliberately deciding not to create a war fever in the U.S.? We decided that, in a nuclear age, it would be just too dangerous. So we didn't have military parades or movie stars selling war bonds. We were trying to do it cold blood at home while our fellas had to do it in hot blood in Vietnam... Vietnam was the first war fought on TV every day. One can only speculate what would have happened if Anzio and Guadalcanal had been on TV [during World War II]. In our next war, Congress will have to decide what to do about censorship from the very beginning. War is the principal obscenity of the human race. To have this exposed on TV weekly, daily, hourly creates special problems.

The Wall Street Journal, 1-14:8.

James R. Schlesinger
Former Secretary of Defense
of the United States

1

During [the war in] Vietnam, the nation's supposed elite, possessed of views then fashionable, was set upon by their children saying: "You led the nation astray." They didn't have the strength of conviction to do what the older generation of an elite have always done when the younger generation acted up: Simply stare back at them.

The Wall Street Journal, 1-14:8.

2

. . . the Secretary of Defense [Caspar Weinberger] has insisted upon domestic consensus before U.S. forces become employed [in hostilities abroad]. Given the circumstances, that is indeed a demanding requirement. Were it to be rigorously implemented, it would virtually assure other powers that they can count on not facing American forces. Much as I personally sympathize with the concerns of the Department of Defense in the post-Vietnam era, I cannot concur with the emerging belief that the United States must only fight popular, winnable wars. The likeliest physical challenges to the United States come in the Third World—not in Europe or North America. If the more predatory states in the Third World are given assurance that they can employ, directly or indirectly, physical force against American interest with impunity, they will feel far less restraint in acting against our interests.

Before Senate Foreign Relations Committee,
Washington, Feb. 6/The New York Times, 2-7:6.

3

I think that one has to be very selective about where one goes [when becoming involved militarily abroad], but when one does decide, one should go in with a strategy quite different from the one that we had in 1965 [in Vietnam]. We were engaged in some kind of signaling, and we were signaling more to the American people that we weren't going to get deeply engaged than we were to the people in Hanoi that we were serious and that they had better back off. If you're going to signal, you'd better have a mailed fist in that velvet glove.

Broadcast interview/
"Meet the Press," NBC-TV, 4-28.

4

All nations love "glorious little wars." Even World War II with its sequential victories was immensely popular in Germany—until 1942. The intelligentsia will no doubt have misgivings, since public enthusiasm sweeps away serious legal and moral questions. But popular support is hardly weakened by such quibbles. Thus, it is useful to have a Grenada to trump a loser like Beirut. But from the national perspective such easy victories resolve remarkably little. If a conflict is sufficiently easy to be a "glorious war," it is certain to be marginal to our interests. Americans historically have embraced crusades—such as World War II—as well as glorious little wars. The difficulty is that the most likely conflicts of the future fall between crusades and such brief encounters as Grenada. Yet these in-between conflicts have weak public support. Even in the best of times—with national unity and at the height of our power—public enthusiasm for Korea and Vietnam evaporated in just a year or two. Indeed, any war that is not a clear-cut winner will not long enjoy public enthusiasm. The problem is that virtually no opportunity exists for future crusades, and those glorious wars are likely to occur infrequently. The role of the U.S. in the world is such that it must be prepared for, be prepared to threaten, and even be prepared to fight those intermediate conflicts that are likely to fare poorly on television. Whether this nation, the leader of the free world, can measure up to such challenges will to a large extent define the future shape of international politics.

Before Senate Foreign Relations Committee,
Washington, Feb. 6/The Wall Street Journal, 7-30:24.

Georgi Shahnazarov
Member, Central Committee,
Communist Party of the Soviet Union

5

In the nuclear age, war cannot any longer be considered as a means for achieving political ob-

George P. Shultz
Secretary of State of the United States

2

In the 1980s and beyond, most likely we will never see a world in a total state of peace—or a state of total war. The West is relatively well prepared to deter an all-out war or a Soviet attack on Western Europe or Japan; that's why these are the least likely contingencies. But day in and day out, we will continue to see a wide range of conflicts in a gray area between major war and millennial peace.

Before Pilgrims Society, London,
Dec. 10/The New York Times, 12-11:6.

(GEORGI SHAHNAZAROV)

jectives . . . In general, one of the imperatives of the nuclear age can be formulated this way: There are no political objectives which could justify the use of means that could lead to a nuclear war.

The Washington Post, 1-5:(A)11.

Eduard A. Shevardnadze
Foreign Minister of the Soviet Union

1

It should be remembered that the higher the level of military confrontation in this nuclear and space age, the more shaky and less secure, even if strategic equilibrium is maintained, become the foundations of world peace. Nuclear war in these conditions may result not only from a deliberate decision but also from attempts at blackmail or from miscalculation by one side as to the intentions or actions of the other; it may also break out as a consequence of someone's reckless behavior prompted by a sudden aggravation of the situation or be caused by malfunctions in computers, which are increasingly relied upon in the operation of modern sophisticated weapons systems. It is precisely for this reason that the Soviet Union has been so persistent in seeking not merely the maintenance, but a lowering, of the existing level of strategic equilibrium, the arms race. We know, and many other states now realize this as well, that there is no more time to waste, for it may become too late.

At United Nations, New York,
Sept. 24/The New York Times, 9-25:8.

Margaret Thatcher
Prime Minister of the United Kingdom

3

Wars are not caused by the buildup of weapons. They are caused when an aggressor believes he can achieve his objectives at an acceptable price. The war of 1939 was not caused by an arms race. It sprang from a tyrant's belief that other countries lacked the means and the will to resist him . . . Our task is to see that potential aggressors . . . understand plainly that the capacity and the resolve of the West would deny them victory in war, and that the price they would pay would be intolerable. That is the basis of deterrence. It is the same whatever the nature of the weapons. Let us never forget the horrors of conventional wars and the hideous sacrifice of those who have suffered in them. Our task is not only to prevent nuclear war, but conventional war as well.

Before joint session of U.S. Congress,
Washington, Feb. 20/The Washington Post, 2-21:(A)9.

Pierre Elliott Trudeau
Former Prime Minister of Canada

4

It is the political leaders in office who will decide whether the possibility of nuclear war will be transformed into a likelihood, and from a likelihood into a reality. It is they who will be held accountable for the success or failure of efforts to turn back Armageddon—not the scientists, not the military commanders, not the arms merchants, not the negotiators; but the politicians. And yet, they are the ones most absent from the discussion and attempted resolution of the nuclear impasse. Why? The subject matter is esoteric; the literature is voluminous, replete with jargon and laced with contradictions. Any government leader who wanted to master the topic completely would have difficulty in discharging all his other duties, particularly when the difficult economic situation calls for so much attention. Hence the temptation to rely on others—be they ministers, ambassadors, chiefs of staff, technocrats or negotiators . . . I am not implying that the leaders on both sides play no role in their respective alliances. On the contrary, where armaments and military budgets are concerned, political will is generally quite apparent. Government leaders everywhere are very

(PIERRE ELLIOTT TRUDEAU)

much involved in the politics of war; they are not very much involved in the politics of peace.

Upon receipt of

Albert Einstein International Peace Prize,
Washington/World Press Review, January:26,27.

Vernon A. Walters

United States Ambassador/
Permanent Representative
to the United Nations

1

War has ceased to be a legitimate means of national policy. I personally do not believe that any of you in your lifetime will see a nuclear war—or even a major war. Those things have become so costly they have priced themselves out of existence. There will be minor disturbances . . . But I think the world has grown too wise to embark on something as risky as [nuclear war].

At Long Island University commencement,
Southampton, N.Y./U.S. News & World Report, 6-3:66.

Fred C. Weyand

General (ret.) and former Chief of Staff,
United States Army

2

There has to be something in between war news censorship and the kind of [news] coverage we had in Vietnam, and I don't know what. "Balance" is one word that comes to mind. There were cameras and reporters on our front lines reporting to our people, but none doing the same to the enemy public. How do we balance this? No, I wouldn't bar cameramen from reporting grisly scenes, but I know it hurt us in terms of support at home. I don't rule out the possibility that less media coverage of Vietnam, less TV coverage delivered into the nation's living rooms, might have led to a more favorable war outcome. Certainly, the dissent from the home front relayed back to troops at the front seriously undermined morale and probably contributed to drug and discipline problems.

Interview/
USA Today,
5-24:(A)11.

357

PART THREE

General

The Arts

Maya Angelou
Author

1

The artist is supposed to see beyond what is seeing. The artist's next job is to learn his or her craft so he can speak—whether through a piece of sculpture or a piece of music. The artist must develop courage to tell the truth in the best possible way. If the artist sees that we are, as a species, moving quite quickly toward the edge of a precipice, then the artist must see it and have the nerve to stand on the edge and say: "This is what I see, everybody." This is art.

Interview/USA Today, 3-5:(A)9.

Thomas N. Armstrong, III
Director,
Whitney Museum of American Art, New York

2

We've [the Whitney] had trustees leave us because they couldn't handle a museum that was making tough decisions and becoming more and more controversial. Being a trustee of the Met [ropolitan Museum] is not controversial. But putting a 100-foot-long Heizer sculpture that's made of cardboard on the fourth floor [at the Whitney] is something you'll have to defend to your peers. Trustees are faced with continuous questions about creativity and the artistic contributions of our time. Can you imagine going to 15 cocktail parties a week and being told, "Why the hell are you on *that* board?" The encouragement to cave in is out there.

The New York Times, 11-26:22.

Gerald Arpino
Assistant director and choreographer,
Joffrey Ballet

3

I like the artist who's vulnerable. The really great artists have that nakedness—physically, emotionally, spiritually—and you can't be naked enough for me.

Interview/Ballet News, November:15.

Richard Avedon
Photographer

4

[In the past,] I felt I could never photograph the common man. I understood beauty, creative power, intellect. I knew nothing about what it was to be a coal miner or a trucker and I couldn't photograph what I didn't understand. Because a portrait is an opinion. You can't feel comfortable with an uneducated opinion.

Interview, New York/
The Washington Post, 10-29:(C)2.

5

A portrait is not a likeness. The moment an emotion or a fact is transformed into a photograph it is no longer a fact but an opinion. There is no such thing as inaccuracy in a photograph. All photographs are accurate. None of them is the truth.

The Washington Post, 12-7:(G)1.

Salvador Dali
Artist

6

Artists are like truffles: There are places where they grow, and others where they don't . . . [Except for Pablo Picasso and Juan Gris,] all the others are losers. All they know how to do is hang their paintings upside down.

Interview, Madrid/USA Today, 2-26:(D)2.

7

Modern art today is a disaster because of an excess of freedom. A boat, like a brigantine, seems to be moving from far away, but up close you see that it depends on a system of rigging. A rope breaks and the deformation comes.

Interview, Figueras, Spain/
The New York Times, 3-19:27.

David Di Chiera
General director,
Michigan Opera Theatre, Detroit

8

[On the Reagan Administration plan to cut the budget of the National Endowment for the Arts]:

(DAVID DI CHIERA)

Even though the support grants are small dollars, they're a kind of signal to the private sector that there's not enough priority on this kind of activity. Government money serves not as a major part of the budget, but as an incentive and catalyst . . . These cuts have a severe economic impact on the communities themselves. A lot of inner cities are benefited by the growth of cultural institutions. When you cut a few million dollars, you're not just cutting a few million dollars. There's a multiplying effect of decreased activity, just as there is of increased activity . . . If opera companies and musical theatre companies don't sell houses to 95 per cent of capacity, they go into financial crisis. There's no financial margin for us, which absolutely precludes experimentation, and this is where the kind of public support one gets from the Endowment is so important.

Jan. 15/
The New York Times, 1-16:16.

Thomas J. Downey
United States Representative, D-New York

[Criticizing planned Reagan Administration cuts in the budget for the National Endowment for the Humanities]: Everyone knows there have to be sacrifices, but the Federal arts and humanities budgets are infinitesimal in the full budget . . . We should understand that when we starve the endowment budgets, we starve our own soul, and that's a bad and stupid thing to do.

The New York Times, 1-18:5.

Martha Graham
Choreographer

Many people [in the arts] don't want the responsibility of deep feeling. You have to go very deep, into the heart and the emotions, and you have to respect the ancestor. People want merely to mimic daily life in the arts, and the arts are a glorification of life, not a mimicry.

Horizon, October:63.

Frank Hodsoll
Chairman, National Endowment for the Arts of the United States

Basically, the arts are an essential component of any society and of the strength and health of that society—and therefore an important aspect of what government should be concerned about. [Government] ought to be supportive of other people doing things rather than undertaking—how shall I say it?—the primary support of the arts or the production of the arts themselves. You need to get very clear about goals. You look at the end result. Not at our bureaucratic processes, not at what we do, but at what is it out there that you want to change. First, you want to encourage more artistic excellence and a climate within which the unpredictable nature of artistic excellence can spring up. And secondly, you want to reach more audiences—that is, all American people. Those are two basic missions . . . I'm only interested in the National Endowment for the Arts to the extent that we are measurably helping the culture of this country. The arts are essential. We [at the Endowment] just help. And if we ever lose sight of that as an agency, we're off on the wrong track.

Interview, Boston/
The Christian Science Monitor,
7-26:6.

Yousuf Karsh
Portrait photographer

Anyone can click a shutter. To capture greatness, don't be overconcerned with lenses, light and film—be a student of life, humanities and mankind . . . I do my homework before I photograph someone. What makes them tick. Why are they creative, which of their talents is so coveted? For Hemingway, it was all revealed in the supreme melancholy in his face; [for] Helen Keller it was the tenderness in her fingers; Einstein showed his wisdom and compassion in his face.

Interview, Ottawa, Canada/
The Christian Science Monitor,
4-12:1,6.

Ardis Krainik
General manager, Chicago Lyric Opera

1

[On the Reagan Administration's plan to cut the budget of the National Endowment for the Arts]: Government support for the arts was a long time coming and a lot less than we needed, and we never got to any level of funding that matched anybody else. Any cut from the already low level of assistance is too much. Cuts are much more difficult for the arts to sustain than for others.

Jan. 15/The New York Times, 1-16:16.

Louis Monreal
Director, Getty Conservation Institute

2

Our enormous cultural heritage will be of no value if it cannot be preserved for future generations to enjoy and appreciate. If, for example, the Acropolis in Athens falls victim to air pollution or if the masterpieces in our museums are mistreated by conservators, what will be left for the future? Nothing. Absolutely nothing . . . Conservation has been an agent of destruction because of lack of knowledge. The improper use of chemical processes is occurring every day in museums around the world, even top museums. In other words, conservators throughout the ages have done as much damage to artworks as the impact of time itself . . . In the 18th century, physicians were forced to experiment on their patients. Today, in conservation, we do very much the same, and in the process we destroy a few masterpieces, even a few hundred. We have a long way to go to bring conservation into the 21st century. Our objective at the Institute will be to transform conservation from an empirical, trial-and-error profession into a more objective, informed practice.

Interview, Paris/
Los Angeles Times, 4-9:(VI)1,6.

Robert Motherwell
Painter

3

[On painting]: I make symbolic expressions of the human experience on flat surfaces, made with burnt sticks, or sticks with chunks of ani-

mal hair tied on one end and dipped in colored liquids. This experience is as primal and natural as moving one's body, or uttering sounds of anger or glee. It is so natural that I am still surprised that children, at the age of 5 or 6 years, give it up . . . The chemistry of the pigments is interesting. Ivory black, like bone black, is made from charred bones or horns. Sometimes I wonder, laying in a great black stripe on a canvas, what animal's bones or horns are making the furrows of my picture.

Upon accepting MacDowell Colony Medal,
Peterborough, N.H., Aug. 18/
The New York Times, 8-19:16.

Bess Myerson
Commissioner of Cultural Affairs
of New York City

4

[On the Reagan Administration plan to cut the budget of the National Endowment for the Arts]: The President will have to reverse this decision . . . The effect of these cuts in New York City would be severe. The $19-million these cuts would save the government is just enough to buy the Defense Department 2,700 new $7,000 coffee pots. However, unlike the situation in the Pentagon, there is no fat in the Arts Endowment. Cuts like this rip through blood and muscle; they cripple and kill.

Jan. 15/The New York Times,
1-16:16.

Gregory Peck
Actor

5

We've come a long way from those days when [the National Endowment for the Arts] only had something like $4-million to haggle over and try to make it count for something. Now there's more than $165-million and a great deal has been done on the Federal and state level to improve the lives of artists. Without Federal and state support of the arts, orchestras would have withered on the vine and museums would have been forced to close. We are beyond the time when a Congressman will stand up and scream

(GREGORY PECK)

about spending taxpayers' dollars for tap-dancers.

*At Governor's Awards for the Arts dinner,
Richmond, Va., May 18/
The Washington Post, 5-20:(C)6.*

Robert Rauschenberg
Painter

You have to be fairly insane to be an artist, or to be an *interesting* artist. If it isn't an adventure, I don't see anything to recommend the profession.

Interview, Washington/USA Today, 5-31:(D)4.

1

Ronald Reagan
President of the United States

In recognizing those who create and those who make creation possible, we celebrate freedom. No one realizes the importance of freedom more than the artist, for only in the atmosphere of freedom can the arts flourish. Artists have to be brave; they live in the realm of ideas and expression, and their ideas will often be provocative and unusual. Artists stretch the limits of understanding. They express ideas that are sometimes unpopular. In an atmosphere of liberty, artists and patrons are free to think the unthinkable and create the audacious; they are free to make both horrendous mistakes and glorious celebrations. Where there's liberty, art succeeds. In societies that are not free, art dies.

*Presenting the National Medal of Arts,
Washington, April 23/The New York Times, 4-29:10.*

2

Arthur Rosenblatt
*Vice president,
Metropolitan Museum of Art, New York*

It's far more entertaining and far less oppressive now to go to a museum than it ever was. A person who visits a museum now is going to be entertained . . . The museums have discovered this renewed interest on the part of the public,

and they are responding. The public's expectations are greater. Having entertained them, now they expect more.

*Interview, New York/
Los Angeles Times, 2-11:(VI)1,6.*

3

William Rubin
*Director,
department of painting and sculpture,
Museum of Modern Art, New York*

There are some artists in their 50s who have had a retrospective and then somehow been dropped out of art-world consciousness. They are overlooked by the publicity mill and the museum mill and art-magazine mill, which are always looking for what's new. But they're still working, and in some cases what they are doing may be better than the work of new young artists. We should have the format to accommodate medium- or small-sized shows to update them.

*Interview, February/
The New York Times, 2-20:19.*

4

Francesco Scavullo
Photographer

I like to photograph people who make me tingle when I see them perform. I know that they will be good subjects if, when I see them on stage, they become big blowups for me. I guess I just like stars . . . It takes a lot of work to bring out magic [in photography]. I can't just walk into the studio and wing it. I have to make something happen, bring all my energy to make the subject perform for me. [Boxer] Muhammad Ali was here, and he just stood there while I clicked and clicked away. Nothing was happening. Then I asked him if he were number two or number one, and he immediately went into a mock fighting position, and I got it.

Interview, New York/Horizon, Jan.-Feb.:69,72.

5

Orville Schell
Chairman, New York City Ballet

[On the Reagan Administration's plan to cut the budget of the National Endowment for the

6

(ORVILLE SCHELL)

Arts]: I believe the amount being cut out of the arts budget could be taken out of the military budget without affecting it a bit . . . We are all out raising money like crazy. It's all very well to say, let the corporations and individuals do it, but they just aren't doing it. My experience is that the money simply isn't going to be forthcoming.

Jan. 15/
The New York Times, 1-16:16.

Arthur Schlesinger, Jr.
Professor of humanities,
City University of New York

1

The idea of public [government] support [for the arts], and with it the idea that the state of the arts is a matter of national concern, are under increasing challenge—ironically not from Congress but from renegade parts of the intellectual community itself. We live in a decade that likes to disparage government and to exalt the market. We are told that, if a cultural institution cannot pay its way, then it has no economic justification and, if no economic justification, no social justification. Art, we are given to understand, must stand or fall by the box-office test, and the devil take the hindmost. To deny the arts a public role is the real *trahison des clercs*. For painters, composers, writers, film-makers, sculptors, architects, orchestras, museums, libraries, concert halls, opera houses contribute indispensably to the pride and glory of the nation. They are crucial to the forming of national traditions and to the preservation of civic cohesion. George Washington wrote: "The Arts and Sciences, essential to the prosperity of the State and to the ornament and happiness of human life, have a primary claim to the encouragement of every lover of his Country and mankind." The arts and humanities serve us all. They are surely as worthy as banks, corporations and other agencies of private profit to the objects of Federal concern, subsidy and even bail-out.

At American Academy and Institute
of Arts and Letters, New York/
The New York Times, 9-20:25.

Martin Segal
Chairman, Lincoln Center for
the Performing Arts, New York

2

[On the Reagan Administration's plan to cut the budget of the National Endowment for the Arts]: To discuss cutting a $200-billion [national] deficit by cutting an appropriation of $15-million or $16-million is preposterous. As it is, the support the National Endowment gets in inadequate for the role the arts have in this country, and to discuss cutting it further as a serious aspect of budget cutting is ridiculous.

Jan. 15/The New York Times, 1-16:16.

Beverly Sills
General director, New York City Opera

3

[On the Reagan Administration plan to cut the budget of the National Endowment for the Arts]: I'm just appalled. I think that to take that enormous percentage off such a miniscule amount in support of the arts is a disgrace . . . I'm just hoping that if enough of us yell and scream and stamp our feet and have tantrums, President Reagan will take another look and say, "My God, that's really very little money."

Jan. 15/The New York Times, 1-16:16.

Kurt Vonnegut, Jr.
Author

4

There's no question about it. [The arts are] an extremely high-risk situation. People are willing to take these extraordinary chances to become writers, musicians or painters, and because of them we have a culture. If this ever stops, our culture will die, because most of our culture, in fact, has been created by people that got paid nothing for it—people like Edgar Allan Poe, Vincent van Gogh or Mozart. So, yes, it's a very foolish thing to do, notoriously foolish, but it seems human to attempt it anyway.

Interview, New York/Writer's Digest, November:26.

Oliver Wright
British Ambassador to the United States

5

Nowhere can serious arts be performed at a profit. In Britain, we tend to look to the govern-

(OLIVER WRIGHT)

ment and the taxpayer to finance the unavoidable operating deficits. In America, it is quite different. The arts could not thrive as they do here [in the U.S.] without the devotion and commitment of private donors, corporations and foundations. We in Britain have a lot to learn from you in this respect.

At luncheon marking 35th anniversary
of Arena Stage, Washington, Oct. 10/
The New York Times, 10-29:12.

Sidney R. Yates
United States Representative, D-Illinois

1

. . . the arts are very much appreciated through the country. The arts are not only the exclusive province of the urban communities or of rich people, as used to be the case years ago. With the impetus of the National Endowment [for the Arts], the value, the benefit and the popularity of the arts have gone through the entire country.

Interview/The Christian Science Monitor, 1-31:36.

Journalism

Jack Anderson
Political columnist

1

I was an investigative reporter back when investigative reporters were pariahs. It was nice to be a folk hero for a little while. Now we're pariahs again. But there is no question that people do not like the messenger who brings them bad news. An investigative reporter is always digging up stories that people in power don't want to see published. When we antagonize the people in power, we also are not really going to please our editors and publishers, because the editors and publishers all too often have a close relationship with the people in power. In any case, they have to respond to the people in power . . . When you write a story that embarrasses a powerful man, he usually has a way of getting through to the publisher of your newspaper, and it causes a problem—a little embarrassment for the publisher. So he isn't all that happy to see the investigative piece. For the editor, he gets denials and has to deal with those. He gets demands for retractions. He gets threats for libel suits. I don't mean to suggest that most editors are ducking investigative stories for this reason, but you've got to admit that it's a lot easier to handle straight stories and to ignore investigative reporting. You don't have to worry about the consequences.

Interview/USA Today, 8-14:(A)7.

Thomas Barr
Chief counsel, Time, Inc.

2

[On former Israeli Defense Minister Ariel Sharon's libel suit against *Time* magazine regarding the massacre of Palestinians in Lebanon in 1982]: This involves a news story about how a horrible, brutal, insensible massacre of women and children took place. That is what the press's job is: to dig at things like this, to pick at things that may not be pleasant or comfortable for the people involved, to try to get as much of the story as possible into the hands of the public so that the public can make decisions about how we want to run our lives.

Summation at trial, New York/Time, 1-21:58.

Ben Bradlee
Executive editor, "The Washington Post"

3

In its lay—or nongovernmental—form, press bashing is most apt to show up in the form of libel suits. The *Philadelphia Inquirer* has no less than 21 libel suits filed against it today. We have had a big one going with the former president of Mobil Oil. Four judges have considered it; two have ruled for him and two for us, but unfortunately for us, the last two were his. It is on appeal now, and our legal bills alone have already topped $1,275,000. Not insured. The chilling effect is considerable, believe me. I consider myself to have my share of guts, but the next reporter who comes to me with a story and tells me it will cost me $1,275,000 to run it, better have himself one hell of a yarn.

At Scripps College commencement/
Time, 6-17:69.

Tom Brokaw
Anchorman, "Nightly News," NBC-TV

4

I know of no more patriotic group than television journalists. But we're not mindless cheerleaders. One of the great strengths of this country is its ability to acknowledge and deal with its errors, its mistakes. Our role is to tell the truth about what, in fact, is going on. Sometimes the truth is elusive. Sometimes truth, like beauty, is in the eye of the beholder. So we work hard, very hard, to know all the facts before we go on the air . . . Sometimes what we report is painful and people say, "You guys only tell us the bad news." Well, check any totalitarian country. You hear only "good news." Our great strength is the courage to hear all sides. Sure, we want people to be excited by achievement—space shots or triumphs of justice or medical breakthroughs. But shouldn't they also hear about malnutrition in America? Shouldn't they be outraged by what big money can get done in Washington?

Interview/
USA Today, 3-18:(A)5.

367

Helen Gurley Brown
Editor-in-chief, "Cosmopolitan" magazine

The secret of editing a successful magazine is knowing your reader. At *Cosmo*, we get lots of stuff submitted that's really wonderful—but not right for us. Too many magazines stray too far. They try to get everybody, and that's not the way it works. Once you establish who you're after, you do everything to please that reader. It's a very specialized form of communication.

USA Today,
9-9:(D)2.

1

Zbigniew Brzezinski
Professor of government, Columbia University; Former Assistant to the President of the United States (Jimmy Carter) for National Security Affairs

[On TV coverage of terrorist kidnappings]: I would say that television has three negatives and one potentially beneficial effect. First, television tends to transform what is essentially a political issue into a personal drama. It prevents the government from dealing with the situation as a political problem and forces it to think of it as a personal problem. Second, television becomes a medium for conveying the kidnappers' demands and for permitting them to appeal directly to the American people, over the head of the government, for the acceptance of the demands. It thus enhances the bargaining capacity of the kidnappers. And third, television humanizes the enemy, thereby also making it more difficult for the government to respond firmly. The only possible beneficial effect is that, in the absence of any contact between the U.S. government and the terrorists, television can fill a void that otherwise would have existed . . . I think there should be some mechanism for voluntary communication between government and the media in these cases. It's done during wartime. A kidnapping or an act of terrorism is something akin to a wartime situation, and I would have thought that patriotism—an old-fashioned word—would have played some role in guiding their decisions.

Interview/
TV Guide, 9-21:22.

2

Warren Buffet
Chairman, Berkshire Hathaway

The smarter the journalists are, the better off society is. If a journalist really wants to know about the insurance industry, I'd want to spend the time with him. To a degree, people read the press to inform themselves—and the better the teacher, the better the student body.

Fortune, 3-4:68.

3

Hodding Carter III
Journalist; Former spokesman, Department of State of the United States

[Comparing the various news media]: Too much of the TV thing consists of the unseen hand with the up-front mouth, and the news magazine's separating the reporter and writer scares me. When you are clearly accountable, it breeds more rigorous reporting.

The New York Times, 1-31:13.

4

[On TV coverage of terrorist kidnappings, such as the recent hostage-taking in Lebanon]: Was television a negative influence in this situation? No. Does it encourage terrorism? No. Terrorism is a product of this age. Was television irresponsible in some of its actions over there? Yes. Does that go with the territory? I'm afraid the answer is yes—the territory being a frantically competitive [journalistic] environment. But I simply cannot buy the idea that television prolongs an agony. The hostages got out about as fast as they were going to get out. And if you read the polls, there is no indication that the American people were deluded by the terrorists. Did television's presence make the [U.S.] President's job tougher? Absolutely. A free press in a crisis situation always makes life more difficult for a democratic government. When I was the State Department spokesman [1977-80], I did what anybody in an official capacity does in moments of stress. I said to the media: Will you kindly shut up and leave us alone. I damn well beat up on the media when I was spokesman. And in retrospect, I was wrong. The interviews with the Ayatollah [during the U.S. hostage cri-

5

(HODDING CARTER III)

sis in Iran] had no more to do with the outcome of that thing than the man in the moon. But they sure made our lives difficult. Some of the best information we got came from those interviews.

Interview/TV Guide, 9-21:23.

Ray Cave
Managing editor, "Time" magazine

1

If you don't have faith in your people [reporters] in the field, you are lost. [But] if that faith is blind faith, then it is not faith at all, just maladministration.

Interview/The New York Times, 1-8:10.

2

[On former Israeli Defense Minister Ariel Sharon's libel suit against *Time*, in which the jury ruled that the magazine told untruths and defamed Sharon, but did not do it with malice]: There's no doubt in my mind that those [first] two pieces of the verdict will raise doubt in the public mind about how careful our [journalistic] processes are. I think that will be a very short-term consideration of our readers. In the long term, this adversity will be negligible.

Interview, Jan. 24/ The Washington Post, 1-25:(A)16.

John T. Chain, Jr.
Director, Bureau of Politico-Military Affairs, Department of State of the United States

3

Unfortunately, it has become customary for some newspapers and journalists to print information which they know to be potentially damaging to the U.S., on the pretext that the public has a "right to know," or that such information prevents governmental abuse of power. Certainly I do not argue with the right of citizens in a democracy to know what their government's policies and actions are, and to oblige the government to articulate and defend its policies. Neither do I question the right of journalists to probe beyond the bland assurances of good intention on the part of the government, to reveal "the true story." But neither our citizens nor the press itself is well served by revealing information . . . which impacts on our national-security capability. In fact, the disclosure of this type of information contributes little to the public's understanding of our nuclear policies and strategies and serves only to aid our potential adversary.

Statement criticizing a "New York Times" article on U.S. nuclear contingency plans, Washington, Feb. 27/ The New York Times, 2-28:6.

John Chancellor
Commentator, NBC News

4

[On his nation-wide survey of local TV news]: [I was] thinking that local television news was filled with glitz and hype, and I found some extraordinary changes around the country. After 30 years, local television news is finally beginning to mature. The agents who handle anchor people are now getting requests for mature and experienced journalists, men and women. Gray hair is no longer a difficulty, and more attention is being paid to professionalism. Local TV news has gone completely beyond the happy-talk idiocy that so damaged it a few years ago.

TV broadcast/"A Portrait of the Press, Wars and All," NBC-TV, 6-15.

5

[On TV coverage of the recent Lebanese hijacking of an American airliner and the holding hostage of its passengers]: You have journalism, which is thoughtful and considered, and you have what I call "electronics," which is the use of our facilities to transmit pictures and words, but does not have a lot to do with journalism. If by some miracle all the world's television networks had magically agreed not to cover the crisis as they did, I suspect that one of the terrorists' demands would have been for a camera.

The New York Times, 7-2:5.

Otis Chandler
Chairman and editor-in-chief,
Times Mirror Company

1

[Newspapers are] a genuine expression of what our society is all about. Because we take snapshots of today, and because snapshots are, in their very nature, candid, we are not always popular, we newspaper people. The temptation of our governors is far greater today than it was . . . to place constraints on that freedom that is so necessary to all of us who are signatories to the social contract.

At Times Mirror Co. annual meeting, Los Angeles,
May 22/Los Angeles Times, 5-23:(IV)2.

Ann Compton
Correspondent, ABC News

2

If the press prints something that is blatantly untrue, unchecked, unfounded and damaging to somebody, why shouldn't the press be as liable for a legal challenge as a doctor who makes a serious surgical mistake, as a business which cheats one of its customers—wittingly or unwittingly? What concerns journalists is that there are gross cases in which a publication has hurt someone maliciously or unmaliciously. But in those cases in which it's a much fuzzier area, the question is whether the legal action is being sought as a means to cut in on the First Amendment. But should the press be responsible for what it prints or what it broadcasts? You're darn right it should.

Interview/USA Today, 11-26:(4)11.

Howard Cosell
Commentator, ABC Sports

3

Don't be fooled: As far as sports is concerned, we don't get truth from the media. It's still mostly celebratory prose and Hollywood gossip, a style of reporting which . . . thrived during the '20s with all the baloney about [baseball star] Babe Ruth—who was nothing but a lush—and [football star] Red Grange. The writers of that era—Grantland Rice, with his Four Horsemen dramatically etched against a grim October sky—created a picture of sports that

persists to this day. The stock of images they built up still forms the basic lexicon of American sportswriting, and the failure to replace those images, or at least to revise the celebratory attitudes they represent, is the essential failure of sports reporting today. Sports journalists are promoters, not reporters.

Panel discussion/"Harper's," September:48.

4

I think it's an absurdity that highly rated schools of journalism are turning out excellent talent, and they are denied an opportunity in sports broadcasting because of this "jockocracy" [the employment of former sports stars as sports broadcasters]. I have never argued that there is no ex-athlete who should be on the air or that they should be barred from an opportunity. But we have broadcasters [employers] who only want to put on a jock. And that has caused a whole new social stratum known as the jockocracy. In no other avenue of endeavor in America, except maybe for prostitution, can you go right in and be at the top. It's just wrong.

Interview/USA Today, 11-7:(4)13.

Philip M. Crane
United States Representative, R-Illinois

5

[Saying there has been a liberal political bias at U.S. TV news organizations:] Any number of independent studies that go back for better than a decade show a liberal bias, especially with regard to CBS [News]. Its coverage in Vietnam leaned disproportionately toward criticism of our policy. In 1972 and '73, the Institute for American Strategy found that CBS quoted the statements of critics 842 times, while those partial to our policy were quoted only 23 times. CBS News has been much more critical of President Reagan than the other networks. In 1983, *TV Guide* looked at pro-Reagan vs. anti-Reagan coverage and found that while NBC was critical 10 per cent of the time and ABC 12 per cent, CBS stood out because it was critical 52 per cent of the time. Then, if you look at CBS and NBC coverage of the political conventions last summer, they used such terms as "right wing" and "hard right" for the Republicans, but rarely

(PHILIP M. CRANE)

used the word "liberal" for the Democrats, and never used the term "left wing," which apparently isn't in their vocabulary.

Interview/U.S. News & World Report, 5-13:64.

Tony Day
Editorial-page editor, "Los Angeles Times"

1

[At news magazines,] the technique is to make a story neater, to point [to] a moral, and come to a neat ending when life isn't like that. Newspapers are truer to the facts at hand, even if it is messy and inconclusive.

The New York Times, 1-31:13.

Michael K. Deaver
*Deputy Chief of Staff
to the President of the United States*

2

[On press complaints of their lessening access to President Reagan]: I understand the media's attitude. But that's a continuing dialogue that we have. The media is never going to be happy unless they sit in the Oval Office 12 hours a day.

*Interview, Washington/
The Christian Science Monitor, 1-3:36.*

Everette E. Dennis
*Executive director, Gannett Center
for Media Studies, Columbia University*

3

[Comparing the various news media]: Broadcasters are storytellers, newspapers are fact-gatherers and organizers of information, and news magazines are kind of a hybrid of both.

The New York Times, 1-31:13.

4

. . . the public doesn't worry as much about confidence and credibility [in the media] as news executives do. For example, there is a perception among editors and broadcasting executives that the public thinks the press is arrogant. The studies show, however, there isn't any evi-

dence that this is so . . . there is a great difference between numbers and noise. Large numbers of people do not worry an awful lot about the media credibility issue, but those who do, do so with great intensity.

Interview/USA Today, 11-26:(A)11.

Sam Donaldson
White House correspondent, ABC News

5

People who are [politically] conservative believe their message isn't getting across [in the press] at this time. Twenty years ago it might have been on the other foot. Twenty years from now it may be some place else. But truth is truth, and it's not something that can be measured in an ideological framework.

Broadcast discussion/"Viewpoint," ABC, 4-17.

6

[Criticizing the proliferation of "soft-news" features on TV newscasts]: It is true that we all strive to do more than just headlines. But I must tell you I think people in Omaha coming home from a hard day's work trying to sell insurance policies want to know what's going on that day— as much or more than seeing a five-minute piece of a three-part series on how to curl your hair without burning it.

Los Angeles Times, 11-22:(I)23.

Osborn Elliott
*Dean, School of Journalism,
Columbia University*

7

I think that any exercise that applies to the press the same critical view that is applied to books, movies, plays, music, etc., would be healthy. Everybody says that nobody's more thin-skinned than an editor or a publisher or a reporter; and I think that's probably true. I think the more critical attention is paid to the performance of the press, the better it would be . . . I think the more the press is discussed, the more it would be understood. The more it is discussed, perhaps the better it would become. The more it admits its own shortcomings and imperfections, the more credible it becomes.

*Interview, New York/
The Christian Science Monitor, 8-15:21,22.*

Katherine Fanning
Editor, "The Christian Science Monitor"

I don't think the public realizes that there is a constant conflict within news organizations between the bottom-liners—those who are responsible for profits—and the journalists themselves. Many journalists deeply want to be responsible, to be public servants. I think that the working journalist has public service very much in mind. So I think there is a continual conflict and a basic schizophrenia in the business that we need to address more than we have.

Interview/USA Today, 11-26:(A)11.

1

Geraldine A. Ferraro
Former United States Representative, D-New York; 1984 Democratic Vice Presidential nominee

[On allegations in the *New York Post*, during her Vice Presidential campaign last year, that her family had connections with organized crime]: The implication they lodged was totally false and unsupported by the facts. Am I unjust in believing that some members of the press are unfair—worse than unfair, that they abuse their power so as to harass, defame and try to defeat a candidate for public office?

Before New York State Press Association, Albany, March 30/The Washington Post, 4-1:(B)3.

2

Mark S. Fowler
Chairman, Federal Communications Commission

. . . the Fairness Doctrine [is] government censorship. There's no room in our society, which is founded on freedom of speech and the press under the First Amendment, to tolerate the Federal Communications Commission acting as a censor over what is broadcast over radio and television stations.

Interview, Washington/ The New York Times, 5-25:7.

3

[Supporting the FCC's declaration against the Fairness Doctrine]: Today's report is an indict-

4

372

ment of a misguided government policy. It is a recital of its shortcomings, both legal and practical. The First Amendment dictates: Choose between the right of the press to criticize freely and the authority of the government to channel that criticism. Today's order is a statement by this Commission that we should reverse course, and head ballistically toward liberty of the press for radio and television.

Aug. 7/The New York Times, 8-8:19.

Pauline Frederick
Former United Nations correspondent, NBC News

[On whether women past 50 or 60 years of age will ever be considered for TV news anchor position]: I think we're suffering from the Hollywood syndrome, and I don't know whether we'll ever get over it—that is, a woman has to be young and beautiful. If a man is older, he's just interesting. We always think of the men as having more authority. When I was being blocked from going on the air early in my career, I was told a woman's voice does not carry authority; therefore, people wouldn't listen to her. I think we have to go through some cultural changes before women really compare with men.

Interview/USA Today, 1-14:(A)9.

5

Fred W. Friendly
Professor emeritus of journalism, Columbia University; Former president, CBS News

Neither television nor print publications are immune from the public perception that editors and producers are insensitive, often arrogant, and unwilling to listen to serious viewers and readers who sometimes believe "they got it wrong."

USA Today, 2-21:(A)6.

6

[On TV coverage of the recent hijacking by Lebanese Shiite Moslems of an American airliner and the holding hostage of its passengers in Beirut]: Terrorism is . . . a species of guerrilla

7

(FRED W. FRIENDLY)

warfare whose battlefield is the television screen and the front page . . . Tragically, the final result of the imperfections of the coverage of Flight 847 is that TV probably inadvertently advanced the cause of terrorism—encouraged another hijacking, while at the same time, parenthetically, saving the 39 hostages.

*Congressional testimony, Washington/
The Christian Science Monitor, 8-1-3.*

George Gerbner
*Dean, Annenberg School of Communications,
University of Pennsylvania*

1

[On the effect on readers of a newspaper strike]: There are a million and one small bits of information that people miss in their daily lives . . . [Reading a newspaper] serves as a ritual occurrence for most people, in which their sense of the world is constantly, periodically reinforced. It confirms people's view of how the world works.

The New York Times, 9-14:6.

Lawrence K. Grossman
President, NBC News

2

. . . I disagree with those who assert that public figures should not have the right to go into court and seek redress when they have been seriously harmed by a mischievous, malicious, inaccurate piece of [news] reporting. They are citizens like everybody else, and, if their reputation has been damaged, they should have some recourse. And I think it is very important for the health of the press that there be recourse for something that we have done irresponsibly.

*Interview, New York/
The Christian Science Monitor, 3-6:15.*

Henry Grunwald
Editor-in-chief, "Time" magazine

3

[On former Israeli Defense Minister Ariel Sharon's libel suit against *Time*, in which the jury ruled that the magazine told untruths and

defamed Sharon, but did not do it with malice]: I'm extremely happy that we won [the malice aspect], but I'm not totally happy with the jury's earlier findings on defamation and on falsity because, with all due respect to the jury, which worked very hard . . . I believe that our story was substantially true [about Sharon being involved in the massacre of Palestinians in Lebanon in 1982], but the important thing is that Mr. Sharon was not able to defeat us in an American court for his own purposes.

*Interview, Jan. 24/
The Washington Post, 1-25:(A)17.*

David Halberstam
Journalist

4

[Journalism] is essentially more a monopoly profession—where there's one dominating paper in every city, so that in effect there's less print competition—and that's a negative thing. Television is now . . . the ballgame. They [TV] respond not to a complexity of stimuli, but to a pure impulse of drama, of the photograph . . . Most of the [media] mergers are counterproductive. They're not about productivity, about making an institution better. They're about driving the stock up. [Media executive] Ted Turner is more important if he gets CBS. It doesn't make CBS better. But it's about ego, and leveraging, and driving stock prices up. It's a Wall Street game. It's not about making this a more productive society.

Interview/USA Today, 7-22:(A)11.

Jesse Helms
*United States Senator,
R-North Carolina*

5

[Criticizing what he calls the "elite media"]: [They are] profoundly out of step with the ideals and goals of the American people. They are produced by men and women who, if they do not hate American virtues, they certainly have a smug contempt for American ideals and principles. The real threat to freedom, the real threat to freedom of speech, and the real threat to our Constitutional system is on our TV screens

(JESSE HELMS)

every evening and on the front pages of our newspapers every day.

At Conservative Political Action Conference,
Washington, March 1/The Washington Post, 3-2:(A)6.

David Hess
President,
National Press Club

1

[On the newly renovated National Press Building]: For us, it is an embodiment of the First Amendment, the place where, over the decades, countless reporters have pecked at their writing machines and attempted to explain to readers and viewers and listeners around the world the mysterious workings of the American democracy. When I think of the Press Building, I don't see a structure of brick and steel and glass. In my mind's eye, I see news men and women exercising a daily vigilance over the government of the most powerful nation in history. As they ply their craft here, they supply the cement that holds together an edifice much greater and more enduring than a building. What they write and broadcast provides the ties that bind an idea—the idea that free people, amply informed, can govern themselves fairly and civilly.

At dedication of the renovated
National Press Building, Washington,
May 21/The New York Times, 5-31:24.

Don Hewitt
Executive producer,
"60 Minutes," CBS-TV

2

TV critics [on newspapers] get their jollies by saying, "Television [news] is in no small part show biz." But it is their newspapers—not *60 Minutes*—which run Sydney Omarr's horoscope, Omar Sharif's bridge game, Garfield the Cat, Blondie, Beetle Bailey, Mary Worth, Ann Landers, Dear Abby, recaps of television soap operas, and a column called Miss Manners that tells among other things when it is proper and when it's not to let guests bathe naked in a hot tub. Constant sniping at us by newspapermen who should know better is unbecoming. And the

374

fallout is beginning to poison all of us [journalists]—high-priced anchor and ink-stained wretch alike. If newspaper publishers spent less time criticizing television news and more time trying to put out a good newspaper, we'd all be richer and the public would be better served.

At symposium, Poynter Institute of Media Studies,
St. Petersburg, Fla., Jan. 24/USA Today, 3-14:(A)10.

3

[Comparing broadcast with print journalism]: What has to make [print] reporters unhappy . . . is if they go out and work their asses off on a story, and find out that people who read their story had seen it closer-up than the reporter did; they were there. Television has taken them there. There was a time when it was kind of exotic to be a reporter. By God, you got to meet Congressmen and go to Bengasi and Tobruk; wow! Now the viewer goes there every night. It's no big deal . . . you've got to realize that the viewers have been everywhere. There's no mystery, I mean, some guy says, "Boy, I was at Cape Kennedy for the launch of the first moon flight," and the guy at home says, "So was I." The Super Bowl was played in your living room; John De-Lorean was acquitted in your living room. It all happens right there. The place of the print reporter in the world is not the same as it once was. That has got to sting. I would be unhappy about that, too. Let any big story break this minute—something big, some catastrophe, or war—in every city newsroom in America the first thing they do is turn on their TV set!

Interview/Playboy, March:160.

4

[On broadcasters, such as CBS, which pay large sums of money to interviewees]: Print reporters, because they deal with the written word, assume that written words are worth money. I mean, they get paid for words they put on paper. But why shouldn't one get paid for the spoken word? I'm in the spoken-word business . . . *The New York Times* paid [former President] Richard Nixon for the right to what he put on paper. And they were outraged that CBS would pay him not for what he put on paper but for what he put on

(DON HEWITT)

video tape. I don't work with paper; I work with video tape. Henry Luce, the publisher of *Time*, was buying news before I was born. That kind of money in this business pays for just a minute-and-a-half commercial. I'm glad CBS spent some of its hard-earned money to inform the public.

Interview/Playboy, March:166.

1

[On the recent libel suit against CBS brought by General William Westmoreland regarding a documentary about his role in the Vietnam war]: I don't look back on [the program] as anything but another very professional broadcast that may have violated some standards and practices at CBS News, which I don't believe should ever have been codified. I think as long as you can say to yourself: "I have never knowingly done violence to the truth; what I am putting on the air is what it purports to be," all those standards-and-practices rules are complete baloney . . . Television news is the first journalistic entity in history to come with built-in checks and balances. There's a reporter, a producer, a tape editor, a cameraman, a soundman. There are too many people watching and looking over other people's shoulders for anybody to play fast and loose with the facts. A newspaper reporter goes out with a pad and a pencil, and the editor has no way of knowing if what the reporter reports is the truth, except that he trusts the guy.

Interview, New York/
The Christian Science Monitor, 3-6:14.

2

[On charges that CBS News has a liberal political bias]: CBS News is neither liberal nor conservative. CBS News is an observer of liberals and conservatives, and sometimes we find them both wanting. We once had a guy on *60 Minutes* who runs a halfway house for drug addicts and criminals who said the underprivileged are "caught in a bind between right-wing nuts who want to hit everybody in the head, and radical-chic creepos who want to kiss everybody's backside." I believe that. I defy anybody

to tag *60 Minutes* as left or right, liberal or conservative. A good story is a good story . . . I lost my left-wing bias when I turned 21. I'm a big fan of both conservative columnist George Will and liberal writer Izzy Stone. I look at 1988, and I'm torn between New York Democratic Governor Mario Cuomo and Senate Republican leader Bob Dole. Now, what kind of liberal bias is that?

Interview/U.S. News & World Report, 5-13:65.

Hu Yaobang
General Secretary,
Communist Party of China

3

Journalism speaks on behalf of the Party and government and makes comments and directs work in accordance with the Party's lines, principles and policies. [The purpose of journalism] is to arouse the people to work with one heart and one mind for the realization of the Party's objectives . . . The slogan "freedom of creation" for literature and art does not entirely apply to journalism, because journalism speaks on behalf of the Party and government, while artists represent themselves and use what they observe to encourage and educate people.

Before Communist Party leaders, February/
Los Angeles Times, 5-7:(I)33.

Bunker Hunt
Industrialist

4

I accept the media for what they are, as they are . . . which is not very favorable where I'm concerned. I don't expect a good press. In fact, I have a saying I think is accurate: the press can make a heel out of a hero or a hero out of a heel. We see this happen every day. That may be overstated or oversimplified, but journalists have the power to paint any picture they desire.

Interview/The Saturday Evening Post, Jan.-Feb.:47.

Bernard Ingham
Press Secretary to the
Prime Minister of the United Kingdom

5

[On criticism that he manages the news and indulges in propaganda]: My crucial stock in

(BERNARD INGHAM)

trade is reliability. Otherwise, I lack credibility and cease to be useful either to the government or the media. I take a skeptical view of anyone's ability to manage the news so certainly and infallibly as to highlight the good and so assuredly as to bury the bad. For one thing, no government in a free society with a free press is in control of events or the news or its management or its presentation. I only wish I were as sophisticated and devilishly clever and Machiavellian as some make out.

Los Angeles Times, 8-4:(I)18.

Richard J. V. Johnson
President, American
Newspaper Publishers Association

3

[On libel suits against the press, such as the recent cases brought by U.S. General William Westmoreland and former Israeli Defense Minister Ariel Sharon]: If there are any changes to be made [in the libel laws], they should be made in favor of the defendants. The plaintiff should be made to pay all court costs if libel is not proven. That would make the plaintiff more responsible. The threat of libel suits has a chilling effect on some smaller papers that absolutely can't afford to be sued . . . What [these two particular cases] did was to give the public an idea of what goes on, which, of course, leads the public to the credibility issues. The Sharon case showed problems with an editor who didn't edit right and how the Sharon article might have been promoted in bad taste. Yet the end result was that the libel case was dropped. In that process, all the warts and all the problems of publishing came out, and that sometimes leads to problems of [press] credibility.

Interview/USA Today, 5-7:(A)9.

Peter Jennings
Anchorman,
"World News Tonight," ABC-TV

1

The great difference between TV [news] and print is that we [in TV] are much, much better at emotion than we are at fact. That doesn't mean that we're always passionate, nor that we are always grabbing for the emotional. But when you add the dimension of picture and sound . . . what comes out of the box is essentially affecting the emotion to a greater extent than it is affecting the intellect. We deal with fact, but sometimes fact is simply overpowered by the emotional equation in that story—even if it's the smallest [part of the] equation.

Interview, New York/
The Christian Science Monitor, 6-12:19.

2

[On whether he thinks the U.S. Reagan Administration tries to manipulate the media]: Of course I do. But every Administration does that. F.D.R. was every bit as manipulative of the media as John Kennedy was, Nixon was, Jimmy Carter was. Every Administration tries to manipulate the media. Sometimes they succeed; sometimes they don't. Sometimes they succeed for longer periods of time. But again, that's not something which need worry us particularly in the long run. The First Amendment does us pretty proud.

Interview/USA Today, 11-5:(A)9.

Edward M. Joyce
President, CBS News

4

[Criticizing U.S. Senator Jesse Helms and his supporters who have attacked the media]: This is not the first time in recent history when we in journalism have been under attack from a group which wants its narrow ideological bias to control the press and ultimately the country. These groups don't just want their voice to be heard; they want theirs to be the only voices to be heard.

March 1/The Washington Post, 3-2:(A)6.

5

[On recent much-publicized libel suits against journalistic institutions]: There is abroad in the land a new mind-set that the mechanisms exist to bring an "errant" press under control. These things represent a collective pattern that I find worrisome . . . Will it be successful? I do not know, but we are determined that it will not be successful at CBS News.

Maclean's, 5-6:56.

George A. Keyworth II
Director, White House
Office of Science and Technology

1

We're trying to build up America, and the press is trying to tear down America. There are several reasons. Number one, for some reason that I just do not understand, much of the press seems to be drawn from a relatively narrow fringe element on the far left of our society. Number two, there's an arrogance that has to do with the power of the press . . . It's easier to achieve power by being negative and tearing at foundations . . . This country is looking toward things like investment in the future, education, respecting people who work hard and well. We have a pragmatic view of the world's competitiveness, not some artificial, ideal world where, for example, foreign policy is dominated by human rights. The American press as a whole is inconsistent with these trends.

Interview/The Washington Post, 2-22:(A)2.

Dave Kindred
Sports columnist,
"Atlanta Constitution"

2

Newspapers are made up of young people who think they're going to change the world. They are dreamers and idealists. They will work for nothing for a byline. Too many people, in fact, have worked too long for too little money. It's not a case of me being overpaid. It's a case of editors being underpaid.

Interview/
Los Angeles Times, 2-13:(III)8.

Jeane J. Kirkpatrick
Former United States Ambassador/
Permanent Representative to
the United Nations

3

One thing I learned in my 4½ years in government about the press was that you say what you want, and they write what they want. And there you are.

Interview/U.S. News & World Report, 9-9:47.

Ted Koppel
Anchorman,
"Nightline," ABC-TV

4

Critics are forever discovering that the press is "out of step with the public," and this discovery is then brandished as evidence of incompetence, or worse. In point of fact, it is, most of the time, neither. It is the natural consequence of a system that grants its press the right to be skeptical.

Broadcast discussion/"Viewpoint," ABC, 4-17.

5

If the question is, should the networks be responsive to the public perception that unfairness has been committed [in a news or documentary broadcast], the answer is unequivocally "Yes." Should the networks feel obligated to make time available to someone whose political appetite is not fulfilled by what we've done on the air? The answer is "No." I do not feel that simply because someone is particularly insistent on laying claim to representing the public or representing other views which he claims are not heard enough on television that that necessarily makes him the acclaimed holder of the title . . . There is simply not the outrage against what appears on TV that so many critics would have you believe. Viewers say: Make your comedy funnier, your mysteries more mysterious. But say to the public . . .: "If you out there feel that there is a particular issue in which we have shown bias, let us know about it," and there is resounding silence.

Interview, New York/
The Christian Science Monitor, 8-8:19.

Bill Kovach
Washington editor,
"The New York Times"

6

The basic policy of [The New York Times] is resist whenever possible "background briefings" by government officials when they are dealing with policy matters for which these officials are accountable to the public. This rule is especially important in situations like that which occurred on Thursday when the briefing begins

(BILL KOVACH)

in the open and then disappears behind the anonymous "background" screen and such large numbers of reporters are present, including reporters for Soviet publications. Under these circumstances, the only people who were being denied information were the American people in general and our readers specifically. By attending the background portion of that briefing, *The New York Times* would have to cooperate in withholding that information from its readers and chose not to do so.

Washington, Jan. 4/The New York Times, 1-5:8.

1

There has been a consistent and organized effort on the part of this [Reagan] Administration to reduce the flow of government information [to the press], beginning with what they consider secret but extended far beyond that. There is no area of government where information is not harder to get for us here, harder to get now than it was when I was here in the Nixon and Ford years. Their whole attitude is that government information belongs to the government.

The Washington Post, 6-10-(4)/4.

Lewis H. Lapham
Editor, "Harper's" magazine

2

Americans seem to want to find truth in the press; they expect to learn how the world really works, why events happen as they do. When they are disappointed in these expectations—as they inevitably are—they become angry and resentful. They tell poll-takers that they "distrust" the press. They applaud when the government excludes reporters from the Grenada invasion. And, more and more often in recent years, they bring libel suits. I think we can conclude that, in general, the public seems to want to criticize, and often to punish, the American press. Now, I think this is somewhat unfair. Certainly there are many things wrong with the press, but to me the punishments seem out of line with the alleged crime.

Panel discussion at New School for Social Research,
New York/Harper's, January:38.

3

. . . I don't think a person is going to become a truly informed citizen by reading nothing more than the American press. If you're serious about trying to find out how your political system works, that will require a good deal of effort. Newspapers tell a story—a very sophisticated one, but a story nonetheless. Read the memoirs of statesmen who have suffered the idiocy of the press over a period of years, and they all say you can't believe what you read in the papers. Historians make exactly the same point. The press is a midden heap, full of bits and pieces of things, some of them true and maybe valuable, but all of them fragments from which the citizen must construct his own distorted portrait of reality. I object to the idea that somehow the press, the media, are going to provide people with all the necessary answers.

Panel discussion at New School for Social Research,
New York/Harper's, January:49.

Robert MacNeil
Executive editor and co-host,
"MacNeil-Lehrer Report," PBS-TV

4

. . . the mass public will increasingly be the captive of television for its [news] information and therefore . . . more manipulatable, and more easily manipulated. And the small, elite, educated public will continue to be consumers of print. And you can almost see that happening [already]. I find television a terrible imposition on time. You can acquire the information you're seeking so much more rapidly through print. I could earn a decent living doing something else, never particularly wanted to be in television. If I'd be dong it. I wanted to be a writer and a playwright and a novelist, and I fell into journalism because—you know how you do in a career—one thing leads to another. I love the opportunity to consider what you're doing.

Interview, New York/
The Christian Science Monitor, 6-12-19.

5

If there is a moral dilemma in broadcast journalism, it has to do with this question: Are the

(ROBERT MacNEIL)

media serving the public well in giving an understanding of the world around them, or are they—especially with increased competition—giving an ever more vivid and encapsulated view of the world that is misleading and oversimplified?

U.S. News & World Report, 12-9:62.

Farouk Muhammed
Editor, "Daily Times,"
Lagos (Nigeria)

1

[On recent much-publicized libel suits against journalistic institutions]: It's very hard, really, to judge the effect of all this on everybody, because people don't talk openly about it. It's hard to know what's in the mind of the other person, or even in your own mind. I would judge there has been an effect [on journalists], but it is hard to measure. Whatever the temporary effect, the best answer to it is to keep on doing good journalism for its own sake. The more of that we do, the better we can obviate whatever effect there has been [from those trials].

The Washington Post, 1-4: (D)4.

2

People like me are increasingly out of date at networks, because we want to take the time to craft journalism, and there is no premium on craftsmanship. There is a perception that the audience wants the kind of editing that [filmmaker] George Lucas made famous in *Star Wars.*

Interview, New York, Aug. 29/
Los Angeles Times, 8-30: (VI)1.

Roger Mudd
Broadcast journalist, NBC-TV

3

Nightly [network] news broadcasts on all three networks have a responsibility to give people a report on what has happened in the previous 24 hours. Generally, they do not have time to take long looks at stories. They just report on conflicts, crises, turmoils. What we don't do is report systematically about the rest of the coun-

try that didn't get on the evening news—transportation, religion, sports, subjects which ordinarily do not supply confrontation and conflict.

Interview/The Christian Science Monitor, 8-2:23.

Farouk Muhammed
Editor, "Daily Times,"
Lagos (Nigeria)

4

[On the international flow of news]: I am very sad about it. The U.S. is a powerful country, and so is the Soviet Union. Both superpowers talk about world peace, but how can that be achieved if there is not understanding among the world's people? And there cannot be that understanding unless there is a true flow of information. If Americans do not know much about the Chinese or the Africans, how can they relate to them? The Western nations control the vast news services—the Associated Press, United Press International, Reuters, Agence France-Presse. It is one thing to have a true information flow; it is entirely another thing to have only one kind of information. The type of information we get is determined basically by what American and European newspapers want. As a result, there is a kind of stereotyping. I do not see how Americans can appreciate the problems and efforts of others to the point that they will say, "Maybe if we push together there will be a better chance for world peace."

Interview/World Press Review, August:31.

Rupert Murdoch
Newspaper publisher

5

The key to what the newspaper business is all about is producing a product that will be read. Please remember that a newspaper, like all your businesses, is a business and not a philanthropy.

The New York Times, 5-7:34.

6

[A newspaper is] a collector and disseminator of news. Beyond that, if it is doing its job properly in the community, it should be drawing attention to issues. It should try to provoke readers

(RUPERT MURDOCH)

into thinking, as long as that doesn't get in the way of telling the news. In doing its job, it is perfectly reasonable for a newspaper to use packaging techniques. That may mean the use of great news pictures or putting in a color magazine on Sunday, such as *The New York Times* does—whatever it takes to reach the maximum number of people with news.

Interview/
U.S. News & World Report, 5-27-73.

1

Sometimes the criticism of the press is justified, sometimes it's not. If you're running a good newspaper and taking part in a community and saying things about issues, you've got to expect to make enemies and be criticized. If you dish it out, you've got to take it. Too many publishers can't take it. They don't mind their editors dishing it out, but when it comes back on them, they run for cover.

Interview/U.S. News & World Report, 5-27-73.

Allen H. Neuharth
Chairman,
Gannett Company

2

Not too many years ago, most print journalists thought futuristic planning was simply trying to figure out what was going to be in next Sunday's newspaper. But newspaper people finally have caught up with the information revolution that was spawned by the electronic media after World War II. That revolution certainly involves satellites and computers and color scanners. But it involves much more. The Information Revolution, like the Industrial Revolution, has changed dramatically not only our lifestyles, but also our attitudes and our expectations. The headline, in terms of the media business, is that people now want their information when they want it, where they want it and how they want it. They want it at home and away, at work and at play, night and day. The bottom line, for the media business, is that people are willing to pay a proper price to get this proper information service properly delivered. That's why the outlook for all forms of media is so encouraging, *if* those of us in this business can properly meet the wants and needs of today's information consumers.

Before Economic Club of Chicago,
Jan. 7/USA Today, 1-8-(B)6.

3

Professional journalists generally spend a lifetime striving to be fair. Narrow-gauged political, philosophical or economic pressure groups or individuals generally work full-time being unfair. Such extremists—whether on the right or the left—are entitled to their views. But they have no business trying to control how those views are presented to the public. Those who control the policies of public media companies should reflect interests as diverse as the audiences they serve. Only from such perspectives can public media companies properly fulfill the public trusts they hold.

At Gannett Co. shareholders meeting,
Rochester, N.Y./The New York Times, 5-23-39.

4

I fully understand that bigness in the media makes some people a little nervous. The potential dangers are there, if there is overconcentration of the media. But I don't believe they are real dangers because people—the readers, the viewers and the listeners—really are pretty sophisticated. They can pick and choose. Large media companies that deliver inferior news products to readers are just not going to get away with it for long.

Interview/USA Today, 9-13:(A)11.

Gregory Nokes
Diplomatic correspondent,
Associated Press

5

[Saying the Reagan Administration challenges journalists' patriotism]: Somehow we're suddenly the enemy—we're representing the [Nicaraguan] Sandinistas, representing the Soviet Union—and that just doesn't make sense. We're part of America, too. We go to church; we go to the softball games; we pay our taxes and serve our time in the military.

The Washington Post, 6-10:(A)4.

Norman J. Ornstein
Resident scholar,
American Enterprise Institute

1

I think the press has become a bogeyman for a lot of bad news that is simply bad news. But I believe the media has contributed to the problem with all its emphasis on scandal and purported conflict of interest by public officials, who are widely portrayed as venal and selfish. It's not surprising that a lot of people thinking about going into public service wind up deciding against it by saying, "What do I need with all this aggravation?"

Interview/U.S. News & World Report, 1-28:54.

Eugene Pell
Director,
Voice of America

2

[On TV news]: We now have Nightlines and Morning Lines, overnight news and 24-hour news, satellite news and local news, hourly news and network news—an endless flow of news. But look closely at the content and you will be struck by its sameness and shallowness . . . two minutes about a dog on a skateboard follows a report of equal length about international terrorism. The broadcast format is loose and linear, flitting rapidly from local to national to international episodes, but telling us little about ourselves or our world. We have an obligation to do better than that. The challenge before us was admirably stated by that revered figure in broadcasting and public diplomacy, Edward R. Murrow . . . : "The speed of communications is wondrous to behold. It is also true that speed can multiply the distribution of information that we know to be untrue. The most sophisticated satellite has no conscience. The newest computer can merely compound, at speed, the oldest problem in the relations between human beings, and in the end the communicator will still be confronted with the dilemma of what to say and how to say it." What to say and how to say it—in the most imaginative, technologically advanced and professional and substantive way possible represents our great challenge.

At his swearing-in ceremony, Washington, June 13/The Washington Post, 6-27:(A)22.

Jody Powell
Former Press Secretary to the
President of the United
States (Jimmy Carter)

3

The cause of excesses by television in reporting [terrorist] hostage situations is not ideological bias. It's motivated by money, which—as St. Paul said—is the root of all evil. Excess tends to play into the hands of the yahoos and people who don't believe in the First Amendment and the free flow of information. It undermines public support for the Constitutional guarantees that journalists need to do the job . . . Some journalists and First Amendment absolutists will argue, in the course of a debate: "It's not our job to worry about the consequences of our reporting. It's our job to report the news." They say that, but most of them don't act that way. Most of them would not report something they knew was going to get somebody killed. It they did, then I might change my view about not favoring government sanctions against the media.

Interview/
TV Guide, 9-21:23.

William Proxmire
United States Senator,
D-Wisconsin

4

What is the most improved institution in America today? Is it the American corporation, the Congress, the Presidency, the American newspaper, our magazines, radio, television, the medical profession, the legal profession, the university in America, the American military forces, the economics profession, American science, our professional sports, American churches and synagogues, our vigorous trade associations, our public schools, the entertainment industry? Some institution I have overlooked? My nomination is the institution that is the most demeaned, insulted and scorned: the American press. Hardly a month has gone by in 200 years when the American press has not been scolded, derided, sneered at, belittled. Today, we have the best system of news gathering and dissemination we have ever had. But there is at least an outside chance that a combination of new corporate takeover techniques and ideological hubris

(WILLIAM PROXMIRE)

may, just may, undermine it. It is worth watching, and closely.

Before the Senate, Washington,
April 2/The New York Times,
4-4:14.

Trygve Ramberg
Co-editor, "Aftenposten,"
Oslo (Norway)

1

[On government subsidization of the press in Norway]: A subsidy was introduced to insure that any citizen, wherever he lives, has access to more than one paper. Any paper with less than 10,000 circulation—or any paper that is losing money—gets financial help. I am ideologically opposed to this, but it has worked. There are no political criteria. The Marxist-Leninist newspaper gets support and so does the most right-wing newspaper, because they meet the circulation and economic criteria. There is a controversy over subsidies only if someone tries to break the rules—for instance, if some members of Parliament say that because of the press subsidy there should be more newspapers writing in New Norwegian or more reports from Parliament. Overall, the subsidy has no political strings and does not invade press freedom. In the U.S., where you have no press subsidy, you have many one-newspaper towns, and outstanding papers have died or are dying.

Interview/World Press Review, July:33.

Dan Rather
Anchorman,
"Evening News," CBS-TV

2

[Evening News executive producer] Lane Venardos compares what we do every day to trying to change a fan belt on a moving Mercedes. And you try to do it without getting your fingers all bloodied and mashed up in the works. If people watch you every night, they can see right into your soul.

Interview, New York/USA Today, 3-5:(A)2.

Harry Reasoner
Correspondent,
"60 Minutes," CBS-TV

3

James Kilpatrick, the conservative columnist, once said that all reporters should remember that even though they're invited to sup at the homes of the powerful, they should remember that tomorrow they may be begging for crumbs at the kitchen door. Your clout is because you're CBS or Playboy or The New York Times. It's not because it's you.

Interview/Playboy, March:170.

David Rubin
Chairman, department of journalism,
New York University

4

Most people, particularly journalists, would like to leave the questions of power and influence [of the press] behind the shield of the First Amendment and not talk about it. But in the areas of East-West relations and the arms race, what the press reports matters because it can affect the climate in which defense budgets are assembled, arms talks are held, and new weapons systems are fitted into an overall strategic concept. Reporters should know somebody's watching them. I think one way—but not the only way—to improve press performance is letting people in the business know that someone is watching.

The Christian Science Monitor, 6-18:25.

Morley Safer
Correspondent,
"60 Minutes," CBS-TV

5

How can they [the subjects of 60 Minutes interviews] know what 60 Minutes wants to do when, most of the time, we don't know what 60 Minutes wants to do? These guys have no understanding of journalism. They have no real feel for what reporters think, what the process is. They think it's all cut and dried: Step A follows step B. Journalism is erratic. It's often irrational. It's the way certain facts fall into place. There is no process.

Interview/Playboy, March:167.

Jonas Salk
Physician, Scientist

1

I hardly use the newspaper as my source of information. I look upon the newspaper as a pathology sheet, analogous to what is seen when you come on to the wards in the hospital in the morning. It reports everything that is sick—everything that has gone wrong the day before. Very little in a newspaper tells you about what's going on that's good.

Interview/USA Today, 9-10:(A)9.

Antonin Scalia
*Judge, United States
Court of Appeals for the
District of Columbia*

2

[On whether there should be tougher laws against the press printing government secrets]: I suspect that the average journalist would not feel free to disregard governmental protestations of compromise of the national security by simply saying, "We can't trust the government." If I didn't believe that, I'd be worried. And I'd be worried if I were a member of the press and didn't believe that, because the fact is, as the British political philosopher Lord Acton put it, that society is the freest which is the most responsible. If you don't have a lot of people in your town spitting in the street, you don't need a no-spitting ordinance. The occasional individual who feels he must spit in the street can be free to do so. But when you have a lot of people who go around spitting, you enact an ordinance. In other words, the First Amendment is a very liberal amendment as it is now applied and interpreted by the courts and implemented by statutes. That liberality depends to a large extent upon the responsibility with which the freedom that it confers is exercised. Since the ultimate law of any society is going to be survival, if that responsibility disappears, other statutes will be passed.

Seminar, Princeton, N.J./Harper's, November:52.

Herbert Schmertz
*Vice president for public
affairs, Mobil Oil Corporation*

3

. . . the American press today is not satisfied with the right to publish without prior restraint.

It wants the right to publish anything without the threat of any consequences whatever, whether legal or marketplace. But the press's actions and what I would call its abuses do have consequences. The most obvious abuse is that the American press often attempts to make policy rather than report it; it seems to see itself as the surrogate of the people. I simply don't buy that. We elect leaders to make policy in this country. When the press departs from its proper role of disseminating information and reporting policy, and begins trying to make or influence policy, then I object. Of course, I exempt from this criticism editorialists and newspaper columnists . . . But when straight-news reporters slant their supposedly objective stories, I object. And I think the American people object, too.

*Panel discussion at New School for Social Research,
New York/Harper's, January:39.*

Patricia Schroeder
*United States Representative,
D-Colorado*

4

[Saying the press reports White House releases as though they are fact, whether true or not]: I do believe that if the White House announced that President Reagan was a giraffe, the next morning's papers would all have headlines, "Reagan a Giraffe, White House discloses." The headlines would be followed by studious analysis on how the giraffe disclosures would affect municipal bond rates, Japanese auto imports and the 1986 elections. Republican Congressional leaders would note that Reagan was a fine-looking giraffe, in good condition for his age. Democrats would complain that he spends too much time ruminating in California. Environmentalists would criticize him for chewing leaves off trees. Meanwhile, somewhere out in the country, someone, most likely a child, would say, "But Reagan's not a giraffe."

*Before the House, Washington,
Feb. 4/The New York Times, 2-6:10.*

Eric Sevareid
Journalist

5

[On the news media]: [Journalist] Walter Lippmann said that the central point is not that

383

WHAT THEY SAID IN 1985

(ERIC SEVAREID)

the full truth is revealed in any one account but that, out of free reporting and discussion, truth emerges. It takes time. And a fairly long attention span. If a story is 50 per cent wrong the first day, it's probably 85 per cent right the second and 99 per cent the third. The news tends to correct itself. And it's the only institution that advertises attacks upon itself. How do we hear about the inadequacies of the press except through the press?

Interview/Business Week, 1-28-5.

1

[On today's TV news coverage of important events]: What we don't have as much of as we used to is leisurely examination of the substance by thoughtful and scholarly people. In part, that may be because the state of mind in the news-production centers is very different from that of the audience at home. There is a kind of controlled frenzy in the newsroom: If you have 4 seconds of silence, you have a heart attack. But people at home just had dinner; they're not all that much in a hurry. TV needs to do more in the way of thoughtful discussion, following more quickly on the presentation of the news.

Interview/U.S. News & World Report, 12-2:33.

Ariel Sharon
Former Minister of Defense of Israel

[On a libel-trial jury's finding that *Time* magazine incorrectly reported that he conspired in the massacre of Palestinians in Lebanon in 1982]: I'm glad that after this long struggle . . . that we have proved . . . that *Time* lied. They lied and they libeled and it was just a blood libel against me, against the state of Israel and against the Jewish people. It is a great moral victory.

To reporters, New York, Jan. 18/
Los Angeles Times, 1-19-(I)3.

Bernard Shaw
Washington anchorman,
Cable News Network

[On news coverage of the recent Lebanese hijacking of an American airliner and the holding

hostage of its passengers]: We [the press] were used. Absolutely. They [the terrorists] wanted a world-wide platform and they got an international stage. The media ought to critically reflect on their role in this story and entertain the question, "To what extent do we cover terrorists in the future?" That would be revolutionary. On the other hand, I fear for the victims of the terrorists if they [the terrorists] are resigned to conducting their acts in private, without the cameras, because their lifeline is media publicity. If they do not get a measure, their frustrations at not being able to speak to the world, and their ignorance of how their demands are being perceived and received, could lead to extreme acts, such as murdering people.

Interview/USA Today, 7-2:(A)9.

Leonard Silk
Journalist, Economist

Reagan is the only President I have never sat down with. Not that I haven't tried. I think the people around Reagan made a shrewd—and possibly correct—decision that the intellectual, or thinking, press really doesn't matter much. As the country became more televisionified, the thinking press diminished in importance.

Interview/Forbes, 1-28:42.

4

Alan K. Simpson
United States Senator,
R-Wyoming

[On what it would be like to have no news reported]: As usual, it was exciting to contemplate there for a minute that we would have no news at all for several days. I was excited about that. Of course, I realize that we do not function, we cannot function, without the news. I always remember what our good librarian, Daniel Boorstin, the Librarian of Congress, said to us. He said, "We are surfeited with information in this country. What we lack is knowledge." I think there is a great deal of truth in that. We are full of information, but sometimes in the glut of information we do not have time to process it and use our good brains and common sense.

Before the Senate, Washington/
The New York Times, 9-13:12.

5

Robert B. Sims
Deputy Press Secretary to the President of the United States

1

[On White House "background briefings" given to the press]: The use of the technique of having Administration officials brief at the White House on a background basis has been a policy of the first four years of the [Reagan] Administration, and I expect it will continue. We like to be "on the record." But there are times, in the interest of informing the press and the public, that "background," and not "on the record," is just the best policy . . . Often times we're trying to explain the nuances of the government's position. Backgrounders are a statement by an informed person in the government trying to explain the government's point of view. It's a diplomatic technique, more than a technique for dealing with the press. For example, after the President and a foreign leader have met and made statements, we have a background briefing on the details of the meeting. Some things are quite acceptable if they're said on background and not attributed. If they are attributed, it becomes an official statement of the U.S. government about relations with a foreign government.

Interview, Washington/
The New York Times, 1-3:8.

Abraham D. Sofaer
Judge in libel suit against
"Time" magazine brought by former
Israeli Defense Minister Ariel Sharon

2

Nothing in the First Amendment requires that the press have absolute freedom to pass off . . . rumors as fact, regardless of how damaging they are to an official's reputation. The Supreme Court has rested its denial of absolute immunity on the fundamental premise that the Constitutional value of free speech does not in all circumstances outweigh the state's interests in protecting the reputations of their citizens.

Instructions to the jury, New York,
Jan. 18/The Washington Post,
1-23:(A)9.

Larry Speakes
Principal Deputy Press Secretary to
the President of the United States

3

[On his de facto role as Press Secretary]: I have some rules. Number one is, always tell the truth. I've got only one currency. That's the truth. There are 10,000 ways to say, "No comment," and I've used 9,999 of them. The second rule is, don't be afraid to say, "I don't know." You may look dumb, but if you don't know, you can't give them [reporters] hot air, because it always shows on your face . . . [At press briefings] it still boils down to a bit of a game of how can they get me to say what I don't want to say. It's a game of checkers where you've got to be three jumps out ahead of your opponents or you can paint yourself into a corner very easily. It is adversarial. I try to deal with that. They know badgering or trying to weasel something out of me really won't work.

Interview, Washington/The New York Times, 2-14:10.

4

[On charges that the Reagan Administration is making it difficult for the press to get information from the government]: Every Administration I have been associated with has tried to focus public attention on a given subject, to expose the President in the best light. Any corporation, including media corporations, do much the same thing, try to present their corporations in the best light. I would say this Administration has been the most accessible as any, so far as senior policy-makers being willing to talk to the press on a regular basis and even a spot news basis.

The Washington Post, 6-10;(A)4.

5

Even as late as the [Gerald] Ford Administration, our press corps was 75 per cent print and 25 per cent electronic. In these 10 years or so, it's reversed itself. Television's influence, both with the public and within the press room itself, is increased extraordinarily. When I was here with [Ford's Press Secretary] Ron Nessen, we'd prepare for 10 or 15 different subjects, any of which might be asked [by the press]. You walk in

(LARRY SPEAKES)

there today, you can virtually prepare for two subjects, many times one. Television almost never does more than one story a day.

Interview/USA Today, 7-29:(A)9.

1

[Defending his integrity as Presidential spokesman]: When you look at an individual and remove everything—money, position, power—you only have your reputation to stand on. And I have spent my lifetime building a reputation, and I've spent 18 years as a press spokesman in Washington building a reputation. That's all I have, is a reputation. Government salaries aren't very high. And I have a reputation for telling the truth, for dealing fairly with people and for hard work and a professional approach to my job. This is a long-term investment. It goes back to Capitol Hill, it goes to the PR business, and it goes to the White House under three Presidents.

To reporters, Washington,
Aug. 7/The New York Times, 8-8:10.

James Squires
Editor, "Chicago Tribune"

2

Newspaper credibility is not in any worse shape than it has ever been, but the problems of media credibility in general are bigger for newspapers. I have to answer for the behavior of *Playboy,* or *Penthouse,* or ABC Sports. That was not true 20 years ago. That, more than anything else, bothers me. I am more bothered by the inability of the public to distinguish the independence of American newspapers from the rest of the media than I am by any sudden loss of newspaper credibility.

Interview, Washington/USA Today, 4-11:(A)9.

Margaret Thatcher
Prime Minister of the United Kingdom

3

I often hear media people say that they hold up a mirror to society. This, I am sure, is what the best and most objective reporters seek to do. But this raises the question of whether the

media . . . accurately reflect the life of the nation, given that the news in their terms is so often of violence, tragedy, conflict, distress—and that a concentrated diet of these things makes it very difficult to see life in perspective.

To regional British television company,
July 17/The Washington Post, 7-18:(A)30.

Helen Thomas
White House correspondent,
United Press International

4

[Saying the Reagan Administration limits the government news and information made available to the press]: They pick the story every day. They pick the one that will almost invariably wind up on the nightly news, and that's the one they answer questions on or give access to information about. A lot of events, we're absolutely blacked out, and if you don't like it, too bad. The whole attitude is, "We will tell you what we think you should know."

The Washington Post, 6-10:(A)4.

Laurence H. Tribe
Professor of law,
Harvard University

5

[On the increase in libel suits by individuals against news organizations]: The burdens of defending a suit remain a powerful disincentive to the kind of adventuresome and forthright journalism that the public has a right to expect from the media.

Los Angeles Times, 2-20:(I)1.

Chris Wallace
White House correspondent,
NBC News

6

[On news coverage of the recent Lebanese hijacking of an American airliner and the holding hostage of its passengers]: We [in the press] must examine what we are doing. Reporters can't constantly think about the social impact of what they are doing. We have to report, even if we think we are encouraging terrorism, or hurting feelings, or causing problems. That is what

(CHRIS WALLACE)

the free press is about. Of course, we were used [by the terrorists]. One of the things that [the] terrorists wanted was to get their message out, to express their grievances. On a more benign level, we are used by public officials, as well as those who want to sell their books or movies. The reporter has to decide whether the story is good, informative and true, and the fact that you are serving someone else's purpose must come second.

Interview/USA Today, 7-2:(A)9.

Mike Wallace
Correspondent,
"60 Minutes," CBS-TV

1

We wince in television journalism at the word "performer" [applied to a broadcast journalist], but the fact of the matter is that there *is* a performance involved. That doesn't mean it's phony or theatrical. But sometimes it's the best way to tell the story of people who are breaking the law.

Interview/Playboy, March:162.

William C. Westmoreland
General, United States Army (ret.);
Former commander,
U.S. forces in Vietnam

2

[On his recent libel suit against CBS in which he charged the network with making false statements about his actions during the Vietnam war]: Consider the plight of a public figure who believes, as I did, that his performance has been unfairly degraded, that his honor has been impugned, that his loyalty has been questioned. The chilling effect of a libel suit on journalistic enterprise is a valid concern. On the other hand, a letter to the editor has little effect except perhaps to satisfy the writer who wants to get something off his chest. There is a need for something in-between . . . The route of the libel suit is not good, either for the plaintiff or defendant. In many cases the legal costs alone are prohibitive, both to the individual and to small publishers and radio and television stations. The rules of evidence, the legalisms of the court system, do

not promote open and free debate . . . I do not believe that either side [in this libel suit] won what it wanted. The time, energy and talent, to say nothing of money, that went into this affair could have been better used.

Before National Press Club, Washington,
March 15/The New York Times, 3-16:7.

Kevin H. White
Former Mayor of Boston

3

[Politicians] are forging coalitions to achieve something . . . and they expect the press to be another audience that gets into that coalition of support. The failure of the press, once educated, not to assume a part in that phalanx is frustrating to a politician—in fact, he almost considers the press traitorous. And yet he fails to understand that the press is reporting what *appears* to be. It isn't that they don't care—in fact, the press more often than not *is* seduced, *is* personal, *is* chauvinistic, *is* patriotic, *does* want to come to the fore. Their role is to report—even if they're wrong. [Theirs] is the perception of reality that the public sees.

Interview/The Christian Science Monitor, 10-7:29.

Tom Wicker
Political columnist; Associate editor,
"The New York Times"

4

. . . when we speak of a free press, I think we necessarily do mean an adversary press, but then we have to explain what we mean by "adversary." The American press is not an adversary in the way that two nations at war, or two neighbors fighting over a boundary line are adversaries. Rather, I think of the press as an adversary in the sense that, in a courtroom, a lawyer is the adversary of a witness as he is cross-examining. The lawyer has a duty not simply to listen to what the witness says and elicit responses from him, but somehow to draw from him as near a true story as possible. Ideally, the press plays an adversarial role by making a similar effort to dig beneath the surface of things, instead of simply broadcasting or printing what appears to be the case, without questioning it.

Panel discussion at New School for Social Research,
New York/Harper's, January:38.

Pete Wilson
United States Senator, R-California

1

I think there is a feeling that the [three broadcast] networks have become so important in terms of providing news. They're a three-way monopoly. And what that means is that they have had conferred upon them enormous power. [Although] it's tough to discharge your responsibilities if you're a television network, a lot of people feel that the networks have not discharged their responsibilities very well.

Interview, Washington, Jan. 28/
Los Angeles Times,
1-29:(VI)3.

Thomas Winship
Fellow,
Gannett Center for Media Studies

2

The way to deal with the [newspaper] credibility problem is to be more accurate—period. Every problem in the newspaper begins and ends with the editor. He has to set the tone. The attack on credibility has to be a frontal attack on improving the accuracy of our newspapers. I would do that by setting up a new fact-checking structure in every daily newspaper, which magazines have done for 50 years. I would also print corrections where errors take place, which includes Page One. I do, however, think soul-searching is always good for us. It just makes us think and discuss the root problems. We have a lot of improving to do.

Interview/
USA Today,
11-26:(A)11.

Timothy E. Wirth
United States Representative,
D-Colorado

3

[Criticizing the FCC's declaration against the Fairness Doctrine]: The question I have for the FCC is why did they want to take the principle of fairness away from the American TV and radio viewer? The Supreme Court has repeatedly said that the right of viewers and listeners to receive information is the paramount right under the First Amendment . . . The American TV and radio audience can rest assured that Congress is not about to take any such action [to eliminate the Fairness Doctrine].

Aug. 7/The New York Times, 8-8:19.

Thomas H. Wyman
Chairman, CBS, Inc.

4

[On U.S. Senator Jesse Helms' urging conservative Americans to buy up CBS stock in an effort to gain control and reverse what he says is the company's liberal bias in news]: I have enough faith in the fiber of this country that this would not happen. The importance of unbiased news is our number-one priority. Senator Helms and his supporters claim that CBS is biased, and they feel that if we do not respond to their demands—which are as yet unspecified—a takeover of the corporation would provide a valid remedy. [But complaining about news coverage] is often an attempt to manipulate the news. And sometimes it is an attempt to intimidate. Whatever the proclaimed goals of such groups may be, their actual agenda is usually the same. It is to manage the news according to standards other than journalism.

At Duke University, Feb. 5/USA Today, 2-6:(D)7.

Literature

Jorge Amado
Author

1

I'm incapable of making a plan [prior to writing a new book]. I know people who construct books beforehand, but I never know what will happen. My stories are construed by the characters that take me along. For me, a book is done when the characters walk and live on their own feet. That's why the beginning of a book is always so hard for me.

Interview, Salvador, Brazil/
The New York Times, 1-12:9.

Maya Angelou
Author

2

[On writing autobiographical works]: If I have done it correctly, then, as a person thinks he or she knows me better, that person knows himself or herself better. That's what I think an autobiographer strives for—to capture that essence of a good humanity and at the same time the temper of the times, to try to bring the reader into the times and make that reader the central character. If the reader so identifies, then the reader becomes the character, and all those things are happening to the reader.

Interview/USA Today, 3-5:(A)9.

3

Hawthorne once said that easy reading is damned hard writing, and that is so true. Writing is not natural. It is very hard work. This does not mean that everybody does not have talent. Everybody in the world is born with it, although we often knock it out of them before they're 4 or 5 years old. But to write well means that one re-writes 20 to 50 times.

Interview/USA Today, 3-5:(A)9.

John Baker
Editor, "Publishers Weekly"

4

Book reviewing in this country [the U.S.] just isn't as good, doesn't have the tradition it does in England. Too many papers just use local academics, rather than real writers and real experts . . . and that makes the reviews pretty dull, not like the wide-ranging, authoritative, thoughtful . . . well-written reviews you get in the [London] *Times Literary Supplement.*

Los Angeles Times, 12-13:(V)14.

James Baldwin
Author

5

A book has a season, and it's a great mistake to think you can write a best-seller once a year. The book behind you is the book behind you; the book ahead of you is the book ahead of you. And a success can be as difficult to survive as a failure. When you're a success, if you believe it, you're finished.

Interview, London/The New York Times, 1-10:18.

Russell Banks
Author

6

I'm really interested in re-inventing the narrator. It's a convention that went out the window in the 20th century. I want to feel I have my arm around a shoulder of this reader and I'm explaining, narrating, telling a wonderful story to this person that I've stopped, like the wedding guest in Coleridge's *The Ancient Mariner.* I'm like the ancient mariner stopping the wedding guest in his rush to tell this wonder to him. And I want to have that sense of intimacy, a face-to-face, arms-around-the-shoulder contact.

Interview/Publishers Weekly, 3-15:121.

John Barth
Author; Professor of English
and creative writing,
Johns Hopkins University

7

[Exiled Soviet author] Alexander Solzhenitsyn . . . comes to the medium of fiction with a high moral purpose; he wants, literally, to try to change the world through the medium of the

(JOHN BARTH)

novel. I honor and admire that intention. But, just as often, a great writer will come to his novel with a much less elevated purpose than wanting to undermine the Soviet government. Henry James wanted to write a book in the shape of an hourglass. Flaubert wanted to write a novel about *nothing*. What I've learned is that the muses' decision to sing or not to sing is not based on the elevation of your moral purpose—they will sing or not, regardless.

Interview, Houston/The Paris Review, Spring:149.

Ann Beattie
Author

1

I don't think that even 20 years ago writers got the kind of attention that I'm likely to get now. Writers weren't considered celebrities. People were more interested in politicians and movie stars. It's still surprising to me and to my colleagues that people want to photograph us and have us endorse products, because writing is such a private act. But the media come after you as though you're interchangeable with any other public figure, which is very weird. When I work I put the notion of media-generated "celebrity" out of my mind. I didn't know anybody who's serious who tries to pitch their work to the media or who thinks about their persona. It's unfortunate for those who can't do that. They become poseurs, and people probably could name some American writers whom that description fits. There are people who play that game, and that goal is to lock into their own images.

Interview/U.S. News & World Report, 7-29:62.

Stephen Birmingham
Author

2

I don't give a damn about critics. I stopped reading reviews of my books a long time ago. The more successful you get, the harder critics are on you anyway. I'm not writing for the critics. I'm writing for my audience, and what the critics have to say doesn't affect the sales of my books one bit. I'm a storyteller. Remember in ancient days, storytellers used to go from village to village and tell tales to people who gathered to listen? When the story was finished, the people gave the yarn-spinner a few coins and then he moved on to the next place. That's how I think of myself. I don't want to change the world. I want to entertain my readers by giving them a good story, by making them laugh and cry, by telling them anecdotes they enjoy.

Interview/Writer's Digest, May:30.

Harold Bloom
Literary critic

3

The social utility of literature and humanistic education is very long-range and an almost invisible affair. That's the way it should be. Any good that gets done, gets done to the single individual. He or she is not a better person for it, but perhaps more aware with a broader range of sensibility . . . The student or reader is to consider himself or herself the text, and all received texts are secondary. Poems matter only if *we* matter. The texts are there for us, not us for them.

Interview, New Haven, Conn./The Washington Post, 8-20:(C)2.

4

Criticism doesn't have to be creative, but obviously criticism is a genre or subgenre of literature. It is part of an art. To say, automatically, that a bad minor poet is part of literature and a great critic is not is obviously preposterous.

Interview, New Haven, Conn./The Washington Post, 8-20:(C)2.

Ray Bradbury
Author

5

I've written some strange, horrible stories, but they've always ended on a high note. Art must do what life can't. We already know a lot about death and dying. My sister died when I was young. An uncle was shot to death. We were so poor I had to wear his suit to my high-school graduation, and it still had the bullet hole in it. [An artist should] tell us what to do next.

Interview, Beverly Hills, Calif./The Wall Street Journal, 10-28:18.

(RAY BRADBURY)

Writing should be as fun and frivolous as sex. If it isn't, why do it?

Interview, Beverly Hills, Calif./
The Wall Street Journal, 10-28:18.

Cleanth Brooks
Author, Critic;
Professor emeritus of rhetoric, Yale University

1

[On the "bastard muses" of literature: propaganda, sentimentality and pornography]: All three are bent on distorting the human dimension. Propaganda does so by pleading, sometimes unscrupulously, for a special cause or issue at the expense of total truth. Sentimentality does so by working up emotional responses unwarranted by, and in excess of, the occasion. Pornography does so by focusing upon one powerful human drive at the expense of the total human personality.

Jefferson Lecture, Washington, May 8/
The Christian Science Monitor, 5-13:23.

Italo Calvino
Author

2

I want to have a relationship with the reader. I want the reader to have fun. I don't want to be a boring writer. At the same time, I want my books to have a meaning and to have a meaning in the culture of our times; to say something that hasn't already been said and to say it in a way that cannot be said except through literature. I believe more and more in literature as a language that says things that the other languages can't say, that literature has full status as a form of knowledge.

Interview, New York/
Saturday Review, March-April:39.

Jackie Collins
Author

3

I'm a street writer who doesn't pretend to be anything else. I'm not grammatical in the way I talk, or in the way I write, and I don't pretend to

be. I'm a high-school dropout who eavesdrops. I don't type, but I once told my typist . . . "All right, you fix my grammar." Well, she did, and I couldn't bear it! "Put it all back the way it was," I told her. Pick up a page, any page, of writing by Truman Capote and you will find that he was incapable of using the wrong word. His writing is timeless, extraordinary. I'm just trying to give people a little piece of 1985.

Interview, Beverly Hills, Calif./
Los Angeles Times, 8-25:(Calendar)3.

Joan Didion
Author

4

In many ways, writing is the act of saying "I," imposing yourself on other people. [Writing] is an aggressive, even hostile, act. You can disguise the aggressiveness any way you want. But there's no getting around the fact that the act of putting your words on paper is the act of a secret bully.

At meeting of PEN, New York,
Nov. 10/Los Angeles Times, 11-13:(V)3.

E. L. Doctorow
Author

5

Fame and fortune [as a writer] aren't something you can take very seriously. And they're certainly nothing you can live on. They're not your inner life. Nothing can help you face the blank page.

Interview,
New York/USA Today, 11-4:(D)7.

6

Writing is very often a desperate act. After I finished *The Book of Daniel,* I was profoundly, emotionally exhausted. But I didn't know it. I sat around for a year trying to write. I wrote endless pages that didn't take me anywhere. I got so desperate that I started to write about the wall that I face when I write. As it happened, that was the wall in my study in New Rochelle, New York. That house was built in 1906. So I started to think about that house and that street and what it must have looked like in 1906. Out of that emerged *Ragtime.* You never know how it's go-

WHAT THEY SAID IN 1985

(E. L. DOCTOROW)

ing to start. But I do know that if I don't write, I feel as if I'm turning inanimate. I don't think of writing as a career; I don't think of it as an occupation. I think of it as the way I'm alive. I don't know how to exist otherwise.

Interview/U.S. News & World Report, 12-16:73.

Margaret Drabble
Editor,
"Oxford Companion to English Literature"

1

You can't complain in the Western world about our freedom to write; we can write whatever we like now. But we do perhaps seem to have lost some link with the people who don't write or read. I am looking for some way of revitalizing things that have dropped out of the novel a bit, and I think other people are looking for it, too: a sense of being rooted in day-to-day reality, social change, history. I think people are looking for a new way of relating the novel to history.

Interview/Publishers Weekly, 5-31:60.

Francine du Plessix Gray
Author

2

While writing non-fiction, you obviously don't learn as much about yourself as you do when writing novels. But, paradoxically, you also don't learn as much about the world. In fiction, precisely because you're working from the subconscious, inventing situations from the substratum of the communal psyche, you're in touch with a mythic reality which is more "real" than the common-sense data of everydayness. I'm talking like a mystic, which I am.

Interview/Saturday Review, Nov.-Dec.:55.

Richard Eder
Book critic, "Los Angeles Times"

3

[There's] a fundamental difference between book reviewing and film or theatre reviewing. When I was a theatre critic [for *The New York Times*], I reviewed just about every play that came along . . . which, by definition, means at

392

Michael Ende
West German author

4

Fifty per cent of my letters are from readers between the ages of 20 and 35—our so-called "alternative" generation. They can't stand the utter lack of fantasy in society. Romanticism is a strong German tradition, and it is part of the German language. We have to take care of our language. The German voice shouldn't get lost in the chorus of nations . . . For decades [in literature], it was considered fantastically clever and progressive to destroy taboos and values . . . I think that it's more progressive, and it takes more courage, to suggest values. People need a balance against the technical world. Fiction should provide that. Without fantasy, the world is just ash.

Interview, Munich/
The Wall Street Journal, 2-28:30.

Joseph Epstein
Editor, "American Scholar"

5

American writers today deal with experience at second remove. They are not holding up our tradition because it means so little to them. I think the '60s damaged the integral nature of our literature with an infusion of politics that caused many talented writers to slide away from seriousness. Our literature became factionalized a generation ago, and it still has not recovered. Which is why, lately, I find myself turning *back*, again with renewed pleasure: Henry James, Evelyn Waugh, Max Beerbohm and E. M. Forster.

Interview, New York/Publishers Weekly, 3-1:82.

Clifton Fadiman
Editor, Critic

6

When I opened and read the first page of a book for the first time, I felt this was

least 80 per cent *dreck*. So I got a reputation as a very tough critic. But there are so many books published every year that a book critic usually reviews only those that interest him. Unless you're an absolute ass, that means 80 per cent of your reviews will be favorable. So now I'm perceived as a very benevolent critic.

Interview/Los Angeles Times, 12-11:(I)16.

(CLIFTON FADIMAN)

remarkable—that I could learn something very quickly that I could not have learned any other way. I grew bug-eyed over the miracle of language. How could a few punctuation marks, plus words made out of 26 letters, be put together so as to create images of people, animals, stories, landscapes, streets, towns and even ideas? Here I was, a rather dull boy looking at an unopened book. Then, within a short time, the dull boy found he was entertained, amused, saddened, delighted, mystified, scared, dreamy, puzzled, astonished, held in suspense—all depending on what was in those pages . . . The first time I read words it seemed like magic. It still does.

*Interview, Santa Barbara, Calif./
The Washington Post, 3-28:(B)2.*

Oriana Fallaci
Author, Journalist

1

People think being a writer simply means having your name on a book jacket. People think that Jane Fonda, Richard Nixon, Henry Kissinger and Shirley MacLaine are writers . . ., that a few years at the White House make [one] a writer . . . The act of writing comes from the result of *being* a writer.

*At University of New Hampshire/
The Christian Science Monitor, 5-31:23.*

Stuart Berg Flexner
*Editor-in-chief, Random House dictionaries;
Former professor of English literature
and linguistics, Cornell University*

2

The charge that English is degenerating into a sloppy and ungrammatical language is not new. It has been made ever since the 17th century. But English is still strong and growing, and we communicate as well as any people ever have. Those who feel the language is declining just don't know much about history. It was never perfect, never followed unchanging rules. We should, of course, try to follow the rules of grammar and usage; but in the search for simpler, quicker, more-direct communication, the human mind is always going to break or ignore

some of them, whether we like it or not. That's how the language evolves. Shakespeare used "pneumonia" to mean "head cold." He used "nice" to mean "lascivious." These words have changed completely, and such changes in meaning and usage are going to continue to take place as long as people use language.

Interview/U.S. News & World Report, 2-18:59.

Frederick Forsyth
Author

3

What I will do after my first draft is hoist in all the criticisms and comments of a very small group—my wife, my editor, my publisher and my agent—and if they all take the view that this needs clarifying, or that is too long, then I will make changes. I've got no literary pretensions. I don't have a highly personalized style. Eighty per cent of my books is story. The other 20 per cent is where I sandwich in the other three components of novels—descriptive passages, dialogue, and character development.

Interview/Saturday Review, July-August:40.

John Fowles
Author

4

After you finish [writing a book], you are intensely depressed. It doesn't much matter whether the reviews are good or not. You feel empty, a field lying fallow, and you must let it stay fallow a while. You love a book when it's being written. You are so close to it. You're the only person who knows it and it's still full of potential. You know you can improve it. Then, suddenly, there's the dreadful day when you have the printed proof texts. You get a feeling of "That's it. This is the final thing and I shan't have a chance to change it." It's a feeling of death, really.

*Interview, New York/
The Washington Post, 9-12:(C)1.*

Dick Francis
Author

5

Writing is actually hard work. The best thing is doing the research, going to different

(DICK FRANCIS)

places . . . Writing about something that you don't know [is hard]. If I'm writing about a character who is doing a job I don't know, I go and research that job. I've learned so much about life since I've been writing the books . . . To win a horse race [the was a jockey before turning to writing] is much more immediately rewarding. Everyone pats you on the back. But it isn't nearly so long-lasting as writing a good book. That goes on for years. You get that satisfaction for a long, long time.

Interview/USA Today, 8-12:(4)9.

Lawrence S. Freundlich
Editor, Publisher

1

[On book reviews]: To get good reviews, you [the publisher] spend a lot of money. You make calls, print extra bound galleys, have parties and invite reviewers, solicit quotes from the authors' friends, hire a big-name public-relations firm—and you let people know you're doing all this.

Los Angeles Times, 12-12:(V)34.

William Gaddis
Author

2

When you come right down to it, [writing] is a massive act of ego, first to get out of The System and say, "I'm not going to go to an office every day if I can possibly avoid it," and then to write a novel. A novel is absolutely one's own creation, on one's own terms. It is one's ego saying, "I want you to read my work, accept my vision and agree. And applaud. And pay—what is it?—$16.95 for this privilege.'" It is a unilateral kind of affront.

Interview, the Hamptons, N.Y./ The Washington Post, 8-23:(B)10.

James Giblin
Author of children's books; Editor-in-chief, Clarion Books

3

Someone once said to a children's book editor, "In adult publishing it's dog eat dog. Is that true in children's books?" And the editor replied, "On, no. In children's books, it's bunny nibble bunny." I think the point is that, though we have to be a business and pay our way, in children's books we can be competitive and idealistic at the same time.

Interview/Publishers Weekly, 7-26:169.

Nikki Giovanni
Poet

4

Writing is, of course, a lonely profession. One of the things that I would urge you to do [as writers] is to find a volunteer project once a year that will take you into people. If you're not careful, you'll spend all of your time with yourself or you'll spend all of your time with other writers. I would urge you not to make friends with other writers because we're all nuts. We are. One of the things that you need to do is to find people who have real concerns because, otherwise, everybody's dealing with similes. Everybody's dealing with "How do you structure this stanza?" What you need is somebody to say, "I know what you're saying about writing this poem, but I have a hell of a time at the grocery store when the woman in front of me has 13 items in a 12-item lane" . . . Sometimes we as artists begin to think that we are so special and so sensitive and so important to the world that we can't do rather mundane, ordinary things like have our cars washed or fill up at a gas station. We forget that there's a real world, and, as we forget . . . we lose touch with the people we're hoping to meet, to reach, to talk to.

Interview, Los Angeles/ Los Angeles Times, 12-4:(V)5.

Rumer Godden
Author

5

[On writing]: An artist has to be ready, as an instrument is ready, to be used. Only, who would choose an instrument like this? This mysterious force picks us up, rushes us along, then leaves us, usually when we're halfway through. It teases us, buffets us, embraces us, hits us, forgets all about us at once, and then wears us out with work. And yet, what is it? . . . I don't

(RUMER GODDEN)

know. I only know its path, its ways—and that always the vision is elusive.

Abraham S. Burack Lecture, Boston University/
Boston Review, September:19.

Don Graham
Associate professor of English,
University of Texas

1

[On the western novel]: It has always been split between two extremes. There's the bus-station western, the paperback original, that's mostly a lower-middle-class literary form—the tradition of Zane Grey, of which Louis L'Amour is the chief practitioner today. Then there's western American literature, by writers like [Larry] McMurtry, William Eastlake, Wallace Stegner. What's interesting is that both forms seem to be enjoying resurgence.

The New York Times, 9-16:19.

Phyllis Grann
President and publisher,
G. P. Putnam's Sons, publishers

2

I'm in the entertainment business, no doubt about it. I don't feel it's my job to educate the consumer; my job is to give him the very best sort of books he enjoys. And that's equally true of literary and commercial fiction. I'm my own best customer. I think certain of these writers are the very best of their kind. The public has a voice, and its voice is heard by this industry. We may not like that voice; we might prefer that the public had different tastes. But my job is to responsibly entertain the public. Isn't it better to entertain people with commercial books than to let them sit mindlessly in their homes watching various screens? Anyway, the real fight against illiteracy involves getting people to read *some-thing*. My daughter started reading commercial fiction, and then she moved up to a better grade of fiction. If people learn to read from Harlequin Romances or westerns, at least they've learned to read, and that's a contribution to education.

Panel discussion, San Francisco/
Harper's, August:42.

Gunter Grass
West German author

3

If an author tries to isolate himself from politics, he will realize, sooner or later, that this is not possible and that he will become a victim of politics. Recall the fate of so-called apolitical authors during the [German] Third Reich. Did the Nazis leave them in peace to their apolitical creativity? Those who rule would like to see writers maintain a distance from the political world because they are afraid that writers might expose the fallacy of their one-dimensional point of view. Writers should stay close to politics and irritate politicians.

Interview/
World Press Review, June:34.

Graham Greene
Author

4

[On writing]: A major character has to come somehow out of the unconscious . . . Because I was psychoanalyzed when I was 16, I have always been interested in dreams and the unconscious . . . The moment comes when a character does or says something you hadn't thought about. At that moment, he's alive and you leave it to him . . . I generally have a character and the beginning of a story and the end of a story. And, in-between, the middle develops in a way I don't foresee.

At Georgetown University,
Oct. 7/The New York Times, 10-9:30.

John Hersey
Author

5

I think the challenge of fiction in dealing with the realities of life is for the author to try to afford the reader identification with the people who took part in the events about which you're writing. Fiction gives that kind of access more deeply than journalism can. The journalist is always a mediator between the material and the reader. And the reader is always conscious of the journalist interpreting and reporting events. If the novelist is successful, he vanishes from the reader's perception except through his voice in the work, and the reader has direct access to ex-

(JOHN HERSEY)

periences. So, to me, fiction is much the more challenging and desirable medium for dealing with the real world than journalism. But there are also things that ask for a direct account while the material is still too hot for fiction. In those cases I resort to reportage.

Interview/Publishers Weekly, 5-10:233.

Wolfgang Hildesheimer
Author

The days of the writers of our generation are gone. They have become silent because they realize that the conventional novel does no longer suffice to carry a message. We have been writing about a world which has long vanished. Every scientist can make fun of us for dealing with problems that have ceased to be problems. And we cannot write about nuclear research, about gene manipulation or biotechnology. [Literature] is ceasing to exist or is already dead. In the foreseeable future all of us [writers] will be without readers because everybody is too busy worrying about survival.

*Interview, Poschiavo, Switzerland/
The Washington Post, 7-11:(B)2.*

1

A. E. Hotchner
Author

Writers like Hemingway had enormous personalities. People like Victor Hugo and Balzac were certainly 10 times bigger than life, and so was their talent. Future generations can read their books, and that keeps interest in them alive. The ones who are most likely to survive in terms of legends are writers.

Interview/USA Today, 3-11:(A)11.

2

Jenette Kahn
President, DC Comics

[On comic books]: There are very few things in kids' literature that really allow you to dream. We all know the ability to dream is the ability to

3

accomplish. Very early on in life, comics tell you there might be other things out there, other possibilities, other kinds of people you could be that may all be in yourself. After all, Clark Kent is Superman in himself. So even the most ordinary person can have someone very, very special inside him or her. That's one of the wonderful fantasies. All the comics that are truly successful can be reduced to some very essential fantasies that touch all of us.

Interview/USA Today, 1-4:(4)9.

Howard Kaminsky
*Publisher and chief operating officer,
trade department, Random House, publishers*

. . . I think critics of publishing tend to exaggerate the commercial aspect of the industry. In my experience, the system of publishing books and getting them out to readers works pretty well. I truly believe that *any* book is a good book—if people will read it. And any book, no matter how "commercial" or crass, might lead a person to pick up another book that is less commercial or crass.

*Panel discussion, San Francisco/
Harper's, August:37.*

4

Garrison Keillor
Author

[On his use of a word processor in writing his latest book]: I'm sure I could have written the book without one, but it would have been such an act of character. I never used a typist all those years. And this machine eliminates all of the retyping. I think word processors can be responsible for producing a good deal of flabby writing. The words come out of you like toothpaste sometimes. There's no shortage of sheer wordage in America; more sentences are not what this country needs.

Interview, New York, Publishers Weekly, 9-13:139.

5

Morton Keller
Historian, Brandeis University

Historians write for historians. The public is bored with the small-scale, highly theoretical

6

(MORTON KELLER)

questions historians ask. But though we need more-general histories, most historians aren't educated to write them.

The Christian Science Monitor, 7-2:36.

Stephen King
Author

1

[On why he writes]: You don't do it for money . . . don't think of it in terms of hourly wage, yearly wage, even lifetime wage . . . In the end, you don't even do it for love . . . You do it because to not do it is suicide.

Newsweek, 6-10:62.

Michael Korda
Editor-in-chief, Simon and Schuster, publishers

2

I flatter myself that I can tell whether a book has the pace, the energy, the subject and the characters that would make it a best-seller. However, if I were right more than half the time, I would be operating somewhere near the genius level. The elements in the market that make for failure are much more dramatic than those that make for success. It's a struggle against considerable odds . . . The most important thing to me is a wonderful first page. I get six thousand manuscripts a year in here, and if somebody can write a first page that makes me say, "Wow, I wonder what happens on the next page?" then there is a chance we've got a winner . . . The advice I would offer to any writer is that, even when you think you have revised your book to the point where you cannot look at it again, it is time to sit down and revise it some more. That's depressing advice, but it's true. I think it was Balzac who said, "A book is never finished. It is only abandoned."

Interview, New York/Cosmopolitan, June:148.

Jonathan Kozol
Author

3

[Criticizing books-on-tape, cassettes with audio recordings of literature]: We will lose some-

thing very stirring in the American tradition when we walk upstairs to find our kids listening to Mark Twain on headsets . . Tapes are one more disincentive to literacy. In the case of serious works of art, there is something precious about the silence that surrounds reading. In the case of books of opinion, it is far more difficult to maintain a fine, critical edge when exposed to the quick-fix, toil-free process of listening.

The New York Times, 7-2:24.

Milan Kundera
Exiled Czech author

4

My biggest problem has to do with the translations of my books: I find them very, very unsatisfying. It gives me much work. In the end, I have little control. People today seem to not mind whether I meant one thing or another, as long as the translation is finished in time and the book published in time.

Interview, Paris/
The Christian Science Monitor, 9-6:(B)5.

Stanley Kunitz
Poet

5

I suppose [an] impulse that dominates my whole activity as a poet is the urgent need to transmit what it means to be alive at this given moment in history. This is one of the great functions of poetry through the ages. To me, that's one of the responsibilities of the poet. And, above all, one has to be determined never to lie, because that's the unforgiveable sin against poetry itself . . . If you write a poem to persuade others to believe or not to believe or to act in such and such a way, if you're trying to convert them to a political cause, you're using poetry as a tool, and poetry resents being so employed. What one tries to do always is to convey the intensity and the truth of one's passions and one's thoughts. Some will listen, and perhaps it will be of help to them in changing their own lives and their own hearts; but the poem cannot deliberately set itself out to do that.

Interview, New York/
Publishers Weekly,
12-20:68.

Lewis H. Lapham
Editor, "Harper's" magazine

When I was a boy growing up in this city, I thought of a book as a precious object and an author as a necessarily obscure figure who seldom earned enough money to pay the rent or hire a press agent. If he or she was known at all, it was by virtue of his or her writing rather than by reason of a persona that could be minted into the coin of celebrity and sold on T-shirts. The times, so I'm told, have changed.

Panel discussion, San Francisco/
Harper's, August:36.

1

John Leonard
Former editor,
"The New York Times Book Review"

As *Book Review* editor, I was inclined—always, every single time—to send a book [for review] to someone who shared my judgment on a book, if I had one. I remember finding one book hateful and obnoxious, and I was going to ignore it, but one writer I was talking to said he hated it, too, so I gave it to him [to review] and he killed it. There's plenty of politics in that job. I was against the [Vietnam] war, and I never gave a Vietnam book to anyone [to review] who was pro-war.

Interview/Los Angeles Times, 12-12:(V)36.

2

William Meredith
Poet; Chancellor,
Academy of American Poets

Poets are professionally committed to telling the truth. And how do they tell the truth? They say something that isn't true. This is the slyness of art: If you tell enough lies, you're bound to say something true. I think my work is only as good as it is honest, but as a data bank it's full of errors.

Interview, Uncasville, Conn./
The Paris Review, Spring:41.

3

James A. Michener
Author

My experience [as a writer] has been that if you do something very well and—this is very important—get the respect of your peers, the word gets around that here's a pro. Here's a guy you can depend on. Here's a girl who knows what she's doing. When that happens, you have an accolade that is priceless. I've seen it happen time and time again. If you do the assignment, get it in on time, don't involve everybody in lawsuits, and editors find you good to work with—gosh, you're invaluable. Being recognized as indispensable—that's the ultimate glory. Everything else just follows.

Interview, Austin, Texas/
Writer's Digest,
February:31.

4

[On writing]: Being goal-oriented instead of self-oriented is crucial. I know so many people who want to be writers. But let me tell you, they really don't want to be writers. They want to *have been* writers. They wish they had a book in print. They don't want to go through the work of getting the damn book out. There is a huge difference.

Interview, Austin, Texas/
Writer's Digest, February:32.

5

A lot of my writing comes from out of the heart, not just from research. I tell young people that that is the best way to write. I don't advise anybody to work the way I do. My method works for me, but there's a better way to write, and that is to write out of one's self . . . I don't know if [writers] have a mission or not. I do know that a writer's work can have a very profound effect. I have a great deal of respect for humorists, as well as for "serious writers," because both have the power to do some good. A book—leaves a record.

Interview, Austin, Texas/
The Saturday Evening Post, September:32.

6

John C. Mortimer
British playwright

It sometimes seems to me that almost the only way we now have of getting in touch with the Russian people is through their marvelous litera-

(JOHN C. MORTIMER)

ture, and perhaps every Western leader should have to pass a preliminary exam in *War and Peace* and *The Brothers Karamazov* before taking office. In the same way, the world might become a safer place if [Soviet leader Mikhail] Gorbachev polished up his knowledge of Mark Twain and Jane Austen.

At Susquehanna University commencement/
The New York Times, 6-17-15.

V. S. Naipaul
Author

1

Literature of real substance finds an original form, and in that sense all great writers are original writers. Second-rate authors write novels that other people might have written. Writers change the form of narrative because every civilization reveals its dynamic in a special way. Writing takes place at moments of crisis, and there are always crises. I have never experienced those peaceful, shady afternoons that people speak of. There is always motion.

Interview/World Press Review, April:33.

Robert Nathan
Author, Poet

2

[On his style of writing]: It is a style at once simple and musical; I trust to the music of words to evoke whatever emotion I wish to evoke. In description, "less is best"; but the exact word, the most evocative phrase, must be used. I look for grace in my style; and always the understatement rather than the over-statement. My vocabulary is small; I use the smallest, simplest words I can. I use as few adjectives as possible. I use, wherever possible, melody and rhythm to create an emotion.

Interview/Writer's Digest, May:36.

3

The publishing industry is, alas, just that—an "industry." The same has happened to it as happened to the corner grocery store: It vanished into a sea of supermarkets. Few publishing houses are still private enterprises; most of them are part of some large conglomerate. Where huge sums are given out and taken in, where books are thought of in terms of millions, there is no place any more for sentiment—for the "small" effort. A book must make an immediate success or be taken out of circulation without delay, to make room for something more successful. There is only so much bookstore space and the competition for it is fierce and unrelenting. Today, the writer himself must help sell his book; he must hawk it about, from talk show to talk show, from department store to drugstore.

Interview/Writer's Digest, May:38.

Amos Oz
Author

4

Writing a poem is like a short love affair; writing a short story [is] like a long love affair; writing a novel is like a marriage. In a novel you have to make a half-million decisions, from the choice of an adverb to where to place a comma. I write my drafts in longhand—I need the sensual contact of paper, pen, ink and my fingers. Then I fight it out on the typewriter.

Interview, New York/
The New York Times, 7-6-13.

Anthony Powell
Author

5

Anyone who writes a long book in which a duke is mentioned is compared to [Marcel] Proust. [Evelyn] Waugh, of course, is of the same generation, but the comparison I always make is between India and Pakistan. A very firm Catholic convert, Evelyn would be Pakistan—a theocracy. I'd be India. India being . . . what? Well, going off in all directions.

Interview, Bath, England/Newsweek, 9-2-69.

Harold Robbins
Author

6

[On his success as a writer]: It can't be talent. It's got to be luck—either that, or the publishers are bribing people to buy the books. Some guy at

399

(HAROLD ROBBINS)

Oxford says, "Harold Robbins tells a story," and that's the name of the game, isn't it? [...] wrote *Vanity Fair*, but they don't give a fig who published it.

Interview/
Los Angeles Times,
12-14:(V)20.

Interview/The Christian Science Monitor, 2-1:(B)2.

Sidney Sheldon
Author

1

[On his becoming a novelist after writing for TV and films]: I never had to do descriptions before. With scripts, you don't describe the character too much. If you describe a tall, lanky man, and Clint Eastwood is not available, the producer might not think Steve McQueen could play it. [But] I enjoyed the freedom of writing a novel. When you do a picture or a play, you have a star who says, "I can't read these lines." A director who says, "We're not going to shoot it in the mountains, but in the valley." The production manager who says, "It's too expensive." You have hundreds of collaborators. Novels gave me the freedom to write what I wanted.

Interview, Washington/
The Washington Post, 2-19:(B)4.

2

I don't believe in formulas [for writing]. When people ask me how to write a best-seller, the answer is very simple: I don't have the faintest idea how you write a best-seller. I firmly believe that when you try to please everybody, you're going to wind up pleasing nobody. I get an idea that excites me, and I write it as well as I know how. It pleases me, and I write a book that pleases me, and I write it as long as it takes to do that. That's the only way I can write.

Interview/USA Today, 9-23:(A)11.

Elisabeth Sifton
Vice president,
Viking Penguin, publishers

3

I like publishing to be transparent. I don't think most people know who publishes what, and I think that's great. They know Thackeray wrote *Vanity Fair*, but they don't give a fig who published it.

4

The cynic's stock definition of a "good book" is a book that sells. In my view, a better definition would be a book that's *read*. . . even at the heart of the commercial activity of bookselling there is still a very private and personal act—reading. The publishing and bookselling business constitutes a continuum between author and reader, a continuum fashioned from dozens of random private experiences of *reading*—from the first reading an editor gives his reading copy to the enjoyment a reader gains from his new purchase. Our rather impossible job is to coordinate all these individual readings into some kind of logical pattern so that the right book gets to the right reader.

Panel discussion, San Francisco/
Harper's, August:36.

Claude Simon
Author; Winner,
1985 Nobel Prize in literature

5

There are no great thoughts, no great metaphysical arguments in my books. I'm no more difficult than a painting by Klee, Miro or Kandinsky. One must not look for an echo of Balzac, Stendhal or Zola in my books, that's all. There is no recipe for reading me. Just start, that's all. If the reader finds pleasure there, let him continue; if not, let him throw the book away. The only criterion in the end is pleasure; all the other arguments are worthless.

Interview, Salses, France/
The New York Times, 11-4:21.

Susan Sontag
Author and critic

6

It is true that the ambition of most of the contemporary North American writers is a small ambition, however long the books. Most North American literature reflects the shallowness and moral paucity of North American society. [It is]

(SUSAN SONTAG)

trivial, selfish, vulgarly psychological, cynical, stupidly sentimental—in short, a consumerist literature, the product of a consumerist society.

At Dialogo de Todas las Americas conference,
New York/Los Angeles Times, 5-15:(V)5.

Peter Straub
Author
1

There is a kind of feeling among readers of serious fiction and reviewers in general—and maybe the public at large—that genre fiction of all kinds is inferior to mainstream fiction. When readers and reviewers discover a genre writer who can write at all acceptably, they go crazy about him and celebrate him as though he were a horse that could count to 20 or a dog that could ride a bike. This does seem unfair, since there are very good and capable and exciting writers who work in genres, though in the main—and this is the reason for the prejudice—writers who work in genres are usually not fully equipped as writers. You can tell that they work in genres, because their sensibilities have been shaped by their genres and can be expressed only in those terms. This isn't to say that genre writers are bad writers, because I think Rex Stout was a great detective-story writer, but he was great only as a detective-story writer.

Interview/Writer's Digest, January:31.

Graham Swift
Author
2

I have as a natural storyteller great faith in the power of story. It is one of the greatest possessions of humanity . . . to transform our experience into stories . . . the story is a way we come to terms with what we suffer.

Interview, Boston/
The Christian Science Monitor, 6-18:26.

Studs Terkel
Author
3

[On his speciality of interviewing ordinary people for oral histories]: I liken myself to a gold prospector . . . When there's someone who's never been interviewed about his or her life, that person opens up like sluice gates open, if that person feels that you are serious, that you really are listening.

Interview, Los Angeles/
Los Angeles Times, 1-2:(V)8.

Lawrence W. Towner
Librarian, Newberry Library, Chicago
4

[On the deterioration of books due to aging]: If we don't correct this situation, we will wind up with a kind of national Alzheimer's disease—mankind's collective memory will be lost. That's a terrifying prospect.

U.S. News & World Report,
4-22:68.

Jeremy Treglown
Editor,
"Times Literary Supplement," London
5

In the early- and mid-19th century, [book] reviewing at its best was a lively, tart and disinterested procedure of high intelligence. Since then, there have been periods of deterioration, when writers were jollying one another along and reviewers were essentially blurb writers. Today, reviewing is in good shape . . . There are two extreme approaches to reviewing. One regards a review as an opportunity for the reviewer to write his own essay and only incidentally, if at all, to deliver some comments on the book. Such a review can, at worst, be a kind of "reader's digest"—a shortcut to reading. You can spend all your time very enjoyably and beneficially reading the *New York Review of Books* and never read the books themselves. The other extreme is the short note that provides information about the book and a critical judgment in it. We steer a course between these. We try to have two or three reviews every week that push beyond the book and make an independent contribution to its subject; and we have many more notices—2,000 or so a year—which stay closer to the work under review.

Interview/World Press Review,
December:34.

John Updike
Author

I had both the happiness and possible misfortune of very early getting into print. And having been a writer now since my early 20s, there is a danger of getting written out and even becoming stale. There is some advantage to doing like [Joseph] Conrad—having a lot of life and then sitting down at 40 to write. You certainly won't run out of material that way, because life isn't long enough to write it all out.

Interview, New York/
The New York Times, 11-21:21.

1

Gore Vidal
Author

The first rule of [book] reviewing is you never review anyone you dislike personally. The second rule of reviewing is you never review anyone you like personally.

Los Angeles Times, 12-11:(I)15.

2

Kurt Vonnegut, Jr.
Author

My books tend to be tightly structured, which makes them short. I was a journalist—you never go for length, you don't tell anything that doesn't belong in the story, and you tell as much as you can up front. The basic principle I have of storytelling is that you don't withhold anything from the reader. If the author should die while writing the story, the reader should have enough information by then to finish the tale.

Interview, New York/
Publishers Weekly, 10-25:69.

3

A book is a work of art; it exists for its own sake. The purpose of art is to make a gift that someone else finds of value. Most beginning writers simply want to tell people off, to present their program for how to save the universe. If you teach creative writing, part of the process is to teach them how to be more sociable, to care about other people and not just to dump on them.

Interview, New York/
Publishers Weekly, 10-25:69.

4

One big problem is that [many writers] don't have anything on their minds. They're not *concerned*—which isn't to say they need an ax to grind. Usually, a person with an ax to grind is a crank of some kind, or a partisan of some kind. So I reject the ax to grind. But you must be passionate about some aspect of life, because it's a high-energy performance to create something the size of a book. It takes energy and concentration. In a way, it's sort of like an athletic event: You have to have the same sort of energy that people are bringing into a basketball tournament, and the same sort of concentration—not an ax to grind. You should have something on your mind. You should have opinions of things. You should *care* about things.

Interview, New York/
Writer's Digest, November:24.

5

Andrei Voznesensky
Soviet poet

[On the fame accorded poets in the Soviet Union]: You can't be alone. Here [in the U.S.], okay; but in Russia, because of TV, they know your face. Even if they don't come to ask you something, they look at you. When people are watching for you, it stops your writing. I don't know, if I am honest, maybe I am very poisoned by this attention—maybe I would be very unhappy if it would stop. Now I want to really, if it is possible, be invisible. The greatest enjoyment in life is to write.

Interview, Washington, Nov. 12/
The Washington Post, 11-13:(B)1.

6

The recent poems you love more because they are alive like a new love. You remember your old mistress or old lovers. But new is the best.

Interview, Washington, Nov. 12/
The Washington Post, 11-13:(B)1.

7

Robert Penn Warren
Poet

Poetry is a clarification, a revision, of life. It's essential to my way of being in the world.

Interview, Vermont/USA Today, 4-26:(D)4.

8

Tom Wolfe
Author

1

There is probably not a single writer on the *Forbes* 400 list, not even Neil Simon, though writers in the theatre have the greatest potential for income. I made a lot of money from *The Right Stuff*, but risked seven years doing it and just scraped by during those years. As writers get older, they wonder, how did I get into this—no money. They go into it for applause, and if they don't get money *or* applause, then they are very unhappy. *Esquire's* Adam Smith once asked me, "Why is it that an inventor can sit in a room for five years with a sheet of paper and a pencil, and when he finally comes up with something, it's capital gain; but when writers do the same thing, it's current income, which is heavily taxed?"

Interview/Esquire, August:123.

Yevgeny Yevtushenko
Poet

2

I always thought that music was the highest genre of art. Then when I met [composer Dmi-

tri] Shostakovich and we became friends, he said that in his opinion poetry was the highest. I asked him why, and he said because poetry contains music inside itself. Poetry, he said, is music with explanation.

*Interview, New York/
The New York Times, 6-14:18.*

William Zinsser
*Writer; General editor,
Book-of-the-Month Club*

3

All writers should strive to deliver something fresh—something editors or readers won't know they want until they see it. That's what makes writing by committee so backward. The minute you try to think about what people want, you're dead. There's no law that says you have to keep 100 per cent of your readers enthralled . . . If you're lucky, you don't have to think about what to put in each sentence. The act of writing pulls things out of your memory that you didn't know were there. I've often been struck by how something comes out of my past that I literally have not thought of since it happened.

Interview/Writer's Digest, September:33,35.

Medicine and Health

Morris B. Abram
Former chairman
of Presidential commission on medical ethics

1

For every illness, there is some procedure that can delay the moment of death. The question is: for how long, at what cost, at what pain, at what suffering?

At a conference on medical ethics,
New York/The New York Times, 1-18:10.

Marcia Angell
Deputy editor,
"New England Journal of Medicine"

2

It's all very well to say doctors should put the needs of the patient first, but who is to define his needs—the physician, the patient himself, the family, an ethics committee, the courts? And do the patient's needs have only to do with the length of his life, or do they include the quality as well? As our technology becomes capable of extending life even when there's little hope of recovery, these questions become increasingly important.

U.S. News & World Report, 12-9:62.

Jerry Avorn
Assistant professor,
department of geriatrics,
Harvard Medical School

3

Sometimes the most compassionate and appropriate care is allowing the patient to die in peace. As a footnote, that happens to be the cheapest. It shouldn't be done as a way of saving money, but sometimes it's the best way to be a doctor. We are in need of learning how to do that.

Interview/The New York Times, 1-18:10.

Christiaan Barnard
Professor of cardiac surgery,
University of Cape Town (South Africa)

4

[On the recently developed artificial heart]: I really can't find any indication for the mechanical heart, except where a very old patient would be satisfied with very limited activity after the operation. It may be an indication for an intermediary device, where you can keep a desperately ill patient alive until the [human-heart transplant] donor arrives. But that has been tried now several times, and it's never been successful because the patients just don't tolerate those two procedures, one right after the other . . . there is no place for the mechanical heart because there is a better alternative. There is no doubt about that. Cardiac transplantation is a better alternative to the mechanical . . . Transplantation will give the patient a much better quality of life. The man with the mechanical heart can't go swimming; I don't know what he'll do with his tubes and his machine to go swimming. However, a patient who had a donor heart transplant *can* go swimming. I don't know how far a man with a mechanical heart can travel. Can he travel overseas in a plane? I don't know. But I *know* that a patient with a cardiac transplantation can travel and, in fact, can live a normal life.

Interview/USA Today, 7-11:(A)9.

5

When you realize that medical therapy can do nothing to give the patient an acceptable quality of life, that then is the end of your duty as a doctor to treat the patient. After that, you must do everything in your power to give the patient a comfortable death with dignity. I've even become much more convinced that *active* euthanasia should become legal, so that doctors can actually actively terminate the patient's life. As I have often said, the goal of medicine is not to prolong life; the goal of medicine is to improve the quality of life.

Interview/USA Today, 7-11:(A)9.

Joseph Boyle
President, American Medical Association

6

[On whether physicians should charge only what patients are able to pay]: When I grew up in medicine, that was the way we dealt with every-

(JOSEPH BOYLE)

body all the time. When I talk to lay people and tell them they ought to talk to their doctors about what kind of fees they're going to charge, they say, "Well, I wouldn't do that. I'd be embarrassed." I don't know why they would be embarrassed. You're not embarrassed to ask a grocer the cost of artichokes.

Interview/USA Today, 2-21:(A)7.

Stephen W. Brown

Professor of marketing,
Arizona State University;
President, American Marketing Association

1

[Saying there is an oversupply of doctors in the U.S.]: There are 500,000 physicians in this country. A majority are viewing marketing [of their practices] as of growing importance, and some view it as a necessity. About four or five years ago, it was very controversial. A few groups even asked if I could keep the word "marketing" out of my title. It used to be equated with used-car salesmen . . . Five to 10 years ago, a new physician could just put out a shingle and they were flocked with patients. [Now] I've had physicians come up to me and say, "Steve, I've been in practice for six months, and I'm seeing three and a half patients a day." That's pretty sobering.

The New York Times, 4-8:9.

Robert N. Butler

Chairman, department of geriatrics,
Mount Sinai School of Medicine,
New York; Former Director,
National Institute on Aging
of the United States

2

[On Alzheimer's disease]: Nothing is more frightening to people than growing old, losing your mind, becoming totally dependent on others and being institutionalized—it's a living death.

U.S. News & World Report, 8-12:46.

Guido Calabresi

Dean-designate, Yale Law School

3

The way we handle [medical] malpractice cases is quite grotesque. Instead of trying to find

solutions for the victims of medical catastrophes, doctors and lawyers are blaming one another and saying each is money-grubbing. It's demeaning to both professions.

The New York Times, 2-21:8.

Barrie Cassileth

Director of psychosocial programs,
University of Pennsylvania Cancer Center

4

[Criticizing the idea that patient attitude can affect the outcome of serious diseases]: For every anecdote about a cancer patient with a good attitude who lived, I can give you 200 about those who had good attitudes and died. We had a 47-year-old department chairman at our university who had lymphoma. He had a very positive attitude. He continued to work even throughout his difficult chemotherapy treatments. He had excellent family support. He wanted very much to live. And he died . . . What bothers me is the assumption that some people want to live more than others. If they don't live, it's not because they failed. It's because they don't have control over an uncontrollable biological process.

Interview/Los Angeles Times, 8-20:(I)1,16.

Gene Cohen

Psychiatrist; Director, Program on Aging,
National Institute of Mental Health

5

A lot of people think, "Gee, I'm old; it's normal to be depressed." It isn't. Depression, anxiety, memory disorders, delusions and hallucinations too often are dismissed as eccentricities of old age, part of an inevitable decline. That's missing the problem. In every case there is some treatment that could improve or alleviate the situation.

Interview/The Washington Post, 1-30:(Health)9.

Denton Cooley

Surgeon-in-chief, Texas Heart Institute

6

I have maintained, since we put in the totally artificial heart, that primarily the usefulness of the device, at present, is as a temporary bridge

405

406

(DENTON COOLEY)

or stage toward cardiac transplantation. We have revealed from our experiences that human life can be sustained by a totally mechanical device. And in those emergency situations where a donor is not available, then the artificial heart has its most practical and logical applications.

Interview/
USA Today,
10-14:(A)13.

3

John Coury
Chairman, board of trustees,
American Medical Association

[On medical malpractice suits]: There is a crisis that is as bad, if not worse, than in 1975. There will be opposition from the legal profession, but the people must be told it is as much their problem as the doctors' problem because the public will have to pay for it in dollars or in quality of care. It is the highly specialized doctors who will stop what they are doing.

Interview/Los Angeles Times, 4-1:(I)1.

1

Norman Cousins
Adjunct professor, School of Medicine,
University of California, Los Angeles;
Former editor, "Saturday Review"

Evidence is abundant that the way we think about life has some bearing on what happens to us. That doesn't mean that attitudes can or should become a substitute for competent medical treatment when we are ill. But a positive attitude about ourselves and our future can help create an environment conducive to effective medical treatment . . . For a patient, the right attitude can be like a bulletproof vest, protecting the body against penalties we otherwise have to pay for panic. Any physician tries to take into account the patient's will to live. If the will to live is strong, the patient's chances may be enhanced; if the will to live is weak or absent, the doctor knows the biological factors will have a clear field.

Interview, Los Angeles/
USA Today, 7-18:(A)6.

2

Alfred Del Bello
Lieutenant Governor of New York;
Co-chairman, National Committee
on Youth Suicide Prevention

We know that more than 6,000 young people are killing themselves each year . . . A psychiatrist who is very active in this field tells me that for every one of those 6,000 kids who kills himself, you can depend on the fact that there are another 15 to 30 who kill themselves. So if I want to be provocative, I'll say to an audience, "We know that somewhere between 5,000 and 180,000 kids killed themselves last year." And I'll suggest that maybe we know more about striped bass or frogs than we do about our own kids.

Interview/USA Today, 1-9:(A)7.

3

Raymond S. Duff
Professor of pediatrics,
Yale University School of Medicine

Today we reward doctors in America for technology, not wisdom; for procedures, not empathy. The rewards are both financial and personal. Physicians can charge a great deal of money for the high-tech aspects of medicine, and a physician's colleagues tend to honor and respect him or her for technical skills and published research. Just sitting and talking to a patient is much less lucrative. Helping patients and their families cope with the emotional and social problems that illness produces is not ranked high on the honors list when physicians discuss other physicians.

Ladies' Home Journal, June:48.

4

Carl Eisdorfer
President, Montefiore Hospital
and Medical Center, Bronx, N.Y.

We spend too much money on dying. If I thought someone had a reasonable chance of restoring function, no cost is unreasonable. I think we have an obligation to try. The thing that troubles me is the case of a miracle. My feeling is if God wants a miracle, he or she will have that miracle. But we can't count on it. We can't spend

5

(CARL EISDORFER)

all resources on keeping alive somebody we know is dead, waiting for a miracle.

Interview/
The New York Times, 1-18:10.

Samuel S. Epstein
Professor of occupational
and environmental medicine,
University of Illinois Medical Center

1

Increasing U.S. cancer rates reflect past and continuing exposure to chemical carcinogens in our air, water, food and workplaces. Industry and the cancer establishment have attempted to dismiss such evidence and attribute any increases to faulty life-style, particularly tobacco and diet. But there are important causes of lung cancer besides smoking, and linking diet to cancer is a tenuous hypothesis at best . . . Millions have died from what should be a preventable disease. Responsibility for this carnage lies in the reckless indifference of the chemical and mining industries, insisting on short-term gains to the detriment of long-term public health and economic interests, and in the cancer establishment's unfounded emphasis on diagnosis and treatment to the virtual exclusion of curbing exposure to environmental and occupational carcinogens.

Interview, Chicago/
USA Today, 7-24:(A)10.

Reva T. Frankle
Adjunct professor on eating disorders,
New York Medical College;
Director of nutrition,
Weight Watchers International

2

[On people who try to diet]: I think they have everything stacked against them. I think our environment is always saying, "Let's eat." Anytime you go out socially, there is a call for food. In addition to that, people around us can sabotage our efforts. The people we trust and love pressure us to come and eat. I call that social

sabotage . . . Another enemy is physical sabotage—the environment, the media, advertisements, television, all saying, "Oh, bake that. Show you really care." The commercials are saying you're going to be a good person if you serve these sweets and high-calorie desserts.

Interview/USA Today, 1-3:(A)9.

Svyatoslav N. Fyodorov
Director, Research Institute
of Eye Microsurgery, Moscow

3

[On those who criticize his "assembly-line" approach to eye surgery in which the patient is moved from one doctor to another during surgery]: Ninety-eight per cent of my colleagues are convinced I'm crazy. They say I'm violating a doctor's personal ties with his patient, eroding tender loving care. But the days of kindly old family doctors sucking on a pipe are over. The modern patient needs a whole range of complex, costly equipment.

During guided tour of his institute,
Moscow/The New York Times, 7-2:20.

Margaret M. Heckler
Secretary of Health and Human Services
of the United States

4

We must continue our absolute commitment to the quality of medical care, but that includes not prolonging treatment when it's of marginal value and at enormous cost. We need a commission to create an ethical framework for making decisions on how to use new medical technologies. Take heart transplants, for example. According to the Battelle study in Seattle, a man aged 47, who will go back to work stands to benefit greatly from this technology. But does that mean everybody should have a heart transplant? There are judgments that will have to be made on the use of life-preserving technologies based on the allocation of resources. I would like to see a Presidential commission for bio-medical ethics, made up of a broad spectrum of people—economists, doctors, hospital administrators and consumers.

Interview/
U.S. News & World Report, 10-14:40.

Jules Hirsch
Professor, Rockefeller University;
Chairman, National Institutes
of Health committee on obesity

1

We want the average American to know that obesity is a disease—it is not a state, like loneliness. It is a disease and carries an increased risk of mortality. It deserves to be treated and considered just as seriously as any other illness . . . Obesity is a killer. It is a killer, as smoking is. Not every cigarette smoker dies of lung cancer, and not every obese person is going to die of these related diseases. But the risk of developing a variety of illnesses has been increased—and obesity is a killer in that way.

Washington, Feb. 13/
Los Angeles Times, 2-14:(I)1.

Jacob K. Javits
Former United States Senator,
R-New York

2

[Saying the terminally ill should have the right to die by voluntarily ending their medical treatment]: Birth and death are the most singular events we experience, and therefore the contemplation of death, as of birth, should be a thing of beauty . . . [Last year, Colorado Governor Richard Lamm] suggested that people with no real prospect of living ought to get out of the way and stop using medical resources to be kept alive. It sounded callous, and probably was, but the Governor was uttering the truth. We have not yet reached the point in this great nation of ours where living or dying has nothing to do with money. That is what makes the right to die with dignity an issue of morality and humanity as well as of policy and law.

Before House Aging Committee, Washington,
Oct. 1/USA Today, 10-2:(A)1;
Los Angeles Times, 10-2:(I)1.

Helen S. Kaplan
Director, human sexuality program,
New York Hospital-Cornell Medical Center

3

[On the AIDS disease]: Too many people are afraid of the wrong things about AIDS, but are not afraid enough of AIDS itself. AIDS could easily wipe out a quarter of the world if it spreads to the heterosexual population—and that's certainly something to be afraid about. Only 65 per cent of those infected with the AIDS virus seem to be immune—they don't get sick. Twenty-five per cent get very sick with AIDS-related conditions. Ten per cent get AIDS and die. So it's not an exaggeration to say that unless we can stop the spread of AIDS, 25 per cent of us may die. But some people are afraid of sitting next to a person who has AIDS. Some are afraid that AIDS will cause our society to become bigoted toward its victims. Both are irrational fears. We know exactly how AIDS is transmitted. If we use the same measures used to eradicate other infectious diseases, we can stop AIDS' spread.

Interview, New York/USA Today, 12-13:(A)12.

C. Everett Koop
Surgeon General of the United States

4

[On whether making cigarettes illegal would be an effective way of limiting their use]: It won't work. The prohibition of alcohol didn't work. It has to be a grass-roots and personal commitment. The smoker today is well educated about the health hazards. Now non-smokers are aware of the dangers they face from others' smoke, and they are becoming more than annoyed. They are becoming militant, and that is a very powerful weapon. The next area that I think is going to be the battleground is the worksite and the economic advantage to the employer, which eventually will be a benefit to the employee. That's where the big battle will be, and we expect to win it with the help of the employers and the assistance of the labor unions.

Interview, Washington/
The New York Times, 12-13:14.

Richard D. Lamm
Governor of Colorado (D)

5

There is a difference between the right to die and the right to be killed. Certainly, most of the elderly I've talked to—and I've always had the strong support of the elderly—don't fear death as much as they do suffering, degradation, help-

(RICHARD D. LAMM)

lessness. So I think medical treatment is fine, but overtreatment or heroic medicine quite often only adds to the pain and prolongs the suffering.

Interview/USA Today, 10-23:(A)11.

1

Our [U.S.] health-care system is one of the most expensive in the world. We spend $1,500 per capita on health care. England spends $400. Singapore spends $200. And we all have the same outcomes. There's no correlation between how much a society spends on health care and what it gets. We're spending all this money on the artificial heart, but we've got many pregnant women who don't have prenatal care; 20 per cent of the kids in America don't have their polio vaccines; 25 million Americans don't have access to basic health care. My God, what are we doing? One of the hard choices we have to make is to announce right now that people don't have a right to an artificial heart until we get some of these higher priorities taken care of.

Interview/U.S. News & World Report, 12-16:59.

Domingo Liotta
Argentinian heart specialist

2

[On the use of artificial hearts and the recent implant of a baboon heart in a human infant in the U.S.]: We do not know if we are on solid ethical ground. We need limits on certain technological developments. [The artificial heart] is still experimental. Medicine, like all sciences, must live in its own time . . . A doctor's first obligation is to save life, but, after a point, death should be respected.

World Press Review, January:46.

Joanne Lynn
Medical director,
Home Hospice, Washington

3

[On hospitals and hospices]: In a busy hospital, a nurse who sees 30 different patients in a week can't know their individual needs. A hospice nurse, on the other hand, is going to know

that when her patient says, "My neck hurts," it may be time for a drug, not a hot-water bottle.

Interview/U.S. News & World Report, 2-11:70.

Sanford Miller
Director, Center for Food Safety
and Applied Nutrition,
Food and Drug Administration
of the United States

4

[On a long-standing proposal that the FDA ban such food additives as red dye #3]: The burden in all safety considerations is on the proponent of the substance to prove safety, not on the agency to prove harm. [However, this] proposal's long delays and debates have had the subtle effect of apparently shifting the burden for proof of harm back to the government.

The New York Times, 2-13:17.

Timothy A. Miller
Professor of plastic surgery,
University of California, Los Angeles

5

I think that advertising and the practice of medicine are mutually contradictory. Advertising is salesmanship; it is selling something. The professional services that a surgeon, in particular a plastic surgeon, should have to offer are something that should have to be sought out by a patient. The problem with advertising is that it tends to appeal to the most insecure listener or reader of that given advertisement. After all, medicine is all about helping someone; it's not about business promotion or a hard sell.

Interview/USA Today, 1-15:(A)9.

Gerald J. Mossinghoff
President,
Pharmaceutical Manufacturers Association

6

[On criticism of the high cost of prescription drugs]: The medicines developed . . . have done more to improve the quality of life than have the products of any other industry. The research-based pharmaceutical industry has discovered, developed and produced the overwhelming majority of new medicines and vaccines that have

(GERALD J. MOSSINGHOFF)

helped to control diseases that were once leading causes of death. In 1976, it cost about $54-million to develop a new drug and obtain approval from the Food and Drug Administration to market it. We estimate that cost today at $94-million.

At hearing, Washington, July 15/
Los Angeles Times, 7-16:(I)4.

Arno Motulsky
Director, Center for Inherited Diseases,
University of Washington

It's important for people to realize that, although we have learned a great deal in medicine in a very short period of time, we are only just beginning to understand basic human biology. Disease has been around for millions of years—science has existed for only a fraction of that time.

U.S. News & World Report, 11-11:47.

1

Ronald Reagan
President of the United States

[On the problem of whether children with AIDS disease should be allowed to attend public school]: I'm glad I'm not [personally] faced with that problem today, and I can well understand the plight of the parents and how they feel about it. I also have compassion, as I think we all do, for the child that has this and doesn't know and can't have it explained to him why somehow he is now an outcast and can no longer associate with his playmates and schoolmates. On the other hand, I can understand the problem of the parents. It is true that some medical sources have said that this [disease] cannot be communicated in any way other than the ones we already know and which would not involve a child being [in] the school. And yet medicine has not come forth unequivocally and said, this we know for a fact, that it is safe. And until they do, I think we just have to do the best we can with this problem. I can understand both sides of it.

News conference, Washington,
Sep. 17/The New York Times, 9-18:14.

2

Donald T. Regan
Secretary of the Treasury
of the United States

My heart cannot bleed for many hospitals hurt by limits on Medicare payments, even those run by Roman Catholic nuns. Their hearts are big, but their heads aren't screwed on tight. Most of them need new management.

USA Today, 2-1:(A)4.

3

Arnold S. Relman
Editor,
"New England Journal of Medicine"

We do have now [in the U.S.] as many physicians as we need . . . and certainly more specialists than we need. [With more specialists,] we tend to see more high technology and expensive procedures than we require and less attention to proven, cost-effective practice. Specialists are trained to practice their specialty to the hilt . . . Most physicians go where the people are. They go where the symphony orchestras are and where the money is . . . [not] to rural areas.

Before Senate subcommittee, Washington,
March 25/USA Today, 3-26:(A)1.

4

If we leave it to the market, you can be sure that 10 per cent or 20 per cent of our citizens will be receiving substandard health care, and many of them virtually no care at all. We will have retreated from our previous commitments to equity in health care and will have a two-tier system, with many of our indigent citizens not even having access to second-class care. That would sow the seeds of a social crisis of major proportions. In that event, health care would become the kind of issue that civil rights was in the late 1960s and early '70s. There are those who believe that we can meet the needs of the poor and still operate our health-care system as if it were an economic marketplace, as long as we assure a decent minimum of care for the poor. I am skeptical . . . I am convinced from nearly 40 years of being a physician that there is something basically different about health care. It is not like anything else that is sold or marketed

5

(ARNOLD S. RELMAN)

... Whether communities will ultimately take the responsibility for meeting the health-care needs of their own indigent citizens, or whether ultimately the Federal government will have to step in with some sort of comprehensive health-care plan, remains to be seen ... This is a decision that will be made in the political arena.

At dedication of expansion of Parkland Memorial Hospital, Dallas, April 23/The Wall Street Journal, 10-23-36.

Harrison L. Rogers, Jr.
President, American Medical Association

1

[On what some physicians call the golden age of medicine—when doctors encountered little interference in the way they practiced in their private offices]: What [older doctors who mourn the passing of that era] are talking about is their own independence. It was not [necessarily] golden [for the patients], but [in a sense] it was from their [the doctors'] perspective. Patients came to you and you told them what to do. That was it. There was no discussion about a second opinion—absolutely none. Patients were so unsophisticated, as far as health care was concerned. You [the doctor] were the absolute oracle. You gave them [the patients] the law and that was it. The current feeling that doctors are paternalistic goes back to some of this. They did come to you as a father. It's hard to say that it's bad that that's changed. But it is harder to accept [for doctors]. For those of us who were there at the time, it was a very nice way to deliver care.

Interview/ Los Angeles Times, 9-3:(V)4.

Jonas Salk
Physician, Scientist

2

[Saying his methods were criticized while he was developing the polio vaccine in the 1950s]: That's true. But that may be how the artists of science work. They advance by leaps and bounds, where others may proceed stepwise. I didn't have the encumbrance of knowing everything that other people knew, or maybe I saw something that others hadn't seen yet. But I had the conviction that it must be possible to immunize against polio with a killed-virus vaccine, having demonstrated this with influenza just a decade before, and having raised the question when I was a medical student in the mid-1930s. At that time, we were told it wasn't possible to immunize against virus diseases with a so-called killed or non-infectious virus vaccine—that one had to experience the infection itself. That was told to us in one lecture, but another lecturer said it was possible to immunize against diphtheria and tetanus with chemically treated toxins. So I knew both statements could not be true.

Interview/USA Today, 9-10:(A)9.

James H. Sammons
Executive vice president, American Medical Association

3

Medical-care quality here [in the U.S.] is the highest of anywhere in the world, yet we have the highest percentage of malpractice suits, and the public is paying for it. In 1984, one of five doctors were named in malpractice suits, whether they deserved to be or not, and the same will hold true for 1985. [It is] a financial crisis that society is paying for. Doctors and hospitals serve as conduits to the bills that are driven upwards by professional liability. The patient needs to understand that a sizable amount of their bill goes toward professional liability.

News conference/ The Washington Post, 2-16:(E)7.

4

Ninety-plus per cent [of medical malpractice suits] are totally without merit. The strange irony of it all is, it's not always the bad guys that get sued, but the super-good guys who get sued, the specialists in the field. They're at the greatest risk. [This has led to] defensive medicine. If you're living under the threat that every time you turn around you're going to get sued, whether it's legitimate or not, you're going to make decisions to protect yourself.

USA Today, 3-7:(A)2.

David Satcher
President, Meharry Medical College,
Nashville, Tenn.

We can improve the management of the Medicaid system. I think everybody would agree that it has not necessarily been well-managed. It has improved over the years, but we can still make it better. We can put more emphasis on prevention; we can put more emphasis on putting people in a system where problems are identified early and people are rewarded for keeping people healthy, not just for treating them when they're sick.

Interview/USA Today, 10-8:(A)11.

1

George Sheldon
Chairman of surgery,
University of North Carolina

When the world's first abdominal operation was done in Kentucky by Dr. Ephraim McDowell in the early 19th century, there was a crowd outside his office wanting to string him up. Advances that have been dramatic have always raised ethical questions—and they should.

U.S. News & World Report, 11-11:53.

2

John C. Shepherd
President, American Bar Association

[On medical malpractice suits]: Some of the problems are traceable to the great advances in medical science that have led the American people to think that doctors can perform miracles. Our jurors have to understand that [TV doctor character] Marcus Welby is not our standard of medical care, that not everyone gets well from illness.

The New York Times, 2-21:8.

3

Cecil Vaughn
Surgeon, St. Luke's Hospital,
Phoenix, Ariz.

[On his implanting an artificial heart in a patient without approval of the FDA]: Part of being a physician is—within reason, and with a reasonable chance of survival—there's a greater law

412

than the FDA, and that is an obligation of a doctor to try to do anything he can to save a life when he thinks that there's a chance.

Broadcast interview/
"Today" show,
NBC-TV, 3-7.

4

Bruce Vladeck
President, United Hospital Fund

It's not big-ticket [medical] items that are killing us. It's the tens of thousands of tonsillectomies. It's the fact that there is three times as much gynecological surgery in one town in Maine as another. We're getting nibbled to death. It's what's being done to healthy people.

Interview/The New York Times, 1-18:10.

5

Henry A. Waxman
United States Representative,
D-California

[On the rising cost of health care]: The truth is, we already have a kind of rationing in this country. But no one wants to admit to it. We stand by and watch people fall through the cracks. The question is: How much bigger will the cracks have to get . . . and how many more people will have to fall through them, before we start acknowledging what is happening to health care in this country?

Los Angeles Times, 4-7:(I)27.

6

[Saying the price of prescription drugs is too high]: Without adequate explanation, one can only conclude that what is going on in this industry is greed on a massive scale. This is an industry that insists on increasing its profits at the expense of the sick, the poor and the elderly . . . One should not be fooled into thinking that most of the dollars pouring in from these price increases are going to R&D. For every additional dollar of sales, the industry is immediately setting aside 13 cents for profit and large amounts for marketing and advertising.

At House subcommittee hearing, Washington,
July 15/The Washington Post, 7-16:(E)1,2.

7

The Performing Arts

Candice Bergen
Actress

1

[On why she is now doing television work]: I love television junk food and I love artful work—to have both is my idea of heaven . . . I want to do more *good* work in my acting, and yet, to be practical, I want to work . . . I don't want to do a lot of *Hollywood Wives* [her new TV movie], but I certainly want to do television, as well as movies and the theatre. And I don't want to sit around for the next 40 years holding on to principle, waiting for another [feature film like] *Rich and Famous*. I don't want to face what so many [in show business] face: Good intentions and no work.

*Interview, New York/
Los Angeles Times, 1-22:(VI)1,6.*

Milton Berle
Entertainer

2

[On whether he would want to do, today, a variety program like the *Texaco Star Theatre*, which he did in the 1950s]: The answer is no. I like to work with an audience and have the rapport of a one-on-one feeling. We don't have that today. And the expenditures are too great [today]. . . if I told you what the first *year* of *Texaco* cost, you'd say, "Milton, you're out of your mind." But with costumes, actors, labor costs, the show cost $15,000. For that price today, you couldn't get Patti Page to sing four bars of a song.

*At Museum of Broadcasting salute to him,
Universal City, Calif., May 13/
Los Angeles Times, 5-15:(VI)5.*

Bruno Bettelheim
Psychologist

3

The media are never very subtle, and that is one of my objections. If they were more subtle, they would force those watching or listening to use their own intelligence. But the mass media don't encourage intelligent processing of information because there's all too little they offer that needs to be processed intelligently. They address themselves to the masses and want to give something that everybody will respond to. A particular problem I have with television is that it deals in stereotypes, and that is devastating to the intelligent development of young people. Television characters go through life unchanged by their experiences. Major things happen to them, and in the next segment they're exactly the same person they were before. In *All in the Family*, for example, Archie Bunker never changes. That tells young people that they don't have to develop their personalities. By contrast, in Shakespeare, Tolstoy or Jane Austen, characters change and develop, just as young people need to do.

Interview/U.S. News & World Report, 10-28:55.

Steven Bochco
Producer

4

One of the distinctive things about TV is that people don't really look at it as something that is *made* by other people. They don't see it as a craft that people work hard at, a craft that demands certain skills. But everyone's a television *maven*. When some viewer is angered by an episode of *Hill Street [Blues]* and dashes off an angry letter, it always shocks them when they get a letter back from me. They're not really writing to me; they're writing to their television set.

Panel discussion, Los Angeles/Harper's, March:52.

Herbert Brodkin
Producer

5

Television is in the worst creative doldrums I've ever seen. You can't get projects through that are different. [The TV bureaucracy is dominated by] the curse of television, the program-

413

WHAT THEY SAID IN 1985

(HERBERT BRODKIN)

ming department—all trained to look for the same kind of show . . . Largely, [the audience has] been trained by the networks to be morons. Instead of giving them anything good, the networks claim to be giving [them] what they want. They have reduced the audience's level of receptivity to a bunch of monkeys asking for the same peanuts. And they are the same organ grinders giving it to them. If that sounds extreme, it's not. It's true.

At gathering in his honor, New York/
The New York Times, 3-19:26.

Peggy Charren
President,
Action for Children's Television

[Criticizing much of children's TV programming]: Comic books belong in a good library, but a good library wouldn't throw everything else out—which is virtually what the [TV] industry has done. Television is one of the most profitable industries in the country, and the vice-presidents for kids' shows are all creatures of the bottom-line people. If executives higher up the ladder told them to turn Saturday morning [TV] into a good children's library, they'd do it with all the diversity and creativity you see in the best of adult programming. But as it stands now—as an *oeuvre,* a set of works that is television's contribution to the children of this country—everybody should be ashamed of himself.

Emmy Magazine, May-June:25.

1

Barry Chase
Vice president, news and public affairs,
Public Broadcasting Service

Children are not being taught to think, because they are not being taught to express themselves. I think that television is part of the reason that that is happening, [because] you don't learn to think visually.

The Christian Science Monitor, 6-13:22.

2

Any program on public television leads a precarious existence. But this is even truer of news and public affairs programs, because added to

414

3

the financial pressures and shortages is the threat of offending some powerful interest that will, in turn, make such programs less attractive to major sources of funding, whether the Federal government, corporations or even the public-TV stations.

Interview, Washington/Los Angeles Times, 1-4:(VI)16.

Bruce Christensen
President,
Public Broadcasting Service

I think PBS audiences will continue to grow, and we may find by the beginning of the 21st century that there is less of a gap between the non-commercial networks and the commercial services. That would mean their [commercial networks] audiences continue to decrease as ours continue to grow. [Our programming] will be based on education, culture, the arts, and they [commercial networks] will have to move more into sports, movies, entertainment, to draw mass audiences. We will continue to reach specific audiences looking for quality programs . . . If broadcasting is around, PBS will be there, too. More and more Americans are discovering each day that PBS is truly a "national treasure" . . . and I have faith that our society simply will not allow this national treasure to fade away because of lack of funds.

Interview, Washington/
The Christian Science Monitor, 8-21:18.

4

Dick Clark
Television personality and producer

There'll be more alternatives to [TV] network programs, but networks aren't going away. They are still going to reach the masses and continue to be the best buy there is. Money is the driving force. When somebody makes a lot of money making Westerns, you'll find a lot of Westerns.

U.S. News & World Report, 5-13:63.

5

Barbara Corday
President,
Columbia Pictures Television

I think that we all would like to see television take more chances—not be all cop shows and detective shows. But this is even truer of news and public affairs programs, because added to

6

(BARBARA CORDAY)

the actors were always wonderful. The problem with television as it exists today is that there are so many hours that have to be made in such a short amount of time that you are always going to get a mix of styles and types and grades of adequacy. I personally think it is amazing that television is as good as it is. I think the amount of product that we turn out in a year is staggering. If people who are making [feature] films had to do the equivalent of a two-hour movie every two weeks, they would be dead at the end of a year. The other side of it is the public. It's all very well and good for us to sit in rooms like this and talk about how television isn't good enough, but I think we have all seen what we would consider to be good shows disappear from television because nobody "out there" watches them. And when people are called on surveys and they say, "Well, we only watch *60 Minutes* and classical music," and the *The Dukes of Hazzard* is the top show on television for five years, somewhere somebody is not telling the truth.

Interview/American Film, August:60.

Bill Cosby
Actor, Comedian

1

[On why he started his family-oriented TV comedy series]: Over the years, I'd seen an awful lot of the same kind of programs. On detective programs, everybody was driving down the block on two wheels, going through glass windows and dropping to their knees with a .357 Magnum. And the shows were rife with stereotypes. Any time you saw a black actor or actress, you *knew* something negative was going to happen. When you saw a beautiful women, you knew that she was the romantic link. Then with the easing censorship, sitcoms could get laughs by having someone say "boobs" or "butt." I felt we should go back to the basics. I'd noticed that people were again enjoying Jackie Gleason and *The Honeymooners*, the old Lucille Ball shows, even Burns and Allen. It was clear that networks were losing viewers to cable. Maybe you could get people to come back if network TV would clean up its act.

Interview, Pacific Palisades, Calif./
Ladies' Home Journal, June:32.

There are certain things that will work on television and certain things that won't work. Who wants to watch a series based on depressing situations? If I am depressed and poor, the last thing I want to watch is myself again at 8 p.m. I don't want to see another kid suffer or another mother and father who are fighting or somebody who is drunk . . . You can't say there was a reality about anybody's life on *Sanford & Son*. You can't say that *Alice* was real. Those were situations thought up by writers. There is nothing on television that is real; it is not meant to be real. As much as it was liked, *M*A*S*H* was not real. It had good acting, good scripts, but it wasn't real.

Interview/USA Today,
9-30:(A)11.

Rick Du Brow
Television editor,
"Los Angeles Herald Examiner";
Former television critic,
United Press International

3

. . . television is a social force more than an art form. To see a film or a play you go out and stand in a line, then sit in a theatre for a couple of hours; and when it's over, you go home and do something else. But TV is not like that; it's just part of the furniture, part of the natural flow of life. When you go to the theatre, or to a movie, something is presented *to* you by the creator. But in television there's a very important creator who isn't critical to the other forms—the viewer. With the vast number of buttons he can press at home, the TV viewer creates his own program schedule—a spectacle that reflects his private tastes and personal history. He can tune in every Sunday night to a fashion show on cable, or watch the Golden State *Warriors* play at four o'clock in the morning, or look at Cable News Network 24 hours a day. Or he can press another button and watch a half-hour program that someone paid 25 bucks to put on the public-access channel. Today, each viewer can create his own TV life. That's why there's an erosion in the network audience. It's a reaction against sameness.

Panel discussion, Los Angeles/
Harper's, March:47.

Dwight M. Ellis
Vice president of minority
and special services,
National Association of Broadcasters

1

Like so many who pray, meditate and give thanks without the benefit of ritual or church, millions of black Americans subliminally celebrate the presence and progress of their heritage daily through the magic of broadcasting. The feelings of pride, awe and sometimes envy at the voices and images of black professionals delivering news, information and entertainment over the airways are examples of celebration. The influence and patterns of popular and contemporary music, reaching even to the soul of country and western, give rise to acknowledgment and nods of knowing that the roots of the black experience run deep. And while the allied industries of film supply television with images and stories too often devoid of the presence and participation of black Americans, when breakthroughs occur, the celebration is real.

The Washington Post, 2-1:(A)18.

Milos Forman
Director

2

[Criticizing how motion pictures shown on TV are edited for television]: What would you think of a guy who chops two feet off Michelangelo's statue of David because the ceiling is too low? Would you think he's barbaric? Uncivilized? That's the same thing these [TV] people are doing.

Interview/Los Angeles Times, 4-29:(VI)9.

Mark S. Fowler
Chairman,
Federal Communications Commission

3

The central focus of our work [at the FCC] has been a desire, wherever possible, to let market forces control program decision-making [in broadcasting] . . . The public's interest should in general determine the public's interest in broadcasting . . . The government's got no interest telling editors or reporters, general managers or talk-show hosts what's unfair or what's offen-

sive. The public has a very good way of dealing with this. It's called changing the station . . . Deregulation, I think, is the right direction for our nation's communications system. It leads to more choice. It gives way to greater diversity. Dealing with all the new choices is daunting. But it's not impossible. And it's a policy that keeps government from controlling what is said or who says it, even if it's wrong.

Before International Radio and Television Society,
September/The Washington Post, 10-15:(A)22.

Fred W. Friendly
Professor of journalism,
Columbia University;
Former president, CBS News

4

Commercial television makes so much money doing its worst that it can't afford to do its best.

On British TV series, "Television"/
The Christian Science Monitor, 3-8:23

5

I watched television last night with an eye to what I was watching, and it's unbelievable. There are more cars being blown up, more alleged sex, more of an amusement-park [atmosphere] than 10 years ago—and 10 years ago was bad.

The Christian Science Monitor, 6-14:20.

Jackie Gleason
Entertainer

6

[In TV today,] they're taking actors and making them comedians, which seems strange to me. I know good comedians who have become good actors, but I've never known the reverse to be true.

To reporters, New York/
Los Angeles Times, 2-8:(VI)27.

Leonard Goldberg
Producer

7

When I became head of programming [at ABC], I got a very simple order. I was told that I

(LEONARD GOLDBERG)

worked for a profit-making organization and my job was to deliver the largest possible audience while spending the smallest possible amount of money. If in the process I could get quality programs, that would be great, but that was not necessarily part of my job. I used to have a *New Yorker* cartoon in my office that illustrated this principle: It showed a scientist rushing into a boardroom with a beaker, shouting, "I've done it, I've done it. I've found a substitute for quality!" It doesn't sound very sophisticated, but that's the way it works [at the networks] . . . What I've found at all the networks in recent years is a lack of emotion. I don't feel any passion or excitement. I talk to network people about new programs, and their eyes wander. I send over scripts, and I don't hear from them for two weeks—and I'm supposed to be a powerful producer. If you happen to hit on an idea they've already thought about, then they listen. Otherwise their minds are miles away. They're going to do what they want to do. If you can execute it for them, fine; if you can't—"Next!"

Panel discussion, Los Angeles/
Harper's, March:50.

Michael Grade
Managing director,
BBC-1 TV (England)

1

[Criticizing proposals to permit advertising on the BBC]: I've worked in the commercial sector in this country and I have no religious objection to advertising. But the way our broadcasting is structured, where you have two channels in the private sector and two in the public sector, they're obviously competitive in terms of program quality and ratings, but they're not competitive for advertising. The day that both sets of broadcasters are chasing the same source of revenue is the day, I think, that standards will fall, inevitably. The chase for ratings, which is now only part of the scene, will become the dominant factor, and the advertisers will get what they've always wanted and what they have in America—which is basic control over their schedules and the quality of programs.

Interview/TV Guide, 5-11:7.

B. Donald Grant
President, CBS Entertainment

2

I believe television today is quite different from what it was in the 1970s and the 1960s. The biggest reason for these changes is the enormous growth in the number of competitors to network television. The TV audience today can choose from among so many different outlets for entertainment, news, information, sports and music. This increased competition has to have an effect on what you see on network television. That's why I believe television today is better than it was 10 years ago. Frankly, I believe the golden age of television is now, and that 10 years from now television will be even better. TV today is dealing seriously with contemporary issues, not only in weekly series but also in movies and miniseries. And the execution is extraordinary. Given the time restrictions, the money restrictions and the restrictions on format, it is astonishing to me that the wonderfully talented people working in television are able to deliver the sheer quality of today's product.

Panel discussion, Los Angeles/
Harper's, March:41.

Lawrence K. Grossman
President, NBC News

3

[On TV "docudramas"]: Much of what constitutes drama is based on reality. The question seems to be, is it okay to dramatize it if it happened 20 years ago, but not if it happened last week? Certainly if it is presented in the guise of news it is unacceptable, and I have no ambivalence there. News should be fact and reality, and nobody should re-enact anything. On the side of drama, I would not like to restrict anything. There's good drama and there's bad drama.

Interview, New York/
The Christian Science Monitor, 3-6:15.

William Henry III
Associate editor, "Time" magazine

4

[On the controversy over television "docudramas"]: The problem is that people look to television for news and they look to television

417

(WILLIAM HENRY III)

for entertainment. They get journalism in print; they get fiction in print—but they don't get it from the same institution.

Broadcast interview/"Nightline," ABC-TV, 2-8.

Glenda Jackson
Actress

[On TV actors]: I actually admire people who can do things like *Dallas* and *Dynasty*). How they suspend disbelief for so long is to me quite extraordinary. That isn't a snide remark. I know it sounds snide, but I actually mean that. I would die of boredom.

*Interview, New York/
The Washington Post, 3-11:(B)8.*

1

Garrison Keillor
Author; Local radio-show host

[Comparing radio with television]: People don't jump off the screen in television the way they jump out of the radio. I never have an illusion of reality from television, ever. And I don't know of anybody who does television for fun. But a lot of people do radio for fun. On radio, the audience isn't so aware of a show being broadcast across the nation because of the intimacy of the medium. [Network radio newscaster] Paul Harvey, and the local announcer who follows him, exist for the listener on the same scale. They are two human beings of the same size. One is not 30 feet high and the other 5½ feet. Radio, thank goodness, is different from television, where the celebrities are. People who come up to me who have listened to the show, with few exceptions, are not awed by meeting me. They don't fall over; they don't stand back. They walk up and say, "Hello."

Interview/U.S. News & World Report, 11-4-75.

2

Norman Lear
Producer, Writer

Eventually, the video cassette will have every kind of programming for any audience. Network

television feels if it doesn't have 20 million, 30 million people watching, it's not a successful show. But 6 million people buying one video cassette—or 2 million people, or 1 million people buying a video cassette—make it an enormous success for everybody involved. So I think the big competition for the networks, for the independent stations and for cable is that video cassette.

Interview/USA Today, 1-17:(A)9.

4

I believe too many programs today begin with people asking themselves, "What do the networks need this season?" And too few begin with someone saying, "I love this idea; I have a crying need to do this program." Too many of the networks' efforts begin with executives saying, "What will rate? How can we win the ratings game very, very quickly?" All of us here know that we work in a business where orders are shorter now than they were 10 years ago, and that they were shorter 10 years ago than they were 10 years before that. In other words, the networks buy fewer episodes of a series at a time than they used to, so they can cancel the program more easily if it isn't an instant success. That means the need to *win* in the ratings is increasingly the only motivating force for writers and studios and producers. Everyone is desperate for a hit, so a successful show like *Dallas* immediately begets—name them—six quick children.

*Panel discussion, Los Angeles/
Harper's, March:41.*

5

. . . I have to say that you can count on the fingers of one hand the number of writers and producers in the last 10 years who have had the freedom to follow their own creative impulses I have had. I wonder what television would be like if more people were able to work freely, to follow their own instincts. That new Paddy Chayefsky who might be waiting out there ready to make brilliant TV programs, that new Rod Serling—I wonder whether any opportunity really exists for them.

*Panel discussion, Los Angeles/
Harper's, March:41.*

3

David Lynch
Director

1

The power of most movies is in the bigness of the image and the sound and the romance. On TV, the sound suffers and the impact suffers. With just a flick of the eye or turn of the head, you see out of the TV stand, you see the rug, you see some little piece of paper with writing on it, or a strange toaster or something. You're out of the picture in a second. In a theatre, when the screen is big and the sound is right, a movie is very powerful, even if it stinks.

Interview/Film Comment, February::56.

Martin Manulis
Producer

2

[Comparing TV's "golden age" of the 1950s with TV today]: I have long since given up the idea that everything was "golden," because that just isn't true . . . The standard of excellence, not only of *Playhouse 90* but a lot of other shows that came right around that time [the 1950s], was very, very good, however crude the technology of it all might have been. In live television, the producers and directors really had more creative control—not because anybody wanted them to; it was just the nature of the beast. Nobody could see the whole show before it was on. Now it's on film, and everybody can play with it. But the good work that's done today is certainly as good, if not better. Didn't you think *Roots* was a good show? I thought *Brideshead Revisited* was one of the best miniseries ever produced. *The Jewel in the Crown* is a very good piece of work . . . I think the good things [done today] are as good or better [than those done in the 1950s]. And the other things have remained what they are; the junk will always come along with the good stuff. It's a giant medium that's just devouring everything. The thing is, we tend to think in terms of *Playhouse 90* as the golden age because all those dramatic shows were grouped under one generic title—*Playhouse 90*—and shown on a weekly basis. That doesn't exist today, except on a show like *American Playhouse* on PBS. The others are all coming out as one-shots. But if you look at the best dramatic shows of the year and put 33 of

them together to match a season of *Playhouse 90*, you would have a series that would be just as good. But it really doesn't make any difference, as long as the work comes out.

Interview, Los Angeles/
Emmy Magazine, Nov.-Dec.::14.

David McCallum
Actor

3

[On censorship in U.S. TV]: It's a form of self-censorship. Ratings are the name of the game in this country and I am told that—New York, Chicago, Washington and Los Angeles—if people are offended by something on television, they turn it off. So you have to make sure you don't offend people on certain levels. Now, life in its true form is wonderful, awful, appealing, offensive, gaudy, pornographic, flimsy and any other adjective there is. People get offended if something is too religious, too ethnic, too loving, whatever, so you tend to eliminate a large part of the spectrum of life [on TV]. It boils down to the world's troubles being eliminated in a one-hour format with a car chase. So I tend to end up doing shows where you don't have to worry about censorship because they're either metaphysical, science fiction, fantasy or history. You're safe there—they can rewrite history but they can't censor it.

Interview, New York/
Los Angeles Times, 12-26:(V)12.

Gloria Monty
Producer

4

[On TV "soap opera" serials]: People are fascinated by serials because they give them a chance to identify with a character. They become part of that person's life. I go back to reading Dickens over and over. I think he really started it all. As Charles Dickens' novels were published in the newspapers in serial form, people would just line up waiting for the next episode. It's, "What's going to happen next?" with people you like . . . I think the viewer has a need for family, community and a center of belonging. In our society today, there are very few large families left. Many of the children and the

(GLORIA MONTY)

parents are apart. There is no longer this very, very strong sense of family, and the soap opera fills that need. The viewers have a family in these people. This family becomes their very close friends. In that sense, it fulfills a great need.

Interview/USA Today, 2-18:(4)7.

Bill Moyers
Journalist

1

After several long and painful months, I have concluded that serious public-affairs reporting in depth isn't going to make it in the entertainment milieu of [TV] prime time. I have to be a grown-up fellow and face the fact that reporting on social issues in depth isn't going to be given a fair shot . . . You spend four to six months of intensive reporting, and then the documentary is scheduled at a poor time, and poorly promoted. The people who would be interested don't watch, and the network says that documentaries can't get an audience.

Interview/The New York Times, 8-14:21.

2

I've never seen a time when a real commitment to the public interest was so sadly missing in television. I think the hottest place in hell will be reserved for the men—and they're all men—who control the networks and don't appreciate the machinery of which they are possessed.

*Interview, New York, Aug. 29/
Los Angeles Times, 8-30:(VI)23.*

Frank Newman
*President,
Education Commission of the States*

3

By the time the typical student graduates from high school, he or she has spent more hours with TV than with teachers. The most important point is not, however, what a child experiences while in front of the television set but what he or she does *not* experience. Increasingly, the child is cast as an observer rather than a participant in life's events.

U.S. News & World Report, 12-9:57.

Wayne Newton
Singer

4

[On the demise of TV variety shows]: Unfortunately, the television camera does not do what the human eye does. Nor does it do what the human ear does when the sound is being fed through a three-inch speaker. When you're dealing with television, you're dealing with a compromise at best, in a variety situation, because it's very difficult to get any flow, any continuity going. So variety television fell into that pattern of blackouts—"Well, here's my guest star, now we're going to sing a song together." I mean, there wouldn't be a 9-year-old or a 6-year-old who couldn't tell you what the format of a variety television show was. And maybe, when it went to tape from being live, it lost the spontaneity that it has to have to survive.

*Interview, Las Vegas, Nev./
USA Today, 2-15:(A)11.*

Neil Postman
*Author; Professor of communications arts
and sciences, New York University*

5

We [in the U.S.] possibly have the most ill-informed electorate in the West because people rely so much on television for their understanding of the world. Television makes Americans know *of* a lot of things, but *about* very little. Knowing *about* implies a historical dimension, an inkling of the implications. Television has become what I call the command center of the culture. It's different from other media in that people don't go to movies to get the weather or find out political information or get the ball scores. We go to television for everything. And the problem that results is that television, because of its entertainment format—its visual nature—turns all forms of discourse into entertainment packages . . . Right now, television has the culture by its throat, and it's not a question of any conspiracy theories. Look, you can't have a 300-pound man run for President of the United States. The Constitution doesn't forbid it; television forbids it. In almost a literal way, television modifies the Constitution. You might as well add an amendment that says, "By the way, as long as we have television—you have to

(NEIL POSTMAN)

be 35, born in the U.S. . . . and under 185 pounds, or you would look gross on television."

Interview/U.S. News & World Report,
12-23:58,59.

Martin Ritt
Director

1

PBS is miles ahead of commercial television. There's no contest because of what they choose to do: material of quality. Commercial television is pap. Absolute, unmitigated, aggressive pap . . .[But] people like me have no choice [but to work in commercial TV]. You try to do the best you can. You don't even think about the other thing. I think there's something ordinary and plain enough in me so that if I really like something, ordinary people will like it. I hate to think of myself as any kind of elitist, which I'm not. When I'm damning television, I'm not damning it on that level. I just think it's lousy.

Interview/Emmy Magazine,
July-August:46.

Sharon Percy Rockefeller
Board member and former chairman,
Corporation for Public Broadcasting

2

The survival of PBS is no longer at stake, this year or next year or in the year 2000. I think that public television is ingrained in most people's lives—almost 60 per cent of the population watches at least once a week. What's difficult is that they don't really know or care how it is structured and funded. It's understandable that all the public cares about is what's on TV. But we have a very curious structure and fragile financing, and that's what keeps the insiders constantly worried. I think we will survive as long as we retain our unique differentness. Public broadcasting has to remain as a real alternative to what else is on TV. It has to be appealing in its separateness. It may at times have to sacrifice some of the entertainment value to retain these other values. That's a very hard balancing act,

because sometimes if you term it "educational" you're more likely not to interest audiences.

Interview, Washington/
The Christian Science Monitor, 8-22:17.

Richard S. Salant
Former president, CBS News

3

The problem with [TV] "docudramas" is that people don't know where docu ends and drama begins . . . If a docudrama involves a current issue, there should be a discussion afterward that looks not at the film as drama but journalistically. When a President speaks, the networks have specials on other points of view. Why should entertainment be immune from an effort to let the public make up its own mind?

The New York Times, 2-14:20.

Eric Sevareid
Journalist

4

Television has a lot of faults. But it seems to be the only sort of national hearth this country has. It brings us together if just for brief moments—as when the prisoners came home from Vietnam or the hostages from Iran. And this is important, because our greatest long-term danger is fragmentation. Television has helped to supplant the principal means of communication, the oldest of all, word of mouth. And word of mouth is a treacherous thing.

Interview/
Business Week, 1-28:5.

Esther Shapiro
Producer

5

I think this whole discussion is hung up on the issue of what "quality"-television is. I love *Hill Street [Blues]* and *All in the Family* as much as anyone, but why should we dismiss entertainment shows, adventure shows, soaps and sitcoms, anything that doesn't "illuminate the human condition" on a weekly basis, as trash? The fact that hundreds or millions of people

(ESTHER SHAPIRO)

make these programs part of their lives every week is easily ignored in a discussion like this one. We're forgetting that television—whether it's *Hill Street* [*Blues*] or *Dynasty*—is the art of *storytelling*. People are buying VCRs so they can tape *Dynasty*. Why should I defend *Dynasty* [which she produces]? I don't think I have to.

Panel discussion, Los Angeles/
Harper's, March:46.

Joel Siegel
Film critic,
"Good Morning America," ABC-TV

It's very tough for actors to go from television to the movies. Movie stars are special—you have to make an effort to go see them. For TV stars, all you have to do is turn your set on and they're right in you home. There's a completely different level of anticipation. That's why so very few TV stars have been able to make the switch. In fact, the only two I can think of are Burt Reynolds and Clint Eastwood, and that's just because people don't remember that they ever starred on television.

Ladies' Home Journal, March:174.

1

Neil Simon
Playwright;
Former television writer

[On writing TV comedy shows]: There's no way you can write 30 half-hour or one-hour shows a year and have them funny all the time. First of all, it's repeating the essential joke—whatever the premise of that particular play is . . . It depends a great deal on the quality of the writers and their dedication to it. But after a while, they'll give it up. They'll say, "I don't want to do this any more." It takes too much out of you. You have to pour everything of yourself into it. Eventually, you would rather put that energy into doing one work that has a lot more to say.

Interview/USA Today, 4-22:(A)11.

2

Christina Hoff Sommers
Assistant professor of philosophy,
Clark University

Teaching values has always been a cooperative effort by the family and the social institutions. Parents could count on honesty being taught in the church or the synagogue, or in the Boy Scouts. Now you have TV instead, but it is hard to see what moral values, if any, are taught by TV. The institutions where moral values are usually reinforced have fallen apart.

U.S. News & World Report, 12-9:57.

3

Aaron Spelling
Producer

[On criticism that his programs are shallow and aim at the lowest common denominator of the audience]: I don't think anybody aims at the lowest common denominator. But if you're a pants manufacturer and pleats are out of fashion, why would you want to make pleats? You can't say to someone who drinks beer that he's stupid because he doesn't like champagne. Besides, there is no such thing as one single audience. There's an audience that needs *The Day After* [about nuclear war] and *Amadeus* [about Mozart], which, by the way, is my favorite film of the last three years. And there's an audience for [Spelling's] *Hollywood Wives* . . . I wish people would remember that I also did *Family*; I had as much joy doing *The Best Little Girl in the World*, which was a film about anorexia, as anything I've done. But that's all right. I'm in the entertainment business. Assuming we want to do a mini-series like *Hollywood Wives*, the question to be asked is, "Was it well done?" It should be judged in comparison to *Malibu Beach* and *Lace*, not in comparison to *Roots*.

Interview, Los Angeles/
The New York Times, 2-13:20.

4

Grant Tinker
Chairman,
National Broadcasting Company

I used to complain that people watched TV too uncritically. Now I'm in a more democratic

5

(GRANT TINKER)

period of realizing that the audience has the right to accept or reject as it wishes. If people want to see *Dallas*, that's not a crime. Our job at NBC is to try to present programming that, by our standards, attempts to elevate the breed and attract the audience. When we do something good that also turns out to be popular, such as *Cheers*, then we are really doing our job. Of course, I can't disassociate myself from the impact and effects of our programs. But I don't lie awake worrying about it in a social-responsibility sense. There are an awful lot of people around here—I am only one of them—who spend a lot of time thinking about what goes on NBC. But we serve many masters, one of whom is commerce. That's something I had to relearn when I came back to NBC. I had gotten into a slightly different frame of mind at MTM [his former production company]. That was a business, too, but somehow we were just having fun making television shows. Here we've got shareholders and all kinds of serious reasons to do our jobs as jobs.

Interview/U.S. News & World Report, 4-8-81.

1

[On whether the quality of TV programming can be improved]: Nightly, perhaps! Sometimes it is extremely unimportant—trivial, witless and forgettable. I'd like to improve the "breed," but we're in an advertising medium that serves a number of masters. Ultimately, the audience decides, and it's harder to grab than ever before. Programs like *Lou Grant* and *Mary* [Tyler Moore]—tasteful, literate comedies—would have difficulty against *Dynasty* and *Falcon Crest*.

Interview/Cosmopolitan, August:106.

2

Mel Tolkin
Writer

In recent years, there [has] been a move to include young writers and women writers in television. It had to happen; it was right and necessary. The results, however, have been somewhat disappointing. They took the reins, and they haven't improved the state of the art. The young writers today learned from television

and not so much from life, and the result has not been as gratifying. I know writers in their fifties with excellent track records who are in serious financial trouble. They can't get a job because they are "old." Nor has the increase of women writers—and their exclusion was a tragic waste of talent—done much to raise the level of TV fare. There simply have to be women writers. But to suggest that women will bring the women's point of view to television is pure bullshit.

Interview, Beverly Hills, Calif./
Emmy Magazine, Jan.-Feb.:9.

3

Gore Vidal
Author

[On his writing plays for TV during the 1950s and '60s]: The great thing about the so-called golden age of television was that the morning after your show was on the air, you'd walk down the street and everybody would be talking about your play. I really began to feel what the Globe Theatre or the Theatre of Dionysus must have been like. Television held the country together in a funny way, and you really felt that you had a role to play.

Interview, Los Angeles/
The New York Times, 12-19:21.

4

Suzanne S. Weil
Senior vice president of programming,
Public Broadcasting Service

Public television has just begun to become a force in this country in a comprehensive way . . . Till now [its impact] has been unmeasurable. The momentum has really gathered, and now I don't think the public will ever let us go. There will always be the need for this other voice . . . When you make something available to 96 per cent of the population, and 5 or 6 million people choose to watch it, it becomes popular culture . . . But elitism is not a pejorative, in my mind . . . What it means is excellence, and what we're trying to do is excellence.

Interview, Washington/
The Christian Science Monitor, 8-21:16.

WHAT THEY SAID IN 1985

Joanne Woodward
Actress

1

[Lamenting the quality of TV programming today compared with that of the 1950s]: I don't know what went wrong, or whether it's anybody's fault, but it certainly all has a lot to do with time and economics. There is no time for rehearsal like there used to be, no time to explore the character, which is the way I originally was trained.

Interview, New York/Los Angeles Times, 5-13:(VI)3.

Stuart Young
Chairman,
British Broadcasting Corporation

2

[Arguing against a proposal to permit advertising on the BBC as a method of raising funds]: If we were to give in to the argument for advertising, then we would start down the slippery slope to destroying the finest broadcasting system in the world.

Los Angeles Times,
1-4:(VI)20.

MOTION PICTURES

Rona Barrett
Entertainment reporter

1

I think people in general look up to leaders. When America was founded, we didn't have that. But when the so-called movie star/celebrity came into existence, we placed them on this exalted pedestal in much the same way royalty was placed on a pedestal in Europe—in England, in particular—and we liked it, because, I think, they are people we like to look up to. I think movie stars can and have at times reflected what it is that society is thinking . . . People look at movie stars or celebrities as testing the lifestyles they think they want but aren't too sure about. So they allow them to do the things they may be doing themselves, or would like to do. If the reaction is more positive than negative, you will then find people picking up on this so-called trend, or starting to adopt the ways of those famous people. I mean, you have seen clothing styles created by movie stars that have been adopted by mass America.

Interview/USA Today, 8-16:(A)9.

Jeanine Basinger
Professor of film, Wesleyan University

2

Film-makers need to realize that making it long is not necessarily making it better. When we go out to a movie, it's not simply to spend time. We're getting our money's worth if we're entertained. They ought to think about it: A film should be good, not long.

Interview/Daily Variety, 1-18:22.

Michael Caine
Actor

3

[On whether he would do a small-budget film if it had a good story]: I would do it if I thought someone would go and see it! I'm not going to do a movie that I can guarantee that no one will go and see. You see, we are in the business of communication, and box-office is not just an instance of greed, but it is an indication of the number of people who go to see the goddamned picture!

*Interview, London/
Films and Filming, January:32.*

Stockard Channing
Actress

4

When [her film] *The Fortune* came out, I felt like I was shot out of a cannon. The kudos, the attention . . . it's all very exciting and intoxicating. But it's also very nerve-racking. And you feel the obligation to sustain it; so you plunge on to the next thing, and the next thing, often when you shouldn't be *doing* the next thing. But everybody urges you to, and often you do it for the money, and it becomes very hard to say no . . . I have nothing against fame, but it's a nightmarish aspect of this business that a lot of very talented people with fame and a familiar face are taken over by an *image*. It all happens before you know it, and it gets very scary.

*Interview, New York/
Los Angeles Times, 6-19:(VI)1,5.*

Chevy Chase
Actor

5

Critics are a lot like children. If you're nice to them and you give them candy, they'll be nice to you. If they don't like what you're doing [as an actor] and you're not nice to them, they will probably kick you when you're not looking. Either way, you have to treat them both very carefully and respect their opinion only part of the time—when you want it to be in your favor.

Interview/USA Today, 12-27:(A)11.

Julie Christie
Actress

1

Acting isn't enough. I guess it should be, but for me it isn't. You are doing other people's work, saying other people's words. I want my own voice to be heard, and the only way you can do that is to choose those areas in which you want to work for change . . . I understand the need for icons. I have had idols and there are still people whom I am in awe of because of their talent, so I try to be understanding. But I so hate being a public person rather than a private person. I'm just not as nice as I should be.

Interview, Washington/
The New York Times, 1-18:24.

Hume Cronyn
Actor

2

There's a law in physics called Kirchhoff's Law of Radiation. It states that the best absorbers are the best emitters. Well, actors are in the business of emitting. You can't give out what you haven't taken in. So it behooves us as actors to open ourselves up to every experience, with a particular awareness of what other people are feeling. Good actors should have very long antennae. They should sense what is going on behind the words. For instance, to some extent right now I'm playing a part with you. I'm trying to say simply and without sounding too pompous something I feel deeply . . . but which I don't much enjoy talking about. I begin to shift my feet and get uncomfortable when I start talking about the craft of acting. My definition of "technique" is "that personal *and private* means by which an actor gets the best out of himself."

Interview, Denver/
Los Angeles Times, 11-17:(Calendar)39.

Tyne Daly
Actress

3

I'm not the sort of actor who tells stories to mollify or take people on a small vacation from their lives. I tend to be of the school of challenging people to think and moving them, either out of the room to make a sandwich or to tears or to laughter or to turn to the next channel. But if I'm making them stay awake for the whole 47 minutes, then I think I've done my job.

Interview, Washington/
The Washington Post, 11-6:(C)2.

Placido Domingo
Opera singer

4

I love opera films. They're terribly important documents. Whatever is done, is there. And the camera, which is the real critic, sees everything. But the pace is completely different from performing on stage. In the opera house, you have to start preparing the mood the day before the show begins, focusing your attention on those three or four hours when the performance, in its entirety, will take place. For a movie, you have to learn to relax. Between the lights and the makeup and the cameras, it can take six hours—mostly of waiting—to shoot a few seconds of film. Luckily, I can fall asleep almost anywhere.

Interview/Ovation, March:38.

Richard Dreyfuss
Actor

5

The problem with most movies today is that, well, it's hard to do a comedy of social mores when everyone in the film is under 18 years old. People still want to see comedies, [but] not "Halley's Comet Goes to High School."

Interview, Los Angeles/
Los Angeles Times, 8-18:(Calendar)44.

Clint Eastwood
Actor

6

The Western [movie] has never died. They just stopped making good ones. A good Western always works.

USA Today, 5-14:(D)2.

7

I've never had a problem dealing with my image. It can become a burden. That's one reason I'm cautious about it. I can't start thinking about

(CLINT EASTWOOD)

how I function within that image instead of how I function as an actor. It leads to a circular thing, worrying about my conception of the audience's conception of who I am. The audience reacts by instinct. So I have to produce the same way they react . . . I'm an actor playing roles; all of them and none of them are me. Sometimes I'm a guy who's animal intelligent like Dirty Harry. Sometimes I'm a dreamer like Bronco Billy. But Dirty Harry gunning people down, that's not me. If people think you are that character, you've really convinced them. That's all an actor really strives for. At least you've moved people in some way.

Carmel, Calif./Newsweek, 7-22:54.

Denholm Elliott
Actor

1

[Comparing acting on stage with acting in films]: I can't bear breaking my heart every night at 8:03 and getting better at 9:10. I prefer film acting. I love the idea of containing all your energy and then throwing it out a minute at a time. If you get it right, it's there forever. If you get it wrong, it's there forever, too.

Interview, London/Los Angeles Times, 6-4:(VI)6.

William K. Everson
*Professor of film history,
New York University*

2

[Criticizing the increasing length of motion pictures]: I'd like to take out a pair of scissors and whittle away at so many movies I've seen in the last few years. I love the old studio system, when they let the story tell it, and that was that. Films are also getting very shapeless, with no beginnings, middle and end—in that order. They all start out with a teaser, since they will end up on TV. Then they try to maintain that pace, and that kills the film, or they can't maintain that pace, which equally kills the film. The film goes into a kind of spiral . . . Every time they remake *The Most Dangerous Game*, they tack on about 10 minutes.

Interview/Daily Variety, 1-18:22.

Federico Fellini
Director

3

That is the happy place, the set where I made my films [where I am myself. Even if I look angry and scream, that is a childish satisfaction I take to appear powerful and play the role of the temperamental movie director. But at that moment, I feel in the center of my story, the center of my existence. It is a great alibi. At the moment I am working nobody can say nothing to me. All the responsibilities—as a husband, as a citizen, as a soldier, as a taxpayer—all are suspended, because I am working. And all my childish vanity, to be boss—of objects, of people, of actresses and actors—is completely gratified. I am happy. That is the reason for which I exist. When you do what is really the reason of your destiny, you are all right.

At tribute to him, sponsored by Film Society of Lincoln Center, New York, June 10/The New York Times, 6-11:24.

Zelda Fichandler
*Producing director,
Arena Stage, Washington*

4

The actor represents us by his deeds, by his presence, by his actions, and by trying to strip away the life mask. It's actors who stand in for us, who take all the risks and engage in speech for people who have no lines, for people who do no dangerous deeds between 9 and 5. Actors take all the risks.

*Interview, Washington/
The Christian Science Monitor, 11-25:36.*

Charles FitzSimons
*Executive director,
Producers Guild of America*

5

A producer has no hours, no working conditions, no health or pension plans, no protection for creative rights and receives no residuals from cassette or pay-television sales. We are the only ones in the movie industry who have none of these benefits. Actors, writers, directors and craft stage workers have all of them.

U.S. News & World Report, 9-16:73.

Glenn Ford
Actor

[On the movie Western]: It's going to come back. It's too much a part of American history not to. And it's so popular in Europe, in the Orient. You don't have to speak English to understand what's going on. But I've always said the talking pictures talk too much anyway. The Duke [John Wayne] proved that: The less said, the better.

Interview/Los Angeles Times, 7-11:(VI)7.

1

Harrison Ford
Actor

I don't choose films on the basis of whether I think they're going to be successful commercially. I'm recalling this bit of advice that Noel Coward gave David Lean. He said, "Do what pleases you, and if people don't like it, get out of show business." I think that is probably the proper attitude.

Interview, Los Angeles/USA Today, 3-13:(D)5.

2

Bob Fosse
Director

[On whether one can be creative in films today]: Yes, of course, but it's not easy. Making movies is so expensive it tends to remove the sense that you should take chances. It heads you down that dangerous "success" road where you stop doing new things. There is a fine line between a movie that communicates and one that turns an audience off. The best are those that entertain but also have something to say.

Interview/USA Today, 8-16:(B)4.

3

James Garner
Actor

I've always said that if motion pictures are an art, it's a collaborative art. And by the time everyone gets done with the script, it's a minor miracle if it's a good one . . . I'm a competitor in everything I do, except acting. I just don't think it's a competitive sport. You have to do

what's right for the film, not just for yourself. That ego business has no place in the movies.

*Interview, Florence, Ariz./
Los Angeles Times, 4-25:(VI)1,4.*

4

Giancarlo Giannini
Actor

[On acting]: It's a game, this profession. Many take it seriously, I know, and I have no quarrel with that. Though I suspect that anyone who keeps claiming he has to act must be an unhappy person. For me, I have no sacred fire for the business of acting. Today, I do it; tomorrow, perhaps not. I act for my own amusement, using my own system, a system which does not touch my brain or create anguish in my life . . . I am my own critic. I learned in the theatre not to pay attention to the critics. After all, how can they help me? They say "the colorful Giannini" or "another triumph by Giannini." What can I learn from that? Nothing. So to read them is a waste of time. Reading "Bravissimo, Giancarlo" means nothing to me. I know when I am good—and bad.

*Interview, Beverly Hills, Calif./
Los Angeles Times, 2-3:(Calendar)19.*

5

Leonard Goldberg
Producer

. . . the top money-making films of all time, all of which were made by Steven Spielberg and George Lucas, are certainly not what we commonly refer to as "quality entertainment." The film critics' awards may have been dominated by *Amadeus* and *A Passage to India* last year, but *Beverly Hills Cop* earned over $36-million in its first twelve days. It's popular entertainment, just like most of television. Interestingly enough, these popular films are being created more and more by film-makers, writers, directors and producers who have grown up on television. Increasingly, movies seem to be imitating the more popular forms of television.

*Panel discussion, Los Angeles/
Harper's, March:47.*

6

428

Alec Guinness
Actor

1

Being a character actor, there are a thousand things to worry about, as opposed to being an actor who plays himself time after time. In fact, one is always very self-conscious at the start, convinced that the shooting will have to be done again and again. Usually, it has to be. People kindly say that it's the lighting or the makeup, but usually it's not. And there's something especially bizarre about playing a Brahmin when you're a Westerner. Playing such parts is always hell.

Interview, New York/
Los Angeles Times, 1-15:(VI)1.

Rex Harrison
Actor

2

The only thing in acting is the truth; you have to be truthful to the situation, whether it's comedy or drama, whether you're in a three-ring circus or slitting your throat. If you go beyond truth, if what you are doing becomes unreal, you get into "ham," very quickly.

Interview, New York/Time, 4-22:65.

Goldie Hawn
Actress

3

[Motion pictures] is a business where people put themselves on show and everybody's got the answer. It's very rare to find people who can throw out their own idea for the sake of a better one—particularly people in omnipotent positions. And because it's such a fragile business, people seem to be protecting their egos and their status all the time. There's a lot of "me, me, me" in our business. There's a lot of cheating to-camera, or not wanting to take a back seat to so-and-so. I feel that the back seat sometimes is not a bad place to be. Being number one is not necessarily the greatest achievement. I would rather be second or third best, because the idea of being on top leaves you nowhere to go.

Interview, Colorado/Playboy, January:76.

Helen Hayes
Actress

4

I was lucky, because in my formative years as an actress I was never allowed to lose sight of why I was there. I was not there to please myself. I was not there as an exercise, an ego. I was there to add something to the lives of that audience out there, to illuminate their hearts, and to arouse and lift their spirits. You don't have to be crazy to be an actor, but it's kind of usual.

At presenation of first Helen Hayes Award,
Washington, May 13/The New York Times, 5-28:10.

Katharine Hepburn
Actress

5

[On acting]: I don't know what the hell I do. I think we're all actors; just some of us get paid for it. I agree with Spencer [Tracy]. If anyone raved about actors, Spence would say, "Remember who shot Lincoln!"

Interview, New York/
Ladies' Home Journal, February:174.

6

I drifted into acting. I think it's a sort of idiot's profession. I would've loved to have been a painter or a writer. Selling my deteriorating self is very humiliating work. If they don't want you any more, they dump you. I know goddam well that's true. I've been dumped and picked up again. I would've liked a more private profession.

Broadcast interview, London/
The Washington Post, 4-15:(B)3.

Ross Hunter
Producer

7

[On the glossy, soap-opera-type films he produced in the 1950s and 1960s]: Who wants to see the ugliness of life? We like to watch the beautiful people. We can live vicariously through them. Escaping for a few hours is more fun than dealing with life's ugliness. We all have to do that enough every day. [Those films] weren't

(ROSS HUNTER)

great, but they weren't supposed to be. They didn't have to be. I gave the public what they wanted—a chance to dream, to live vicariously, to see beautiful women, jewels, gorgeous clothes, melodrama.

Los Angeles Times, 6-7:(VI)14.

Glenda Jackson
Actress

1

There isn't a line of parts that actresses can play, from adolescence to old age, as there is for actors. They [actors] can go from *Hamlet* to *Lear*, and there's something all along the way. When you get to my age, the good parts become less and less. But you can't dictate to a creative being what they find interesting to write about.

Interview, New York/
The Wall Street Journal, 2-15:20.

2

[On acting]: . . . I certainly take the work seriously, and I expect it to be taken seriously. I don't believe that acting is a sort of day-care center for the emotionally disabled. I think it is a serious profession with seriously minded people. I don't believe we're necessarily hiding our personal failings behind every character.

Interview, New York/
The Washington Post, 3-11:(B)8.

3

You have to work, and if you're going to work constantly [in Hollywood] you are going to have to work in rubbish—at least about 90 per cent of the work is rubbish. And if you don't work, you're going to involve yourself in an external life-style there—all of which would drive me crazy. This is not meant as a condemnation of those who do this—they have to work—but of the studios. The work they produce is so bland and unremarkable . . . They don't accept the initial truth that none of us really know what people want to see [in films], and so they get embroiled in ambitions for success, rather than in quality. And if the formula for success is of supreme importance, then you cut away the trappings of a root that is good and could be great. Greatness doesn't come out of a vacuum—there has to be work at it. This is a shame, because Hollywood once did intelligent films, even films of real social protest and commitment.

Interview, New York/
Los Angeles Times, 4-6:(VI)6.

Derek Jacobi
Actor

4

[Actors are] always watching people, watching what they're doing physically, and how they're doing it. And also what thoughts must be going through their heads to make them do that. Most of the time actors are scavengers—any little thing that helps, you put into your bag of tricks. Even with other actors, you see another actor do something on stage and you think, hmmmm. Acting is about making a choice. How did he *think* of doing it that way? Wonderful! And suddenly in rehearsal one day you say, "Yes, that's what I need, that's it." I do think acting is a magical mystery tour. But it's also sleight of hand, it's also the art of the conjurer. It has to be.

Interview, Washington/
The Christian Science Monitor, 3-13:26.

Pauline Kael
Film critic,
"The New Yorker" magazine

5

Movies are terrible now . . . There's an elation I used to feel about going to a movie; only a fool would be elated now . . . Why are movies so bad? One hates to say it comes down to the success of [fantasy-film director] Steven Spielberg, but—. It's not so much what Spielberg has done as what he has encouraged. Everyone else has imitated his fantasies, and the result is an infantalization of the culture. Spielberg, with his TV series (*Amazing Stories*), now rips off his own things. I can't think of any other director who's started paying homage to himself so early. [But] he's still young, so there's time.

Interview, New York/
Los Angeles Times, 12-22:(Calendar)3.

Fay Kanin
Writer; Co-chairman,
National Center
for Film and Video Preservation

1

[Calling for the saving and preservation of old motion pictures]: We all say a great film will last forever, but the physical materials from which it was made just don't. Nitrate film turns to goo, then to dust—that is, if it doesn't burn first.

Los Angeles, May 22/
The New York Times, 5-23:16.

Gene Kelly
Actor, Dancer

2

It is still very hard to explain the difference between dancers who work in films or in theatre and dancers who work with dance companies. You see, we [who work in films] are rightly called song-and-dance men. We have to play a role . . . Then we have to interpret the role with the composers and the musicians . . . and then try to choreograph that role so it fits whatever character you are playing. So choreographing for that kind of thing really should come out of the character, and the character should dance in the spirit of the person he is playing . . . [But] I must say, without being derogatory, that until the late thirties, this wasn't the way musicals happened. Every once in a while they accidentally happened, but songs and dances were interludes; they could be lifted from one picture and put in another.

Interview/American Film, March:24.

3

I always wanted to be a director, not an actor . . . I always wanted to be a choreographer, not an actor. My joy and my fun is creating. It is not performing. If you ask me to get up and do two choruses, and people applaud, fine; but I really don't enjoy it that much. I would just as soon sit in a room and, say, pull things out of thin air and put them on paper or onto the screen, or whatever. That to me is the fun in life. I became a performer because there was nobody else around dancing the way I danced.

Interview/American Film, March:26.

Akira Kurosawa
Director

4

My creative method is to let things flow naturally, to be completely open to whatever is going to come out of you—not unlike the martial arts. I never construct a story-line and then come up with characters to fit into it. I allow my characters to have a life of their own, so much so that I can't predict their behavior. They end up creating their own story and you have to chase them through your movie . . . They control you.

Interview, New York/
Los Angeles Times, 12-29:(Calendar)40.

David Lean
Director

5

I'm a picture chap. I like pictures. And, when I go to the movies, I go to see pictures. I think dialogue is nearly always secondary in a movie. It's awfully hard when you look back over the really great movies that you see in your life to remember a line of dialogue. You will not forget pictures.

Interview, Los Angeles/
Film Comment, February:32.

Christopher Lee
Actor

6

An actor or an actress is only offered worthwhile parts and paid a worthwhile salary because of the commercial value that he or she actually has to the company that makes the picture and handles the distribution. I am also perfectly well aware of the fact that I am not necessarily employed on a picture because of my dramatic abilities. Regardless of whether it was Bogart in a raincoat or me in a cape, or something else, if you take any name actor or actress of the last 30 or 40 years—or in the present day and the forseeable future—and really dissect the reasons as to why they have played this and that, it's quite obvious that it is not necessarily because of their "talent."

Interview/Films and Filming, September:29.

WHAT THEY SAID IN 1985

Claude Lelouch
French director

1

Hollywood [film] budgets baffle me. I just cannot imagine a film costing $40-million. My 27 films put together haven't cost that. In France, we cannot make films like that because our small budgets make special-effects out of the question. In any event, we make very different pictures in France; ours are still geared toward an adult market. Here [in the U.S.], everything seems aimed at children.

Interview, Los Angeles/
Los Angeles Times, 6-23:(Calendar)27.

John Lithgow
Actor

2

Reviewers were constantly asking me, "Don't you ever want to play the guy who gets the girl?" And what they're really asking is, "Don't you want to act out your fantasies in plays and movies?" But I see that as the thing to watch out for. The most insidious thing about this profession is the longing to succeed in a movie or play in the way you're not succeeding in life.

Interview, Palm Beach, Fla./
USA Today, 3-6:(D)5.

3

[On playing "bad guys"]: Acting is wonderful for me because it's an anonymous discipline. It's a matter of persuading people to forget about *you* and just to accept the character that you temporarily are. And that, to me, is the liberation of playing the villain occasionally—"Fine, I'm an actor; I'll play the cello this time instead of the violin." I just love that dark sound, anyway.

Interview, Los Angeles/
Los Angeles Times, 11-4:(VI)3.

David Lynch
Director

4

The closer I get to finishing a movie, the more I start projecting my fears onto it. Not only have I seen it all over and over, I start seeing where I've made mistakes. I see my fears

432

Louis Malle
French director

5

. . . basically, I prefer making movies over here [in the U.S.]. The American film industry is more honest than the European one. Here, they make it quite clear that it's all about money; in Europe, they're still pretending it's about art.

Interview, Los Angeles/
Los Angeles Times, 3-31:(Calendar)20.

Bette Midler
Actress

6

The hardest thing to do in this business is to get some momentum going—to keep rolling. I've gotten to the point where I believe in myself. One of the things I do great is be funny. I can sing passably and I can dance a little. But the one thing I've learned is that if you fail, you can't stop. If you fall on your face, you've got to pick yourself right up and get going again. Because, in Hollywood, you can't wait around for someone to come by and pick you up off the pavement. If you just wait around, you could be down there on your face for a long time.

Interview, Los Angeles/
Los Angeles Times, 8-18:(Calendar)45.

Robert Mitchum
Actor

7

The main secret of acting is to not look like you're acting. If you can master that, you have the whole ball game down. Then it's just fun and good pay.

Interview/USA Today, 10-21:(D)2.

Jeanne Moreau
Actress

8

Like anybody's life, my life is an adventure. But it has a special quality because I am an ac-

double-exposed with the images on the screen. And it just keeps getting worse until I can't stand being in the screening room. I can't see it—I just see fear, and horror.

Interview/Film Comment, February:56.

(JEANNE MOREAU)

tress. Sometimes I allow myself to say that I'm a great actress. I can say that because I don't think I'm responsible. Oh, I'm responsible for the work. But the gift? The poise? The capacity for concentrating, for bringing out things you don't even know you have inside yourself? Where does that come from? I don't know.

Interview, New York/
The Washington Post,
10-14:(B)10.

Eddie Murphy
Actor, Comedian

1

. . . I have a talent and it works for me. I don't think there are such things as "geniuses" in this business. I think people like doctors and scholars who have to learn things fast are the geniuses. If a guy can sing real good or can tell a good joke or can write a good song, that's a *talent*. I don't think you label a person a "genius" for that. A lot of people can sing and dance. You can be very entertaining, but I don't think you can be a genius.

Interview/
Ebony, July:42.

Nick Nolte
Actor

2

In a way, it's part of an actor's life-style to be out of the mainstream. I think the problem is that the role almost always rubs off on you. But that's almost what you want to happen—to work toward creating some of that confusion. Let's face it: we work in a make-believe world that's actually real—the film's really in the camera. That's why I used to go home and never go to sleep after work. I didn't want to lose that edge. I didn't want things to get too slick. It's better if you stay off-balance a little. I mean, being an actor, you've either got to have lots of confidence or guts, or just blind foolery.

Interview, Los Angeles/
Los Angeles Times, 8-18:(Calendar)27.

Chuck Norris
Actor

3

[On criticism that his films are too violent for younger viewers]: You will never see me playing a character that I think could be harmful to kids. There are good guys and bad guys in my movies. What I really make are modern-day Westerns. The kids know that, and so do their parents. They know my films are okay because I don't get into heavy-duty sex scenes. As far as I'm concerned, it's sex scenes that can harm a kid. That's a tension thing; sexual tension is something they can't release. But when you watch a fight scene, and start yelling and getting into the action, that's tension you *can* release.

Interview/
Los Angeles Times, 5-19:(Calendar)31.

Gregory Peck
Actor

4

[Saying that the film industry is owned today by conglomerates]: Now you have a bunch of cold sharks running the studios. They're brokers between the conglomerate and the talent. They'll decide if they open up the purse strings and let you make this or not make that. That's a big, big change. It has taken out a lot of the humanity, a lot of the passion. It's a colder business now. The executives are faceless. They have no personality. They're holding on to their perks. They're holding on to their offices up in the tower, and they are playing it safe. They are jumping on each other's bandwagon. When the one trend wears out, then someone comes up with something new, and they all jump on that. Every now and then a good film will sneak through.

Interview/USA Today, 3-22:(A)11.

Anthony Perkins
Actor, Director

5

Some people have already begun referring to me as a director. But being a first-time movie director is a bit like being a first-time bullfighter. You can find out all about the ring and the people who'll assist you and the outfit you wear—but

(ANTHONY PERKINS)

until you get into that ring with the bull, you can't call yourself a bullfighter . . . Anyway, there's a theory that the first movies of most directors are among their best. It's when they're at their most inventive, when they're willing to listen. I think that's a good theory. In fact, I'm clinging to it.

Interview, Los Angeles/
Los Angeles Times, 4-28:(Calendar)27.

Sidney Poitier
Actor, Director

[Saying he is now primarily a director]: I had a weird, peculiar view of the work I did [as an actor]. For me, acting was a way of self-definition. And unless the work could distinguish me from a dishwasher, I had no need for it . . . I made 38 or 40 movies [as an actor], and in that body nestles a little group of rather remarkable films—more than a couple with a kind of immediacy that hasn't been dulled too badly by the years. I would rather leave them alone rather than [return to acting] at a level unbecoming to them.

Interview, New York/USA Today, 3-5:(D)5.

1

Sydney Pollack
Director

I don't think there is an awful lot you can do to influence [the film media's social conscience] other than to be careful about who becomes a film-maker. You hope that the responsibility of making movies will fall into the hands of essentially moral people.

Panel discussion, Aug. 28/
Los Angeles Times, 8-30:(VI)1.

2

Making a movie is a network of decisions that keep multiplying as you go. You leave a trail of decisions behind you and that's how you start to see the shape of what you've done. When you get far enough, you turn around and say, "Ha, that's the movie." It's only then that you find out if it's going to work or not.

Interview, Universal City, Calif./
Los Angeles Times, 12-8:(Calendar)3.

3

Frank Price
Chairman, MCA Motion Picture Group
(Universal Pictures)

A sequel [to a successful film] has the great advantage of being familiar. We spend millions of dollars to make something unknown into something that is known. A non-sequel starts from zero. A sequel is a guaranteed reward. If you enjoyed Sugar Pops last week for breakfast, you're probably going to want them again. But you can certainly manage to screw up a sequel by making it very different from the original in terms of the story or the actors.

The New York Times, 7-8:15.

4

I think there have always been more women involved in the [motion-picture] business than the perception may have indicated. Costume design was for women to a great extent. Story department, that was literary—so it was considered all right. But society's view of women's roles has changed, and I think there has been more of a response to that in Hollywood than anywhere. For example, our production staff is about 50 percent women . . . There was a time when the common misconception was, "Those rough male crews won't respect a woman director. She won't be able to control them." Clearly, nothing to that . . . People forget that Ida Lupino was directing here—she had her own production company. And certainly the female stars could be pretty rough . . . you know, Joan Crawford, Bette Davis, and that group. You want to see a male crew member get intimidated? Just let him get in trouble with one of those ladies . . . If someone wants in [in the film industry], there is only one way to get in, and that is to persist, persist, persist. If you've got talent and drive, this is the most tolerant business in the world. If you're the female Steven Spielberg, just tell me . . . and I'll make you comfortable.

Interview, Universal City, Calif./
Cosmopolitan, November:166.

5

David Puttnam
Producer

I find myself running counter to many of the pressures and many of the aspirations of the film

6

(DAVID PUTTNAM)

industry. I mean, I certainly feel that the films I do have an ethical, as opposed to a show-business, base. And I like that idea . . . The sanctity of the individual is the idea that's most important to me. I could never go along with acts [in my films] that violate the individual.

Interview, London/
The Christian Science Monitor, 2-13:23,24.

Steve Randall
Vice president of marketing,
Tri-Star Pictures

1

We used to have "bankable" actors. Now the most bankable thing going is the sequel to a successful movie. Once a movie is successful, the concept of the movie itself becomes a star.

The New York Times, 7-8:15.

Robert Redford
Actor

2

We need to get away from this whole idea of having to release films that will be instantly viewed by the entire nation. There are great stories to be told about regional subjects, but they aren't being told. The independent film-makers are the ones to do it.

To reporters at United States Film Festival,
Park City, Utah, Jan. 20/USA Today, 1-22:(D)5.

Carl Reiner
Actor, Director, Writer

3

[On comedy]: People laugh primarily because they are sharing a sense of identification. If you're a comedy writer, you bring to comedy who you are and what your environment and family influences are. You take your genes into every theatre you enter, and when the comedy writer touches those chords, you laugh . . . The only thing you can do as a creator of comedy is make *yourself* laugh and hope that you're the norm, so more people will laugh at what you laugh at because you see things that most people see. Comedy is a success if you leave the theatre feeling good. A couple of belly laughs is all you

can expect. And those are very satisfying . . . And then, too, hopefully, you've spent some time with people [characters] you liked.

Interview/Films in Review, December:549.

Karel Reisz
Director

4

An American "star" tends to be convinced his own personality is in itself admirable and interesting. That's not true of Britain. A lot of our [British] stars are slightly ashamed, I think, [of doing commercial films]. There's the feeling, "I'm doing this for the money, but what I should be doing is *Coriolanus.*" They don't think it's such a marvelous thing to be—a star . . . I do think we take things much too seriously now. It's so boring. Every time you make a movie, there's so much riding on it that people become neurotic; they feel their entire career depends on its success. There was a time, you know, when, if you directed a film, the producer or perhaps some studio executive would come to the set to give you encouragement. Now it's completely the other way around. Now, because of the huge investments involved, *we* have to calm *them* down, saying, "Don't worry, it's going to be all right."

Interview, Los Angeles/
Los Angeles Times, 9-15:(Calendar)21.

Jason Robards
Actor

5

Acting is make-believe. There's nothing else to it. All the rest is crazy self-analysis that means nothing to the audience. If you make-believe well enough, they make-believe, too.

Interview, Washington/
The New York Times, 7-23:21.

Nicolas Roeg
Director

6

I suppose I am outside the mainstream of British cinema. But then, I have to watch the films I make. I can't make films to please the organizers of a film-year, or whatever. I'm not ac-

(NICOLAS ROEG)

tually complaining, but it seems that the result of refusing to compromise is that one simply has to survive as best one can.

Interview/Films and Filming, July:16.

Eric Rohmer
Director, Screenwriter

I do feel a little ashamed that I have always been able to make the films that I wanted to make when I wanted. Somehow, they make their money back and I am lucky to have producers for friends. I think the best reason for that is that I am a very economical director. I only start filming when we are absolutely ready, and I normally never do more than one take. I think the great plague of the cinema is waste; waste of money, of ideas, of time.

Interview/World Press Review, May:59.

1

Maximilian Schell
Actor

The big difference—for actors—from earlier times is that they wrote *for* Humphrey Bogart, *for* Marlene Dietrich, *for* Gary Cooper. The studio put on a writer and said, "This is Max Schell, let's do a film for him, modeled to his personality." Today, everybody's struggling for himself, even Dustin Hoffman.

*Interview, Los Angeles/
Los Angeles Times, 1-14:(V)6.*

2

Sissy Spacek
Actress

Right now, I just hunger for a role that you normally wouldn't think of me playing—something that I'd really have to work on not to blow. I want to knock people's socks off! You know, a role that even *I'm* sure ahead of time that I can't do, a role that's a shot in the arm. It's like an addiction. You never want to admit to yourself that you're not going to get better, because if you aren't getting better, it means you're getting worse. I want to peak on my deathbed. But I want it to be a *long* peak, understand.

Interview/Esquire, February:99.

3

Steven Spielberg
Director, Producer

I dream for a living. Once a month the sky falls on my head, I come to, and I see another movie I want to make. Sometimes I think I've got ball bearings for brains; these ideas are slipping and sliding across each other all the time. My problem is that my imagination won't turn off. I wake up so excited I can't eat breakfast. I've never run out of energy. It's not like OPEC oil; I don't worry about a premium going on my energy. It's just always been there.

Interview/Time, 7-15:56.

4

Sylvester Stallone
Actor

I understand the critics' dilemma—I really do. But the critic should also understand the actor's dilemma. His job is to convey what he's feeling inside, to the largest number of people. They call it commerciality. I call it communication. I could go out and make a film that no one goes to see—a film that is hard-edged, insightful, painful, controversial. But I would rather do something that is meaningful to the masses.

*Interview, Pacific Palisades, Calif./
The Washington Post, 5-22:(F)4.*

5

Mary Steenburgen
Actress

[In the beginning,] I was offered a lot of roles, and everybody in Hollywood told me to take them. But it would have been pretty stupid of me to indiscriminately grab the first role that came along. I have never worried about the one that got away . . . That is a problem for idiots. Maybe I haven't worked as much as I could have, but I wouldn't have wanted it any other way. This may all sound egotistical, but actually it's quite practical. I want to be working when I'm old, and it wouldn't serve your career in the long run if you set your sights too low. You have to go for quality . . . People are very happy to pigeonhole you in this business, and why not? It's a *business*, and they figure if you do it well once, you'll probably do it well again.

*Interview, New York/
Los Angeles Times, 12-26:(V)3.*

6

Peter Strauss
Actor

1

To the British, the screenplay, the teleplay, is a very important, highly detailed blueprint. What happens in America is usually that the writer is gone by the time the picture goes into production. So a lot of other people start altering the screenplay. That doesn't happen on Broadway, and it doesn't happen in London for the most part. Where the writer is still the revered figure, the end result is most often good . . . or at least is the culmination of somebody's vision.

Interview, New York/
The Christian Science Monitor, 10-31:28.

Richard Thomas
Actor

2

As an actor, you want to know you've worked hard and that you've arrived. And then when you've arrived, you want to think that it's never going to change. So you erect this edifice around yourself, and it's a perfectly natural thing to do. You're just protecting yourself, because to be an actor means that you must be given permission to work. You're constantly in a posture of supplication. Constantly. I mean, I spent my entire childhood working as an actor. I auditioned for everything. I got up and did whatever they asked me to do. I went out on the stage of those dark theatres and sang and read those scenes, and believe me, at the age of 10, 11, 12, that can be a very terrifying experience. But I did all that. And then you get to the point where you think you have a position, a job, a reputation, and you say to yourself, "I don't ever want to go through that again. I don't have to put myself through that humiliation. I've paid my dues." And that's an incredibly dangerous crossroads. Because that's the day you decide your own security is more important than the impulse to be an actor.

Interview, Washington/
The Washington Post, 5-16:(B)1.

Liv Ullmann
Actress

3

It's amazing to me how little realms of human contact are available in movie houses right now.

The current rage in film has nothing to do with real emotions. They don't even involve real people. We are in an era of robots and ghosts and make-believe people. Or we have a lot of silly comedies with characters nobody knows. Film should tell us about real people, real feelings. I am so disappointed with what is going on now, with what passes off for art.

USA Today, 1-21:(D)2.

Bud Yorkin
Director

4

[On the difference between directing drama and directing comedy]: In directing a drama . . . there can be many interpretations to each scene. I might interpret a scene differently from the actor, and you, as an audience, could have yet a different interpretation. And they all could be equally valid! In a comedy, when you ask an audience to laugh at a given moment, you're saying, "When I tell you to laugh, you're going to laugh." You want no other emotion, and that's the difference.

Interview/
American Film, October:18.

Saul Zaentz
Producer

5

[On how to determine what audiences want to see]: We don't really worry about what they want to see, because I think anyone who thinks he can outguess the market is a fool. I don't know what people want to see. I think you have to go by what you can do. Starting your career, you may have to work in pictures that are not pictures you really want to make, but that doesn't mean you have to be bad on that picture, no matter what job you do. But we're lucky that we can make pictures we *want* to make, rightly or wrongly. We may make the wrong choices. And we may not make so may films . . . You spend a long time on a film, and if you are to spend that time intelligently, I think you have to take a little time to decide what you want to make.

Interview/American Film, Jan.-Feb.:68.

MUSIC

Paul Anka
Singer, Songwriter

[On whether today's song lyrics promote drug-use and anti-social behavior among audiences]: I would not like to believe that deep within someone's soul they are overcome by the power of a song to where it would instill some kind of detrimental or negative posture in them. Even though it certainly does have an inspiring aspect to it, it is only music. I would not like to think that music is responsible for a lot of negatives. I think it should be taken for what it is, and if certain people are weak in fiber and need some kind of a crutch to lean on, they of course have turned to music. But I think that certainly you could look to the positive side—rock people have realized that they have a certain commitment to society and have found there is more of a powerful meaning to what they do, to be able to raise the amount of money that was raised by [the charitable] *We Are the World* and the Live Aid concert. I think that is an incredible commentary on pop music.

Interview/USA Today, 8-27:(A)9.

1

Emanuel Ax
Pianist

There are advantages and disadvantages to doing contemporary music. You have to put in an enormous amount of time and work before you really come to know the piece—and then what happens . . . ? [Very likely, a single performance.] Still, it's exciting, and it's new. And, you know, there are so many valid performances of Beethoven and Brahms, and so many people who can talk all night about the *forte* in measure forty-nine—or something like that. Come on, the message has come across. It's too much already—like comparative literature. We need *new* novels! It's *enough!* And besides, when people hear a piece that they don't know so very

2

438

well, their attention focuses on the music, not on the performance. And that's nice.

Interview/Ovation, April:10.

Susan Baker
Leader,
Parents Musical Resource Center

[Saying there should be a classification system for records with sex and violence in their lyrics]: Parents have been yelling about rock-and-roll forever, but they don't know that the lyrics have changed, and a line has been crossed . . . You're always going to find sex in music. It's there from the beginning, and we're not trying to do something about it. But now, instead of being suggestive and creative, they're describing the act in detail, and they're describing rape and violence in detail.

The New York Times, 9-18:26.

3

Tony Bennett
Singer

I grew up in an era when there were real geniuses around. Not that there aren't some brilliant guys today; but it's going to be hard for anyone to compete with Art Tatum or Duke Ellington, Benny Goodman, Frank Sinatra, Billie Holliday, Woody Herman, Stan Kenton, Fats Waller—they were all around us, the great entertainers. It was the best era of music in the United States. And right before that was the '30s, which is really the kind of music that I love—the songs of Jerome Kern and George Gershwin and Irving Berlin and Harry Warren and Harold Arlen, the great composers era that came out of Richard Rodgers . . . Now the accent's on money, where years ago it was on money plus integrity. It's impulse now; impact; let's see how much money we can make from this. In the late '50s, the major record companies started imitating the Detroit syndrome. They went for obsolescence rather

4

(TONY BENNETT)

than quality—let's get everybody hot on something and two weeks later come out with the next thing; let's just keep whipping the public rather than waiting to find out what the public likes.

Interview, Washington/
The Washington Post, 7-9:(C)9.

Montserrat Caballe
Opera singer

1

I am nervous [onstage], maybe more nervous than the others. They are more quiet. Some are more relaxed, or at least look to me more relaxed. But I cannot be relaxed before going onstage. I am in tension that I try to cover with a smile, with something, but inside it's incredible! And more and more and more—every time I sing, more. Coming to the Met [ropolitan Opera] . . . and before beginning to sing to receive an ovation like I receive these days, it makes me shake in all my body. I think, "Oh, they're going to expect something very special, but I can only be me—maybe today not *even* me. I don't feel well, but let's see" . . . As I say, you go on the stage and the public sees a myth. They don't see Caballe; they see something out of this world. And I look at this hall and say, "What can I give tonight?" I always can hear that word *truth*. It's the only thing you can offer; and I think it's the only thing you understand.

Interview, New York/Opera News, 3-2:12.

Elliott Carter
Composer

2

One of our dilemmas today is that we have this extraordinary legacy of classical music produced under conditions which cannot now be duplicated. Music in Haydn's time was encouraged and supported by the musical members of an educated aristocracy and leisured members of the upper bourgeoisie. In the 19th century, many such people had a lot of time to practice the piano, learn music, as servants took care of so many practical problems, and the fading aristocracy established the idea of what a cultivated life should consist of. Now all this is past, although

we still have the musical repertory from that time setting a high standard of accomplishment for composers, a standard that one often feels the present-day listener is hardly aware of. As composers, many of us try to carry on this old level of musical skill and imagination, and this poses very serious problems, since only a very small part of the public is likely to treasure such skills, at least at first, and this small part seldom has much say in the larger musical world.

Interview, Banff, Canada/
Music Magazine, Nov.-Dec.:33.

3

Johnny Cash
Singer

[On "dirty lyrics" in today's songs]: I don't think it's necessary. I don't know how damaging it is to our youth . . . I never have seen that it leads our youth into decadence. If they want to become decadent, they will. There are a lot of things in our lives that suggest everything under the sun all day long. If you read the newspapers and watch television and commercials, you'd be drinking beer all night . . . I don't think these rock 'n' roll songs are message songs that are trying to make the kids do anything anyway, except to listen to the songs and be entertained. If they're going to go astray, they will, and rock 'n' roll lyrics won't have a thing in the world to do with it. Personally, I would not record a song with profanities and obscenities in it now. I might have back years ago when I was feeling a little cocky.

Interview/USA Today, 11-8:(A)11.

4

Ray Charles
Musician

I think there is something for all of us in music. The great thing about it is that we don't have to all like the same thing. I remember back in the 1950s when people were saying what I did was vulgar. Many people were annoyed with it. When Elvis Presley came out, people said, "Oh, my God, he's going to destroy the world out there, wiggling and carrying on." Of course, black people were doing that long before. That's

WHAT THEY SAID IN 1985

(RAY CHARLES)

where Elvis started from. But, in any event, many people thought I was a degradation.

Interview/USA Today, 11-1:(A)11.

Kyung Wha Chung
Violinist

1

. . . as a performer, I really feel that we are just filling the gap. I know that when I perform, people do appreciate it and enjoy it. For the next generation there will be another performer to fill that gap. A composer, on the other hand, is forever living. I don't believe that performers are *the* most important. All I believe is that I have a certain talent and that I always crave to express it.

Interview/Music Magazine, February:9.

Dick Clark
Host and producer,
"American Bandstand," ABC-TV

2

[On the beginnings of rock 'n' roll in the 1950s]: Anybody could tell that it was youth-oriented music. It was there because parents hated it, and it was something that the younger generation grabbed and made their own. So if you could have been far-seeing enough, you could have seen that it would be the music of the future. It was extraordinarily difficult, because the music was universally hated by older people, almost without exception . . . This was music created by people who sometimes couldn't even write it down, many of whom had no formal musical training, and many of whom were black and who were country-oriented. So it was a totally alien invasion. And they set up a concerted effort to nip it in the bud, to kill it. It didn't work, fortunately.

Interview/USA Today, 8-2:(D)6.

Aaron Copland
Composer

3

Some composers have been able to lend themselves to a great many different styles just by na-

ture. They have that gift. I think it's hard to create a musical style of your own through sheer will. Either you have your own thing to say and it comes out on your own terms in a natural way without putting forth too much effort, or you don't have your own style. There are composers —good ones—who don't have any particular style of their own. But most of the great ones you can recognize when you hear their music.

Interview/USA Today, 12-9:(A)15.

John Corigliano
Composer

4

The thought that means the most to me on the 300th anniversary of [Johann Sebastian] Bach's birth is the image of the composer as a member of society who works for a living—and not some alienated, misunderstood creature on a pedestal. Bach was a real composer who had to work to compose real pieces for every Sunday's services. He was a family man, a religious man, a working man—and music was his craft. It's important that we remember that—not just composers but people who listen to our music. Bach was not just a great composer but also a professional who did his job. I think the more that's illuminated, the healthier the world will be.

Interview/Ovation, February:21.

5

As far as I'm concerned, a composer's job does not end when he puts the double bar at the end of the piece. That's only half the job. Before a concert with one of my works, I'm addressing envelopes, making sure people who I think should hear the work know it's being played. And after the concert, if I have a good performance tape, I make copies and send them, with a score, to performers I know. I find that once a conductor has played one of your works and has had success with it, you can always go to him with the next one and be reasonably sure that your score won't end up on the pile of unopened envelopes from other composers. And if you don't do that, you're naive. Yes, it does take away from composing, but so what? If you have spent a year writing a piece, spending a day mailing these things is not very much.

Interview/Ovation, November:18.

Bruce Crawford
General manager,
Metropolitan Opera, New York

1

[On running the Metropolitan Opera]: You always have to worry about waste. Waste in a creative enterprise is different from that in other areas. In other words, what is waste, what is investment, and what is good experimental money? In a creative enterprise, you can't run everything so tightly that people can't make mistakes. You'll never achieve anything if you *have* to be right! And you can't run everything for the short term. If you try to run an entirely safe creative enterprise, you will run a very dull operation, and you will not achieve artistic success. In the long run you'll be out of business, because you didn't provide a high enough quality product for your constituents.

Interview, New York/Opera News, September:14.

R. Serge Denisoff
Professor of sociology,
Bowling Green State University

2

People have a very simple-minded view that [today's] music corrupts the young. It's never been proven. I don't think it does, because if you take the music of the '30s—*Love for Sale*—there was scandal about that, then about swing, then about [Elvis] Presley, the Beatles and Led Zeppelin. Now MTV is the big villain.

USA Today, 3-14:(D)3.

Placido Domingo
Opera singer

3

[On his recent forays into conducting]: The two jobs [singing and conducting] take different kinds of energy. With singing, you have to pamper yourself in a very special way. You have to be quiet the day before. You have to have all your energy. The voice has to be fresh, and so on. For conducting, you need to be physically and mentally relaxed, like I am the day after I sing. Then you have to go out there and really give energy from beginning to end, because it is you that is directing the performance.

Interview/Ovation, March:10.

Jacob Druckman
Composer-in-residence,
New York Philharmonic Orchestra

4

[On being a composer-in-residence]: My particular prejudice is that I love to know for whom I'm writing: who'll be conducting, playing alto flute, and so forth. Knowing these people as I do, I can lean on their strengths and perhaps avoid weaknesses . . . It's not so much a matter of squeezing out the last drop of virtuosity. It's just that when I know who the performer is, when it will be performed, and more or less who the audience will be, I find myself writing a much more communicative piece than if I'm writing in the abstract . . . The aim isn't necessarily to embrace the listener; to know the audience is not necessarily to love it. I think in general I do, but I'm not about to write a piece in order to please their taste. That's pandering. Then again, I won't go out to upset them. Except on given occasions—the way Haydn still surprises people with his *Surprise Symphony!*

Interview, New York/
The Christian Science Monitor, 9-19:27.

JoAnn Falletta
Music director, Denver Chamber Orchestra
and Queens (N.Y.) Philharmonic Orchestra

5

Many people still cannot seem to make the conceptual plunge of accepting a woman in the role of conductor. Audiences, once they get over the initial surprise, respond very well. Younger people don't find it so difficult at all. But some older players are used to the old dictatorial, tyrannical type of conductor, which I am not. I feel that conducting styles have changed and that conductors no longer feel the need to throw Toscanini-like temper tantrums and fire musicians on the spot. I think musicians should be protected, and never at the mercy of one person.

Interview, New York/
The Christian Science Monitor, 8-15:25.

6

In Europe, a music director is more apt to spend most of the year with his orchestra, so his personality, his concept of sound and tempos,

(JoANN FALLETTA)

become part of the orchestra. In a way, the orchestra begins to think as one person. In general, American orchestras don't develope a sound of their own, and they don't develop the concept of playing together as an ensemble as well as European orchestras do. This is because European orchestras play together every day—hours and hours of rehearsal. European orchestras have the money to allow them that leisure. We [in the U.S.] don't.

Interview/Music Magazine, Nov.-Dec.:17.

Lukas Foss
Composer; Music director,
Brooklyn Philharmonic and
Milwaukee Symphony orchestras

I'd have to say that my long love affair with [Johann Sebastian] Bach, which has influenced a lot of my music, is due to many aspects of his music. One, in particular, is the way Bach shows, most eloquently, the fallacy of thinking that music is either emotional *or* intellectual, a case of either/or. Something like the *Saint Matthew Passion*, for example, is both a most romantic work and an extremely brainy, structural work. That's why Bach, like Mozart and Beethoven, never goes out of fashion—for, as the fashion changes, you merely look at another side of him. The 19th century looked at one side of Bach, and we today look at another.

Interview/Ovation, February:22.

1

Ira Glasser
Executive director,
American Civil Liberties Union

[Arguing against a government classification system for records with sex and violence in their lyrics]: It is entirely improper, and we think unConstitutional, for the Congress to be making an inquiry into the content of published material with a view toward classifying or regulating that content by legislation. And legislation is the only reason to hold a hearing. What they are doing is using the threat of legislation to force voluntary compliance. And the threat of legislation doesn't exist, since no such legislation would survive a Constitutional challenge. The only purpose is to try and create self-censorship in the music industry.

The New York Times, 9-18:26.

2

David Gockley
General director,
Houston Grand Opera

I'm not content with opera as a museum. I want to attract a whole new crowd at our performances—people who consider themselves in the avant-garde—who like dance, the visual arts and film. Opera has always been a little too old and stodgy for these people, and I'm trying to dispel that image.

Interview, New York/Ovation, February:74.

3

Benny Goodman
Band leader; Clarinetist

[The trouble with today's music business is that] a bunch of lawyers and CPA guys are running it, looking for a jackpot. They aren't interested in music. It's as simple as that. The music doesn't mean anything to them. They don't look for talent; wouldn't know it if they heard it. They sit waiting for some miracle to happen, like [rock star] Bruce Springsteen.

The Washington Post, 12-9:(C)3.

4

Nikolaus Harnoncourt
Orchestra conductor

For me, the [musical] instruments of Western culture—from the earliest surviving ones to the most modern—are a great continuum and offer a great possibility of sound. I see a composer choosing the best sound from what he has available in order to express what he wants to express, and—like Bach and Beethoven and Berlioz—he pushes the development of instruments. A composer hears his composition in his mind in the best possible way; he pushes the instrument makers, who respond and develop new possibilities for the composers, who then take the next step and repeat the process. But, at the

5

(NIKOLAUS HARNONCOURT)

same time, I deeply believe that you cannot just make improvements. I don't believe that humanity always goes forward. You have to pay for everything that you gain with a corresponding loss. I call it *knodeltheorie*—the dumpling principal. You have only so much dough; when you add to one side of the dumpling, you take from the other. Take the flute, for example. In increasing the range and improving the quality of the semi-tones, the artist instrument makers had to pay for it with sonority, with changed sound quality. You also have to consider the changes in people. We hear with totally different ears. We are accustomed to traffic noise. We know all the music that has been written since Bach and Mozart. We cannot erase that from our experience.

Interview/Ovation, May:10.

Antonio Carlos Jobim
Composer

2

Writing music is more a matter of perspiration than inspiration. The hardest part is the art of throwing stuff into the garbage.

Interview, New York/
The New York Times, 3-29:15.

Quincy Jones
Musician

3

. . . you can't go somewhere and learn how to write a good song. It's a gift. The bottom line is divine inspiration. It's innate, pure inspiration from upstairs, because the structure of a song—the sequence of notes, the intervals, the patterns, etc.—there's no school that can teach you how to put all that down on paper. It has to come from inside. You have to have "the gift," and that comes from God . . . Some [of today's instant superstars] are really tragic. For one thing, they won't listen to anybody. They just won't listen. When I was a young musician I learned to shut up and listen to people like Ray Charles and Clark Terry, Billy Eckstine, Count [Basie], Duke [Ellington], Dizzy Gillespie . . . people like that. You can't beat that kind of education from people who know what they're talking about. But many of the youngsters today don't want to listen to what they consider "old fogies." All they want to do is get a hit record and earn enough money to get a pound of cocaine . . .

Interview, Los Angeles/
Ebony, October:38.

Marilyn Horne
Opera singer

1

[On being an opera singer]: Concentration is the biggie. It's the whole ballgame after breath support. At times, I've had to *drag* myself to wherever I'm singing because I was not in a great mood, had problems in my life or was tired. But when you go on that stage and start concentrating, everything else leaves your mind and it can even become a superlative performance. I've never had to describe my feelings when it all comes together in performance. Certainly there is some kind of joy. Usually, I'm aware of special emotional rewards during the quieter, more precious moments of a recital, and, even then, the experience is rare and fleeting. It happened once when I was singing a particularly beautiful Schumann song about evening. Suddenly I had this incredible feeling that I was in the right place at the right time, the audience and I were communicating, my accompanist and I were together and the world was wonderful. I felt nature, God and the whole spiritual thing. If anything, music makes me believe there is some great force out there.

Interview, New York/
Music Magazine,
May-June:10.

Edwin Lester
Founder,
Los Angeles Civic Light Opera

4

The music that was written around the turn of the century, and up until 1930 or 1940, was written for very good singers. And those singers were drawn from the operatic realm. Grand opera, which through the years has been the most successful surviving musical form, has thrived. And it has thrived, not from the new operas, but from revivals, revivals, revivals. Those are the things people still go to. They want familiar mu-

WHAT THEY SAID IN 1985

sic, and it's hard to get familiar with music in the modern vein.

(EDWIN LESTER)

Witold Lutoslawski
Composer

My element is the symphony orchestra, though it's anachronistic because all the instruments in it are in a way museum specimens. I find it's a rather strange situation in which satellites can turn around our earth, and we still play bassoons.

Interview, Los Angeles/
Los Angeles Times,
4-7:(Calendar)37.

1

Lorin Maazel
Orchestra conductor

The true musician must be at home with every kind of music. I've had periods when I worked with one composer, but whenever I felt I was too closely associated, I moved out of it. Finally, people accept me, but not as a jack of all trades and master of none. I've tried to master everything.

Interview, Pittsburgh/USA Today, 10-1:(D)5.

2

Henry Mancini
Composer, Conductor

[On electronic music synthesizers]: There is an evolution of sound, and we're right in the middle of it. The art world and the business world and the commercial world are all banging their heads together, and we don't know where it's going . . . It is technology versus the human element. It's happened in many industries. It's happened in newspapers. As Charlie Chaplin said, it's "Modern Times."

Interview/Los Angeles Times, 12-6:(I)1,26.

3

Eva Marton
Opera singer

What is important for me is finding what the composer wants in the character—what is deep in the character. I see it like an empty house. When I move into this house, I give it my character. I feel this true for roles, too. I put my personality into the role, and that is very important. When you have character and personality, you can *feel* the roles.

Interview, New York/
The Christian Science Monitor, 2-13:24.

4

James McCracken
Opera singer

If there's a high-school quarterback that's worth anything at all, all the colleges know where he is and they keep their eye on him. If there's a college quarterback that's any good at all, the pros all have their eyes on him. There are [opera] singers out there, but who is finding them, nurturing them, and giving them the opportunity? When I've done my master classes—and I've only done about 10 in my life—I say that if there is anything that I say here in this class that can discourage you, then you'll never make it anyway, which is true. So I tend to be a little pessimistic when I do master classes, because what else is there? I'd just be painting a rosy picture that isn't there.

Interview, New York/
The Christian Science Monitor, 1-2:23.

5

I enjoy what I'm doing now so much because I know my roles so well. Today, I don't have the kind of fear, the kind of sweaty palms that come from doing the first few performances of a role. After you've done a role many times, there's nothing that's really going to bother you. You have nerves—but for a different reason. You're worried about making the performance as good as your last. After a performance, I don't feel that I did it better 10 years ago. If I did, I probably wouldn't continue.

Interview/Ovation, September:30.

6

Carlos Moseley
Former chairman of the board,
New York Philharmonic Orchestra

1

There are still many people who are very en-
thusiastic about music, but audiences today are
different from what they were in 1930, or even
1955. When I first started going to concerts in
the late 1920s, when Toscanini had become conductor of the [New York] Philharmonic, there
was a European orientation to the audience.
They had a different feeling than today's audiences; they were more knowledgeable about music.

Interview, New York/
The New York Times, 11-7:24.

Riccardo Muti
Music director, Philadelphia Orchestra

2

I am not too well-understood. When someone
visits me in my dressing room before I conduct
the Verdi Requiem and he says "Enjoy," we're
like two people from different planets. No comment could seem more absurd to me. And after-
wards, when I'm still judging a performance and
mulling it over, they come again to intrude with
unwanted opinions. I am proud. My career was
not made by kissing hands, and making small
talk is disagreeable to me. Not for arrogance or
wanting to be a *primo uomo*. But because I am
serious about the work. In the 20 years I was in
London, no one asked me to honor this obligation. I try to be as gracious as I can—when necessary.

Interview, New York/
Los Angeles Times, 2-3:(Calendar)48.

Luciano Pavarotti
Opera singer

3

[Today,] there is no more *fight* to reach the
great [opera] theatres of the world. Everything
[for young singers] is too easy, too fast. The audiences today are more flexible, less fanatical
and demanding. Their big defect in the past was
to be inflexible, and they would boo. Okay, it
was bad, but if you came through that, you knew
you had done something. Now if the critic is

writing well, even if you don't make the public
crazy, you are success.

Interview, New York/
The New York Times, 9-24:20.

Itzhak Perlman
Violinist

4

I began to notice how audiences responded at
my recitals to the spoken word. First, I just announced encores and then I began to add little
anecdotes that I remembered. They almost
sighed with relief that I could actually talk. But
none of it is planned in advance. I do what
strikes me as being natural. If it's natural to talk,
I do. There are no rules I subscribe to.

Interview, Santa Barbara, Calif./
Los Angeles Times, 8-13:(VI)3.

Rinaldo Petrignani
Italian Ambassador
to the United States

5

[On his helping raise funds for the Washington Opera]: I often think what would opera be
without Italy and what would Italy be without
opera? As Ambassador, and as an Italian, I am
both delighted and proud to see this longstanding
association between the mythical muses and my
country so brilliantly perpetuated on the stage of
the Washington Opera.

The New York Times, 6-1:8.

Joseph W. Polisi
President,
Juilliard School, New York

6

There's no question but that, in the past 20
years, there has been a decrease in the amount
and quality of music teaching taking place in the
elementary and secondary schools of the United
States. You've got relatively large audiences in
concert halls today. I'm just asking the question
out loud: "Is this trend going to continue?"
. . . What percentage of young people will we
attract in the future? I'm not just bringing this up
from a marketing and audience point of view, but
from a cultural, sociological standpoint. There

(JOSEPH W. POLISI)

really is an intellectual content to classical music which, in my opinion, is not contained in popular music . . . I deeply believe that if most of our society rejects traditional Western culture [as expressed in classical music, dance, drama], we will become a weaker society and a more blemished place.

Interview, New York/
The Christian Science Monitor, 9-25:28.

Andre Previn
Music director,
Los Angeles Philharmonic Orchestra

1

The music of our time that we play doesn't have to be tried and true. We must take changes . . . I have a definite cut-off point, though. I like music that is written out. I don't like things left to chance. I don't like performing pieces where the explanations for the symbols in the score take up more space than the music. I won't do music that tells a player to stand on his head and hit the cello with a Coke bottle.

Interview, Beverly Hills, Calif./
Los Angeles Times, 9-29:(Calendar)57.

Leontyne Price
Opera singer

2

[On her decision to retire from singing]: On February 10 I will be 58 years old, and it is thrilling to be asked why I am retiring, rather than why not. There is nothing in the world more embarrassing, more pathetic than the artist who can no longer give his best. I did something right. I took care of the most extraordinary thing I have: my voice.

Time, 1-14:67.

3

[As a singer,] the performance begins from the first instant you leave your home to go to it. You should be in it then. [It is important] how to present yourself to show you at your very best. Now I look around, and it's changed. People do not dress to go to the Metropolitan [Opera]. I *am*

446

a snob, I am. You're not supposed to sound elite, but I am. I mean, it's the place. Where else are you going to be right if you're not going to be in the Met ambience? In the '60s, we felt it was an honor to be a part of it. I'm sure that still exists, but I'm not sure it's as serious as we used to take it. It was an *image*. It would bother me even to *listen* to this quality art-form not properly dressed. I must sound terribly conservative, but I feel strongly about that. And it's not being a diva so much as just living up to that image of your own pride, of being a part of this particular institution. Pride is what makes a diva . . . pride combined with the performing.

Interview/Opera News, August:47.

Simon Rattle
Conductor, City of Birmingham
(England) Symphony Orchestra

4

If an orchestra can be trained to play by listening to each other—playing as if in a kind of transfigured string quartet—then you've got a chance to go somewhere and you can do more than just hold it all together. It took me a long time to learn that *I* wasn't playing the notes—the orchestra plays! Any conductor who thinks he is making the impulses can cripple an orchestra for life; with such a conductor no one is allowed to play, nothing can be spontaneous. I don't like the sound an orchestra makes when it's being forced. I can hear when something is being conducted autocratically—it may be easier to get certain things quickly, but I feel a rigidity and a lack of breathing that worries me. It's interesting to me to see what an orchestra will have to offer, of itself.

Interview/Ovation, June:10.

Mstislav Rostropovich
Cellist; Music director,
National Symphony Orchestra, Washington

5

When I go to a rehearsal [as a conductor] I have already a model in my mind for the sound of a piece, for the shape of the interpretation. Maybe I'm wrong, but if there are no special acoustical problems in the hall, I produce *exactly* what I want. If there is a choice, I would

(MSTISLAV ROSTROPOVICH)

rather have ideas and some difficulties of technique, than a perfect technique and no ideas.

Interview, New York/
The New York Times, 10-11:20.

Julius Rudel
Music director,
Buffalo Philharmonic Orchestra;
Former music director,
New York City Opera

1

Conducting is something you have within you and needs to be focused, corrected in certain areas. It's partly instinctive and part experiences of knowing what causes what and how you get what you need. You acquire that technique by doing it . . . When you work with a fine orchestra, you don't have to keep stopping all the time, because something will correct itself. The players have seen what can happen, so you don't waste time by stopping for things that take care of themselves. You have to feel that, judge that. It's a constant testing process.

Interview/Opera News, 1-19:35,46.

Ken Russell
Film and opera director

2

[On opera]: The whole thing's a happening. From the usherette to the guys pulling the scenery up and down, they're all part of that happening. It depends on a million possibilities. If the audience is looking for explanations, they're going to be terribly disappointed. It's about something that's inexplicable, and you just go along in the hope that it's going to happen to you—that mystical experience. You can go many times when it doesn't; but when it does, you know you're on another plane—not here, but somewhere else. And that somewhere else is a very nice place to be. Opera is the last sort of believable religion. It's like the mass, but without the overtones of suffering. So being a sort of acolyte mixed up in this funny old religion is exciting. And you're an acolyte if you're part of the audience. If you go to the cinema or watch television, you're not.

Interview/Opera News, 2-2:42.

Andras Schiff
Pianist

3

Contemporary music is divided into popular and serious. The popular is not worthwhile—although it could be. And today's serious music is done in a kind of intellectual ghetto. Occasionally, an orchestra will sandwich a new piece between two war-horses, but these works rarely get second performances. And many of them should not. There is no musical language or style today. There are just a bunch of "isms." This isn't music. It's not honest, either, because it is just trying to be original. Bach, you know, was not very original, but he synthesized all those elements of the music of his time, and from them formed a meaningful language.

Interview/Ovation, July:12.

Gunther Schuller
Composer, Conductor

4

[Today's] conductor—this packaged product, not untalented, obviously, but maybe not ready to be a music director—will be wanting to have four other orchestras, several recording contracts and more weeks away from the orchestra than with it. The [orchestral] board usually doesn't have the knowledge or the guts to stand up against these ambitions. The conductor/music director should be made to stay put and get to work on the care and feeding of that one orchestra, to develop its special personality, its uniqueness. He should be the central figure of the community, as Koussevitzky was here in Boston, and like the other great ones: Stokowski, Mitropoulos, Toscanini, Steinberg, Goossens, Dorati, Abravanel. But, of course, this new type of conductor can make 20 times as much money, and get a lot more media coverage, by jetting around the world with his handful of memorized programs than by staying put. So what happens is that American orchestra players—no question the finest in the world—are deprived of playing together under a powerful unifying force to forge a collective personality differentiating one orchestra from another. Classical music is becoming more and more synthetic and homogenized, just like international pop.

Interview, Boston/Ovation, November:26.

WHAT THEY SAID IN 1985

(GUNTHER SCHULLER)

1

More than 95 per cent of the American population has never even heard a Beethoven symphony, has absolutely no idea what a symphony orchestra is! For them, it's [rock stars] Michael Jackson and Madonna—pop, rock and schlock all the way. And not only teen-agers; it's their parents, too. Classical music simply doesn't exist for them. But neither do [jazz musicians] Duke Ellington, John Coltrane, Charlie Parker, Charlie Mingus—even good bluegrass music doesn't exist for the overwhelming majority of our population. And make no mistake about it: The smartest, shrewdest, richest people in the business are at work in those commercial studios, grabbing even larger pieces of the financial and media pies.

Interview, Boston/Ovation, November:26.

Peter Sellars
Artistic director,
American National Theatre,
Kennedy Center, Washington

2

[Opera] audiences are being trained to accept mediocrity. They are told this is what they should get. Because opera connects to social climbing and pretension, these people don't know any better, and they say, "I guess this should be it." The really deadly thing about opera nowadays is that very few people, especially stage directors, know anything about the music.

Interview, New York/Opera News, July:11.

3

Opera is able to be the only important form of political theatre to my mind. In it, because of music, people are never reduced to slogans. Yet all the great operas are really aggressive, alarming, very precise political diatribes.

Interview, New York/Opera News, July:13.

Peter Serkin
Pianist

4

[Saying that continuous playing of only the old classics detracts from their performance

quality]: Why have these pieces lost their vitality? There's nothing jaded about the works themselves. It's up to us performers to bring a fresh outlook to them . . . I believe that playing *new* music, where there are no reference points other than one's personal experience with those notes, stimulates that process.

Interview, Lenox, Mass./
The Wall Street Journal, 9-3:18.

Ravi Shankar
Sitarist

5

My music is a religious act; there is still that feeling. When the music is not written down and you learn by an oral tradition, that attitude remains the same. What is transmitted by the guru is not merely a technique but a feeling. My guru taught me that the best way to worship is by music.

Interview, Washington/
The Washington Post, 6-13:(D)1.

Artie Shaw
Jazz-band leader

6

The band is great but the world is terrible. Many people have to be told that what we play is jazz, because we don't come up there sweating and we don't come in old dashikis and we don't do all this weird video stuff. We live in a video world where everything is for the eyes. People say, "I'm going to see your show." I say, "You're going to be disappointed—we don't do a show. We're going to play a concert." They say they can't dance to our music. I'm not interested in a dance band. All you need for that is a windshield wiper. If they want to dance, it's their business. My business is to play music that is very, very hearable. Mozart wrote dance music, but nobody dances to it. It's a question of training an audience . . . It's a tremendous pleasure for me when I can get up in front of that band when it's sounding right. I think there's nothing better than a guy can do. You're playing music that nobody's ever played before, because every night it's different. The element of surprise is there. That's certainly a part of jazz.

Interview, New York/
The New York Times, 8-16:20.

Russell Sherman
Pianist

1

I never lost my sense of puzzlement and wonder and mystery and anxiety over how to handle the instrument [piano]. There are those who love the possibility that in some unearthly paradise the piano can be played without making one harsh sound. The side I covet and adore, though, is the piano that is the abbreviation of *all* musical possibilities, the aliveness of it. That is what is so endearing about Schnabel's records, especially when we hear them today in the context of "flawless" recorded performances. His records sound absolutely live, and every one of his mistakes is ravishing—like spitting cherry pits and missing the receptacle, like going for the brass ring and falling off the horse.

Interview/Ovation, June.:14.

Beverly Sills
General director, New York City Opera;
Former opera singer

2

I miss singing. I miss the sessions with my coach, cracking the score for the first time and the rehearsal periods, which were always the most creative time. But I don't miss performing. I don't want to go back to the arena again and fight the bull—in *every* sense of the word.

Interview, New York/USA Today, 4-4:(D)4.

3

When I look at the house, I don't worry about the most expensive seats; they are usually bought by corporations and other organizations and rarely get to the public. I worry about the one thousand $29 seats downstairs and the inexpensive seats at the top of the theatre. Our audience is part of the general economy—they aren't the ones who are unaffected by economic changes. If the $6 seats aren't filled, I start to worry . . .

July 12/The New York Times, 7-15:16.

Leonard Slatkin
Music director,
St. Louis Symphony Orchestra

4

Being a guest conductor is definitely schizophrenic! At home, you're under scrutiny; the au-

dience is evaluating you most of the time. When you're on the road, you're not responsible for any administrative work or for anyone else's programs. You just take pieces you think you can do consistently well and you try to enjoy yourself as much as you can. It's like being a guest in someone's home: Your job [as a guest conductor] is not to go into that house and move the furniture about. Your job is to enjoy what is already there.

Interview/Music Magazine, Nov.-Dec.:17.

Kiri Te Kanawa
Opera singer

5

The best [opera] singers come from a very ordinary background most of the time. There is often mixed blood in them, like a dog that's all sorts of bits and pieces—a mutt—which often turns out to be the healthiest and strongest. I don't think singers are made from fine breeding lines. A few, a very few. But most of them have had good educations and "By the way, they sing,"—and suddenly they are back at their other job of being a doctor or something. I think you've got to be pretty smart to have a career as a singer, but the blood stock has got to be pretty ordinary.

Interview, Oyster Bay, N.Y./
Ovation, September:13.

Virgil Thomson
Composer, Critic

6

[On writing music reviews]: You explain how it went, and, as far as you can figure out, how it got that way . . . The description and explanation is the best part of music reviewing. There is such a thing, and you know it too, as a gift for judgment. If you have it, you can say anything you like. If you haven't got it, you don't know you haven't got it. And everything you say will be held against you.

Interview, Boston/
The Christian Science Monitor, 2-12:31.

Michael Tippett
Composer

7

Any considerable [symphonic] work, or one with a text, requires a long period of cogitation

(MICHAEL TIPPETT)

and digestion [before the composer puts it on paper]. Composing is rather like the poet's work—you force it bit by bit until it has a kind of bone structure.

Interview, Houston/
Los Angeles Times,
1-11:(VI)10.

Andre Watts
Pianist

3

I'm a little bothered by musicians who say they don't want to hear anyone else's performance. If you don't have the ability, imagination or creativity to develop your own musical interpretation, or if your listening to someone else is going to mess up your creativity, then you are in the wrong business. I don't think anybody questions that Picasso was influenced by the great artists who preceded him. Rather, I'm sure he was. I think he would have found it ridiculous if someone said he shouldn't look at Rembrandt or Van Gogh because it would mess up his creativity. The same applies to music. So many concerts are played, but how many can you personally hear? You have to listen to records. I don't understand why you should only hear your own playing—it's so narrow. Take a recording of Artur Schnabel playing Beethoven. Often you can learn from something he plays very beautifully. You may go back to the score and search for why he plays that part so beautifully, and find something you hadn't noticed before. On the other hand, Schnabel might be playing something slower than is indicated in the score, and your reaction might be, "I want to make sure I don't slow that part." A pianist doesn't play in a vacuum.

Interview, Suffern, N.Y./
Music Magazine, Sep.-Oct.:18.

Anna Tomowa-Sintow
Opera singer

1

Every singer should know his limit. I am completely against the kind of circus that happens when a singer goes beyond his or her voice. All my colleagues who know me well know how much consideration I give to the offer of a new role . . . I must be convinced that a part is for me. Sometimes I have been shocked by the proposals of roles that I have received. When one has the right voice, the right technique and style, whatever flexibility is required and, of course, the courage, the belief in one's self, that is the time to say yes.

Interview/Opera News,
2-16:17.

Giorgio Tozzi
Opera singer

2

Some young singers think that learning a few tricks of the trade will enable them to build a career. That just isn't so. Becoming a singer is like becoming an athlete: You have to be trained into it. That means you enter the training, and part of the result is that your voice develops. But it's only total commitment that gets any results at all. I believe ballet dancers understand this better than most young singers. They know that no matter what you do artistically, you always have to come back to the barre. You have to develop your muscles continually.

Interview, North Malibu, Calif./
Los Angeles Times,
5-28:(VI)2.

Robert White
Singer

4

[On being an Irish tenor]: There is a special timbre, a plangent quality, a lightness—but a lightness with a bit of heft. It's a lovely sound with great flexibility, a sound that in classical music is wonderful for Mozart and for Baroque music. It's much more than a matter of simply singing ballads in a folksy style—the Irish timbre is fine for Italian bel canto, for instance. But you can't altogether overlook the birth factor. I can't think of a single Irish tenor of quality who wasn't Irish. Maybe your readers will be able to name one, but I can't.

Interview/Ovation, October:20.

Pinchas Zukerman
Violinist; Conductor,
St. Paul Chamber Orchestra

1

For the last year or so, conducting has been second nature to me. It will never be as second nature as playing the fiddle. Because with the violin or viola you are physically in control of your sound; on the podium, you are producing it in the abstract. You have to internalize the sound, and that takes awhile. As [conductor] Zubin Mehta says, we conductors practice in public . . . Conducting becomes—it has to be—a repetitive act. You always find yourself achieving a *piano* in the same way: You tell the orchestra, "No, it's too loud." When I play the violin or viola, I don't have to ask them, "Can you please articulate?" I just look at the music and articulate on the instrument. So you find yourself [as conductor] standing in front and cueing people for no apparent reason except, sometimes, their own laziness; it's like being the coach on a football team. Yesterday, I rehearsed the Mozart *Jupiter* Symphony. The St. Paul and I have played it together umpteen times. The players know my gestures; they have my markings in their parts. Even so, I had to start the opening phrase four times. Why? No reason, except that's the nature of the animal. It's just one of those things you have to do. Orchestra musicians look for leadership.

Interview, Chicago/Ovation, December:14.

451

Judith Anderson

Actress

[Comparing acting on stage with acting on TV]: I never liked playing for the camera—so cold, cold. It's the people out there [in the audience] that makes acting fun—and it *is* great fun, getting on a stage and showing off; that's what it is, you know. It's the people, and when the people couldn't come to New York to see our plays, we took the plays to them—to Kansas City and Seattle and Tulsa and Tucson.

Interview, Santa Barbara, Calif./
Los Angeles Times,
4-22:(VI)2.

1

Gerald Arpino

Assistant director and choreographer,
Joffrey Ballet

Dance represents life at its fullest. When you decide to dance, you alienate yourself from your family, your church and society. There can be pain, but nothing substitutes for a *grand batte-ment* or *double tour*.

Interview/
Ballet News, November:12.

2

Elizabeth Ashley

Actress

[On being a stage actress]: I love the work. I need that whole backstage ritual. I love the order of it—the makeup, the five-minute calls. When I sit down and stare at my mirror, I don't see myself; I see the character coming out. It's as if you become a medium. You're like a surfer riding a wave: If you think about it, you lose it.

Interview, Los Angeles/
Los Angeles Times, 4-4:(VI)4.

3

Maurice Bejart

Choreographer; Director,
Ballet of the 20th Century, Brussels

If you are not subsidized at all, life is an aching hell: You have to be commercial and you cannot do the real creation of your mind. [But] if you get too much money, you lose contact with reality. The Royal Ballet [of Britain], Bolshoi [of the Soviet Union] and Paris Opera companies are heavily subsidized, so they can live in a dream—make a production for one week and then take it away. We are only partly subsidized. We have some money, but sometimes we have to struggle to live. And I think that's very good and very important.

Interview, Ottawa, Canada/
Los Angeles Times, 2-10:(Calendar)52.

4

Milton Berle

Entertainer

Comedy never changes. There are only eight or nine formats of jokes . . . Funny is funny. There is nothing new that's old. There's nothing old that's new. Everything has been done before, with switches. If it sounds like a new joke, it's been taken from some place.

Interview/
USA Today, 12-20:(D)2.

5

Ann Blyth

Actress

Most actors who have done theatre dearly love getting back to it. It's exciting . . . Once you start, that's it. Nobody's going to say, "Cut; let's try it again." You must continue, but that's part of the excitement.

Interview/Los Angeles Times, 2-28:(VI)8.

6

Robert Brustein
Founder and artistic director,
American Repertory Theatre,
Cambridge, Mass.

1

The American theatre, like American society, is most healthy when it is most pluralistic. All forms of culture are important in this country, whether commercial or non-commercial, conventional or experimental, popular or advanced. This means that any decline in the quality of Broadway offerings adversely affects everyone working in the theatre. It also means that the not-for-profit theatres centered in so many American cities must incessantly try to maintain their identity in the face of mounting pressures to change them. Only by adhering to our original goals can we continue to provide help for each other and preserve the diversity that becomes a great culture.

Upon accepting Jujamcyn Theatres Award,
New York, Nov. 25/The New York Times, 11-26:22.

Yul Brynner
Actor

2

I never thought about missing a performance [in a play]. It must be a special event for the people who've made the effort to come to the theatre. Every time, I must be fresh. That keeps me going.

Interview, New York/USA Today, 3-6:(D)1.

Fernando Bujones
Ballet dancer,
American Ballet Theatre

3

[Saying the "star system" should have a place in dance]: The present administration at ABT is trying to underscore the idea of equality among dancers, but this is just not true—certainly not at the box-office! Dancers are not interchangeable, as they would have us believe; their individual qualities as performers are important and should be acknowledged for what they are—those very qualities that have drawn the audience into the theatre in the first place. If the star system is not important, however, then where would that tour be that [Mikhail] Bary-shnikov himself led this summer, using many of ABT's dancers? Without Baryshnikov, *the star,* would box offices across the country be able to sell tickets? If the star system is dying, then why would ABT bring in a star from the Royal Ballet—Alessandra Ferri—for the current season at the Met? Furthermore, I don't think that all the younger dancers at ABT think that the star system is dying. If you ask some of them—young ones, new to the company—you'll find there are many who aspire to being stars, who would like someday to become ballerinas and danseurs . . . Dancers still need role models. It's an important part of learning your art, that which is handed down from generation to generation, that which older dancers give to younger dancers. Unfortunately, that isn't being encouraged.

Interview/Dancemagazine, September:67.

Michael Caine
Actor

4

[Comparing films with the stage]: I always find that I tend to watch comedy in the theatre, because if I go and see a drama I'm inclined to want to laugh when someone's serious on stage, because for someone brought up in movies I can see that the walls are made of canvas; and I very often get into awkward situations during a dramatic piece, when I'm the only one who's sitting there laughing! In the movies, you know that a tree is a tree and a person better be a person, and I've set myself the task of . . being accepted just as a person rather than as an actor, so that you are just watching a person, not a performance. You're watching a living person, the trees are real, the curtains are real, the spiders are real; and on stage, you suspend disbelief the minute you walk on. Or you better, otherwise you're going to think it's a load of crap. In movies, you don't suspend disbelief; the movies do that to you if they work.

Interview, London/
Films and Filming, January:28.

Liviu Ciulei
Artistic director,
Guthrie Theatre, Minneapolis

5

At the moment, it plays a very great role, the regional theatre. It's a theatre where things hap-

(LIVIU CIULEI)

pen. Things don't happen on Broadway at the moment. But they happen at the American Rep Theatre [in Cambridge, Mass.]; they happen in Washington at the Arena and at the National Theatre; and they happen in other places—maybe sporadically still. We have started it now . . . It will have a great impact on Broadway—theatre which represents an image of what we are today, and not just entertainment, not just a garage where you bring in show after show.

Interview, Minneapolis/
The Christian Science Monitor, 10-11:25.

Paul Connelly
Conductor, American Ballet Theatre

1

I have many reservations about the relations of music to dance. I wish that the repertoire were more interesting musically. And it would be nice if the attitude of some of the dancers and ballet masters toward music was on a higher level. Several people have been spoiled and think they can do as they please with music. Sometimes you hear a choreographer or ballet master say "Listen to the music!" But that's as far as it goes . . . The ideal is that there be a point of view established by the choreographer or ballet master, and that he or she have the necessary discussions with the conductor. You don't need cold, hard-and-fast rules. You just need to trust the people in charge.

Interview/Ballet News, June:24,25.

Jim Dale
Actor

2

[On acting on stage]: We only exist in people's memories. We don't exist on film or tape and we can't be played back. What happens tonight will never happen again . . . You rehearse and listen to the director, but finally, in the end, you're out there on your own. Your performance isn't being edited or added to by soundtracks, as in films.

Interview, New York/
The New York Times, 4-5:15.

Bob Fosse
Director

5

[On whether a show constantly changes during its run]: Unfortunately, yes. You build a cast emotionally, psychologically, physically to a

Dana Elcar
Actor

3

When you're younger, the fantasy life that theatre affords gives you a certain perspective, it makes you feel good. But as you get older, fantasy isn't enough. Theatre began to speak to me of freedom, beauty, love, not like other institutions such as the church . . . But it's also fun. My God! Still is! To do a play, get a group together—"What? You wanna do a play?"—it takes doing.

Interview, Los Angeles/
Los Angeles Times, 1-10:(VI)7.

Suzanne Farrell
Ballerina; Dance teacher,
School of American Ballet

4

[In teaching dance,] I'm interested in seeing something that is interesting to look at. Some people need more life in the arms. Some need them toned down. But that's the easy part. What they need most to learn is musicianship. But there is something else that is even harder to teach and to learn. You can call it "soul" or whatever you like. But it has to do with your identity as a dancer, the thing that is specifically you. "It's up to you to find that," I tell them. "I can't show you how to be special. What's special about you is distinctly yours." This gets a little heavy, but it's something they have to learn. I think that whatever value there is in my teaching has more to do with how I talk to them than what I tell them to do. I got that from Mr. B [George Balanchine]. I learned less from him about dance technique itself than about things that could apply to dancing. It didn't matter if it was about cooking or the Bible or whatever. It had to do with how to live and therefore, for a dancer, how to dance.

Interview, New York/Dancemagazine, June:42.

(BOB FOSSE)

peak for opening night. After that, things creep in you can't control . . . say your best dancer gets pregnant. The audience still sees a good show that's maybe 90 per cent, but I feel guilty because I know what it is at 99 per cent.

Interview/USA Today, 8-16:(B)4.

Martha Graham
Choreographer

1

Technique [in dance] is a joy and a terror, a bore at times, and a necessity always. Those who do not have order and discipline can never be dancers . . . If a student comes to me and asks, "Should I be a dancer?" I tell her, "If you have to ask, you should not."

Interview/Horizon, October:61.

A. R. Gurney
Playwright

2

Is play writing the toughest form? I think it *is* tough for those who are not happy under its restrictions. Some of us need those rules. Great playwrights—Shakespeare, Ibsen—redefined the rules under which other playwrights then played.

Interview, New York/ Los Angeles Times, 1-14:(VI)2.

Julie Harris
Actress

3

When I used to think of theatre, it was New York. Now producers almost can't afford to do it [there] and people really can't spend $40 and $50 for a ticket. That's not theatre any more. It's something else . . . But when you ask me where my allegiance is, my allegiance is first to a good play, and I don't care where I do it as long as somebody's there to see it. [In television,] it's different. I don't have any control. I hardly have any input. You work very fast. It's a little like vaudeville . . . [The stage is] where I started and where I've been the happiest overall. I can believe in a play, in the characters, in the prose or,

if it's Shakespeare, it's the language that I love, the sound of it and the ideas—and the performance being *live*.

Interview, Pacific Palisades, Calif./ Los Angeles Times, 9-5:(VI)6.

Rex Harrison
Actor

4

Theatre was extraordinary when angry young men came in and hated everything . . . But nobody hates anything anymore. The '80s are strange . . . That's why I do revivals.

Interview, New York/USA Today, 4-29:(D)1.

5

. . . I've always enjoyed playing [the light] sort of English comedies, which aren't written any more. I like the style of acting; it enables one to assume a naturalism that has gone totally out of style. Well, it's in style, but no one can do it. Naturalism is appearing to be perfectly natural. Of course, you're not; if you were, nothing much would happen. You have to have a very strong degree of energy to *appear* to be acting natural. But I think this kind of thing is coming back into vogue. I think people got absolutely sick of having messages thrown at their heads.

Interview, New York/ The New York Times, 5-8:24.

Marcia Haydee
Ballerina

6

Onstage you should never be just what you are. You have to find the essence of the thing. It is the essence of youth. It is the essence of maturity, even of aging. To have true power on the stage, one must know all of that. No, I never think about the physical risks [of dancing] because I believe that with the mind one can do anything. It's the mind that blocks us. If you get scared of doing something, then you won't be able to do it. But if you believe, you can do anything. When one reads Gandhi, one sees what you can do with the power of the mind. I believe that while the mind is young, while you believe that you can help people, believe that you can

455

(MARCIA HAYDEE)

bring something beautiful into the world, well, then you will be able to go on performing. It is only when you start thinking about being a star, or being a "great dancer," that things go wrong.

Interview/Ballet News, March:13.

Helen Hayes

Actress

1

You don't have to be crazy to be an actor, but it's kind of usual. Or to be in the theatre in any capacity, I guess. We're gypsies and we're odd; we're different. But we have some kind of wonderful impulse that draws us to this theatre and I say "Wonderful!" because it is the most rewarding thing I can think of that happens. An actor once gave me a verse written on the back of a menu at the Players Club in New York, and I want to say it for you because it sums up all of what I think about theatre. It's called "A Theatre Speaks to the Actor."

I will give you hunger and pain,
and sleepless nights
and happiness known to few.
Beauty, glimpses of the heavenly light.
All of these things you will have not continuously;
And of their coming and going
you shall not be foretold.

That's an actor's life and a good one and a rich one.

At presentation of first Helen Hayes Award, Washington, May 13/The New York Times, 5-28:10.

Glenda Jackson

Actress

2

[Acting in the theatre is] not a life that I like. I find it deeply unnatural to go to work when most people are coming home. The physical conditions of the work are usually painful and unpleasant and cold and drafty. And why do it? The only reason for doing it is the work itself, and if that doesn't have some quality, then forget it.

Interview, New York/ The Washington Post, 3-11:(B)8.

Bob Hope

Entertainer

3

Comedy is just about impossible to explain. You have the different formats—ridicule, satire, tearing down the dignity of a king or a President; but when you try to explain timing . . . I've seen civilians [non-show business professionals] with a wonderful sense of timing—knowing how to lob it in there at the right time with the right speed. But it's so hard to explain. It's a combination of mind and mouth that you have to master.

Interview/TV Guide, 12-14:32.

Milton Katselas

Director

4

I still feel inhibited when I interrupt an actor. But I think anyone's motive for wanting to do a play is that you see something in it you want to articulate. If you teach or direct, it's the same thing—you set out to say something. I never like to stop actors, but you have to step in.

Interview, Los Angeles/ Los Angeles Times, 1-22:(VI)4.

Gene Kelly

Actor, Dancer

5

The thing that I do [dancing in film] is not the same as my friends [choreographers] Peter Martins or Jerry Robbins, because they're with dance companies and they use dance with music to express a certain idea in the context of a complete dance that includes music. The dancer in film for years has not done that. He takes a role. He gets a group of songs sometimes and interprets the role. If he is a truck driver, he cannot come out and dance in fifth position. Everybody would laugh. If he is a prince consort, he would have to dance a certain way. If I played a pirate in the early 19th century, I certainly couldn't tap dance. So the role of the dancer is subject to the role he's playing and often very subject to the song that's composed. This doesn't happen in a dance company. The question is who has the greater freedom.

Interview, New York/ The New York Times, 1-17:16.

(GENE KELLY)

1

Without doubt, dancing onstage is much better than dancing on film. Onstage, you not only have the personality of the performer impinging on the audience's reactions, but the dancer's kinetic force as well. The kinetic force elicits a muscular response from the audience, and you can't get that on the screen. The other thing that happens when you dance on film is that you're only seen by one eye—the camera eye. You negate all the peripheral vision that an audience has in a theatre, where the dancer's environment is a factor.

Interview/Ballet News, April:15.

Robert La Fosse
Ballet dancer,
American Ballet Theatre

2

Today, the "stars" are choreographers [rather than the dancers]. And that's as it should be. Yes, I suppose the star system was wonderful in its day. It brought a lot of money to ABT and it's what the public seemed to want. But the dance world has changed. I think people are coming to see the ballets. I don't think they're coming to see *me* . . . or anybody else. Of course, it's nice when they do come and see us, but I look at it this way: When I hear there's a revival of a Tennessee Williams play, I want to go and see it because I've never seen it. To me, it makes no difference *who* is starring in it. That's the way it should be in ballet. It's the ballet that counts.

Interview/Dancemagazine, May:102.

Robert Linowes
Head of the board
of Folger Shakespeare Library Theatre,
Washington

3

Why should we care about classical theatre? Because we need it—this city [Washington] needs it, the nation needs it, and so does the world. We need classical theatre not simply because classical theatre educates, enlightens and entertains, which it certainly does, and not simply because it makes us laugh and weep and wonder and dream and believe, and sometimes even suspend belief. We need a strong, vibrant classical theatre because theatres are essential to the cultural well-being of any community, especially ours, and because classical theatre featuring the work of Shakespeare, Moliere, Chekhov, Ben Jonson and the like embodies the finest of our collective heritage . . . In a cultural atmosphere anesthetized by television, where the average household watches about eight hours a day, the intellectual challenges of classical theatre provide essential stimulation. In a society increasingly caught up in trivial pursuits, classical theatre has the courage to take on more lasting and universal themes. When [TV's] *Dallas* is held up as the paragon of drama, when [TV's] *Laverne and Shirley* is considered the height of comedy, when [TV's] *The Gong Show* models human behavior, the value of classical theatre as an essential antidote cannot be overestimated.

At celebration of Folger Theatre's
recent fund drive, Washington, Sept. 10/
The New York Times, 9-17:12.

Natalia Makarova
Ballerina

4

We don't have many ballerinas any more. A ballerina must have personality. She is not just a principal dancer. Being a ballerina takes more. She must say something. She must make a mark. She must approach the ideal image of the choreography. Or, like me, she must grab everywhere to try to achieve something.

Interview, San Francisco/
Los Angeles Times, 3-3: (Calendar) 50.

5

What does the word "star" mean? It's just a word. People become stars because they did something in art. They said something. They left a mark. Ballet is not Hollywood. It comes through a lifetime of work. Ours is a different type of stardom. In ballet, stardom doesn't come overnight as it does in Hollywood. It's not the same as being a movie star, because we work every single day of our lives to improve ourselves. It's constant, continuous work, and it's a question of growth—personal, emotional and artistic growth. So if a dancer becomes a star, that

WHAT THEY SAID IN 1985

(NATALIA MAKAROVA)

stardom has been won through the sweat of our brows. To say that the star system is dead is to speak empty words.

Interview, Dancemagazine, August:46.

Bruce Marks
Artistic director, Ballet West;
Artistic director-designate, Boston Ballet

1

I think the San Francisco Ballet looks like San Francisco—it's glitzy; it loves any kind of controversy and newness; it's just like its city. And then you see Ballet West [of Salt Lake City], and they're all dancing with this big open style, wide-eyed. No one puts their nose in the air. You go to—excuse me—New York companies sometimes, and you see people with their chin lifted just a little bit higher that says: "We're the best. We live in New York". . . . Each company has to find its own face, and that's hard to do in this day and age when everyone's dancing the same repertoire.

Interview, Boston/
The Christian Science Monitor, 5-1:7.

Elizabeth McCann
Producer

2

[On the Broadway theatre]: We're dealing here with an art form in transition, an industry in aesthetic turmoil . . . We need to be more theatrical, innovative. We need to face the fact that we have to reach a mass entertainment audience. Maybe if the [economic] situation gets bad enough, we'll all put our heads together and start dealing with the problems. I think we're beginning to. We have to remember that what affects Broadway affects the theatre in general.

Los Angeles Times, 5-29:(VI)2.

Mike Nichols
Director

3

I passionately believe that in art, and certainly in the theatre, there are only two questions, and just like in life or analysis, if you've ever been through either of those, the same thing

458

is learned over and over and over—it's always the same thing and you keep thinking, "Why didn't I remember it from last time?" But you don't. The first question is: "What is this really when it happens in life?" Not what is the accepted convention, not what do we always do when this comes up, but what is it really like? And the other question we really have to ask is, "What happens next?" . . . "What happens next?" is a question I really urge you all to ask yourselves in any kind of work, if you're writing or working on movies or anything that expresses our lives. Then it will be you and it will never have happened before and therefore, because it's accurately you, everyone will recognize it and say, "Oh, yes, that's me, too."

Libby Zion lecture, Yale University;
April 18/The New York Times, 4-20:12.

Al Pacino
Actor

4

You bend your psyche if you are an actor, and it really is a relief when it's over. Even after *Richard III* closed, around 8 at night I'd find myself walking with a limp. The body doesn't know a role is over until the mind tells it.

Interview, Beverly Hills, Calif/
Los Angeles Times, 12-29:(Calendar)24.

Joseph Papp
Producer

5

Last season I had 14 or 15 shows [at the off-Broadway Public Theatre]. None of which—thank God—I had to take the risk of bringing to Broadway this season.

New York, June 2/USA Today, 6-3:(D)2.

6

I've never lost faith in theatre. And even though I have a very successful film out now . . . I would still rather have a hit show, in the park, off-Broadway, on Broadway, anywhere. There is nothing in the world of entertainment like a cast of characters doing a play or a musical on stage right then and there. That moment, that evening, will never be replaced.

(JOSEPH PAPP)

Every performance is a once-in-a-lifetime for a performer and the audience. God, I love it.

Interview/USA Today, 10-21:(D)2.

Robert Preston
Actor

1

I'm still reading plays, because something might really grab me and break through the series of objections I have to the [Broadway] theatre today, first among them being the ticket prices. My audience—the ideal audience—can't afford the theatre any more. By and large, you're playing to an expense-account audience.

*Interview, Los Angeles/
The New York Times, 2-20:18.*

Harold Prince
Producer

2

There are two propositions with which I totally and absolutely disagree. The first is that if people want to see a play, they will pay almost anything to see it; and the second is that Broadway has no problems that a blockbuster hit won't solve. Ticket prices are too high, period. Not only do we need a greater mix of prices at the box-office, we must have lower top prices. I don't subscribe to the notion that kids pay huge prices for a Bruce Springsteen concert and, they'll pay the same on Broadway. A rock concert is a once-a-year thing. Broadway should be a habit, with people going every month or six weeks. But they'll never do that at today's prices.

The Wall Street Journal, 10-8:28.

Edvard Radzinsky
Soviet playwright

3

The theatre is not just an art, it is one of the most mysterious and important of the arts. It is part of culture, of education. Why does it have to survive with such difficulty in such a rich country [the U.S.]? Why do great actors have to work as waiters? I don't understand this. [It is marvelous that] these [theatre] people maintain this

wonderful fanaticism. From the point of view of normal people, they must be a little crazy. But only the mad can make art. And I would wish that normal people would help these crazy people a little. Because if they suddenly ceased being mad, something very important would die in this world.

*Interview, New York/
The Christian Science Monitor, 9-25:23*

Vanessa Redgrave
Actress

4

It's in theatre that you [as an actor] really stretch, because you have to sustain and re-create for an audience, communicate each night. All actors who want to develop as actors will turn to the classics, as musicians [do].

*Interview, Los Angeles/
Los Angeles Times, 3-19:(VI)1.*

Christopher Reeve
Actor

5

Given the temptation of the movies, we actors who were trained on the stage can often lose touch with that dream—that the stage is, after all, the ultimate place to be.

USA Today, 5-20:(E)7.

Jason Robards
Actor

6

[Saying he dislikes many of the works of current playwrights]: I don't see why I have to pay $50 to see people taking cocaine in Hollywood [referring to David Rabe's *Hurlyburly*]. And if you took out all the profanity in [David Mamet's] *Glengarry Glen Ross*, you'd have a 25-minute play. It means nothing, looking at a bunch of scum all the time. Playwrights are a dime a dozen. But as Mrs. O'Neill [widow of writer Eugene O'Neill] said, "Eugene is not a playwright, he's a *dramatist*." There are very few. Shaw, Shakespeare, O'Neill. Marvelous, wonderful roles, very specific for the actor . . . roles that give you a helping hand, not something that you have to dream up. It's all about serving the play. It's not about serving yourself. People get

459

(JASON ROBARDS)

this mixed up. It's an era of television, big stupid stars, imagery, and they forget what the hell it's all about.

Interview, Washington/USA Today, 8-12:(D)1.

Murray Schisgal
Playwright

1

When I started writing in the early '60s, it was possible to be a professional playwright and earn a living in the theatre. That's no longer possible; there just aren't enough opportunities. Consequently, I appreciate my theatre work so much more. I love the idea of not having to fill a 1,500-seat house, get tacky or jokey or schmaltzy or raunchy so that it appeals to a wide audience. For me, that keeps theatre special.

*Interview, Los Angeles/
Los Angeles Times, 9-30:(VI)5.*

Neil Simon
Playwright

[On the plays he writes which chronicle his life]: I think you discover things by writing; it can be therapeutic. And I wanted to know how this extremely shy, not enormously well-educated boy came to do what I consider a very hard thing to do—write plays. I wanted to see how I became the person I am. I seem to be, in my own mind, a very unlikely candidate for success. It's like when I see [actress] Joan Collins on the Johnny Carson show, I say, "Yeah, she was made to be on the Johnny Carson show." But when I see myself there, I say, "What are you doing there? You belong in the Bronx playing stickball." I don't feel like that all the time; I can go to an opening night and deal with all the cameras. But then I go home and I'm depressed somehow, because I don't understand how this all happened.

*Interview, New York/
The New York Times, 4-1:16.*

Peter Sellars
*Artistic director,
American National Theatre,
Kennedy Center, Washington*

2

[On his plans for the new American National Theatre]: The theatre is the most depressed art form in America. Either we continue with quick fixes, or we recognize that we've got to rethink the whole thing from the bottom up. That's what we'll be doing over the next five years—radically re-thinking the way theatre is done. I see it as five years of research and development. Kodak and Polaroid recognize the value of research and development and know that after five years they'll come up with a better camera. It should be the same for theatre. In this charter season, we'll be floating balloons and testing a wide range of work.

*Interview, Washington, Jan. 23/
The Washington Post, 1-24:(D)1.*

3

Theatre is political; it always will be. In ancient Greece, the politicians all knew that the theatre put them in touch with what the country

460

was thinking. In Elizabethan England, Shakespeare's plays let the Queen know where she stood in the context of history. His great plays about kings were really about where England was going. Policy-making tends to be done in the abstract. But theatre puts you in the other guy's shoes for 2 hours; you suddenly realize how he or she feels. There's no distance; you're in the room with the person. Most people in policy-making positions don't get that in real life. When they do, frequently their lives are in danger. In theatre, there is no personal threat; everybody lives. The audience faces death, and at the end the curtain comes down and everyone can applaud and go home. The actors don't just lie there and keep bleeding. You can make policy decisions—and nobody dies. That's a luxury politicians usually don't have.

Interview/U.S. News & World Report, 3-4:91.

4

[On writing comedy plays]: It's the hardest writing there is, because it's relentless. The audience becomes extremely greedy. There's a play called *Noises Off*, which may be the funniest

5

(NEIL SIMON)

farce ever written since, let's say, *Three Men on a Horse*. If that had 10 minutes out of its two hours of playing time that just were not funny, the audience would be terribly disappointed. But if you were to do a dramatic picture, and if there were 10 minutes in the picture that were slow, but the picture built to this enormous impact and a terrific climax, the audience wouldn't mind that. They'd sit and watch it. But with a farce, the audience is as greedy as can be. They want to laugh all the time.

Interview/USA Today, 4-22:(A)11.

1

In the beginning, I had a lot of critical success plus popular success. Then the critical success sort of dropped away. It was mostly popular, bolstered by enough good reviews to get the play out to the audience, and the audience then made up their own minds. But the critics started to head away from me in other directions, saying, Here comes another whizzbang comedy, and we're not interested in whizzbang comedies. I never thought that they were whizzbang comedies, and the audience didn't take them that way. And then, suddenly, everything reversed with *Brighton Beach* [*Memoirs*], and on top of that, *Biloxi Blues* even more so. And so, like the Gershwin song—*They Can't Take That Away From Me*—I've written them now. At least I've been to that place where I wanted to get to in my search to become a better playwright, and I've achieved it in some measure. It's not that the critical reaction has changed me. It's just pointed out to me that I have broken through another barrier as a playwright. I mean, they used to write about how much money I was earning and things like that. If you already have success, they aren't very eager to give you more success.

*Interview/
Horizon, June:60.*

Paul Taylor
Choreographer

2

[When conducting rehearsals,] I usually don't yell, but I can become terribly threatening. I've

actually hit dancers. I've bitten little fingers that stuck out too much; I've slapped wrists; I've threatened to throw people out of the window. People don't usually learn unless there's a little pain involved. When a new dancer joins the group, he feels he has to prove himself; he's somewhat insecure. So I sometimes intentionally see what a little stress and strain will do to him, at what point he's going to break. Naturally, each one is different. Dancers are like animals that you train: While you don't usually do it by bullying them, you don't necessarily do it by giving them little yummies, either. Still, I find that one very effective thing, in bringing out the best in them, is encouragement—judiciously administered.

Interview/Dancemagazine, April:57.

Twyla Tharp
Choreographer

3

I never paid attention to the writings on my work when everyone hated it, and now I don't pay attention to them although they tend to be very positive. I would describe your [dance critics'] enterprise as futile. Dancing is done precisely because it is not something that can be described through writing . . . Writers cannot dictate to the public what to see and what to avoid. The public must learn to make up its own mind. Too many dance writers make their opinion the dominant element of the dance. I think, How dare they! And yet it's undeniable that the dance press is a strong contingent in the arts. I'm certainly not advocating war between dancemakers and dance writers. For me, the bottom line is that I don't need the approval of writers, though I'm still concerned about the effects of bad reviews on my dancers. I tell them just to keep going, to follow through with what feels right for them.

Interview, New York/Dancemagazine, August:41.

Kurt Vonnegut, Jr.
Author

4

. . . there have been virtually no novelists who have written good plays, and also there have been virtually no playwrights who have written

461

WHAT THEY SAID IN 1985

(KURT VONNEGUT, JR.)

good novels. I think a young writer comes to a fork in the road very early and becomes one sort of a writer or the other. When I was young, there were a lot of very good playwrights, people like Tennessee Williams and William Saroyan, and, God, I would get to New York to see what they were doing. That sort of thing is happening now . . . I envy those people. I'd rather be a playwright than a novelist now, because it seems to me that they're doing a lot more.

Interview, New York/Writer's Digest, November:27.

Lanford Wilson
Playwright

1

[On rewriting revivals of his plays]: It's almost impossible to go back and . . . put your head in the same place it was 15 years ago. When you're writing a play, its whole universe is in your head—the history of every character, the stagecraft. When you try to fix things later, you solve one problem, but then five other things are thrown out of synch.

Interview, New York/
The New York Times, 12-26:16.

Philosophy

Walter Annenberg
*Former United States Ambassador
to the United Kingdom;
Owner, "TV Guide" magazine*

1

As I've grown older, I earnestly believe that people who are not subjected to some adversity usually end up as well-fed housedogs.

*Interview, Rancho Mirage, Calif./
USA Today, 11-5:(D)7.*

David Attenborough
Author, Naturalist

2

Some of the greatest pleasures that come from life come from the natural world. Nothing gives me greater pleasure, in terms of beauty, than birds of paradise or hummingbirds or butterflies. I don't know anything that gives me a greater sense of drama than an exploding volcano or a migrating wildebeest. I don't know anything that I find more riveting than trying to follow the life history of a complicated insect. The natural world is of the greatest interest to small children of three and professors of 93, to bankers of 50 and coal miners of 30. This is one of the most primary and fundamental pleasures in life.

Interview/USA Today, 2-1:(A)7.

William J. Bennett
*Secretary of Education
of the United States*

3

Happiness is like a cat. If you try to coax it or call it, it will avoid you; it will never come. But if you pay no attention to it and go about your business, you'll find it rubbing against your legs and jumping into your lap. So forget pursuing happiness. Pin your hopes on work, on family, on learning, on knowing, on loving. Forget pursuing happiness. Pursue other things. And, with luck, happiness will come.

*At Assumption College commencement/
Time, 6-17:69.*

Rose Elizabeth Bird
*Chief Justice,
Supreme Court of California*

4

My own personal feeling . . . is that being a vegetarian makes one much more pacific as a person. I'm not quite sure whether that's psychological or whether in fact there is something psychological involved. But, through getting in touch with your inner sea of calm, you also get in touch with nature and with the beauty of all aspects of the planet.

Interview/The Washington Post, 10-23:(A)3.

Fernand Braudel
French historian

5

I believe in the progress of humankind—in intelligence and character. But history advances like a Spanish procession: two steps forward, and one, or even two, back. Every accomplishment creates new problems. Material comfort, for example, has been purchased at the expense of a rise in criminality. In the structures of history, there is not only God; there is also the Devil.

Interview/World Press Review, March:32.

Cleanth Brooks
*Author, Critic; Professor emeritus
of rhetoric, Yale University*

6

[On the importance of individuality]: Computers are programmed by human beings; but human beings move toward the state of being computers when they allow themselves to be programmed by other human beings.

*Jefferson Lecture, Washington, May 8/
The Christian Science Monitor, 5-13:23.*

George Bush
Vice President of the United States

7

Democracy is necessary, as Abraham Lincoln once explained, because "no man is good

463

(GEORGE BUSH)

enough that he should rule another without his consent"... The plain truth is that mankind longs for freedom and democracy, and if we underestimate that fact, we will misunderstand the significance of the great political events going on around us.

At Wheaton (Ill.) College commencement/
USA Today, 6-3:(A)11.

Sid Caesar
Comedian

1

Nobody is completely happy. I don't look for perfection any more. Right now is perfection. I don't have to be the best or the biggest any more. The greatest joy is appreciation. Once you have something in life and almost lose it and manage to get it back, you learn about appreciation.

Interview, New York/
The Christian Science Monitor, 4-17:23.

Fidel Castro
President of Cuba

2

Money does not motivate me; material goods do not motivate me. Likewise, the lust for glory, fame and prestige does not motivate me. I really think that ideas motivate me. Ideas, convictions are what spur a man to struggle in the first place. When you are truly devoted to an idea, you feel more convinced and more committed with each passing year. I think that personal selflessness grows; the spirit of sacrifice grows; you gradually relinquish your personal pride, vanity... all those elements that in one way or another exist in all men. If you do not guard against those vanities, if you let yourself become conceited or think that you are irreplaceable or indispensable, you can become infatuated with all of that— the riches, the glory. I've been on guard against those things. Maybe I have developed a philosophy on man's relative importance, on the relative value of individuals, the conviction that it is not the individual but the people who make history, the idea that I can't lay claim to the merits of an entire people. A phrase by Jose Marti left in me a deep and unforgettable impression: "All the glory of the world fits into a kernel of corn."

Interview, Havana/Playboy, August:58.

3

...I think the cruelest people on earth are the ones who are indifferent to social injustice, discrimination, inequality, the exploitation of others—people who don't react when they see a child with no shoes, a beggar in the streets or millions of hungry people. I really think that people who have spent all their lives struggling against injustice and oppression, serving others, fighting for others and practicing and preaching solidarity cannot possibly be cruel. I'd say that what is really cruel is a society—a capitalist one, for instance—that not only is cruel in itself but forces man to be cruel. Socialism is just the opposite. By definition, it expresses confidence and faith in man, in solidarity among men and in the brotherhood of man—not selfishness, ambition, competition or struggle. I believe that cruelty is born of selfishness, ambition, inequality, injustice, competition and struggle among men.

Interview, Havana/Playboy, August:66.

Ray Charles
Musician

4

I'm not into the money thing. You can only sleep in one bed at a time. You can only eat one meal at a time, or be in one car, or be in one place at a time. So I don't have to have millions of dollars to be happy. All I need is to have some clothes on my back, eat a decent meal when I want to, and get a little loving when I feel like it. That's the bottom line, man.

Interview/USA Today, 11-1:(A)11.

Howard Cosell
Commentator, ABC Sports

5

The focus on [baseball player] Pete Rose's quest to beat Ty Cobb's [hitting] record typifies what's going on [in society today]. It's as if that's more important than achieving a nuclear peace. The answer to all of society's problems is not lodged in the game. A society that thinks

(HOWARD COSELL)

otherwise—a society whose values are so disordered—cannot prosper or even long survive.

Interview/U.S. News & World Report, 9-16:74.

Jacques Cousteau
Explorer, Environmentalist

1

I have made friends with death. I mean that I have accepted it not only as inevitable but also as constructive. If we didn't die, we would not appreciate life as we do. So it's a constructive force.

Interview, Washington/
Los Angeles Times, 6-13:(V)27.

E. L. Doctorow
Author

2

Being a child is a time we don't want to remember, usually, because it's too painful. What we remember about our childhood is the humiliation of it, a state of almost constant humiliation, of terrors and fears and nightmares and powerlessness and shame.

Interview, Los Angeles/
Los Angeles Times, 12-11:(V)1.

Robert J. Dole
United States Senator, R-Kansas

3

[On his 62nd birthday]: I find I am always glad when the birthday is over. Then you have another whole year. The most difficult ones are the ones that end with a zero—20,30,40,50,60, whatever. Those are the hard ones. The others are sort of rest periods between the zeros.

Before the Senate, Washington, July 22/
The Wall Street Journal, 9-24:32.

Clint Eastwood
Actor

4

There's a rebel lying deep in my soul. Anytime anybody tells me the trend is such and such,

I go in the opposite direction. I hate the idea of trends. I hate imitation. I have a reverence for individuality. I got where I am by coming off the wall.

Interview, Carmel, Calif./Newsweek, 7-22:54.

Nikki Giovanni
Poet

5

Hopefully, we communicate with each other; we share with each other; we learn to love somebody some time, recognizing that nothing is permanent. But we would not stop the sunset because we cannot see it every day; we would enjoy it when it comes. We would not decide that we don't want a full moon because we only get 12 of them a year. Beauty is its own reward. And no matter how transitory it is, it is nice to know that there is something beautiful or something lovely or something we can take joy in.

At Loyola Marymount University,
November/Los Angeles Times, 12-4:(V)5.

Martha Graham
Choreographer

6

I'm not sure what genius is. Edgard Varese, the composer, once told me, "Everyone is born with genius, Martha. The sad thing is that most people only keep it for a few minutes." We exist in space—that is the energy of the world, and each of us is a recipient of that energy if he so wills. Some people get old and sit on the porch [in their minds] at 16, and other people are willing to seek out the energy of the world at 60 and beyond. There has to be about you a transparency to receive the energy around you—maybe that's what genius is; I don't really know.

Interview/Horizon, October:64.

Katharine Hepburn
Actress

7

I go mad when I read about kids cheating on exams in school, and now even in the Army and Navy. When I was at college at Bryn Mawr we had an honor system, and if any girl was found cheating, she was kicked out. The point is, if

465

(KATHARINE HEPBURN)

you're going to cheat as a kid, and they let you get by with it, you begin to join the criminal classes, don't you? Either you're honorable or dishonorable. The distinction is very clear in my mind, though apparently not to a lot of other people.

Interview, New York/
Ladies' Home Journal, February:176.

Glenda Jackson
Actress

1

One knows one's done one's job as a parent properly if one's children reject everything one stands for.

Interview, New York/
The Wall Street Journal, 2-15:20.

John Paul II
Pope

2

The ultimate determining factor is the human person. It is not science and technology, or the increasing means of economic and material development, but the human person, and especially groups of persons, communities and nations, freely choosing to face the problems together, who will, under God, determine the future. That is why whatever impedes human freedom, or dishonors it, such as the evil of apartheid and all forms of prejudice and discrimination, is an affront to man's vocation to shape his own destiny.

Nairobi, Kenya, Aug. 18/
The Washington Post, 8-19:(A)21.

Milan Kundera
Exiled Czech author

3

. . . all I can see as expressions of cultural life [today] are TV soaps, vulgar articles in the press, clever ads for consumer goods, and a preoccupation with one's physical shape—like jogging. Over here [in the West], like over there [in Eastern Europe], a cultural vacuum. Obviously, the end of an era. Perhaps the beginning of a new

barbarian age? The point is not so much *how* this is happening—whether through Communist police brutality, Nazi coercion, gradual alienation in Western democracies—but *what* is happening. What deep, common process is at work that lowers man, that leads him back to tribal behavior, that crushes spiritual and humanistic values?

Interview, Paris/
The Christian Science Monitor, 9-6:(B)3.

Ernst Kux
Swiss political scientist; Foreign editor,
"Neue Zürcher Zeitung," Zurich

4

Communist economies are losing the competition with capitalist economies. From the days of Marx, the main aim of Communism has been to supplant capitalism and provide a better economic system. Twenty years ago, [the late Soviet Premier] Nikita Khrushchev predicted that the Soviet Union would overtake the United States. But today the economic gap between the two countries is greater than ever . . . Marxism-Leninism just doesn't fit a modern industrial society. It has proved incapable of adapting to the scientific-technological revolution of our time. So has the Stalinist model, with its stress on centralized planning, heavy industry and tight controls over labor. Even Soviet leaders are now beginning to recognize this.

Interview, Zurich/
U.S. News & World Report, 2-4:43.

Andrew Lytle
Author, Editor

5

No man creates. God creates. [Man gives] a special view to what was always there.

At Southern Literary Festival,
Nicholls State University/
The Christian Science Monitor, 5-8:28.

Carlos Manini Rios
Minister of the Interior
of Uruguay

6

Democracy is a bit like that old Spanish story of a boy and his grandfather walking home with

(CARLOS MANINI RIOS)

their burro on a hot afternoon. The grandfather rides until a passer-by scolds him for abusing the child. Then the child rides until somebody complains he is not showing respect for his grandfather. So they both ride, until another busybody asks how they could be so cruel to the burro. Somehow, they get home. Democracy never pleases everybody. But nobody has yet come up with a better recipe for governing free men.

Interview, Montevideo, Uruguay/
Los Angeles Times, 6-10:(I)14.

Marcello Mastroianni
Actor

1

I work all the time. It gives me the illusion that I am younger and will not die. And what else can I do? I am ignoramus. I don't like music, I don't like reading, I don't like to work in the garden, I don't like to take trips. So I act. Anyway, I need money. I spend everything I make. To me, my career is a sort of dream, one that will end some day. Someone will tap me on my shoulder and say, "It's over. Give us back what we've given you." When that day comes, I want to be able to say, "Aha, there is nothing left; I spent it all."

Interview, Los Angeles/
Los Angeles Times, 11-3:(Calendar)16.

Edwin Meese III
Attorney General
of the United States

2

[On a commission he named to study pornography and recommend ways of dealing with it]: Formation of this commission reflects the concern a healthy society must have regarding the ways in which its people publicly entertain themselves. The commission is an affirmation of the proposition that the purpose of a democracy involves . . . the achievement of the good life and the good society.

News conference, Washington, May 20/
The Washington Post, 5-21:(A)16.

George Michanowsky
Archives chairman,
Explorers Club, New York

3

[On what kind of person becomes an explorer]: One in a hundred. That is the rarity of the person who possesses the spark that ignites the spirit of exploration. What caused [Robert] Peary to run for the [North] Pole or Amelia Earhart to circumnavigate the globe? Chalk it up to the essential human drive to see what's over the next hill. The life of an explorer is an inconvenient life, a crazy life, but it is this inspired absurdity that moves human history off center.

The Christian Science Monitor,
7-5:19.

James A. Michener
Author

4

I think it's much more difficult to be a kid now than when I was a boy. Drugs. Violence. Confusion. The escalation of things causes young people to be drawn into situations before they're ready. I see little girls nine and 10 being put into beauty pageants. What in the world are they doing in beauty pageants? As for little tots being thrown into that sort of thing—now, that's disgraceful. I think it's important to remember that it's not the primary job of the young person to make his parents happy. His primary job is to reach his potential.

Interview, Austin, Texas/
The Saturday Evening Post,
September:32.

Bill Moyers
Journalist

5

The great enemy of understanding is imprecise language. Yet the pollution of our language spreads everywhere, like great globs of sludge crowding the shores of public thought.

At Lyndon B. Johnson School
of Public Affairs commencement,
University of Texas, Austin/
U.S. News & World Report, 6-3:66.

Francine Patterson
President and research director,
Gorilla Foundation; Adjunct professor
of psychology, University of
Santa Clara (Calif.)

1

Despite the evidence that apes have intelligence, many people just dismiss it as impossible. We have a very human-centered view of the world, and ascribing intelligence to animals is threatening to some people. We don't like to admit that we are animals, too, and we share many behavioral characteristics with the great apes. If we do realize that animals have intelligence and emotions, it changes our whole relationship to the natural world. Instead of being above it and dominating over all, we have to treat animals and their homelands in a more respectful way.

Interview/U.S. News & World Report, 7-22:72.

Neil Postman
Author; Professor of communications arts
and sciences, New York University

2

When a population becomes distracted by trivia, when cultural life is redefined as a perpetual round of entertainments, when serious public conversation becomes a form of baby-talk, when, in short, a people become an audience and their public business a vaudeville act, then a nation finds itself at risk; culture-death is a clear possibility.

Interview/
The Christian Science Monitor, 11-25:29.

Ronald Reagan
President of the United States

3

At the start of this century, there were only a handful of democracies, but today more than 50 countries, one-third of the world's population, are living under democratic rule. One of the engines of this progress is the desire for economic development—the realization that it is free nations that prosper and free peoples who create better lives for themselves and their children. This realization is growing throughout the world, and in some nations it is causing conflict

and disorder. In a sense, then, Marx was right—economic progress is leading to clashes with old, entrenched political orders. But Marx was wrong about where all this would occur; for it is the democratic world that is flexible, vibrant and growing—bringing its peoples higher and higher standards of living even as freedom grows and deepens. It is in the collectivist world that economies stagnate, that technology is lagging, and that the people are oppressed and unhappy with their lives. So everywhere we turn there is an uprising of mind and will against the old cliches of collectivism.

Before Portuguese Assembly of the Republic,
Lisbon, May 9/
The New York Times, 5-10:6.

4

One of the most damaging lies of our era is the falsehood that people must give up freedom to enjoy economic progress, which makes me think of a story . . . about three dogs: an American dog and a Polish dog and a Russian dog. And they were all having a visit, and the American dog was telling them about how things were in this country. He said, "You know, you bark; and if you have to, you bark long enough, and then somebody comes along and gives you some meat." And the Polish dog said, "What's meat?" And the Russian dog says, "What's bark?"

Before Council of the Americas,
Washington/The New York Times,
5-28:10.

Jonas Salk
Physician, Scientist

5

When we understand ourselves and our motivations, we might then be able to bring these under some restraint and begin to engage in more self-restraint and in a more disciplined way of dealing with each other. That would be to everyone's advantage . . . I use as thinking tools many of the ideas that come from my understanding of how life works—how nature works. Wisdom is beginning to emerge out of necessity.

Interview/
USA Today, 9-10:(A)9.

Jack Santino
Assistant professor of popular culture,
Bowling Green State University

1

[On fads]: Fads, no matter where they occur, create a certain kind of status. Those who buy a Pet Rock, Cabbage Patch doll or Trivial Pursuit game often have a sense of being part of an in-group. Fads also appeal to people's desire to be part of something that is new, creative, avant-garde. It seems that part of the American mentality is the idea that if there isn't constant change, something must be wrong. If you feel blue, go out and buy a new hat. Your 5-year-old car may be perfectly good, but you yearn for this year's model with its fresh styling. But I don't want to give the idea that fads are purely an American phenomenon. Any country with a large technological base and a consumer-driven economy, such as Japan and Britain, is susceptible to fads. Just look at the swift changes in fashion and popular music in Britain down through the years.

Interview/U.S. News & World Report, 2-11:44.

Victoria Secunda
Author

2

America is the worst country as far as youth obsession is concerned. It's very difficult to ignore those ads that say, for instance, "Does everyone at work suddenly look younger than you?" "Do you see your mother in the mirror?" There is no question that this is insidious—this pervasive insistence on viewing signs of experience as akin to laundry stains. If you have a wrinkle, the only way the cosmetics industry is going to succeed is to tell you that wrinkle is a terrible, terrible flaw that must be fixed by buying something. You cannot be both seasoned and 22. So why should we be ashamed of the evidence of that seasoning? We're taught to be ashamed. So we're filling in our wrinkles with silly putty and covering our gray hairs with hair dye. Just as we're living longer than ever, we're trying to get rid of the evidence of experience on our faces.

Interview/The Christian Science Monitor, 2-25:23.

Albert Shanker
President,
American Federation of Teachers

3

Power is a good thing. It is better than powerlessness. But there are two ways to use power—by having control over people or by leadership.

The Christian Science Monitor, 2-25:28.

George P. Shultz
Secretary of State
of the United States

4

As we head toward the 21st century, it is time for the democracies to celebrate their system, their beliefs and their success. We face challenges, but we are well poised to master them. Opinions are being revised about which system is the wave of the future. The free nations, if they maintain their unity and their faith in themselves, have the advantage—economically, technologically, morally.

Before Senate Foreign Relations Committee,
Washington, Jan. 31/The New York Times, 2-1:4.

Frank Sinatra
Entertainer

5

I don't know what it means when people call me a legend. What is a legend? King Arthur was a legend, I'm told. I can't relate to it. People say you are a legend if everybody is talking about you. How do I know who's talking about me? Maybe longevity makes a legend. If you last long enough, are around long enough, you are a legend.

Interview, Washington/USA Today, 1-28:(D)2.

Page Smith
Author, Historian

6

The average historian sees history as a particular problem that he or she is dedicated to solving. Not for me. Everything that I write about history must, at the heart of it, be inexplicable . . . just as life is. The historian's ultimate responsibility is simply to tell what happened. The drama of history is with the involvement of

470

(PAGE SMITH)

individuals. I don't believe that there are remote, impersonal forces. I don't believe in dialectical materialism, obviously, or that economics dictate our behavior. I believe that it's the response of people to each other and to history as it develops that above all determines the course their future has taken. I want readers to feel that more than anything else, so I talk about history as biography.

Interview/Publishers Weekly, 6-21:107.

Stephen Spender
Poet

[On the definition of "quality"]: Three parts natural grace, one part sense of period and two parts eccentricity.

Time, 1-28:79.

1

Rod Steiger
Actor

It drives me absolutely mad out of my mind that I am getting older. Do you know what it feels like to turn on the television and see yourself 30 years younger? Suddenly, there is no de-

2

nying that you are just another member of the human race, even though all your life—especially because of the attention you receive as an actor—you thought you were touched with something special.

Interview, Malibu, Calif./USA Today, 2-13:(D)5.

Ben Wattenberg
*Senior fellow,
American Enterprise Institute*

3

The club of democratic, modern nations now accounts for about one seventh of the global population. At the end of World War II, these nations had about a quarter of the world's population. If present trends continue, Western countries will go down to one tenth or one twelfth of the global population by the middle of the next century, and lower than that as the century progresses. On balance, it's a lot more difficult to have a dominant culture when you're one fifteenth of the world than when you're one fourth. The history of civilization is one of nations and cultures growing and then dying. There were Greeks and Romans who dominated the world; the Austro-Hungarians, the French, the Spaniards, the Portuguese. There's nothing to say that our particular democratic club will last forever.

Interview/U.S. News & World Report, 12-16:67.

Religion

William J. Bennett
*Secretary of Education
of the United States*

1

[Criticizing the strict interpretation of separation of church and state]: The attitude that regards "entanglement" with religion as something akin to entanglement with an infectious disease must be confronted broadly and directly . . . Our values as a free people and the central values of the Judeo-Christian tradition are flesh of the flesh, blood of the blood. Was George Washington wrong when he argued that "reason and experience both forbid us to expect that national morality can prevail in exclusion of religious principle"? Was Thomas Jefferson wrong when he asserted that the liberties of a nation cannot be thought secure "when we have removed their only firm basis—a conviction in the minds of the people that these liberties are of the gift of God"? Has subsequent history made the wisdom of our founders obsolete? I do not believe so. No one demands doctrinal adherence to any religious beliefs as a condition of citizenship, or as proof of good citizenship here. But, at the same time, we should not deny what is true: that from the Judeo-Christian tradition come our values, our principles, the animating spirit of our institutions. That tradition and our tradition are wedded together. When we have disdain for our religious tradition, we have disdain for ourselves.

*Before Supreme Council of the Knights
of Columbus, Washington, Aug. 7/
USA Today, 8-12:(A)8.*

Charles Bergstrom
Executive director, Lutheran Council

2

[Agreeing with a Supreme Court ruling against permitting school classroom time specifically for silent prayer]: It may sound like hair-splitting to separate silence and prayer, but theologically it's very important. To be silent is one thing, but for a state or teacher to add comments that there could or should be prayer is a

problem, because it could mislead people on what prayer is.

June 4/Los Angeles Times, 6-5:(I)12.

Cleanth Brooks
*Author, Critic; Professor emeritus
of rhetoric, Yale University*

3

Our Constitutional separation of church and state forbids the teaching of institutionalized religion in state-supported schools and colleges. Yet [in a technological age] the problem of the inculcation of ethical standards and ultimate values becomes more and more urgent.

*Jefferson Lecture, Washington, May 8/
The Christian Science Monitor, 5-13:23.*

Philip R. Cousin
*President, National Council
of Churches of Christ*

4

[Saying more Americans are turning to religion]: So many are seeking answers. And they are finding out that the only lasting answer comes through an inner peace . . . the anchoring of life that religion gives. [A] threatening world situation, domestic difficulties with economics, [disenchantment] with the drug culture, and various social concerns [have prodded many people to return to religion]. The turning to absolutes helps us understand how to relate to all areas of life. Religion cannot be isolated; it is necessary to have in the marketplace as well as the pew.

Interview/The Christian Science Monitor, 4-5:1.

Amy Eilberg
Rabbi

5

[On her becoming Conservative Judaism's first female rabbi]: The years of struggle, of pain and of exclusion are at an end. Our movement faces a new beginning, a new era of equality and vitality, and a beginning of a healing process that will bring us all to a new kind of

(AMY EILBERG)

unity, in which all may be included and to which all must contribute.

At Jewish Theological Seminary commencement, New York, May 12/The New York Times, 5-13:12.

Jerry Falwell
Evangelist

[Criticizing a Supreme Court ruling against permitting school classroom time for silent prayer]: The Founding Fathers did not intend separation from God and state—only church and state—and they [the Supreme Court Justices] don't seem to understand that.

June 4/USA Today, 6-5:(A)1.

1

Louis Finkelstein
Chancellor emeritus, Jewish Theological Seminary, New York

Judaism is very demanding. It demands of its people what other religions demand of those in religious orders . . . Because Judaism demands so much, it never gets 100 per cent. The fact that it gets any is remarkable. A rabbi today has his work cut out for him, but he should not despair if people do not do as much as they should. Every parent has that with children. God is merciful.

Interview, New York/The New York Times, 9-2:13.

2

John P. Foley
American priest; President, Pontifical Commission for Social Communication

The Vatican is not only the center of a world religion, but it's also the repository of tremendous cultural works of art and literature. So the church not only speaks for the spiritual aspirations of human beings, but also for the highest achievements of human beings—the artistic, the musical, the literary, the highest expressions of the person.

Interview/USA Today, 11-27:(4)13.

3

Mary H. Futrell
President, National Education Association

. . . the NEA is not opposed to individual prayer in school. What we oppose is group-led prayer in the school, which is un-Constitutional. Can Johnny say a prayer before a test? Absolutely. Can Jane say grace before eating lunch? Absolutely. Do we ever try to stop the basketball team or the football team from saying a prayer before a game? No, we don't. But you have to realize that when we look at the makeup of our individual classrooms, we see different national-ities and different religions. There is, therefore, no one religion that should be imposed on such a captive audience.

Interview/Christianity Today, 3-15:32.

4

George Gallup, Jr.
Public-opinion analyst

We do see signs of new interest in religion on the part of young adults in this country [the U.S.] There's a slight upturn in churchgoing among young people. And when we survey college students, we find that a higher proportion than in the last five or six years say that religion is very important in their lives . . . The interest in religion is across the board. And students are interested in religion in general. Religious-studies courses in colleges are oversubscribed. They [young adults] are searching for spiritual moorings. But it's not necessarily within a traditional religious framework [such as church membership] . . . The vast majority of Americans would like prayer in the schools. By the same token, most Americans say that spiritual [teaching] takes place best in the home or church. That's where they feel religious background and interests should be built up.

Interview, Princeton, N.J./The Christian Science Monitor, 12-6:27.

5

Billy Graham
Evangelist

[Criticizing religious figures who were involved in the 1984 U.S. Presidential campaign]:

6

(BILLY GRAHAM)

In the political area, I think there were pastors and evangelists who went too far, from my point of view, both from the left and from the right . . . If that is the way they feel led to do, I'm not going to debate with them. My own position is that I will not get involved in partisan politics . . . I suppose there was a time that it was assumed because of a friendship with a President [Richard M. Nixon] that I got involved [in partisan politics]. But I really have never endorsed a political candidate and do not intend to in the future.

Interview, New York, Jan. 2/
The New York Times, 1-3:20.

1

The latest Gallup Poll indicated that about 94 per cent of the American people believe in a personal God. Seventy-four per cent believe in a personal devil. Now, this would have been laughable 35 years ago when I started. We have more people now in church and synagogues on a weekend—15 times more—than all the sporting events put together in an entire week. [Why?] We've become afraid of the future. Young people are afraid because, when they face the future, they're not sure they're going to get a job; they look at this [Federal] deficit and they read that they're going to have to pay for it; or the atomic bomb is out there waiting for them. About 5,000 teenagers committed suicide last year and 500,000 tried. We're going to see a growth in spiritual interest. There are thousands of Bible classes and study groups and parent-church organizations that nobody ever hears about.

Interview/USA Today, 5-15:(A)9.

Orrin G. Hatch
United States Senator, R-Utah

2

[Criticizing a Supreme Court decision prohibiting schools from setting aside time specifically for prayer]: The tragedy of this opinion is that it transforms neutrality toward religion into hostility toward religion.

The Washington Post, 6-6:(A)7.

Jesse Helms
United States Senator,
R-North Carolina

3

[Criticizing a Supreme Court ruling prohibiting schools from setting aside time specifically for prayer]: [It is an] unwise and unjust decision, delivering a slap in the face to the vast majority of Americans who favor school prayer . . . It's time for Congress to stand up to the Supreme Court [and to] withdraw Federal jurisdiction over school prayer. This is a matter that clearly should be left to the states, which is where it was until the 1960s when the Supreme Court first began its intrusion on this issue.

The Washington Post, 6-6:(A)7.

Bunker Hunt
Industrialist

4

I'm no great church historian, but the pendulum swings, and right now there's a tremendous acceptance for the gospel. [Evangelist] Jerry Falwell told me the other day that his theological school is producing 250 graduates a year and each graduate will go out and start a church or school . . . In this country we had gone so far toward the agnostic and atheistic side that we had to experience a revulsion. I think a lot of politicians are surprised at the depth of the religious interest and beliefs. If America survives, it will be because of its return to Christian beliefs.

Interview/The Saturday Evening Post, Jan.-Feb.:45.

Wojciech Jaruzelski
Prime Minister of Poland

5

[On the church in Poland]: Remnants [of the Solidarity independent trade-union movement] today are trying to exploit the great authority of the Catholic Church in Poland, as if they were hiding under its umbrella. It is not secret that the church itself has a critical appraisal of such behavior. There are many cases in which people who never believed in any religion, or believed in the Jewish religion, go to church and get baptized when they are 50 or 60 years of age. I do believe that these are not religious conversions, but political conversions. The percentage of

(WOJCIECH JARUZELSKI)

those who believe is very high, and we respect that. But a new category has emerged: the non-believing but practicing churchgoer.

Interview, New York/Time, 10-28:57.

John Paul II
Pope

There are sectors in which social progress and well-being manifest themselves in a luxurious egoism, while other sectors remain in poverty, on the fringes, and illiterate. The church, committed to man, especially with the most poor and alienated, cannot ignore these situations. It must not resign itself passively to leave these things as they are or, as often happens, to degenerate into worse situations.

Before priests and nuns, Caracas, Venezuela, Jan. 28/The New York Times, 1-29:3.

1

[Criticizing radical church practices by some evangelists]: Evangelists have the undeniable duty of a strict and loving loyalty to the teachings of Jesus—because evangelists are not owners of the word God, but its ministers and its servants.

Homily, Piura, Peru, Feb. 4/ The Washington Post, 2-5:(A)11.

2

I am convinced, and I am happy to state it on this occasion, that the relationships between Jews and Christians have radically improved in these years. Where there was mistrust and perhaps fear, there is now confidence. Where there was ignorance and therefore prejudice and stereotypes, there is now growing mutual knowledge, appreciation and respect. Anti-Semitism, which is unfortunately still a problem in certain places, has been repeatedly condemned by the Catholic tradition as incompatible with Christ's teachings and with the respect due to the dignity of men and women created in the image and likeness of God.

To American Jewish Committee leaders, Vatican City, Feb. 15/The New York Times, 2-16:3.

3

Indulgence does not make people happy. The consumer society does not make people happy, either. If the church makes unpalatable pronouncements, it is because it is obliged to do so. It does so from honesty. Being a Christian has never been an easy choice, and it never will be.

At meeting with young people, Amersfoort, Netherlands, May 14/ The New York Times, 5-15:6.

4

Hans Kung
Theologian

[Criticizing the Roman Catholic hierarchy for limiting the theological independence of its priests]: The Vatican is, unfortunately, very similar to a lot of totalitarian states that are always demanding human rights abroad but refuse to give them to their own people.

The New York Times, 3-22:3.

5

James W. Malone
Roman Catholic Bishop of Youngstown, Ohio; President, National Conference of Bishops

[Supporting "collegiality," the consultation among members of the church hierarchy, which some criticize as eroding the power of the Vatican]: The expressions of collegiality in the episcopal conference of the United States are not just instances of those gimmicks and pragmatic contrivances for which Americans are thought to have a penchant. We see collegiality embodied in our conference as an important service to evangelization.

At synod, Rome, Nov. 26/ The New York Times, 11-27:3.

6

William McCready
Sociologist, University of Chicago

There are really two Catholic churches in this country [the U.S.]: those [who] identify with the institutional church and are active in their parishes, and those—probably a majority—who never darken the door, yet still call themselves Catholics.

Newsweek, 12-9:68.

7

Edwin Meese III
*Attorney General
of the United States*

1

[Saying the framers of the Constitution wanted only to prevent government from favoring one religion over another, not to totally separate church and state]: Strict neutrality between religion and irreligion would have struck the founding generation as somewhat bizarre. The purpose of [barring government establishment of religion] was to prohibit religious tyranny, not to undermine religion generally.

*Before American Bar Association, Washington,
July 9/Los Angeles Times, 7-10:(I)6.*

2

There are ideas that have gained influence in some parts of our [U.S.] society, particularly in some important and sophisticated circles, that are opposed to religious freedom, indeed that have an attitude of hostility toward religion in our country. By gradually removing from public education and public discourse all references to traditional religion . . . and by substituting instead the jargon and the ritual and the morality of cult and of self, we run the risk of subordinating all other religions to a new secular religion . . . In its application, the principle of neutrality toward all religions has often been transformed by some into a hostility toward anything religious. The danger is that religion, which has been such an important force in our country, could lose its social and historical, indeed its public, character. There are nations, we should remind ourselves, where religion has just this status, where the cause of religion, and its expression, has been reduced to something that people can only do behind locked doors.

*At prayer breakfast for members
of Christian Legal Society, San Diego, Calif.,
Sept. 29/Los Angeles Times, 9-30:(I)16.*

Langhorne A. Motley
*Assistant Secretary
for Inter-American Affairs,
Department of State
of the United States*

3

[Criticizing churches for taking sides on foreign-policy issues]: Religious persons should

not use the credibility they enjoy because of their religious roles to market personal secular ideological and philosophical beliefs. The pulpit, I believe, is misused when devoted to secular political causes. Marxist groups in Latin America have consciously sought out clerical groups to use as window dressing . . . I believe that the growing involvement of religious groups in international politics has generally been driven by well-meaning people, both lay and clergy, many of whom have devoted their lives to fighting misery and poverty. [But] the issue of whether they're correct or not correct is not debated. It appears to be a "no-no" subject . . . I think it should be debated.

*To reporters, Washington,
June 27/Los Angeles Times, 6-28:(I)5.*

Francis J. Mugarevo
*Roman Catholic Bishop,
Diocese of Brooklyn, N.Y.*

4

[On the "priestless day," he called for, on which churches were closed so that priests in his diocese could attend a conference to dramatize their declining numbers]: A priestless day is a powerful sign to people of the need for prayer and concern over this issue. It is also a dramatic symbol to all of us as priests of the importance of the priesthood and our need to sustain each other in it. . . . In 1960, we ordained 32 men to serve the Diocese of Brooklyn as priests. Last year, we ordained 4. The vocation crisis is hitting us full force.

*At the "priestless day" conference,
New York, March 7/The New York Times, 3-8:18.*

Ronald Reagan
President of the United States

5

[On criticism of his citing Scriptures when discussing his policies]: I don't think I've ever used the Bible to further political ends or not. But I've found that the Bible contains an answer to just about everything and every problem that confronts us, and I wonder sometimes why we won't recognize that one book could solve a lot of problems for us.

*News conference, Washington,
Feb. 21/The New York Times, 2-22:10.*

WHAT THEY SAID IN 1985

(RONALD REAGAN)

You can judge any new government, any new regime, by whether or not it allows religion to flourish. If it doesn't, you can be sure it's an enemy of mankind, for it is attempting to ban what is most beautiful in the human heart.

To religious leaders, Washington,
April 16/The Washington Post, 4-17:(A)10.

1

Pat Robertson
Evangelist; President,
Christian Broadcasting Network

[Criticizing the U.S. Supreme Court's ruling against prayer in schools]: I am opposed to the idea of a formal prayer in school and a dictated prayer by officialdom or school authorities or anyone else. What I am in favor of is eliminating a court decision that tells a generation of young people coming up through our schools that prayer is unacceptable in certain public areas. The Congress of the United States opens with a prayer. I think the Supreme Court went beyond its province there.

Interview/U.S. News & World Report, 11-18:32.

2

I don't think that there should be an influence from the government upon the church, nor do I think there should be influence by the church as an institution in regard to the government. But I do think that there should be moral influences, and I do think that those who are deeply dedicated, religious people of all faiths, should be involved in the governmental process. I certainly don't think the [U.S.] Constitution in any way intended to protect the government from religion. I think religion is a very vital part of the morality of our life in this nation.

Interview/U.S. News & World Report, 11-4:71.

3

Robert A. K. Runcie
Archbishop of Canterbury

[On bishops who openly question the church's teachings]: [Bishops must steer a course between] mindless dogmatism [and] root-

less individualism. Clearly, such a path is fraught with difficulty and danger, and it's a wise bishop who treads with care and reverence . . . The church is not like a school-teacher who must expel a boy from school lest he influence the others to wickedness. We need shepherds not only to repel wolves from the fold but also to lead the flock to new and more fertile pastures.

Before governing synod of the Church of England,
London, Feb. 13/Los Angeles Times, 2-14:(I)4.

5

Alexander M. Shapiro
President,
Conservative Rabbinical Assembly

[Calling for reconciliation of the various branches of Jewry]: In the long run, in order for Judaism to survive in America, there must be an outreach to all of the disaffected and the alienated, to all those thirsty for the word of God, even if we interpret that word in a different way . . . We need rabbis who are able to see the spark of holiness in each other, without necessarily agreeing with one another; we need rabbis able to sit around the same table, to study with one another, to learn from one another, to accept the fact that each is created in the image of God and that each is consecrated to the task of saving the souls of our people. How much more ready will you find groups of Jews around the country ready to accept the loving quality of *halacha* if you are perceived by your colleagues not as haranguing, judgmental human beings who care, apparently, more for power in the Jewish community than anything else, but rather those who can be depended on to sustain each other with love and compassion.

Before Orthodox Rabbinical Council of America,
Spring Glen, N.Y., April 30/
The New York Times, 5-1:17.

6

Charles F. Stanley
President, Southern Baptist Convention

A liberal theology does not grow churches. You see no great evangelical churches from liberal pastors, or great mission churches from liberal pastors. They create doubt among the members. When you say the first eleven chapters

4

(CHARLES F. STANLEY)

of Genesis are allegory or myth or this, that and the other, you've cut the foundation out of the Bible. Or when you say that Jesus Christ did not bodily rise from the dead, or when you say you don't believe in the devil or you don't believe in the Virgin birth of Jesus Christ, you're sending a crack right through the heart and core of theology. We don't believe this is what God wants in our seminaries. We don't believe this is what the majority of Southern Baptists want. We think it's an issue worth fighting for.

Interview/USA Today, 6-11:(A)11.

Cal Thomas
Columnist;
Vice president, Moral Majority

1

[On the increasing popularity of fundamentalist religion, especially among young married couples]: This group has been a sleeping giant ever since the Scopes trial. Now they are getting involved, and it's not the old-style fundamentalists in polyester and white socks. The torch has passed to another generation that looks and acts different. People who never knew they existed are pretty surprised.

Los Angeles Times, 5-15:(I)1.

Lowell P. Weicker, Jr.
United States Senator, R-Connecticut

2

[Arguing against legislation permitting organized prayer in schools.]: The more times it's voted on, the more times the television preachers talk about what Congress ought to do, the more people realize it's these people [the New Right] who are bringing government into religion, and they don't want it.

The Washington Post, 9-11:(A)3.

Science and Technology

John Ashworth
Vice chancellor,
University of Salford (England);
Member of committees advising
the British Prime Minister on technology

1

In a sense, there has been a gap in technological capabilities between the U.S. and Europe at least since the end of the second World War. What's happening now is that different kinds of gaps with different characteristics are opening up. In what I call "heroic" technology—space exploration, for instance—undoubtedly there is a wide gap now, largely because Americans backed a defense program and Europeans did not. But in addition to heroic technology, there is manipulative technology—things like microelectronics and biotechnology—which essentially involves fiddling about with control mechanisms. In these areas, Europe did not lag in the past, but it is today—not only in relation to the United States, but also to Japan.

Interview, Salford, England/
U.S. News & World Report, 5-27-47.

Isaac Asimov
Science-fiction writer

2

Science is the only human activity which always [is progressive]. It's progressive while virtually all other cultural endeavors are cyclic. Even the Middle Ages contributed such scientific advances as horseshoes, the compass, printing, clocks and gunpowder.

Interview/USA Today, 2-15:(B)4.

Jerry Berman
Legislative counsel,
American Civil Liberties Union

3

The computer is giving government and business whole new ways of keeping track of behavior [at a time when] privacy laws are completely ineffective . . . Congress has got to look at what is happening to privacy in the age of computers and start giving citizens some control over information kept in homes that now, to bank for ex-

ample, you have to share with government and business entities.

The Washington Post, 3-9:(A)10.

Roger Brinner
Senior economist, Data Resources, Inc.

4

The risk of cheap computing is the assumption that the machine can provide the intelligence. Researchers make the error of failing to test competing theories against each other; instead, you spend all of your time plugging away at the [computer] terminal, trying to get your data to fit your theory.

The Atlantic Monthly, February: 78.

Iben Browning
Author, Scientist

5

Being a scientist, I have a great leaning toward data. Data cannot be ignored. Computer models may or may not be right. They are oversimplified, because a computer is smaller than the world. I think masses of money are being poured into computer models that are certainly entertaining, but not very real. I am a tremendous believer in people getting out and wading in the mud. You should not just try to simulate things in computers.

Interview/USA Today, 1-23:(A)9.

Loren Graham
Authority on Soviet science,
Massachusetts Institute of Technology

6

[On Western technology leaks to the Soviet Union]: The Soviet Union is a very sophisticated country and they can do pretty much anything they want to. They may not be a leader in technology, but they're pretty good followers. Anything we get, they're going to get in a few years, and I don't think whether they steal the technology is going to change that picture very much.

The New York Times, 1-2.25.

Paul Gray
President,
Massachusetts Institute of Technology

1

[Criticizing scientific secrecy and national restrictions on the flow of technological information]: The quality and integrity of research are anchored in its nature as a dispersed, interdependent and cumulative enterprise. Research is dispersed in the sense that work at the frontier in most fields is carried on simultaneously in several locations. It is interdependent in the sense that different investigators, or groups of investigators, rely on work done elsewhere to validate and extend their own work. The closer work is to the frontier of knowledge and the more swiftly a field is developing, the more the researchers are dependent on open and rapid communication with colleagues working on similar problems elsewhere. And research is cumulative in the sense that many small steps, taken by individuals working in many different places and under different auspices, contribute to knowledge. Scientific research is also, and increasingly, an international undertaking. Talent and creative energy and world-class research are found throughout the globe and do not respect political and national boundaries. The scientific community *is* an international community.

At University of Cairo (Egypt)/
The Christian Science Monitor, 1-24:19.

Thomas Hughes
Engineer; Professor,
University of Pennsylvania

2

Most Americans are keenly interested in this country's history, and I think there is general agreement that, especially in the 20th century, our country has been as much influenced by technology as by any other single force. If we wish to understand ourselves as Americans, we need to know about our political, ethnic and economic history—but we also need to know about our technological achievements. Because if you scratch an American, you will find, somewhere beneath the surface, a person shaped by technology, a person who is living in a mainly technological society. There are may other societies in the world today that are not nearly so deeply influenced by modern technology as we are. In dealing with technology's history, we are dealing with an American characteristic. We have expressed ourselves magnificently, as a people, through technological achievements. You might compare this recent search for our technological past to a psychiatrist's effort to find in an individual's biographical past events that deeply influenced her or him, events the patient is not consciously aware of today. Technology has, for better or worse, deeply influenced us, for very complex reasons. Strangely enough, we have not celebrated or critically scrutinized our technological roots as much as we have, say, our political roots. I think it's time we got to know ourselves better by exploring all aspects of our technological character.

Interview, Philadelphia/
American Heritage, October:66.

John Paul II
Pope

3

Technology can become—and has become—alienating and manipulative to the point where we must morally reject the presence of a certain ideology of technology because it has imposed the primacy of matter over spirit, of things over the human person.

At mass, Ciudad Guayana, Venezuela,
Jan. 29/Los Angeles Times, 1-30(I)6.

James Joseph
President, Council on Foundations

4

The case for foundations is that, historically, they have been willing to take risks and support innovation and research. They provide the seed money for the development of many of the cures to illnesses and new technology. Foundation money is the society's research-and-development money. One of the problems we have now is cutbacks in government funds. What used to be innovative money is becoming survival money, and when a society loses its innovative money, it becomes analogous to the corporation that no longer has R&D money.

Interview/USA Today, 5-1:(A)11.

Michael Kenward
Editor, "New Scientist" (Britain)

[In science,] the U.S. leads in many things, but it depends who you read. The American press gives the impression that nothing goes on outside the U.S. This annoys most scientists outside the U.S. . . . American scientists are much better at getting their message across to the media. Scientists in Britain and Japan are not as adept at publicity. India is another country getting too little recognition for its work. Israel has a strong public-relations operation behind its scientists. And Italy has been good in publicizing some energy research—solar energy, for example. English-language scientists get too much attention in the media. There is a lot going on in the Soviet Union that needs to be reported more thoroughly . . .

Interview/World Press Review, November:27.

1

George A. Keyworth II
Director, White House Office of Science and Technology Policy

Basic [scientific] research is funded primarily by the government for a very good reason—because who else is going to do it? And, also over the years it has paid off, and, [not only] in absolutely unpredictable fashion, but also in an absolutely unpredictable huge way. And as time evolved, and it has evolved, I think we have felt that it was essential to do two things—which was to sustain the government's role in basic research and, more importantly, to strengthen it—because we are entering an era of even greater dependence on technology. And basic research is the absolute base.

Interview, Washington/
The Christian Science Monitor, 1-22:16.

2

Patrick J. Leahy
United States Senator, D-Vermont

[On the loss of personal privacy due to advances in technology]: Technology leaps ahead, and the law stands still. Technology eats away at

480

3

Kageyu Noro
Professor, University of Industry and Medicine (Japan)

A robot [in the workplace] acts just like a human, taking over the work that a human was doing before. But a human chatted with you, told you to wait while he took a break and went out drinking with you. The robot doesn't do any of that. That makes for a forlorn existence for the human working beside it.

The Wall Street Journal,
9-16:(C)77.

4

Seymour Papert
Professor of mathematics and education, Massachusetts Institute of Technology

[Supporting the use of computers to teach schoolchildren]: What's most important in physics is the laws of motion—how they affect the stars, atoms, gravity—but it's almost impossible to study this even in high school because the mathematics is just too complicated. Or was, until the computer. With the computer, it's now possible for elementary schoolchildren to manipulate motion in quite a formal way. Moving objects on the screen can be related, say, to throwing balls, so that what is fundamental in science can be brought into relationship with what is most natural to children—moving about . . . Computers cost more than pencils, but they cost a lot less than the wasted time of teachers or the consequences of children who are turned off by schools, drop out and end up with drugs. In New York it costs about $40,000 of taxpayer money to educate each child for the whole area. You can go to the stores and buy a pretty powerful computer for less than a thousand dollars.

Interview/The New York Times, 7-2:22.

5

what we assume are our protections in the Constitution . . . Within a decade, our privacy is going to be as rare a commodity as the old hand-cranked telephone.

Los Angeles, 5-14:(I)1.

Frank Press
President,
National Academy of Sciences

1

American science is at a peak of activity and progress that's unprecedented. Now, all of this is happening at a time when the nation faces a $200-billion deficit. And so the question that's on everybody's mind is what will be the resources under these conditions available for science, because everybody agrees that with the opportunities available, marginal increases will reap big returns . . . The great success story of American science in the past 30 or 40 years rests in the research university—a peculiarly unique American institution. It doesn't exist anywhere else in the numbers [in which] it exists here. For many reasons, the research universities are in trouble. And that means basic science has some problems . . . I don't mean necessarily that these are Federal problems. They might be internal problems, investment problems, maybe decisions that they themselves made. But we have to understand the nature of the distress and see what the appropriate roles of the private and public sectors are and address those issues.

Interview, Washington/
The Christian Science Monitor, 3-25:8.

Ronald Reagan
President of the United States

3

We have seen the success of the space shuttle. Now we are going to develop a permanently manned space station and new opportunities for free enterprise. In the next decade, Americans and our friends around the world will be living and working in space. In the zero gravity of space, we could manufacture in 30 days life-saving medicines it would take 30 years to make on earth. We can make crystals of exceptional purity to produce super computers, creating technologies and medical breakthroughs beyond anything we ever dreamed possible.

State of the Union address, Washington,
Feb. 6/The New York Times, 2-7:13.

Chester A. Sadlow
Executive vice president
of advanced production technology,
Westinghouse Electric Company

4

[On automation in the workplace]: I think it's . . . important to remember that you really don't automate to replace labor. That's the wrong mission, because in many companies labor is only 5 per cent to 15 per cent of your costs, whereas more than 50 per cent of your costs are for materials and equipment. The biggest contribution of automation is producing a quality product. The robot does it the same way every time.

Panel discussion/
Wall Street Journal, 9-16:(C)11.

Carl Sagan
Professor of astronomy and space science,
Cornell University

5

The stuff of life is everywhere. It's easily made. There's nothing magic about that. When we look at time scales, we see that there are a large number of stars that are much older than our sun and planets. We see there's an enormous amount of time for evolution to occur . . . Putting all that together, it seems to me very plausible that there's a great deal of life, and even a great deal of intelligent life, more advanced than we. But that's just the plausibility argument. That says it's not nonsense to search. It doesn't say that it's guaranteed we'll find something.

Interview/USA Today, 10-11:(A)11.

Harley Shaiken
Professor,
Massachusetts Institute of Technology

6

[On the introduction of automation into the workplace]: . . . the quality of the job clearly de-

2

The new technologies are fueling a new industrial revolution . . . The symbol for the second industrial revolution is the computer. I believe that 10 years from now we'll look back at this time and realize that the computer was only in the kindergarten stage, insofar as its ubiquity and importance is concerned.

At University of Pittsburgh commencement/
U.S. News & World Report, 6-3:66.

(HARLEY SHAIKEN)

teriorates as a result of automation. I visited one welding shop in the automobile industry that had 300 or 400 workers prior to automation. After robots were introduced, they were left with 150 workers. Prior to automation, workers were responsible for a certain fixed production at the end of the day, but they largely controlled their own pace on the assembly line. Afterward, everyone was linked to the final line, so they couldn't work ahead or fall behind a little. They felt their jobs were far more desirable before the robotics system was introduced. I've also seen this happen with highly skilled machinists when they're put on computerized numerical-control machines. Often they feel that they're no longer participants, but only monitors.

Panel discussion/
The Wall Street Journal, 9-16:(C)11.

Eduard A. Shevardnadze
Foreign Minister
of the Soviet Union

1

Space, until recently the realm of science-fiction writers, has now become an area of man's practical activity. Peaceful exploration of space holds out for mankind truly limitless prospects of utilizing scientific and technological achievements to promote the economic and social progress of the peoples and to solve the vast problems that face mankind on earth. However, these truly cosmic dimensions, and I am not speaking figuratively, also present new requirements to the inhabitants of the earth and, above all, to the leaders of states. There should be no repetition of the mistake made four decades ago, when the states and peoples of the world were unable to prevent the great intellectual achievement of the mid-20th century, the release of the energy of the atom, from becoming a means for the mass annihilation of human beings.

At United Nations, New York,
Sept. 24/The New York Times, 9-25:8.

Sultan Salman al-Saud
Saudi Arabian Prince and astronaut

2

[On the view from the U.S. space shuttle]: Looking at [the earth] from here, with trouble all over the world, not just the Middle East, it looks very strange as you see the [national] boundaries and borderlines disappearing. Lots of people who are causing some of these problems [on earth] ought to come up here and take a look.

News conference, aboard U.S. space shuttle,
June 23/The New York Times, 6-24:1.

Sherry Turkle
Associate professor of sociology,
Massachusetts Institute of Technology

3

Different people use the computer in contrasting ways to profoundly different psychological ends. Some use the computer to build a world where everything feels very much in order, a world of safety and structure. But others build a world characterized by the pleasures of risk. For them, working with complex computer systems is the joy of walking a narrow line between winning and losing. They build a system where they feel almost out of control, and the pleasure is in the magic of grabbing control back. So one dichotomy in style of computer use is between risk and reassurance. There is another very important one. Today, the dominant computer culture stresses a style of programming that looks at the machine in terms of structured planning and domination. A program is seen as the imposition of will over the machine. But there is another approach that involves more of a give-and-take with the machine. It is less like domination than negotiation; it's more a conversation than a monologue.

Interview/U.S. News & World Report, 1-14:67.

Michael Turner
Theoretical physicist,
University of Chicago

4

Right now, [cosmic] theorists have gotten a little bit ahead of themselves. Cosmology is not a smooth progression where scientist "A" thinks up a theory, proposes an experiment, which then either agrees or doesn't agree with the theory. It moves in jerks, and right now there's been a lot of theoretical activity. The experiments have to catch up, and they will.

The Christian Science Monitor, 3-7:21.

Ezra Vogel
Professor of sociology,
and director of U.S.-Japan program,
Harvard University

1

As I talk to people in the forefront of technology, they're shocked to find that the Japanese are pulling ahead in broadly diverse fields. We tend to underestimate the Japanese. We used to think they could make junk but not good products; then they could make radios and transistors but not big things like televisions; then they could make televisions but not automobiles; then automobiles but not high technology. The latest phase has us saying they aren't creative enough

to be good at software, and they can't handle the service sector. I wouldn't bet on that.

Interview/U.S. News & World Report, 9-2:45.

Steve Wozniak
Designer of first Apple computer

2

[As to when home computers will be found in half of U.S. households]: I don't think home computers will become that commonplace. It's difficult to justify why that many homes would need one. It's like asking: How many homes need a typewriter? They have a presence correlated with their need right now.

Interview/USA Today, 9-23:(E)3.

Sports

Muhammad Ali
*Former heavyweight boxing champion
of the world*

[Saying the movement to ban boxing is racist in nature]: Black people are now in control [of boxing] . . . All the champions are black. Many of the promoters and managers are black. When we had all white champions, they never talked about stopping boxing.

*News conference, Peking/
USA Today, 5-15:(C)2.*

Mario Andretti
Racing-car driver

Second means nothing. Especially here [at the Indianapolis 500]. When you get to a certain stage in your career, winning seems to be the only thing. You get spoiled, and I guess I want to stay spoiled. This is a very selfish business.

*Indianapolis, May 26/
Los Angeles Times, 5-27:(III)4.*

Arthur Ashe
Tennis player

The average sports fan doesn't get as emotionally involved in a tennis event as he does the team sports, because the players don't belong to a particular city. When people come out to watch tennis they say, "I think I'd like to watch Mayotte win," or "Sadri has a nice serve, I think I'll root for him." But, if you go to a New England Patriots football game, there's no question—you're unequivocally cheering for the *Patriots.*

The Christian Science Monitor, 9-6:20.

The U.S.A. will always produce its fair share of [tennis] pros in the top 50. But we are indeed in danger at the top, because we don't have a national effort by our governing body of the sport, as other countries do. In every other country, the best young players are put on a national team,

Interview/The Christian Science Monitor, 1-7:22.

and the team pays all the expenses. Here [in the U.S.], you're left to fend for yourself. It costs so damn much to produce a top player.

Interview/USA Today, 9-24:(A)11.

Don Baylor
*Baseball player,
New York "Yankees"*

Hitting is contagious and so is defense. When someone gets a big hit, another guy wants to get a big hit, too. If someone makes a great play, another guy wants to contribute by making a great play.

*Interview, New York, April 16/
The New York Times, 4-17:20.*

Yogi Berra
*Former manager,
New York "Yankees" baseball club*

[On his just being fired as manager by Yankee owner George Steinbrenner]: He's the boss. He can do what he wants. I'm used to this. This is the third time I've been fired. That's what this game is—managers are hired and fired. I know it's an old saying, but that's what it is.

*To reporters, Chicago, April 28/
The New York Times, 4-29:1.*

Larry Bird
Basketball player, Boston "Celtics"

You can talk about the breaks or injuries, or players losing their desire, as contributing factors to a champion [team's] downfall. But I think the biggest obstacle to winning successive titles is mistakenly believing that you can do it again the same way you did the previous season, and with the same personnel. You can't. You have to make yourself a better team the second year, and for recent NBA playoff winners that hasn't been happening.

484
1
2
3
4
5
6
7

Lou Brock
Former baseball player,
St. Louis "Cardinals"

1

Base-running arrogance is just like pitching arrogance or hitting arrogance. You are a force and you have to instill [that] you are a force to the opposition. [Pitchers] Don Drysdale and Sal Maglie would throw a ball close to the hitter to let you know they were out there. That's pitching arrogance, because now he's coming at you. He's just driven you to your very best. And he wants to challenge you. Base running is the same thing, with one exception. The runner gets to first base and stands out there 9 or 10 feet off the base. The question then becomes, how do I act, how do I respond? Do I challenge them or do I back away? If you're arrogant, you are presenting a presence that tells the opposition, "I am ready for the test."

News conference after being named
to Baseball Hall of Fame, New York,
Jan. 8/USA Today, 1-9:(C)3.

Herb Brooks
Former hockey coach,
New York "Rangers"

2

[On his being asked to run for Governor of Minnesota]: I can't imagine that 15 years in the locker room prepared me for a position as lofty as that. We didn't talk about the issues of the day in the locker room. I've always said that coaching is like being a king: It prepares you for absolutely nothing.

Interview/Los Angeles Times, 7-26:(III)10.

Lou Carnesecca
Basketball coach,
St. John's University

3

The most important thing for a coach to do is to give hope. You cannot be an emissary of doom. You can do an awful lot of teaching—not just basketball—when things don't go well. You lost a game. So what?

Interview, New York/The New York Times, 3-4:32.

M. L. Carr
Basketball player, Boston "Celtics"

4

Everybody in sports is on an ego trip to a certain degree. We all grew up being patted on the head and pampered and told how great we were. But when you get into that green [Celtic] shirt, even if you were a shooter, you become a "passer." Bob Cousy and Bill Sharman passed it on to K. C. and Sam Jones, and they passed it on to John Havlicek and Jo Jo White, and some day Larry Bird and Kevin McHale will have to pass it on, too. That's what I'm doing now. I'm 34, still competitive in practice, still running as hard as I can, pushing players from behind, but without causing them to look over their shoulders. It's just my turn to pass it on.

Time, 6-10:72.

Gary Carter
Baseball player, New York "Mets"

5

Drug involvement in sports takes away from what can be a good thing, like being part of a World Series. A lot of us have been blessed by God to be able to play this game; it's amazing to me that some would risk ruining that experience. I may be a bit old-fashioned that way, but if you're doing drugs, it takes away from the whole team—you're hurting the other players . . . But these ballplayers [who abuse drugs] aren't criminals. They were victims who fell into a bad thing and couldn't get out of it. With time, a lot of them realized they had the strength to get out and get help . . . I not only love to play the game, I'm a fan. I'd hate to see it tainted by this thing. I want fans to again look at baseball as being up there with apple pie, mother and Chevrolet.

Interview, New York/USA Today, 9-13:10.

Bob Chandler
Former football player,
Buffalo "Bills" and Oakland "Raiders"

6

[On playing with injuries]: There's an adjustment period after each injury that requires an operation, when you say, "This is ridiculous; nothing is worth this; I'm tearing myself apart." For some reason, at least for myself, that was always a very short period. I loved catching the ball and running patterns. I didn't like getting hit and having operations, but I loved football . . . [Playing with injuries is] expected of you. But the pressure is indirect. You know someone is going to come in and take your job. That's the biggest pressure.

(BOB CHANDLER)

Interview/USA Today, 1-3:(C)2.

Michael Cooper
Basketball player,
Los Angeles "Lakers"

Defensive players are like garbage collectors: You don't notice them unless they don't do their job. You handle the messes and the stinky stuff. Defense is dirty work.

Interview/Los Angeles Times, 5-16:(III)1.

3

Howard Cosell
Commentator, ABC Sports

My place in the history of the industry is obviously secured. Who have been the largest figures in American television? In news, Walter Cronkite. In entertainment, Johnny Carson. And in sports, Howard Cosell . . . I never sought fame. I never sought celebrity status. It came to me because of the puerile field I was in, where I was different, where I had opinions and could state them and backed it up with an abundance of background and knowledge and the trust and respect of everybody who mattered in the field I was in. So I became a celebrity who also happened to be a multi-faceted person with lots of talent.

Interview, New York/
The Washington Post, 5-21:(D)1,4.

4

In my view, sports is a deeply perverted element in American society. The frequently touted uplifting qualities associated with sports have become but a murky blur in a morass of hypocrisy, corruption and deceit that I like to call the sports syndrome. Of course, the inherent rewards of sports are the same as they have always been: the fulfillment of discovering one's own athletic skills, of taking part in a team effort, of learning one's physical limits and pushing those limits back. But these values have become subservient to the sports syndrome, which has at its heart a number of very doubtful postulates that in my view delineate the problems facing sports today. First, sports is a wholly separate and deeply necessary refuge from the daily travail of human existence—a charmed, magical world. Second, victory is cosmetically important. To-

5

Eddie Chiles
Owner,
Texas "Rangers" Baseball club

I don't know why it has become the standard procedure in baseball to fire the manager if things are not going well. I don't think that makes much sense. There are so many things that contribute to a team's performance. You can't blame the field manager for everything that happens on a baseball field. In other businesses, you don't do that. You look for what's causing the problem and you make a correction. Many times that deficiency might be in the ownership, the financial structure, or somewhere else in the organization. So just because the team might not do well doesn't mean we'd blame [the manager]. And it certainly doesn't mean that he'd be fired.

Interview/
Los Angeles Times, 5-26:(III)4.

1

Jimmy Connors
Tennis player

[Saying U.S. tennis tournaments should use playing surfaces that are good for American players]: Europeans and South Americans just mostly play on clay anyway, but players from the States and Australia are the ones who go and fight it out on everything. Our national championship, the U.S. Open, has gone from grass to clay to hardcourt, so we've been trying to satisfy everyone, except the Americans. If the best players from Czechoslovakia played well on cow dung, do you think they'd change it?

Los Angeles Times, 8-13:(III)2.

2

(HOWARD COSELL)

day, winning is truly the only thing—a phrase [the late football coach] Vince Lombardi, by the way, never uttered. Third, these games are so utterly complex that only those who have played them can possibly transmit their mysterious essence to mere mortals. Finally, the fan is an entitled being, with inalienable rights not set forth in any constitution; he pays the price of admission and is thereby entitled to enter the stadium and do whatever the hell he wants, including commit violent acts. Of course, our great player-commentators don't deign to discuss these trivial matters. Instead, they analyze grave issues like the deportment of one tennis player or another. I, for one, can think of nothing less consequential in the scheme of human existence than whether or not a goddamn tennis player loses his temper with an umpire.

Panel discussion/"Harper's," September:47.

Doug DeCinces
Baseball player, California "Angels";
Member, executive council,
Major League Baseball Players Association

1

[Criticizing club owners' proposals to put a cap on player salaries]: I don't want to see the game hurt. I'd be the first to go to bat for baseball if it was proven to me that it was in financial jeopardy; but I haven't seen figures that would justify changing the structure as the owners are proposing. They've studied long and hard and come up with something that would obliterate free agency and rising salaries while doing nothing at all to help the poorer clubs, and that's all we ever hear about. [The proposed salary cap is] so bizarre, my reaction was, "What's happened to the free-enterprise system?"

Interview/Los Angeles Times, 5-21:(III)7.

Joseph E. diGenova
United States Attorney
for the District of Columbia

2

[On the drugs-in-baseball trial in Pittsburgh]: Nothing that I say here should be misconstrued as criticizing my good friend Jerry Johnson, the U.S. Attorney in Pittsburgh. He has to give these [testifying] players immunity to get at the pusher. But that said, let me add that that means that these players have already gotten their break, the biggest one of all—a free pass criminally. They are entitled to no more breaks. They got the big one; they won't be going to the slammer. The contempt that these players have shown for the game of baseball, for the American people and, most importantly, for American youth, the boys and girls who play baseball, must be answered roundly and unequivocally by baseball, its owners and its commissioner. These players should be thrown out of baseball.

To lawyers, Arlington, Va./
The New York Times, 9-27:27.

David F. Dixon
Founder,
United States Football League

3

In football, at least, the traditional owner is obsolete . . . Let the fans own the teams . . . Let's say we have a $12.50 football ticket. That ticket will contain a "stock-stub" for, say, $2.50. Thus, every spectator in every stadium at every game will own a share of Class A, common voting stock the minute he buys a ticket. Man, does everyone here grasp the significance of that? If you think the Notre Dame student body is wild, if you think Harvard students get worked up against Yale, try out a stadium with 60,000 owners! We'll have to build moats around the fields.

Before Harvard Business School, May/
The Wall Street Journal, 7-9:32.

Larry Doby
Former baseball player

4

[On the current controversy over drug abuse in the major leagues]: I don't really know what's going on in the drug world, but I do know it's not just a baseball problem. You hear it happening everywhere in society. It's an American problem, an athletic problem, and a black and white problem. It especially hurts me to see any kid in sports involved; I mean, it hurts me a little more because athletics is my fraternity. I've always been a part of it . . . I can tell you this: if

(LARRY DOBY)

[former baseball players Jackie] Robinson or [Roy] Campanella or [Larry] Doby did anything like some of [the] things you see [in sports] today, we wouldn't have been playing on teams, and maybe a lot of people after us wouldn't have gotten the chance to play. You wonder about some of those athletes who are risking their careers—even their lives—in these drug activities. You wonder why, when they're making enough money to live well for the rest of their lives. What do they need it for?

The New York Times, 8-22:25.

Julius Erving
Basketball player, Philadelphia "76ers"

1

I admit to liking the feel of things being in context, the sense of the familiar waters. Out of one hundred moves I make, I've made ninety-nine before, at one time or another. Sure, that one new one gives me a hit, but actually I get as much or more out of doing the other ninety-nine, because when I do something I've done before, it means that I've compiled this information in my mind and selected the right action for the proper situation. That gives me a lot of pleasure.

Interview/Esquire, February:118.

Don Fehr
Acting executive director,
Major League Baseball Players Association

2

[On fans who criticize baseball players for considering labor strikes despite their high salaries]: I would like them to think about the facts they already know: that baseball is a short career, one requiring a lot of skill, drive and determination just to get to the major leagues, and a lot of luck to get to stay there. I would also want them to realize that the top people in every profession in this country make that kind of money, yet no one ever suggests that they should forfeit the right to pursue their trades in a free-market economy. They say that only about ballplayers. A baseball player is far closer to normal physical stature than any other athlete . . . There's a tendency to watch a major-league game and say,

488

"That could've been me, and I'd do it for free, because it's not really a job." Well, it *is* a job, and you wouldn't do it for free either, once you've played for a year. But that's the perception we face, and I frankly don't know how to deal with it.

Interview, New York/USA Today, 6-27:(C)2.

3

[Criticizing proposed mandatory drug tests for players, saying that would presume guilt until proven innocent]: The way the clubs are putting it now, they're saying, "I don't suspect you of anything, but unless you agree to take a test any time I want, I'm not going to hire you." If you're a 20-year-old kid, they're saying, "We're going to test you for the next 20 years." So you're going to have to prove them wrong again and again.

USA Today, 12-4:(C)11.

Charles O. Finley
Former owner,
Oakland "A's" baseball club

4

[On the impending player strike]: There's no question players have too much power. If they force the owners to give in again, they are going to kill the goose that lays the golden egg. The baseball union is no different than any other. In autos and steel, the unions have hit the industry so hard that they've put some firms out of business and caused others to suffer immeasurably—and things are moving the same way fast in sports . . . There's also the idiocy of the owners. I don't blame the players for the astronomical salaries. If I was playing today, I would take as much as the boss would give. The owners have been stupid, and now they are hollering: "Hey, baby, you're hurting me. Look at my books. I'm about ready to go out of business."

Interview/U.S. News & World Report, 8-5:56.

Bill Fitch
Basketball coach, Houston "Rockets"

5

Any time you set out to build a winner, you try to get people you know will play well to-

(BILL FITCH)

gether, and then you let the rest of the problems take care of themselves. The toughest thing is the patience you have to exercise until that [championship] title arrives, because there is always the tendency to think you can speed things up by making changes.

Interview/The Christian Science Monitor, 2-6:20.

William Friday
President,
University of North Carolina

1

In our country now, sports has taken the form of a religion. All these forces have generated enormous pressures on the schools [with sports programs] . . . There are allegations that colleges and universities are in the entertainment business, that they mold themselves and their existence to accommodate that pressure and that demand. All of these circumstances raise questions that deal with academic requirements, recruiting abuses, scheduling abuses, impact of commercial television, ineffective sanctions, salary excesses and the ultimate abuses—gambling and cheating that we have witnessed.

Los Angeles Times, 6-23:(III)1.

Steve Garvey
Baseball player,
San Diego "Padres"

2

Whenever I go up to the plate, no matter who the pitcher is, I always think I can get a base hit. I've come to the conclusion that for players with big-league reflexes, hitting is 60 per cent physical and 40 per cent mental their first couple of years in the majors. But once they establish that inner confidence where they know how to adjust to situations, while also continuing to protect the strike zone, then the reverse is true. I have my slumps at the plate like everyone else, but over the years I've learned to deal with them, and I've never struck out much.

Interview, San Diego/
The Christian Science Monitor, 5-13:22.

Ira Glasser
Executive director,
American Civil Liberties Union

3

[Criticizing the Commissioner of Baseball for suggesting the testing of baseball players to detect drug abuse]: The question it raises is whether or not it is permissible to invade the privacy of thousands who are innocent of drug use in order to find a handful of drug users. There's an old Southern song—"If you hang 'em all, you get the guilty" . . . It's like shooting a fly with a cannon. And when you do that, a lot of innocent people get hit by the shrapnel . . . The whole idea to allow people to search whoever they want is the type of thing done in a totalitarian country . . . [As for the commissioner's view that testing will bolster the sport's integrity,] people in power always say things like that, as if violating the rights of innocent people increases integrity. He's not being tough on drug users—he's being tough on innocent people.

Interview, New York, May 8/
Los Angeles Times,
5-9:(III)10.

Jeffrey H. Goldstein
Professor of psychology,
Temple University

4

[On the increase in fan violence at sporting events around the world]: The people watching an aggressive sport are likely to become more aggressive themselves, thus the sequence of events tends to perpetuate itself—the fans themselves feel aggressive, they sense or see aggression, and then they act aggressively . . . Social class or economic considerations are not the main roots—it's nationalism, pure and simple. In an era of instant communications, people increasingly are making nationalist issues of international sporting events, and the people are abetted by the actions of the press, sports officials, politicians and the athletes themselves. Rightly or wrongly, international sporting events have become tests of the rightness or wrongness of ideology, and everyone seems to be contributing to the notion that "it's us against them."

Interview, May 29/The New York Times, 5-30:6.

Scott Hamilton
Former Olympic skating champion

The greatest feeling in skating is the 10 minutes after you win. Because you see that everything you've done—all the work and all the time that you've put into it, injury and everything else—was worth it. The feeling of accomplishment. The ego inflation you get from just winning a competition. That 10 minutes is the greatest thing in the world. That's what you work all year for, that 10 minutes. Then you have it, forever, the fact that you did it, and you won it, and you proved yourself. I'm going to miss those 10 minutes for a long time.

Interview/The New York Times, 1-26:15.

1

Ken Harrelson
Executive vice president,
Chicago "White Sox" baseball club;
Former player

I firmly believe a [baseball club's] farm system is like a candy store. Everyone thinks there are always all kinds of goodies in the candy store, and all you have to do is plunk down your cash and you have instant gratification. The truth of the matter is, farm systems do supply players for the majors, but to rely solely on this method of winning a pennant is ridiculous.

USA Today, 10-8:(C)2.

2

Marv Harshman
Basketball coach,
University of Washington

There used to be a great deal more loyalty in coaching on every level. Forty years ago, a coach was a teacher first and a coach second. A coach could stay as long as he wanted to. The bottom line wasn't wins . . . Now the bottom line is money. Everybody needs money to run their programs. It's simple: The more you win, the more people turn out and the more money you make so you can finance those other programs that don't make money.

Interview, Seattle/The Washington Post, 2-20:(F)6.

3

Jack Hartman
Basketball coach,
Kansas State University

[On the pressure of being a basketball coach]: If you choose this profession, you accept the stress. There's no way you can say, "Don't take it so seriously. The hell with that." You'll be a loser.

Interview/USA Today, 2-20:(C)4.

4

Whitey Herzog
Baseball manager,
St. Louis "Cardinals"

No team can afford to be one-dimensional, and that ought to be obvious to everyone. If you look at us defensively, we've got a lot of people who can catch the ball and throw it straight. Of course, I like speed because the opposition can't defend against it without weakening itself somewhere else. But you can't win without balance, either. Anyway, no matter what kind of surface you play on, the key is always pitching. Sometimes, when we discuss possible pennant-winners, I don't understand why we talk about anything else.

Interview/The Christian Science Monitor, 8-5:24.

5

Larry Holmes
Heavyweight boxing champion
of the world

When [another] fighter's out partying, I'm at home sleeping. When a fighter's in the bed, I'm doing roadwork. When a fighter's drinking wine, I'm drinking milk. And when a fighter's having sex, I'm thinking about it. This is what makes me better than everybody else.

To reporters, Las Vegas/
The Washington Post, 9-19:(B)8.

6

Boxing is always going to survive because it has got that human interest. People like violence. They like to see people bleed. They like to see that. People don't go to a football game to see a guy score; they want to see a guy get car-

7

(LARRY HOLMES)

ried out. They don't go to see a race car win a race; they go to see accidents. That's the way it is. They go to a rodeo to see the guy get thrown off the horse or stepped on by the bull. You can't sell love. You can't sell happiness, because people want no part of that. Your [news] paper can't sell none of this unless they write violence in there.

Interview/USA Today, 9-20:(A)11.

Lou Holtz
Football coach,
University of Minnesota

1

A "lifetime contract" for a coach means if you're ahead in the third quarter and moving the ball, they can't fire you.

The Wall Street Journal, 10-28:20.

Steve Howe
Former baseball pitcher,
Los Angeles "Dodgers"

2

[On his cocaine-addiction problem which led to his release from baseball]: My sole existence, of what I did in life, was what I did on the ballfield. When nothing else matters and you don't feel that you're going to be able to perform up to your capabilities and someone gives you an avenue to deaden that pain [cocaine] . . . you're going to do what you can do, so that people are going to like you and accept you.

Broadcast interview/"Nightline," ABC-TV, 9-12.

Gary Hulst
Basketball coach,
California State University, Hayward

3

Losing is a terrible experience. What they say about athletics building character isn't true. Athletics magnify character. When you win, that's great. But when you lose, the alibis really come out.

Interview, Hayward, Calif./USA Today, 1-8:(C)7.

Reggie Jackson
Baseball player, California "Angels"

4

[Saying he prefers not to be a designated hitter]: I haven't been a successful DH. My mind wanders . . . If you're the DH and you make the last out, you've got a full half hour—30 to 40 minutes—before you hit again. You go back to the clubhouse, read books, magazines, think about the problems you had during the day. You don't want to think about the last strike-out you made or the last pop-up you had. If I hit a home run, I want to go out the next inning and tip my cap. Or if I strike out, I want to go out there and take the blame. I don't need to hide. I'm not afraid of dealing with failure. You do poorly, you face the music. It's worth it.

Interview/Los Angeles Times, 3-11:(III)13.

5

When you get in the later years of your career and you go 0-for-20, they say Reggie's getting old. He's not getting around on the ball. His days are numbered. That's pressure. But in those years of 27 to 32, the prime years like Jim Rice and Eddie Murray are having right now, you own the world. You have proved you belong. You are the big gorilla. Those golden years, you call the shots. You talk and others listen. Then, if you don't hit for a couple of days, so what? You know you will.

Interview, Boston/
The Washington Post, 5-11:(C)3.

6

[Saying he approves of management testing players for drug abuse]: One of these days, I'm probably going [to] wind up in someone's baseball front office. Okay, I bust you two or three times with drugs, I send you to a rehab center, I hold press conferences for you, I take people's time. I sit down and converse with you. Try. I send you to a psychiatrist; I send you to a doctor. I pay for your medical bills. And I pay you $500,000 a year. Gee, do you think once in a while I can test you, to make sure you're clean? Now you want to sue me for your personal rights. Don't *I* have rights? I'm paying you half a million a year, ain't I? So, yes, I do believe in

(REGGIE JACKSON)

testing. I think if you're going [to] test a guy like Rod Carew or Brian Downing, a model citizen, no, you shouldn't do that. But if I give you reasonable cause, I don't think there's anything wrong with it. When you've shown me that you've lied to me, deceived me, don't I have a right to test you?

Interview, Palm Springs, Calif./
Los Angeles Times, 9-10:(III)3.

Deacon Jones
Former football player,
Los Angeles "Rams"

[The late football coach] Vince Lombardi said it: "You've got to hate in the game, but it has to be controlled hate." You have to hate for 3½ hours on Sunday, drop that hate and pick up some more hate for another team the next week. It's a hell of a mind-trip that you go through.

Interview, Studio City, Calif./
Los Angeles Times, 9-16:(III)10.

1

Joe Kapp
Football coach,
University of California, Berkeley

You put a team together, a group of people, and then it's a series of strokes. It's like a painting that you're constantly working on, and it's finally finished only at sundown, when the gun goes off. The difference between winning and losing is an inch, a breath, a blink. If enough people in this painting—in this group effort—do a little bit more, you're liable to win. It's a fine, fine line.

Interview, Berkeley, Calif./
Los Angeles Times, 1-20:(III)19.

2

Jack Kemp
United States Representative, R-New York;
Former football quarterback,
San Diego "Chargers"
and Buffalo "Bills"

In football, [a quarterback has] to make decisions every second, on the margin. You're either winning or losing, and everything is calibrated. And you not only have to have the ability to make a decision, you have to take responsibility for it. You're either a success or you're not. I think, well, that most quarterbacks have natural leadership qualities.

Los Angeles Times, 5-16:(I)15.

3

Billie Jean King
Tennis player

Maybe the best thing we can do to clean up sports in this country is to reduce the hypocrisy that underlies the whole system . . . Think of our romance with so-called amateur sports. Look at the Olympics, for God's sake—the biggest, grandest spectacle of hypocrisy imaginable. None of those kids are amateurs! They all live on "athletic scholarships," a misnomer if there ever was one. Colleges want top athletes because they help build winning teams. And winning teams fill the stadiums, make the television deals more lucrative, and put the alumni in a generous mood. But do we tell our young athletes, children the truth? No, we tell our young athletes, "You must win a gold medal at any cost. You must set records and make the pros at any cost. Meanwhile, of course, you have to attend classes and get an education—which, after all, is why you're in college in the first place." That's a lot of baloney. Colleges want these kids because they're highly skilled in a particular sport, pure and simple. Why keep lying about it? What's wrong with it? Athletic scholarships should be called contracts: You have a contract with this college to play this sport, period.

Panel discussion/"Harper's," September:52.

4

Bobby Knight
Basketball coach,
University of Indiana

My players put up with me because they know that when I do things, even when I do things that I consider distasteful, I do it because I'm trying to help them be the best thing they can be, whatever it is. And I have enough of an ego to think I know better than anyone—professors, girlfriends, the guy in the dorm—what's best for

5

(BOBBY KNIGHT)

them . . . I talk to our players about being warriors, because that's what I want them to become as players. I know when I recruit them, they're not warriors. But what I would like them to do eventually is to reflect my personality on the court, because there's never been any doubt that I'm a warrior.

Interview, Feb. 22/
Los Angeles Times, 2-27:(III)6.

Jake LaMotta
Former middleweight boxing champion
of the world

1

I don't believe in stopping fights. Even if a guy is getting too much of a beating. You shouldn't be prolonging a guy's career. If he's done, let him be done. It's like mercy killing.

Interview/USA Today, 4-10:(C)3.

Gord Lane
Hockey player,
New York "Islanders"

2

It's not how good you are that counts any more. It's how old you are. The [National Hockey] League's gone from experience to youth. Teams used to say, "Wait for our team to be experienced." Then, when you're finally experienced, they say, "Wait 'til you see these young kids." Well, by the time this season's over, I'll be 32. It's not old . . . But it's old.

Interview/The New York Times, 1-24:21.

Tom Lasorda
Baseball manager,
Los Angeles "Dodgers"

3

The best thing in the world is to manage a winning game. The second best thing in the world is to manage a losing game.

Interview, Miami/USA Today, 4-1:(D)2.

4

A lot of people pass off drug-taking [by baseball players] as a sickness. It's not a sickness,

it's a weakness. As far as I'm concerned, anybody who takes drugs is weak, very weak. Players need to be role models. Not very often do you see a 12-year-old youngster who wants to grow up to be a governor. He wants to be a ballplayer. The recent [drugs-in-baseball] trial in Pittsburgh really hurt baseball. We got to try to clean out the guys who do drugs. But the Players Association seems like it's trying to protect those players [by not allowing drug tests]. Are we running a rehabilitation center in baseball? I think we should really clamp down on those guys. Drugs are harmful, they're illegal and they lead you down the path to destruction.

To reporters, Phoenix, Dec. 5/
Los Angeles Times, 12-6:(III)4.

Sugar Ray Leonard
Boxer

5

The outcome of [a] fight will be determined by who wants it too much. By that, I mean one fighter will be quicker to leave his game plan because he desperately wants to beat the other guy. The one who does that will make more mistakes and will lose . . . [When I lost to Roberto Duran,] that's the only time I left my game plan. I let my emotions get the best of me. I tried to prove my manhood, so I fought his fight. He taunted me. He cursed my mother, my children, my wife. He said unbelievable things, and I let them get to me. Now we are good friends and I have learned that that was his game plan, so to speak. He got to me. That was very stupid of me, but emotions are a part of life. Up to that time, I always thought I could separate them from my work.

Interview/Los Angeles Times, 4-2:(III)2.

Don Leppert
Former baseball coach,
Houston "Astros"

6

[On his being fired as coach]: The *Astros* want everyone to be a gentleman, to look nice on airplanes and to have no beer on the bus. Sometimes I feel they think that's more important than winning games. All that Mickey Mouse stuff is okay if you're at a prep school. [But] they think

WHAT THEY SAID IN 1985

(DON LEPPERT)

being clean-shaven is more important than winning. They want to make this a Sunday-school church game. I want to win.

Los Angeles Times, 6-9:(III)6.

Chris Evert Lloyd
Tennis player

1

Everyone dreams of going out on top, of winning Wimbledon or the U.S. Open, and then waving goodbye. But I think it may be more normal not to go out on top. That may be reality.

Interview, New York, Jan. 29/
The New York Times, 1-30:21.

Vince Lombardi, Jr.
General manager,
Oakland "Invaders" football team

2

[Saying the USFL is not pursuing NFL players as much as in the past]: We don't feel the need to sign NFL players. The high-priced defensive end or defensive back doesn't put fannies in the seats. Some teams who spent a lot of money the last two years have learned that.

USA Today, 1-25:(C)1.

Kevin Loughery
Basketball coach, Chicago "Bulls"

3

[The NBA has] become a three-level league. Teams like Boston, Philadelphia and Los Angeles win almost every night. Houston, Milwaukee and Detroit have the ability to knock on the door of the elite. The rest of us are capable of winning or losing on any given night.

The New York Times, 1-16:19.

Lee MacPhail
President, baseball owners'
Player Relations Committee; Former president,
American (baseball) League

4

[Saying baseball clubs are in economic trouble and the players should bear that in mind

494

during owner-player negotiations]: . . . the situation [is] bad and [is] getting worse. If anything further happened that would be adverse to baseball's economics, it could be disastrous. The players have as much at stake as the clubs. We have to look at the whole basic system we're working under. We're not playing any games. This is no delaying action. This is no public-relations ploy to get a better deal. We're concerned about the welfare of the game, the financial structure of the game. We asked [the players] to sit down together with us and work out joint solutions. We can't go in and cure everything by cutting back what players get. We'll have to take a look at costs and revenues from all sources. It's not a position that anybody is pleased to have to come to.

Feb. 27/The New York Times, 2-28:22.

5

[On a possible player strike]: It's the union's state of mind that bothers us. I'm not saying that the players have to publicly say we [the owners] have financial problems, but I am saying that they have to recognize it in framing an agreement. I mean, they keep saying that all they want is the status quo, but the status quo represents a $45-million increase in their pension fund and a $35-million increase in salaries. That's $80-million from an industry already deep in the red. I don't know where they think we're going to get the money.

July 15/Los Angeles Times, 7-16:(III)4.

Pete Maravich
Former basketball player

6

No matter how much money you make, no matter how many things you have, you still are going to try to get more. And that "more" is usually what is going to self-destruct you as a player; more wealth, more money, more success, the right parties, the right cars, the right clothes, the right houses. We [players] live in a fantasy world. It's not what most athletes think it is. We think we live in a fishbowl and that everybody knows who we are and this is what's happening. This *isn't* what's happening.

Interview/Los Angeles Times, 1-28:(III)12.

Billy Martin
Baseball manager,
New York "Yankees"

1

[On the courtroom testimony of several base-ball players about drug use in the major leagues]: They're giving those squealers too much immunity, and you can quote me. I hate stool pigeons, and these guys are copping on their own pals. The government is plenty to blame, too. Why do they need a dozen players to turn state's evidence when two or three would do? They made a parade out of it. That last thing, John Milner stooling on Willie Mays, re-ally upset me. Those guys who admit they've been using the stuff should be on trial, and ain't. They're bringing in other names and hurting other people. Let me tell you how I stand on drugs, cocaine and all the rest. First time a player is caught on coke or anything, give him a year out of baseball right away. If he blows reha-bilitation, give him life. Let's let our country know how strong we are on this.

Interview/Los Angeles Times, 9-16:(III)2.

Johnny Mathis
Singer

2

Golf, for me, has always been a great social lubricant. You meet many people in my busi-ness. But you get to *know* them on a golf course. It's a great game. No, make that *the* great game. I think it appeals to singers because it's some-what the same thing, a medium of self-expression. In singing, you strive to make certain muscles do the same thing over and over again to produce the same effect. Ditto golf. It's the pursuit of perfection. It's never boring. It's a challenge to perform up to your best in public.

Interview/Los Angeles Times, 3-26:(III)8.

Gene Mauch
Baseball manager, California "Angels"

3

I don't know what all the ingredients are to managing in the majors, but I do know you can't do it without enthusiasm, without excitement . . . If obviously caring, as I do, rubs off, that's great, but I don't even think about what I con-tribute in that area. I don't handle people, I level with people.

Los Angeles Times, 4-1:(III)16.

4

General managers are more important than ever in baseball today, because they are the ones who ultimately seem to decide who gets the big money and the long-term contracts. You give the wrong players that kind of deal and you've tied up your ball club financially for years. The min-ute some players grab that much security, their drive simply disappears. I'm not saying that most players today don't want to win as much as they did in the old days. In fact, I've got several like that on the *Angels* . . . [who] make so much money that they are playing strictly for pride and to get us into a World Series. Even if we win it all, Uncle Sam is going to take almost all their money. The point is, in the old days teams had to win pennants for their players to get raises, and sometimes they didn't get them even then. But today, players know they can get the super con-tract just by having a big individual year. Today, before you sign anybody to a multiple contract, you do as close an inspection of his character as you do his talent.

The Christian Science Monitor, 7-30:18.

John McEnroe
Tennis player

5

[On his reputation for being arrogant]: I keep my perspective on reality. I don't have entou-rages. I call and make my own airline reserva-tions; it's a small thing, but I do it. I'm excited about meeting people and I listen to what others say. I never feel that I'm bigger than life because I can hit a tennis ball over a net. When I sit there and think of what I have, I say this is unbeliev-able. I'm very lucky. But I do feel I should get more respect than I do . . . Everyone is inse-cure, and my personality is that I'm not totally secure. When you go out there to play, you're not sure you can do it like you did the last time. So I'm reluctant to change the way I've been. I might lose the competitive edge.

Interview, Glen Cove, N.Y./
The New York Times, 5-6:45.

1

(JOHN McENROE)

[Criticizing the effect TV has on the way tennis tournaments are scheduled]: I think it's a major injustice to have us play for two straight days in a major championship. You know that the semis and the finals are going to be the two toughest matches and they're going to take the most out of you. It's a shame that TV controls what we'd do at this point. I'd rather take less money and screw TV, for all I'm concerned. It's more important to see the best tennis, not seeing two tired players out there. That's what happened the last couple of years . . . Unfortunately, that's a part of tennis right now. We don't have enough cohesion as a player's group, and the USTA's too afraid of TV to make any changes.

New York, Sep. 8/
Los Angeles Times, 9-9:(III)17.

Al McGuire

Sports commentator, NBC-TV

2

I've often wondered why basketball coaches dress like business executives rather than jocks. A coach is moving almost as much as his players. I'll bet you the [sportswear manufacturers] Nikes, Converses, Pumas and Adidases of the world would love to see these coaches in a nice, classy warmup suit, with their marquee. Some kind of leisurely jogging suit, maybe. The way it is now, they all look like they're running for office. But I have yet to see a Senator or Congressman campaigning with a sport shirt on. The whole coach's outfit runs counter to what he's doing. He's all dressed up and he's going into dirty, old locker rooms, and gyms and arenas. What would be wrong with a nice jogging suit for coaches?

Interview/Los Angeles Times, 2-8:(III)2.

Steve McMichael

Football player, Chicago "Bears"

3

[On the sophistication of modern-day football]: All the computers and genius coaches aren't worth a thing on Sundays if you don't have a bunch of guys who go out and play as though somebody called their mommas a nasty name.

Los Angeles Times, 12-26:(III)2.

Howard Metzenbaum

United States Senator, D-Ohio

4

[On football antitrust regulations such as those governing the movement of franchises from city to city]: The nation faces a $200-billion deficit. The arms race is hot and unemployment is up. Why are we holding hearings on sports teams moving from one town to another? The marketplace is the best way to decide these things. Government regulation only leads to more regulation. Some of the most successful business people in the U.S., and some of the most ardent supporters of this [Reagan] Administration, are owners of NFL teams. They say, "Keep government out of business, except when it affects me." Then they yell, "Congress get in and regulate us." Let's get Congress out of the business of football . . . Let 'em fight it out . . . Fans would benefit from *real* competition. But the real benefit would be on Capitol Hill, where we could get back to unimportant issues such as war and peace.

At Senate Judiciary Committee hearing, Washington, Feb. 6/The Washington Post, 2-9:(D)1.

Barbara A. Mikulski

United States Representative, D-Maryland

5

. . . we find that sports teams come to the government [state and local] for the sole purpose to ask for guaranteed, fancy, often lavish, luxurious sports arenas. They want guaranteed ticket sales. They want state and local exemptions. And in the case of Louisiana [the New Orleans Saints], they even wanted the state legislature to put up a substantial amount of money. Then, they come to us [the Congress] for an antitrust exemption, and they call that free enterprise. I don't call that free enterprise. We think that's looking for a free ride.

The Washington Post, 2-21:(B)7.

Marvin Miller

Former executive director,
Major League Baseball Players Association

6

[On fan reaction if there is a player strike this year]: What people lose sight of is that in 19

(MARVIN MILLER)

years of collective bargaining, we've negotiated 12 contracts and had work stoppages of only eight days in '72, and 50 in '81. That's a 19-year average of only three days per year, which is rather remarkable. People also forget that baseball set an attendance record in '82, then signed a national TV contract in '83 that was four times larger than the previous contract. The strike didn't seem to hurt that much.

Interview, Chicago, May 23/
Los Angeles Times,
5-24:(III)16.

Martina Navratilova
Tennis player

1

[On why she is so businesslike in her matches]: The main reason I find it difficult to joke around and laugh it up is because I'm beating people 99 per cent of the time. And I wouldn't want somebody beating me and joking around about it. When I used to lose, it was easy to kid around and have a good time. When you're down 5-2, you can lighten up because you're obviously going to lose. You can sit on the lineman's lap, or whatever. But I've been very conscious of not rubbing it in my opponent's face when I'm winning because I know it would hurt. I would love to celebrate and jump around, but that's not right.

Interview/Los Angeles Times, 1-24:(III)2.

2

[On John McEnroe's losing the Wimbledon championship]: He was just having one of the best years anybody could have. [But] it finally got to him. Having to be on the top, putting yourself on the line every time you go out there, it wears you down. It wore me down and it had to wear him down. And with the men, it's so much different, because so many men are capable of beating the McEnroes or the [Jimmy] Connorses . . . In women's tennis, there are just not that many players who can overpower me.

Interview, New York,
July 9/USA Today, 7-10:(C)1.

John Nerud
Hall of Fame race-horse trainer

3

People who aren't close to the sport [horse racing] think it's dishonest. They think a trainer is a fellow in a plaid jacket who steals chickens at night. And they have some good reasons, because the game is changing. More and more, your owners are just money people, and they're looking to get rich in a hurry.

Los Angeles Times, 2-11:(III)14.

Jack Nicklaus
Golfer

4

The worse you're performing on the course, the harder you must work at the game mentally and emotionally. The greatest—and toughest—art in golf is "playing badly well." All the true greats have been masters at it.

The Christian Science Monitor, 5-14:20.

5

[On the increase in non-U.S. golfers winning major world tournaments]: There are just more non-U.S. players that have become good players. That is a development of other tours and is no reflection on our [U.S.] tour. And they are good players. The U.S. is not the only place that is developing good players. We did have sort of a monopoly on that. Britain dominated it 60, 70 years ago before the balance of power shifted over here [to the U.S.]. Then, in the last 20 years, the foreign tours have developed and so the players on those tours have improved. They are competitive on any tour now, and when they peak for the major championships they are going to play well. If they win on those tours, why shouldn't they feel confident going into a major?

The New York Times, 7-15:32.

Phil Niekro
Baseball pitcher,
New York "Yankees"

6

I just keep my arm as healthy as I can and try to keep myself mentally prepared for the whole season. That's the toughest part. That's where a

(PHIL NIEKRO)

lot of guys probably break down—the mental end of the game. You can either throw a ball, or you run, or you can't. You can catch a ball, or you can't. That's cut and dried. But the mental end of the game—162 games a year and six weeks of spring training, the ups and downs, the good games and the bad games—that's the toughest part a lot of players have to deal with.

Interview/Los Angeles, 5-29:(III)7.

[On his being, at 46, the oldest active baseball pitcher]: That's the biggest thing—why everybody keeps referring to the age all the time. There's a lot of guys in baseball that are a lot younger than I am right now, having worse years than I am. No one brings their age up. Nobody ever says they're getting too old, that they're over the hill. What's wrong with them? They're just having pitching problems, the same as I was there for a while. Someone has to be the oldest pitcher in the game. Unless there's twins, or something. And someone's got to be the youngest. It just has to be that way. I don't think age has any meaning in the game. It's the best man for the job. If I'm not doing my job, someone will take my job away from me.

Interview/The New York Times, 7-23:24.

1

Hank Peters
General manager,
Baltimore "Orioles" baseball club

[On high player salaries]: Any club that has not won will have a low payroll until they do win. Then they'll have to pay the price. It's the Catch-22 of salaries.

USA Today, 12-5:(C)3.

2

George Plimpton
Editor, "The Paris Review";
Former professional athlete

We hear a great deal about corruption in sports. Hardly a week goes by that some college coach is not accused of bribing a star high-school athlete to come to his school, or of paying his supposedly amateur players under the table, or that some professional athlete isn't arrested for possession of one controlled substance or another. Sportswriters seem more concerned with drugs, gambling and corruption than with won-lost records or hard-fought championship games. Many Americans persist in thinking of sports as a heroic realm where brave men and women battle for glory; but this realm seems to have been invaded by the sordid facts of everyday life.

Panel discussion/"Harper's," September:46.

3

John Pont
Football coach,
Hamilton (Ohio) High School;
Former football coach,
University of Indiana

[Comparing coaching high-school football with college football]: I've only found one real difference. You have to exercise more patience in high school—a lot more. Everything else seems the same to me. My practice schedule is the same. I teach the same things. There are as many demands on a coach here as there are on the college level. The strategy of the game is the same. But if you don't have the patience of Job, you can't make it as a high-school coach.

Interview, Hamilton, Ohio/
Los Angeles Times, 11-25:(III)4.

4

Chris Raymond
Former football coach,
Colby College

[Saying Colby fired him after he refused their request that he resign]: I talked with my father [Delaware's football coach Tubby Raymond], and his advice was, "Make them fire you." My thinking is that being fired in this profession is like a red badge of courage. But if you go to a convention of coaches and say you've resigned, you'd better have a real good reason.

The New York Times, 11-22:29.

5

Joe Robbie
Owner,
Miami "Dolphins" football team

1

[On football-team owners]: I think many of them are in this for different reasons than I am. I am, because I'd rather compete than do anything . . . I'm in football to win championships. If I ever lost that verve I'd be in something less strenuous . . . It may not be the fun it once was. You can't pass out envelopes saying how much everyone is going to get; I mean, [the players] talk back now. I've said there are only 26 guys on earth [the owners] who can destroy professional football—and here we all sit. We've caused a number of our own problems.

Interview, Oakland, Calif./
Los Angeles Times, 1-20:(III)11.

Darryl Rogers
Football coach, Detroit "Lions"

2

I think there's a very fine line between a great football team and a good football team. A lot of it is mental. So, play like you have a chance to win it and a lot of things even out in a hurry. And you have to play and have a good time. I don't think football is any different than any other job. If it's drudgery, you don't perform very well.

Interview, Pontiac, Mich.,
Sept. 16/USA Today, 9-17:(C)8.

3

What's tough for most new coaches is that they almost always come into a losing situation. While looking at old films to pinpoint problems is helpful, final decisions can't really be made until you start working with your players in practice, and that takes weeks.

The Christian Science Monitor, 11-13:22.

Pete Rose
Baseball manager and player,
Cincinnati "Reds"

4

Medical people tell me I have the body of a 30-year-old. I know I've got the brain of a 15-year-old. You got both, you can play baseball.

Interview/Los Angeles Times, 4-4:(II)2.

5

You don't realize it, but a baseball manager has a game-plan similar to a football coach. You know who you'll put in in relief in the fourth or the sixth or the ninth. And then you know who you'll substitute in other situations if you need them. You're not going to put in a fat guy to pinch-run. You're not going to put in a singles hitter if you need a home run.

Interview, San Diego, Calif./
The New York Times, 8-16:22.

6

[On his philosophy of managing]: It's simple. I treat the players as men. I do not have a lot of rules. All I want them to do is give 110 per cent, and be on time. The thing I have going for me is I'm also a player and I know what their needs are, what their thoughts are. I want baseball to be fun for them. I want them to enjoy winning, because that's the only way you can truly enjoy this game . . . My father taught me that. He said if you only give 100 per cent, the other guy might also be giving 100 per cent, and you won't win. The extra 10 per cent makes the difference.

Interview/USA Today, 8-30:(A)9.

7

There is no doubt that [Ty Cobb] was the best hitter who ever lived. Look at his lifetime average of .367, and then he leads the league in hitting for nine straight years, misses once, and leads it again for what, three more years? But I think the best baseball player who ever lived was Babe Ruth—for hitting, for pitching, for fielding, and I understand that he was so popular he actually saved franchises. When he came into a city, even teams that were dying at the gate filled up the stands. He just may have saved baseball altogether. And when he walked into a room—it's the same with Joe DiMaggio—you don't have to turn on the light switch. Those guys light up a room by just walking in.

Interview, Chicago/
The New York Times, 9-9:52.

8

[On his breaking up emotionally after he got his 4,192nd hit, breaking Ty Cobb's all-time

(PETE ROSE)

record]: I was okay until I looked up in the sky and I saw my father and Ty Cobb looking down at me. They took care of me. I wish everyone in baseball could experience this . . . It was the first time I was ever on a baseball field and I didn't know what to do. All I could do was stand there . . . I don't think something has ended. A milestone has ended, but I'll come back tomorrow night and try to do my job.

Interview, Cincinnati,
Sept. 11/USA Today, 9-12:(C)6.

Pete Rozelle
Commissioner,
National Football League

My theory is that people turn to sports as they do movies—as an outlet, enjoyment, entertainment. When that entertainment becomes something they read about on the front page or on the editorial page—holdouts, strikes, litigation, drugs—it detracts . . . We've had our peaks and valleys [in the NFL]. I've seen them for 25 years. Ten years ago, we had three anti-trust suits going at the same time . . . People were saying football had peaked and [then] we had the World Football League. But we're still here, aren't we?

Interview, New York/
Los Angeles Times, 1-14:(III)8.

1

[On pro football's declining television ratings]: I think it's due to a glut of football on the tube, and the USFL with its spring football is part of the problem. During the fall, there are eight or nine college games on TV every Saturday. On Sunday, we [the NFL] take over. Then, after our season, comes the USFL. Despite their [low] ratings and their [poor] attendance, they still get attention in the media. I think people need a rest from football. That's why the USFL's move to a fall schedule in 1986 might actually help the situation.

News conference, Palo Alto, Calif./
The Christian Science Monitor, 1-21:20.

2

The biggest change [in football over the past 25 years] is, you have bigger, faster players running into each other now. In 1952, when I started working for the Los Angeles Rams, I don't recall all the injuries. Artificial turf makes it a faster game. It's like if you shoot a BB into the wall, it won't do the same thing as a howitzer.

Los Angeles, 8-6:(III)2.

3

Charles F. Rule
Acting Assistant Secretary, Antitrust Division,
Department of Justice
of the United States

[Saying that sports leagues should be free of antitrust oversight in determining whether teams be allowed to relocate to other cities]: At times, courts and government enforcers have inappropriately applied the antitrust laws in a way that interfered with, rather than protected, the marketplace, with the result that the antitrust "cure" was worse, in terms of the marketplace, than the competitive "disease" at which it was aimed. Such is necessarily the case with efforts by the courts to second-guess a league's decision concerning franchise relocations . . . Professional sports have become so popular precisely because the entrepreneurs who own teams have been able to respond to market forces. Indeed, professional team sports in this country represent a triumph of capitalism. We would be unwise to ignore the importance of private economic decision-making in that success.

Before Senate Judiciary Committee,
Washington, June 12/
The Washington Post, 6-13:(B)9.

4

JoAnne Russell
Tennis player

[Saying women players don't show their tempers while on the court, as some men players do]: Society disapproves of angry, belligerent women. If a woman gets mad, people say, "That's so un-ladylike." But when [John] McEnroe goes crazy, nobody says, "That's so

5

(JoANNE RUSSELL)

un-gentlemanly-like." When McEnroe and [Jimmy] Connors get wild, people say, "What a man! What a guy!" If I did it, nobody would say, "What a woman!" . . . It happens all the time in juniors. When the boys carry on, people say they're just being boys. But if a girl curses on a sidecourt somewhere, 83 guys in armbands will come sprinting out to wash her mouth out with soap.

Interview/
Los Angeles Times,
1-20:(III)21.

Johnny Sain
Pitching coach,
Atlanta "Braves" baseball club;
Former pitcher

1

I start with the idea that every pitcher is different and that he has to have something going for him, or he wouldn't be in the majors. I let him know right away that I'm for him—that I want him to succeed—and that I'm not fussy about how he does it. If a guy's going well, I don't bother him. If he's got a problem, I try to get him to talk to me. It doesn't have to be about baseball at first. I've farmed, sold cars and flew airplanes, and lived in lots of towns, so I have things in common with everybody. A pitcher knows himself best, and usually he'll have an idea what's wrong. Then we'll discuss how to correct it. Mostly, it's nothing major. A lot of pitchers don't realize that, and when they hit a really bad stretch they'll start looking for something radical, like a new pitch. I usually discourage them. Not many guys can make a living throwing a forkball or screwball—they're too tough to control. A guy doesn't have to have five or six pitches; two are enough if he can control them and change speeds . . . One thing I've found is that if you change a pitcher against his will, you'll hurt him ways you never thought. Pitching is a heck of a lot more complicated than it looks.

Interview, West Palm Beach, Fla./
The Wall Street Journal, 3-19:30.

Tom Sanders
Assistant director, Center for
the Study of Sport in Society,
Northeastern University;
Former basketball player
and coach, Boston "Celtics"

2

Athletes in general see themselves as protected from the world. Most of them, particularly the very good ones, have been protected all their lives. Basically, they've learned how to sign their names on the dotted line. They are only too happy to avoid the reality they've been helped to avoid. When I was playing for the *Celtics,* I had roommates who refused to discuss *anything* political. What do you think about politics, drugs, this or that issue? "Sorry, man, I don't get into that."

Panel discussion/"Harper's," September:56.

Ted Sator
Hockey coach,
New York "Rangers"

3

[On coaching]: [Chrysler Corporation's chairman] Lee Iacocca's philosophy is that any idea that's worth an idea is worth putting down on paper. You can't be too organized. You have to have a plan that takes precedence over how you might be feeling from day to day. That helps you lock in. Ego is not part of my personality makeup. People envision a pro coach as a Knute Rockne type, but 80 nights a year—that's too demanding on the physical component. Ego is a negative energy focus.

Interview, Rye, N.Y./
The New York Times, 9-30:40.

Mike Schmidt
Baseball player,
Philadelphia "Phillies"

4

There's a lot of God-given [baseball] talent around that winds up being mediocre. The only difference between greatness and mediocrity is dedication. You have to eat, drink and sleep baseball when you're young if you want to be great. You have to be married to it. Young players aren't willing to pay that price any more. Maybe the money comes too quickly.

Interview/USA Today, 7-16:(C)2.

Howard Schnellenberger
Football coach,
University of Louisville

1

A head football coach of any school, by his position, has the ability to have a major impact [in the community]. It's a person's responsibility to use that position to make positive steps. Fortunately or unfortunately, college football coaches are a status symbol in a city unlike anything else. You're non-political and you're looked up to by alumni and people who never went to college. If I ask the community to support our team, I have to support the community. A successful program goes a long way to establishing a city. I don't think anything that happened in Miami during my years there had the dramatic positive effect that winning the national championship did.

Interview, Louisville, Ky./
Los Angeles Times, 9-3:(III)6.

Marty Schottenheimer
Football coach, Cleveland "Browns"

2

People ask if confidence or winning comes first. In my opinion, winning comes first. After you win one, winning becomes a habit.

USA Today, 12-4:(C)4.

Vin Scully
Baseball announcer,
Los Angeles "Dodgers" and NBC-TV

3

You can't compare sports. You can't compare baseball, for instance, with basketball or football. Basically, basketball is like playing 21: two cards. Hit me. Bingo. You made it or you didn't. Constant action. Action. Action. Turnover. A lot of people like 21. Other people like gin rummy; it takes some more thinking. Then there's that group that loves chess . . . If you're a gin rummy player, baseball might be gin rummy. But if you're really into it and you're looking to see "Are they holding the runner on?; this might be a hit-and-run play," then suddenly it's chess. It's like beauty: It's in the eye of the beholder.

Interview/Los Angeles Times Magazine, 10-13:19.

Tom Seaver
Baseball pitcher,
Chicago "White Sox"

4

One of the things a pitcher must know is that there are usually four or five times in a game when the game hinges on the next batter. You have to be able to recognize those instances—a lot of pitchers don't—and if you do, you have to be able to understand it mentally, decide what to do, and execute it physically.

Interview, Chicago/
The New York Times, 7-1:34.

Eric Show
Baseball pitcher,
San Diego "Padres"

5

[On the possibility, which came true, that he would be the pitcher when Cincinnati's Pete Rose got his 4,192nd hit, breaking Ty Cobb's all-time record]: When time passes, Lord willing and assuming the earth continues to exist as we know it, I might be a trivia question. But in the eternal scope of things, who really cares? . . . I don't mean to be a fuddy-dud about it. Uh, scratch that word. I mean, I don't mean to be a kill-joy.

Interview just before game
in which Rose broke the record
with a hit off Show, Cincinnati,
Sept. 11/Los Angeles Times, 9-12:(III)12.

Don Shula
Football coach, Miami "Dolphins"

6

I think the first essential of the good coach is that he or she be a good teacher. All the principles of good teaching can be found in good coaching . . . You must impart into your player all you know about the game. You must have the ability to make it work for the player, to make him understand what you know and to then apply it in game situations. Add to that the good motivator. Any leader must be able to motivate those under his charge to rise to their best efforts.

USA Today, 1-21:(D)2.

Ken Singleton
Former baseball player,
Baltimore "Orioles"

1

To the fans, baseball looks easy. But it looks easy only because major-league players are that good. It's said baseball is a little kid's game, but in the majors it's a little kid's game played at a man's level. The players earn their money. They earn it by being away from home on anniversaries and birthdays, by traveling the country at 3 a.m. to get from one game to the next, by having to abruptly pack up and move when traded or reassigned, by giving up any chance to establish roots. And a lot of fans tend to think everyone plays 23 years in the majors, as Brooks Robinson did. But very, very few have careers that are anywhere near that long.

Interview, Baltimore/USA Today, 8-2:(A)8.

Ozzie Smith
Baseball player,
St. Louis "Cardinals"

2

[Saying he is paid his high salary for his fielding rather than his hitting]: Baseball has always been an offensive-oriented game. That's the thing that people have always gone to see. Yet it's defense that puts your offense in position to win. It's okay to pay a pitcher, who is basically a defensive player, so why not somebody like me? . . . The most important word associated with the game of baseball is consistency. To be able to make the next play that comes to you, you have to forget that one, great play you just made. The thing that separates the good from the average or the good from the great is the degree of consistency with which you perform. I don't necessarily believe I'm the greatest. I just want to maximize my God-given talent. Every night when I leave the ballpark, I ask myself this question: "Did you do your very best?" To this point, the answer has been yes.

Interview/Los Angeles Times, 7-23:(III)6.

Warren Spahn
Former baseball pitcher

3

I didn't get to manage [a major-league team] for two reasons: I was a pitcher, and a good one.

There's a prejudice in baseball against pitchers as managers in the big leagues, and against guys who had good playing records. It's spread by all those little bench-warmers who get the managing jobs. They'll tell you that things came easy to the stars, so we're no good as teachers. That's bull. We got good because we studied the game and ourselves and did what it took to excel. When a manager's job comes open, who gets it? Some ex-catcher or utility infielder. They're supposed to know strategy. Hell, who knows more about the steal or the hit-and-run than a pitcher? He's in the middle on both those plays. He knows the most about pitchers because he was one, and about hitters because it was his job to get them out. If I owned a club, I'd have nothing but pitchers for managers.

Interview, Atlantic City, N.J. /
The Wall Street Journal, 8-2:11.

George Steinbrenner
Owner,
New York "Yankees" baseball club

4

[On player drug-abuse]: If a player wants help, I'm willing to help him. But if he's not, I'll keep him out of baseball as long as possible. And I'll fight it all the way to the Supreme Court. These kids are going to learn quick. They're going to feel the full fury of getting into that sort of thing. I want to get the message across that we won't tolerate drugs. It may cost us some prized players along the way, but I'm willing to accept that. If we don't nip this thing in the bud, it's going to hurt this game something terrible.

April 22/Los Angeles Times, 4-23:(III)5.

5

The problem is, today's player has too many interests other than baseball. With many of these athletes, these interests are taking up too much of their waking hours. The discipline on this club is going to be put back to the extent where they're going to devote their waking hours to baseball. If they don't think that's fair, perhaps they should go out and drive a cab in New York City or work as a policeman or fireman, where they don't know if they're going to come home to

(GEORGE STEINBRENNER)

their families at night. These players have a great deal, a hell of a job. They're going to be made to earn their money.

Interview, Ocala, Fla.,
April 29/USA Today, 4-30:(C)9.

Margaret Thatcher
Prime Minister of the United Kingdom

[On a riot by British fans at a soccer game in Brussels, which resulted in deaths and injuries]: No words can adequately express the horror and revulsion which I and millions of British people felt at the scenes of violence which we witnessed at last night's European Cup final in Brussels. These terrible events have brought shame and disgrace on those responsible and on their country. They never should have happened. It is the thugs who destroy football [soccer].

London, May 30/
Los Angeles Times, 5-31:(I)15.

1

John Thompson
Basketball coach, Georgetown University

. . . success is the hardest thing to manage, because with success comes complacency, or at least the danger of it. To tell you the truth, I've never really trusted success.

Newsweek, 2-11:74.

2

[On his keeping a low public profile]: I don't care whether they know me. That's what the problem is. If I don't know you, I don't put a label on you. The problem is, people know a lot more about personalities than they know about basketball, so they deal with the personalities and not the basketball. We play basketball. People pay admission to watch us play, and we play hard. I don't want to go out of the way to expose myself.

Interview/
USA Today, 3-29:(C)5.

3

Donald Trump
Owner,
New Jersey ''Generals'' football team

[Arguing against greater antitrust exemptions for the NFL, such as allowing its teams more freedom to move their franchises]: The USFL, as a new league, must have the NFL subject to the laws of the state. We [in the USFL] must have protection. The NFL must be subject to antitrust, as any other business.

Before Senate Judiciary Committee,
Washington, Feb. 6/USA Today, 2-7:(C)3.

4

Thomas A. Tutko
Professor of psychology,
San Jose (Calif.) State University

[On the increase in fan violence at sporting events around the world]: It's certainly good that we don't have more wars, but in their relative absence it has been the athletes who have taken the identities of warriors, especially so at international sports events. I see a progression of events in the international sports world that is getting worse, which at its center involves the over-identification of ways of life with athletes. Thus the bottom line is the final score, and a loss leads to great embarrassment—and fights in the stands. The [violent] happenings at the matches in Brussels, and most recently Peking, lead to great national and international embarrassment, but the riots go beyond soccer in that many fans sense that coming under challenge—and perhaps defeat—is their whole concept of what they stand for and agree with.

Interview, May 29/The New York Times, 5-30:6.

5

Peter V. Ueberroth
Commissioner of Baseball

[On his handling of last year's umpire strike]: Easy decision. Baseball just had a bad attitude toward the umps. They're good people . . . working stiffs . . . underpaid . . . You give 'em a raise. Done. Next subject.

Interview, Miami/Los Angeles Times, 3-17:(III)1.

6

[Calling for testing of baseball players to detect drug abuse]: One way to rid baseball com-

7

(PETER V. UEBERROTH)

pletely so we can hold our heads up high is to test—and if there are problems, to get help. This should not be a subject of confrontation between the Major League Baseball Players Association and the owners. We're trying to cure a problem, not persecute people. When I took this job, I said I would fight drugs and not players. If we protect the privacy of individuals and attempt to help those who are damaging themselves and using illegal substances—and we are helping them—I think everyone should support that effort. Starting mandatory drug testing for baseball personnel is not a calculating or mercenary act. I'm doing this because I don't think baseball can take the risk of not doing it. It just can't.

Interview/USA Today, 5-13:(A)8.

1

[On a possible player strike]: A strike is a failure. They [the players' union] are going to set a date which is being called a strike date. It's not a strike date—it's a failure date. It means both sides have failed to come together. It's not a victory for anybody. The fans lose, the players lose, the owners lose—everybody loses . . . Baseball teams are losing money. I don't take the owners' position; I don't take the players' position. But I think both sides at the table are beginning to get serious about "Let's not have an industry that's going to be going down the tubes," having terrible problems that they can't recover from.

Broadcast interview/ "Meet the Press," NBC-TV, 7-14.

2

Gene Upshaw
Executive director,
National Football League
Players Association

[On the current relationship between the owners and the players union following a long player strike in 1982]: We're all trying to promote the game back to what it was in the 1970s; we're all trying to find the solutions. What we wanted, and what we've gotten, is respect. What I've tried to do is create an atmosphere we can co-exist in. This business is not like a football game where there's a winner and a loser. You give, they give, and we find what's fair.

Interview/USA Today, 1-8:(C)2.

3

[Criticizing an owners' decision to cut player rosters from 49 to 45]: Basically, according to the collective-bargaining agreement, I guess they have the right to reduce the rosters. But from the standpoint of what it would do for the game, I think it hurt. We're talking about the injury rate increasing, about younger players not getting a chance to learn. I think the quality of play, the quality of the game, is going to be hurt. Plus, I think it just looks bad.

May 22/The New York Times, 5-23:26.

4

Harry Usher
Commissioner,
United States Football League

[On the very high salaries being offered by USFL teams to attract player talent]: If you're going to have a league that's not going to go right out of sight, you have to say, "Let's curtail some of this incentive to buy the biggest and the best all the time." There's a continual pull and tug between the finances of the individual clubs and the competitive aspect of the league itself. The league is only as strong as its weakest member, and it can't allow an economic policy to develop where the wealthiest clubs buy everyone out.

Los Angeles Times, 2-10:(III)18.

5

Lanny Wadkins
Golfer

[Criticizing slow-playing golfers]: I don't know what they're doing. They're walking around, lining up a putt they've lined up 12 times before. Nobody wants to see a player walking around the green for 20 minutes, and that's what we're getting. They're tossing grass in the air and they're looking over the shot. I don't know what they're looking for. It's something I've never seen . . . It's a problem. It's something we on the tour need to deal with. I don't know what the solution is. It's not for me to say. But something definitely needs to be done to speed up play.

Interview, Pebble Beach, Calif./ Los Angeles Times, 1-31:(III)2.

Darrell Waltrip
Auto-racing driver

We know how it feels to win and how it feels to lose, and believe me, winning is better no matter how much character they say the other builds.

Interview/Los Angeles Times,
11-15:(III)14.

1

Earl Weaver
Former baseball manager,
Baltimore "Orioles"

There's a difference between playing and managing. Playing is fun. If I was a player, I'd be like the rest of them; they'd have to carry me out. But managing—that was work. W-O-R-K.

Interview, Miami/The Washington Post, 3-21:(E)4.

2

Hoyt Wilhelm
Former baseball pitcher

Nobody ever really masters the knuckleball. I started throwing it in high school, used it for seven or eight years in the minor leagues and 21 years in the majors, and still I never knew just what it was going to do. There's no way you can throw the pitch that it will do exactly the same thing twice in a row . . . The knuckleball isn't as hard on the arm as some pitches. You don't twist your arm, and you don't have to throw hard. On days when I was getting a good spin on the ball, I just lobbed it in there. It was just like playing catch.

Interview/The Christian Science Monitor, 3-1:18.

3

Pat Williams
General manager,
Philadelphia "76ers" basketball team

Basketball is the sport that can truly be influenced by one man. Baseball and football can't, and hockey no one understands, anyway.

Los Angeles Times, 5-13:(III)2.

4

Max Winter
Owner,
Minnesota "Vikings" football team

Money has never won a championship. The fact that you pay a player $50,000 more doesn't make him a better player. A good player plays the game as well as he can all the time. You have to keep salaries down in order to keep everyone on the team happy. You can't pay one guard $200,000 when the guy next to him is getting $100,000. That's dissension.

Interview, Eden Prairie, Minn./
Los Angeles Times, 10-3:(III)8.

5

John Wooden
Former basketball coach,
University of California, Los Angeles

In the 88-game [winning] streak, my players were never bothered until we got close to 60, which was then the record. Near 60, I sensed them getting a little tight. But once we tied the record—even before we broke it—they were no longer tight. There was no longer any pressure. I think the notion that a long winning streak puts more pressure on you is wrong. It puts more pressure on your opponent. I have always liked to be in the spot where teams that played us were ready to celebrate when they even came close to beating us. I told my players it was to our advantage that teams felt they had nothing to lose by playing us. That meant they put us on a little pedestal. I wanted to keep it that way.

Interview/Los Angeles Times, 2-1:(III)2.

6

Bob Woolf
Professional sports player agent

I've lived through the demise of the World Football League, the American Basketball Association, the World Hockey Association, because the [player] salaries rise at such a rate that the encumbrances overwhelm them. Even in baseball, it's ultimately going to prove impossible to sell these teams with all the deferred [player salary] liabilities they will have. Believe me, despite what anybody says, it represents an incredible danger in organized sport.

Los Angeles Times, 1-7:(III)11.

7

The Indexes

Index To Speakers

Index to Subjects